Corruptions of Empire

The Haymarket Series

Editors: Mike Davis and Michael Sprinker

The Haymarket Series is a new publishing initiative by Verso offering original studies of politics, history and culture focused on North America. The series presents innovative but representative views from across the American left on a wide range of topics of current and continuing interest to socialists in North America and throughout the world. A century after the first May Day, the American left remains in the shadow of those martyrs whom this series honors and commemorates. The studies in the Haymarket Series testify to the living legacy of activism and political commitment for which they gave up their lives.

Already Published

Corruptions of Empire

Life Studies & The Reagan Era

———◆———

ALEXANDER COCKBURN

VERSO

London · New York

Note to illustration on front of jacket: In August 1814, a British raiding party led by Admiral Sir George Cockburn launched an attack on Washington. They set fire to the Capitol, then proceeded to the White House and, before setting fire to it, consumed a meal set out by Dolly Madison which had been abandoned by the fugitive President and his family. Cockburn next proceeded to the offices of *The National Intelligence* to avenge himself on the press which had abused him. He ordered his men to destroy the paper's printing types, saying 'Be sure that all the Cs are destroyed so that the rascals cannot any longer abuse my name'. Cockburn then laid siege to Balitmore, the unsuccessful fusillades prompting the composition of 'The Star Spangled Banner', whose reference to 'the hireling and slave' in the British force alludes, as Robin Blackburn points out in *The Overthrow of Colonial Slavery*, to the fact that Cockburn had offered freedom to all slaves who would join him in his attacks of 1813 and 1814. According to a British report these slaves conducted themselves very well and 'were uniformly volunteers for the Station where they might expect to meet their former masters.' Some of these black recruits were in the party that burned the White House.

This collection first published by Verso 1987
Paperback edition published by Verso 1988
© This collection Alexander Cockburn, 1988
All rights reserved

Verso
UK: 6 Meard Street, London W1V 3HR
USA: 29 West 35th Street, New York, NY 10001-2291

Verso is the imprint of New Left Books

British Library Cataloguing in Publication Data

Cockburn, Alexander
　　Corruptions of empire: life studies and
　　the Reagan era. — 2nd ed.
　　I. Title
　　081
　　ISBN 0-86091-940-4

US Library of Congress Cataloging in Publication Data

Cockburn, Alexander.
　　　Corruptions of empire: life studies & the Reagan era / Alexander
　　Cockburn. — 2nd ed.
　　　　p.　　　c.
　　　ISBN 0-86091-940-4 (pbk.) : $12.95
　　1. United States — Politics and government — 1945-　　2. Corruption
　　(in politics) — United States — History — 20th century.　　3. Political
　　culture — United States — History — 20th century.　　4. Press and
　　politics — United States — History — 20th century.　　I. Title.
　　E839.5.C63　　1988
　　973.927—dc19

Printed in Finland by Werner Söderström Oy
Typeset by Leaper & Gard Ltd, Bristol, England

CONTENTS

For a complete list of titles in this section, see p. 525

ACKNOWLEDGEMENTS

'Heatherdown' © Alexander Cockburn 1985, from *Grand Street*. 'Home Town' © Alexander Cockburn 1985, from *Atlantic Monthly*. Introduction to *Beat the Devil* © Chatto & Windus 1985, reprinted by their permission. 'The Scoutmaster' © Alexander Cockburn 1986, from *The Nation*. 'The Secret Agent' © *American Film Institute* 1987, reprinted by their permission. 'The Underclass' © Alexander Cockburn and James Ridgeway 1982, from *Village Voice*, reprinted by permission James Ridgeway. 'Edward James: At Home in Xilitla' © Alexander Cockburn 1987, from *House and Garden*. 'Culinary Conquests' © Alexander Cockburn 1985, from *House and Garden*. 'Seint's Sanctuary' © Alexander Cockburn 1985, from *House and Garden*. 'Assault on Miami's Virtues' © Alexander Cockburn 1982, from *Village Voice*. 'The Circulation of Commodities' © *American Film Institute* 1986, reprinted by their permission. 'Militarizing the Tortugas © *Wall Street Journal* 1986, reprinted by their permission. 'Battleship America' © Alexander Cockburn 1983, from *Vanity Fair*. 'Top Gun' © *American Film Institute* 1986, reprinted by their permission. 'The Truth About the Blue Lagoon' © Alexander Cockburn and James Ridgeway 1982, from *Village Voice*, reprinted by permission James Ridgeway. 'How to Be a Foreign Correspondent' © Alexander Cockburn 1976, from *More*. 'The Pundit' © Alexander Cockburn 1980, from *Harpers*. 'The Tedium Twins' © Alexander Cockburn 1982, from *Harpers*. 'Vagabonds and Outlaws' © Alexander Cockburn 1981, from *Harpers*. 'Blood and Ink' © Alexander Cockburn 1981, from *Harpers*. 'The Boss' © Alexander Cockburn 1982, from *Grand Street*. 'Prizes' © *Wall Street Journal* 1984, reprinted by their permission.

'P.G. Wodehouse: The Road to Long Island', 'The History of Mr P', 'Gastro-Porn' and 'The Need to Tell: The Psychopathology of Journalism': Reprinted with permission from *The New York Review of Books*. Copyright 1975-82, Nyrev, Inc.

The material in Part II, An Archive of the Reagan Era, 1976-1988, is from *Village Voice* © Alexander Cockburn; *The Nation* © Alexander

Cockburn; *The Wall Street Journal* © and reprinted by their permission; *Mother Jones* © Alexander Cockburn; *House and Garden* © Alexander Cockburn; syndicated column distributed by *L.A. Weekly* © Alexander Cockburn; *Zeta* © Alexander Cockburn; *Interview* © Alexander Cockburn; *New Statesman* © Alexander Cockburn. The following are exceptions: 'Reagan in New Hampshire', 'Reagan in Detroit', 'Bring Back Prohibition', 'Interview with Israel Shahak' and 'The Death of Herman Kahn' © Alexander Cockburn and James Ridgeway, from *Village Voice*, reprinted by permission James Ridgeway. 'The Left, the Democrats and 1984' © *The Nation*, reprinted by permission *The Nation* and Andrew Kopkind.

Where appropriate in terms of historical and stylistic congruity, I have made minor emendations to the text and sometimes shortened the material in the interest of brevity. Very occasionally I have restored material deleted from the previously published version.

It would be less than gallant to omit a final work of gratitude to all the editors, copy editors, researchers, typesetters, designers, photographers, receptionists and accounting departments I have worked with down the years and who are for me the people who give meaning to the phrase *esprit de corps.*

INTRODUCTION

I came to the United States in June of 1972, the month Nixon's burglars broke into the Watergate. Fifteen years later I was assembling this collection as Colonel North lectured Congress about the role of executive power in the Iran-Contra scandal. Looking at North's cocksure, edgy, ingratiating profile I was reminded of his precursor: the 'can do' guy in Nixon's White House, Gordon Liddy. The contrast was a good measure of the political and social distance the country had traveled between the two scandals.

Liddy, endlessly testing his 'will' and firing himself up with Nietzschean vitamins, had the beleaguered paranoia of a sworn foe of the sixties counter-culture. Bad fellow though Liddy was, there was always an element of Inspector Clouseau about him. He held his hand over a candle to prove his fortitude against pain, and when the time came, he stood by the 'can do' guy's code of *omerta* and served his time in Danbury federal penitentiary without a whimper.

Back in the Watergate hearings you could look at the burglars, at their sponsors in the White House, at Nixon himself and see that despite noises of defiance and protestations of innocence they knew they had been caught on the wrong side of the law and, though they would do their utmost to keep clear of the slammer, it would not come as a shock to them if the slammer was where they finally ended up.

North was as true a memento of the Reagan era as Liddy was of that earlier time. North had Reagan's own capacity for the vibrant lie, uttered with such conviction that it was evident how formidable psychic mechanisms of self-validation, in the very instant of the lie's utterance, convinced the liar – Reagan, North – that what he was saying was true. But if Liddy embodied the spirit of fascism at the level of *grand guignol*, North had the aroma of the real thing, eighties all-American style: absolute moral assurance that his lawlessness was lawful; that though he was there to 'get things done', he was following orders; that all impediments in his path, legal or moral, were obstructions erected by a hostile conspiracy.

North proclaimed that he had been ready to take the fall, just as Liddy had been ready fifteen years before. But North, unlike Liddy, lost his taste for martyrdom as soon as he saw it might involve criminal indictment, and forthrightly confessed as much to Congress. Arrogant to the largely deferential senators and representatives on the Congressional committee, North and his associates entertained thoughts of the slammer only in the outrage they genuinely felt at the thought that anyone might think the slammer an appropriate place for them to be. Liddy bore marks of a losing fight with the counter-culture. North had the jaunty physical and spiritual mien of a man to whom the culture had, for the preceding decade, been a friend.

The texture of the political and journalistic culture and how that culture has changed between the two scandals is one of the prime themes in this collection which, so far as America is concerned, takes as its point of departure the intimations of the Reagan era in the mid-1970s. Here was a moment rich in opportunity for a journalist to get everything wrong. A president had been driven from office and the mainstream press was preening itself on its resourceful vigilance and investigative powers. The covert activities of the CIA were under congressional scrutiny. Liberals and even radicals in the United States could gesture towards avenues of social progress beckoning the incoming Carter administration.

This, after all, was a period when a bill to break up the oil companies was only narrowly defeated in the US Senate, when it seemed that legislation guaranteeing full employment would pass, along with laws making the Federal Reserve accountable to Congress, introducing progressive tax reform and a national health service and ratifying arms control agreements with the Soviet Union. It took about a year to scuttle these notions and by 1979 the spirit of liberal reform was dead in mainstream American politics. The mainstream press was Reagan's election agent and held true to that supportive role until over-extended lines of communication caused Reaganism, expressed in this instance as constitutional and bureaucratic coup d'état, to falter in November 1986.

This role of the press in articulating and hence validating the concepts and imagery of the Reagan era is the story of the second part of this book – an informal archive of those years, concluding with the campaign for the Democratic presidential nominations, the role of Jesse Jackson and the political character and psychological make-up of Michael Dukakis. In the section called 'Terms of the Trade' I deal in more discursive essays with the operating assumptions of the journalism business, the psychopathology of its practitioners and such totemic fixtures as the pundit, the foreign correspondent and the search for 'balance'.

Reaganism is shorthand for a particular culture of consumption, a reverie of militarism, of violence redeemed; of a manic, corrupted and malevolent idealism. The priorities of this culture at the directly political level were simple enough: the transfer of income from poor to rich, the expansion of war production and an 'activist' foreign policy, traditional in many ways but as Noam Chomsky has said, 'at an extreme end of the spectrum: intervention, subversion, aggression, international terrorism and general gangsterism and lawlessness, the essential content of the "Reagan doctrine"'. Beneath the political, at the level of everyday life, there were the trends and shifts that every journalist or historian tries to identify; the section called 'Tastes of the Times' contains work addressing itself to this theme.

I arrived in America in 1972, having spent the preceding 30 years of my life amid the relics of an empire corrupted far beyond the reach of the popular indignation that discomfitted Nixon and then Reagan. I came from a family whose earliest connection with America had been the brusque torching of the White House and Capitol by Admiral Sir George Cockburn in the War of 1812, and I spent some of my earliest years in a house, Myrtle Grove in Youghal, shadowed by souvenirs of the birth of that earlier empire and its engendering of the later one: four Irish yews under which, by tradition, Sir Walter Raleigh had sat and smoked his first pipe of the tobacco he brought back from Virginia.

The implied narrative of this collection is the journalist's background, the imperial myths that helped to shape him, the impulse to exile and his encounter with the Reagan era. The background, the myths and the impulse to exile form the first three sections of this book, whose overall architecture will, I hope, give some sense of the terms in which I have viewed my trade.

July, 1988

PART ONE

◆

Life Studies

DEEP
BACKGROUND

A childish soul not inoculated with compulsory
prayer is a soul open to any religious infection.

Heatherdown

One morning in Manhattan, when fall was still holding winter at bay, my daughter Daisy called from London in some excitement. The casting director for a TV movie had been holding some auditions in her school in Hammersmith; she and two schoolmates had been selected for major parts; filming would begin almost at once. Then my former wife came on the phone. She had read the script. Certain scenes could, in the hands of an unscrupulous director, exploit the thirteen-year-old child. Vigilance was necessary. Besides, there was the matter of what Daisy should be paid ...

A few days later Daisy called again to report. With the help of a lawyer, proper safeguards had been established and adequate sums guaranteed. It turned out that the director of *Secrets*, one in a series of films generically entitled *First Love*, was to be Gavin Millar. He had been at Oxford at the same time as I had and in my recollection had not seemed then to be an embryonic pornographer.

Daisy added that filming would start in ten days at a recently closed prep school near Ascot. My heart tripped. What was the name of the school? 'Hold on while I find the address.' The wind outside was stripping golden leaves off the trees in Central Park and I waited, foot poised on the threshold of memory. Daisy picked up the phone again. 'Heatherdown. It's called Heatherdown.' The past welcomed me in.

In the hard winter of 1947 we moved from London to County Cork, Ireland, and after several months my parents decided that I had better start going to some sort of local school. I would have been happy to go on spending my days playing with Doreen French, the sexton's daughter, and my evenings listening to my father read *Don Quixote*. I was shy and already felt awkward in Ireland, where social divisions were much more transparent than in London. To walk out of the gates of my grandparents' big house and walk along Main Street where the unemployed men lounged all day in front of Farrell's was bad enough. Staring idly at everything, they stared at

5

me too. School meant ridicule at closer quarters.

But my parents were adamant. I was seven and it was time to retrieve the education abandoned when we had left London. They proposed to send me to the Loretto Convent, a large red building overlooking Youghal Bay. My grandmother was horrified. The Loretto Convent was a Roman Catholic institution and we, as members of the Anglo-Irish class were, however notionally, Protestant.

My parents pointed out there was no Protestant school in Youghal. My grandmother was scarcely a bigot but in the late 1940s the gulf between Protestants and Catholics was still fixed and deep – as it is in our town no longer. Brought up in the government houses of varying British colonies from Jamaica to Hong Kong, she took certain social and religious proprieties absolutely for granted. She discovered that there was a tiny parochial school for Protestant children. It was about to close since attendance had just dropped below the quorum of seven children which the Church of Ireland reckoned as the minimum its budget would permit.

There had been, before the achievement of Irish independence, a substantial British garrison in Youghal. St. Mary's Church, whose ancient bell tower loomed behind the wall of my grandparents' equally ancient Tudor house, could hold a congregation of three thousand. Back at the turn of the century certain tradesmen, eager for the business of this garrison, had thought it opportune to convert to Protestantism. They changed ships on a falling tide. The garrison left in 1922 and a quarter of a century later we could see the descendants of the apostates, beached on the shoals of history. Their stores were ill favored by the overwhelmingly Catholic population of Youghal and they had the added misfortune, as members of the shrunken congregation of some sixty-odd souls attending St. Mary's, to have to endure the Reverend Watts's annual Christmas sermon. Peering down from his pulpit at the shopkeepers who were making a couple of shillings out of the Christmas buying spree, Watts would savagely denounce the gross commercialization of a holy festival celebrating the birth of the Savior. Then he took to attacking the atom bomb too and the shopkeepers saw their chance. They complained to the bishop and Watts was demoted and became curate of Watergrass Hill, a desolate hamlet twenty miles inland.

The shopkeepers had children, still officially within the Protestant fold, and these were the cannon fodder in my grandmother's campaign. Their parents were told firmly that attendance at the parochial school was essential. A few weeks later a donkey and trap, purchased by my grandmother, made its rounds, depositing me and my new companions at the parochial school, a grey stone building just down the road from the Loretto Convent. In the last months of my sojourn at the school workmen erected a little shrine across the street. There was a statue of the Virgin and under it some lines, the first of which read 'Dogma of the Ass'. The next line continued with '-umption of the Virgin Mary'. The shrine and plaque celebrated the dogma promulgated by Pope Pius XII in 1950, which asserted that Mary had been bodily assumed into the bosom of the heavenly father. We used to wonder what archaeologists of the future would make of the plaque, if it got broken and only the top line survived.

My grandmother rejoiced that I had been saved from priestcraft and the donkey groaned as he dragged us through the town. A few months later my parents bought a house of their own three miles from Youghal, a distance beyond the powers of the donkey. A new pony, trap and gardener's boy took me to school in the morning and then would return home. In late morning my mother would drive the trap in again for shopping and to take me home for lunch. The gardener's boy would drive me in again to school after lunch and at the end of the afternoon make the final trip to take me home once more. Blackie thus trotted or walked twenty-four miles a day. Once the gardener's boy forgot to fasten Blackie's reins to the bridle but buckled them to the shoulder collar instead. It made no difference to Blackie, who started, stopped and swerved left or right at all the proper points. A photograph of Main Street in Youghal in 1948 would have shown that eighty percent of all the transportation was horsedrawn. Fifteen years later the proportions were reversed. We got our first car in 1958 when I turned seventeen, got a license and was thus able to chauffeur our family into the twentieth century.

Secure from popish influence, my education did not noticeably improve. The problem was that though Rome was held at bay, the Irish state played an important part in our instruction. It was mandatory that we be taught Gaelic and much time was set aside for that purpose every day. Thus after two years I was the regional champion in Scripture knowledge and could say 'Shut the door' and some other useful phrases in Irish.

My parents pondered the alternatives. They could send me – over my grandmother's undoubted resistance – to the Christian Brothers school. Its reputation was bad aside from the brothers' savage recourse to the pandybat. Besides, it would be of little help in the overall strategic plan of my education, which was to get me into Oxford.

Though only recently disengaged from the Communist Party and still – as always – of stout radical beliefs, my father held true to his class origins in pondering the contours of his plan. The route march to Oxford or Cambridge was well established: at the age of eight the raw recruits would go to preparatory – or prep – schools and there obtain the rudiments of an education sufficient to get them, at the age of fourteen, into a 'public' (that is, private) school such as Eton, Harrow, Winchester, Westminster and so forth.

The alacrity with which parents of the recruits dispatched them from home at the age of eight has often been noted with bemused concern by foreigners. From that year forward the child would be at home for only four months in the year. Of course many parents are far happier to see the back of a son than they may care to admit and boarding school was as good an excuse as any. Besides, these schools allowed the recruits to the system to cluster with members of their own class rather than go to a local school where contact with the lower orders might be inevitable: in sum, these prep and public schools were – and are – the training camps in the long guerrilla war of British social relations.

The form was to put down your child for a prep school as soon as he entered the world. (Girls were less of a problem and might never, at least in those days, be put down for anything at all.) My parents and I had spent a portion of 1941, the year of my birth, sitting in St. John's Wood underground station as the German bombs and rockets rained down overhead. My father was on the Nazi blacklist and in the event of an invasion they certainly would have shot him if his plan to escape by boat to Ireland had failed. The British authorities, scarcely less hostile to Communists than to the Nazis – and in many cases more so – were vacillating on how to deal with Reds. At first they reckoned it best to draft them, sending them to the front and hope that the first Panzers they met would do their duty. But then, amid the stunning exhibitions of British military incompetence, it was feared that the Reds would foment discontent and even mutiny. In accord with this dogleg in government policy my father first got a set of peremptory call-up papers and then, almost at once, a countermanding set of instructions. Later a German V-2 rocket landed on our house and reduced it to rubble. Perhaps understandably my father had not got around to the business of putting me down for a prep school. One way or another it did not seem, in the early 1940s, that there would necessarily be prep schools to go to.

But of course the prep schools survived and the 'public' schools survived and the British class system survived. For that matter, many of those who had engineered the destruction of our house in Acacia Road survived too. My brother Andrew found one in Washington, D.C., in the late 1970s. He was called Dieter Schwebs. He had been one of the designers of the V-2 and had gone to work for the U.S. after the war. By the time Andrew met him, Schwebs was in the General Accounting Office, rootling out fraud and waste in the Defense Department. Andrew told him about our house and Schwebs was full of concern: 'Oh my heffens, nobody hurt I hope?'

I was nine, already one year late for prep school. It was July 1950 and the start of the school year was menacingly close. No suitable place willing to accept me had been found. Old friends to whom my father had not spoken in years were pressed into action and that filiation of patronage and mutual back-scratching called 'the old boy network' was shaken into action. One midsummer day my father dismounted from the bicycle he used to go into the town of Youghal to dispatch articles, make telephone calls and have pleasant conversations in one of Youghal's quiet, dark bars. 'Well, we've got you into Heatherdown. It's supposed to be one of the most exclusive and expensive prep schools in England. In a couple of weeks we'll take the boat train to London, and then go to Ascot and have a look at the school. If it seems alright we'll get the uniforms and so forth and you'll start there in mid-September.'

The inspection trip was pretty bad. There were no boys about, naturally, but the headmaster described the amenities with a relentless glee which was unnerving. He tried to show my father the cricket pitch, of which he was plainly very proud. My father, who had no views on cricket pitches, tried to offset his lack of interest or knowledge by asking to inspect the kitchens and dormitories. The headmaster, confronted with this aberrant scale of priorities, began to form what became an increasingly dubious opinion of our family's values. There followed an expensive trip to Gorringes, school outfitters, and I was fitted out in the black and red colors that were Heatherdown's motif.

On a grim September morning I stood on the platform at Waterloo Station. Prep schools were clustered thickly around Ascot, perhaps drawn by the magnet of Eton in nearby Windsor, and there was a rainbow of other school uniforms, of Earlywood, Scaitcliffe, Ludgrove and Lambrook. I kept my eyes alert for the red ties and caps of Heatherdown and soon saw these colors adorning a small boy who was sobbing quietly. His equally stricken mother made a lunge to cover his tear-stained face with kisses but he fought her off. Excessive displays of emotion by one's parents were a matter for great dread. In fact any display of originality or character by them, apart from a humdrum sort of parentness or hitting a six at the father's cricket match, was thought to be bad form. The train whistle sounded, my mother began some final gesture of valediction which seemed ominously tinged with sentiment. I scuttled into the same compartment as the sobbing child, the door slammed and we chugged into the home counties.

Daisy called. They had started filming and, 'Daddy, we've found your photograph.' Every boy leaving Heatherdown had his photograph taken. It was then framed and put up in the corridor outside the classrooms. There were all the boys who had ever been to the school, right back to Hely-Hutchinson, who had his photograph taken in 1914, which meant that he may just have escaped being killed on the Western Front by 1918. About a thousand boys had gone through Heatherdown since his time. In any given year about fifty-five noisy little creatures inhabited the place, along with masters, matron, maids and gardeners.

Daisy reported that my photograph was on the top row, near the music room. I could see in my mind's eye where it was. Next to me there was probably Miller-Mundy and next to him maybe Piggott-Brown or Legge-Bourke. Legge-Bourke's father was a Conservative member of Parliament who once flipped a coin at Prime Minister Attlee during question time, shouting 'Next record please.' By the time I reached Heatherdown the first postwar Labour government was slipping from power and no one at Heatherdown was particularly upset about this. Parents of boys at Heatherdown were very conservative; masters were very conservative and the boys were very conservative too. Word got around that my father was a Red. This was not quite as bad as being identified as Irish, even though I had no brogue. Six years after a war in which De Valera had kept Ireland neutral, feeling still ran high. In argument the ladder of escalation was soon well known to me: 'Cocky's Irish, Cocky's a dirty pig. . . . Cocky helped Hitler in the war. . .' and so on.

The Attlee government had just survived the election of 1950 but when another election loomed in 1951 excitement ran high. There were endless jocular references to groundnuts – the well-intentioned but ill-fated scheme of the Labour government to cultivate peanuts in west Africa, thus providing employment for the locals and nutrition for British schoolchildren. Cost overruns and mismanagement brought the scheme low and the word 'groundnuts' could be guaranteed to arouse derision at any Conservative gathering between the years 1949 and 1964.

The night of the 1951 election a large electoral map of the United Kingdom was placed on an easel in the doorway of our dormitory. As the results came in over the radio a master called Hall would color the relevant constituency blue in the event of a Conservative victory and an unpleasant puce if Labour won. Legge-Bourke was in our dormitory and we naturally rooted for his father Harry, who carried the Isle of Ely by about six thousand votes. When we awoke in the morning an extensive portion of the map was colored blue – some of this being because Conservatives tended to win the large rural constituencies. A rout of Labour and of socialism was proclaimed. Actually Labour won the popular vote by about a quarter of a million, but gerrymandering saw the Conservatives win a clear majority of twenty-six seats over Labour. Thus began thirteen years of Tory rule which lasted clear through the rest of my education and ended only in 1964, just after I had left Oxford. More people, nearly fourteen million, voted for Labour in 1951 than for any British political party before or since, though this was not at all the sense of the situation one got at Heatherdown.

The headmaster was very pleased. At that time the entirely groundless fear that the Labour Party would somehow attack private education was still very great. At each Labour Party conference the rhetorical thunder against it outstripped even the tremendous bellowing against 'tied cottages', the feudal system whereby farm workers dwelt in their cottages only at the pleasure of their employers and, at the end of a lifetime of ill-paid labor, were evicted to the local almshouse to make way for younger muscles.

Jokes about the Labour Party were a staple among boys and masters. I was a supporter of the Labour Party – partly because I had the reputation of being Red hellspawn to maintain and partly because it seemed sensible to oppose anything favored by most of the people at the school. But I felt – amid my support – the disappointment of a fan who knows that his team is making a bit of an ass of itself and that improvement is unlikely in the near future. The innate conservatism of British schoolboys in private institutions was always impressive. At my next school, sometime in the late fifties, there was a 'mock election.' My friend Freddy Fitzpayne ran as the Communist and got one vote. I ran as the Labour candidate and got one vote. The Scottish Nationalist got eighty-three and the Conservative ninety-five.

Fitzpayne and I represented that school in debates. Each team had its own topic on which it spoke throughout the debating tournament, no matter what the other team was talking about. Fitzpayne and I used to speak to the motion, Great Britain Must Leave NATO Now. When I sat down after proposing the motion, our opponent would rise and, depending on what school we happened to be debating, would reel off a speech about the monarchy, Scottish independence or, in the case of one debate with Dollar Academy, a spirited defense of some controversial form of pig breeding. Fitzpayne and I got as far as the semifinals with our seditious topic before losing to some polished orators from Edinburgh Academy. We were photographed in the local Blairgowrie paper toasting each other with pints of beer and narrowly escaped being expelled.

The ground squelched wetly underfoot as I walked across Central Park, brooding about groundnuts, Heatherdown and the autumn reek of Berkshire bonfires. The idea of a quick return flight to yesterday, courtesy of trans-Atlantic standby, was growing on me. If the premise of the voyage was commonplace in one respect – to see how exactly the child had become father to the man – there would be the unusual twist of being there as father of the child.

Three days later I was standing on Waterloo platform, just as I had with my mother over thirty years before. Daisy had been nervous of the idea and I knew well her familiar fear: I would somehow make a fool of myself, embarrass her in front of her friends and the entire production crew of *Secrets*. She reminded me of the Poppy Day Affair, a tale I occasionally told to show what I had had to cope with when I had been a boy, worried, just like her, about the embarrassment parents can cause. Even now the memory causes me to sweat and stamp about a bit.

Back in the early 1950s Armistice Day – or Poppy Day – was taken a great deal more seriously than it is now. At precisely 11 A.M. there would be two minutes' silence in memory of those killed in the two Great Wars. The service in the little mock Tudor chapel at Heatherdown had an extra piquancy because the headmaster would bring in a small radio, just to make sure that we all fell silent at exactly 11 A.M. We didn't associate God with radios, machines that contradicted the high-toned nineteenth-century flavor of our Anglican observances, in which diction was so etherialized that very often it was hard to tell whether we were praying for peace or for good weather on the sports day coming up next week.

As we gathered in the chapel upstairs waiting for the Greenwich Mean Time pips, parents who had traveled to Heatherdown to take their children out for the afternoon would assemble downstairs in the headmaster's study. Since my parents lived in Ireland they rarely appeared. Other boys would occasionally invite me out for tea in Maidenhead, or to their homes if they lived relatively close by. These were the very early days of television and often the parents' idea of an uplifting yet amusing afternoon was to assemble in front of the TV on which the BBC would run a dignified Sunday afternoon quiz show called 'Twenty Questions.' The contestants were the usual British salad for such enterprises, containing a couple of academics, someone known to be waggish, and a socialite in relatively decent moral standing. At the beginning of each round a voice, audible to all but the participants, would give the answer. It was a deep voice, tranquil with the power of absolute knowledge, and it would intone, 'The answer is *porridge*; the answer is *porridge*.' I always thought the voice of God would sound like that; unruffled and awful as He asked me why I did not believe in Him unreservedly.

On Armistice Day in 1953 my father, in London on business, traveled down to Heatherdown to take me out. He arrived downstairs just as we heard the GMT signal on the radio and fell silent. Obliged to remember and revere the fallen in war, I would think of my Uncle Teeny who had died of malaria in Italy in 1944. I had never known him but I would do my best to imagine him fighting bravely; then, after about thirty seconds, I would just concentrate on dead British soldiers generally and say thank you. Along my pew, past Walduck who was fat and who claimed his family name was Valdrake and had come over with William and Mary, I could see out of the corner of my eye MacLean, whose father had been killed in the war. Each year, about fifty-five seconds after eleven, MacLean would start crying. I think he felt he had to. There were about six boys whose fathers had died in the war and usually they all cried, chins tucked in and shoulders shaking a little. Though 'blubbing' was normally despised, it was regarded as fine for MacLean and the others to cry on this particular occasion.

A few minutes later the service was over and I went downstairs to meet my father. He lost no time in hurrying me into an ancient taxi waiting outside and we rattled off to Great Fosters, a ghastly mock-Tudor establishment not far off, where we would while away the rest of the day. Even before we got into the taxi my father seemed to have a furtive, slightly hangdog air. Other parents seemed to be glaring at him. I surmised with a sinking heart that he had somehow attracted unwelcome attention – not perhaps as bad as the times he would barrack the actors in London theaters ('Perfectly sound tradition; Elizabethans did it all the time') but still alarming.

In the taxi he confessed all. He had arrived at about ten to eleven and had joined the other parents in the headmaster's study. 'The conversation was a bit stilted and after a bit I thought I would try to jolly things along by telling them a couple of funny stories.' My father was a very good storyteller, throwing himself into the anecdotes, which were often long. He used florid motions of his hands to accentuate important turns in the narrative. 'After a bit,' he continued, 'I noticed that the other people didn't seem to be following my story with any enthusiasm. When I got to the punch line they were all looking down and no one laughed at all.'

'Oh Daddy, you *didn't!*'

'I'm afraid so.' So he had told jokes all the way through the two-minute silence – a silence no other parent would break even in order to ask him to shut up, and meanwhile MacLean and the others were weeping upstairs. Most of the parents knew by now that Cockburn's father, Claud, was some sort of a Red and here were their darkest fears confirmed, with the scoundrel polluting the memory of the dead with his foul banter.

The train ambled along and the conductor cried, 'Next stop Ascot!' The station looked relatively unchanged. On the far side of the main London road was Ascot race course. Ascot race week loomed large on the school calendar. Fathers, magnificently arrayed in morning coats and top hats, mothers with amazing summer confections on their heads, would arrive to take children for picnics of cold salmon and strawberries in the enclosure. All morning long on the Saturday of the big weekend we could see those great summer hats of the women as they drove in open cars to the race course a couple of miles up the road.

But now it was October, the track was bare and the enclosure empty. My taxi driver said that he had heard that Heatherdown was to be sold for real-estate development once the film crew had gone. The driveway, fringed with fateful rhododendrons, looked much the same and at last I entered the front door. Heatherdown had actually been built as a school just before the First World War, unlike many of the prep schools round about which were simply converted Victorian country houses with maids' rooms converted into diminutive dormitories. All such schools were divided into the boys' zone of activity – classrooms, dormitories and the like – and the headmaster's private quarters. The room of concern to us was the headmaster's study, thickly carpeted, fragrant with tobacco and terror. It was here that we were summoned for interrogation and punishment. In exact evocation of Freud's essay on *Haemlichkeit* – 'homeliness' with a sinister and uncanny core – the study was both the closest echo of distant home and a parent's love but also the Colosseum for the unleashed superego. My own father never beat me. The closest he ever got to it was saying once that had any other father endured such injury (I had let down the tires of his bicycle to stop him from going into town one evening), this other father would have thrashed his son savagely. But here, hundreds of miles from the security of my own father's study, was this ersatz study, inhabited by the father-substitute who did indeed – on a few occasions – beat me with a clothes brush, once for repeatedly trying to conceal from Matron the fact that I had again wet my bed.

It was here too that the headmaster – a bouncy, bantam cock of a man called Charles Warner – interrogated me fiercely about the reason for my father's lateness in paying the hefty school bills. I knew the reason: not enough money. But this seemed a humiliating confession and I blubbed copiously as Warner plowed on remorselessly about the need for financial promptness. At least he didn't beat me for that, unlike Mr. Squeers in *Nicholas Nickleby*: 'I have had disappointments to contend against,' said Squeers, looking very grim, 'Bolder's father was two pound ten short. Where is Bolder?' 'Here he is, please Sir,' rejoined twenty officious voices. Boys are very like men to be sure. 'Come here, Bolder,' said Squeers. An unhealthy-looking boy, with warts all over his hands, stepped from his place to the master's desk, and raised his eyes imploringly to Squeers's face; his own quite white from the rapid beating of his heart. ...'

When I read accounts of the early explorers surrounded by natives who 'seemed friendly' but who suddenly 'attacked without warning,' I know just how those natives felt and I sympathize with them. To this day I have only to hear the words 'X wants to see you in his office' to be thrown into the state of hatred and fear with which I used to approach Warner's study, knock on his door and hear that falsely jocose voice cry, 'Come in.' Sometimes as I entered to my doom his wife, Patsy, used to scuttle out, giving me a cheery Hello, though she and I both knew the sombre nature of the occasion.

This fear and hatred has colored my relationship with authority, both privately and officially vested, and I count it as one of the major consequences of my education, just as my father's Micawberish struggle, pursued with heroic tenacity to virtually the very moment he died – he dictated to my mother a column for the *Irish Times* almost with his last breath – to keep clear of financial disaster greatly conditioned my attitude to credit.

Early in life in Ireland I learned to appreciate the color of the envelopes containing the day's mail. White envelopes were good. Brown ones weren't and my father would leave them up on the mantelpiece unopened. Over the months they would gradually get demoted from this high station to his study and then to the bottom drawer of a desk in his study. We would all laugh heartily over the form letter to creditors my father threatened to send: 'Dear Sir, I am in receipt of your fourth communication regarding my outstanding account. Let me explain how I pay my bills. I throw them all into a large basket. Each year I stir the basket with a stick, take out four bills and pay them. One more letter from you and you're out of the game.'

The whole school seemed silent as I walked towards Warner's study. Presumably they were filming elsewhere. I pushed open the door of his study. It was bare. Two film electricians were sitting on milk crates, drinking out of beer bottles. They said that the company was having lunch in the canteen out back.

I wandered upstairs and found myself facing the door of the school chapel. It used to have a thick curtain in front of it, as if to separate spiritual affairs from the coarse business of an English prep school. The curtain was gone and the door was ajar. Here I had begun my career as a choirboy, nicely done up in a sort of long red tunic and white surplice. I had a reedy alto. As the years progressed I rose to become a bass in the choir in Glenalmond – my public school. Thus, from the age of nine to the age of eighteen, my schoolmates and I had about thirty minutes of prayer each morning and each night – about three hundred hours of public worship a year. On Sundays, at Glenalmond, we had at least an hour each of matins and evensong. During these prayer-choked years I acquired an extensive knowledge of Scripture, of the Book of Common Prayer and of *Hymns Ancient and Modern.* It is one of the reasons I favor compulsory prayer at schools. A childish soul not inoculated with compulsory prayer is a soul open to any religious infection. At the end of my compulsory religious observances I was a thoroughgoing atheist, with a sufficient knowledge of Scripture to combat the faithful.

There was a hymnal still in one of the pews and I leafed through it. 'As pants the hart for cooling stream/When heated in the chase ...' This had always been popular, owing to the fervor with which one could hit the D in 'cooo-ling.' 'Eternal Father strong to save ...' wasn't bad either, with its mournful call to the Almighty: 'Oh hear us when we cry to thee/For those in peril on the sea.' But the big hit each term was undoubtedly 'Onward, Christian Soldiers,' with Sir Arthur Sullivan's pugnacious tune. 'At the sound of triumph,' we sang vaingloriously, 'Satan's host doth flee;/On then, Christian so-o-oldiers,/On to victoreee!' The general religious line at Heatherdown was that Victory was more or less assured for one, unless very serious blunders let Satan squeeze in under the door. We did not spend much time worrying about damnation, except after a serious bout of cursing God's name on a dare to see what would happen. I had once got a tummy ache after cursing God and believed in Him for at least a week. I went on leafing through the hymnal. Here was a particularly chipper one, 'All things bright and beautiful,' with its reassuring verse – omitted from most American hymnals, as I later discovered:

> The rich man in his castle,
> The poor man at his gate,
> God made them high and lowly,
> He ordered their estate.

The class system was never far away. My father said that his own radical beliefs had come as much from the words of the Magnificat as from the works of Marx and Lenin. You could see why. Even when chanted dolefully as a canticle the words carried a serious charge:

> He hath scattered the proud in the imagination
>   of their hearts;
> He hath put down the mighty from their seat
> And hath exalted the humble and meek;
> He hath filled the hungry with good things
> And the rich he hath sent empty away.

At Heatherdown Christ was depicted as a limp-wristed pre-Raphaelite with tepid social democratic convictions, urging a better world but shunning any robust means to achieve it. Habituated to this version of Christ, I was startled at Glenalmond when the Bishop of Dundee, preaching for an hour one Sunday evening, reported on his own personal conversations with Christ from which it had emerged that He had powerful revolutionary views. 'He meant what He said,' the Bishop roared. 'The furrrst sh-aall be last, and the last sha-all be furrst!' I was all for this in principle, though the town boys – who presumably would go to the front of the line while I dropped back – frightened me greatly.

I went downstairs and found Daisy and the others in the canteen, which had once been the carpentry shop. I had half-expected coarse film hands, rabid with cocaine and intent on debauching the girls temporarily at their mercy. To the contrary, they seemed a proper and restrained lot. To make up for lost school time a teacher had been imported and she would barely allow Daisy to talk to me before hurrying her away to her books. Daisy quickly steered me back to the main school building, along a corridor, and then pointed up. There I was in my farewell school photograph, looking rather like Daisy and exactly the same age as she was now. My eye wandered along the row: Piggott-Brown, who later founded a fashionable clothes store called Browns in South Moulton St., Walduck, Cordy-

Simpson, Miller-Mundy, Lycett-Green. I gazed along the corridor and saw another, slightly less familiar face; that of Sebastian Yorke, Daisy's mother's first husband, who had gone to Heatherdown some five years before me.

Daisy was full of gossip about the school. It had closed very suddenly. Boys going home for the summer holidays had fully expected to return. Mr. Edwards, who had taken over from Warner, had suddenly decided to sell up. A rescue bid mounted by another master and parents had only just failed. Now local real-estate interests were about to take over and had already announced the school's closure. Heatherdown would cease to exist – unless perhaps as a private nursing home. The photographs – the institutional record, as it were – would be thrown on the garbage heap.

It was the work of a moment to take my own photograph down, along with Sebastian's and one of the art dealer and historian Ian Dunlop, of whom I had no memory at Heatherdown but who was a friend of mine in New York. 'Daisy to make-up,' a voice shouted and she hurried away. I wandered along the corridor. A cupboard door was ajar and I peered in. The books were large and dusty and after a moment I realized with a shock that I was looking at the collective sporting memory of Heatherdown across half a century: the detailed record of every game of cricket played by Heatherdown's First Eleven between 1952 and 1978. The records of soccer and rugby went back to 1935.

I pulled out *The Unrivalled Cricket Scoring Book* covering the years 1952 to 1956. A note on the cover said that Heatherdown had played 52, won 22, lost 11 and drawn 19. I opened it and stared down at two pages detailing a game played between Heatherdown and Ludgrove on June 26, 1954. Ludgrove had won easily, by eight wickets. I remembered the game vividly. Ludgrove had a very fast bowler. Here he was in the book – Jefferson. He was vast and hurled the cricket ball down the pitch with horrifying speed. Our champions went out to bat and trailed back almost at once, out for 0, a 'duck.' Then our captain, Watson. Out for a duck too. I was last man in, and walked out slowly. There was a thunder of Jefferson's feet, a hard object swooped like a swallow down the pitch, hit my bat and spun away. 'Run,' screamed Lawson-Smith from the other end and I scampered to the other wicket and safety. Lawson-Smith was out next ball. Here it all was in the book, Cockburn 1 not out; Heatherdown all out for nineteen. 'Lost by 8 wickets,' Warner's notation across the page said gloomily.

The Queen's second son, Andrew, had gone to Heatherdown in the early 1970s and I turned to the score book covering 1971 to 1974 to see how he had done. The prince, flanked in the First Eleven by such revered names in British financial history as Hambro and Kleinwort, seems to have had his best game against Scaitcliffe on 19 May, 1973, when he had bowled and got three wickets at a cost of fourteen runs. But in a needle game against Ludgrove on 7 June of the same year he was bowled by Agar for a duck and Ludgrove won by four runs. I dare say the memory haunts him to this day, and – should he ever assume the throne – will no doubt affect his overall performance. I found his brother, Prince Edward, battling for Heatherdown four years later. He doesn't seem to have done much better.

I turned to the book filled with soccer and rugby scores. Warner had started filling in the exercise book in 1935. His writing did not change in over thirty years. His last entry was for 1965 at which point he must have dropped dead, because another, more childish hand starts with the Michaelmas term of that year. I was good at rugby football, being left-footed and thus having an inbuilt advantage if I played in the position known as 'hooker.' Here was our great season – the Lent term of 1954 – when we lost only one game. Because I had this aptitude for being a hooker in the 'scrum' I could be regarded as 'good at games,' which was a great help at school. At my next school it meant that every other week we got in a bus and went off to Edinburgh or Aberdeen to play. At the age of eighteen I stopped playing rugby, stopped hunting at home in Ireland and never took any exercise ever again. It is as though, having had cold baths and gone for early morning runs for nearly ten years, one has paid in advance the physical rent check for the next thirty years.

Daisy came back from make-up in the school uniform called for in the script. It slightly reminded me of the uniform worn by the girls at Heath-field, a well-known prep school for girls right next door. My aunt had gone there in the early part of the century and almost the only other fact I knew about it was that David Niven had been expelled from Heatherdown – or said he had – for climbing over the Heathfield wall to steal a cabbage out of its garden. It seemed an odd piece of flora for a person who relished the reputation of a lady's man to pride himself on having stolen. I suppose he thought that no one would believe him if he had claimed to have taken a rose. Heatherdown had absolutely no contact with Heathfield all those years I was there. Our school was very definitely in the non-coed tradition, holding to the view that juxtaposition of the sexes would lead instantly to debauch. Aside from the Heathfield peril, women were successfully kept at bay. Heatherdown was not as purely masculine as Mount Athos. There were Patsy Warner and Matron, a steely creature who maintained an insensate interest in our bodily functions but who – perhaps for reasons of what Herbert Marcuse later called repressive desublimation (rare was the week in which she did not seize my private parts in a chill grip as part of some diagnostic test) – did not inflame our imaginations. There were the older sisters who came and were ogled on Visitors' Day, and that was about it.

Daisy reported that Gavin Millar had agreed that I could watch a scene being shot and that although my presence might make her feel awkward she did not really mind. I followed her up to the old school library, where the technicians were setting up the next scene.

I had read the script of *Secrets.* It was about bonding rituals among teenage girls, and a great many scenes consisted of Daisy and a couple of her schoolmates parodying Masonic rituals. The scene in preparation was simple enough. It involved the same girls making moderate nuisances of themselves during a Latin class. I waited, eyeing the film crew. As always with movies, the setup went on interminably, and my attention wandered to the shelves of the library. The books seemed to be mostly the same as in my day: G.A. Henty, W.E. Johns, Baroness Orczy, W.W. Jacobs, Sapper, Jules Verne, John Buchan, P.G. Wodehouse, and for more sophisticated tastes, Nevil Shute and A.J. Cronin.

So far as politics goes these authors were all stoutly counter-revolutionary, whether it was some lad in Henty trying to thwart the Indian Mutiny, a Buchan hero heading off a black nationalist upsurge in *Prester John* or Bulldog Drummond and his 'Black Gang' murdering Bolsheviks. Drummond could break a chap's neck like a twig and laugh while doing it. He dropped Henry Lakington into an acid bath, telling him as he did so that 'the retribution is just.' No author in our library had much time for the French Revolution or for Napoleon. Henty did not care for them and neither did C.S. Forester. The Scarlet Pimpernel devoted his entire professional life – if 'professional' could be linked to so quintessential an amateur as Sir Percy, who yawned a lot and laughed down from under lazy eyelids – to the outwitting of the Committee of Public Safety and the stalwart revolutionary M. Chauvelin. And then there was Dickens too, with *A Tale of Two Cities* and the great sacrifice of Sidney Carton. In my case this ideological saturation bombing did not have much effect. One did a form of double-entry political bookkeeping – hoping for the victory of Sir Percy, Hornblower, Hannay or whoever, while simultaneously approving the deeds of St. Just, Danton, or Napoleon.

And of course the library permitted us to seek in literary guise the woman we were denied in bodily form. In Henty and Verne, women barely existed. Orczy tried harder. Sir Percy Blakeney concealed beneath his foppish nonchalance the tenderest emotions towards the Lady Marguerite and would, after she had swept away, lower his lips to the stone balustrade and stair where her hand and foot had rested but a moment before. In Sapper and Buchan women had literary utility as good little troopers – like Matron, only younger. The moment of greatest sexual tension in Buchan is when Hannay realizes from the effeminate nature of the furniture that Von Stumm is homosexual ('I was reminded of certain practices not unknown in the German General Staff') and, in a panic bordering on hysteria, knocks him down.

Nevil Shute and H.E. Bates, powerfully represented in the school library, permitted certain intimacies. There was a strong scene in the latter's *The Purple Plain* in which the hero nearly persuades the Burmese girl Anna to bathe naked with him. In the end after many sufferings he gets into bed with her, with the imprimatur of Mrs. McNab. I wandered along the shelves and found the book – no doubt the same one I fingered excitedly thirty years before. Here it was: 'Go in and lie down and sleep with her. Nothing will be said in this house about that sort of sleep together.' *What* sort of sleep? I spent a lot of time puzzling about this. Couples in those sorts of books used to embrace, then there would be some tactful punctuation and then, 'Hours later they awoke.' I used to think sex and sleep were indivisible, just as everyone at my next school thought that one's virginity would expire just as soon as one contrived to be alone with a French girl. Words would be unnecessary, given the torrid and impulsive morals of these women, though just to be on the safe side we would complacently rehearse the words *Voulez-vous coucher avec moi.* It was curious, in the late sixties, to meet French adolescents rushing eagerly the other way, certain that Swinging London would be the answer to their problems.

It's hard to know where these illusions about French morals started. There was the French kiss and the French letter. Brothels were legal over there too. In Ireland there were no legal brothels, no legal French letters and the rules of censorship prevailing at that time did not permit French kissing in films. The great heads on the screen of Horgan's cinema would approach with lips puckered and then suddenly spring apart, lips relaxing after raptures excised by the scissors of the Catholic hierarchy. It was all very frustrating and I would retire to the adventures of my great hero, the shy, brilliant, and – to women – irresistibly attractive Horatio Hornblower. Who could forget the long-delayed embrace with Lady Barbara Leighton in *Beat to Quarters* or the spasm of passion with the Vicomtesse Marie de Graçay in *Flying Colors*? There were three copies of this book still on the Heatherdown shelves and soon I found the well-worn page: 'It was madness to yield to the torrent of impulses let loose, but madness was somehow sweet. They were inside the room now, and the door was closed, There was sweet, healthy, satisfying flesh in his arms. There were no doubts, no uncertainties; no mystic speculation. Now blind instinct could take charge, all the bodily urges of months of celibacy. Her lips were ripe and rich and ready, the breasts which he crushed against him were hillocks of sweetness. ... Just as another man might have given way to drink ... so Hornblower numbed his own brain with lust and passion.' C.S. Forester wasn't much given to this sort of thing, but he knew how to lay it on when he had to.

Sex was mostly literary at Heatherdown. Homosexuality, at least in my cohort, was unknown. My own psychosexual development was erratic. I liked to dress up in the holidays and would occasionally come down to dinner in long dress and carefully applied make-up. Years later David McEwen described to me the scene in some grim Scottish fortress when the son and heir of the house, then in his twenties, swept into dinner in long dress and white gloves. The aged butler muttered apologetically into the ear of the stricken father, 'It's no' what I laid oot for him, my lorrrd.'

Whatever unease my parents may have felt at such appearances would, had they known of it, been balanced by the news of my engagement to Adrienne Hamilton. At the age of ten I proposed and was accepted in the course of a stay with Adrienne at Blarney Castle, owned at the time by her mother. Next term at Heatherdown Adrienne's cousin Henry Combe made a laughing stock out of me by publicizing the fact that I was 'in love' with Adrienne. This was thought to be very ridiculous. Our engagement was cancelled. I never forgave her for the betrayal and the experience no doubt has powerfully colored my relations with women ever since. When next I met her, thirty years later in New York, she laughed prettily when I reminded her of her treachery. No matter. They laughed lightly at the Count of Monte Cristo too, when he reminded them of a long-forgotten fellow called Dantès.

I put down the Hornblower. By now the technicians had set up the scene. My daughter was sitting more or less exactly in the position that I was long ago when Warner had announced that all boys in the school – some fifty-five – were doing well, except for one. This one was slacking. 'Cockburn,' Warner was a great finger-crooker, and his finger now crooked horribly. 'Come here, boy.' He had a habit of getting one by the short hairs right behind the ear and pulling up sharply. 'Some of us aren't working hard enough, are we?' Jerk. 'No, Sir.' 'Some of us are going to work harder, aren't we?' Another savage jerk. 'Yes, Sir.' A final jerk and Cockburn, blubbing with pain and humiliation, stumbled back to his place.

Gavin Millar kindly gave me a script. 'Miss Johnson' is teaching a Latin class and the girls are not behaving. Millar cries 'Action' and the girls, Daisy included, start making furtive animal noises. Amid their snickers Miss Johnson tries doggedly to explain the structure and importance of the Latin grammatical construction known as the ablative absolute. Finally, peering irritably at one fractious girl, she says with heavy sarcasm, 'Louise having been blessed with such talent, we don't have to bother to teach her,' and goes on to outline the benefits of a classical education. 'Ablative absolutes could be the key to your whole future. Think about it, Louise.' Louise tries to look thoughtful and Millar says, 'Cut.'

Could it be that my classical education, commenced at Heatherdown, is at last going to be of some immediate, practical utility?

I raised my hand and saw, out of the corner of my eye, Daisy freeze with horror and embarrassment. It was clear to her that I was about to make a public ass of myself and, by extension, of her too.

'Gavin,' I said quietly, 'I don't suppose it matters, but your scriptwriter doesn't know Latin.' I saw a tough-looking young woman bridle at this and realized that Noella Smith, scriptwriter, was in the room. I pressed on. 'The clause "Louise having been blessed with such talent" is really in apposition to "her," which in turn is the object of "teach" – all of which makes it a participial accusative construction, not an ablative absolute. You could make it better by omitting the final "her," which would sequester the Louise clause as an ablative absolute.'

Millar recognized superior fire power and 'Miss Johnson' was instructed to drop the final 'her.' She kept forgetting and the scene was reshot five times. Millar pointed out the substantial sum my quibble had cost them. Daisy, having concluded that I had not made a major fool out of myself or her, hastened away to make-up and wardrobe, and the room emptied. Still pondering ablative absolutes, I looked along the library shelves till I found *Latin Course for Schools, Part One,* by L.A. Wilding, first published in 1949.

'The study of a foreign language,' wrote Mr. Wilding in his introduction, 'is an exciting matter; it is like a key that will open many doors. ... By a knowledge of Latin we are introduced to a great people, the Romans. The Romans led the world as men of action; they built good roads, made good laws, and organised what was in their time almost world-wide government and citizenship. At their best, too, they set the highest examples of honour, loyalty and self-sacrifice.'

I leafed through the book. Exercise 65: '"By means of justice and kindness Agricola wins over the natives of Britain." Translate.' This must be Tacitus. Tacitus, married to General Gnaeus Julius Agricola's daughter, wrote a toadying biography of his father-in-law. Wilding's textbook was strewn with what I could now see was heavy propaganda for the benefits of imperial conquest, whether Roman or British. Exercise 171: 'Render into Latin, "It is just," they say, "to surrender our city to the Romans: such men know how to keep faith even in war. They have conquered us, not by force, but by justice, and we and the Roman people will hand down a good example to the human race."' Exercise 65: 'Render into Latin: "By means of justice and kindness Agricola wins over the natives of Britain. He then hastens beyond Chester towards Scotland. He rouses his troops to battle and to victory. At first Agricola wastes the land, then he displays to the natives his moderation."'

It is summer in 1952 and Mr. Toppin has us penned in, even though the bell has gone for morning break. We are in Latin class and Mr. Toppin is trying to give us a sense of occasion. 'This is the speech of Calgacus to his troops before the battle at Graupian Hill in A.D. 84. Calgacus is the name Tacitus gives the Scottish general. *"Hodie pro patria adhuc libera ..."*

Cockburn? "Today ..."' 'Today you will fight for a country still free against the Romans. ...' 'Good. "*Patriam vestram in dextris vestris portatis*"?' 'You carry your country in your right hand. ...'

Wilding left it in no doubt, in his simplified and polite version of Tacitus, that the Roman victory at Mons Graupius was a good thing. Ten thousand Scots fell that day, the blood of kerns flowing in the heather near Inverness, not so far from where I was born. The Romans slaughtered till their arms were tired. Night, as Tacitus put it, was jubilant with triumph and plunder. The Scots, scattering amid the grief of men and women, abandoned their homes and set them on fire. The day after, bleak and wet, disclosed more fully the lineaments of triumph: silence everywhere, lonely hills, houses smoldering to heaven.

Resolute to favor Roman imperialism over British nationalism – Viking imperialism was a different matter – Wilding suppressed the eloquence of Calgacus's appeal to his troops, as conceived by Tacitus. Back in London the next day I looked it up in the Loeb translation: 'Here at the world's end, on its last inch of liberty, we have lived unmolested to this day. ...' Calgacus gestures down the hill to where the Romans – in actual fact Provençal French, Spaniards and Italians – stand with their German auxiliaries: 'Harriers of the world, now that earth fails their all-devastating hands – they probe even the sea: if their enemy have wealth, they have greed; if he be poor, they are ambitious; East nor West has glutted them; alone of mankind they behold with the same passion of concupiscence waste and want alike. To plunder, butcher, steal, these things they misname empire: they make a desolation and they call it peace.'

Ubi solitudinem faciunt, pacem appellant. They make a desolation and they call it peace. The phrase has echoed down the ages as the tersest condemnation of Rome. Nothing of this in Wilding.

Those were the days in the early 1950s when the British Empire was falling rapidly apart. On Sundays boys at Heatherdown had to write a weekly letter home ('Dear Mummy and Daddy, I am very well. How are you ...') and many of the envelopes at our school were addressed to army posts in Kenya, Malaya, Aden, Cyprus and other outposts of shriveling empire. At school I would hear grim tales of the Kenyan Mau Mau and then go home to hear my father consider such events in a very different way.

Both my father and I, forty years apart, studied classics. A significant portion of this study was spent considering the birth and practice of democracy in Athens in the fifth century B.C. It seemed to be the consensus of our teachers that between fifth-century Athens, the senate under the Roman Republic and nineteenth- and twentieth-century Westminster, nothing much of interest by way of political experiment had occurred, and that the virtues and glories of ancient Greece and modern Britain were essentially the same.

There was a problem, of course. One of the first words to be found in Wilding was '*servus*,' meaning 'slave.' In our Greek primer the word '*doulos*' soon obtruded itself. Our schoolmasters could not conceal from us that Athenian 'democracy' was practiced on the backs of hundreds and thousands of these *servi* or *douloi*. The fact of slavery was acknowledged, but with that acknowledgement the matter was closed. Thus the statement 'Athenian democracy was a great and noble achievement' was accompanied by the footnote, 'Athenian democracy was based on slavery.' But the footnote remained a footnote and two people being given a ruling-class education in Britain at either end of the first half of the twentieth century were taught that democratic achievement and slavery were not mutually contradictory. This sort of instruction was helpful if one was to continue to run the British Empire with a clear conscience. (Twentieth-century British classics teachers were not the only people to remain somewhat silent on the matter of slavery in the ancient world. The great classical historian G.E.M. de Ste. Croix has written that he knows 'of no general, outright condemnation of slavery inspired by a Christian outlook before the petition of the Mennonites in Germantown in Pennsylvania in 1668.')

I left the library and walked down to the old dining room, now changed by the set designers into a school laboratory. Daisy was hurrying through, on her way to another bout of tuition. At her London day school she had decided against Latin and in favor of German, despite some dutiful lectures from me on the merits, even if only from the vantage point of etymological comprehension, of a classical grounding. This was, for the second time in my life, my last day at school, though devoid of that immense spiritual and physical rapture connected to 'ends of term' back in the fifties. In those days I would go up to London on the school train and there be met by my father who would take me off to a treat, usually lunch at some restaurant such as Rules, Simpsons, or Chez Victor. Once we went out with Gilbert Harding, a noted radio 'personality' of the day. This 'personality' was of the choleric Englishman, perpetually raging against poor service and so forth. We were never able to get through lunch because Harding, in order to keep this income-yielding 'personality' at full stretch, would burst forth after about ten minutes with curses at management and waiters and we would have to leave. Then, later in the day, my father and I would board the boat train at Paddington in the company of about four thousand other Irish passengers. It was so crowded that once my father could not even get his hand into his upper pocket to get out a whiskey bottle and had to ask the man on his other side to help him.

In these more sophisticated times Daisy and I discussed our Christmas rendezvous in New York after her term was over. I had hoped to persuade the set photographer to take a picture of her standing in front of the same rhododendron bush as I, when I had my farewell photograph taken. But by now the novelty of the old-Heatherdown-boy-with-daughter-in-film was wearing off. I remembered how revisiting fathers, trying to find the initials they had carved in their school desks, had seemed vaguely ridiculous to us and decided not to outlast my welcome. The taxi took me off down the drive past the empty swimming pool, and I had carefully on my knee my old portrait, saved by my daughter from the wrecker's ball.

Grand Street, Summer, 1985

Home Town

Where are our missing twenty millions of Irish should be here today instead of four, our lost tribes? And our potteries and textiles, the finest in the whole world! And our wool that was sold in Rome in the time of Juvenal and our flax and our damask from the looms of Antrim and our Limerick lace, our tanneries and our white flint glass down there by Ballybough and our Huguenot poplin that we have since Jacquard de Lyon and our woven silk and our Foxford tweeds and ivory raised point from the Carmelite convent in New Ross, nothing like it in the whole wide world! Where are the Greek merchants that came through the pillars of Hercules, the Gibraltar now grabbed by the foe of mankind, with gold and Tyrian purple to sell in Wexford at the fair of Carmen? Read Tacitus and Ptolemy, even Giraldus Cambrensis. Wine, peltries, Connemara marble, silver from Tipperary, second to none, our far-famed horses even today, the Irish hobbies, with king Philip of Spain offering to pay customs duties for the right to fish in our waters. What do the yellow-johns of Anglia owe us for our ruined trade and our ruined hearths?

– James Joyce, Ulysses

Squeezed between the estuary of the Blackwater River and the steep hill behind, squeezed too – harshly so – by human decisions of more recent vintage, the town of Youghal, in County Cork, Ireland, advertises as succinctly as you might wish the facts of life in a poor country in the middle of this decade. There's no need to go below the fiftieth parallel to encounter what are often sedately described as 'problems of underdevelopment.'

It's not as though each time I go home there the place hastens to disclose the changes in its fortunes. Seen in the pale morning light from across the river, the quays and gray stone houses surely look much as they did to Sir Walter Raleigh, who was mayor of Youghal in 1588; to Cromwell, who made the town the base for his rampages in 1650; to Michael Collins, who sheltered near there during the Civil War of 1922. From the middle distance, at least, Irish towns like Youghal do not conspicuously display the fingerprints of change, which is no doubt why John

26

Huston and his film crew settled in Youghal for a few uproarious months in 1954 to re-create Melville's New Bedford for the film *Moby Dick*.

A 35-year-old photograph of North Main Street looks very much like a 75-year-old one of the same view, to either side of the great Clock Gate. When I was driven to parochial school in a trap in 1948, I can remember horse-drawn transportation outnumbered automobiles ten to one and knots of unemployed men lounged away their days in front of Farrell's grain store. But by the early 1960s the carts and traps were mostly gone and a prosperous Youghal was forced to import labor from the surrounding countryside. Amid the increasing (but still modest) affluence of Youghal's population of five thousand the town council faced a parking problem, and the odd BMW and even Mercedes announced the spending power and great expectations of a growing managerial class.

Today, a drive down North Main Street suggests that Youghal remains an emblem of this post-war boom, which, for Ireland, surged in the 1960s.

Just for an instant at the turn of this year Youghal seemed unchanged from those glory days. Home from abroad to visit the old place and the old folk, one is loath to dwell upon intimations of mortality creeping across the features of one's parents or one's town. But after a day I knew well enough that even if the three new little high-tech plants on the edge of town represented a reversal of the desperate crisis of four years ago, the situation was still pretty bad. 'Youghal's fighting back,' the locals said to me each day, but from the anxious way they put it I knew that for a time the place had been lying awfully still on the floor.

Enter Youghal along the Cork road from the west and you see on your left, just on the town's outskirts, the textile factory built in the 1940s to house Seafield Fabrics. There had been no substantial manufacturing employment in Youghal till it went up, just a poor retail economy – an economy that, after the British garrison had left, following the Treaty of 1921, had limped along on the tourists coming down in the summer from Cork and beyond to spend a day or a two-week vacation on the town's fine beaches.

'In 1946 I and some other young fellows agreed that we had our freedom, all right,' Paddy Linehan, owner of the Moby Dick saloon and one of Youghal's better-known citizens, remembers, 'but we didn't have freedom from want, from hunger, from unemployment, from malnutrition. There was tremendous emigration.' So he and his fellows hunted about to try to get some investment in their town. They found out that a Cork man called Bill Dwyer was looking for some land for his weaving factory, and they made sure that Youghal offered Dwyer a hearty welcome. Up went Seafield Fabrics, and a few years later Blackwater Cottons, its subsidiary, went up alongside it. By the mid-1960s the two plants were employing 600 people between them. An enterprise started in the center of town by John

Murray in the mid-1950s became the flourishing Youghal Carpets, employing 850 at its peak. Add in a work force of 120 at Murray's Kitchens and Youghal had nearly 1,500 manufacturing jobs for an employable 2,500 in the town. Small wonder that workers were being bused in from as far afield as the late Mayor Richard Daley's ancestral town of Dungarvan, fifteen miles east along the coast; that emigration came to a halt; and that, local history has it, there were only forty incorrigibly unemployed people in the whole place.

The Irish economy as a whole was changing gear from the protected, mostly agricultural system presided over by Eamon de Valera in the 1930s and 1940s. By the 1950s the long-range course was set: credits, tax breaks, and training grants to make Ireland alluring to foreign investors, particularly United States manufacturers looking for a base whence to attack European markets. From 1960 to 1973 manufactured exports increased fivefold and accounted for under half of all exports; by May of 1972 more than half the fixed assets of Ireland's industry and service firms were foreign-owned. So much for the nationalism of an earlier time: in the 1930s de Valera had put through a law limiting foreign ownership to 49 percent.

Those three high-tech firms, all of them U.S.-owned, came in 1981 as a glimmer of hope to a desperate town. For by then the town, like Ireland, was in deep trouble. Seafield had gone, along with Blackwater Cottons, and, worst of all, Youghal Carpets had closed down. The reasons were not hard to find; indeed, one of them nestled next to my neck after I bought a sweater in Merrick's clothing store. MADE IN MACAU, said the label. Youghal had got on the wrong end of what theorists of underdevelopment call the economics of comparative advantage – the comparative advantage of those sweater-makers in Macau being their ability to work for wages far lower than what the sad weavers and spinners of Youghal required to preserve life and limb. Youghal had got on the wrong end too of the consequences of free trade. Ireland's entry into the Common Market, in 1973, rendered the local factories vulnerable to competition. Describing the low productivity and slack practices of Seafield Fabrics, Paddy Linehan reached for an image of Babylonian luxury: 'They had *colored* toilet paper. It was like the Shah of Iran.'

'It's very bad,' said Tom O'Connell – or, in the Irish version of his name painted over the front of his shop, Tomas O'Conaill. Tom is on the left end of Youghal's political spectrum, a Labour town councillor, formerly in Sinn Fein. As we stood chatting by his shop counter, children and a surprising number of adults slipped in and out, buying tiny amounts of candy. Remembering how much candy the Irish eat, I joked to Tom that he must be getting a kickback from the local dentists. 'It's one of the few little luxuries people can afford,' he remarked. 'Meat once or twice a week, maybe. No vacations. Remember, we lost not just the jobs in the factories but as a result also about 75 percent of the service jobs, in the shops and pubs. You couldn't give a pub away today in Youghal. People are barely existing.'

A girl in her late teens, looking badly scared, came into the shop and muttered to Tom. He gave her a name and address and she trotted out, hauling her three-year-old after her. 'The ESB has just cut off her electricity,' Tom said, 'and she's trying to find someone from St. Vincent de Paul. A lot of people are depending on charity.' I could sympathize with the girl's problem with the Electricity Supply Board. Back in the 1960s, when the lights used to go off in our house outside Youghal, we used to run outdoors to see if there was a blackout at the Cunninghams' farm, half a mile away across the stream. If lights blazed at the Cunninghams', we knew the ESB was forcefully indicating its differences with us alone on the nature of consumer credit.

Over at the Allied Irish Bank I had another illustration of Ireland's woes, as graphic as the label from Macau. I wanted seventy-five Irish pounds – or punts, as they are properly called. The cashier worked out that to get this sum I needed to write a check for $77.96 on my own New York branch of the Allied. The two currencies are at par: one dollar gets you one punt, meaning that the punt has halved in value against the dollar in the past five years. This is very nice for a firm like Waterford Crystal, which exports to the United States, but not particularly helpful in paying dollar-denominated interest charges on Ireland's swag-bellied foreign debt. This debt in per capita terms is three times that of Mexico. In a leap familiar throughout the Third World it has gone from $161 million in 1970 to about $8 billion – more than half the country's GNP – in 1984.

In absolute terms, of course, this sum doesn't look so huge these days, and international bankers and kindred purse-string minders seem to take a benign view of Ireland. 'You Irish have got the economy of Jamaica and the credit rating of Holland,' one such banker once remarked to a friend of mine, by which I suppose he meant that the all-important though unstated bottom line is that Ireland is white, English-speaking, and part of European culture. Bankers wouldn't admit it publicly, but they associate profligacy and possible default or debt repudiation with banana- rather than potato-eating republics.

After a doleful chat with local bankers about high taxes, low land prices, and 17¼ percent interest rates on personal overdrafts, I headed off to see some of the few rays of light amid the darkness – salvation dressed as high tech.

Paddy Linehan says that when he became chairman of the Youghal Council, in 1980, he held an all-night prayer vigil on June 21 of that year. By May of 1981 three U.S.-owned firms were committed to setting up shop in Youghal. It's the kind of employment people mean when they use words like *post-industrial.* Doret and Bryant, the two factories alongside the main road to Waterford, just outside town, are small and clean and don't have smoke hanging over them. They make 'documentation products' and rubber mouldings and employ about thirty people each.

Inside another tidy factory, looking like a health clinic up on top of Cork Hill, is Power Products, which employs 120 people in the manufacture of power converters for electronic equipment. Its parent company is in Fort Lauderdale, and it has a brisk thirty-five-year-old Irishman named Barry Kelleher as managing director.

It may be that in the wake of the Linehan-led prayers God was the ultimate sponsor of high tech's arrival in Youghal, but Kelleher's account of why the men in Fort Lauderdale decided to set up an operation in Ireland left me in little doubt as to the executive agent. To firms like Power Products the Irish people, in the form of their vested instrument the Industrial Development Authority (IDA), offer 45 percent of the cost of setting up shop and also basic-training costs (including trips to the United States) and a waiver of corporate taxes on profits generated by exports. The gamble, as the economist Jeff Frieden describes it in his forthcoming survey of the Irish predicament, is with money borrowed abroad to give to the IDA, which in turn gives it to industrialists. The gamble may eventually pay off in cash terms by indirectly increasing government tax receipts from an enlarged wage bill, and it may pay off in balance-of-payments terms by increasing Irish exports. A further incentive to U.S. investors is that the Irish education system offers a bountiful supply of technically well-trained graduates prepared to start off at $10,000 a year, less than half the opening price for their American equivalents. From Youghal the U.S. firm has a springboard into European markets, without the ball and chain of the strong-dollar costs of a purely domestic U.S. operation. And none of the software and manuals generated in the United States has to be translated.

There's a catch of sorts, at least as far as any thirty-five- or forty-year-old person who used to work at Youghal Carpets, earning $200 a week, is concerned. The jobs at a plant like Power Products tend to go to the school-leavers and preponderantly to women, and the pay is about half what the old factories used to offer top-scale workers. As Tom O'Connell put it, 'These new companies want seventeen-year-olds, new and fresh, and they want them for ten years. The thirty-five-year-old is obsolete.' I've heard the same thing from unemployed steelworkers in the Mahoning Valley, all washed up at forty. It makes for a lot of stress around the house when the wife, the younger sister, or the daughter is the one bringing home the wage.

This shift in wage scales points up the great problem for any Irish government. (There have been four governments since 1977, all vainly struggling with crisis, three duly turfed out after inevitable failure.) To keep exports competitive, wages have to be low, lest the guest company take off for Portugal or Greece or even Morocco, which is itself trying to join the Common Market. But the lower the wages the less the inhabitants of Youghal can afford to buy clothes in Merrick's, or drink in Paddy Linehan's bar, or eat candy from Tom O'Connell's shop, and the more the domestic economy stagnates. As Tom said, 'There'll be a lot of window shopping this year.' This is not surprising, since real unemployment in Youghal approaches 50 percent – even allowing for the 'foxers,' or that substantial part of the Irish population that at one time or another works off the books, in the underground economy.

I walked out toward the Strand, where the old villas and lodging houses have names like Railway View, in honor of the invention that gave them their nineteenth-century prosperity. Tourism kept Youghal going in the old days, and the people of Youghal know well enough that even if new plants are coming in on the urging of the IDA (two more, making floppy disks and nappies for old folks, are on the way), they may in the end go the way of the textile factories. But people will always want to go on holiday. Youghal is remembering how to be a tourist resort. A 'draft development plan' has reviewed Youghal's historical and picturesque assets: thirteenth-century church, fifteenth-century Tudor house, Cromwell's arch, the old town walls. For years many Irish people thought (correctly) that if accurately deconstructed, the 'picturesque' – whether it was a color-washed cottage or a venerable shopfront – spelled poverty. Thus they rejoiced in pebble-dash bungalows and plastic shop signs. But tourists do not always appreciate the aesthetic properties of upward mobility from nineteenth-century squalor. The draft plan says somberly, 'We in Ireland have a great tradition of very good handpainted signs, but, unfortunately, many new signs are brash, gaudy, and in poor taste. It is vital to remember that an otherwise very good shopfront or commercial premises can be completely ruined by brash, vulgar signs; therefore, stringent controls should be given to the size, color, texture, and position of all these signs.' So much for leprechaun schmaltz. This is a town that has to lure subsidiaries from the factories on Boston's Route 128 and tourists from the Ring of Kerry.

I wandered along the promenade in the company of some of the town's unemployed, who have little else to do with themselves each day. There on my right was Perks' Amusements, where as a fifteen-year-old I had helped run a local version of Bingo, tossing tennis balls into a rack. In my day the big prizes were worth $5 or $10.

I went in, and Sal Perks Tivy, who, along with her husband, Phil, has taken the place over from her father, Jumbo, said that it's now a matter of $1,000 prizes and that the Bingo boards are of course electronic. No more

Showboat Saturday Night Dance, either. Bands cost too much, and people have television these days anyway. Sal went on to describe Youghal's Walter Raleigh Potato Festival, designed to extol Sir Walter's importation of the sacred tuber to Youghal four hundred years ago.

On my way home I gave a lift to an earnest young man from Dungarvan who was studying marketing at University College Cork. The Irish, he said, were short of good marketeers of their produce. He said some friends of his had emigrated to Australia.

That evening I went to the Choucas Restaurant, outside Youghal, which had been opened in the late 1970s to cater to the new managerial class. As I ate the fine Lyonnais cooking of chef-proprietor Raymond I listened to his wife, Kendra, spiritedly explain the grotesque horrors and injustice of the 'value-added' sales tax, and, more generally, the rising cost of getting by.

It was my last evening in Youghal and the sixth straight day that I had not heard the North mentioned even once, nor any politician referred to without uniform derision.

Later, an old friend from Galway, who had laid aside a turbulent political life in favor of white-collar stability, did at last mention the North in the course of a succinct résumé of the Irish situation: 'In less than twenty years we've seen capitalism promise much and then fail; looking North, we've seen the nationalist mythology of Finn MacCool and Patrick Pearse end with little old ladies being blown up in shopping malls; the old ruling ideology of church and state has gone. The kids are all well educated and there's no hope for them. In the old days they didn't know it and now they do.'

No one is painting nationalist slogans on Youghal's new plants. The *fin de siècle*, this time around, is no time for dreaming. Be thankful to have a plough, and let the stars look after themselves.

Atlantic Monthly, April, 1985

Beat the Devil

My father wrote *Beat the Devil* in 1949, some of it in the house we had just acquired three miles outside Youghal, County Cork, and some in a summer cottage taken for August in the tiny village of Ardmore, which was all of eight miles away, across the Blackwater in County Waterford. These were the years immediately after his departure from London and from the Communist Party in 1947 and the name Cockburn did not have benign associations for the publishers and magazine editors crucial to our well-being. Since my father had left the Party without fanfare it took a while for his absence to register; then finally the security forces, in the form of the Special Branch and the *Daily Express*, sent men to investigate. In the absence of nutritious commentary from either my father or the locals the investigators concentrated on my father's locomotive resources. The man from the Special Branch established by zealous questioning – all subsequently related to us – that boat, train and car had been the various means assisting my father's translation from London to Youghal, while all the *Express* man could report was that the ex-Red was now using a bicycle to get about, 'head down against the wind and,' he asked dramatically, 'against the Party line?'

Neither my father nor my mother could drive and, for that matter, we wouldn't have been able to afford a car. But Ireland, or at least our particular part of it, was still essentially a nineteenth-century rural society and the cost of living was negligible by present-day standards; and anyway the pretensions of genteel poverty have never been part of the Anglo-Irish sensibility. You could be flat broke with rain pouring through the roof and bailiffs pouring down the drive and still hold head high – in our case, above the handlebars of the famous bicycle or in the horse and trap which was our alternative means of transportation. This was just as well because we were indeed flat broke, even though my father, banging away on his elderly Underwood, had developed a whole family of pseudonyms to try to confine the wolf at least to the hallway of our spacious and draughty Georgian house.

My father later wrote in his memoirs that a guest had described in the visitors' book what he called the 'literary colony' at Youghal:

He claimed to have met Frank Pitcairn, ex-correspondent of the *Daily Worker* – a grouchy, disillusioned type secretly itching to dash out and describe a barricade. There was Claud Cockburn, founder and editor of *The Week*, talkative, boastful of past achievements, and apt, at the drop of a hat, to tell, at length, the inside story of some forgotten diplomatic crisis of the 1930s. Patrick Cork would look in – a brash little number, and something of a professional Irishman, seeking, no doubt, to live up to his name. James Helvick lived in and on the establishment, claiming that he needed quiet with plenty of good food and drink to enable him to finish a play and a novel which soon would bring enough money to repay all costs. In the background, despised by the others as a mere commercial hack, Kenneth Drew hammered away at the articles which supplied the necessities of the colony's life.

'James Helvick', the name under which *Beat the Devil* was originally published, had been my mother's suggestion. Across the bay from Ardmore the long green finger of Helvick Head poked out into the sea and in the end its borrowed name decorated my father's first three novels – *Beat the Devil, Overdraft on Glory* and *The Horses*. These were all written in the 1950s. When my father returned to fiction with *Ballantyne's Folly* in 1970 and *Jericho Road* in 1974, they were launched under the true colors of his own name.

Beat The Devil was published at the beginning of the fifties, in England by Boardman and in the US by Lippincott. Both are now defunct, at least as houses publishing trade books. The advance against royalties provided by Boardman was, to my mother's recollection, somewhere between £200 and £300, and the sum for American rights was $750. This sort of money, though not as paltry as it now appears, did not long stay the bailiffs and things were looking bad as we went off to stay, for the Dublin Horse Show week, with Oonagh Oranmore at Luggala, her house in the Wicklow mountains.

Quite apart from the simple comfort of not having water on the floor and bailiffs at the gate, Luggala was a wonderful place to go in the early and mid-1950s. Writers and artists from Dublin, London, Paris and New York drank and sang through the long hectic meals with a similarly dissolute throng of politicians and members-in-good-standing of the café society of the time. And during this particular Horse Show week Luggala was further dignified by the presence of the film director John Huston and his wife of those years, Ricky. My father was a friend of Huston – from his stint in New York in the late 1920s perhaps, or maybe from Spanish Civil War days – and quite apart from the pleasures of reunion there was *Beat the Devil*, ready and waiting to be converted into a film by the famous director of *The Treasure of the Sierra Madre.*

My father spoke urgently to Huston of the virtues of *Beat the Devil,* but he found he had given, beneath fulsome dedications, his last two copies to our hostess and to a fellow guest, Terry Kilmartin. These copies were snatched back and thrown into Huston's departing taxi. A week later Huston was in Dublin again, shouting the novel's praises. He and Humphrey Bogart had just completed *The African Queen* and were awaiting the outcome of that enormous gamble. I can remember Huston calling Bogart in Hollywood and reading substantial portions of the novel to him down the phone – a deed which stayed with me for years as the acme of extravagance.

By the time Huston and his wife came down to Youghal to talk more about the screenplay he couldn't read *Beat the Devil* down the phone, not ours at least, because it had been cut off for non-payment of bills. Telegrams shuttled back and forth between Youghal and Hollywood and finally the offer came: £3,000 for rights and screenplay, or a lesser sum up front, against a greater, but as yet insubstantial reward – the famous 'points' – in the distant future. My father naturally took the lump sum on the barrel, used some of it to plug the roof and appease the bailiffs and then went to work with Huston on the screenplay.

The film had a sumptuous cast: Bogart, Peter Lorre, Gina Lollobrigida, Jennifer Jones, Robert Morley. When it finally got to Youghal there was a great to-do in the form of a grand screening at Horgan's Cinema. The people of Youghal, not entirely without reason, found it incomprehensible but applauded heartily, none more so, I imagine, than the bailiffs and other representatives of the commercial sector of the town.

Though not an immediate success, the film of *Beat the Devil* has developed a cult following over the years, and in the US quite often bobs up on late night TV. One aspect of this cult caused some irritation to my father and indeed to the rest of the family. The film's credits announced the screenplay was by Truman Capote, from a novel by James Helvick. Admirers of the film professed to find evidence of Capote's mastery in every interstice of the dialogue and over the years Capote did nothing to dissuade them from this enthusiasm. But in fact his own contribution was limited to some concluding scenes, for it had chanced that during the final days of shooting in Italy the end had suddenly to be altered: as far as I can remember, the locale of the scenes had to be changed in a hurry. In the emergency, with my father back in Ireland, Capote, who happened to be visiting the set at the time, was drafted to do the necessary work and his name – more alluring than that of the unknown Helvick or the ex-Red Cockburn – scrambled into the credits. Although reissued as a paperback in 1971 *Beat the Devil* has been, till now, almost unobtainable and it's not the least of my pleasures that admirers of the film may now see that the inspiration for that dialogue came not from Capote but from my father.

As a comedy-thriller of manners *Beat the Devil* has lasted well. Aside from a short story published by Ezra Pound in *The Dial* in the 1920s my father had previously written no fiction. From a writer whose chief occupation for twenty-five years had been political journalism, set at high volume, the lightness and poise of the novel are remarkable. Sententiousness, let alone sentimentality, is never, even surreptitiously, imported into the rapid dialogue in which most of the action is expressed. There is no interior monologue, nor are any thoughts ascribed to any of the characters. I can remember my father once explaining his formal resolve to set forth the story in the modalities (ineluctable, no doubt) solely of the visible and the audible.

Only recently departed from England himself, my father chose to tell a story of exile in which the keynote was moral illusion. The raffish bunch gathered in a hotel in the south of France are all fragrant with imperial decay: the adventurer Dannreuther, fixit-man for the crooks hoping to make a killing in Kivu province in the Belgian Congo; Mr O'Hara, the Pomeranian con-man; Jack Ross, the murderous Major; and of course the Chelms, haughty Harry and the lovely liar Gwendolen.

Everyone knows that so far as England is concerned, the shot is no longer on the board:

> 'What I feel is,' explained Chelm carefully, 'that in England under present conditions ...'
> 'Absolutely right. You can't beat the game. I tell you, England ... Europe ... the game's up.'
> Before this assertion Chelm decorously hesitated.
> 'I don't know that I'd exactly lump England and the rag-tag and bobtail of Europe together. There are certain qualities which ... Of course,' he repeated like a ritual, 'under present conditions ...'
> But Dunnreuther was paying no attention. Emphatically he developed his view that Europe as a paying proposition was finished. He quoted figures, voluminously and with gusto. It came out as a statistical funeral chant.
> 'But the Americans,' said Chelm.
> 'The Americans fiddlesticks,' shouted Dannreuther. 'Anything that's going, they'll get.'

Having spent a considerable part of his formative years in central Europe my father had a highly developed ear for the British national fantasy, expressed in *Beat the Devil* usually either by Chelm or by Dannreuther's Hungarian wife Maria, who proudly boasts of her liberalism: 'In Hungary you know, my family were great liberals. That is why they were beloved. My father could ride from our own gates right down to the village, even after dark, without risk of being shot at.' Maria, brought up to esteem all things English, is attracted to obtuse Chelm, just as Dannreuther is drawn to the adventurous Gwendolen:

> 'You know,' said Mrs Dannreuther, lying on the bed and playing with her big bracelet, 'if I ever leave you it will be for someone of the type of Harry Chelm ... that type of Englishman is like a story my father once told me long ago in Hungary. We were in the garden of our country place there, and my father told me about a gardener, an English gardener in England, at Oxford, I think it was, who was showing some Americans one of those wonderful English lawns, and of course they wanted to know how to make a lawn like that, and this English gardener said ...'
>
> 'I know damn well what the gardener said,' shouted Dannreuther ... 'He said all you had to do was get some good grass and then roll it every day for some six hundred years or some such howling nonsense. I heard that gardener thing before you were born. English people tell it when they feel poor.'

The paradox of good intentions was something that preoccupied my father in much of his work in fiction – most finely in his last (and I think best) novel, *Jericho Road,* where the generous impulse of the Good Samaritan in rescuing the waylaid traveller provokes such unpleasant consequences. The same paradox is studied in *Ballantyne's Folly* (which Graham Greene has set beside Chesterton's *The Man Who Was Thursday*) and it is present in *Beat the Devil.* The befuddled Chelm, impelled by notions of what would be the 'British thing to do' tries to get the *Nyanga's* engines going again, with unfortunate results; Gwendolen tells lies to improve her husband's fortunes, once again with results quite the reverse of her expectations.

The reason for my father's long engagement with this paradox is not hard to find. A reformer – in his case a revolutionary reformer, given his long activities in the international Communist movement – must inevitably ponder the consequences of his high intentions. But now the temptation for my father, flat broke in 1949 and writing *Beat the Devil,* was to write the familiar 50,000 words denouncing Communism and his Party associates. Given the offers he was being made to do just this, to have succumbed would have been richly rewarded. But as his father used to quote to him from Juvenal, 'Nec propter vitam vivendi perdere causas' (Just for the sake of living, don't lose the reasons for living) and my father never flirted with the notion for a moment. In *Beat the Devil* the character of Billy Dannreuther is a sour commentary on good intentions, temptation and, in a double twist, on the paradox of bad intentions too. O'Hara puts it this way to Dannreuther:

> 'You ... have had many imaginary objectives. Partly real, mainly imaginary ... People said you were a second Lawrence. You believed you were absorbed in

organizing some good forces against some bad ones ... Not so very far from
where we now sit. Dannreuther-Lawrence ... running guns to Spaniards. But you
quit in the middle.'

'It was the end,' said Dannreuther ...

'Quits,' pursued O'Hara, 'and here he is the adviser of quite a different kind
of expedition. Much simpler. Hunting money and nothing else. And this you will
not quit because all along, you see, through all these illusions, your real objective
has been something different from what you thought.'

'Do tell,' said Dannreuther.

'It has been,' said O'Hara 'the same as my own. Money and peace. So simple.
Nothing more. Money and peace.'

O'Hara's is that same voice of the tempter who urged my father towards
the broad path of betrayal. But by the end of the novel O'Hara himself
gives the answer, when Dannreuther asks him if he will go on looking for
money and peace: 'At my age this must be seen to be an illusion. There is
no such possibility.'

Against the illusions and velleities of the voyagers to Africa is set the
character of the Spanish police chief, prototype of a much more ample
version in *Jericho Road.* Here there are no paradoxes – merely the raw,
uncomplicated search for money and the peace that money brings. As
Dannreuther is trying to get his group out of the police chief's jail, he
finally approaches the matter of the actual bribe:

> It came in earnest to the money at the next interview. Money for the ruthless
> and passionate, for the superior man with his own opinions and moral judge-
> ments. Money for a villa in the hills behind Buenos Aires, money for the attrac-
> tion and subjection of gorgeous Argentine women who with passion, and a
> sophistication unknown in the villages of Andalusia, unknown in the brothels
> even of Granada, even of Málaga, even, by God, of Madrid, would expend them-
> selves in ministering to the desires of the superior man, the super-man who with
> ruthless intelligence saw and seized opportunity, rose above his fellows, marched
> forward, did not miss the bus. Dollars and women danced and twisted back and
> forth across the desk of the Chief of Police.
>
> 'There is a point,' said he, 'on which I would like your opinion – as a man of
> the world ... would you say, yourself, that in, for example, Buenos Aires, among
> smart people, the Packard or the Cadillac is considered the more chic?'
>
> 'In your position,' said Dannreuther, 'there will be no need for you to decide.
> You will, I imagine, have one of each.'

In his next novel, *Overdraft on Glory*, my father studied the glory and
greatness of good intentions. It was a much warmer affair than *Beat the
Devil* with its dégagé nonchalance. But *Overdraft on Glory* was, to my
father's sorrow, one of his less successful books and its fate contributed to
his return to weekly journalism through the 1960s.

It is heartening to see *Beat the Devil* published again. The sight of it provokes some vivid memories. One is of Huston. I had never met an American so theatrical in so grand a manner before. He could turn everything into an occasion. When he entered a room he would rearrange people, as though in preparation for a camera shot. There was a tiresome chore at our house outside Youghal, which was swinging a hand pump to and fro for about forty minutes a morning (an hour if more than two baths were taken) to fill the tank upstairs from the old well. Huston contrived that he and my father would swing the pump together, somehow transforming the task into one of archetypal grandeur. One would have thought they were Moses and Yahweh himself, rising water from the desert.

We saw a good deal of him because after the completion of *Beat the Devil* he returned to Youghal, having decided to recreate New Bedford there for his version of *Moby Dick*. By this time he had bought a house in Galway and was very much the grand squire. When he would appear at hunt balls in full ceremonial hunting rig and foxes' masks embossed in gold thread on his pumps the Anglo-Irish gentry would snigger, but he hypnotised them all the same. When Jean-Paul Sartre visited him in Galway in 1959 to work on his script of *Freud*, he sent back two extremely funny letters to Simone de Beauvoir, later printed in *Lettres à Castor*, about Ireland and about aspects of Huston. He found the bare Galway countryside to be a moonscape and remarked:

> This is exactly what makes up the interior landscape of my boss, the great Huston. Ruins, abandoned houses, wastelands, marshes, a thousand traces of the human presence, but the man himself has left, I don't know where ... Almost every night he invites the strangest sort of guests: the richest heir in England, a rajah who is also an innkeeper (a big hotel in Kashmir), an Irish master of foxhounds, an American producer, an English director. And he says *nothing* to them. Arlette and I came into the drawing room at a moment when Huston was chatting languidly to the master of hounds, a broadbacked young man with a red nose, *très* gentleman farmer. We were introduced and the 'major' said that he didn't know French. Huston banged him on the shoulder and said, 'Well, I'll leave you to practise your French,' and went off, leaving us there feeling stupid. Panic-stricken, the major rolled his eyes and finally said, 'Churchill is funny when he speaks French.' I said 'Ha, ha' and silence fell until we were called into dinner.

I remember at about that time seeing Huston ride in a re-creation of the first steeple chase, which was run between Buttevant and Doneraile, in County Cork. He was doing well on a horse called Naso, until he saw a television camera team. Although he was in the middle of a tricky jump onto a bank he turned towards the camera, smiled and doffed his cap. Off balance as the horse rose, he took a most tremendous toss and crashed heavily to the ground.

Aside from Huston and the little house in Ardmore facing Helvick Head (a view enjoyed by my father until the day he died – for in the end we moved to Ardmore permanently, to a house right across the road from that one where he had written *Beat the Devil* thirty years before), I can remember with extraordinary clarity a moment in London. After my father had agreed with Huston to take the money up front we traveled to London for a couple of weeks. I remember sitting in a hotel room with my mother and father and their friend Maurice Richardson, waiting for the cheque to arrive. I don't think we could go out till it did. There was a call from downstairs and in came a waiter with an envelope on a tray. There was silence as my father opened it and then volleys of cheers as they danced about, passing the cheque from hand to hand and shouting for champagne. I was ten and not interested in champagne.

'Does this mean I can have a new bicycle?' I shouted up.

'Yes, yes,' they beamed down. 'Of course you can have a new bicycle.'

Introduction to a new edition of Beat the Devil, *published in the UK by Hogarth Press, 1985*

IMPERIAL
EMBLEMS

*'The worst part of slavery is, as a rule, the
hardships entailed in the slave-caravan marches,
which have to be conducted at a forced pace over
desert and devious routes, in order to avoid
the good intentions of the European
anti-slavery forces.'*
Lord Baden-Powell

The Scoutmaster

The anxieties and preoccupations of the imperial nation into which Lord Baden-Powell introduced the Boy Scout movement some seventy-five years ago have a familiar look to them. Prominent citizens bewailed something it would be fair to call post-Boer War syndrome, variously defined as a lack of national resolve, declining military ardor, physical degeneration of the island race, reluctance to face global responsibilities, shortfall in spunk, pluck and kindred vitamins. The Japanese were keenly admired. 'If we look at the causes of Japan's success,' wrote Baden-Powell in December 1904, 'we find it very largely in the soldierly spirit and self-sacrificing patriotism of the whole of the people.' Easily as great as admiration of the Japanese example was gloom at Britain's own lack of military preparedness, supposedly caused by the lack of a universal draft and by the machinations of the pacifist, white-feather crowd. Invasion scenarios, dismissed by Winston Churchill as being 'confined to the inmates of Bedlam and writers for the *National Review*,' poured off the presses and were neatly parodied by young P.G. Wodehouse in *The Swoop*, published in 1909:

> Not only had the Germans effected a landing in Essex, but, in addition, no fewer than eight other hostile armies had, by some remarkable coincidence, hit on that identical moment for launching their long-prepared blow. England was not merely beneath the heel of the invader. It was beneath the heels of nine invaders. There was barely standing room.

For every outcrop of today's blend of malaise-mongering and profit-through-panic, one can find a parallel in those agitated times. The producers of ABC's forthcoming *Amerika* (a Commies-are-here fantasy) should study William Le Queux's best seller of 1906, *The Invasion of*

43

1910, serialized by the *Daily Mail,* whose proprietor had the sound judgment to insist that Le Queux alter the route of the invading Huns so that they would pass through areas where his newspapers enjoyed a high circulation. For every Podhoretz lamenting moral decline and the pullulation of homosexuals in the State Department, there was a Buchan similarly keening over Albion's accelerating moral turpitude; for every Vidal shouting for a U.S.-Soviet entente against the yellows, there is a premonitory echo, as from the National Council of Public Morals, which announced, 'It behoves the white races to end their differences and to unite in establishing durable civilizations.'

Protectionists complained that the very body of John Bull had been infiltrated by alien matter. 'The flour for his bread is probably American, his eggs are possibly French, ... beef from Argentina pasturage. ... There is little British in his composition in a physical sense,' wrote James Cantlie in 1900. Sidney Webb worried that the most prolific breeders were coming from the wrong end of the social spectrum, that the country would 'gradually' (Webb, after all, was one of the founding Fabians) fall to the Irish and the Jews and that 'the ultimate future of these islands may be to the Chinese.'

Then, as now, the analysis and the conclusions were absurd. The fundamental problem was domestic economic stagnation, induced by a class structure that constricted the development of adequate internal markets. At the time Le Queux was fearfully prophesying German rampages in the home counties, the chances of a British working-class boy getting to university were about one in a million, a statistic of considerably more moment to the decline of empire than the ingestion of alien foodstuffs.

Of the innumerable members of this Edwardian preview of the Committee on the Present Danger it is hard to imagine anyone more paradigmatic than Robert Baden-Powell. Despite Michael Rosenthal's excellent and unsparing portrait of his personality, his obsessions and the national preoccupations from which they derived, Baden-Powell – or B.P. as he liked to be called – will no doubt survive in collective memory as the kindly, generous figure in the legend he so zealously fostered. Certainly when I was a Wolf Cub in the early 1950s he was constantly invoked as role model by Patsy Warner, the amiable wife of our headmaster. She would deploy us round her in a circle beneath a chestnut tree and tell us of B.P.'s exploits on the veld, his woodcraft, his jousts with the obstreperous Boers; and I listened with a pleasure terminated only when the use of bad language caused me to be stripped of my green jersey and expelled forever from the magic circle.

A big moment in the popular fiction of Baden-Powell's contemporaries such as John Buchan or 'Sapper,' was the occasion of unmasking. Before the startled gaze of the hero the kindly features of the parson or retired army major would suddenly recompose into the lineaments of villainy, whether of the man who hooded his eyes like a hawk in *Thirty-Nine Steps* or of the Absolute Evil of the dying Carl Peterson in *The Final Round*, so physically repugnant that 'what that face truly was no man can ever tell.' The same sort of thing happens in *The Character Factory*. Just as down the decades many a Scout has discovered that the ardent gaze and intrusive hands of his Scoutmaster portended more than innocent zeal to convey the rudiments of woodcraft, so too, in Rosenthal's account, does the hearty mien of B.P. – or Grey Wolf, as he also liked to be known – dissolve into a pathology of racism, militarism and sexual repression.

Until the lifting of the siege of Mafeking, on May 17, 1900, at which point he became a national hero, there was no indication that Baden-Powell would be more than a typical officer of empire. His father died when he was 3 months old, and from his earliest years his mother, struggling to raise seven children on sparse means, taught him the importance of 'grouping,' her word for what would now be called networking, whereby Baden-Powell toadied to his superiors and spent long and anxious hours pondering how to turn every circumstance to his own advantage. Few saw through him, though Angus Hamilton of *The Times* once invoked 'the steel manacles of his ambition, which had checkmated the emotions of the man in the instincts of the officer.'

His army service in India was distinguished chiefly by his passion for pig-sticking, on which he wrote an authoritative treatise. With that characteristic British talent for rationalizing a victim's agonies as being somehow for his own good, Baden-Powell said that the pig, at least until it got terminally stuck, had a good time too. Thus far B.P. was an entirely conventional case of arrested mental and emotional development. Mafeking was his breakthrough, the apotheosis of a demented school prefect. Managing to be comfortably besieged for 217 days by a Boer force only slightly superior to his own, he became a symbol of valor for a nation humiliated by the dour resistance of a few thousand Dutchmen. The care with which B.P. attended to what he regarded as his prime military duty – the preparation of modestly vainglorious communiqués for domestic consumption – is reminiscent of Gen. Douglas MacArthur, another chill self-promoter. The more journalists found out about MacArthur, the less they liked him, and the same was true for B.P. Newsmen in Mafeking soon noted that there was little risk from the besieging enemy, whose passions had been most deeply aroused by B.P.'s impiety in playing polo on Sunday. They also noted that in order to assure the material comforts of the white inhabitants of Mafeking, B.P. was systematically starving to death the several thousand Africans in the town.

As befits one of the greatest of the great communicators (Rosenthal reckons him to be the best-selling British author in history, after Shakespeare), B.P. learned and remembered the promotional values of Mafeking. He expressed them with appropriate cynicism to some journalists, in the course of a few tips about self-advancement based on his own experiences as a correspondent:

> I thought it the sure road to success to strike out a new and original line for myself, and found – I was quite wrong. That instead of taking my powers to be original my business was to write what, at the moment, the public wanted to believe.

The public wanted a victory, which B.P. supplied them from the squalid realities of a militarily unimportant siege. The public, as B.P. brilliantly sensed, also needed reassurance about the 'youth problem,' a vast reserve army of juvenile discontent – pimply, thriftless, physically unfit for war, insufficiently respectful of authority and the imperatives of empire, potentially seditious.

B.P. brought to his self-appointed career as youth organizer some essential attributes. His verbal and syntactic data base was uncannily apt for his role, a bluff lexicographic universe peopled with chaps and bricks ('If you are discontented with your place or with your neighbours or if you are a rotten brick, you are not good to the wall. ... Some bricks may be high up and others low down in the wall; but all must make the best of it') and straight talk and manliness and short sentences administered with avuncular good cheer. He knew the virtues of absolute and continued self-assurance, of being decent to the other fellow, of giving a firm handshake and looking someone straight in the eye. B.P. brought to perfection the art of homespun, jovial demagogy, in which the very candor of expression carried his audience pleasantly through such reflections as:

> The worst part of slavery is, as a rule, the hardships entailed in the slave-caravan marches, which have to be conducted at a forced pace over desert and devious routes, in order to avoid the good intentions of the European anti-slavery forces.

One can imagine Ronald Reagan reading out this passage with great conviction, allowing a friendly, chuckling pause at the words 'good intentions.'

Another important quality was his sure instinct for plagiarism. B.P.'s purpose in founding the Boy Scouts was simplicity itself. He wanted to found, as he put it, a Society for the Propagation of Moral Attributes, the attribute in question being primarily obedience. Seeking to add allurement to his design, he brazenly stole the woodcraft system of Ernest Thompson Seton, an English artist and naturalist living in the United States, and when Seton wrote furiously to complain – as he did for many years – B.P. gave him an epistolary clap on the back and thanked him for being so awfully decent about the whole thing.

To the gifts of demagogy and plagiarism B.P. added a keen political sense of alliances. The usefulness of a movement inculcating patriotism and obedience did not escape the generals, politicians and newspaper proprietors who backed Baden-Powell to the hilt, aware that B.P. always had the adroitness to share their agenda while preserving the fiction that Scouting's chief injunction, 'Be Prepared,' had nothing to do with war.

B.P.'s ideal Scout was prepared for war, prepared to defend empire and, literally, propagate it. An ardent admirer of the eugenicists, B.P. shared their concern about the adulteration of national blood lines by coarse genetic material. This concern prompted, at least in part, an obsession with the perils of masturbation. He was strongly against the practice, urging cold baths and exercise of 'the upper half' of the body as antidote. One unpublished draft unearthed by Rosenthal stated flatly that the result of self-abuse 'is always – mind you, always – that the boy after a time becomes weak and nervous and shy, he gets headaches, ... and if he still carries it on too far he very often goes out of his mind and becomes an idiot.' B.P. plainly felt that each unproductive emission from a public-school lad meant a loss of sound ruling-class stock. Although he couldn't publicly advocate a class-based policy on wanking, there is evidence that he would not have been unduly upset by lower-class lads spilling their seed on the ground. He didn't want them to breed at all, and spoke fondly of bees, who had the good sense to 'kill their unemployed.'

When it came to sex, B.P.'s imaginative landscape was surrealist in contour. His volumes of instruction are thickly populated with sudden fires, runaway horses, oncoming trains, drowning women and venomous snakes. According to Rosenthal, the 'most intense relationship of his life' was with an officer named Kenneth McLaren, nicknamed, on account of his youthful good looks, 'the boy.' It's not known whether actual beastliness occurred. B.P. was married very late, long past what he called 'the dangerous rutting period,' to Olave Soames, whom he described to his mother as 'the cheeriest girl possible,' with the added virtue of an income of £1,000 a year from her father.

Far more sinister – because more plausible – than Sir Oswald Mosley, B.P. was the *echt* British fascist, from the crest of his Scout hat to the soles of his sensible brogues. He hated 'niggers,' Jews and trade unions with a zeal matched only by his enthusiasm for Mussolini and the Hitler Jugend, which he considered emblematic of the finest ideals of Scouting. When a certain Herr Riecke, a German youth leader trying to form an alternative to the Hitler Jugend, was sent to a concentration camp, B.P. rallied to the Nazis' defense, saying that Riecke had been sent there 'not for international tendencies, but for homosexual tendencies!'

Following B.P.'s career forward from World War I, where his instilled qualities of obedience, reverence for authority and associated family values helped account for the death of millions, we can see all the necessary attributes of British-style Nazism, simultaneously expressed by the brutish figure of Bulldog Drummond and his 'Black Gang' in Sapper's books. Having won the war, Britain could export this fascism to the colonies, where Scouting's traditions were boldly exercised until the end. The final joke on B.P. was that the surviving spirit of Scouting is the more pacific woodcraft element he stole from Seton. This would not have bothered B.P. too much. Born again in the United States today, he would, I imagine, soon be forming alliances with the survivalists, General Singlaub, Secretary of Education Bennett, Nancy Reagan and the other great communicator, and working hard for national regeneration.

Review of The Character Factory: Baden-Powell's Boy Scouts and the Imperatives of Empire, *by Michael Rosenthal; The Nation, May 10, 1986*

The Secret Agent

The most successful saga in postwar popular culture got off to a conscientious start after breakfast on a tropical morning in Jamaica on 16 January, 1952. Ian Fleming, forty-three years old and ten weeks away from his first and last marriage, knocked out about 2,000 words on his Imperial portable claiming (falsely) that he was just passing time while his bride elect, Anne Rothermere, painted landscapes in the garden. In fact Fleming had been planning to write a spy thriller for years and he kept up the regimen of 2,000 daily words until, two months later, he was done, with Commander James Bond recovering from a near lethal attack on his balls from Le Chiffre's carpet beater, Le Chiffre finished off by a Russian, Vesper Lynd dead by her own hand, and a major addition to the world's cultural and political furniture under way.

On 16 January, 1962, ten years to the day after Fleming had typed those first words of *Casino Royale* ('The scent and smoke and sweat of a casino are nauseating at three in the morning') filming began on *Dr No* at Palisadoes airport in Jamaica, with the British Secret Service and the CIA duly represented by Sean Connery and Jack Lord. That was fifteen Bond films and a quarter of a century ago. Fleming lived long enough to see only two of them, *Dr No* and *From Russia With Love*, before dying in August, 1964 of a heart attack helped along by his seventy or so Morland's Specials a day.

He has much to answer for. Without Fleming we would have had no OSS, hence no CIA. The cold war would have ended in the early 1960s. We would have had no Vietnam, no Nixon, no Reagan and no Star Wars.

Let those dubious of such assertions study the evidence. It was Fleming, assistant to the director of British naval intelligence during the Second World War, who visited Washington DC in 1941 and wrote a long memo of advice for General 'Will Bill' Donovan, President Roosevelt's Co-ordinator of Information, whose duties included the collection of intelligence and the planning of various covert offensive operations. According to Ivar Bryce, a lifelong friend of Fleming's who was working at the time for Sir William Stephenson, the director of Britain's intelligence operations in the Americas, 'Ian wrote out the charter for the COI at General Donovan's request.... He wrote it as a sort of imaginary exercise describing in detail all the arrangements necessary for financing, paying, organizing, controlling, and training a secret service in a country which had never had one before.'

Fleming's memo was dashed down in long-hand over two days in the British Embassy with the diligence later exhibited in his imaginative stints after breakfast in Jamaica. It impressed Donovan, who gave him a .38 Police Positive Colt inscribed with the words 'For Special Services' and went on to build the COI which later evolved into OSS and later still into the CIA.

So, you see, it was all Fleming's fault. He had a riotous imagination utterly unsuited to serious intelligence collection and analysis, and the offices of the British Admiralty often rang with laughter at his mad schemes. It was Fleming who suggested that British sailors be entombed in a giant lump of concrete off Dieppe, from which they could keep watch on Dieppe through periscopes. It was Fleming who proposed to send a cruiser into Nazi waters with a transmitter beamed to the German Navy's wavelength which would, in his words, 'keep up a torrent of abuse, challenging the German naval commanders by name to come out and do something about it. No sailor likes to be accused of cowardice, and Germans are always particularly touchy.'

Fortified by such boyish fantasies, the officers of OSS never wrought much damage to the foe, but, from Donovan and his subordinate Allen Dulles downwards, learned to exploit romantic public fantasies of what a secret service should be. Thus they ensured their survival, if not in the field then in the crucial bureaucratic battlegrounds of Washington.

At the end of the war the future of the OSS hung in the balance. Alert to the importance of publicity for their supposedly secret organization, Donovan and Dulles lent every assistance to Hollywood producers racing to be first in the theaters with an OSS movie. Paramount's man in this race was Richard Maibaum, who, with Alan Ladd produced *OSS*. Donovan's aid was later responsible for turning the Bond novels into film scripts. Maibaum recently recalled that 'before we got done we had literally about ten technical agents all telling us marvelous stories of what had happened to them all over the world which we incorporated into the plot. There were foreshadowings of things in the Bond films, – the pipe that was a gun, and other gadgets. There were some things we couldn't use, such as foul smelling stuff like an enormous fart that the OSS agents used to spray on people they wished to discredit, and thus cause them to be socially humiliated. It was called Who, Me? We could never get it in, because the

Johnson office would never let us use it.'

Soon the postwar audiences were enjoying Maibaum's *OSS* along with *Cloak and Dagger* from Warner's and *13, Rue Madeleine* from Twentieth-Century Fox. This spy hype helped the OSS resist bureaucratic extinction and instead metastasize into the CIA.

Having engendered the OSS, Fleming now began to lure Anthony Eden down the path of fantasy. Like many in the small but enthusiastic fan club for Fleming's early thrillers, Sir Anthony Eden rejoiced that in Fleming's pages, if not in the real world, a Briton was capable of decisive, if ruthless action. Eden, as prime minister, resolved that the fortunes of 007 would be reflected in bold deeds, undertaken by himself. In concert with France and Israel he invaded Egypt in 1956. He had not studied the works of his friend Ian with sufficient care. Bond and his master, M, placed the highest priority upon acting at all times with the approval of the United States. In the case of Suez, President Eisenhower said the invasion had to stop and it did. Twelve days later Eden had an attack of what his spokesman called 'severe overstrain' and his doctors urged him to spend a few weeks in absolute seclusion and repose.

Once again Eden was overwhelmed by the fantasies of his friend. After the war Fleming had bought a plot of land on Jamaica's North Shore and built a small house on it. To acquaintances trembling with cold in English winters Fleming would body forth 'Goldeneye', his Caribbean paradise. In the crisis, seeking rest, Eden and his wife decided to go to Goldeneye. Fleming was delighted, since it raised the rental value of the place and he was badly in need of cash. But for the Edens the trip was unfortunate. The quarters were unalluring. Gazing into the rafters of Goldeneye, the prime minister, already suffering bouts of paranoia, fancied he saw rats. He was right. He consumed days chasing them in the company of his two body-guards. Finally, harrowed by lack of sleep, broken in health, he returned to London, announced he was 'fit to resume my duties' and resigned three weeks later.

In 1958, Fleming wrote *Dr No*, which advanced the novel notion that Cuba, as the local representative of the international Communist conspiracy, had perfected a reactor-based instrument capable of sabotaging US missile tests, thus explaining the Soviets' apparent advantage in space technology, as evidenced by the launching of the Sputnik.

Having proposed a fictional Caribbean missile crisis, Fleming followed up in person. In the spring of 1960 he was taken to dinner at the Washington home of Senator and Democratic presidential candidate-elect Jack Kennedy. The conversation turned to the problem of Castro. How should he be dealt with? Fleming's imagination sprang into action. As Fleming's biographer, John Pierson, reported the conversation, he told the assembled company, which included a CIA man called John Bross, that 'the United States should send planes over Cuba dropping pamphlets, with the compliments of the Soviet Union, to the effect that owing to American atom-bomb tests the atmosphere over the island had become radioactive; that radioactivity is held longest in beards; and that radioactivity makes men impotent. As a consequence the Cubans would shave off their beards, and without bearded Cubans there would be no revolution.'

Everyone, including Senator Kennedy, laughed at the scheme. The next day Allen Dulles, director of the CIA, telephoned a friend of Fleming's to express regrets that he had not been able to listen to Fleming's plans in person. Within two years the Kennedy brothers, along with Allen Dulles, director of the CIA, were hiring gangsters to help in either the murder or humiliation of Castro, with the latter being attempted by a dust which would cause his beard to fall out. The subculture of sabotage and assassination coaxed into being by the Kennedys finally, on 22 November, 1963, turned back on the President.

Just as Eden helped raise the real estate value of Goldeneye, so did President Kennedy augment the fortunes of the fantasist. On 17 March, 1961, an article by Hugh Sidey in *Life* announced that President Kennedy read at a rate of 1,200 words a minute and had ten favorite books. *From Russia With Love* was ninth, just ahead of Stendhal's *The Red and the Black*.

Bond became the embodiment of western discourse on the cold war. The men who would later construct the Reaganite view of the universe turned, time and again, to their Bond for edification. From him they learned that the Russians use Bulgarians as 'proxies' and thus the legend of the KGB-Bulgarian plot to kill the Pope was born. They watched *Thunderball* and conceived that terrorists, probably Libyans, would steal atomic bombs and attack American cities. They worried about germ warfare when they saw *On Her Majesty's Secret Service* and about weather modification when they saw *The Man With the Golden Gun.* But it was the lasers in *Goldfinger* and *Diamonds Are Forever*, along with the space station in *Moonraker* that made the deepest impact. Could missiles be destroyed in space? Could there be such a thing as a space shield? They brooded. To hand was a Bond sequel by John Gardner called *For Special Services* in which the villain announces on page 222 that 'The Particle Beam – once operational – will prevent any country from launching a conventional [sic] nuclear attack. Particle Beam means absolute neutralisation.' On March 23, 1983, President Reagan proposed a space-based defense system, known as SDI, which would use lasers and particle beams. Star Wars was born. As I said, Fleming and Bond have a lot to answer for.

In late January 1987 I drove out to Pinewood Studios outside London to spend the day on the set of *The Living Daylights*, fifteenth in the series of

Bond films produced by Harry Saltzman and Albert (Cubby) Broccoli, or by Broccoli alone, and distributed through United Artists. A spoof, *Casino Royale*, was put out in 1969 through Columbia, starring Woody Allen and David Niven, and a remake of *Thunderball*, called *Never Say Never Again*, starred a *revenant* Connery and was put out through Warner Brothers.

The original nucleus of Pinewood Studios was Heatherden Hall, a fashionable weekend retreat for politically influential members of the upper class, owned by Grant Morden, a Canadian speculator and member of parliament. He died a bankrupt in 1934, and in 1936 Charles Boot, eager to build a studio to rival Hollywood, joined forces with a rich Methodist flour miller, militant Christian and film enthusiast, J. Arthur Rank, and founded Pinewood Studios.

The moment of truth that struck Anthony Eden when President Eisenhower told him to call off the Suez adventure afflicted Pinewood nine years earlier. The postwar Labour government, wishing to fortify cultural nationalism and repel invasion by Hollywood, imposed a 75 percent tax on the box office earnings of Hollywood films. The tax was to be paid in advance, on the basis of estimated revenues. Hollywood promptly placed Britain under embargo, causing a potentially disastrous shortage of product. Rank announced that to fill the breach he would undertake the production of 47 films at a capital outlay of £9 million, the largest commitment to film making ever made in Britain.

But the Labour government was buckling under tremendous pressure from the United States. The 75 percent levy was abandoned and replaced by a ceiling to the profits that could be repatriated to Hollywood, with the balance to be reinvested in Britain. The Hollywood films came flooding back, just in time to sink the hastily produced and cheap material being put out by Rank.

By 1952 the situation had improved. Social democracy in the Attlee variant, so impotent in the face of the United States, had also fostered a new audience for middlebrow comedy. *Genevieve* came in 1952, *Doctor in the House* in 1953, launching a long and profitable series. In 1954 Norman Wisdom made his first comedy at Pinewood, *Trouble in Store*. To the Doctor series and the Wisdom comedies was added, in 1958, the first of the *Carry On* films, *Carry On Sergeant*, launching a cycle of twenty-eight comedies, of immense popularity in Great Britain and Australia.

Then in 1962, to a Pinewood shuddering from the great *Cleopatra* disaster of 1960 (it rained all the time and the costly Egyptian sets had to be torn down and reassembled in Rome), came *Dr No*, a production modestly budgeted at $1 million and starring an unknown leading man. In the ensuing quarter of a century Bond became the backbone of Pinewood. A generation of technicians have grown up on the saga, and low cost productions (there were 42 films produced at Pinewood in 1962 and 1963, including two Bond movies and three *Carry On* films) have given way to the blockbuster projects of today, in which the average Bond movie costs around $30 million. Two films can take up all eighteen stages, as happened in 1982 with *Octopussy* and *Superman III*.

The British film industry, as embodied in Pinewood, has been sustained since the fifties as much as anything else by preoccupations about social control, authority, security and reveries, comic or serious, of omnipotence: *Carry On Sergeant,* Norman Wisdom's *On the Beat,* Peter Sellers's *Pink Panther* series, the Bond films and, at the extreme level of fantasy, the *Superman* cycle. The progression indicates thirty-five years' worth of increasing integration of world capital and culture in the journey from the provincial particularism of a Norman Wisdom to the globally totemic late Bond.

The question of globally totemic late Bond, of the simultaneously mutable and immutable nature of our hero, is very much on the minds of Cubby Broccoli and his associates at Eon and United Artists these days. After five tours of duty, Sean Connery gave way to George Lazenby, who was swiftly replaced, after only one turn in *OHMS,* by Connery and then by Roger Moore, who made seven Bond movies over thirteen years, culminating in *A View To a Kill,* made when Moore was in his late fifties. The new Bond is a forty-year-old actor, Timothy Dalton.

In the dining-room of Heatherden Hall, Charles Jurow, marketing director of the Bond films and long associate of Broccoli's, brooded about changing Bonds.

'People who saw their first Bond with Sean never took to Roger, and people who saw their first Bond with Roger never took to Sean. Roger's movies grossed more than Sean's, and in fact *A View To a Kill* broke all records. Roger really came into his own with *The Spy Who Loved Me,* it took a change of directors really, from Guy Hamilton to Lewis Gilbert. Hamilton saw the character of Bond so much in terms of Sean, and Roger just couldn't do the things required of him, like slapping a woman or being a vicious killer. Now John Glen has made the last four, but he'll allow an actor, particularly one he respects, to develop a character in his own persona and not have too many fixations on the way it was done before.'

The unit publicist, Geoff Freeman led me to the sound stage. There was a tremendous racket of a wind machine and we rounded the corner to observe Dalton clinging to a net and being kicked in the face by Andreas Wisniewski. A few moments later the noise stopped, Dalton sat down in his chair and Wisniewski went back to reading *The Agony and The Ecstasy.*

John Glen took me over to a viewing machine to show what was going on. The net is hanging out the back of a plane flying some thousands of feet above Afghanistan, piloted by Maryam D'Abo. A time bomb is ticking away and Bond and Wisniewski are battling it out on the net which holds bales of drugs which ...

Glen started his professional life at Pinewood as a sound man, running up and down stairs to recreate the noise of Harry Lime's feet as he fled down the Vienna sewers in *The Third Man*. He'd made his mark in the Bond series as editor and action unit director, most memorably in the ski chase and parachuting sequence in *The Spy Who Loved Me*. He said that somewhat as a consequence of Dalton's arrival, *The Living Daylights* will be straighter than the high period Moore. 'Dalton is the best actor we ever had, and we're probably slightly more adult in the approach we're taking. Tim is certainly a great mover.'

I went over to talk to Dalton, and asked him how he was enjoying the film. He said very much, thank you, adding rather earnestly that 'if you enjoy work then you enjoy all movies.'

We started talking about Fleming's novels, with Dalton maintaining that the first, *Casino Royale*, was the best: 'It was the melting pot out of which the series evolved, but much more disturbed and psychological. Bond says clearly that he's in a state of moral and ethical confusion. He looks back on people he has killed and realises they were just guys on the other side, doing their job. Then there's a marvelous moment when his friend the French agent says that if Bond is confused he should forget about people and just go after the evil that creates the necessity for spies.' Dalton stopped, brooding raptly, then plunged on.

'In the same book he fell in love with a woman who in turn fell in love so deeply with him that she couldn't tell him she was a double agent and committed suicide, but at the same time by committing suicide she betrayed her love to him. How does a man deal with that?'

Dalton's name has been linked with that of Vanessa Redgrave and since Redgrave is a committed member of a Trotskyist groupuscule it was tempting to enquire whether Dalton himself was a Trotskyist and thus, whether, in a manner of speaking, 007 had been politically compromised. 'As a species, secret agents aren't looking too good these days,' I said. 'No, but then who has looked good of late?'

The wind machine started up again. Dalton went back to the net and a few seconds later was being kicked by Wisniewski in the face again.

He was right about *Casino Royale*. Bond was in poor ideological shape at the beginning, running badly to seed in a way that would have aroused the contempt of his fictional antecedent, the fascist Captain Bulldog Drummond. In the exchange with the Frenchman Mathis, alluded to by Dalton, Bond unburdens himself of the following:

> 'The villains and heroes all get mixed up. Of course ... patriotism comes along and makes it seem fairly all right, but this country-right-or-wrong business is getting a little out of date. Today we are fighting communism. Okay. If I'd been

alive fifty years ago, the brand of conservatism we have today would have been damn near called communism, and we should have been told to go and fight that.'

It didn't take too long for Bond to straighten himself out and declare unending war on evil in the manner prescribed by Mathis. As Maibaum puts it, 'the basic success of Bond is Ian Fleming's James Bond syndrome: a ruthless killer who is also St George of England, a modern day combination of morality and immorality. In the age of the sick joke it clicked.'

Of course the Bond of the books was a bit of a sicko, held together mostly by his sanction from the state: *licensed to kill.* He could never keep any relationship together, and if Vesper Lynd hadn't done herself in with a handful of Nembutals before they got married she probably would have got around to it in the end. What a prissy old autocrat of the breakfast table he would have been, howling for his perfectly brown egg, boiled for three and a third minutes and then put in its Minton cup, next to the Queen Anne coffee pot and the Cooper's Vintage Oxford marmalade! There was something a bit common too in all this insistence on the very best, as though Bond knew that in the end he was, as the elegant Dr No put it in Maibaum's line in the movie, 'nothing but a stupid policeman,' on hire to the ruling class. Hence the great scene in *From Russia With Love*, when the class impostor Bond, played by a working-class boy from Edinburgh with a Scots burr in his voice, comes up against the other class impostor and psychopath Red Grant, played by Robert Shaw. 'Red wine with fish,' says Connery, 'I should have known.' 'I may take red wine with fish,' Shaw hisses viciously, 'but you're the one on your knees now.'

Bond was in urgent need of a shrink. Fleming himself had the good fortune to be cared for in his troubled teens at Kitzbuhel in Switzerland by a couple called Forbes-Dennis, who were much influenced by Alfred Adler. Mrs Forbes Dennis, who wrote under the name Phyllis Bottome, thought the young Fleming proof of Adler's theories, his impressive elder brother Peter being the Adlerian *Gegenspieler*. 'The *Gegenspieler*,' wrote Bottome in her book on Adler, 'is a contemporary brother or sister by whom the child felt dethroned ... in almost any intimate relationship that follows, the child as he develops into the man will build up the same perpetual antagonism between himself and any beloved person.' The subject, said Adler, pushes aside the world by a mechanism consisting of 'hypersensitiveness and intolerance ... the neurotic man employs a number of devices for enabling him to side-step the demands of reality.' If Adler had lived long enough to visit Pinewood in 1982 when they were making Octopussy and Superman III he would have surely felt vindicated.

Somewhere along the line, in their post-imperial fantasy life, the British got muddled about secrets and spying and sex and identity, and the confusion has been causing them endless trouble ever since. The week I was in England the newspaper headlines were replete with spy and sex scandals. Thatcher's government was claiming that national security had been 'compromised,' by a *New Statesman* article about a British spy satellite. Another story concerned Mrs Payne, a woman on trial for running prostitutes, about whom Terry Jones, of the Monty Python crew, has produced a film. According to the account in *The Independent,*

> A tall man who dressed as a French maid at Cynthia Payne's parties told yesterday how he was 'touched up' by a man he later learned was a 'boisterous, tall and very fat' undercover policeman. Keith Savage, with short cropped hair and a Geordie accent, told a jury that the bearded officer put his hand up his skirt and fondled his bottom. 'I was a bit upset about the police bursting in and I thought this man was trying to console me. But he got a bit overfriendly ... I think he had a motive of a sexual nature.' Another policeman, he claimed, was dressed effeminately wearing eye make-up and a monocle.

The titular villains in the Bond books are always grotesques. Le Chiffre, in *Casino Royale*, set the tone, weighing in at 252 pounds at a height of 5'8", with his 'small, rather feminine mouth', small hairy hands, small feet, small ears 'with large lobes, indicating some Jewish blood', 'soft and even' voice and white showing all round the iris of each eye, 'large sexual appetites' and 'flagellant' tastes. This, in admittedly baroque form, was our old friend the Father Figure, as evinced in the scene where Le Chiffre goes to work on Bond's balls with the carpet beater and promises to chop them off with a carving knife. Fleming inaugurates the torture scene thus: '"My dear boy" – Le Chiffre spoke like a father – "the game of Red Indians is over, quite over. You have stumbled by mischance into a game for grown-ups, and you have already found it a painful experience. You are not equipped, my dear boy, to play games with adults, and it was very foolish of your nanny in London to have sent you out here with your spade and bucket."'

But when Bond, manhood spared by the Russian executioner who dispatches Le Chiffre, recovers in hospital and then prepares – with Vesper Lynd's help – to check that all physical systems are in working order, he discovers that she too is a villain. This is less surprising when we realise that Bond's women are often men, thinly disguised. This is progress from Buchan and Drummond, where they were often horses. Vesper is introduced with the news that 'her eyes were wide apart and deep blue and they gazed candidly back at Bond with a touch of ironical disinterest which, to his annoyance, he found he would like to shatter, roughly. Her skin was lightly suntanned and bore no trace of make-up except on her mouth which was wide and sensual. ... the general impression of restraint in her appearance and movements was carried even to her fingernails, which were unpainted and cut short.'

Of course there was dutiful mention of Vesper's 'fine breasts' but Fleming does not seem to have been too interested in them. Four years later, in *From Russia With Love*, Fleming scurries past Tatiana Romanova's breasts with a mumbled 'faultless' before assuming a hotly didactic tone on the matter of her ass: 'A purist would have disapproved of her behind. Its muscles were so hardened with exercise that it had lost the smooth downward feminine sweep, and now, round at the back and flat and hard at the sides, it jutted like a man's.' A year later, after publication of *Dr No*, Noel Coward wrote to Fleming, saying that he was 'slightly shocked by the lascivious announcement that Honeychile's bottom was like a boy's. I know that we are all becoming progressively more broadminded nowadays but really, old chap, what *could* you have been thinking of?'

Fleming didn't address the point in his response, but there is an answer in one of his notebooks from the thirties, a period when he looked, in one description, like someone who had walked out of the pages of *The Romantic Agony*: 'Some women respond to the whip, some to the kiss. Most of them like a mixture of both, but none of them answer to the mind alone, to the intellectual demand, unless they are men dressed as women.'

For Bond there were father figures lurking behind every shrub, none more imposing than old M, with his damnably blue eyes, whom Bond tries to kill in an Oedipal spasm at the start of *OHMS*. But here too we find that ambiguity discovered by the very fat policeman when he slipped his hand up Savage's skirt. Fleming's father was killed in the war when he was a boy. The dominant figure in Ian's life was his formidable mother, Mrs Val. Like Holmes and Moriarty locked together over the Reichenbach Falls, mother and son maintained vigorous psychic combat until they died within two months of each other in 1964, Mrs Val going first in July. Fleming often called his mother M.

Always this terrible confusion! The real 'M' in the war was the head of MI5, a man called Maxwell Knight. He was loved by his secretary, Joan Miller. She died in 1984 but her daughter fought, over the desperate efforts of MI5 to suppress them, to publish her memoirs, which are now available in Ireland. There is a poignant passage in which Miller describes the object of her doomed love: 'As I sat there watching this avowed opponent of homosexuality mince across the lawn, a number of things became clear to me ... His tastes obviously inclined him in the direction of what, in a phrase not then current, is known as "rough trade". It was plain that he'd taken himself, that time, to the cinema tea room, instead of spending the afternoon with his wife in Oxford, in the hope of effecting a suitably scrubby pick-up.'

If Bond's women were men in the books, in the movies they are fish, starting with Honeychile who comes up out of the sea in *Dr No* in one of the most successful associations of woman with water since Botticelli stood Venus up on a clamshell. In the movies Bond is often to be found down in cold water or up in the snow. The problem for Maibaum and for the various directors was no doubt to find scenery to match or compensate for the distraught psychic landscapes of the books. They found the answer where Jules Verne so often did, in the soothingly amoral underworld of the sea. It didn't always work. The underwater sequences in *Thunderball* are numbingly slow. But at their best, in the explicitly Verne-like *Spy Who Loved Me* with Curt Jurgens' Atlantis on its tarantula legs, or in the lesbian fantasy, *Octopussy*, the movies do take on the surreal texture of a Max Ernst painting.

They also lightened everything up. The only time Bond really behaves like a licensed killer is at the start of *Dr No*, when he studies the renegade Strangeway's empty gun, says 'You've had your six' and then kills him in cold blood. Maibaum gave Bond a sense of humor. The idea was to present the cold war as a necessary, but humorous – in the case of Moore, frivolous – ritual.

Right from the start the film series stood in marked contrast to the books in being pro detente. The only bad Russians are renegades, part of SPECTER, intent on sowing distrust between the great powers, as in *The Spy Who Loved Me*, where Jurgens schemes to arrange mutual assured destruction of all great powers other than his own. Maibaum says now that starting with *Dr No*, 'for some reason, looking at the very, very long-range future, United Artists did not want the Russians to be out and out villains, so we made Dr No come from SPECTER rather than SMERSH. That was really done for reasons of motion picture distribution, thinking that maybe some day Bond might go to Russia.'

Michael Wilson, producer and co-writer of *The Living Daylights*, and also Broccoli's stepson, sounded a dignified political note to match whatever commercial considerations United Artists may have been nourishing, saying that 'I think that if we do have an influence in the world it's an influence of moderation. Our films are seen by 250 million people in the first five years after they are made, right across the world, and because of that we are mindful that we have a responsibility. You can't be spewing out a lot of venom.'

Dr No set the high standard for Bond villains. The best of these villains was probably Gert Frobe in *Goldfinger* and Maibaum gave him one of the best lines. 'Do you expect me to talk?' Connery grits as the laser slices towards his crotch. 'No Mr Bond, I expect you to die.' On the whole one feels rather sorry for the villains, cultured and bold but thwarted in their schemes for world conquest by so mean an intellect as Bond's. But they don't have the juice that Fleming's cold war fifties political stance gave the novels, which is no doubt why the films got more and more fantastical, as sea, snow and travelogue became substitutes for Fleming's paranoid verve. So Dalton may talk of a return to the Bond of the books, but how can that be done in the age of Gorbachev?

It is not surprising, given the length of the Bond series, that the audiences now take so much pleasure in the expected, in Bond as ritual: the pre-credit sequence established in *From Russia With Love*; the encounter with Miss Moneypenny; the throw-away lines and polished dialogue; the gadgets produced by Q.

Ah yes, the gadgets: the briefcase with knives and gold sovereigns, the Aston Martin DB5 with ejector seat and saw-blades in the wheel hubs ... In the mid 1960s Umberto Eco wrote an interesting essay about Fleming in which he discussed the author's stylistic technique. 'Fleming takes time to convey the familiar with photographic accuracy,' Eco wrote, 'because it is upon the familiar that he can solicit our capacity for identification. Our credulity is solicited, blandished, directed to the region of possible and desirable things. Here the narration is realistic, the attention to detail intense; for the rest, so far as the unlikely is concerned, a few pages suffice and an implicit wink of the eye.'

Fleming, and through him, Bond, was acutely aware of commodities, mundane objects of desire. No previous thriller writer had ever accommodated himself to such an extent to the psychology of acquisition, of envy, to the spiritual rhythms of the advertising industry. The makers and marketers of Bond movies understood this aspect of Fleming's appeal very well, and soon the world grew used to Bond's pedantic lectures on Taittinger and Q's proud demonstrations of the latest in British gadgetry.

The movies are full of tie-ins, from Cartier watches to vodka to the trusty Aston Martin itself. Backdrop becomes commodified too, as the Bond producers scour the world for fresh locations, and ministers of tourism plead for a visit.

In this matter of commodities the Bond films have been a somewhat ironic reverie of British omnipotence. The cycle of Bond films began just when the Labour prime minister Harold Wilson was urging the nation to cast aside the archaic vestments of the past and bathe itself in the 'white heat of technology'. Things worked in Bond movies but they didn't work in Britain, and as Kingsley Amis once sadly remarked, if Bond had really had to use his mini-submarine in combat conditions it would have surely taken him straight to the bottom. In 1983, just when Q gave Bond a staggering number of gadgets in *Octopussy*, Britain became for the first time in its history a net importer of industrial goods.

Noel Coward put the contrast between fantasy and reality well. 'One of the things that still makes me laugh whenever I read Ian's books is the contrast between the standard of living of dear old Bond and the sort of thing Ian used to put up with at Goldeneye. When Bond drinks his wine it has to be properly *chambré*, the tournedos slightly underdone, and so forth. But whenever I ate with Ian at Goldeneye the food was so abominable I used to cross myself before I took a mouthful. ... I used to say, "Ian, it tastes like armpits." And all the time you were eating there was old Ian smacking his lips for more while his guests remembered all those delicious meals he had put into the books.'

I headed back into London from Pinewood and, late in the evening, turned on Channel 4. There was my friend Robin Blackburn, editor of *New Left Review*, addressing the nation on the paramount necessity of Britain becoming truly socialist if it is to get out of its present mess. 'The social horizon,' Robin said, 'is still defined by institutions which serve British capital but which are not specifically capitalist and are not found in any other capitalist country. Our ruling institutions are the products of oligarchy and empire. Consecrated by time and custom they are like a dead weight on the imagination and aspirations of the living. Britain has become a living museum of obsolescence, whose most splendid trophy is nothing less than the world's last ancien régime.'

Under prime ministers stretching back to Churchill, 007 has done his best to put Britain's foot forward. He himself is, with the happy assistance of United Artists, one of Britain's most successful exports. But if Bond is a fine example of world cultural integration at the level of kitsch, things are not in good shape on the home front, as bad under Thatcher as it was under her predecessors: productivity down, exports poor, rate of returns lousy, per capita income half what it is in France. What has improved strongly is the coercive apparatus of the state. 'You're nothing but a stupid policeman,' Dr No told Bond. If he had not had the misfortune to drown in his own nuclear well, the doctor would have been unhappy to discover that Bond's trade – policing the British state — has fared better than most of the other props in the old museum. In this respect at least, the fantasy came true.

American Film, July, 1987

The Underclass

I think that from the police point of view . . . my task in the future, in the ten to fifteen years from now . . . that basic crime such as theft, burglary, even violent crime will not be the predominant police feature. What will be the matter of greatest concern to me will be the covert and ultimately overt attempts to overthrow democracy, to subvert the authority of the state, and to in fact involve themselves in acts of sedition to destroy our parliamentary system and the democratic government of this country.

– James Anderton, Chief Constable of Greater Manchester, October 16, 1980

Once begun, the disorders on the Friday and the Saturday [April 10–11, 1981] soon developed into a riot. The common purpose of the two riots was to attack the police. But the riots were neither premeditated nor planned. Each was the spontaneous reaction of angry young men, most of whom were black, against what they saw as a hostile police force.

– Lord Scarman's Enquiry into the Brixton Disorders, November 1981

The riots, or uprisings, which erupted in 30 British cities last spring and summer did not merely register the rage of blacks against decades of police harassment and brutality. They represented, too, a rising of whites, mostly youths, against the police, against a desolate environment and zero expectations. What they registered, most fundamentally, were the effects of Britain's shift – stimulated by sharply rising unemployment and social discontent – from a 'liberal' to an 'authoritarian' democracy. Unemployment throughout the 1980s promises to be vastly more severe, with perhaps a third of the work force permanently unemployed. The uprisings of 1981 may be an intimation as much as a verdict. How the British state and the political parties respond – whether Conservative, Labour, or Social Democrat – is of more than passing relevance on this side of the Atlantic, where similar crises – often magnified – exist.

On the government agenda of every advanced industrial nation, in the ebb from the great postwar boom, is the simple question: amid vast structural unemployment and diminished social expectations, how best can the alarm expressed above by Chief Constable Anderton be assuaged? In the 1960s – as the British wistfully point out – the US was able, with the proper mixture of straightforward violence, to try to buy its way out of trouble from the underclass. Today, by ideological inclination or fiscal crisis, the buy-out formula is gathering dust. The crisis, most sharply expressed in relations between the police and blacks, caught up with Britain last year.

The Police

It is the devout belief of foreigners, a belief sedulously maintained by the British press, that the British police are the best in the world. It is not a belief that has ever been firmly held by the British working class or even substantial sections of the middle classes.

In the face of enormous popular unrest the London Metropolitan police force was set up in 1829. It was viewed then as the strong left arm of state supervision of discontent. The strong right arm was the army, which, between 1872 and 1908, was called in no less than 24 times to quell political and trade union demonstrations. Only with great difficulty – never with total social acceptance – was the consent of the working class won, by the 1920s, for policing by the 'bobby,' now etherealized as the arm of a 'neutral' state, acting for the benefit of the community as a whole.

By the end of the 1960s, as Britain settled fractiously into continuous economic decline, this compact was beginning to disintegrate. A number of scandals banished the legend of the incorruptibility of the British policeman and kindred fantasies about his disinterested pursuit of justice. Social unrest produced coercive policing of a sort long known to the Irish and other inhabitants of the old Empire.

The British Special Branch (broadly, the political police) increased sevenfold between the early 1960s and 1978. And in 1978 Merlyn Rees, the (Labour Party) Home Secretary, defined 'subversion' against the state as 'activities which threaten the safety and well-being of the state, and are intended to undermine or overthrow parliamentary democracy by political, industrial or violent means.' The word 'industrial' was not included by accident.

Unremitting efforts by successive British governments to curb trade union militancy produced, in 1971, the Industrial Relations Act, restricting picketing and various forms of strike action. In 1972, 30,000 miners and other industrial workers picketed the coal depot at Saltley. Their successful action led to the fall of the Heath government. It also accelerated the 'modernizing' of policing in Britain, in an echo of the overt and savage techniques being deployed in Northern Ireland.

The Special Branch, MI5, and military intelligence were all beefed up, with the latter's role being broadened to include internal affairs. Computer analysis of the population was extended and refined. In 1974, Heathrow airport just outside London was occupied by the army and the police four times. *The Guardian* reported that these operations were designed as 'public relations to accustom the public to the reality of troops deploying through the high streets.'

Riot shields were used for the first time in mainland Britain in Lewisham in 1977. In the winter of 1977-78 the army – for the first time in British history – replaced an entire work force, taking over from 20,000 striking firemen.

Two new police techniques developed. One takes the form of 'fire brigade' trouble-squelching, with patrol cars backed by a central mobile reserve – highly trained Special Patrol Groups and Police Support Units, replete with modern enforcement technology and firearms. These units are the equivalent of the CRS in France, Marechausee of Holland, or the Bereitschaftpolizei in West Germany. Their overtly repressive function even caused unease among some police chiefs who saw, in the words of Chief Constable Alderson of Devon, that 'Social pressures tend more and more to seduce police thinking and public awareness ... towards a quasi-military reactive concept.' Alderson's solution: 'Whereas preventive policing tends to put the system on the defensive, pro-active policing sets out to penetrate the community in a multitude of ways. It seeks to reinforce social discipline and mutual trust.' Put less politely, community control. Alderson saw the police as 'better placed than most organizations for providing social leadership of that kind,' working with the media (in 'an open and trusting' relationship), and breaking down barriers between themselves and other social, probation, and educational agencies.

Such was the twin-pronged approach developed through the 1970s, which failed utterly to predict or control the uprisings of 1981. Reactive policing down the years had taken too heavy a toll, notably on blacks.

The Blacks

There are today about three million Afro-Caribbean and other black people as well as Asians living in Britain. In the years after World War II, Britain, like other European countries, was desperate for labor and eagerly sought an immigrant labor force. As late as 1956, London Transport was recruiting from Barbados. There was as yet no officially sanctioned government racism – merely unofficial racism in housing, jobs, education, unionism, and so forth. In 1958, the Notting Hill Gate riots broke out, and

Justice Salmon sent nine white Teddy Boys to long terms in prison, saying 'We must establish the rights of everyone, irrespective of the color of their skin ... to walk through our streets with their heads erect and free from fear.'

Twenty years later, in 1978, Judge McKinnon ruled that Kingsley Read, head of the fascist National Party, was not guilty of incitement to racial hatred when he said publicly of 18-year-old Gurdip Singh Chaggar, set upon by white youths and stabbed to death, 'One down, one million to go.'

In the interval British governments, both Conservative and Labour, falteringly, with occasional remissions and bouts of bad conscience, proceeded down the path to racism – or more technically a 'guest-worker' economy. The revered totem of British citizenship was uprooted. Between the late 1940s and the late 1960s the chance of establishing a multiracial society was squandered. Immigration and policing policies grew harsher.

The year 1962 saw the Immigration Act regulate labor intake from 'colored' Commonwealth and colonial outposts. Racial discrimination was officially institutionalized. Police harassment increased accordingly. Most shamefully, in 1968 a Labour government devised and passed in one week the Kenyan Asian Act, barring free entry – guaranteed on their passports – of those of its citizens in Kenya, if they were Asians; if they could not prove, that is, that they had a parent or grandparent 'born, naturalised or adopted in the United Kingdom.'

The Immigration Act of 1971 stopped all primary immigration in its tracks. Only 'patrials' (i.e. someone with at least one grandparent born in the UK, and of British descent) retained the right of abode. 'Guest workers' were given special permits for a specific period. Rigorous rules blocked families from joining immigrants already settled in Britain. Police and immigration officers were empowered to arrest without warrant anyone who had entered or who was suspected of entering the country illegally or who had overstayed his or her visit.

It requires little imagination to see that such powers gave the police *carte blanche* to harass any black or Asian person they might encounter. The police were, in addition, equipped with laws that aroused enormous resentment and hatred in the black community, known as the 'Sus' laws. Section 4 of the Vagrancy Act of 1824 permitted a policeman to arrest anyone 'on suspicion of loitering with intent to commit an arrestable offense.' The police used the Sus laws to create virtual off-limits areas for blacks in certain sections and to control them elsewhere. The 1824 Sus law was repealed in 1981. Substituted, with masterly sleight of hand, was Section 9 of the Criminal Attempts Act which creates a new offense: 'to interfere [the word is undefined] with a motor vehicle with the intention of theft of the vehicle, or of theft of anything in it, or of taking and driving it away without consent.' Subsection 2 further adds, 'And, if it is shown that a person accused of an offence under this section intended that one of those offences should be committed, it is immaterial that it cannot be shown which it was.'

By the end of the 1970s Britain was – and still is – moving toward a pass-law society, in which the government could insist on passports and identity checks before providing services. The Thatcher government is still attempting to formulate an Act which will, definitively, keep blacks out and let whites in.

The Uprising

Overweening police power and a racism of the state fueled unofficial racism, with innumerable murderous attacks on blacks, in a Britain ravaged by Margaret Thatcher's economic politics, which struck at white and black alike. In April 1980, riots began in the St. Paul's area of Bristol, with some 130 arrests. At the start of April 1981, the police launched Operation Swamp '81 to combat street crime. More than 1,000 people were stopped and questioned in the first four days. The uprising in Brixton began on April 9 and lasted through Sunday, April 11. There were 4,000 police in the area, and 286 people arrested. The uprisings of July began on the 3rd in Southall. A day later Toxteth was in flames. By the weekend of July 10-12, 'riots' were taking place in 30 towns and cities – black and white youths together and in some cases white youths alone. They were scenes, as Lord Scarman said of Brixton 'of violence and disorder ... the like of which had not previously been seen in this century in Britain.'

'A New Ethos'

In the heart of Brixton, just off Railton Road where the April uprising began, are to be found the offices of *Race Today*. Its editor is Darcus Howe, a 38-year-old Trinidadian. Howe is one of the best-known black activists in Britain; we talked with him at length about the uprisings, about developments in the Afro-Caribbean and Asian communities, and about his perspective of political options, both for blacks and whites.

DH: 'We were persuaded, encouraged to come to Britain, to be hewers of wood and drawers of water. The perception of this new section of working people went as follows: we would rigidly concern ourselves with work: we would have no leisure; we would, without deviation, get there in the morning, come home in the evening, go to bed, go back there in the morning, come home in the afternoon, go to bed. Any relaxation of that discipline would undermine the exclusive reason for why we were here. So when West Indians held parties in their homes to ease the tensions of the working day, the police would raid them, to suppress them. Any form of leisure activity at all that we were involved in, anything other than on the way to work, we were harassed. So if you were unemployed and weren't working and you were found around the streets of London, there was a charge which they resurrected called 'Sus,' 'being a suspicious person,' a charge going back centuries, when they sought to curb the unemployed in the early period of British industrialization.

'It is necessary to identify these reasons because we tend to get carried away by this exclusive question of race, without taking into consideration the fundamental reasons. Of course race is used to justify it, once it takes place. It gives it an extra impetus, but it is not fundamental. That's the first point.

'The second point is this: we have come up against – in posing the question of the behavior of the British police – a formidable hurdle. I describe it in this way: it's a myth, all the more powerful because it contains elements of truth, that the British police are the best in the world. It is truth turned on its head. What is the case is that the mass of the British population, having neutralized a very powerful monarchy and having established parliamentary democracy, developed – I believe – a very strong democratic instinct and a very strong sense of freedom that ensured that the British police were hemmed in by a set of rules and regulations. But whenever those constraints are absent, the British police are capable of all the excesses which can be perpetrated by modern police forces. All.

'And the Caribbean peoples, who are always reminded of slavery at the slightest hint of oppression, have revolted in a way that no one has seen in Britain in the last hundred years. It is an historical moment of extreme significance, not only for ourselves but for society as a whole.'

'*Why did this historical moment occur in 1981?*'

'Several factors. The major one is a change in composition in the black community. Those of us who came here in the late '50s and early '60s were constrained by the myth that we were going home sooner or later, that we would earn some money and go, and therefore tended to put up with things that we knew were wrong and discussed with each other as being illegal and against any conception of human rights. But there are young blacks who were born here, who have grown up here, who eat bangers and mash, egg and chips with the same ease as their white counterparts, who sit in the same classrooms with them, who know that whites aren't in any way superior to them, and once the police encountered that generation, they met with a completely different attitude.

'Because the older West Indian population had been separated socially from their white counterparts – they didn't mix – they had no measure of what they thought. All assessment of your white fellow workers was governed by myth and prejudice. But the younger ones went to school with those kids. One of the myths that constrained us was that there would be a white backlash if we acted. The younger ones know that that isn't so. They know that the young whites have the same problems.'

'*So, concerning the police what would you specifically advocate?*'

'There's a new and very dangerous tendency which creeps into all these matters. They now invest the police with political powers. We don't vote for them. We don't elect them, but suddenly we are asked to have discussions with them on social and political questions. I am against that, for this reason: they have a tremendous amount of power and I have none, so it's an unequal discussion.'

'*... which institutionalizes the inequality.*'

'Absolutely. I will talk to them if a burglar comes into my house. That's when I speak to them. If I want some direction. Those areas in which you speak to the police must be so strictly defined that they won't be able to creep out of that into general discussion.'

'*So what you want are laws to curb the police. It's as simple as that.*'

'Absolutely. The reinstitution of civil power over institutionalized, coercive power. Heavy discipline.'

'*So what is going on, socially and politically, in terms of black organization?*'

'The riots opened up an entirely new political ethos. To understand the organizational stages that we are moving to, it is essential to know that in the late 1960s there were black-power organizations in almost every city in this country. A combination of repression – not as sharp as in the United States – but repression British-style and Harold Wilson's political cynicism undermined that movement. What he did was to offer a lot of money to the black community, which set up all kinds of advice centers and projects for this and projects for that. So, in some black communities, if you have a headache somebody is onto you saying, 'Well, look, I have a project for blacks with headaches.' That paralysed the political initiative of blacks. It was done for you by the state and, as you know, Britain is saturated with the concept of welfare.

'The riots have broken through that completely, smashed it to smithereens, indicating that it was no palliative, no cure for the cancer.'

'*You are looking toward a black/white mass organization?*'

'Black/white mass movement. But one always must point to what we are heading for. What are we aiming for? Are we aiming for the vulgarity of a better standard of living? I think a passion has arisen in the breasts of millions of people in the world for a kind of democratic form and shape which would equal parliamentary democracy in its creativity and innovation.

'The competition for jobs leads two ways. In meeting each other in the competition, we either decide not to compete anymore or we take that competition to its logical conclusion. What prevents you from taking competition to the logical conclusion is that Britain has a sense of class. The working class have a sense of themselves, and when you go to America you know how important that is. Working people in Britain tend to see being working class as a virtue. In *Great Expectations*, Dickens had a character called Joe Gargery. He wasn't contented, in that he accepted tribulations as though they were designed for him, but he had a certain pride in his class. So when Pip wanted to get up he said, Well if you want to go that way, go your way, but I'm going to remain here and I'm going to carry on my life and improve my circumstances, but nevertheless I'm not leaving here. Gargery seems to me to be the reflection of what British working-class people are like. Everyone talks about Pip and Miss Havisham, but never has an artist fashioned such a historical character as Gargery.'

'*So class is dominant over race in Britain?*'

'Dominant. It could cease being so, you know. One has to fight to keep it that way.'

'*But let's look at a likely future for Britain: enormous structural unemployment, the creation of a permanent underclass . . .*'

'Permanent unemployed, that is what is on the agenda, with the revolutionizing of production, with the microchip. Now what the British working class has to do is to break out of this demand for jobs, which characterized the 1930s, the Jarrow marches, and so on. They will have to lift themselves to this new reality, which will of course call for the merciless shortening of the working day, the working week, and the working life, and a concentration on leisure and the quality of work. That is the debate that is going on and that is the debate missed by a lot of the old-style trade unionists and the old-style institutions like the trade union bureaucracy and the Labour Party.

'I look at young blacks. If you look at the development of Rastafarianism on such a massive scale, this cannot be separated in my view from the material basis and creeping consciousness that one will not work again and one must now be concerned with what is life? Is there a God? Who is he? What is the relationship between yourself and your kind? That is the creeping development of Rastafarianism.

'The first set of people to know that there ain't no work anymore were ex-slaves. From the moment we came off the plantation, labor-intensive, and you started to present us with factories, there was no work ever again. That is new to the advanced countries, but to the underdeveloped countries . . . I could take you to Port of Spain now and point to him, him, and him and say he is a grandfather and he never worked in his life. This is a grandmother who never worked in her life. We come easy to it. But here, they say "March for Jobs." What jobs?'

'*It's stimulating to hear you say this, because the left seems to have a lot of illusions about this. The slogan should really be "Less work," not "More Work."'*

'"Less work, more money." And that's a vulgarity too. "Less work, more leisure." We have built up over the centuries the technological capacity to release people from that kind of servitude.'

'*So then you have to talk about redistribution of wealth.*'

'Free distribution. A completely new ethos. And we are on the verge of it.'

'*Don't you think that pathological symptoms, including racism, will increase as people fight on the scrap heap, as the economy goes down?*'

'I agree. Something else increases too. Side by side, living in the same atom with pathology, is the possibility to lift. You can't reach the lifting stage without the pathological stage.'

'*So the oppositions are a client populace, battling for a little bit more of a slice.*'

'Crabs in a barrel. Or you leap. The leap depends on what dominant political ideology is presented to the population.'

'*You view the current decline of the Labour Party with considerable optimism?*'

'Considerable optimism. The Labour Party is a creature of a certain moment in the material organization of society, and the forces which arise from this. It's work, it's welfare. It's getting some things to the ordinary working people, which of course I understand. When you read, especially in the novels, I think there you get much more penetrating insights into life and society than those offered by politicians. The poverty of the mining population when people would have to wrap cloth around their feet to keep warm – that doesn't exist in Britain anymore. Nor will people permit it. Either they are driven back to that, or something else happens. My view is that the Labour Party is an instrument that was necessary for that period.'

A Sudden Shout

It was six in the evening and outside the *Race Today* offices people were sloshing through the puddles on the way home from work, or standing about in doorways. Howe got up and stretched, then picked up a document.

'Listen to this,' he said. 'After the uprising in Moss Side last July they appointed a local Manchester barrister called Hytner to enquire into what happened, and how it started. Here's what he writes:

'"At about 10:20 pm a responsible and in our view reliable mature black citizen was in Moss Lane East, and observed a large number of black youths whom he recognized as having come from a club a mile away. At the same time a horde of white youths came up the road from the direction of Moss Side. He spoke to them and ascertained they were from Withenshawe. The two groups met and joined. There was nothing in the manner of their meeting which in any way reflected a prearranged plan. There was a sudden shout and the mob stormed off in the direction of Moss Side police station. We are given an account by another witness who saw the mob approach the station, led, so it was claimed, by a nine-year-old boy with those with Liverpool accents in the van." '

Howe smiled: 'Whites from Withenshawe, blacks from Moss Side, no prearranged plan. They gather. There is a shout, "On to Moss Side police station." That gives you some indication. You must have a convergence of interests in order for that to happen.'

Village Voice, January 6, 1982

COUNTRIES LOST
AND FOUND

*History may be irrevocable, but there is always
the self to be discovered.*

P.G. Wodehouse:
The Road to Long Island

Somewhat as if Robinson Crusoe tried to tell Man Friday about Yorkshire pudding, it's hard to explain Wodehouse to the uninitiated. He evolved a comedy of manners and a mannered style that came into perfect fluency and equilibrium by the early thirties. In the early fifties that tautness of control began to slacken. I myself believe that he reached the summit of his careful art with *The Code of the Woosters*, published in 1938, and *Joy in the Morning*, largely written as the Germans were preparing to invade France, polished as they bore Wodehouse off from Le Touquet to internment in Germany, and published after the war. His latest biographer, Frances Donaldson, believes the peak came earlier, with *Thank You, Jeeves*, in 1934. Wodehouse himself preferred *Quick Service*, published in 1940.

It is not a dispute of much importance. By the mid-thirties Hilaire Belloc was broadcasting to America his view that Wodehouse was 'the best living writer of English' and there are at least half a dozen books in the decade surrounding that dictum to which admirers can reach, if asked to furnish proofs of Belloc's veracity.

Cultism – and there has long been a Wodehouse cult with powerful adepts guarding the mystery – often leads to facetious overstatement. A bad sign is when worshipers start calling the object of their veneration 'the Master.' But Belloc had it right all the same in stressing Wodehouse's virtues as an artificer of language, rather than as the creator of Jeeves, Bertie Wooster, Emsworth, Mulliner, Ukridge, Psmith, and the rest of them. Few writers were so self-conscious in the refinement of language. Wodehouse loved to read trash, just as in his later years he loved to watch it on daytime TV, and in the dense allusive utterance of Bertie Wooster one can find a meditation on the banality, coarsened *tempi*, images, and conventions of late Victorian and Edwardian literary discourse which scarcely suffers from being set next to the great explorations of cliché in Joyce's *Ulysses*. Wodehouse was as determined a mannerist as Wilde in the guying of conventional discourse. His best books are the apotheosis of the artificial, yet like Wilde his fluency and ease of idiom rendered this artifice natural and altered English diction, hence British culture.

It is instructive to read aloud dialogue from *The Importance of Being Earnest* and follow with exchanges between Bertie Wooster and Jeeves or Bertie and Gussie Fink-Nottle, et al. The rhythms are remarkably similar. Both writers get their effects – Wilde much more sharply – from reversals of conventional idiom and conventional attitude (e.g., 'Was your father born to ... the purple of commerce or did he rise from the ranks of the aristocracy?'). For the more conventional and conservative Wodehouse the critique was more narrowly of language than of society, so the paradoxes and parodies were more technical whereas in Wilde's case they were more substantive.

I do not recall Wodehouse discussing Wilde in his letters, which is surprising, given the extent of his stylistic debt. My own view is that Wodehouse's almost pathological prudery in sexual matters, a reticence sublimated in the jocular male partnerships employed in his fiction and the loyal epistolary male friendships of his life, caused him to shy away in extreme nervousness from mention of Wilde.

Wooster says there are those who like to find girls in heliotrope pajamas in their beds and those who don't. He belonged to the latter category, and Wodehouse seems to have thought that was the sensible outlook to have. The girls esteemed by Wooster – e.g., Stiffy, Bobby – were boys, to all intents and mentionable purposes. Girls of the other type – Madeline Bassett – were boys too, only 'wets,' reading poetry and no doubt ending up as dissidents in Thatcher's Cabinet. There is a third, Amazonian category – Honoria Glossop springs imposingly to mind, as indeed does the present British prime minister herself. Donaldson's remarks about Wodehouse's sexuality – quoted below – are pertinent.

One way to evoke Wodehouse at his best is once again to remember Wilde at full stretch in *The Importance of Being Earnest*, where skill of exposition, mastery of structure, combined with fluency and inventiveness in idiom, carry the reader at top speed and without pause through farcical imbroglio to ultimate resolution. *The Code of the Woosters* contains a main plot, three subplots, two separate love interests, two major villains. Yet there is no moment when the reader is left hanging as Wodehouse switches scenery and redeploys. The language, all of it contained within Bertie's first-person narrative, is at full tension throughout, with the famous similes resplendent. The beauty lies in the deftness, pacing, linguistic aplomb: early Waugh with better manners and without the edgy madness and social bad faith.

But then Wodehouse was more poised because, unlike Waugh (or indeed another admirer, Orwell), he did not like England very much and consequently had a better prose style. In his *Life of Raymond Chandler* Frank MacShane quotes Chandler's little essay in his notebook on English and American style:

> [American style] is a fluid language, like Shakespearian English, and easily takes in new words, new meanings for old words. ... Its overtones and undertones are not stylized into a social conventional kind of subtlety which is in effect a class language. It is more alive to clichés. Consider the appalling, because apparently unconscious, use of clichés by as good a writer as Maugham in *The Summing Up*, the deadly repetition of pet words until they almost make you scream. ... English, being on the defensive, is static and cannot contribute anything but a sort of waspish criticism of forms and manners. ... The tone quality of English speech is usually overlooked. This tone quality is infinitely variable and contributes infinite meaning. The American voice is flat, toneless and tiresome. The English tone quality makes a thinner vocabulary and a more formalized use of language capable of infinite meanings. Its tones are of course written into written speech by association. This of course makes good English a class language, and that is its fatal defect. The English writer is a gentleman (or not a gentleman) first and a writer second.

Chandler went to the same British public school (Dulwich) as Wodehouse. Both of them made most of their money in America and had to take care of audiences on both sides of the Atlantic. Wodehouse made his first crossing in 1904, broke into the US magazine market in a big way in 1915 and into the theater shortly thereafter. Wodehouse got the best of both worlds: the fluidity, the alertness to cliché, the detachment that held him free of waspishness. Wodehouse's style was highly formalized, yet he certainly remained always a writer first and a gentleman second. Oddly enough, Chandler made Marlowe a gentleman in the end, which proved his stylistic undoing. At a critical moment Wodehouse behaved like a writer and not at all like a gentleman, which nearly proved his undoing too.

This moment had to do with Wodehouse's notorious broadcasts from Berlin in 1941, an episode that takes up a substantial portion of Frances Donaldson's book, and provides it with nearly all of its drama. Aside from the matter of the broadcasts, Wodehouse's life and professional career were of a simplicity and general uneventfulness that would not, in a rational world, provoke a critical and biographical industry. Enthusiasts already have Richard Usborne's work, in *Clubland Heroes* and two other volumes; a biography and bibliography by David Jansen; and a respectable covey of other studies. Frances Donaldson's biography avails itself of new letters provided her by relatives and friends. She sets forth the known facts conveniently enough, excavates new ones, uses what memories she has as a family friend and as a particularly close acquaintance of Wodehouse's beloved stepdaughter Leonora. She falters only when she attempts critical appreciation of Wodehouse's work – a subject on which she has nothing particularly illuminating to add.

Born in 1881, Wodehouse lived through a moderately unpleasant childhood when he was separated from his parents for long intervals, delightful schooldays at Dulwich which he later described as the happiest time of his life, and a brief sojourn in a bank before becoming a full-time writer. He published his first novel, *The Pothunters*, in 1902 and his last, *The Cat Nappers*, in 1975. Only in 1911, 1941, and the years from 1943 to 1945 did he fail to provide either his British or his American audiences with a new book in the intervening seventy-three years. In the first half of his career he was also collaborating, mostly with Guy Bolton and Jerome Kern, in a profusion of musical comedies put on in the teens and twenties. A wife, a few close friends, and an unending succession of pets – mostly Pekingese dogs – refreshed his emotional life, but from the end of his teens to his ninety-fifth year he devoted almost every day of his prolonged existence to writing or to thinking about writing, and there is no evidence to suggest that he had much interest in doing anything else.

The immensity of his literary production is not perhaps as unrivaled as Donaldson appears to believe. Simenon's output – until his retirement – was similarly prodigious. But it is hard to think of another writer who worked so tranquilly with such copious success within so narrow a range, unless we are to consider a detective-story writer such as Agatha Christie, whose entire *oeuvre* scarcely contains a single memorable line.

Wodehouse lived to work, well beyond the point where he had to work for a living. He had a vast contempt for writers 'with only one book in them' and believed with Arnold Bennett that an audience could be won and retained only if the author's name, on a new dust jacket, was constantly obtruded upon the readers' attention. Just as another great producer and hero of Wodehouse, Arthur Conan Doyle, scribbled in railway stations, trains, and cars so too did Wodehouse never stop working. Briefly arrested by the French at the end of the Second World War, he occupied some of his time in the police station polishing off another chapter.

He described himself as an 'objective' rather than a 'subjective' writer, perceiving his task as the satisfaction of magazine editors, publishers, and readers. He regarded prattle about 'artistic self-expression' as disgraceful egoism. Indeed nothing Wodehouse said about himself can be regarded as particularly trustworthy. He readily made up stories, or fabricated views, when pestered by interviewers and admirers about such matters as the origins of Jeeves or his verdict on this or that writer or book. Publishing some of his correspondence with his friend William Townend, he had no compunction in smartening it up for the reader. For him it was all a matter of professionalism, and if his critical judgment told him that his audience would prefer to hear that Jeeves was based on a real-life butler called Robinson rather than a stock type in the British comic tradition he would alter the truth with just the same alacrity as he would obey the editors of the *Saturday Evening Post* when they asked him to restructure the first chapter of *The Code of the Woosters.*

What Wodehouse admirers really need is an edition of the complete letters, even including the innumerable tedious and prolix passages on his beloved Pekes. These letters, notably the ones to Townend, Dennis Mackail, and Guy Bolton reveal him as a professional literary technician of enormous self-assurance and rather intolerant perspicacity, quite different from the records of his conversations and interviews, where he usually displayed a self-deprecation and an innocence partly natural but sometimes contrived.

Wodehouse presents a challenge to any biographer in that he was productive for three quarters of the twentieth century but with one exception held all potentially troublesome parts of this period expertly at bay. By the 1930s he was one of the highest-paid writers in the United States, suffering endless disputes with the IRS in consequence. But long before these years he had won a financial security and hence latitude in existence which any writer could envy. Success brought none of the usual vices. He did not drink to excess. Donaldson carefully writes that '... one would not expect to find him capable of intense, passionate love. His relationships with women, including his wife, have been speculated upon in the idle, gossipy way in which people speculate on the intimate affairs of their friends and of public characters about whom a good deal is known. Wodehouse may or may not have been inhibited sexually as well as emotionally, and this inhibition may have been partial or complete.'

He married a widow called Ethel Rowley in 1914. They produced no children. The management and enjoyment of his large earnings were, as Donaldson delicately indicates, chiefly the preserve of Lady Wodehouse, who kept her husband on a tight allowance and who was an enthusiastic investor and gambler besides.

Given tolerable and sometimes considerable comfort Wodehouse seems to have been relatively indifferent on the matter of where he should live. Perhaps appropriately for a writer who spent much of his time evoking an England which dwelt only in his imagination, he spent the larger portion of his life outside the jurisdiction, in New York, Hollywood, Le Touquet, Cannes, and ultimately Remsenburg, Long Island, where he spent his last twenty-odd years.

The version of England disposed by Wodehouse would probably have lost its refinement if he had spent all his time scribbling in the Cotswolds or some grim hamlet in the Home Counties, rather than snugly ensconced in the neutral terrain of New York or the suburban-pastoral of Long Island.

The muscle-bound Anglophilia, blending into dogged reaction, which captures most British writers in the end was held at bay, and Wodehouse himself stayed decently remote from the invented Wodehouse of admirers such as Auberon Waugh, middlebrows beetling as they bear down on the moderns and anything so noxious as culture or the world of the intellect.

Wodehouse's indifference to England may have been rather more profound than he cared publicly to let on. *Author! Author!*, the American edition of the letters published in England as *Performing Flea*, has some reflections on the British class system omitted from the earlier version, presumably because he did not wish to offend his British audience.

A letter to Townend dated May 11, 1929, mentions a meeting with H.G. Wells and goes on:

> What do you think happened when we met? We shook hands, and his first remark apropos of nothing, was 'My father was a professional cricketer.' A conversation stopper if ever there was one. What a weird country England is, with its class distinctions and that ingrained snobbery you can't seem to escape from. I suppose I notice it more because I've spent so much of my time in America. Can you imagine an American who had achieved the position Wells has, worrying because he started out in life on the wrong side of the tracks? But nothing will ever make Wells forget that his father was a professional cricketer and his mother the housekeeper at Up Park.

There is mention of Wells's remark in *Performing Flea*, in a letter written three years later; but the comment about ingrained English snobbery is nowhere to be found.

Donaldson quotes from a couple of revealing letters Wodehouse wrote in the mid-fifties. To Townend: 'I'm being egged on to become an American citizen. Do you think it would hurt me in England if I did? I don't want to let Jenkins [his publisher] down by suddenly ruining my sales ...' And to Mackail, just after he had received his US citizenship: 'The morning after the proceedings I was rung up on the telephone by the *Mail*, the *Express*, *The Times*, the Associated Press and others. They all wanted to know why I had done it, and it was a little difficult to explain without hurting anyone's feelings that, like you, I don't feel it matters a damn what country one belongs to and that what I really wanted was to be able to travel abroad without having to get an exit permit and an entrance permit, plus – I believe – a medical examination.'

Now spending much time and ingenuity preventing the black inhabitants of their former dominions from enjoying the perquisites of citizenship in the UK, the British have always found it inexplicable when a full-fledged white member of the race opts for another passport or seems indifferent on the matter of whether he should or shouldn't. It's why the British are always so peculiarly astounded by what they care to call treachery – a word much in vogue in the recent Falklands affair – and spend much foolish time trying to divine the motivation of Oxbridge undergraduates, subsequently elevated in public life, who thought that mass unemployment in the thirties was a bad thing and that Marxism might be the best answer to the problem. Discounted by these plodding analysts of the roots of treachery is that there was a lot to feel treacherous about.

Wodehouse was accused of treachery because he broadcast from Nazi Germany in 1941. Donaldson, using all available documentation, gives a complete account of the affair. The circumstances surrounding Wodehouse's supposed treachery and certain bad judgment appear to be as follows.

He was working on *Joy in the Morning* in Le Touquet, perhaps oblivious of the approaching Germans, perhaps confident they would leave him alone. After a short interval he was marched off to an internment camp in Upper Silesia, where he spent eleven months. Internees were routinely released when they reached sixty, but shortly before he reached this particular birthday Wodehouse became the beneficiary of pressure applied by American friends who had become alarmed at a photograph of him taken at the internment camp, in which he appeared somewhat emaciated.

He was released and taken to Berlin. Waiting to meet him in the Adlon Hotel were a Major Erich, Baron von Barnekow, an old friend from the United States, and a man from the German foreign office called Werner Plack, whom Wodehouse had known slightly in Hollywood. Plack suggested that he make a broadcast to America, recounting his experiences during internment. Wodehouse readily agreed and shortly thereafter recorded five talks.

While Plack seems to have made the correct calculation that Wodehouse's material would be lighthearted in vein and therefore display the Third Reich in a kindly light, Donaldson convincingly shows that Wodehouse had not bargained release from the internment camp against the broadcasts. He seems to have been guided by four professional instincts: it was an assignment which by nature and training he was conditioned to accept; the broadcasts were a way of keeping his name before his American audience; they were additionally a way of thanking his American admirers for their support; and, as Wodehouse rather touchingly confessed later, he thought they would reveal him as having borne up spunkily under trying circumstances.

By no stretch of the imagination can the five broadcasts themselves (sequestered from public view by the British authorities for many years after Wodehouse gave them to a British intelligence officer in Paris at the end of the war and printed by Donaldson in their entirety) be regarded as Nazi propaganda. They were slightly labored, knockabout, jocular reminiscences of internment camp life, as first jotted down by Wodehouse in an internment camp diary which formed the basis for the manuscript 'Camp Book', which he readied for publication after the war (his *Ballad of Reading Gaol?*) but which either he or Lady Wodehouse finally destroyed.

The fact is that Wodehouse seems to have rather enjoyed internment, perhaps unsurprisingly for someone who thought public school to have been the happiest season of his life. Nor did he seem to have the remotest idea of what the war was about, as the reminiscences of Harry Flannery, a CBS correspondent who interviewed him at the Adlon at the time, make clear.

> Among other things I planned to ask him what he thought of the Russian Campaign. Wodehouse [the two were rehearsing the interview] proposed saying: 'The bigger they are, the harder they fall.' I cautioned him against that. 'That predicts a Nazi victory,' I said. 'You can't do that.' 'Why not?' he asked. 'We're fighting the Nazis. Any such reply would be propaganda or worse, coming from you. You can't say that.' Wodehouse thought for a moment. 'Do you know,' he said, 'I wouldn't have thought of that.'

We either have to suppose that Wodehouse was a devious pro-Nazi, which in the face of all the evidence (including the important passages on fascist and lingerie-designer Sir Roderick Spode, leader of the Black Shorts in *The Code of the Woosters*) is absurd, or we must conclude that Wodehouse's detachment from inconvenient realities included political and military developments from the onset of the war. This absence of focus accounts for his foolishness in making the broadcasts, his ill-taste to accept a small payment for them (which he later lied about), and for the fact that it was not until the fifties that he seems to have realized that he had made a terrible mistake. It is indeed not entirely clear whether he ever thought in his heart of hearts that he had made a mistake at all, or whether he merely came to the conclusion that he better say he had, just to placate general ill-feeling. In the years immediately following the war he regarded accusations of treachery as ludicrous – in which view he was most famously supported by George Orwell – and derogatory of a nicely judged piece of writing.

In Britain, of course, right from the moment he announced his intention to broadcast, he was in the soup – understandably so. Most people never heard the actual talks and concluded after a vicious press campaign led by the *Daily Mirror* columnist 'Cassandra' (William Connor) and stimulated by Duff Cooper, minister of information, that Wodehouse had become the willing pawn of Goebbels. As the bombs crashed down on Coventry and London, it is not hard to see why many regarded Wodehouse with scant esteem. And he was, after the broadcasts, having a reasonably comfortable time of it, 'interned' in a succession of pleasant German country houses and the Adlon Hotel, before moving to Paris in 1943.

In Paris at the end of the war he was interrogated by the British, and finally – after some menacing talk in the British Commons about the possibility of prosecution for trading with the enemy (that former Mosley henchperson Harold Nicolson was particularly venomous) – he removed to the security of the United States, where he spent the rest of his days, receiving full pardon from the British in the form of a knighthood awarded in 1975, two months before he died.

So detached, so selfish, so tenacious in achieving the tranquil isolation necessary for his art, Wodehouse paid a heavy price for his insouciance in the face of history. The revisionists have tried to suggest that Wodehouse actually behaved well in Berlin in 1941, or at least did not behave badly. This is too kind to Wodehouse. His performance was discreditable, the hysteria at his broadcasts equally so. The governors of the BBC tried gallantly to prevent Cassandra from broadcasting his calumnies in 1941. They were overruled by Duff Cooper. Forty-one years later Prime Minister Thatcher ventilated similar fury at the BBC for having the bad taste to regard the Argentinians as human beings, residents of the planet Earth in equal standing with the citizens of the British nation. Charges of treachery were leveled, revenge plotted. The Britain that Wodehouse fled and that he purified in art lives on.

Review of P.G. Wodehouse: A Biography, *by Frances Donaldson; The New York Review of Books, September 23, 1982*

Edward James:
At Home in Xilitla

The sun climbs over the rim of some mountains 200 miles north of Mexico City and gleams like a poached egg through the milky morning mist. Three miles away across the valley the little town of Xilitla takes shape and color, nowhere more strikingly than in the antic cupolas and Venetian colonnades of the house of Plutarco Gastelum, part Yaqui Indian, part Basque, self-taught architect. Down on the valley floor the sun begins to disclose the work of Plutarco's late associate, sometime employer, and longtime friend Edward James, who was part English, part American, probably the grandson of Kind Edward VII, most assuredly a millionaire, and, when it came to architecture, as self-taught as Plutarco.

The transition to James's concrete dreamscape comes abruptly a few hundred yards down a rutted track off the road up to Xilitla. Pairs of columns forty feet high and crowned with wings lead to a triumphal arch, an echo of the Borromini false perspective in the Palazzo Spada. The red, tan, and gray scoops in its abruptly narrowing vault begin to glow in the sunrise with an ironic salute to European tradition from the Mexican hillside.

Round the corner from the arch there is a narrow door in what looks, at first glance, like a gatehouse. A column, bulging at its midriff like the royal palm next to it, carries a frill of steps up to the concrete mezzanine of what James called the House Destined to Be a Cinema. Here is the symbolic furniture of the Surrealists, of Hollywood montages of the unconscious: windows on nothing, doorways to nowhere, spirals that beckon one up to arches that end in air. A few yards farther on, orange doors of iron, shaped like the oval tunnel entry to a mystery ride in a funfair, lead to a vista of leaping serpents, seven feet high, inlaid with turquoise mosaic chips and with iron reinforcing rods darting from their mouths, hissing across the path at giant concrete toadstools buttressed by swans' necks rising from clusters of stone leaves stained green and blue.

In five minutes we have gone from Borromini to Dali to Disney and now we are on the flagged pathway of an English country churchyard with a mossy wall, winding uphill through the jungle. In the temple of dark green, with the help of sunbeam spotlights, the eye gradually picks out the hopes, the whims, the afterthoughts of James and his builders.

It's a dream in which nothing ever comes to a conclusion. There are houses without floors, floors almost without houses, electric cables for a nonexistent lighting system snaking out of walls and pillars. Everywhere there are impedimenta of the dreamscape: a cavernous cellar with a concrete couch, a stone hand four feet high, a Gothico-Hindi ocelot cage with a magenta floor, a concrete screen of Regency bamboo. The paths are almost blocked by immense leaves of *Philodendron giganteum.* Columns abound: bulbous, slender, hexagonal, Ionic, Corinthian, Oriental, square. There are fat columns in the Homage to Max Ernst, columns like a coast-guard's watchtree, columns half-buried by vines amid the pale pink phlox, stippled with lichen and the fading tints of violent Mexican colors.

Up the hill one goes through vistas of Gothic, reminiscences of Angkor Wat, Bangkok, and the Brighton Pavilion, till at last one reaches the crystal pool at the bottom of the sixty-foot falls that give the *finca* its name, Las Posas. Here's the little Temple for the Ducks, crowned with pale mauve wildflowers, water splashing past it through mysterious stone courses and great whale ribs of concrete, a half dam with a Dali cartwheel set into it. The butterflies swoop to and fro and one can hear distant laughter from the pool down by the Borromini arch where the people from Xilitla go. Here, as everywhere in Las Posas, there are signs of mighty work in progress, trace elements of some civilization long gone or brusquely interrupted. But this is an illusion, partly deliberate and partly prompted by the jungle's own rapid reclamation project. At Las Posas, the Age of James only began in the 1960s. There are scarcely any structures here older than the New Frontier.

Edward James is one of our century's minor cult figures. The path that led him to Xilitla winds back through the century past such landmarks as Dali, Magritte, and Kurt Weill to the Oxford of the late 1920s and ultimately to a large house in Sussex, where he grew up amid every appurtenance of luxury, having been born near Edinburgh in 1907. His paternal grandfather had solidly anchored the family's fortune in the American lumber and mining empires resumed in the names of his two wives, Phelps and Dodge. James's mother brought her son misery rather than money, but also the distinction of having almost certainly been the consequence of a Highland fling between her mother, Helen Forbes, and the Prince of Wales, later Edward VII.

With Saxe-Coburg blood pulsing in his veins and Phelps-Dodge income coursing through his bank account James fashioned a life of conspicuous idleness, undistinguished versifying, and sometimes brilliant patronage and collecting. His meandering romantic and sexual interests reached their greatest notoriety with his brief marriage to the Viennese actress and dancer Tilly Losch. To further her career he sponsored Balanchine's first company, Les Ballets 1933, for which he claimed later to have written a scenario with music by Weill, lyrics by Brecht, best known now in the form of *The Seven Deadly Sins*. The marriage to Tilly was a disaster. She sued for a divorce, alleging homosexuality and cruelty on his part. Against the etiquette of the time he countersued, charging her with infidelity, most notably with Serge Obolensky, though once James's maid had entered the drawing room of their house in London to find her in flagrante on the sofa with James's friend Randolph Churchill. The sensational court case ended with James's getting his decree nisi as well as the cold shoulder from most of his friends, who thought he'd behaved like a cad. The experience seems to have pushed him towards exile.

From the early 1930s he had become close friends with the Surrealists and a patron of Dali and Magritte. He built up a fine collection, most notably of these two – the back of James's head features in Magritte's *La Reproduction interdite* – but also including such artists as Paul Delvaux, Christian Bérard, Leonora Carrington, Pavel Tchelitchew. The collection was successfully sold in the late 1970s, thus permitting the construction at Las Posas to continue till James's death in 1984.

After offering to buy the Republicans a bomber in the Spanish civil war, in return for first pick of some Spanish paintings he was keen on, James set course for Los Angeles, where he spent a good portion of the next twenty years. He frequented the Vedanta circle fostered by Gerald Heard, was a friend of Krishnamurti and Aldous Huxley, and began in 1945 to make a series of trips to Mexico. In that year, driving south in a Lincoln Continental with a U.S. army sergeant, he first saw the curving thumb of the mountain crag of Huestmolotepl, and two years later, with the help of Plutarco Gastelum, he bought some steep jungle land along the waterfalls in the shadow of this same thumb.

At first James planned to grow orchids at Las Posas. The weather changed his mind for him in 1962 when a rare frost killed thousands of plants. By this time he had taken Plutarco and his wife, Marina, on a tour of Europe and on his return Plutarco, fired with the glories of Venice and Florence, decided to build something serious in Xilitla. As Plutarco's structure rose with its colonnades and cupolas, James embarked upon his strange version of a home across the valley.

The two projects progressed, both accurate reflections of their makers. Plutarco domesticated his imagination sufficiently to make a home. James, as befits an exile and a dilettante, supervised an architectural résumé of his life and travels: a folly in the eighteenth-century manner, a Surrealist manifesto in poured concrete, homage to Lewis Carroll, Ernst, Dali, Miró.

If Las Posas is in the tradition of eighteenth-century landscaping, it also owes much to two great naive architects: Le Facteur Cheval, whose Palais Idéal in the French Drôme was an icon of the Surrealists, and Simon Rodia, whose Watts Towers in Los Angeles James helped save from destruction in the 1960s, just as he started work at Xilitla.

Las Posas looks to the fantastic and to the light-hearted in architectural history, from Eastern temples through Gaudí to Juan O'Gorman. In his only other architectural enterprise, a semi-surreal rehab of the Lutyens-built Monkton House on his Sussex estate which he supervised in the 1930s, James did his best to transcend the spirit-squashing tedium of the well-bred English country house.

To start with, he painted the place purple, added wooden palm trees either side of the front door, molded plaster drapery below the bedroom windows to look like towels hung out to dry; the sitting room was resplendent with the famous bright red Mae West's lips sofas by Dali. All this was outré but still within the ambit of conventional good taste. In Mexico, several thousand miles west of the well bred and a few hundred miles south of the nearest planning commission or neighborhood association, James could really let go.

Of course, he did have a neighborhood association in the form of the people who worked for him and among whom he lived. Over the years James was the major employer in Xilitla with anywhere from fifty to seventy locals on his payroll, heaving sand, concrete, and reinforcing wire and rocks up and down the hill. Quite obviously they regarded him as a rich madman whom God had chosen to drop on Xilitla, but after a generation, like his structures, he had become a pleasantly regarded fixture. James was diplomatic, too. He took care to soothe local sensibilities by such enterprises as raising the great stone walls and dams of the public swimming place.

As well as being a one-man relief program, Las Posas was a collective endeavor. Like the butterflies fluttering up and down the hill, James would dart from one half-finished fantasy to the next, calling for his builders to follow him, and one suspects that much of the work got done in the seven or eight months of the year when James was not there. It all came down to the carpenter, José Aguilar. James would scribble his vision – a fleur-de-lys, a broken pediment like a snail's horns, a shape from Miró – on a scrap of paper and give it to Aguilar who would retire to his workshop and painstakingly convert James's sketch into a wooden form or mold for the concrete.

The workers cooperated in the creative enterprise, and James rejoiced that when asked to produce an iron gate, they would forge one of vigorous and attractive design. But did it bother them that they were building something absolutely useless, an architectural equivalent of Keynes's mine shafts sunk only as public works to provide employment and redistribute wealth, in this case a portion of the Phelps-Dodge profits? The young Mexican art historian Xavier Guzmán, who visited Las Posas in 1983 and talked to several of the people who used to work there, says it did bother them that none of the work was ever finished. For James, I imagine, part of the point of Las Posas was that it was never finished according to the sedate concepts of the land he'd left behind.

Plutarco describes an occasion in which James supervised the mixing of liquid concrete and color. First he asked for a streak of yellow, and the worker poured in the color and stirred it with infinite care. James instructed him to add some blue and then, across the tint that was now green, a streak of red 'like an arrow', then some brown. As the tint darkened to orange, Plutarco remembers, James expressed every sign of jubilation. Then he asked for black to be added to the mix. Everyone around fell silent. The black would overwhelm the other tints. Was he mad? Then James said to Plutarco, 'Haven't you ever seen a jungle sunset as the darkness finally overwhelms all the separate threads of color?' So Las Posas becomes a Surreal joke, a great cock-snooking at the Modernists' house-as-machine-for-living, a hymn to the nonfunctional.

Not only Las Posas but also Xilitla stands at a slight angle to the universe, as E.M. Forster once said of the poet Cavafy. The second night we were there schoolchildren from miles around gathered for a dancing and singing competition in the town square. The children performed against a fretwork of lightning that silhouetted the open vaulting, which was all James had ever managed to complete of a projected house next to Plutarco's, where he actually stayed in Xilitla. In the midst of a spirited dance the rain poured down, the children fled, and we returned to talk to Plutarco. He's 73 now and badly afflicted with Parkinson's disease. We sat looking at the graceful ellipses of his swimming pool over which a magnolia stands lifeguard. One passage leads to a Surreal mural by Leonora Carrington, another to a cavernous sitting room filled with the enormous pieces of fifties furniture which were Marina's dowry.

The man of the house now is really the son, also called Plutarco, a charming young person of 26 who told us that everyone in Xilitla is pretty crazy, as witness the ongoing drama in the town square. Xilitla is divided into four bitter factions, which cannot agree on the design of this square. The 25 years of Don Eduardo have turned them all into architectural dreamers. Or maybe not. Maybe it was James who was overwhelmed by Xilitla. Young Plutarco explained that he and his three sisters had been left Las Posas by 'Uncle Edward.' There had been a trust fund for them, but James had died suddenly and there was no money in it. He loved Las Posas and liked to go there and read. In the late 1960s, James had tried to deed Las Posas to the Mexican park system, which deemed it too small but nonetheless tried to settle some landless peasants on it. In angry retaliation James made it more private than ever, even though it does now have a somewhat mysterious, word-of-mouth reputation in artistic circles in Mexico. Young Plutarco would like it to be completely secret, which – given the speed with which the jungle is advancing – it may soon be.

Plutarco led us back up the hill to another gate. Halfway down the hill one comes to the most enchanting structure, which James called Jungle Regency; no walls, but three floors, stained a pinkish maroon, looking down on the House with a Roof Curved Like a Whale. Across a little gulch hangs the delicate bridge James built for the Indians who live above Las Posas to preserve their ancient right-of-way and across which they totter fearfully when tipsily heading for home.

On the top floor of Jungle Regency, beneath open Gothic vaulting twined with wild roses, James would sleep contentedly, master of all he surveyed. He had hated his childhood. In *Swans Reflecting Elephants*, the memoir he dictated to George Melly, he says, 'The only escape I achieved was when I went all alone into a wood ... and ... ran and ran and ran, weeping and weeping and weeping, sobbing and sobbing because everything was awful. The housemaster at Eton was awful and life during the holidays was worse than school, and I longed to kill myself, and then the wood overwhelmed me, and nature became a protective mother.' Atop Jungle Regency below his Gothic vault and behind a screen of concrete bamboo James could enjoy a rosy dream of childhood: an open-air bath like a peacock's eye; a wall garden without cabbages but with mauve plantain blossoms bursting from their green hearts; ocelots, ducks, and parrots as his neighbors; and in the forest the imported boa constrictor whistling in frustration as it searched for its lost mate. Here in the jungle, heeding the lessons of the Surrealists, James brought back his horrible childhood and gave it a happy ending.

House and Garden, May, 1987

Robert Laughlin:
Lost in a World of Words

The days turned into months, and the months into years. He started as a poet and ended up as a lexicographer. Now he sits in the Natural History Museum in Washington, DC, flushed with a triumph he says is absurd. He has compiled the largest dictionary of a native language ever assembled in the Western hemisphere. He thinks often of poor Praharaj, the great Indian lexicographer who lived to witness his mammoth quadrilingual dictionary, the fruit of twenty-five years of labor, carted off in wheelbarrows to be sold by the pound as scrap paper.

But at least he finished it, and in January 1976 he approached the chief magistrate of Zinacantan in southern Mexico, sank to his knees and held up the book which had lost him fourteen years of his life. Falteringly he started to chant in Mayan couplets: 'k'usi yepal li yo kee / li yo hti'e/ kahval' ('This is the sum of my humble mouth, my humble lips, My Lord'). He muffed some of the words and the magistrate tried to cut him short. 'Then,' as he later said 'I heard a person who was watching me say that I must be a shaman. The couplets just came tumbling out.'

Robert Laughlin first visited the Tzotzil, otherwise known as the 'People of the Bat' back in 1961. These Indians, about 120,000 of them, live in the province of Chiapas and speak one of the thirty Mayan languages still in common usage. They are depressed and drink a large amount of cane liquor. They grow corn but are themselves under intensive anthropological cultivation. Their capital town of Zinacantan is an entrepôt for scores of American anthropologists saturating the province of Chiapas.

Among these academics was young Laughlin. In the early 1960s he started to record Tzotzil dreams and found they were mostly nightmares. The madness, slowly at first, started to engulf him and he recorded some Tzotzil words and their English equivalents in a small black notebook. In 1963 he wrote to Washington that an extensive dictionary of the Tzotzil language had not been compiled since the eighteenth century. He proposed to amend this lack. 'It is hoped that this material will be ready for publication in a year's time.'

'The Great Tzotzil Dictionary of San Lorenzo Zinacantan' was finally published in December of 1975. Now Laughlin sits in his Washington office. The day I saw him he was studying a map of the world. Marked on it with large dots were the institutions to which the dictionary had been sent. There was an extra large blob over Novosibirsk. That's where Professor Kaladnikov lives. Not that Kaladnikov cares about Tzotzil. It's just that all anthropological publications from the Smithsonian Institution – which is what pays Laughlin his salary – go to Kaladnikov.

Laughlin, very thin and sad, with bare feet in Tzotzil sandals, stops thinking about the mysterious Kaladnikov.

'At what point did you realise that your little dictionary was going to take fourteen years?'

'I suppose it was in the first fourteen weeks, when I realised there were so many words I didn't know existed.'

'Were you always compulsive about collecting information?'

'I suppose so, yes. And compulsive about detail. I remember criticism of my work when I was at boarding school. Too much concentration on detail. My father is an expert on American pewter, which I suppose influenced me because if you do something you do it as completely as you can. He spent years and years studying American pewter.'

'Had you had much training before you started?'

'None, no. I didn't know how to do it. I just did it. When I started I adopted a method where you just go automatically through AA, AAB and so on.'

'But that could lead to infinity.'

'I know. I had bak, so I knew there could be a suffix bak-um. Then is there a word bakumtasvan? Is there a word bakumtasvanan? Sometimes the Tzotzil helping me would get so they couldn't remember if words they told me really existed. They sounded like good words. I worked mainly with two men. One of them is an alcoholic now. I don't know that I can say I am responsible. They became more sensitive to language. And there was one woman whose grammar seemed much more sophisticated. Like lacework. I don't know why. She was a very smart woman, very aggressive and out-going.'

'Were you living alone?'

'In the beginning, then I got married. One of my sons was drowned there. He fell in a swimming pool. I have two others.'

'What were the effects of working on a dictionary for fourteen years?'

'Well, a dictionary is like stone soup. It fed us, my family and me for years. It prevented my wife from doing creative writing because she thought she oughtn't to be doing it while I was immersed in the dictionary. Which I didn't realise and she didn't realise till the dictionary was finished.'

'Why?'

'Well, she thought it would be difficult for me if she was writing away and there I was enmired in the words.'

'Did she hate the dictionary?'

'I don't think she liked it.'

'Did you find yourself getting very monomaniacal?'

'Yes. But I thought I should exhaust all the possibilities.'

'What do you feel the whole function of the enterprise was?'

'That's the problem. Because it is an obvious absurdity. Here's a dictionary published in letters that are so esoteric that no one can read them, in an Indian language that almost no one can read, translated into English, which is not the language of Mexico.'

Laughlin's voice was getting rather high and thin. He has long, graceful fingers which were shaking a little. 'It's totally absurd. I was going to do it into Spanish, but I got tired.'

'Did you think it was necessarily a bad thing that it was all absurd?'

'What? No, I don't. Oh, I think it's amusing. I had the kind of feeling too that if I'm going to be an academic, then by God I'm going to be an academic and I'm going to do it to the point of absurdity.'

'Did you want to be an academic?'

'No, not really. In a way I want to be, in a way No. I want to be a freer person.'

'Did you want to be something else; a writer, an aviator ...?'

'No, not an aviator. Yes, I had wanted to be a writer, but I could never think what I had to say. I thought of this dictionary as being similar in a way to someone playing chess with himself as the city crumbles.'

'Do you still feel depressed that this 595-page dictionary doesn't matter much?'

'Yes, sometimes. Sometimes not. Then I say, Ha ha, I've done it and who cares? Also I'm consoled by the thought Levi-Strauss defined in his first book, *Tristes Tropiques*. How do you define civilisation and what are its ultimate goals? There are people like the Nambikwara, who no one knows about but whose style of living is perhaps as great as great civilisations. I was thinking of this creation of mine as truly having no utilitarian value. So I was influenced by *Tristes Tropiques*.'

'Well, what are your claims for the Great Tzotzil Dictionary?'

'It's the largest dictionary of any native language of this hemisphere. It gives more of a context to the words than others do. It has more accurate scientific information than any other dictionary. It may be bigger than any other dictionary of a native language in the world. I don't know what else to say. Hopefully it will help in translating Mayan glyphs.'

'How many people could review it properly?'

'Well, I've had the thought at times, wouldn't it be fun if this dictionary was a complete hoax. Really, there's hardly anyone in the world who would know, apart from a Zinacantan. And he wouldn't know the English. In fact no one knows these 30,000 words. You can take the logical extensions of the language and create a word which may or may not exist. A linguist could tell if there were errors, but he couldn't tell if I had padded it greatly or not.'

We worked out the implications of the hoax on a paper napkin in the Smithsonian canteen: $238,000 total salary over 14 years, plus $50,000 publication cost plus $70,000 in extra grants. Total: $358,000.

'Was there a time when you thought you were really going mad?'

'I thought I'd throw myself off the cathedral of Notre Dame at one point. I happened to be there. The dictionary was in the computer and nothing was getting out. There seemed to be no way of getting at it. There was this feeling of total helplessness. One operator resigned because she didn't want to print the word shit. She kept putting in 'unprintable word'. The people at the Smithsonian, when it was nearly finished and I only needed $15,000 more, stopped giving me money. They called it the Great Tzotzil Disaster. My chairman here was doing everything he could to stop it. Internal politics. He is properly memorialised in the dictionary, if you know where to look.'

'What is the genius of Tzotzil?'

'I realised how much the Mayan languages concentrate on shape and movement, and sound. All that is totally foreign to us. There's a word for the noise a pig makes when it is chomping peach pits. It's a very puritan, repressed culture. The word for to talk to a girl means to have an affair with her. The girls are watched all the time.'

'How did you feel when you finished?'

'At first I felt nothing. Then I began to feel liberated. I went to Seville to look for the Spanish original of a Tzotzil translation. It wasn't there. I got back here and found it right here in the Library of Congress. My wife and I would like to write, but we don't come from very self-confident families.'

It's all finished now, even though no one can actually obtain the Great Tzotzil Dictionary from government bookshops, because one of the reference numbers was omitted from the final copies. Laughlin is toying with all the many, many Tzotzil words describing what people do and feel when they are drunk. Fiddling with some index cards he went back to the day in January when he presented the Great Tzotzil Dictionary to the magistrates in Zinacantan.

'I wanted to do it on the Fiesta of San Sebastian. It's the biggest Fiesta of the year. And there's one account of its background that tells how once there was a book of knowledge that St Sebastian had and that it was lost. And the Indians say that is how the Ladinos, the non-Indians, are rich today because they had the book of knowledge and we lost ours. So I said to the magistrate, if any Ladino comes and says you are stupid, asinine Indians, please show them this book, show them the 30,000 words of your knowledge, of your reasoning.'

June, 1976

Bwana Vistas

The travel writer seeks the world we have lost − the lost valleys of the imagination. There is no joy more profound than that of the British explorer of old setting foot where no man trod before: that which has been hidden, except to savages and the beasts of the field is found by him alone, gazing upon the uncompromised fruits of God's creation. The eighteenth and nineteenth centuries rang with the exultant howls of British explorers laying claim to virgin vista. Listen to James Bruce describe his emotions on November 4, 1770, when a guide pointed out to him the long-sought source of the Nile:

> I stood in rapture. ... It is easier to guess than to describe the situation of my mind at the moment, standing in that spot which had baffled the genius, industry and inquiry of both ancients and moderns, for the course of near three thousand years. ... Though a mere private Briton, I triumphed here in my own mind, over kings and their armies.

The operative words here, as so often in travel literature, are 'in my own mind.' Alan Moorehead, describing this sadly comic scene in *The Blue Nile*, observed that Bruce, amid the mountains of central Ethiopia, was a thousand miles from the actual source of the Nile, which is Lake Victoria, and seventy miles south of the wellspring of the Blue Nile, which is an overflow from Lake Tana. Nor was Bruce even the first European to arrive at the spot that suffused him with such joy. The Portuguese priest Pedro Paez anticipated him by 142 years and came to the same erroneous conclusion, boasting that he 'saw, with the greatest delight, what neither Cyrus, the king of the Persians, nor Cambyses, nor Alexander the Great, nor the famous Julius Caesar, could ever discover.'

The joy of the pioneer encountering the primal scene quickly passes. The missionary, the soldier, the slaver, the anthropologist, the Orientalist, and kindred men of commerce soon go to work. Then we hear the lament of the returning traveler venting elegies to a world on the wane. The tone becomes one of desperate nostalgia, beautifully diagnosed by Claude Lévi-Strauss in *Tristes Tropiques*, one of the greatest travel books of the postwar period:

> Journeys, those magic caskets full of dreamlike promises, will never again yield up their treasures untarnished. A proliferating and overexcited civilization has broken the silence of the seas once and for all. The perfumes of the tropics and the pristine freshness of human beings have been corrupted. ... Our great Western civilization, which has created the marvels we now enjoy, has only succeeded in producing them at the cost of corresponding ills. ... The first thing we see as we travel round the world is our own filth, thrown into the face of mankind. So I can understand the mad passion for travel books and their deceptiveness. They create the illusion of something which no longer exists but still should exist, if we were to have any hope of avoiding the overwhelming conclusion that the history of the past twenty thousand years is irrevocable.

The travel writer voyages toward a past beyond his reach. Amid the wreckage of the twentieth-century world, his mode must be one of irony. Round the next bend may be Eden, but Eve will have endemic syphilis and live in a tarpaper shack, while Adam will work at a construction project downriver. But even irony is too exhausting, and so the mode shifts to dilettantism, variously self-deprecating or mock-heroic but always ego-centric. History may be irrevocable, but there is always the self to be discovered.

This is the phase of travel writing discussed by Paul Fussell in *Abroad*: the Brideshead generation overseas – not just Evelyn Waugh but Graham Greene, Norman Douglas, T.E. Lawrence, Cyril Connolly, and (much overestimated by Fussell) Robert Byron. Fussell is a conservative fellow, and he seems rather too easily impressed with the noise of the British upper-middle classes telling their travelers' tales. Class is important here, not just because the mythic pattern is, as Fussell points out, a version of pastoral (so was a lot of the left-wing fellow-traveling prose of the time about visits to the Soviet Union, as is much of the right-wing fellow-traveling prose today about China), but because the classy traveler is conducting a whimsical mime of the old imperial appropriation of the world. And just as the mythic prince would explore his kingdom in disguise, so does the British traveler, with his love of fancy dress, emblem of anxieties and desires, come usefully into play as a way of confronting the world. The fancy dress could either be Maugham's dinner jackets in the jungle (a detail Englishmen adore precisely because it rubs them so firmly the right way) or the Arab vestments in which Sir Richard Burton fancied he was slipping through the souk unperceived. The trouble came when one could no longer be exactly sure who was disguising what – which is why T.E. Lawrence, perhaps ravished by the Turk, remains an object of suspicion to this day.

Almost the only acceptable place to 'go native' – or at least get near it, for syzygy was preferred to full mutation – was in the South Seas. Ever since the days of Captain Cook, Loti, and Gauguin, the South Seas have spelled sex, and lots of it. Free. Sex in the Orient, as we have seen with Lawrence and in Flaubert's cavortings with the courtesan described in his *Voyages* (admirably situated in Edward Said's *Orientalism*), was always a nervy business. The whole syndrome is resumed in Lucy Irvine's recent *Castaway*, in which two whites try to mime the legend. A British writer advertises for a 'wife' to share solitude with him for a year on a desert island in the Timor Sea. Irvine sets up camp with him, but he wants a companionship to ripen into romance; she doesn't, and finally he bellows, 'If you had behaved the way you do in the days when I had my Jaguar I'd have kicked your arse out of the door. I sometimes wonder if what you need is a bloody good hiding'. Thus do the suburbs meet the Blue Lagoon.

The joy of Thor Heyerdahl's *Kon-Tiki* was that it married two congenial essences, Vikings and the South Pacific. The Boy Scout charm of Heyerdahl and his jolly Norwegian crew almost atones, in one's imagination, for Captain Cook, Captain Bligh, and the horror-stained reality of what the First World has done to that particular part of the globe, most notably, at the time, with the atom bomb tests at Bikini and Eniwetok – which virtually coincided with Heyerdahl's pastoral.

Heyerdahl 'went native' in the relatively beneficent sense of going to the islanders to learn how to float a raft across the Pacific. It was probably the most trouble-free transaction between the First and Third Worlds in the modern era. Just over a decade later the First World went to the natives again – this time to obtain testimony from the Third World against itself. The *Schadenfreude* with which Britons and Americans read V.S. Naipaul's *An Area of Darkness* is hard to overestimate. Indians are dirty and shit in the streets. *See, here's Naipaul saying so, and he should know.* Naipaul has been a one-man cultural Rapid Deployment Force ever since, the Third World's answer to Joan Didion and with the same fastidious conservatism, so comforting to their admirers.

Somewhat influenced by Naipaul, but spiritually descended from Fussell's group, are those now hailed as the new school of travel writers. Many of them are to be found in the tenth issue of the British literary magazine *Granta*, a number devoted to travel writing. Here are Jonathan Raban, Paul Theroux, Bruce Chatwin, James Fenton, Redmond O'Hanlon, and – slightly older – Jan Morris and Norman Lewis.

This is Thatcher's England: postmodern imperialism, no doubt about it. Sometimes the tranquil conservatism is hallucinatory. Redmond O'Hanlon plans to travel into the jungles of Borneo with his friend James Fenton.

Why they want to travel into the jungles of Borneo is never disclosed by O'Hanlon, but the better to be prepared they visit a British Special Air Services training camp near Hereford: 'We were in the company of a soft-spoken major,' recalls O'Hanlon. 'A veteran of Special Forces campaigns in Occupied Europe in the Second World War, of the war in Malaya, of Jebel Akhdar, Aden, Borneo and Dhofar, he was huge. ... And his office, hung with battle honors, SAS shields emblazoned with the regiment's motto, *Qui ose gagne* ... was an impressive place.' O'Hanlon, embarking on his Rousseauian project, seems to see no irony in getting some tips from this veteran of counterinsurgency and despoiler of Third World aspiration.

The silliness of the whole thing becomes apparent when O'Hanlon gives an admiring description of Fenton as they head up a Borneo river in a canoe:

> James, sitting opposite me on the duck-boards in the center of the canoe, facing upstream, our equipment lashed down under tarpaulins to front and rear of us, was reading his way through Pat Rogers's new edition of the complete poems of Swift. A straw boater on his bald head, his white shirt buttoned at the neck and at the wrists, his trousers no less and no more disgraceful than the ones he wore in Oxford (being the same pair), he would be, I thought, a formidable figure for the jungle to conquer.

This arch prose is the last self-regarding whimper of the once heroic rhythms of exploration.

To get O'Hanlon's dilettantish prose out of my head I took a quick dose of Henry M. Stanley's *In Darkest Africa*, the *Kon-Tiki* of its day, albeit a bitter chronicle of endurance and privation that reminds us how seriously travel and travel writing were taken in the high Victorian age of colonial expansion. Listen to Stanley brood as his party nears death from starvation on the Ituri River:

> Vain was it for me to seek for that sleep which is 'the balm of hurt minds.' Too many memories crowded about me; too many dying forms haunted me in the darkness ... the stark forms lying in links along the path, which we had seen that afternoon in our tramp, were things too solemn for sudden oblivion. The stars could not be seen to seek comfort in their twinkling; the poor hearts around me were too heavy to utter naught but groans of despair; the fires were not lit, for there was no food to cook – my grief was great.

But then Stanley was an American, and the best American travel writing is, even today, a more serious affair, usually because it's engaged upon a mission of national inquiry. It's not that Americans are innocents abroad or at home; just that they never quite know who they are or where they are at; therefore much of their travel writing is a strenuous effort to find out.

Potted essence of Englishman has been on sale for over a century and is part of the tourist industry, as declaimed by Robert Morley. It's hard to turn out good travel writing in such conditions. Of course American writers are fortunate in having the road, as apt a formal device in this century as the river was for Twain in that best of all travel books, *The Adventures of Huckleberry Finn*. For our own times we have Kerouac's *On the Road*, and Clancy Sigal's *Going Away* – both of them significant missions of inquiry, as are Edward Abbey's books about the Southwest. Today we have the immensely popular *Blue Highways*, by William Least Heat Moon. Moon's appeal is that he suggests that despite interstates, Howard Johnsons, and other appurtenances of auto culture, America is still full of people worth talking to, and that driving across the country is still a satisfactory way of meeting them.

People enjoy Moon, if only because the chief alternative is the Mobil series of travel guides, whose volumes are useful enough if you want to know the address, telephone number, and price of every tolerable motel room in America, but not if you want to know much else. It is a fact of great interest that America has not produced a satisfactory series of guidebooks since the WPA guides of the 1930s, some of which Pantheon has recently reissued.*

Roland Barthes spoke to the problem of most guidebooks in his attack on the Blue Guides:

> Generally speaking, the Blue Guide testifies to the futility of all analytical descriptions, those which reject both explanations and phenomenology: it answers in fact none of the questions which a modern traveller can ask himself while crossing a countryside which is real *and which exists in time*. To select only monuments suppresses at one stroke the reality of the land and that of its people; it accounts for nothing of the present, that is, nothing historical, and as a consequence, the monuments themselves become undecipherable, therefore senseless.

The Blue Guides postulate Art (usually religious) as the fundamental value of culture and, piled up in museums, as a reassuring accumulation of goods.

But already by the mid-1950s, Barthes noted, the myth of travel embodied in the Blue Guides was on the wane. 'Notice,' he wrote, 'how already, in the *Michelin Guide*, the number of bathrooms and forks indicating good restaurants is vying with that of "artistic curiosities"; even the bourgeois have their differential geology.'

America has not got a satisfactory guide because no one knows what we should look at, beyond the hardy standbys of the picturesque, the heroic, or the artistically OK. Mobil makes a stab at it and has the resources to do

---

*Joy Williams's wonderful *The Florida Keys* (1987) should be a model for guide-writers.

better. But how could Mobil do a truthful guide to that great monument to oil-based, auto-carried civilization – the New Jersey Turnpike? When I drive around America I carry the *American Guide,* which is a boiled-down version of the WPA guides; the Mobil guides; the Rand McNally *Road Atlas* and the Rand McNally *Guide to Campgrounds*; and the *Atlas of Cancer Mortality for US Counties: 1950-1969,* put out by the National Institutes of Health. This gives one a sense of real-life travel in the late twentieth century. Driving north from southern Florida I pass through Dade County, which the NIH atlas tells me has a high rate of cancer of the brain and of other parts of the nervous system, in women but not men. The men in Dade County have a high rate of bladder cancer, but not the women. So it goes. In southwest Wyoming there's a county that seems altogether unafflicted by cancer. I drove through it last year – a high plateau cut through by Interstate 80. There was no one there, which explains the map.

Harper's, August, 1985

Karl and Fred:
Driving into the Sunset

Riverside, Calif. – Halfway between those twin poles of the American Fantasy, Disneyland and Palm Springs, and 50 miles due east of the Beverly Hills Hotel is the city of Riverside where I've been spending the past few days contemplating the future of capitalism. All Marxists should pay regular visits to Southern California and ask themselves what Karl would have said about the inevitability of crisis as he cruised the freeways and sauntered through the boutiques of La Jolla with his good friend Fred.

Riverside is a pretty good vantage point from which to observe the fortunes of the Reagan economy. The city, with a population nearing 200,000, is rich in history and cultural tradition. It was in Riverside that Richard and Pat Nixon enjoyed their honeymoon at the beautiful Mission Inn; in Riverside that a baboon heart was implanted in the chest of Baby Fae; in Riverside, on the local University of California campus that Christopher Boyce, later to sell to the Soviet Union some of America's most cherished secrets of satellite communication, acquired the rudiments of higher education; in Riverside that the shock troops of the Animal Liberation Front took the laboratories of this same campus by storm and turned loose the beasts previously doomed to the scalpels and electrodes of forward-marching science.

Today, Riverside is a boom town. Three years ago Chase Econometrics noted that population growth in Riverside and neighboring San Bernardino counties was leaping ahead of the Sun Belt magnets such as Miami and San Antonio. I drive along Iowa Avenue and see the bulldozers crunching up the orange trees as the groves and pickers move farther east. In place of these groves are rising the Type V houses – stick construction with spray-on stucco to evoke the Spanish tradition – typical of the real-estate boom surging through the area.

Who are the denizens of the new Riverside economy? Some are refugees from Rust Belt America, from declining industrial towns where they could once earn $15 an hour in a factory and who now look for jobs in the

101

service sector of Southern California at $4 an hour. Some are refugees from real-estate inflation along the Southern California coast. Others, at a lower level of subsistence, are Mexican refugees from the debt crisis, once again filling out every crevice of the service economy. Others are beneficiaries of the pulsing engine of the Reagan economy, military spending, on which the prosperity of Riverside heavily depends. In Riverside County is March Air Force Base and 10 minutes north on route 215 is Norton AFB in San Bernardino. Each day Highway 91 and Route 60 are clogged with commuters heading toward the plants of Lockheed, TRW, Rockwell and McDonnell Douglas. Back from the aerospace and defense research and development complexes of Los Angeles and Orange counties, they return to Riverside with the dollars to sustain the real-estate boom and the service economy.

Riverside, in short, is what the Reagan economy is all about, in bad ways as well as good. Even here, amid the boom of Southern California, these new residents ensconced in their Type V houses are groaning beneath the weight of their variable-rate mortgages as the interest payments soar from the seductive 8.5% initial three-month rate to 13% and 14%, as the repo man begins to lick his lips. These Riversiders, like millions of others, are finding that through variable interest rate mortgages the burden of risk is on their shoulders as opposed to those of their lending institutions. The rate of mortgage delinquencies, across the country and even in Riverside, was higher in the first quarter of 1985 than at any time in the past 30 years, evidence of the fragility of the Reagan economy, which, as Business Week remarked a year ago, rests on the financial equivalent of the San Andreas fault, a geological fissure that in fact happens to run right through Riverside County.

How wide is the fault? Wide enough to set Karl and Fred licking their lips? With my Riverside host, Robert Pollin of the UC economics faculty, I took a quick overview of the situation. The rate at which the nonfinancial economy – households, nonfinancial corporations and government – depends on debt to finance expenditures is higher than it has ever been since they started collecting the numbers a century ago. Everyone talks about government borrowing but the borrowing by the private sector, less publicly lamented, is also historically unprecedented.

Something else that has Karl and Fred nudging each other is the fall in real wages, about which there has been some comment lately. The fall actually began at the end of 1973 when real wages peaked in the postwar period. And of course these declining real wages are the reason the freeways around Riverside, like many other commuter arteries in America, are filled with women commuters who have left home and joined the work force to keep the family afloat. But despite the two-wage household, family incomes peaked in the early 1970s and have been drifting down ever since.

According to the Federal Reserve's major 1983 Survey of Consumer Finances, real median family income was 16% lower in 1982 than it was in 1969, and despite an upturn in 1984 there is no evidence of a return to the prosperity of the late 1960s.

So much for the householders of Riverside. Not too many of them probably have copies of 'Das Kapital' beside their beds (always excepting those of the distinguished economics department of the UC campus here, where the Marxists are thick enough upon the ground to give Reed Irvine a heart attack). But if the Riversiders were to pick up a copy of Karl's book and push through to Volume III and his discussion of the falling rate of profit, they might realize the benefits of Marxist analysis. Despite the upturn in profitability in the 'defense'-led recovery of 1984, profit rates of nonfinancial corporations remain at roughly half their postwar peak in the mid-1960s. This has led nonfinancial corporations, just like households, to rush to the financial markets and borrow at an unprecedented clip.

All this borrowing – private as well as governmental – puts increasing upward pressure on interest rates, thus inhibiting any efforts of the Fed to push them down, even if the urge were there to do so. And of course real interest rates, despite their decline over the past year, remain at a historic high. What has emerged, with the allure of these high rates, is the go-go financial supermarket of the Roaring '80s, where fortunes are gained and lost overnight in an Aladdin's cave of ever more baroque financial mechanisms wherewith to borrow and to lend.

So if President Reagan were to take Karl for a helicopter ride over Riverside and the rest of Southern California he would doubtless point out the building boom, the swimming pools and all the other elements of the American Dream come true. Marx would pull thoughtfully at his beard and nod politely, but then he would point out to the president the rest of the story: long-term decline, faltering living standards, a crisis of profitability in the nonfinancial sector; everywhere the signs of financial fragility, even in Southern California and the dream fortress of world capitalism spread among Disneyland, Palm Springs and the Beverly Hills Hotel.

Wall Street Journal, October 24, 1985

TASTES OF THE TIMES

*'Consumption is the sole end and purpose of all
production.'*
Adam Smith

The History of Mr P

Reich and the other crazies used to think that sex, proper orgasms, and so forth constituted a challenge to power, to the bourgeois order: a freer fuck means a freer world. Plodding along the trail marked out by the high priest of the orgone box comes Gay Talese with the same assumption.

Orgasms as such do not interest him too much, as against the property/possession/power relations amid which the O, big, little, copious or casual, takes place. The smut-hound, dipping into his book *Thy Neighbor's Wife* in bookshop or library, won't find much to induce tumescence. Though the book purports to be a saga of sex liberation, of society's journey upward toward the light, Talese is not interested in sensuality, the erotic, or the perverse.

In fact the book is terribly sedate. He has a concept of sex as 'recreation,' rather like the other great postwar bourgeois obsession, tennis. Singles, or doubles, a good fast serve, netplay, game, set and M-A-T-C-H.

The dark god can be found in the index, wedged between 'Peeping Toms' and 'Pennsylvania.' This is Mr 'Penis' who has the modest distinction of getting three references. Talese's normally lackluster prose takes on a modicum of energy when dealing with Mr P.

... it does indeed seem to have a will of its own, an ego beyond its size, and is frequently embarrassing because of its needs, infatuations and unpredictable nature. Men sometimes feel that their penis controls *them*, leads them astray, causes them to beg favors at night from women whose names they prefer to forget in the morning. Whether insatiable or insecure, it demands constant proof of its potency, introducing into a man's life unwanted complications and frequent rejection.

Talese's contemplation of Mr P then takes on the rhythm of a job application.

Qualifications: 'Sensitive but resilient, equally available during the day or night with a minimum of coaxing ...'

Previous Experience: '... it has performed purposefully if not always skillfully for an eternity of centuries, endlessly searching, sensing, expanding, probing, penetrating, throbbing, wilting, and wanting more.'

Character Testimonial: 'Never concealing its prurient interest, it is a man's most honest organ.'

Hired! Mr P, our society has had its troubles with your sort in the past, and frankly some members of the screening committee here think we'd be better off without you. But we're a forward-looking company, and I'm sure you'll fit in.

Though Mr P gets the job, Talese is still bothered about him. 'It is also symbolic of masculine imperfection. ... It is very vulnerable even when made of stone, and the museums of the world are filled with herculean figures brandishing penises that are chipped, clipped, or completely chopped off.' This sentence, parsed literally, must mean that there are statues where Mr P, broken off from the crotch, is being hoisted aloft in the hand – which slip nicely illustrates the true story that Talese's book avoids. Mr P, so frisky and troublesome in the past, is in the mid-twentieth century in middle-class American society being socialized, brought under control, jerked off into repressive desublimation and if necessary snapped off at the root altogether and brandished aloft as the captive object, six inches of stone under control.

What about Mrs V? One gets the impression that Talese is more of a tit man really, since there's a fair amount of to-do in the book about breasts being presented in swelling, pointed, creamy or simply 'large' guise for the delectation of Mr P. Near the end of the book there's a sort of 'Honor Mrs V' day, when Talese reports on the efforts of some women to give Mrs Vagina and her close relative Mrs Clitoris a modicum of civil rights, bring them out into the noonday of progress amid inspection and approval.

Mrs V's triumphant social integration in full civil rights status is signaled by Talese's report that 'One woman who, like [Betty] Dodson years ago, believed that her genitals were deformed and ugly, was persuaded by Dodson's color slides of female genitalia that she was as attractive as most other women; and the next day in her office, reassured and confident, she demanded a raise – and got it.'

This is splendidly helpful of Mrs V, but on the whole Talese's book, though purportedly about liberation and the escape from the Puritan heritage, is not about the liberation of women or of Mrs V into emancipated hunter-gatherers of sexual gratification. Mr P is the hunter, home from the hill to the womb. 'For a man,' says Talese obliquely quoting 'a recently divorced husband of a famous European actress' of whose views he seems to approve, 'there is no substitute for the warm, welcoming place between a woman's legs, the birthplace to which men continuously try to return.' Mrs V hangs around as receptionist and, if she's lucky, gets to know Mr P really well and settles down.

'Quite apart from the potential danger involved in picking up stray men in public places, the average sexual woman did not enjoy intercourse without a feeling of familiarity or personal interest in her partner. If it was merely an orgasm that she sought, she would prefer masturbating in her bedroom with a penis-shaped vibrator to engaging the genuine article of a male stranger.'

This is Talese reproducing without demur the views of 'men who were well qualified to comment.' We must assume – since the passage occurs on page 530 in the final section – that this is what he tends to think.

'*If it was merely an orgasm she sought.*' The hunt for the big O used to be central to chronicles of sex liberation. The idea was that you masturbated until, in the fullness of time and good fortune, you obtained proper fulfillment for yourself and your employee Mr P by meeting up with Mrs V. The most virtuous course was then to discipline Mr P until with skill and practice the supreme objective of simultaneous orgasm could be achieved.

There were endless tracts on how to achieve this satisfactory condition. They roughly paralleled in the fifties and sixties the strategic concept, espoused in the Pentagon, of Mutual Assured Destruction, which proposed that all bombs would go off pretty much together if one side made an aggressive move against the other. Both sides would shin up the escalatory ladder in tandem until prodigious emissions of radioactive material were jointly achieved.

Mutual orgasm is less fashionable these days, as the desired objective of congress. And in parallel the Pentagon strategists have shifted emphasis to preemptive strikes, flexible targeting options, and the view that one side could emit at least some radioactive material without necessarily causing the mutual assured destruction deemed the inevitable, proper terminus in earlier decades. The MX system even envisages Russian missiles speeding toward what may or may not be *dry holes*, a sort of cock-teasing ritual very alien to the manly 'Let's All Go Off Together' Big Bang approach of yesteryear.

Quite in keeping with his interest in finding Mr P satisfactory conditions of employment in late capitalist society, and describing Mr P's efforts to attain same, Talese is not particularly interested in mutual orgasm or whatever Mr P might do when he gets stuck into his job. He's interested in Mr P's basic rights – notably for Mr P's owner to obtain freely a magazine or photograph (if necessary purveyed through the public mails) over which he can masturbate, and in the property/power relations in which Mr P can have a good time. Mr P covets Thy Neighbor's Wife (his ox or his ass or anything else that is Thy Neighbor's are tastefully omitted, since this is a good clean book), and Talese tries to describe how Mr P can enter into at least temporary owner-occupancy with a minimum of social disruption.

The overall assumption of the book is that Mr P is having a better time these days. Talese noticed this almost a decade ago and thought he would write a book explaining how and why.

Various techniques are mustered for the enterprise. Least successful is Talese's nonchalant blend of instant-history, which crops up intermittently – reeking of scissors, paste, and the hot breath of the editor: 'In this Freudian age, Americans were opening up, acknowledging their needs, and, because of automation and the shorter working week, they had more time in which to ponder and seek their pleasure. The newly developed birth-control pill was being anticipated by women. The bikini bathing suit, imported from France, was beginning to appear on American beaches. And there were newspaper stories about the existence of mate-swapping clubs in several suburban communities. Jukeboxes across the nation were throbbing with the music of pelvic-thrusting Elvis Presley, and audiences gathered in nightclubs to hear a shocking new comedian named Lenny Bruce.'

Thirty-three pages later Gary Powers lands his U-2 in the Soviet Union and 'this was one of many incidents that contributed to growing public doubts about the integrity and supremacy of American leadership. ... Multitudes of younger Americans [were] now disregarding the codes and inhibitions that had influenced their parents. ... While most of these and similar acts of defiance would be associated historically with the mid-sixties and later, the initial tremors were felt years before, when Eisenhower was still the President; and many early signs of this schismatic trend were sexual.'

A couple of pages after this we have the inauguration of Jack Kennedy whose 'personal popularity was of course enhanced by his fashionable young wife, Jacqueline, who became the most photographed young woman in the world and, parenthetically, the masturbatory object of numerous male magazine readers.'

So there was even a place for Onan on the New Frontier, admittedly well back in the pecking order of the great Kennedy circle-jerk but given increasing status in the capitalist circulation of goods and services. Talese takes care to write earlier in the same sequence that 'by 1960 the multiplying fortunes of Hugh Hefner permitted him to purchase for $370,000 a forty-eight-room Victorian mansion near the exclusive Lake Shore Drive, and to spend an additional $250,000 on renovations and such furnishings as a large circular rotating bed that would become the center of his expanding empire.'

Talese deals with Hefner at length. His function in the book is twofold, as illustration of how Americans were provided with a better class of wank, and as emblem of the great success story: how Mr P shook aside his early inhibitions, grew rich and successful, lived in a lovely home, possessed Mrs Vs by the hundreds, if not thousands, without truly paying the price demanded by nineteenth-century morality.

In describing the growth of the sex-service industry in the last decade or so Talese does not confine himself exclusively to the accommodation and pleasuring of Mr P via pictures of desirable women in magazines. Al Goldstein, inventor of *Screw* magazine, receives due recognition as the Ralph Nader of the massage parlor. But there's no doubt that his greater interest is in Hefner, whose magazine, *Playboy*, allowed the humble wanker dignified, if lonely, participation in the consumer world where the fetishization of consumer durables and Miss April were nicely combined by the manipulation of Mr P over the coated stock and color spreads of this monthly advertisement for the better life.

Masturbation has come a long way since Onan first spilled his seed upon the ground. Characteristically, Talese maintains a tone of uplift about the practice, as if in the end society would be working nicely were all its individual members wanking away in autotelic equilibrium, appropriating each other without the trouble and fuss of actual contact. Poor Schopenhauer. He held the view that 'the collected love affairs of the present generation, taken together, are ... the human race's serious meditation on the composition of the future generation on which in their turn innumerable generations depend.' He would presumably have been much distressed about the apotheosis of Onan and concomitant evidence of considerable aversion among the citizenry to the notion of 'the future generation,' as attested by the increasing social stature and self-confidence of buggery and the blow-job in American life.

Schopenhauer did at least have a theory of instinctive natural selection, in which the buggers simply disqualified themselves, after a process of unconscious self-assessment, from the high task of composing the future of the species. Talese isn't interested in buggery at all, whether of women by men or men by men. This is a pity. Perhaps his publishers could commission a companion volume to be called 'From Suburb to Sodom' which would study the fall of the wife-swapping suburbs and the rise of the homosexually gentrified inner city, in which such thoroughfares as Columbus Avenue, New York, attest to the integration of 'perversity' into the social-industrial complex. Nice, decent, suburban Mrs V, organizer of consumption for Mr P, promoter of the more rapid circulation of commodities and the greater glory of capitalism, enters – 'liberated' – the workpool of surplus labor and surplus pussy, while Mr P now no longer has to busy himself with procreation of the suburban way but can do just exactly what he wants, can fit in anywhere, in any orifice, amid growing social approval, sterilely 'recreating' to his heart's content.

Hefner is symbol of the triumphant career of Mr P. Talese devotes many pages to his good fortune, culminating in the return of Mr P, original sin satisfactorily disposed of, to Eden. Eden in this case is in Holmby Hills, Los Angeles, whither Hefner transported himself from Chicago in 1970:

> In 1970 he purchased for $1.5 million a Gothic-Tudor chateau on a lush estate near Sunset Boulevard. ... For many months architects and workmen reshaped the surrounding five and a half acres into gently rolling hills and lawns, built a lake and waterfall behind the main house, and also created a stone grotto that sheltered a series of warm Jacuzzi baths in which guests could bathe in the nude. Music was piped into the steaming grotto, through the surrounding forest of redwoods and pines, across the sprawling green lawns on which dozens of Hefner's newly acquired animals were allowed to roam. ... On other parts of the property there was a greenhouse filled with rare flowers and plants; guest cottages furnished with antiques; a game house in which was a pool table, pinball and Pong machines, and small private bedrooms with mirrored ceilings. There was also built within a wide clearing of trees a step-down tennis court that was overlooked by an outdoor dining area where lunch or dinner could be served, and where black-tied waiters would provide on trays to each arriving racket-carrying couple *two* unopened cans of tennis balls.

The italicised *two* is Talese's typographical gasp at the *ne plus ultra* of human felicity: balls in never-ending profusion. I remember visiting Holmby Hills a few years ago. The ventilation system had gone wrong so Eden smelled strongly of chicken soup. The birds stood sullenly in their own shit and the master bedroom, stuffed with cardboard boxes full of newspaper clippings, dominated by two enormous television screens arranged before an unmade and not particularly magnificent bed, suggested that Mr P had not entirely shaken off the memory of adolescence, of the nervous youth whose occupation was to make pornographic drawings of Dagwood and Blondie.

Since *Thy Neighbor's Wife* is really about property rights and power over them, it is instructive to follow Talese's account of Hefner's relations with Karen Christy, who arrived in Chicago from Texas to become a bunny in the Playboy Club, was espied by Hefner, and – though Hefner was conducting an official liaison with Barbi Benton in Eden West in Los Angeles – made *maîtress en titre* in Chicago.

Qualifications of Mrs V:

> 'Though shy in a crowd, Karen was uninhibited in private; and during his [Hefner's] vast and varied erotic past, he had never known anyone who could surpass her skill and ardor in bed. The sight of her removing her clothes thrilled

him; and after he had covered her body with oil – which she seemed to enjoy as much as he – the smooth, soothing, glistening lovemaking on the satin sheets aroused him to peaks of passionate pleasure.'

Character reference for Mrs V:

'Unlike Barbi, who was often tired in the evening after rehearsing in studios, and who disliked it when oil got into her hair on those nights when she had auditions on the following morning, Karen was not ambitious about a career and she had many free hours during the day for the washing and drying of her hair.'

Reward for Mrs V:

'During their first month together, he had given her a diamond watch inscribed "with love"; and his Christmas gift to her in 1971 was a full-length white mink coat. In March 1972, on her twenty-first birthday, he gave her a five-karat diamond cocktail ring from Tiffany's. He also gave her an emerald ring, a silver fox jacket, a Matisse painting, a Persian cat, a beautiful metallic reproduction of the *Playboy* cover on which she was featured; and for her Christmas gift in 1972, she received a white Mark IV Lincoln.'

Final fate of Mrs V, following departure from Hefner:

'While she continued to drive her white Lincoln [around Dallas], she had no use for her furs and expensive jewelry. Around her neck she was soon wearing a gold chain given her by her new boy friend; and suspended from it was a fourteen-karat price tag on which was printed: "Sold."'

Karen did, as we can see, contribute magnificently to the circulation of commodities. Talese does not even assuage the envious disciple of Onan, studying Karen and Hefner's career, by assuring him that Mr P came to a bad end. Talese dutifully recounts how the Playboy Empire fell briefly upon bad days – amid cruder offerings to Onan by *Penthouse* and *Hustler* – but concludes with a rousing corporate testimonial and considerable emphasis on the successful ascent of Hefner's daughter, Christie, up the business ladder at Playboy Enterprises. Since it is implied that truly liberated, successful Mr P can never get married – which would assume some measure of fealty and submission to home-loving Mrs V – we are left with the father-daughter alliance in managing Mr P's commercial affairs. Talese has as much disdain for incest as he does for buggery, but there have been some valiant attempts in recent years to integrate even this sturdy taboo into the proper desire and pursuit of the whole – the nuclear family's last gasp together, you could say – and so perhaps Talese's evocation of familial union in property management is an effort to penetrate the *Zeitgeist* in a tasteful way without approaching sexual incest directly. In the end the only orifice that matters is the bank teller's window.

Specific barter arrangements, when couples take it into their heads to start compounding the conjugal P = V, can cause no end of trouble. Take Sally Binford: '... in real life, when she and one of her husbands tried to experience group sex by answering an advertisement in a swingers' periodical, the only result was a rendezvous in a restaurant-bar with a portly burgher wearing a Goldwater button on his lapel, and his timid wife, who wore a plastic daisy in her hat. After moments of awkward amiability, during which the couple explained that they were not interested in a foursome but wanted to swap partners in private, they all shook hands and the couple disappeared into the balmy summer night.'

Small business Republicanism meets the conglomerating spirit. Eventually Sally Binford meets up with an actor called Jeremy Slate who, after breaking his leg and living in 'virtual isolation in his Laurel Canyon apartment, brooding and meditating, smoking pot and masturbating,' reads some Reich and hauls his ass up to the Sandstone Retreat in the Santa Monica mountains, at which sex facility he meets Binford. P = V, first in the 'recreational sex' context of the public ballroom, but this 'was mainly an excuse for them to be together and to explore within their embrace the deeper intimacy that they both sensed was there.' Later Sally teaches women's studies at Goddard College and 'Jeremy conducted a male consciousness-raising seminar in which he disseminated Sandstone's equal-rights sex doctrine, getting a positive reaction from many men who shared his view that the elimination of the double standard would be liberating for men as well as women.'

The 'double standard' is of course the old male theorem that whereas P may equal V^2, the reverse is intolerable. Sandstone was a sex resort dedicated to the refutation of this traditional formulation, where every P could merge with every consenting V and vice versa, and Talese devotes much space to the intentions and adventures of its original inhabitants.

Put in elemental terms the story tells what happens when the insurance business meets up with the military-industrial complex. John Bullaro, an executive of the New York Life Insurance Company, is – when we first encounter him – married to Judith Palmer, daughter of 'a top executive with a Los Angeles aeronautics firm' with 'personal connections in the industrial-military complex that was investing billions into the California economy.' Though, in their early days together, Judith had on occasion 'performed fellatio with uncommon skill and ardor,' the marriage is not what it was and Bullaro is keeping Mr P in good shape during brisk lunch-time rendezvous with Barbara Cramer, a business colleague. Talese says that Cramer has 'large breasts ... firm thighs and buttocks,' which he should know about, since he has P/V relations with her 403 pages after Bullaro, on page 541.

Cramer, however, marries John Williamson, formerly an employee of Boeing, then of Lockheed, in Florida, before setting up his own electronics firm in Los Angeles. The capital realized in the sale of this business finances the acquisition of Sandstone, which is therefore a remote consequence of the space program. Before he buys Sandstone, Williamson, a student of Ayn Rand, decides to test Barbara's 'tolerance of sexual variety within their marriage' by taking her off on a weekend during which he leaves her in the next room and sleeps with a former airline hostess who now works in his electronics firm. The next day, to even things up, he introduces Barbara to David Schwind, an employee of Douglas Aircraft, and $V^2 = P^2$.

Aerospace now starts to proselytize insurance. Soon we find Bullaro sitting on a sofa in the Williamson house in Woodland Hills between Barbara and Arlene Gough (Hughes Aircraft), listening to group chat about Krishnamurti and responding manfully with the latest news on medical malpractice insurance. Bullaro knows the group to be 'liberated' and as he eyes 'the upturned breasts and dark nipples' of Oralia Leal ('a nude Nefertiti' of unstated corporate origin) he clearly hopes that $P = V^2$ will soon result. Life deals the cautious insurance man a whack when the demonic Williamson invites Judith Bullaro to join her husband for a soirée in Woodland Hills. Judith has no knowledge that free love may accompany the martinis and pretzels, or that Bullaro has previously been in P/V contact with Barbara.

A truth séance follows in which the wretched Bullaro has to confess the facts of his liaison with Barbara. Judith is most upset, and Williamson, disposer of property relations, makes the crucial suggestion: Judith 'should return to the Williamsons' home and actually watch her husband walk off to a bedroom with another woman to make love, and perhaps in this way she would realize that an open act of physical infidelity was less threatening than one that she might suspect and embellish with emotion.'

This too comes to pass. Then a few days later the Bullaros and the Williamsons set forth on a weekend to Big Bear Lake. As Bullaro emerges from the bedroom from a P/V session with Barbara he sees 'two naked bodies together.'

The woman was on the bottom, lying on her back with her eyes closed, her blonde hair touching the floor, her legs spread wide and held high with her toes pointed to the ceiling. She was sighing softly and edging her hips forward as the broad-shouldered man who hovered over her was penetrating her with a penis that in the firelight looked like a burning red rivet ... for the briefest moment he regarded the sight as beautiful. But then he recognized the familiar shape of his wife's thighs and saw the foreign fetid penis oozing in and out of her, provoking her pleasurable sighs, and pounding back her buttocks, and ripping into Bullaro's guts with such violent force that he suddenly felt disemboweled. Bullaro fell back, stumbling as he turned quickly toward the bedroom. He felt Barbara reaching out to him, trying to embrace and comfort him, but he abruptly slapped her hands away, no longer wanting to be touched by her, or by anyone, as he slammed the bedroom door behind him and collapsed crying on the bed.

The rivet, appropriately enough, belongs to engineer Williamson. $P^2 = V^2$.

This is the only moment in the entire book when you get some sense of human pain. (The only convincing literary conveyance of a sense of pleasure comes courtesy of a letter of James Joyce printed in *Screw* and quoted by Talese – 'I would love to be whipped by you, Nora. ... The smallest things give me a great cockstand – a whorish movement of your mouth, a little brown stain on the seat of your white drawers. ...' Old-style fetishism. Joyce would not have liked Sandstone.) The pain presumably stems from Talese's empathy with the travails of Bullaro. Stylistic energy here contrasts strongly with the dutiful rhythms of Talese's account of Barbara's emotions the morning after Williamson had abandoned her in a Lake Arrowhead bedroom for noisy P/V next door with Carol the former airline hostess: 'Her awareness that her husband had been sexually engaged the previous night with another woman was, after she recovered from the shock, not really shocking ... his railing against covert adultery and sense-less sexual possessiveness and jealousy had culminated last night in a defiant act against a centuries-old tradition of propriety and deceit.' Cha cha cha.

The truth is that there are two Taleses hard at work, telling two stories at cross purposes to each other. Advanced, 'recreational sex' Talese hawks the free fuck/freer world line of goods, with plenty of bouncy stuff about the joys of $P^2 = V^2$ and the merry times enjoyed by all down on the old sex farm. Ur-Talese, New Jersey Catholic with a size 16 superego, comes lumbering along behind with intimations that Bullaro wanted to kill Williamson; that Williamson was Mr P(rimus) inter P(are)s, group guru and power fucker; and he hints that unlike John Humphrey Noyes's boast about the nineteenth-century experiment in P/V multiple equations at the Oneida Colony ('We made a raid into an unknown country, charted it, and returned without the loss of a man, woman or child') there were some psychic victims of Sandstone. Oneida was a manufacturing facility with an emphasis on eugenics, hence was the self-confident progeny of nineteenth-century industrial capitalism, whereas Sandstone was, in the appropriate late capitalist mode, devoted to sex servicing (voluntarily engaged in by the adepts), being finally bought in 1974 by an ex-marine and social worker whose first act was to double the couples-club rates. Surplus sex = surplus value. Neither manufacturing nor eugenics was of interest to the Sandston-istas. Talese's book is almost devoid of any mention of children. The P/V reportage steers clear of them, presumably on the grounds that recreation and re-creation are not the same thing.

Ur-Talese and Advanced Talese, toiling through the nine-year travail of *Thy Neighbor's Wife*, never quite sorted things out between themselves on matters of basic attitude, but they are at one in extolling the book's high importance. In the May *Playboy* (a wankfest, incidentally, for those with a preference for airline hostesses) Talese is asked, 'Why do you believe this is an important book?'

Talese: 'As a work of nonfiction it is pioneering because, for the first time, it reports what really happens in bedrooms, what really happens in the most private moments of real people's lives, and it stands behind the reporting. It presents the real names. It gives you information you can verify.' Bullaro is *real*. You can call him up on the telephone and ask if he or maybe Barbara likened Mr P (Bear Lake appearance) to a rivet.

Talese: 'The book is an invasion of privacy, no question about it. Those people became pioneers when they gave me releases to write about them.'

Buttressing the invocation of the 'real' is the traditional New-Journalist Author's Note at the back citing tape-recorded interviews with 'hundreds' of people, 'some of them more than fifty times each.' Familiar problems at once intrude. Since Talese excises his own questions from the interviews and sometimes transfers direct into indirect speech, you can never be sure who is saying what. Did Hefner really proclaim, in one go, that 'after I had covered her body with oil – and she seemed to enjoy it as much as I did – the smooth, soothing, glistening lovemaking on my satin sheets aroused me to peaks of passionate pleasure. In all my vast and varied erotic past, Gay, I have never known anyone who could surpass Karen's skill and ardor in bed'? Maybe Hefner does talk like this. Maybe Mr P himself gave an opinion on a deep background, nonattributable basis.

This stress on the 'real' is enhanced by Talese's appearance, as 'Talese,' in the final section of the book before a concluding bow as Talese in the author's note. Talese tells us that 'Talese' worked in massage parlors, visited Sandstone, and caused great pain to 'Mrs Talese' by reason of the P/V activity involved in R&D for the book. Meanwhile newspaper interviews with Mr and Mrs Talese confirm the problems of 'Talese' and spouse and indeed children incurred over the nine years of preparation, composition, and concluding publicity. Thus the book, in the oldest of journalistic traditions, is 'A True Confession' given majesty by the gigantic sums of money expended upon it by Doubleday and Hollywood; pathos by Talese's indication in interviews that he is uncertain how Mrs Talese will react to public discussion of what Talese and 'Talese' got up to; and absurdity by the last lines of the book in which Talese says that 'Talese' returned to his childhood haunts in New Jersey, stripped his clothes off in a nudist colony on the shores of the Great Egg Harbor River and, regarded by bourgeois mariners, 'looked back,' with Mr P presumably pendent and unashamed.

The shabbiest thing about this sad book is Talese's view of it as pioneering because it tells what 'real people' do in real bedrooms. It is as though the prime sexual discourse of the twentieth century – psychoanalysis and 'the cast study' – let alone the far older juridical confession, had never been.

Talese's function as a journalist in this particular project is quite other than he proposes. His ambition was to describe a struggle against puritanism, and his belief seems to be that though puritanism still threatens and menaces the liberation of Mr P and Mrs V, all will be well and at least the middle classes will evolve to more natural sexual mores, confounding the repressive instincts of the state and other powers that be. Back to Reich and the crazies: freer fuck means freer world.

Reich was wrong, and Michel Foucault right when he said, 'We must not think that by saying yes to sex, one says no to power.' At the end of the first volume of his *History of Sexuality* Foucault says:

> We are often reminded of the countless procedures which Christianity once employed to make us detest the body; but let us ponder all the ruses that were employed for centuries to make us love sex, to make the knowledge of it desirable and everything said about it precious. Let us consider the stratagems by which we were induced to apply all our skills to discovering its secrets, by which we were attached to the obligation to draw out its truth and made guilty for having failed to recognize it for so long. These devices are what ought to make us wonder today. Moreover, we need to consider the possibility that one day, perhaps in a different economy of bodies and pleasures, people will no longer quite understand how the ruses of sexuality, and the power that sustains its organization, were able to subject us to that austere monarchy of sex, so that we became dedicated to the endless task of forcing its secret, of exacting the truest confessions from a shadow.
>
> The irony of this deployment is in having us believe that our 'liberation' is in the balance.

Talese, or at the very least 'Talese,' should have pondered his actual achievement as a journalist here. In his meandering package tour he has ratified the fresher forms of subjugation of Mr P and all his friends in these late capitalist days. With the true instincts of the social-issues liberal he touts the trip as a journey toward liberation and a better world, with 'real life' stenciled on the side of the suitcase.

Review of Thy Neighbor's Wife, *by Gay Talese; The New York Review of Books, May 29, 1980*

Afternote: These reflections came on the eve of the onset of AIDS, which disease has markedly inflected the political economy of desire. Sexuality in the Reagan years pertains to a discourse that Foucault – himself an AIDS victim – would have seen as an ironic pendant to his reflections quoted here: Schopenhauer and Onan in the ascendent over Reich and Sade in a veritable apotheosis of regulation.

Gastro-Porn

They came and told one of the more recent dukes of Devonshire that in the interests of economy and general modernmindedness Chatsworth really ought to dispense with the pastry chef. 'What,' cried the duke, aghast. 'Is a man no longer to be allowed his biscuit?' Somehow things never seem to get better in the world of eating. Indeed, if we are to believe Marvin Harris's version of prehistory in *Cannibals and Kings*, things have gone more or less downhill since the upper palaeolithic period when the hunter-gatherers enjoyed high quality diets with plenty of free time too.

But those times are gone, alas – and are unlikely to return, since analysts of the connections between energy and food such as David Pimentel have reckoned that the land mass of the present United States could only support 750,000 hunter-gatherers before overcrowding would force agricultural settlements and the whole ghastly trend toward Earl Butz, General Foods, and liquid protein diets.

Cookbooks with certain very rare exceptions, such as Marinetti's futurist cookbook, almost by definition try to appropriate the past, at least those bits of it that seem palatable. And so usually they become versions of pastoral, with the urban masticator being whisked into a world where kitchen and garden coexist in harmonious union instead of being mediated by the Safeway, the can, the freezer, and the poison list on the back of every package. Here's a fairly representative swatch of pastoral from Richard Olney's *Simple French Food*:

> Comforting also are the fantastic, crowded out-of-door morning markets, of which that in Toulon is exemplary, bearing ample witness to the fact that people still want fresh garden produce and seafood and to the certainty that, on the whole, the French willingly spend a great deal more on food than a similar budget in any other part of the world would permit. The banks of fruits and vegetables, freshly picked (depending on the season), baby violet artichokes, tender young broad beans, tiny green beans, peas, tomatoes, fennel, squash, and zucchini squash with its flower still clinging; creamy white cauliflower the size of one's fist,

giant sweet peppers, and asparagus – white, violet, and green; figs, cherries, peaches, strawberries, raspberries, and medlar; the endless tresses of garlic and wild mushrooms of all kinds (including the divine amanita of the Caesars); and crates full of live snails and crabs, both of which constantly escape and wander in a wide circle around the vendor's stand. There are the odors of basil and *pissaladière*; the mongers' cants [*sic*], melodic and raucous; and the Renoiresque play of light through the plane trees' foliage, an all-over sense of gaiety and well-being ...

Provence is of course the heartland of cookbook pastoral, and we can set Olney down on the shelf next to Elizabeth David, who began her great *French Provincial Cooking* with a reverie in her London kitchen:

... now and again the vision of golden tiles on a round southern roof, or of some warm, stony, herb-scented hillside will rise out of my kitchen pots with the smell of a piece of orange peel scenting a beef stew. The picture flickers into focus again. Ford Madox Ford's words come back, 'sometimes between Vienne and Valence, below Lyons on the Rhône, the sun is shining, and south of Valence Provincià Romana, the Roman Province, lies beneath the sun. There there is no more any evil, for there the apple will not flourish and the brussels sprout will not grow at all.'

By the time *French Provincial Cooking* was published in 1960 Elizabeth David had been conducting her elegant propaganda for French regional peasant and bourgeois cuisine for a decade. And it was having considerable and generally beneficial effect – at least in England. By the early 1960s, when I was there (and eating cheap Indian food most of the time), half the academic kitchens in north Oxford had earthenware pots in them, simmering *queue de boeuf aux olives noires* or a *daube du béarn*, or indeed the fearful *cassoulet* itself; this last produced with prodigious effort and damage to digestion and the thought processes generally.

(Students of Provence cookbook pastoral will know that *cassoulet* invariably stirs the writer to protracted analysis and counsel. The normally pithy Elizabeth David spends three pages on this dish; in the first volume of their *Mastering the Art of French Cooking* [1961], Julia Child et al. take six pages, or rather eight if you include their preliminary advice on how to roast pork in a casserole; and even this barrage of advice omits a recipe for *confit d'oie*, which only makes its appearance on two pages of their second volume [1970]. I'm glad to see that some sense of brevity is restored in Paula Wolfert's excellent Braudelian *Mediterranean Cooking* [1977], which cuts the saga down to three pages, although she does shirk the *confit* business. By contrast Escoffier's *Cook Book*, which had to cover more ground than just Provence, takes just three-quarters of a page.)

These cookbook pastorals have some pretty consistent formal rules. There is the customary invocation to Escoffier's edict *Faites simple* and usually a doff of the toque to Brillat-Savarin, though I'm glad to see that Olney denounces him for the gormandizing old bore he was. And there's the insistence that only the best ingredients will produce the best results. This apparently self-evident piece of counsel is actually a crafty pastoral ruse, since the cookbook reader is usually nowhere near Olney's Toulon market or some equivalent haven and thus is damned before he begins. You can of course try to interview a fish in the local store to see whether its eyes are clear, its gills red, and its scales in prime condition, but fish-mongers have a limit to their patience and so you are left with the unspoken recommendation of the cookbooks – namely to get up at four in the morning and go to the local wholesale market where you will be trampled to death by the retailers and restaurateurs, and despised by the wholesalers to boot.

In keeping with the pastoral genre, many cookbooks are in fact moral tracts about gastronomic good behavior in which the reader-consumer's best strategy is to fall into line without too much fuss. Sometimes, in a confusion of genres, amateur cookbook writers attempt a jocose tone, hoping to inveigle the reader into a shared ritual. Thus, in her *The Carter Family Favorites Cookbook*, Ceil Dyer attempts some advice on the preparation of coleslaw: 'Cut the cabbage in quarters, place in a large bowl of well-salted cold water, and let stand for at least one hour. This is to make sure any possible "critters" emerge – nothing spoils good slaw like a many-footed friend. Once soaked, drain and place the cabbage on a large chopping board and chop away like mad ...' This is all wrong, and the reader backs cautiously away from Dyer, somehow associating her with the critter instead of with the healthy strips of slaw.

Far superior to the Dyer approach is the pastoral-aristocratic strategy of Pamela Harlech, whose *Feast Without Fuss* invites the reader to consume, in a simple act of transubstantiation, aristos and their camp followers. Lady Harlech, as the book jacket takes good care to term her, announces in her acknowledgements that:

> The following recipes are reproduced by kind permission of Condé Nast Publications Ltd – Miss Fleur Cowles's Jerusalem artichoke soup; Mrs John Hay Whitney's oyster stew; Madame Jacques de Beaumarchais's *oeufs chimay*; the Earl of Gowrie's *oeufs en cocotte* with duck jelly; Mrs Anthony Lund's *taramasalata*: Mrs Rory McEwen's avocado and caviar mousse; Peter Coats's Mr Briggs's avocado ramekin; Baroness Dacre's curried melon and shrimp; Mrs Arthur Schlesinger's spinach quiche; Lady Elizabeth von Hofmannsthal's poached bass; Fiona Charlton-Dewar's *kedgeree*; the Honorable Mrs James Ogilvy's deviled pheasant; Anthony West's good chicken recipe; Mrs Jeanette de Rothschild's special stuffing; the Earl of Gowrie's cold steak au poivre; Derek Hart's stew; Mrs Ralph F. Colin's baked Virginia ham; Mrs Anthony Lewis's veal goulash; Anthony West's veal roast; Anthony West's kidneys in cream and Calvados. ...

But I'll stop here, for the merging of person and product goes altogether too far with the thought of West's innards (or 'variety meats' as they are called) being bathed in cream and apple-jack and served up to the would-be gourmet.

There are, as a matter of fact, some pretty disgusting things in the Harlech anthology. We need go no further than 'Peter Coats's Mr Briggs's avocado ramekin' listed above. Lady Harlech confides that she was given the recipe by Coats, who presumably got it from Briggs. What this man Briggs apparently did – unless either Coats or Harlech got it wrong – was to put three ripe avocados in a blender along with three quarters of a can of Crosse & Blackwell clear consommé, some lemon juice, and two table-spoons of cream. Half the resultant gunk is then put into the ramekins and allowed to set in the refrigerator. A little later chopped walnuts are added, then more gunk, then a little bit more Crosse & Blackwell, and finally some bits of crisp bacon. The stuff, says Harlech, should then be kept in the refrigerator until it is finally unleashed on unsuspecting guests. Harlech, naturally, does not mention guests unsuspecting or not, but I do not imagine the ramekins were destined for anyone with the least capacity for resistance, such as children or pets. Guests will eat almost anything.

However even the Coats/Briggs/Harlech effort pales in comparison with a recipe from another volume in the pastoral-aristocratic mode. This is *Irish Countryhouse Cooking*, edited by Rosie Tinne. Miss Tinne, who seems to run a restaurant in Dublin called Snaffles (which gives the whole game away), has put together one of those cookbooks where each page is a simulation of the letterhead of the relevant recipe provider, thus allowing the reader almost to imagine that 'Lindy Dufferin and Ava' (facsimile signature) is sending her 'Clandeboye chicken' to him personally from Clandeboye House, Bangor, Co. Down.

On page seventy-seven of this dreadful volume, beneath the letterhead 'The Glebe, Leixlip, Co. Kildare' we find a recipe for 'Cold curried fish.' An indecipherable signature which appears by process of elimination to be that of Lady Holmpatrick is attached to the following:

½ lb spaghetti – cooked and cold	GARNISH
1-2 lb white fish – cooked and cold	
1-2 pt white sauce – cold	parsley
1 (or more) tin shrimps	paprika
1 dessertspoon curry powder	
chopped chives	
1 teaspoon lemon juice	
1 teaspoon redcurrant jelly or apricot jam	

Mix all ingredients gently together, sprinkle with parsley or paprika. Chill and serve.

I wonder what the hunter-gatherers of the upper palaeolithic period would have made of this. Short of lowering one's naked foot slowly into the weeds at the bottom of a pond it is hard to imagine a more depressing experience.

Indeed Irish cooking, justly maligned, does badly in the current crop of cookbooks. *Paul Bocuse's French Cooking*, one of the fancier productions of the season, has a recipe for *Ragoût de mouton à l'irlandaise* which defiles the divine purity of Irish stew by urging a bouquet garni, lamb shoulder and lower ribs (instead of just best end of neck), and celery. And Bocuse omits the pearl barley which is the whole point and without which life – so far as Irish stew is concerned – lacks all meaning. There should only be the meat, potatoes, onions, and barley. Bocuse is not alone in his errors, and indeed was possibly influenced by Escoffier, who gives virtually the same recipe. Prosper Montagné, in his *Larousse Gastronomique*, adds insult to injury by calling his version of Irish stew '*Ragoût d'agneau à blanc (à l'anglaise)*.' There may be a problem here. On the old packet boat which used to ply between Fishguard (Wales) and Cork (Ireland), the dishes on the menu were rendered on either side of the card in both Irish and English. Except for Irish stew, which appeared only in English and which apparently defeated the best efforts of Gaelic scholars.

Be that as it may, for a long time after the war it seemed the English country house pastoral cookbooks had been vanquished by the pro-French school and that the daube had triumphed utterly over Lancashire hotpot. (If the Julia Child wave is anything to go by, something of the same sort seems to have occurred in the US – France's revenge for the Marshall Plan.) In England, particularly in the sixties, little inns sprang up, often run by retired naval officers, in which zealous renditions of bourgeois French cuisine were offered and painstakingly evaluated in the Good Food Guide, an extremely pallid and tolerant version of the Michelin.

But gradually, perhaps as the horrible memory of rationing and whale meat receded and with them the immediate appeal of Continental good eating, a reappropriation of the English, Scottish, even Cornish (though not Welsh) past seemed to take place, more or less at the same time as the devolutionary movements. In 1968 a slimmed-down version of the great Eliza Acton's mid-nineteenth-century *Modern Cookery for Private Families* was issued, with a prideful introduction by Elizabeth David. Acton's delicate yet properly austere recipes were made available to a wider public by Penguin in 1974 and the reputation of the cheerless Beeton as the Escoffier of England at last was under serious assault. By 1970 David herself had published the first volume of 'English Cooking, Ancient and Modern' under the title *Spices, Salt and Aromatics in the English Kitchen.* By the mid-1970s several exercises in national gastronomic excavation had appeared, including Elisabeth Ayrton's *The Cookery of England*, published by Penguin this year. 'Let us cook and eat our traditional dishes,' Ayrton's introduction concluded, 'remembering that the food of France should be a treat not because it is better than our own but because it is different.' Hurray for the Cornish pasty rather than Olney's *pissaladière*; down with *bourrides* and *bouillabaisses*, and up with grilled herrings with mustard sauce.

There were signs of counter attack against Gallo-gastromonopoly in the United States too. John and Karen Hess's polemical *The Taste of America*, published earlier this year, paid unstinting tribute to French cuisine, but mercilessly belabored gastrosnobbery and also attempted to excavate an authentic American cookery from beneath the heavy footprints of Fanny Farmer, the nutritionists, the home economists, the food processing companies, and junk food.

The French were not idle amid such signs of mutiny from the periphery, and over the last few years a tremendous counter attack has rolled off the presses. First it was labelled *la nouvelle cuisine française* and latterly *cuisine minceur*. The premises of these self-proclaimed advances in the art of cookery are simple enough: that modern times and modern arteries no longer permit the sauces of nineteenth-century French cooking, that cooking is a revelation of the inner and spiritual essence of each ingredient rather than a decorative assemblage of flavors. The watchwords are authenticity and purity.

Much of this has to do with the history of publicity and the demands of the French tourist and restaurant industry rather than with gastronomy. Sometimes, indeed, it seemed as though the whole movement had to do with a war between various French guidebooks – such as the Kleber or the Gault-Millau – each discovering a new tradition and a new pantheon of chefs, and each assailing the ancient monopoly of Michelin.

Certainly the wretched American reader was placed at an even greater disadvantage than usual; purity and freshness were stressed ever more unremittingly, and the distance to the French country market seemed altogether unbridgeable, despite encouraging noises from visiting French chefs who were reported to take sackfuls of Idaho potatoes back across the Atlantic with them.

Paul Bocuse's French Cooking is a fair example of the new genre. The American introduction by Colette Rossant makes a customary stress: 'Quality is the most important criterion in the choice of ingredients. As he explains in his introduction, in Lyons, Bocuse himself goes to the market every morning to choose his menu for the day. Whatever he finds fresh and in season is what will appear on his table for lunch or dinner.' The sense of the unattainable is rendered even more palpable with the news that 'In the book, there are numerous recipes for small game birds that usually are not found in United States markets. ... Bocuse asked that these recipes be retained in the book, because he hopes that readers will enjoy them, and when traveling in France, recognize these dishes on the menus and be tempted to order them.'

It turns out really that the book is not actually a guide to practical cooking but rather a costly exercise ($20.00) in gastro-porn. Now it cannot escape attention that there are curious parallels between manuals on sexual techniques and manuals on the preparation of food; the same studious emphasis on leisurely technique, the same apostrophes to the ultimate, heavenly delights. True gastro-porn heightens the excitement and also the sense of the unattainable by proffering colored photographs of various completed recipes. The gastro-pornhound can, in the Bocuse book for example, moisten his lips over a color plate of fresh water crayfish au gratin à la Fernand Point. True, you cannot get black truffles in the U.S., three tablespoons of which, cut into julienne, are recommended by Bocuse. No matter. The delights offered in sexual pornography are equally unattainable. Roland Barthes made an equivalent point about ornamental cookery in *Mythologies*, when he was discussing the recipe photographs in *Elle*:

> This ornamental cookery is indeed supported by wholly mythical economics. This is an openly dreamlike cookery, as proved by the photographs in *Elle*, which never show the dishes except from a high angle, as objects at once near and inaccessible, whose consumption can perfectly well be accomplished just by looking. It is, in the fullest meaning of the word, a cuisine of advertisement, totally magical. ...

Alongside Bocuse, who offers full-blooded gastro-porn along with the traditional pastoral, are the exponents of *cuisine minceur*. The premise of *cuisine minceur* is that you can have your cake and eat it with a clear conscience; that French inventiveness has brought relief to gastronomes eager for fine nosh but fearful of high blood pressure, cholesterol, not to mention cancer of the colon. Virtually banished are butter, cream, other fats, starches, sugar, flour. This Gallic answer to the McGovern senate committee's report on dietary goals for the United States (less fat, less sugar, less salt, more complex carbohydrates) is certainly a saner strategy than the traditional pattern, namely abandoned consumption of rich food followed by brutal dieting on the morrow; two huge American industries shackled together. And again it is a form of tourist advertisement for Americans making their Continental holiday plans: eat like a hog and stay healthy. Roy Andries de Groot's *Revolutionizing French Cooking*, published last year, is really a catalogue of suitable French restaurants where the chef will not tip a pint of cream into the sauce while your back is turned.

The gastro-porn that accompanies this style is far more restrained than the Rubensesque excess of the Bocuse genre. The photographs in *Michel*

Guérard's Cuisine Minceur, which crept into Christmas stockings last year just when people were bracing themselves for the Yuletide high-fat blow-out, stress the healthful simplicities of nature. Bocuse's crayfish (about forty all told) swim in cream, cognac, wine, truffles, and even two table-spoons of flour: Guérard's photograph has just a very few crayfish resting chastely on leaves of trevise lettuce ('It is picked very young in the vegetable garden at Eugenie les Bains'). The plate rests on earth, next to a bunch of primroses. The other photographs are in a similar style and plainly owe much to Japanese traditions of food presentation and arrange-ment. The entire cuisine, indeed, owes a good deal to the Orient, to which the *minceur* gang pays fervent tribute. Cooking and eating here become exercises of the good, balanced life in an age of recession, energy shortages, and high food prices.

And indeed essays in an interesting volume edited by K.C. Chang and titled *Food in Chinese Culture* make the parallel quite clearly. The Sung period produced the world's first great cuisine. The Hangchow visited by Marco Polo bulged with restaurants, fast food joints, ritual feasts, and general gormandizing. But, as Michael Freeman makes clear in his essay, *minceur* morality was also abroad in the land. Freeman quotes Su Shih's essay in praise of Tung-po's soup:

> 'Tung-po's soup is a vegetable soup that he cooked when he was living in retire-ment. It did not contain fish or meat or the five flavourings, but it had a natural sweetness. His recipe was this: he took *sung* cabbage, rape-turnip, wild daikon, and shepherd's purse and scrubbed them thoroughly to get rid of the bitter sap. First he took a bit of oil to coat the pot, then he put in the vegetables with water, along with a bit of rice and fresh ginger.' ... For Su Shih [Freeman continues] and for many others of the intellectual elite, naturalness was itself a value, and their interest in mountain herbs and peasant dishes reflected a broader concern for health, society, and self-definition. The praise of simple food, held up in opposition to the elaborate cookery and costly ingredients of the city, was attuned to common intellectual concerns. ...

The cook, to return to the modern *minceur* school, thus appears as a moral guide, appropriating not only the natural pastoral virtues but world gastronomy in an effort to lead the consumer toward the balanced life. (Just how ludicrous this catholic appropriation can get is demonstrated in Armand Aulicino's *The New French Cooking.* One of his specimen '*minceur* menus' suggests the following: 'Appetizer: Guacamole Salad. Main Dish: Swedish Pot Roast. Alternate Main Dish: Steak with Tomatoes and Oregano. Accoutrement: Spinach and Pear Puree. Dessert: Bahamian Banana Soup.' Aulicino does not make one feel much better by starting many of his recipes 'Applying cookware spray to a skillet. ...' I much prefer the older, though no doubt perilous, 'Throw a lump of butter the size of a hazelnut into a pan. . . .')

But at whom are all these adjurations and recipes leveled? You cannot read many of the cookbooks mentioned above without starting to feel that Bocuse's claim that his book is really a novel is not so wide of the mark. De Groot, for example, presents 'An American adaptation of Chef Roger Vergé's Almost-Melted Leg of Lamb Layered with Eggplant and Tomato à la Moussaka.' It is of immense length and complexity and indeed de Groot says sympathetically that 'perhaps it should be a weekend project with some help from family or friends.' I'm not so sure about the family or friends. Food preparation in fact becomes a solipsistic ritual, almost infinitely protracted. The ritual accords with certain well-known trends in American life: to wit, gradual decomposition of the home, exit of the wife to work, dwindling number of tiny mouths agape to receive the junk contents of the local supermarket. Gradually the domestic kitchen of the postwar period is cleared of female/child oriented appurtenances of domestic management and becomes instead the temple of the modern gastronome, male and at peace with himself and his Cuisinart.

I do not mention the Cuisinart idly. Just as the wife leaves the gastronome's sanctuary this device makes its entry, a mechanical drudge instead of the human one at last making good her escape. In orderly silence the onion, pastry dough, meat, suet, herbs can be submitted to its implacable blade. And it is indeed a fine, labor-saving tool, with only the paradox that modern ritualistic gastronomy demands a reverence for process, for the tender adaptation of natural materials to human requirements, whereas the Cuisinart is an abrupt instrument of domination, attacking and ravishing food, smashing it into small pieces or even pulp. The old pestle and mortar were servile adjuncts of the (usually female) hand and wrist, whereas the Cuisinart (itself set in motion by rapid jerks of the wrist rather than by pressing a button) is a mode of assault and subjugation.

Cooking thus becomes a lonely pastoral idyll amid the rising tides of liquid protein, McDonald's hamburger, taco chains, and the active pursuit of the better beefsteak. The pastoral implies an entire scheme of life revolving around the gourmet store, the spice parlor, the trusted market, and even perhaps in the end the small family farm where critters can crawl out of cabbages unpolluted by insecticides. Man is restored to the kitchen, in a modern rendition of the good life of the old hunter-gatherers.

The New York Review of Books, December 8, 1977

Culinary Conquests

We drove south on the San Diego Freeway, past the neon sea of LA International Airport, through the purple twilight to Manhattan Beach and the restaurant they call the Saint Estéphe. I was well armed, for beside me at the wheel of the Nissan Sentra was a man I'll call Mercator, a professor of political science at UCLA, undiluted in his radical convictions, awesome in appetite, his palate trained in Mexico, Paris, Budapest, Moscow, and the Upper West Side of Manhattan; in the back seat was his wife Augusta, a child of Portuguese colonialism, nourished on the *caldo verde* of Lisbon, the *muamba* of Angola, the *feijoada* of Brazil.

We'd heard of the Saint Estéphe a few weeks earlier, with reports filtering in of a successful fusion of New Mexican with New French cuisine. As we rolled along the freeway I brought reports of the food frenzies of New York, of gastrofads bursting like comets in the twilight, gone in an eyeblink: the mustard mania, the vinegar madness, the peppercorn frenzy; American tongues darting at the spinning globe, at Szechwan, Osaka, Bangkok, Hanoi, and now, most recently, at Mexico and the great American Southwest.

Mercator addressed the inside of the Sentra as though it were a lecture hall. 'You ask, why this frenzied food faddism, this orgy of gastroglobal eclecticism? Consider. There is a familiar pattern in which food in the imperial, mother countries is influenced by, even replaced by, food from annexed, or colonial, or even neo-colonial areas: Algerian or North African or Vietnamese food in France; Indonesian or Surinamese food in Holland; Indian food in Great Britain. In pre-revolutionary Russia, the best food came, still comes, from the Transcaucasus, from Armenia, Azerbaijan, Georgia, and central Asia. Why?'

Augusta answered: 'Food from imperial countries is inherently bland. Being in temperate areas the imperialists are less likely to be using interesting condiments and spices, and besides they're so busy imperializing the world that they have no time.'

'What about French food?'

'Stolen from Italy via the cooks of Marie de' Medici, when she crossed the Alps to marry Henry IV. The cuisine of France is oversold. English food? Bland beyond belief. Think of it, the least imperial countries in Europe have the best food: Italy and Hungary, which is the crossroads of eastern Europe.' Augusta fell silent, and Mercator, peering for the exit sign to Manhattan Beach, resumed:

'How else can we account for the mania here for Third World food? I could point to the ready availability of cheap raw materials as an essential component of colonialism. As a student of our political culture I could cite liberal guilt over colonial repression, the frumpies – formerly radical, upwardly mobile professionals – saying to themselves, "If we can't fight for their causes, the least we can do is eat their food."'

Mercator suddenly swerved the car into the exit ramp and there was a startled blare from behind as a Buick wooshed past us into the red ribbon of taillights streaming south. I thought of the cult of Vietnamese food, of the success in lower Manhattan of two restaurants, dowdy Saigon and modish Indochine. 'Don't trust liberal guilt,' I said. 'It's always two-edged. What could not be conquered in the Mekong Delta is consumed at the table; in an anthropological paradox the defeated devour, symbolically, the victors.'

We drove down Sepulveda Boulevard. The Saint Estéphe was in a shopping mall and at last, to our left, we saw the gray expanse of Manhattan Village Mall. Obedient as only California drivers are, Mercator obeyed the NO U-TURN, NO LEFT TURN signs. As we searched for a legal left turn Augusta brooded further on the appeal of Third World cuisine: 'It is the exoticism of the subordinate. You and I read qualities into a culture that conform to the stereotypes and reinforce our dominant position vis-à-vis that culture. The English, for example, eat Indian food. They tell each other that the true Indian eats fiery curries to make himself cool in a hot climate. What they are really saying is that the Indian is impervious to pain and hence can be treated abominably, because they think that the Indian must be silly to think he can get cool in this way. The Dutch say that the Indonesians eat such mountains of *rijsttefel* that they cannot work hard, proving they must be lazy. Take this craze for Mexican food ...'

But at last Mercator had made his legal turn, gone back along the boulevard, and was parking in front of an undistinguished concrete structure labeled Saint Estéphe.

The cooking was modern French in technique, *nouvelle* in presentation with some polite, though restrained bows in the direction of the American Southwest, mostly in the higher hucksterism and bad faith of the menu's language. It spoke of the Sangre de Cristo mountains, the civilization of the first American Indians, the small villages of Hispanic settlers and the natural foods – corn, chile, beans, wild herbs, pumpkins, piñon nuts, squash – that had 'blended together to make America's first historic cuisine.' The Saint Estéphe, the menu suggested, has concocted 'a modern Southwest cuisine' by taking these raw materials and adding 'new interest, inspiration and refinement.'

We ordered blue corn tortillas 'served with smoked salmon and two types of American caviar.' They were cocktail canapés, resting on white plates and set off against a trim of small red peppers. A snap of Mercator's jaws and they were gone. We had a tiny cassoulet of sweetbreads with pinto beans and wild rice. The only element here the Southwest could claim for its own would be the pinto beans, but the dish was good. As our third hors d'oeuvre we had 'New Mexican style raviolis stuffed with *carne adobada*, served with a cream garlic chèvre sauce' – four pale squares, a mini-UN of ingredients: Southwestern filling, Italian envelope, sauce from a peasant product of the eastern Mediterranean.

Contented as we waited for the main dishes, perched in the western edge of one of the largest Spanish-speaking cities in the world, we debated the fashion for Mexican food and the meaning of the Saint Estéphe.

'After all,' Mercator pointed out, 'though Mexico has some of the most sophisticated food in the world, in the United States we basically eat what the cowboys have round the campfire: beans, enchiladas, rice, and tacos. What's being enforced is the peasant stereotype, a version of pastoral. The classic Mexican leftover dish is *ropa vieja*, literally "old clothes." You tell us it's on the menu of the Cafe Marimba in New York for $14.95. That's like selling a hot dog with sauerkraut for $10. Now the colonized are not only exotic but also threatening. Mexico conjures up an image of illegal immigrants flooding across the Rio Grande, of perilous external bank debt, of drug smuggling. It has these dual connotations – quaint but threatening. Hence you get attempts at domestication and cultural pacification via a pastoral version of Mexican cuisine and, even less threatening, the notion of New Mexican food. New Mexico isn't going to threaten America. It *is* America.'

'Yes, it is the very image of repressive tolerance!' said Augusta, who had just been reading Marcuse. 'The proliferation of Third World food is a concession to immigrants, allowing them a toe hold in the American dream. You integrate the Third World into American cuisine while at the same time segregating it from American society. As an immigrant you have the vicarious pleasure of seeing your food move out of the gastro-ghetto into middle-class respectability in a fancy restaurant where you might be lucky to work as busboy.'

The main dishes came: the menu's 'fresh prawns from Arizona served Southwest bouillabaisse style, flavored with nopalitos and chile pods'; though entirely unrelated to bouillabaisse in any style the prawns were great and the little bits of nopal cactus served as signifiers of the Southwest as surely as an ox skull on a whitewashed wall signifies Georgia O'Keeffe. Signifier of the Southwesternness of the *suprême de volaille* was *jicama,* Mexico's retort to the daikon radish, this year's crisp texture of choice though, in the Saint Estéphe's presentation, pointlessly shredded. The saddle of lamb had its signifying *posole,* and the New Mexican *carte d'identité* of the veal chop was established by a *sopaipilla* – a square pouch of puff pastry from which one tears a corner to pour in honey.

We ate and we drank and as we did so parties of sober-looking men in suits and ties came in to eat, straight from the office evidently, even though it was now well past nine – Hughes engineers, aerospace executives, traders and guardians of the Pacific rim. As the hefty bill arrived I told Mercator and Augusta of the feeding frenzies of the East Coast: bogus regionalism disguised as the 'new American cuisine.' In New York at Jams, for example, Norwegian salmon with *jicama* and green-pepper *concasse*; sautéed foie-gras salad with *jicama,* sherry vinaigrette, and deep-fried spinach; red-pepper pancake with salmon and Oestra caviar.

Mercator raised his hand. 'Stop, please! It's the same here in Los Angeles, as you well know. Probably worse.' But it was my privilege to give myself the final word. 'The last refuge for an elite frantic to define itself, yet with nothing creative to say, is conspicuous, relentless consumption of commodities of which the most basic is food. The British elite, at the height of their empire in the late nineteenth century, conspicuously consumed meals which were vast in size and, amid their belches, proclaimed, "We gorge, therefore we exist." Today, the conspicuous consumer in the United States knows that to gorge is to die. He renders his orgies of consumption – hugely expensive to be sure – more theatrical. He nods to the humble New Mexican pueblos with a blue corn tortilla. He winks at the Orient with a cumin seed, at China with a water chestnut, at Siam with some lemon grass, at Japan with a dried *bonito* shred. He consumes the world by symbols and the more he eats down the more he pays up. Ideally our conspicuous consumers must ingest all these symbols at the same time, for then truly they can fold their napkins with a contented sigh and say, "We are the world."'

House and Garden, December, 1985

Seint's Sanctuary

A man we shall disguise here, in homage to Huysmans, as Mr. Des E. Seint wanted, in the rolling country a few miles northwest of Philadelphia, a *fin de siècle* womb – the *siècle* in question being the twentieth. Mr. Seint desired a house commanded by computers and served by all the electronic apparatus of modern life. Though Mr. Seint mostly lives alone he wanted to be able to retreat to his private second-floor quarters and there behind a Tutankhamen slab of a door some thirty inches thick at the hinges, indulge his tastes: yoga, whirlpool bathing, the finest sound system, the largest video screen. Never for a moment, in upstairs bath or downstairs atrium, need Mr. Seint be beyond the range of speakers deployed about the house; never need a sound or image fly into the void uncaptured. What Mr. Seint sees or hears on his TV and video screens can be recorded. When he sits down at the piano a microphone can receive the notes, record them and, while he climbs up the mirrored staircase, Mr. Seint can hear what he has been playing a moment before.

The original house on the fifteen-acre property was built in 1740, with add-ons down the years. Georgian columns advertise the pretensions of a former time. Mr. Seint, I suspect, wanted the best of both worlds, old and new. He gave the designer, Eric Bernard, a long list of his domestic wishes, from live-in computers to wing chairs and a fourposter bed. He agreed to buy the house only when Bernard promised him a main staircase of stately grandeur. In the event Bernard, with experience in television set design, gave him at least the illusion of just such a staircase, doubling the visual, if not actual, width of the stairs by lining the inner wall with the mirror mentioned above.

Aside from the staircase, Bernard and his men ripped out the entrails of the old building and went to work. The result is *le style Star Trek*. Bernard says that 'everything had to be very sensuous. He said it was very important that if he were a blind person everything he touched would be soft.' And indeed almost the only hard-looking thing in the sitting room is the black piano. Everything else is in the squishy syntax of camel wool carpet, camel leather banquettes, camel cashmere from the men's suiting industry on the walls and, overhead, a chromatic cantata of camel. 'The room,' Bernard explains, 'was very low – seven and a half feet. What I did was bring it down six inches and make six elevations, with each panel edged with silver leaf and getting a lighter shade of camel. You get a tremendous feeling of height and grandeur.'

Across the hall is what Bernard calls 'a sort of contemporary Alistair Cooke traditional space. When we talked about the den he said he wanted something like Alistair Cooke sits in, with the wing chair in that color.' The result, as accurately described by Bernard, is an ecstasy of library Morocco: 'We ended up doing a den of all bordeaux color, bordeaux wool carpeting, bordeaux leather sofas. All the cabinetry is bordeaux-colored lacquered wood and the ceiling is bordeaux lacquer. The room – which he felt was very Alistair Cooke – is very today, very current, not old English. But the feeling is the same. You get that masculine ...' Bernard uncharacteristically groped for words and then hit happily upon the just parallel: 'It's like opening up a new bordeaux Rolls-Royce.'

The dining room tilts forward in time from Alistair Cooke contemporary to the idiom of Star Trek – a board room for the Intergalactic Governing Council: eight-foot circular glass table resting on a leather-covered plinth, itself sustained by a six-inch steel post resting on the concrete floor of the basement below. Round the table are Bernard's evocation of wing chairs and above is a large circular light hovering just under the ceiling like a UFO and capable of multifarious functions, from diffuse unearthly glow to specific spotlighting of the contents of a single plate.

The kitchen is modified Star Trek too – curves and planes of brass metal surfacing – and about as far from rural cook-nook as you can get. As Bernard put it: 'If I were to build what I considered the ideal kitchen it would be similar to the inside of a Kitchen Aid dishwasher, all stainless steel. Close the kitchen door, push a button, and it should be able to wash itself out through a drain in the middle of the floor. This kind of stuff is available now, and is ideal for the lady who works and comes home at the end of the day. In the urban cities these days, with all the wonderful catering around, it's nothing to be able to put together a fabulous dinner. Go by horse and carriage if you believe in chintz. But it's a false front. They're living one way and saying, This is the way you should live, with tons of curtains. Do you know what it's like, to live in New York City with tons of curtains, taking them down, sending them to the cleaners, getting someone to put them back up? It's impossible. Have Riviera blinds, dust them once a week and that's it.'

The four second-floor rooms in the old house were fused to make Mr. Seint's most private retreat. Camel, our old friend from downstairs, is here too, in leather covering the king-size bed, in the massage stretcher next to it, on the leather-covered columns which were Bernard's response to Mr. Seint's expressed yearning for the fourposter of yesteryear. Bernard gave him columns attached to the wall and to the ceiling over the bed. There's mirror on the ceiling over the bed too, contrived so that no seams mar the reflected image.

Opening his eyes of a morning and looking left from his king-size, Mr. Seint can see an Intergalactic Gateway, portal to the domain of his apparel: scores of suits, shirts, sporting rigs, and kindred accessories keyed to color and function. The idea was that Mr. Seint could punch the code for Florida weekend beachwear in on the keyboard and the dry-cleaning racks would trundle round and offer them to his hand. Forty feet away, after a soak in the four-person-size sunken bath or a dousing under the speaker-equipped shower Mr. Seint supposedly could weigh himself, and a kitchen computer hooked to the weighing machine would decree meals – Mr. Seint eats health foods – guaranteed to maintain fitness and the trimmer waistline. Thus far none of this gadgetry is working. As Bernard complains, 'The equipment is there, but no one ever told me you had to have a live-in programmer.' That's the *fin de siècle* for you. When you build a $2 million house with the help of a consultant from the space program, don't expect the place to be maintenance-free.

Behind his thirty-inch door Mr. Seint can perform yoga exercises on his mat, tone up on his Marcy gym equipment, or loll in front of his giant video screen. The world outside beckons? At the press of a button Riviera blinds rise and he can step forth onto the balcony of his two-floor atrium, embrace the shining cylinder of his fireman's pole, and slide to the bar, itself equipped with TV and sound system. There is no chink in the electronic envelope.

Mr. Seint wanted 'tremendous security' and his designer approached the task with zeal: 'What we really tried as a total environment was to take care of all a human being's needs, the need to be warm and to have the acoustical problems solved. Hunger was taken care of. There's a refrigerator on every floor. Everything in his oasis is the right temperature. It had to be this total nurturing, in a sense returning to the womb. This he explained to me and this is where I come from anyway, because I really feel that's the ultimate.'

It isn't clear whether, as part of 'total nurturing' Mr. Seint includes the realms of literature and art, beyond tape, disc, tv and stereo. It seemed possible that all the books in the den might have been acquired from the Strand at the same time, and as Bernard explained, 'The art is not his. He's not about to collect all that art so fast. Whether he'll ever collect anything I don't know. He's intimidated by it. He feels it interrupts his privacy.'

But as Bernard says, 'Who needs portraits all over the bedroom of ancestors who never existed?' What does *fin de siècle* man need? Bernard broods. 'A lot of young people today are very involved with drugs, but the reversion back to a period that doesn't exist – the false representation of heirs and family you don't have, along with your grandmother's secretaire whose drawers stick – is more of an artificial stimulant than the toot of coke that someone in a current apartment might take before going out. I'm very interested in producing environments that allow you to live with the tensions of work and career and the fear of nuclear war. It's important with the pressures of today to have an environment that works for you, just as the womb worked for you.'

In the space he designed for Mr. Seint, Bernard has not omitted primal sanctuary. From the foot of the fireman's pole it is only a few short steps to the basement stairs and down to a ten by six by five foot padded cell, entirely dark and lined with 6″ foam rubber. As I peered into the cell, through the dim light admitted by the open door, there came, from the far corner, the friendly gleam of a teddy bear's eyes.

House and Garden, April, 1985

Assault on Miami's Virtues

What is man before beauty lures him from his free enjoyment and tranquil form tempers his wild life? Eternally uniform in his aims, eternally shifting in his judgements, self-seeking without being himself, unfettered without being free, a slave though serving no rule. At this period the world to him is merely destiny, not yet object; everything has existence for him only insofar as it secures existence for him; what neither gives to him nor takes from him, is to him simply not there ...

Ignorant of his own dignity, he is far removed from honoring it in others, and conscious of his own savage greed, he fears it in every creature that resembles him. He never perceives others in himself, only himself in others; and society, instead of expanding him into the species, only confines him ever more closely inside this individuality. In this dull limitation, he wanders through his twilit life. ...

Friedrich Schiller's *Letters on the Aesthetic Education of Man*

Any fool can see that although Schiller, being a high-minded eighteenth-century German, talks about 'man,' he is in fact referring to real estate developers, a body of creatures who should be chained to a pile of Westway environmental-impact statements and thrown into the Hudson. They could, alternatively, be marched to the site of the late Morosco Theater, given a last cigarette or a last telephone call to Mayor Koch, blindfolded with old theater bills, and then shot.

These real estate developers are of course swarming all over New York like cockroaches, seeking out, with intent to destroy, any structure with the least pretensions to dignity and grace. New York citizens, numbed by their ravages, may feel that in other parts of the country such barbarism is restrained by some vestige of human decency. Such citizens would be wrong. The wrecker's ball now hangs over one of the loveliest neighborhoods in the United States: the Deco District of Miami Beach.

Like the Goths massing before Rome, or Bomber Command proceeding toward Dresden, real estate developers are now poised to destroy a square mile of Miami Beach and obliterate the most ample reliquary of the Art

Deco era. If it were the Pentagon threatening such destruction by aerial bombardment, there might be a shred of hope. In all likelihood the projectiles would fall far from their targets and merely disintegrate an unoffending hospital or school. But with real estate developers, we do not even have the comfort of this uncertainty. Comes the demolition order and the wreckers march at dawn.

Visitors to London may have noticed, in years gone by, the Firestone Factory on the left side of the road in from Heathrow Airport. It was a perfect example of Deco industrial architecture – streamlined, uplifting amid the gray horror of the western approaches to London. It uplifts no more. At five o'clock one dark evening a couple of years ago, the developers obtained a demolition order from a suitably compliant government authority. Under cover of night, the bulldozers took up position. At dawn, before the horrified eyes of preservationists rushing too late to the scene, the Firestone Factory succumbed into a heap of rubble. And as trucks carted away its remains these same government officials politely began to ponder, and even embark upon, the last alibi of bureaucracy, an Inquiry.

Just the same fate awaits much of an entire square mile of old Miami Beach.

'During the Depression, people needed to let go. ... They became wild on Miami Beach. ... They didn't watch their nickels. You would think nothing of ordering something you couldn't pay for because you'd figure, 'Maybe they'll carry me or maybe I'll wash dishes.'

'[Architects] were determined not to use any older styles like the Spanish. ... They didn't quite know where they were headed; but they wanted something modern, so they smoothed out all the Spanish things. They smoothed the balconies, they smoothed everything until you got the feeling that life was smooth. The buildings made you feel all clean and new and excited and happy to be there.' (Leicester Hemingway, author, Miami Beach.)

'I just came back from staying in New Orleans. The French Quarter is wonderful, very historic. I love old buildings. But these Art Deco buildings are 40, 50 years old. They aren't historic. They aren't special. We shouldn't be forced to keep them.' (Abe Resnick, Miami real estate developer and member of the Miami Beach Planning Board.)

The square mile of Miami Beach now awaiting the rapine of Resnick and his co-conspirators stretches from Sixth Street north to Lincoln Road and east of Washington Avenue, and as far north as 23rd Street. Before the First World War much of it was part of a coconut plantation, bought by a Pennsylvanian called Henry Lum from the U.S. Government for 35 cents an acre. Miami Beach was incorporated in 1915. By 1921 there were three hotels, and the building boom lasted – largely in the Mediterranean Revival tradition – until 1927.

The second great building boom, establishing the Deco District now under imminent sentence of death, lasted from 1935 to 1945. Sun, sand, and architecture conspired to create an escape from the Depression. The spirit was one of gaiety, lightness, the swoop of the streamline, and the soothing tonic of ice cream and pastel colors.

'Are any of these buildings masterpieces?' John Perreault asked in an article about art in Miami in *Art International* last year. 'Probably not. Yet the Miami Beach Deco District in its entirety *is* a kind of architectural masterpiece, the work of virtually anonymous designers and architects, created quickly and largely by chance. It comprises an unparalleled street-scape that not only reflects a particular time, climate and economy, but also offers lessons for those seriously committed to a more humane urban environment. ... The Miami Beach hotels are Pop Deco, a mass art mani-festation, that includes give-away refrigerator ware, costume jewelry, window displays, Flash Gordon rocket ships and much much more. What the hotels lose by lack of rare materials and traditional craftsmanship, they gain in vitality. ... Miami Beach's Pop Deco hotels epitomize a 30s dream of progress.'

And not just the hotels. Throughout the square mile are apartment houses ranged along the streets and boulevards, affording glances of inti-mate courtyards and tropical comfort on a human scale. Amid condo madness, the lava-like concrete torrents of horror carving their way along the coastline of Florida – prison houses of loneliness, emblems of the inhumanity of most architects and developers toward their fellow creatures – Deco Miami is the emblem of a gentle, proper sense of proportion.

Miami Beach, like much of Florida, is filled with elderly people: prob-ably more than 70 per cent of the inhabitants. But in the square mile they are not penned into high-rise concrete fortresses, locked into terror-stricken solitude. Nor are there the ghastly plazas – griddle irons of dis-comfort which planners often throw in as a belated concession to the desire of humankind to sit in the sun. The architecture and disposition of the district is a paradigm of how the elderly might like to live: beachfront promenades, safe hotel parlors and cafes, apartment house courts – inti-mate yet not concealed from that public, social vigilance which is the best protection for the elderly against more youthful predators; community and social interaction for old people rather than solitude.

There is a certain seediness, still well this side of terminal decay. Particu-larly since the arrival of what residents refer to with trembling hatred as 'the Mariel scum' from Cuba in 1978, the district's southern approaches have become more menacing. It is in short an area which energetic civic and government action could save – not as a Disney museum piece, nor as yet another swatch of high-priced gentrification loaded down with Deco Stores and high-income time-sharers perched in '30s nostalgia for a month in the year, but as a lesson in how an aging country with an aging population could deal with age and transcend the graveyards known as Sunset Cities.

'At night, when the Miami full moon is overhead, the residential streets of the Art Deco district take on that stagey, solemn simplicity of another era. Moonlight and neon articulate the stripes and circles of the small apartments on Euclid or Jefferson and the swaying palms cast shadows on the curving walls. This is the night world that Thomas Wolfe wrote of in the 30s – the decade of our District's revival – nights filled with the far-hooting of trains, the nearer sounding of great vessels moving into port, the mysterious rustling of trees. ...

'The daytime world of the Art Deco district, when the sun shines on the faceted corner windows and glistens on the white stucco walls is the world of hope and promise and the future. ... In the bright daytime world of the Art Deco district, these buildings have become the basis for heady plans now plummeted into the future by the Historic District designation – the scene for active restoration.'

These words, alas so over-optimistic, were written by a true heroine, Barbara Baer Capitman. She and her family moved to Florida in 1973 from New York. In 1976 she was instrumental in helping to form the Miami Design Preservation League. The League forthwith began agitation to have the square-mile district listed on the National Register of Historic Places. And on May 14, 1979, the more than 800 buildings in the area were indeed formally entered on the Register as the first 20th-century district to become officially part of the preservation movement.

Like many things in the United States, the Register is an outcropping of the tax codes, designed to save beauty through greed. Under tax laws (which have now changed in the Reagan era) inclusion in the Register entitled owners of such buildings to accelerated depreciation on rehabilitation work, and qualified them for various federal programs. There were tax disincentives to demolition, and demolishers would have no equivalent access to federal funds. But it should be emphasized that inclusion on the Register is not a formal prohibition against the destruction, or sale and consequent destruction, of any such designated building.

While the Preservation League, energetically led by Capitman, enjoyed its triumph, laid plans, and commissioned architects to produce schemes for the area's revival, the city of Miami Beach – in the form of its elected representatives – remained opposed to any consistent attempt to save and restore the area. The developers, naturally well-represented in the city's power structure, brooded and waited.

The forces of darkness gathered their nerve, and finally, in 1981, tore off their whiskers and pounced. Anyone who wants to see what might happen to the Deco Square Mile need only glance north of 23rd Street, where architectural barbarism is on the rampage and the condomaniac, behemothic tide marches down via the Fountainbleau and other signposts of Babylon.

Last year, starting in January – a month of infamy – destruction of the New Yorker Hotel, a creation of the genius of Henry Hohauser, was begun as hirelings of the forces of darkness marched up and down with signs reading 'Deco Shmeco' and 'New is Beautiful.' There is nothing new on the site now, just a horrible hole.

The developers had another reason for ripping off their whiskers and pouncing. A Miami Metro ordinance, which would become a Miami Beach ordinance this July unless the city passes its own, presented a possible hindrance to their designs: it would create a historic preservation board, composed of three architecture and three real estate representatives to designate the historic district. It would allow the board to designate any building it chose. It would allow the board to delay demolition for six months without the owner's consent while a preservation-minded buyer was sought.

Thus it was that the city of Miami Beach promulgated its own proposal, a hypocritical scheme mistakenly imagined by some naive souls to have something to do with preservation. It is of course a recipe for destruction. It would create a historic preservation board composed of three architecture and six real estate representatives to designate the historic district; it would crucially require the board to *have an owner's written consent to designation of his or her property as 'historic'.* And the Miami Beach ordinance would of course take precedence over the Metro ordinance.

Result: nothing would prevent the rapid destruction of the Deco District. Already the developers are calling for a whittling down of the original square mile to a few blocks. The few blocks will no doubt be whittled down to one building, and in the end all that will be left will be a Deco mailbox well pissed on by the local dogs. In another era it was called salami tactics.

The Miami Beach ordinance was given a reading in March and passed unanimously. Capitman came in for much abuse, as did her son Andrew. Andrew had founded a limited partnership in March of 1979, with the intent of buying up half a dozen or so of the small hotels in Miami Beach, and reviving them as Deco monuments.

After the March meeting, the city council, in a traditional bureaucratic move to mask barbarism, created an Ad Hoc Committee on the Historic Preservation Ordinance. It looked as though it was heavily manned by enthusiasts for the wrecker's ball, including Resnick associate Dov Dunaevsky who, along with Resnick, tore down the New Yorker Hotel. Foes of the preservationists, accusing the Capitmans of self-serving deeds, have been somewhat discountenanced by disclosure of the fact that one of the city officials most belaboring Barbara Capitman had his campaign partly financed by Resnick concerns.

Recently, the Ad Hoc Committee has been showing some signs of independence, of possibly slipping out of the control of the forces of darkness. It may even produce a possible compromise, to be presented to Miami Beach Mayor Norman Ciment in time for the second fateful reading of the Miami Beach ordinance on May 5.

The Miami Design Preservation League has been battling gamely. Young artists at the University of Miami organized a rally on April 13 in the north and most threatened end of the Deco District. Fourteen-hundred district residents – 80 per cent of them elderly – showed up, helping to expose the developers' line that the preservationists have little local support. There have been mailings and increasing pressure on Mayor Ciment.

If the ordinance to be voted on May 5 is passed unchanged, it will be a dreadful deed. As one who was recently escorted around the district by Barbara Capitman, I can say that it would strike me as forcibly as the permanent submersion of substantial portions of Venice.

Village Voice, April 27, 1982

Afternote: By 1987 a visitor to Miami Beach could see that Capitman's efforts succeeded. Deco revivalism was in full swing, in a riot of pastels. Salvation, albeit only partial, has come at a price: Disney deco is on the upswing, in a pell mell commodification of the sensibility of Streamline. Across southern Florida real estate developers, starting in 1983, began to build 'art deco' communities, as a break from pervasive Mediterranean or California designs and Cuban caca brown. If restoration is the goal between Miami Beach's 6th and 23rd streets, urban renewal is the target below 6th, altogether a grimmer area. But in the preservation district the wrecker can still rampage. By 1987 the Royale Group, which now owns the Cardozo, Leslie and Carlyle hotels wanted to knock down the Senator, one of the more significant deco buildings in the district. The group says it needs parking space for the other hotels. So Hohauser lives, but in the moral shadow of *Miami Vice*, anomic emblem of cocaine culture, cruel to the old and poor, appropriating the *zeitgeist* on a cash basis.

The Circulation of Commodities

> A game show is reality, not fiction. Except for sports and news, game shows
> are the only reality left on television.
> – Giraud Chester, executive vice-president of Goodson-Todman Productions

I visited 'Wheel of Fortune' on the first day of spring. The radio told me
that it had been another good day for the Dow and that the House of
Representatives had just rejected President Reagan's request for $100
million for the Contras. With uplifted heart, I swung into the NBC parking
lot in Burbank and made my way towards Studio 4, outside of which was a
long line of people waiting to get into 'Wheel of Fortune', the most popular
show on television, source of pleasure and excitement for forty-two million
Americans each day.

Inside, they were starting to tape a show. The wheel spun and disem-
bodied voices squealed, 'Whee-e-e-e-l of Fortu-u-u-ne!' A blonde nymph,
vestal virgin in the Temple of Mammon, raised her slim arms in a gesture of
demonstrative worship towards a Mazda light truck and a revolving platform, partitioned into three rooms crammed with consumer durables. A
curtain fell swiftly in front of her and her temple, and the camera shifted to
'our host', Pat Sajak, who smiled pleasantly and then introduced the
nymph, emerging radiantly from behind the curtain, as 'our co-host',
Vanna White. Then Sajak introduced the three contestants, each backed by
a great sun painted red and yellow and blue. There was Phil Loper, a
sophomore from the University of New Mexico; Heather Daly, a psychology student at UCLA; and Mark Steimer, an administrative assistant in a
communications company – as nice a bunch of young people as you could
hope to meet.

The atmosphere was of a mutuality of good feelings so pervasive that
even in its forced moments it had an innocent authenticity much like
Vanna's smile and eager cries as she urged on the players. The studio
crowd was encouraged to applaud, but they seemed to want to applaud
anyway. Only the players themselves appeared a bit self-conscious as they

shouted, 'Thousand dollars!' at the wheel and clapped resolutely as it revolved. (It soon became apparent that Mark, the loosest of the three, was going to do the best. Early in each game, either Phil or Heather started well, building up their dollar holdings, calling out correct letters on the great puzzle board so zealously tended by Vanna. But then they stumbled, and there was Mark, ready to clean up. It was Phil or Heather who got as far as THE E---T--N P-R---DS, but somehow it was Mark who rose to fortune on their honest toil by guessing THE EGYPTIAN PYRAMIDS.)

With each victory came an implacable ritual: Sajak announced to Mark the dollar value of his win – say, $3,000 – and attention shifted to the heaped-up prizes, as Mark peered at an off-camera billboard listing the available goodies and their dollar values.

'I'd like the Caribbean cruise.'

'Now we're talking,' said Sajak gleefully.

'And for $1,999, the pine bookcase.'

'Fine with me, and that takes you down to $495.'

'Uh, for $400, I would love the mantel clock.'

'And that leaves you $95 in gift certificates. And now, let Jack tell you what you've got.'

And then came, with anonymity from the heavens, the deep voice of Jack.

'They're beautiful, Pat. Mark, we start with Hamilton's Monticello mantel clock, key wound, eight day, walnut solids and veneers, gentle triple chimes, furnished by Hamilton, retail value $400. Now, this impressive arch-front bookcase is a reproduction of an early Spanish design. It's carefully crafted in pine with panel doors at the bottom. And, finally, we'll fly you and your guests to Miami, to a new superliner, the fun ship *Holiday*, cruising seven days to Saint Martin, Saint Thomas, and Nassau, all furnished by Carnival Cruise Lines, retail value $2,900.'

Jack's voice kept us company as the evening wore on.

'Next, a solid maple serving cart with butcher-block top which slides open to reveal an ice well with cutlery drawer, hanging stemware rack, slatted bottom shelf, rolling casters that lock in place, all for just $450. And next is a trip to San Francisco, where you may enjoy the warm hospitality and friendly services furnished by Western Airlines. In San Francisco you'll spend two nights and three days at the Holiday Inn at Fisherman's Wharf, where you'll receive special attention and service, making your stay in this delightful and scenic city a memorable one, at a total retail value of $606.'

'Wheel of Fortune' shows are taped for about twelve days each month, with sometimes as many as five half-hour shows recorded per day. Mark was a three-day winner, so he didn't look too upset when he lost a bonus-round chance to win the $7,000 Mazda light truck. He already had $15,120 worth of prizes in his possession, including two vacations. With a final radiant smile, Vanna bade him and his girlfriend, Danna, farewell as they stepped out into the night.

* * *

A commodity appears, at first sight, a very trivial thing, easily understood. Analysis shows that in reality it is a queer thing, abounding in metaphysical subtleties and theological niceties.
– Karl Marx, *Capital I*

How long does it take to pick up a dollar bill? – Arthur Laffer

Las Vegas police set up a decoy operation in a skid row area. An officer disguised himself as a vagrant and slumped against a palm tree pretending to be asleep, prominently displaying a ten-dollar bill from his jacket's breast pocket. The purpose of the operation, the decoy said later, was 'to provide an opportunity for a dishonest person to prove himself.' Oliver, a derelict, walked by the decoy, then turned back, nudged him with his foot, and warned him that the police would arrest him if he did not move on. When Oliver noticed the ten-dollar bill, he reached down and took it, saying, 'Thanks, home boy' as he did so. The decoy and two watching officers arrested him. Convicted of larceny, he was sentenced to ten years in jail. The court finds that Oliver was entrapped.
– Nevada Supreme Court proceedings, July 31, 1985, as reported in *Criminal Law Monthly*, March 1986

Ours is a society, the vagrant Oliver would surely agree, with a most refined sense of discrimination about what constitutes the legitimate proceeds of luck and application, and what pertains to the less wholesome pursuit of getting something for nothing. And it is no small part of the genius of Merv Griffin, inventor of 'Wheel of Fortune', that he understood this sense of discrimination.

Griffin has said that the game developed from his memories of long car trips with his family when he was a little boy. He and his sister would play hangman, the game where you guess the letters of someone's name (and concurrently fill in the macabre outline of a hanging man). In the early seventies, Griffin blended an element of hangman with the old carnival wheel, thus fusing what the French essayist Roger Caillois once isolated as two of the four basic types of play: the *agon*, or contest, and *alea*, or chance. The *agon* category includes games of skill, such as chess, tennis, football. *Alea* includes roulette, cards, dice – games of fate. (Caillois's other two categories were *mime* – the assumption of another's identity, as in charades and, ultimately, shamanism – and *ilinx*, the pursuit of vertigo and loss of consciousness, as in dancing, acrobatics, whirling, roundabouts, and the use of psychotropic drugs.)

Each 'Wheel of Fortune' program opens with both the image and reality of chance as the great wheel is spun. The player finds, most often, that the wheel has bestowed somewhere between $150 and $1,000 in the opening round, and the chance to call a consonant. Decryption and gambling then march forward arm in arm, as the player presses his luck with the wheel – thus racking up dollars to make appropriate inroads into the pile of commodities – while filling out the puzzle board with intuition and common sense, occasionally buying a vowel (for $250) to help things along.

Pat Sajak, Vanna White, and producer Nancy Jones (who has been with the show since its inception) all expressed uncertainty when asked to account for the show's extraordinary success. 'I'm really at a loss as to why it works,' Sajak said. Vanna took the view that 'it's a fun game that everyone of all ages can play at the same time, instead of watching all the murders and crime.' Nancy Jones separated out three elements: First, the game allows for strong home viewer participation. Second, she was determined at the outset that the prizes had to be things people would really want: 'We were the first show offering top-quality luxury prizes. We thought in terms of Tiffany, whereas it used to be stuff from the basement of K-Mart.' Finally, Jones said, the staff took great pains to find contestants from outside the usual Southern California pool.

The game itself has changed hardly at all through the years, though Jones said people are getting better at it. Griffin and Jones make up a lot of the puzzles, with input from the rest of the unit, and Jones keeps a very close eye on the prizes. She buys some of them directly, while others – after she's indicated what she has in mind – are handled by PIC-TV (a company that writes a separate contract with the manufacturer for each product and establishes the description that Jack will read out in his reverent tones). The objects thus sponsored are, of course, donated in exchange for their endorsement.

The selection of contestants in an unending process. Each month Pat, Vanna, Nancy Jones, and staffers Harv Selsby and Peggy Lavell take off for a new city to find players. In a two-day stint in Atlanta at the start of April, they conducted four interviews a day of 150 people each, thus winnowing down 1,200 of Georgia's finest puzzle solvers to the tiny group that would finally be invited to travel, at its own expense, to Burbank. Once in lift-off mode at Burbank, waiting for the final call, the contestants are given a series of briefings by Harv and Peggy, by the 'compliance and practice' people ever alert to the possibility of cheating, and by PIC-TV on the all-important topic of the prizes.

What does the staff look for in contestants? 'Well,' said Peggy, 'we ask ourselves, do they have energy, personality, a sense of humor? Are they having fun? We don't want to have people who are introverted. Not that they aren't people, but on the game show it's that little extra spark the contestant brings that adds a lot to the game.'

Just as Peggy and Harv were rounding off their account of the *rites de passage* of competitors, I could see three of them being shown this particular day's stock of prizes. No unauthorized contact with contestants, preshow, is allowed, but I joined Karen Griffin, assistant to the producer, as she wandered around the prizes making sure everything was just so. Merv Griffin has said that 'Wheel of Fortune' gives Middle America the excitement of a shopping trip along Rodeo Drive. Actually, the prizes are dead-center middle class, exactly what the average rational American would buy if God suddenly bestowed an extra fistful of dollars. Karen said that audiences use the show like a sales catalog, calling up to ask where that bookcase or brass lamp came from.

The lights went up, the crowd filed in, the wheel began to spin. When all goes well, a 'Wheel of Fortune' show builds, across the half hour, to a climax and dramatic resolution through the substantial victory of one contestant over Fortune's Wheel. That night it was the turn, and the triumph, of Dolores Rovnack, a young housewife from Redondo Beach.

At the end of the first half hour alone, she had won Le Creuset of America blue cookware, $350; Krups small kitchen appliances, $358; a Taylor Woodcraft Gourmet Serving Cart, $450; a service merchandise gift certificate, $142; a pair of tea caddy lamps, $280; a Hitachi compact disc player, $450; a Suzuki portable keyboard, $532; a Van Cleef & Arpels eighteen-carat gold and diamond scalloped-shaped ring, $1,300; and, finally, what Jack's oleaginous tones announced as a guarantee to 'fly you and a guest from Los Angeles to New Orleans, where you may long remember your week's stay at the Bienville House in New Orleans's French Quarter. It's close to historic sights and sounds, furnished by the Bienville House, retail value $2,238.' In the next two games, Dolores won another $15,460 worth of prizes, including a RCA video camera and recorder, $2,320; a Sony stereo cassette, $400; a Sharp video recorder, $600; and airline tickets and a three-day stay at the Hotel Coronado in San Diego, $960.

Finally, the bonus round. Sajak asked Dolores to give him five con-sonants and a vowel, and Dolores offered L,N,R,S,T,E. Up on the puzzle board went -E--- R-RE, with indications that the puzzle was a phrase of two words. Dolores had fifteen seconds, and after about eight she cried out, 'MEDIUM RARE', thus winning a Mazda hatchback with a/c, radio cassette, floor mats, freight, tax and license, $9,079.

I saw Dolores right after the show as she was busily signing forms put in front of her by someone from PIC-TV. On one of them I noticed a sinister little note saying, 'Income Tax Information: Please understand that the retail value of the prizes listed above are manufacturer's suggested Retail Price and are not necessarily the fair market value which must be reported to the U.S. Internal Revenue Service for Federal Income Tax Purposes ... You may forfeit any prize won for income-tax purposes. Notification of such forfeiture, however, must reach us three days after tape date.'

Dolores was understandably excited.

'What do you do, Dolores?'

'I'm a homemaker.'

'What does your husband do?'

'He's an electrical engineer for a major aerospace company, here in L.A.'

'How come you're so good at "Wheel of Fortune"?'

'I watch it in the morning. I watch it in the evening. For over ten years. I practice a lot, ever since I was in junior high school and high school. It's my favorite game show. I tried [to become a contestant] a little over a year ago and I didn't pass the written test. So I was discouraged. I came back, made an appointment to come for an interview in July of '85. I passed the test. I played the game and they liked me. I didn't think they'd call me but they did, out of the blue, just when I was getting ready to call them back and make another appointment.'

'How'd you guess MEDIUM RARE?'

'I like to eat. When I saw R, blank, R, E, I knew. Have I got room for all this stuff? Well, I'll give some to my mother. I've got several sisters-in-law. I'm sure they could use some of the stuff. Thirty thousand dollars in prizes. Boy, that's twice what I was making when I worked as an accounting assistant at Hughes Aircraft.'

It was the end of taping for the day. Vanna passed by, sighing. 'I'm exhausted. When I go home after doing five shows I usually die.' She bathed me in a wonderful smile and moved on. Security guards paced watchfully round Dolores's prizes. The puzzle board went dark and the wheel came to rest.

* * *

Consumption is the sole end and purpose of all production.
– Adam Smith, *The Wealth of Nations*, Volume II

Wheel has revived good, clean American greed.
– *People* magazine

The appellant shot his seventy-two-year-old grandmother, Pearl Plemmons, with whom he lived, through the heart. He robbed her of several thousand dollars, which she carried in a pouch in her brassiere, and took change belonging to her which he found in the house. ... The testimony was uncontradicted that the seventy-two-year-old Pearl was so drunk immediately prior to her murder that she was sitting on the living room floor, leaning against the sofa, without her glasses on. Although she was seen shouting, cursing, and pointing her finger at the appellant because he had allowed her sixteen-year-old mentally retarded protégé to attend a Christmas parade, this conduct would not constitute legal provocation for a killing. In fact, the

appellant told the sixteen-year-old that he killed Pearl because she had a demon and he needed money.
– South Carolina Supreme Court, June 3, 1985, death sentence affirmed, as reported in *Criminal Law Monthly*, March 1986

'Wheel of Fortune' isn't about greed. Greed is young Plemmons robbing and murdering his granny, capitalism at its worst. 'Wheel of Fortune,' by contrast, is a stately mime of capitalism at its best, celebrating that *sine qua non* of the system, the circulation of commodities. It is a Keynesian parable about the creation and satisfaction of demand in an egalitarian society in which all competitor-consumers are created equal in the eyes of Pat Sajak and, with the appropriate injection of capitalist good luck and capitalist hard work, earn the right to the prizes, which are sanctified in their life-enhancing, economy-boosting properties by the divine Vanna. ('Wheel of Fortune' became an evening as well as a daytime show in 1983 – the eve of the biggest growth year for the American economy in a generation. Another growth year in the same league was 1955, one of the host years to that emblem of greed and bad faith, 'The $64,000 Question.')

The competitors I saw were not crazed with greed; indeed, both Mark and Dolores seemed much more excited by the fact that they had won than by what they had won. Dolores referred to her treasures rather disparagingly as 'stuff', and was plainly relieved that she would be able to dump much of it on her in-laws. Indeed, she had a positively Brechtian objectivity about the mime: her account of her efforts to get on the show was couched exactly in the idiom of someone trying hard to get a job ('So I was discouraged. I came back, made an appointment to come for an interview. . . .'). This objectivity was sustained when it came to the prizes, as though Dolores recognized that it was absurd to have both an RCA and a Sharp video recorder, yet simultaneously accepted the entirely correct proposition that, as presently constituted, American capitalism (and Japanese capitalism, too, for the show's ideology is internationalist and antiprotectionist) can survive only if the consumer buys as many video recorders, microwave ovens, et al. as the home will hold. There's no hoarding on 'Wheel of Fortune', no obeisance to the exigencies of capital formation, the need for thrift, and other virtues dear to the heart of the Chamber of Commerce.

The game – because it is an idealized representation of the proper motions of the economy – does not pit competitors against each other: it's all against the wheel and the limitations of their own skills. Even the losers don't seem too upset. Many of them have won something nice, and even the complete losers go home with a bottle of carpet cleaner (or some similar reminder that consumerism has its dreary side). For all the talk of prizes, Sajak was right when he said, 'Ours is not a big money show, relatively speaking. We've had a few instances where people have lost a huge amount of money, but usually it's a few hundred dollars. You get bankrupted, you lose a microwave oven. It's not a matter of life and death.' The show is not vulgar. As Vanna has said, 'It's not hysterical, like "The Price is Right." Who wants to look at screaming women at 7:30?'

In this orderly mime, there's no room for double entendres or the leers and heavy breathing of many other game shows. The theme is: Young and old, Pat and Vanna, Dolores and Mark, all are in this together, advertising – right down to the clothes Pat and Vanna wear – this demonstration-only model of the way life ought to be. And if there are people like Plemmons out there shooting their grannies, who, as Vanna so rightly asks, wants to watch that?

American Film, July/August, 1986

WAR
FEVERS

*'I will say this, though. If I were given a choice
to be aboard one ship during a nuclear attack, I
would pick this one.'*

Captain Fogarty of the New Jersey

Militarizing the Tortugas

I clambered into a tiny seaplane on Memorial Day and, since it seemed to be a suitable occasion on which to ponder the role of military thinking and planning in American life, flew 69 miles west from Key West, where the Florida Straits meet the Gulf, to inspect one of the most striking military follies of the nineteenth century, still enduring testament to the acts of madness to which the concept of 'national security' can drive an idle mind.

Today Fort Jefferson is a hexagon of 16 million bricks, 50 feet high and 10 acres in extent. The vast interior expanse, which once echoed to the shout of command and the babble of those stricken by yellow fever, is now silent and bare, except for stray linden and buttonwood trees. When Ponce de Leon first came upon the anchorage and sandy shoals he named the Tortugas, in 1513, he did not seem to have considered them of any consequence. For the next three centuries his opinion was shared by most mariners, including Commodore David Porter, who, in 1825, reported to his superiors in Washington that the Tortugas could be 'easily blockaded' and furnished 'scarcely land enough to place a fortification.' Furthermore, Porter added, if such fortifications were attempted, the land would probably give way under them.

Porter had sound engineering judgment but a bad sense of political timing. After the War of 1812 and Adm. Sir George Cockburn's rampages through Washington, the big vogue in military thinking was shield defense, and the Army Corps of Engineers was hard at work planning the 'Third System' of coastal defense, a boondoggling mother lode that was still tunneling its way through annual military budgets by the time World War II broke out. In 1829 Commodore John Rodgers visited the Tortugas and although the phrase 'force projection' was still mercifully unknown, he did his best, predicting that if the Tortugas were fortified, 'the commerce of La Habana and even the homeward bound trade of Jamaica would be subjected to its grasp.' History would have been a more congenial affair if such vagrant mariners had kept their mouths shut. But navy men always want a base they can sail to, an outpost they will have to protect, so Rodgers and his colleague Josiah Tatnall pronounced the Tortugas 'a magnificent resource' and the damage was done.

Shield defense steadily fortified the East Coast of the U.S., leaving a trail of cost overruns and contented contractors. By 1846 work had begun on Fort Taylor in Key West, and the following year Horatio G. Wright of the Army Corps stepped onto a Tortugan islet and commenced the planning of Fort Jefferson. It was a momentous hour for the Army Corps, since construction of the fort entailed its first big sub-marine construction, a foundation 14 feet wide, 2 feet thick and a mile in circumference. So stout an underpinning was essential, since the plan called for three tiers, housing no less than 400 guns and quarters for 1,500 men.

Pay ran from $3 a day for master workmen and $1.12 for common laborers. Slaves came at $20 a month to their owners. The sun blazed down mercilessly on the lonely site and the work was unpopular. The torpor spread to the Army Corps lobbyists and in 1851, with the fort still only 5 feet above ground, Congress cut off funding.

The peril was awful and the War Department sprang to life. Congress was treated to lurid scenarios of revolutionary Cubans only a few days' sail from New Orleans, of menacing British fleets, of a Central America threatening to erupt, of a Mexico bursting with menace to the Republic. Only a fleet anchored beneath the great guns of Fort Jefferson could stop them. Funding flowed once more.

Urged forward by warnings of frightful peril from the south, the builders labored on. As yet, no gun dignified this Gibraltar of the Gulf and by 1857 the inhabitants became more vulnerable than ever to the foes feverishly imagined in Washington. To cope with the dry Tortugas' well-known lack of fresh water, the Army Corps had devised a system of collecting rain water in no less than 109 cisterns, but in 1859 Commodore Porter's suspicions turned out to be correct. Fort Jefferson was built on sand and not on coral rock. The higher it got the more it weighed and the more it sank – a foot in 1859 alone. The walls cracked and salt water began to seep in. Most of the system became useless.

Such omens were dismaying, but great was the joy of all when in 1861 guns arrived. Ultimately the great 15-inch Rodman smoothbores were mounted on the tiers: 25 tons of cast iron that could lob 315-pound shells up to three miles. Prudent would be the enemy warships on their way to ravage New Orleans and Pensacola that gave Fort Jefferson wide berth through the leagues of undefended ocean on either side! The gunners daily refined their skills so that a seven-man crew could load and fire the Rodman in 70 seconds and traverse it 90 degrees in just twice that time. They moved fast, but technology moved faster. Robert Parrott had invented his rifled cannon. In one Civil War demonstration its shells smashed through the 8-foot-thick walls of Fort Pulaski in nine hours.

Built, like an aircraft carrier, essentially to defend itself, Fort Jefferson was obsolete. In 1863 it became a military prison. In 1865, fearing that added weight would cause disastrous sinking, engineers halted construction. By this time Fort Jefferson had reached its full height. Its immense galleries and barbicans were monuments to the bricklayers' art. But its active military service was over. The great magazine in the parade ground stood unfinished. No gun at Fort Jefferson had ever been fired in anger. It had deterred no foe, except in 1861 when, invited to surrender by the state of Florida, the union officer in command invoked imaginary batteries and scared the foe away. In 1875 the fort was largely abandoned.

In 1896 a new generation of navy men tried again. Familiar phrases rolled off their tongues: 'the only harbor between the Chesapeake and the Rio Grande deep enough for battleships'; 'here a fleet could renew its sinews of war.' In 1898, the Maine anchored there, then projected itself into Havana Harbor, where it duly blew up. With the new century the navy said Fort Jefferson would be ideal as a coaling station. At great expense piers were built and channels were dredged, 30 feet deep and 300 feet wide. It was a brave stand but the last, and in 1908 the navy gave up and handed it over to the Department of Agriculture as a bird preserve. Two years later a hurricane wrecked the coaling docks anyway. For a while it served as a quarantine station. In 1935 President Roosevelt declared it a national monument.

Though militarily impractical, as Commodore Porter had instantly divined, the fort made a useful contribution to the gross national product. Such is the function of almost all 'national security.' Between 1846 and 1860 it cost $1,259,113 – about $16 million in today's money remembering that the consumer price index has gone up 1,118% since 1850. (For that year the military budget was $17 million, about 0.3% of GNP.) The fort's total costs, when the navy turned it over, amounted to $53 million in today's money. It had brought profit and joy to quarries, lumbermen, masons, sutlers from Maine to Louisiana. It had injured no foe. To this day it affords pleasure to visitors, who can gaze upon the ruins and listen to the exuberant squawk of the sooty tern, nesting happily in the sanctuary that is the main consequence of such prodigious human labor.

Wall Street Journal, May 29, 1986

Battleship America

No firmer symbol of Reaganite foreign policy – minatory, explosive, and antique – has established itself this alarming year of 1983 than the USS *New Jersey*. This forty-one-year-old battleship was prominent in the mighty armada summoned by President Reagan to stand off the shores of Nicaragua and terrify the Sandinistas. Then the tocsin sounded in the Mediterranean in September and the *New Jersey* lumbered off toward Beirut to menace the Shouf and the Druse. If the U-2 evokes the age of Eisenhower and the AWACS that of Carter, the whiskered dreadnought now prowling the oceans of crisis nicely encapsulates Reaganism's armor-plated relationship to the modern world.

Six weeks before the *New Jersey* was told to go waggle its great guns at the Nicaraguans, it was making a portentous entry into Pearl Harbor, which from an altitude of 1,000 feet is where I first caught sight of that venerable vessel.

As the great ship stood off Diamond Head and our helicopter dropped delicately toward its deck, the famous sixteen-inch guns were indeed the ship's most conspicuous feature. Nine of them poked grimly forward some sixty-six feet from their armored turrets. In the whole of the Second World War they had fired 771 times; 6,671 times in the Korean War; 5,688 off the coast of Vietnam. A salvo from all nine, the briefing material on my knee heartily informed me, 'will level almost anything standing within an area the size of one square mile.' Like almost all such boasts about the capabilities of the world's only active battleship, this assertion is certainly untrue. But, even so, it seemed an occasion for gloom that in the summer of 1983 the guns were on the loose again and, though the ship had been hauled out of mothballs during both the Korean and Vietnam wars, that this was the first time the sixteen-inchers had been reloaded at a time when the United States was supposedly at peace.

Hours later, ship at anchor and light slowly draining from the wide Pacific sky, I looked west toward the Waianae range. Through a notch in those hills, forty-two years before, had come the first wave of Japanese planes. Commander Mitsuo Fuchida, leading the attack, had looked down on Pearl Harbor stirring in the December dawn and radioed back the thrice-repeated code word *tora* – 'complete surprise.' The day of infamy had begun. Ten minutes later an armor-piercing bomb had penetrated the forward powder magazine of the battleship *Arizona*. She sank in nine minutes, and her remains lie just beneath the surface of the water, a few hundred feet from where I now stood, with 1,102 skeletons still on board.

The *New Jersey* had spent a good hour earlier that June day inching its way in from the mouth of the harbor toward the *Arizona* memorial off Ford Island. Peering curiously at the landscape after a week's trip from Long Beach on the shakedown cruise, the bulk of the crew manned the rail in their whites, most of them lightly armed with cameras. Thick crowds of U.S. personnel from the base waved pleasantly, and on top of a warehouse a waggish gang of submariners held up a hand-lettered sign reminding the *New Jersey* that to them the battleship was STILL JUST A TARGET.

Standing level with the memorial behind them, the senior petty officer and the youngest man aboard jointly held a wreath as the ship's chaplain addressed the Heavenly Father: 'Strengthen us, that we may also be solely dedicated to duty, honor, and country, loyal to shipmates and service, your loyal and obedient sons. Amen.' The plastic wreath, upside down in the water, bobbed away to stern as the *New Jersey* moved toward its wharf. A civilian standing next to me pointed at the lonely marine band tootling out a welcome on the wharf and burst into passionate complaint. 'This is a shame! Where's the greeting committee? There's nobody here! The mayor didn't even come and we've known about the *New Jersey*'s arrival for weeks.'

He was a Navy Leaguer, and introduced himself as Kurt Laubscher, president of Hawaiian Financial Insurance Systems. After brief formalities my neighbor continued his lament: 'This is one of the black days of Hawaii. I thought we would have a welcoming committee, dancers, local color. This is a big event in the state of Hawaii. The armed forces represent 30 percent of our income in the state, yet a current governor just doesn't care. He's not here either.'

I asked a midshipman what he thought the point of a battleship in the modern age was. 'The point of it? To show the flag,' he answered promptly. 'It's like when a person drives up in a big Rolls-Royce. He's showing off. You drive up in a battleship and it's got a big American flag. It's the same thing, showing how powerful you are, what you can do.'

I was leaning on the rail, thinking about the flag and the dead men on the *Arizona*, when Commander Willenbrock, public affairs officer on the *New Jersey*, brisk and trim with dress whites all agleam, drew alongside. Captain Fogarty was hosting a small reception and Willenbrock's team, aghast at the prospect of pictures displaying roistering tars swigging down wine cup, had rigorously expelled all photographers and indeed most journalists. Partly because of the navy's extreme reluctance to admit any unreliable observer to this revel, I had allowed my imagination to get seriously out of control. I pictured an aquatic jamboree of the sort favored by Lord Mountbatten when he was directing naval operations in the Far East during the Second World War: the cream of Hawaiian society, flirtations over the daiquiris, a symphony of gold braid, service whites, and summer dresses as the Ava Gardner of the islands flirted outrageously with Captain Cary Grant.

This was not quite how things turned out. The affair breathed all the style and romance of the annual office picnic of a small-town bank. A fair slice of the visiting civilians did indeed seem to be bank managers, though I cannot be sure about the Japanese gentleman I found sitting in the captain's chair, looking thoughtfully toward the Waianae range. The extreme decorum of the proceedings was ably preserved by the pinkish, almost transparent fluid ladled out sparingly to the sparse assembly. The band played a jaunty tune, visiting navy officers congratulated Captain Fogarty on his command, and the sailors' voices echoed up cheerfully from the quayside as they headed toward the coarser comforts of Honolulu. Willenbrock eyed with almost tangible pride the *New Jersey*'s magnificently scrubbed teak deck spreading away for hundreds of feet, the towering superstructure bristling with the latest in electronic gadgetry and the mighty sixteen-inch-guns. He laid a hand on my arm with the complicity of a man certain that his sentiments are shared: 'Off the record, Mr. Cockburn, you do agree that she's a *beautiful* ship, don't you?'

There was an unprofessional intensity in his voice, an almost excessive flash of ardor in his eye. Like so many of the all-volunteer crew I had spoken to that day, Willenbrock simply felt terrifically proud of the *New Jersey*, with all the ingenuous enthusiasm of the person who had announced in the press kit Willenbrock had stuffed under my arm that each of the great guns could hurl the equivalent of a Volkswagen twenty-three miles. The comical symbolism of Battleship America, besieged by foreign imports, firing back salvo after salvo of automobiles at its tormentors from the gun muzzles of a forty-one-year-old dreadnought had evidently not occurred to the publicist.

But then, large ships, and particularly battleships, have long had an allure that seems to vanquish critical faculties. Nikita Khrushchev, lamenting the desire of his own naval commanders for unnecessarily large craft, had a cynical reason: 'Our naval commanders thought they [large ships] were beautiful and liked to show them off to foreigners. An officer likes to hear all the young sailors greet his command with a loud cheer. That always makes a big impression.'

It was true that Captain Fogarty did not seem dissatisfied with his situation, as each visitor got a snappy salute from the sailor at the head of the companionway. But in fact the navy had not been particularly keen on this third recommissioning of the *New Jersey*. Its original attitude to the proposal had been closer to that of a curator of the Metropolitan Museum, were he asked to go riding in Central Park in one of the equine armor sets from sixteenth-century Germany.

The third recommissioning of the *New Jersey* was in fact the brain spawn of a former pilot and Washington defense 'consultant' called Charles Myers, who began pushing his cause back in the dog days of the Carter administration. But for the Reaganauts, massed beneath the banners of Renewal and Making America Great Again, one can see that the *New Jersey* must have had particular appeal. Swathed in armor a foot thick, its very structure spoke of an era when there was full employment in the mills around Pittsburgh, and the Volkswagen little more than a gleam in Hitler's eye. Its guns retrieved an age of simple percussive prowess, innocent of basing systems, silo vulnerability, and the provisions of arms limitation treaties.

Although he gave every appearance of being an intelligent fellow, I feared, during his allocution, that Captain Fogarty had fallen victim to the complaint called 'battleship mind-set.'

The occasion was a small press conference in his cabin, convened once the ship had been safely brought to anchor. After some pleasantries about the arrival in Hawaii the conversation turned to what military men like to call the 'survivability' of the *New Jersey* under conditions of war.

Now the one thing firmly lodged in the minds of journalists about the realities of modern naval warfare is that during the Falklands war the Argentines fired an Exocet missile at a British destroyer called the *Sheffield,* and gutted it.

Captain Fogarty was ready. 'The question is asked, what would I do if an Exocet missile were to hit the ship. Before I answer that, let me precede it by telling you that there is not a more survivable ship in the world than the *New Jersey*. As for the Exocet, I would not worry about it at all. It would be like a bee sting to me. I recall Admiral Halsey's statement when he was asked, What would you do if a kamikaze were to hit your ship? He replied, I'd probably pass the word: Sweepers, man your brooms. It's similar. I'm not worried about Exocet missiles.'

It seemed, from the answers that followed, that Captain Fogarty stoutly believed that the *New Jersey* was indestructible by any force devised by man or God. 'God forbid, Captain,' a man from a local television station finally burst out impatiently, 'would one nuke take care of the *New Jersey*?' Captain Fogarty took the shot without blinking: 'I don't know. That is a question that is hypothetical and hard to answer because we haven't really tested it.' Before we could absorb the full implications of this remark he hurried on. 'I will say this, though. If I were given a choice to be aboard one ship during a nuclear attack, I would pick this one.'

It's a modest comfort to think that in the event of outbreak of the Third World War at least 1,527 men aboard the *New Jersey* will feel that they could not do better by way of shelter, but even the Pentagon and Congress might have had reservations about spending $240 million in refitting a floating bomb shelter. So, what, in the last analysis, is the *New Jersey* for?

Captain Fogarty had a rather cryptic way of putting it, when I asked him. 'I think perhaps we have been a little too defensive in our concept of operating ships. This ship is an addition to our fleet that is offensive. ... This ship is built to go in harm's way.' Charles Myers has put it more bluntly, with the two words 'forcible entry.'

As Myers has explained it and as Captain Fogarty was perhaps delicately hinting, one of the tasks the navy may be needed for in the 1980s is intervention in third world countries. Assuming that the locals were not terrified into submission by the mere sight of the *New Jersey*, the battleship would lie offshore and pump rounds of protective fire over the heads of the marines splashing up the beach. Enemy marshaling yards, bridges, troop concentrations, and warehouses further inland would be hostage to these same big guns, and targets beyond their twenty-three-mile range could fall victim to the Tomahawk cruise missiles, tipped with either nuclear or conventional warheads.

Myers went about Congress with a fine model of a battleship of the *Iowa* class, to which the *New Jersey* belongs, in his briefcase. To senators such as Jeremiah Denton of Alabama, who had the misfortune to be shot down while trying to knock out the Thanh Hoa bridge in North Vietnam, Myers indicated that the bridge was within range of the *New Jersey*'s guns and there should have been no need for fifty U.S. planes, Denton's among them, to be shot down.

Some congressmen may have been interested, but the navy was far from enthusiastic. For one thing, a number of weapons designers and engineers opposed to the Myers scheme had a rather different estimate of the power of the *New Jersey*'s sixteen-inch guns. By the time of the Vietnam War the myth had grown up that the mighty projectiles lobbed onto the Korean coastline from the *New Jersey* had been almost mininuclear in their devastating effect. Far from it, the critics said. Both shore-bombardment shell and armor-piercing shell tended to burrow into the ground on impact; the result was a deep crater and not much else.

The next problem was accuracy. Gunnery skills had been in decline since the Second World War, and the low trajectory of shells fired from sea level did not improve matters. A ship constantly shifting in position could not accurately adjust its fire, either. U.S. planes may have taken from 1965 to 1972 to drop the Thanh Hoa bridge – unused by the Vietnamese for the final three years anyway – but there was no record that naval gunnery had performed any better against such targets.

One of the arguments in favor of recommissioning the *New Jersey* for Vietnam had been the cheaply available stockpile of shells left over from Korea and World War II. When these cratermakers turned out not to be quite as useful as originally conceived, the navy started buying anti-personnel cluster shells, costing about $30,000 a round, which did kill a lot of civilians, thus firming up enemy morale, while leaving the soldiers secure in their foxholes. Meanwhile the navy was growing increasingly nervous at the thought of having nearly 2,000 men aboard a major ship within range of the Russian-supplied Komar fast boats with which the North Vietnamese were equipped. These boats had Styx missiles, which, whatever Captain Fogarty may say about the Exocet, could do the *New Jersey* a great deal of damage. After only six months' active duty the *New Jersey* was once again inactivated, on December 17, 1969.

As it now patrols the high seas, alert for 'forcible entry,' the *New Jersey* seems prey to illusions about the past and the future. The forcible entries, that is, the contested landings of the Second World War, did not demand just one battleship firing a stately two rounds a minute from its big guns. Even after a curtain of softening fire from an entire fleet, the Japanese would emerge from their foxholes and wreak fearful destruction on the landing marines.

The future is embodied in the fancy electronic wares which eventually won the support of the navy and the large arms contractors for the recommissioning of the *New Jersey*, an event which finally occurred on December 28, 1982: the Tomahawk missiles, the Vulcan-Phalanx Close-In weapons system, the AN/SLQ-32 electronic warfare system, SPS-49 radar, and so forth. Festooned with the costly wares of General Dynamics, McDonnell Douglas, Martin Marietta, Raytheon and other concerns, the *New Jersey* may now be an emblem of the military-industrial-intellectual complex, but its actual prowess – both aggressive and defensive – may not have been significantly enhanced. It is now becoming widely accepted that complex and hence expensive electronic weaponry does not work particularly well, and the stuff aboard the *New Jersey* is no exception. The Vulcan-Phalanx, for example, is designed to fill the air with lead, 3,000 rounds of 20mm projectiles a minute, and thus explode an incoming missile. It's a chancy business at the best of times, and matters are not improved by the fact that the relatively light ammunition can strike the incoming missile, ignite but not detonate it, and thus cause a flaming explosive warhead to hit the ship.

The vaunted Tomahawk cruise missile has performed dismally in its tests. The nuclear version relies on a TERCOM guidance system to steer it toward the target. This system, which relies on contour mapping programmed into its computer, becomes sadly confused over such featureless terrain as snow or thick foliage. The conventional warhead version needs a TV guidance system with image matching to home it in satisfactorily on the target. This has been causing the manufacturers dreadful problems, as has their inability to get the missile to rise near the end of its trajectory before taking a terminal dive into its target. A recent letter from the General Accounting Office to Secretary of Defense Caspar Weinberger remarked, apropos of the TLACM/C conventionally warheaded Tomahawk, 'We recommend you direct the navy to limit its acquisition of these missiles to the forty-four already funded until an effective terminal maneuver capability can be demonstrated.' As things stand at the moment, the Tomahawk with conventional warhead can only hit the target horizontally, which means that the enemy has only to surround its target with chicken wire or trees – which will cause the warhead to detonate.

It seems slightly unfair to belabor the *New Jersey* with all these criticisms, rather like taunting a stately old bull. As the sailors aboard confessed, its purpose is essentially histrionic: to show the flag and strike terror into the foe. In a press conference on October 19, Ronald Reagan was repeatedly asked about the security of the marines in Beirut. The interrogator likened their situation to the French at Dien Bien Phu in 1954. 'Maybe,' Reagan replied, 'the French at Dien Bien Phu, in that terrible defeat, didn't have a *New Jersey* sitting offshore as we do.' Four days later over 240 U.S. marines were blown up, and the *New Jersey* couldn't do a thing about it. If a symbol has to be found for Reaganism in mid-course, plying the high seas of nostalgia and grim intentions, the recommissioning of the *New Jersey* serves well enough.

Vanity Fair, December, 1983

Top Gun

The July sun beamed hotly upon San Diego, upon West Market Street, and upon assorted members of the *Top Gun* film unit hanging about outside the BBQ Beach Bar. Inside the bar, director Tony Scott was giving advice and encouragement to Tom Cruise and Kelly McGillis. Cruise plays the part of Maverick, a headstrong young pilot going through Top Gun, a rigorous training program for navy pilots. McGillis plays Charlie, a civilian instructor. They were enjoying themselves at the BBQ Beach Bar with Maverick's good buddy and flying partner, 'Goose,' known in real life as Tony Edwards, and Mrs. Goose, *aka* Meg Ryan.

Actually, no one inside the bar was particularly enjoying themselves, since the premises were filled with smoke, wafted by fans, belching from strategically placed hoses, all in the interest of the 'look' planned by Scott, noted for his stylish work in *The Hunger*.

Outside on West Market Street, I was waiting for a talk with producer Jerry Bruckheimer, and brooding on the similarities – from the journalist's point of view – between covering a film on location and a political campaign. The most evident similarity is, in fact, exactly what I was doing outside the BBQ Beach Bar – waiting and watching someone do the same thing over and over again. On the campaign plane or bus, one waits for the interview and watches the stump speech; on the film location, one waits for the interview and watches the retakes. In both situations, the journalist is eyed with mistrust by the objects of his attention: Politicians and film-makers tolerate his presence only because they hope for favorable publicity, even though realism and bitter experience mostly persuade them that the journalist will do all the harm he can and only the good that he must. The journalist joining a campaign or a shoot will find himself excluded by a web of intimacies, shared jokes, and allusions built up by the campaign team or unit. Mostly he can't even tell who's sleeping with whom, and can have only the haziest idea of what is really going on. And the journalist must know that the nicer his behavior and the more

163

deferential his questions, the more the politicians and the filmmakers will despise him.

There is one big difference all the same: You eat a lot better on a film location than on a political campaign. If film crews had even to look at the swill served up to journalists on a campaign plane, they'd be on strike in a minute.

To understand the full background to *Top Gun*, we could, of course, go as far back as Ho Chi Minh's time as a pastry cook in the Ritz Carlton Hotel in London, but all you need know is:

1. The years 1944 and 1945 saw the births of, respectively, Jerry Bruckheimer and Don Simpson, thus launching careers that in the fullness of time intertwined and led the men to coproduce *Flashdance* and *Beverly Hills Cop*.
2. By 1968, U.S. fighter pilots were having an unexpectedly hard time of it in the skies over Vietnam. (Not as hard as the people underneath, but that's another story.) The 'exchange ratio' was one to three, meaning that the U.S. Navy and U.S. Air Force were losing one plane for every three enemy planes downed.
3. The U.S. Navy sent Captain Bud Ault to figure out what was going wrong. Ault's report said that the pilots, over-reliant on the hi-tech equipment with which their planes were laden, didn't know the fundamentals of air-to-air combat, otherwise known as dogfighting.
4. Consequent upon Ault's report, in the spring of 1969 some instructors with the F-4 Phantom training group at Miramar Naval Air Station just north of San Diego set up the U.S. Navy Postgraduate Course in Fighter Weapons Tactics and Doctrine, renamed later the Navy Fighter Weapons School, and familiarly known as Top Gun.
5. When the air war over Vietnam resumed again in 1972, Top Gun teaching got results. The exchange ratio went from an official one to three to an official one to twelve.
6. In May of 1983, *California* magazine published an article about Top Gun by Ehud Yonay. At a point in time not long thereafter, Jerry Bruckheimer flipped through this same magazine to page 95, saw a full-page photograph taken by a Top Gun instructor called Lt. Comdr. C.J. 'Heater' Heatley, and, after due consultation with Don Simpson, determined that this was a project in which they might take a professional interest. As Bruckheimer puts it: 'I opened this page, and I saw this helmet streaking across the sky and it said, "Top Guns." Don was on the phone and I flipped it to him and he said, "We've got to buy this."

It was now mid-1985 and much had happened since Bruckheimer had first spied Heater's photograph in *California*. He and Simpson had gotten the go-ahead from Paramount, and secured a story from Jim Cash and Jack Epps, a screenplay from Warren Skaaren, and full cooperation from the U.S. Navy.

The one thing on my mind as I waited for Bruckheimer was the whole Post-Vietnam Syndrome, New Patriotism, Us versus the World fever then in its psycho-terminal *Rambo* phase. I'd just heard an audience in Key West, Florida, shout 'U-S-A' for five minutes as Rambo mowed down the yellow men. Bruckheimer, slight and pleasant, came up and we sat down in the shadow of one of the laden catering trucks.

'Why did you want to make *Top Gun*?'

'It just intrigued us. Don and I both grew up in Middle America. Our tastes are what other people want to go and see. So we see this as a kind of our *Star Wars* on earth. We just shot a scene in the radar room of the USS *Ranger* and they have all this wonderful technology, and it looks like something George Lucas created.'

Bruckheimer beamed affably and sipped at his can of soda. An American Airlines jet, plunging down over Interstate 5 onto a runway of the San Diego airport, roared horribly as Bruckheimer made a series of remarks that seemed to end with the words 'sex in a car wreck.'

'I thought you said sex in a car wreck.'

'I did. I said the Top Gun pilots all have this wonderful bravado – the way they talk and walk and stand. When I went to college, I sat in a class-room with bright, handsome kids: I was always envious. That's what these pilots remind me of. I think the public should know about these guys. The public should know what it's like to do a night landing on an aircraft carrier. The pilots say it's like sex in a car wreck. That's why we picked the navy – because their pilots have to land on those carriers.'

'But Jerry, don't you think there's a *Rambo* element in all this, making this kind of movie right now?'

Bruckheimer seemed to be expecting the question. At least, he glanced meaningfully at Marsha Robertson, the publicist who was sitting with us, and answered with emphasis.

'That's not what we're trying to do. We see something that interests us. We don't follow trends. *Flashdance* was very risky. It was a fairy tale. Here we're trying to tell a story about a really strong character who has to test himself, and when he does, he loses his courage and then regains it. Also there's a wonderful romance and ...,' Bruckheimer paused for a moment, '... a pursuit of excellence. That's what the story's about: nobility of purpose, how to compete against each other to be the best. It's not jingo-istic.'

'You don't think people will stand up and shout "U-S-A" when the

MIGs get shot down?'

'It could be MIGs; it could be anybody. It could be Darth Vader. You have to have competition in films. We're really not trying to make a jingoistic movie. The audience is going to enter a fighter pilot's world. We call this a process movie because it gives the public an insight into something they would otherwise never see. When I was growing up I wanted to be a photographer, but the only photographers I ever saw were the guys who did weddings and Bar Mitzvahs. We'd like to educate the public.'

Bruckheimer talked some more about excellence and the foolishness of any comparisons with *Rambo,* and then asked me if I was staying around for Animal Night. It was not the first time I'd heard about Animal Night. It had been item one on the agenda when Peggy Siegal, New York publicist for *Top Gun,* had given me my original briefing on what to expect. 'And then there's ANIMAL NIGHT,' Siegal had shouted into the phone. 'These Top Gun pilots, who are the elite of the elite and everyone looks up to them, have this club night and girls from all over Southern California come and it's completely incredible. 'YOU'VE GOT TO GO TO ANIMAL NIGHT.' I told Bruckheimer I'd try to make it to Animal Night and wandered back into the BBQ Beach Bar.

'This film has nothing to do with *Rambo* or Reagan or war fever,' said Tom Cruise with even more vehemence than Bruckheimer. 'I'm not interested in making a propaganda film. This is not about the F-14; it's a film about the men who fly the F-14. These guys get up there and it's terrifying. They're not sitting in their seats hoping for a war. They love to fly. This film's about relationships, about independence, about understanding – about excellence.'

Bruckheimer had said that they had never wanted anyone but Cruise to play Maverick and, sitting at the back of the bar, amid the smoke, Cruise seemed indeed to be *echt* pilot, in a flying jacket designed to set up the same sort of cultic vibrations as Jennifer Beals's torn sweat shirt in *Flashdance.*

'They're a breed of their own,' Cruise went on raptly about the Top Gun pilots. 'It was interesting to me, their passion for flying, because they don't get paid a lot of money. They do everything 150 percent. One of them said to me, "There are only a few jobs worth having – actor, rock 'n' roll star, president of the United States, and a jet fighter pilot. Landing on a carrier at night – that's sex in a car wreck."'

Cruise returned to the question of what *Top Gun* was all about.

'In *Risky Business,* Joel was questioning capitalist society, asking himself, "Do you want to help anyone or do you just want to make money?" So he became an extreme capitalist [turning his parents' home into a brothel]. He became kind of understanding of capitalism, but still having compassion. My character in *Top Gun*, Maverick, he goes through real extremes, and he's not real worried about death. He likes to live on that edge. Now, if you have a bad day, you can go home. These guys, if they have a bad day on a carrier, they're dead. They go out there and risk their lives just for the passion of flying the F-14. Maverick's got a passion. So the message is that fighter pilots do die, not necessarily in war, but in carrier landings. The character goes through that. He's a better person. ...'

That afternoon, we drove up to Miramar to talk to the pilots. The base is wedged in the triangle above the convergence of Interstates 5 and 805. A large sign on the side of the hangar said, 'Fightertown U.S.A.' The sticker on the back of the car next to us in the parking lot, with someone who looked like a Special Forces man getting out of it, announced, 'I'd rather be killing commies in Central America.'

Air war, so far as my next half hour inside the Top Gun hangar was concerned, seemed to be closely related to an electronic video arcade. They showed me the screen on which computerized simulations of their dogfights and training runs over the California and Arizona deserts are displayed for retrospective discussion. Three little green dots appeared on the left of the screen: F-14s. On the right, five more green dots: MIGs. Up over the desert, they had been roaring toward each other at a combined speed of well over a thousand miles an hour. As they turned, the pilots were blacking out under the pressure of gravity. Down here, the little green dots inched forward. Even smaller green dots, shaped like bullets, appeared. 'Phoenix missiles,' my guide explained. The missiles crept forward, found their mark. Down went a MIG. They put me in the cockpit simulator to make my night landing on a carrier. Sex in a car wreck at last! I gripped the stick and looked at the tiny television screen in front of me, tried to line up, pulled sharply on the stick, and plunged – so I was informed – straight into the Pacific.

Reality scampers after myth, which, in the case of *Top Gun*, rolls off the tongues of producers, actors, writers, publicists, and navy pilots with the authority of scripture, to the general effect that before Top Gun, no one taught advanced dogfighting skills. In fact, the mid-fifties, which gave us Elvis Presley, the Chrysler 300A, and many other good things besides, also gave us the first extensive formulation of air-to-air tactics, by John '40-Second' Boyd. Boyd, veteran of many missions over Korea, arrived as an instructor at the Air Force's Fighter Weapons School at Nellis Air Force Base in Nevada, and advanced what had previously been a bag of dogfighting tricks to the level of chess. He taught move, countermove, and counter-countermove, and naturally no one would have listened to his theories except for the fact that Boyd had a standing offer to let anyone start on his tail, and if he didn't have them in his gunsights in forty seconds, he would pay them $40. If not, then the loser would pay him the $40. Boyd never had to pay out, and in due course formalized his tactics into the standard manual on the theory and practice of dogfighting. But Ehud Yonay wrote about Miramar, not Nellis. The air force had *The Right Stuff.* Give the navy a break.

The pilots, *noms de guerre* Jaws, Flex, and Jambo, described their first meeting with Cruise.

'Initially, we were very skeptical,' said Jaws. 'The first time any of us saw him, he showed up with a ponytail and we thought: Oh, no. But he's very responsive and a really professional actor. We went out drinking. He wanted to know about flying, and we wanted to know about parties and all the Hollywood stuff.'

'So who debriefed who?'

'We both lied to each other. The grass always looks greener on the other side. I think at this moment he'd do anything to do what we do, and around here, well, I'd like to get paid what he's getting paid.'

Jaws, Jambo, and Flex, all twenty-nine years old and at the peak of their flying careers, were making about $37,000 a year. I asked them what it took to be Top Gun instructors. 'Extremely large penises,' said Flex. He thought some more. 'You have to be able to fly your plane absolutely perfectly and also think what the other guy is going to do to you and how you can counter. It's like brain time-sharing.'

'Do you think about war?'

'We have to. It's part of our job. People say, "Are you warmongers?" and I say, "No, for the most part, we're not." On the other hand, we're on a football team that's always practicing, but never gets to play. We work hard to be able to do something we don't want to do. But there is that frustration, because you want to test yourself.'

'We have to keep emotionally cool and not let anything cloud us,' said Jaws. 'It's so complicated up there. If you start letting waves of patriotism rule your actions up there, it's really going to cause problems.'

Talk about patriotism led back into the *Rambo* business and the whole context of *Top Gun.* 'The intent of the movie is maybe a little bit to take advantage of the newfound – what's the word – patriotism. And that's great. It's good for the navy. We can't complain about the glamorization. We have an image. I think this is the first place and the only place I'll ever be in the navy where people ask me for my autograph. So we do have the Top Gun image, but it's an awful lot of work, and ninety percent of this work is paperwork, preparing lectures, and so on.' Jambo paused, and collected his thoughts. There was a thunderous vibration as an F-14 landed. The sign outside said, 'The sound of freedom.'

'To be perfectly honest with you,' Jambo concluded, 'this is the best job in the universe and the ultimate in motor sports, as far as I'm concerned.

It's the most expensive motor sport there is. It's very fast and it's very competitive. It's like a chess match and sex in a car wreck at the same time.'

Where does art meet life? Who is starring in whose movie? Jambo, Flex, Jaws, and the other Top Gun instructors plan and fly the combat sequences in the film. The only actual military engagement in which navy pilots have been involved since the Vietnam War has been over the Gulf of Sidra, where in 1981 two Top Gun graduates shot down two Libyan planes. When Ault delivered the report that prompted the establishment of Top Gun, these three pilots were twelve years old. For all the computer simulations, the training flights, and the night carrier landings, the men at Top Gun are increasingly remote from actual combat – war. 'The man who can say, "I've been there" is extremely important,' said Jambo. 'That's something we can't impart.'

I waited for Don Simpson in the Fort Rosencrans National Cemetery on Point Loma. The view was ridiculously sublime: The sparkling Pacific curved into the perfect harbor into which Juan Cabrillo sailed on September 28, 1542 – now filled with much of the United States' Pacific fleet. Around me stretched the memorial markers, 'the final resting place,' so a Veterans Administration brochure told me, 'for the Americans who were willing to fight and perhaps, to die to preserve American beliefs and ideals.' Due to the 'high burial activity,' the brochure added, 'Fort Rosencrans National Cemetery [is] closed to interments, except for those in reserved grave sites.'

Outside in the road loomed the familiar catering trucks. In another bit of the graveyard beyond the road, the unit was tinkering with the Kelly McGillis character's Porsche, mounted on a flatbed truck.

Simpson came across the grass toward me, stamping down angrily on the earth as though he suspected it of trying to steal his shoes. He launched into immediate explication of his troubles. 'There was supposedly a communication from the studio. They wanted two critical lines changed and Tom didn't feel it was right. It turned out to be a misunderstanding.'

Simpson bounced up and down on his heels, a squat exclamation point among the grave markers.

'Why make the film? I like them, I like heroes. *Flashdance* was fabulistic, about overcoming your fears. The girl in *Flashdance* is a hero. Eddie Murphy in *Beverly Hills Cop* is going to avenge the death of his friend, risk his life and career to do it, and be heroic. *Top Gun* is definitely about nobility, incredible nobility, dedication to excellence.' Simpson looked at me sharply. 'It has nothing to do with jingoism, nothing to do with war.'

'But Don, it does have to do with war. They're in planes which kill people.'

'It's about character. If you want to talk about politics, a left-wing movie is about peace and a right-wing movie is about war. This isn't a right-wing or a left-wing movie. Jerry and I happen to be apolitical. I'm not exactly proud of it, but I've never voted in my life. I'm a hard-core libertarian, born and raised in Alaska, third generation. This is a libertarian movie. Maverick is an iconoclast of the first order. I believe in iconoclasts. I'm not the sort of person you'd find in the military. I got out of the military on purpose. I wrecked a motorcycle and, shall we say, I managed to stay out of the military, even though I have a lot of guns around my house. That's the Alaskan in me. However, I like people and this is what this picture's about.'

As Simpson stopped for breath amid this torrent, an assistant came up with news of some fresh crisis demanding his immediate attention. He trudged off, promising to be back in ten minutes. I leaned against the cemetery wall, happy to sun myself in peace for a while. A member of the film unit went through his martial exercises with disciplined ardor in front of a plaque with the Gettysburg Address on it. Three workers from the Veterans Administration appeared and began to arrange some folding chairs, seemingly in preparation for a ceremony. One of them approached me.

'When are you guys finished filming here?' he asked.

'I don't know. Why?'

'We're waiting to bury someone.'

'Who?'

He looked at a scrap of paper. 'Jack Stern. His relatives will be here soon.'

I said I supposed that the film would no doubt be over without much delay and Stern's last rites could commence on time. Simpson came stamping back. The navy, he said, was favorably disposed to his movie. 'They'd said no to cooperation over *Officer and a Gentleman*, and it was an enormous success. According to them, the recruiting level in the navy went up over twenty percent when the movie came out. With *Top Gun*, they'd be in from the start. And the film is about character, not hardware.' Simpson glared at me meaningfully. 'This led to them being favorable. And we are spending lots of money.' Simpson explained that the navy had established a complicated formula with the Paramount accountants to figure out how much to charge for use of fighters, pilots, aircraft carrier, and so on. Later, I had a report of how this had worked out in one particular instance.

Out on the aircraft carrier, Tony Scott and his crew had everything lined up for a sensational shot of an F-14 coming in to land against a backdrop of the setting sun. As the last-minute countdown proceeded, Scott noticed with horror that the carrier's bows were veering off and that, in fact, the ship was changing course by a factor of ninety degrees. He rushed to the captain and explained that it was vital to proceed in the original direction.

After a brief calculation, the captain remarked that it would cost Paramount $25,000 to resume the original course. Scott hastily scribbled a check to the Defense Department and, in the nick of time, all was well.

Outside the cemetery, on Cabrillo Memorial Drive, a small line of cars, headed by a Volvo, had formed. From them stepped mourners who headed purposefully in our direction. It seemed likely that they were the relatives of the late Jack Stern. Simpson peered glumly at them and said, 'It was very important for us to show death in the film. We wanted to show reality. Up at Miramar, people die in Top Gun training. We're not interested in cartoon movies.'

The day wore slowly on. At last, Tony Scott said he was ready to see me. I rushed to his office. He began to explain the precise look he and Bruckheimer were after. He began to discourse on the role of smoke in manipulating light. An aide rushed in and whispered. I heard the words 'crisis' and 'admiral.' He said he would be back in a minute. I never saw him again.

Waiting vainly for Scott, I remembered it was Animal Night. I drove north to Miramar with Marsha Robertson. Marsha put the top down on her Mustang and we whizzed along listening to Patsy Cline. It was the high point of the evening. Surveying the O Club with a practiced eye, Marsha announced that the Top Gun elite were elsewhere. So were the scantily clad dancers I'd read about in Yonay's article. There were lots of very clean-cut younger persons drinking beer in a restrained fashion. We drove back gloomily to the Travel Lodge, where a sound man gave me a precise and expert account of regional politics in Mexico.

Back in Washington, D.C., I had a long talk with a weapons designer. 'One thing the public isn't going to learn from *Top Gun*,' he remarked finally, 'is that the F-14 is sluggish and poor performing. So what you have here is a $50 million fighter defending a $5 billion carrier, which is already being defended by $10-$15 billions' worth of escort ships, and so the carrier's main mission in life is to defend itself. It has only got thirty planes on board which can harm the enemy, and all that these attack planes – A-6s and F-18s – can do is drop bombs, that is, attack villages and cities, stiffen the enemy's will to resist and lengthen any war. It's true enough that the guys at Top Gun are pretty skillful, but even so, on the one hand, they've gone back to the long-range Phoenix radar missile, and on the other, a gross overemphasis on head-on encounters, which is not the way combat happens. So the pilots are being taught to fly a total turkey of a fighter and being given totally inadequate equipment. And they're flying from a floating fortress that's as obsolete as cavalry, and which will be at the bottom of the sea in the first three days of any war.'

So much for sex in a car wreck. But then, as Jerry and Tom and Don all said, *Top Gun* is about character and nobility and heroism, and the fact that these virtues are associated with fighter pilots in Top Gun ten years after the United States left Vietnam, in the era of the new patriotism, is entirely besides the point.

American Film, June, 1986

The Truth About the Blue Lagoon

About five hundred miles north of the equator and nearly twice the distance (as the missile flies) from California to Hawaii is the atoll of Kwajalein. Some 90 islands with a total land mass of five and a half square miles enclose a 900-square-mile lagoon.

This lagoon lies at the heart of U.S. nuclear strategy: all the plans and scenarios for 'massive response' or 'counterforce' strikes against the Soviet Union rely on the testimony of Kwajalein lagoon, which is at the far end of the test range for land-based ICBMs launched from Vandenberg Air Force Base in California.

The islands scattered along the boomerang-shaped curve of Kwajalein lagoon have a similar historical significance. In the dreadful experience of their inhabitants – even though spared the horrors of some other Marshall islanders – is etched a living history of the postwar nuclear age. Kwajalein atoll, part of a trust territory of the United States, is a monument to the cruelty and folly of the trustee.

The Islands

In January 1944, 18 months before the first atomic bomb exploded over Hiroshima, American troops came to Kwajalein to liberate the Marshall Islands from the Japanese. In brief but bloody battles, the islands were quickly taken, with the help of 100 pounds per square foot of shells and bombs. When it was over, not one tree or shrub remained.

After the war, atomic tests were conducted in other parts of the Marshall Islands, notably Eniwetok and Bikini. In 1950, the U.S. Navy summarily set up a base and evicted the inhabitants of Kwajalein, at 700 acres the largest (slightly smaller than Central Park) and most populous of the entire atoll group. The inhabitants were dispatched to Ebeye island, four miles to the north and only 65 acres in size.

In 1959, the Navy abandoned its base, and the U.S. Army took it over as a site for ABM testing. The army swiftly claimed more islands in the atoll, again sending their inhabitants to Ebeye, which today has about 8,000 people. The U.S. taxpayer was not unduly burdened by these seizures. The army paid 10 cents a year for the whole of Roi-Namur, $5 an acre for other islands, and a premium price of $10 an acre for Kwajalein itself.

Ebeye now suffers in conditions scarcely to be found outside the slums of Calcutta. There is no grass and few trees. The roads are unpaved. There are no drains and the gray, muddy sand is covered with raw garbage and sewage, which also sometimes pours from the taps of shacks housing from 15 to 40 people, who are forced to sleep in shifts. There is no drinking water, save what is brought across in buckets from Kwajalein. A planned sewage-treatment works was abandoned in 1973. Because of budget restrictions, there are no coffins to bury the dead.

Three quarters of a million cans of beer per year play their part in anesthetizing the inhabitants – half of whom are under 14 years of age – from their misery. Visitors report seeing 10 year olds too drunk to walk and 11 year olds working as prostitutes for the U.S. personnel on Kwajalein.

Education is not among Ebeye's most distinguished features. The one elementary school (there are no high schools) can accommodate only a third of the eligible students and they are taught in shifts. Epidemics have occurred.

Against the slum that is Ebeye, the island of Kwajalein presents a dramatic contrast: clean, with luxurious beaches, swimming pools and other recreational and health facilities, including a country club called the Kwaj Lodge, another called the Yukway Yuk, and a PX known as Macy's East.

To this paradise, formerly their own, some denizens of Ebeye are permitted to come and work for $1.50 an hour, with each worker supporting an average of 15 family members back on Ebeye. U.S. servicemen can buy chickens at 50 cents a pound on Kwajalein. The Micronesians pay $1.55 for gizzards, and on their return to Ebeye are searched. Unauthorized purchases and even gifts are confiscated.

The relationship between Kwajalein and Ebeye is well evoked by the following account of Dr. William Vitarelli, former trust territory liaison officer for Ebeye. During an epidemic of gastroenteritis, he testifies, 'the Ebeye hospital ran out of intravenous fluids needed to sustain the lives of the Marshallese children, severely dehydrated from the profuse vomiting and diarrhea. I took one Marshallese child who was very ill and put her on a skiff, and motored four miles to Kwajalein where the Americans live. We also needed to borrow some intravenous solution to take back to Ebeye.

'We were stopped at the beach by an American guard who would not let the child enter the island. ... She was Marshallese. The Marshallese nurse pleaded with the guard that the child was dying, and she could not receive appropriate therapy on Ebeye. The guard did not permit the child onto the island. She died on her way back to Ebeye. ... I went to the Kwajalein hospital. There I met with an American M.D., and asked for the intravenous fluid that we needed. He also refused my request. I then went to the medical warehouse in Kwajalein and stole several cases of intravenous fluids and took them back to Ebeye.'

The Lagoon

Since the days of the Titan II, the Vandenberg/Kwajalein test range has been the only such facility for the Air Force's landbased intercontinental ballistic missiles. Every few weeks or months, a missile will arc above the atmosphere on its east-west trajectory, and then plunge down into the lagoon. From the test results are constructed the data that are the currency of nuclear 'deterrence' and 'war-fighting' plans. Thus, when a nuclear strategist refers to the CEP (circular error probable) of a Minuteman III with MK 12A warhead as being $\frac{1}{5}$ of a nautical mile, he is saying that half the warheads from that missile will fall within a radius of 200 yards, with an alleged 70 per cent 'probability' of 'busting' a Soviet missile silo. These entirely hypothetical figures are all derived from the evidence of the test range and the lagoon.

What happens is this: the missile is fired, and its course and the performance of its onboard instruments are monitored. The missiles then drop into Kwajalein lagoon after their 5000-mile flight at varying distances – closely measured and held in deepest secrecy – from the target beacon. This process is regarded as ideal testing for a 'real war' situation.

There are serious differences between the test and the real thing (no ICBM has ever been successfully launched from an operational silo), which produce something colloquially known as the 'bias factor.'

The test results are built up after a series of corrections in trajectory and instrumentation, even though in real war, the first launch will be the only launch. The missiles speed over a track which is probably surveyed with more precision than any other equivalent portion of the globe. The surveying is useful, for a missile is affected (drastically, if silo-busting accuracy is desired) by the varying gravitational pulls of different portions of the earth's surface and by atmospheric variations such as jet streams and surface winds. Even under the carefully controlled and surveyed conditions of the Vandenberg/Kwajalein range, missiles have displayed unpredicted biases over years of testing, veering off-course because of unexpected variations.

Yet all predictions of ICBM performance are based on the Kwajalein figures, and the Russians draw similar deductions from the performance of their missiles tested between Tyuratam and Kamchatka. In a real war situation, the missiles will be traveling over unsurveyed terrain, north instead of west. The biases will be, and must theoretically *always* be, unpredictable.

But supposed accuracy is the motor of all modern debate about nuclear strategy. The MX and indeed Reagan's latest arms 'reduction' proposals are similarly premised on accuracy: the notion that the Russians could launch 2000 warheads which would land within 600 feet of their objective, all at the same moment. The U.S. 'response' or even 'launch-on-warning' preemptive strikes are similarly based on such delusions of accuracy.

In 1974, Secretary of Defense James Schlesinger, the apostle of limited nuclear war-fighting, denounced such suppositions of accuracy, and the nuclear theology constructed on them. On April 30 of this year, he returned to testify before the Senate Foreign Relations Committee, and once again stressed the all-important point. No newspaper saw fit to reprint his testimony.

'Happily, no one has ever fought a nuclear war. Not only have ICBMs never been tested in flying operational trajectories against operational targets, they have not been tested flying north, and this may or may not introduce certain areas of bias in the estimates of accuracy. Nuclear weapons have never flown 6,500 miles through space, with the accompanying acceleration and deceleration, and, therefore, we have no real test data regarding failure rates. Consequently, neither the Soviet Union nor ourselves has appropriate test data to buttress the estimates regularly made about either nation's strategic forces. For leaders on either side that may be enticed into considering the utility of a major nuclear strike, I would hope there would always be somebody there under such hypothetical circumstances to remind them of these realities.

'For these reasons, perhaps the dominant element in measuring nuclear forces against each other is the unknown and immeasurable element of the possibility of major technical failure. It would tend to dominate any outcome. Given the spotty Soviet history in dealing with modern technologies, one would hypothesize that this must be a constant worry of the Soviet leaders – regardless of what others abroad may say about the supposed superiority of their forces.'

In such careful language did this indisputable hawk say that no one could have the slightest idea of what would happen to missiles in a real war situation, and that the Russians (any more than the U.S.) do not realistically have the capacity for first-strike silo-busting assault that has prompted the Reaganite scramble to close the 'window of vulnerability' against their SS-18s.

Islands and Lagoon

Driven from their islands around the lagoon upon which the ludicrous edifice of nuclear strategic war-fighting theory has been reared, the inhabitants of the atoll are crammed onto Ebeye. And by 1982 they have had enough.

The Marshall Islands, which include Kwajalein are currently trying to change their status from a trust territory to a 'compact of free association.' This boils down to the semblance of independence, with the U.S. entirely responsible for military and foreign policy, and essentially running everything. Kwajalein itself, which boasts of some of the most powerful political families in the Marshalls, is run by a body called the Kwajalein Atoll Corporation, a quasi-public organization that acts as the representative of all the inhabitants. It is made up of some 5,000 landholders, mostly on Ebeye.

The Kwajalein Atoll Corporation has a separate agreement with the U.S. for interim use of the atoll by the U.S. military. The agreement comes up for renewal this fall, and, given the mounting intensity of feeling on Ebeye, the corporation has decided to put the status of the atoll to a plebiscite of its members in August. Feelings against weapons-testing are running high, and the legacy of the nuclear age has engendered a powerful movement across the Pacific to clear the whole region of nuclear weapons and weapons-testing.

It is therefore quite possible that the plebiscite could result in demands by the inhabitants of Ebeye for the U.S. to quit testing in the lagoon, and that they be allowed to regain their former islands. The tension has been aggravated by recent comments by Fred Zeder, U.S. envoy at the talks, on the status of the Marshalls. Zeder said the plebiscite was 'at best a cheap shot,' 'unconscionable tactics,' and he openly threatened that any attempt to disrupt operations at the Kwajalein missile range 'would be dealt with as any other cases of civil disturbance are dealt with when our national security is at stake.'

Inhabitants of the Marshalls know what demands U.S. national security is capable of making on them and their environment. The evidence is inscribed on Ebeye, Bikini, Eniwetok, and one other island, which was the site of the first H-bomb test. Looking down from a plane, all you can see of that island's previous existence is just a deeper shade of Pacific blue.

With James Ridgeway, Village Voice, June 1, 1982

TERMS OF THE TRADE

Remember that the world turns slowly and that almost without exception what was true about a country ten years ago is still true today. Life goes on as usual. *Bear in mind Lord Northcliffe's sage advice to journalists: 'Never lose your sense of the superficial.'*

The Need to Tell:
The Psychopathology of Journalism

Early in his memoirs the great Victorian journalist Henri de Blowitz refers to his 'uncontrollable desire to get at the bottom of sensational reports.' He was trying to explain why he became a journalist, instead of remaining a sober businessman in Marseilles. This was the best he could do. In a later chapter he discusses what was in 'universal opinion, the greatest journalistic feat on record, ... the publication, in *The Times*, of the Treaty of Berlin at the very hour it was being signed in Berlin.' Needless to say, de Blowitz was the person responsible for this triumph. But plainly he felt some puzzlement about exactly why it was such a feat.

> To have published an important document before anybody else does not make you a great writer or even a great journalist. ... Any journalist by profession might have done what I did if he had said, 'I *will* do it,' and had thought over the ways of accomplishing his scheme. It was a feat in which neither talent nor science stood for anything. The story I am about to tell must not therefore be ascribed to vanity, but should merely be considered as the fulfilment of a duty to my journalistic profession, to which I am devoted.

Evidently de Blowitz could see that detached readers might well have asked what exactly was the point of a feat in which *The Times* of London managed to print a document on a Saturday only through prodigious efforts and enormous expense, whereas this same document was freely distributed to every journalist in Berlin shortly afterward.

At the heart of de Blowitz's confusion was his difficulty in confronting the fact that his sense of pleasure and triumph was that of the gossip, the person first with the news, suffused with the satisfaction of having slaked that 'uncontrollable desire to get to the bottom of sensational reports.' Such, in essence, was the duty he felt towards his profession.

Now, journalism has always been fair game for abuse and though they may have made a fuss about Spiro Agnew, most members of the profession readily concede the fact. Indeed the more seasoned of these members will invariably commend Evelyn Waugh's novel *Scoop* to novices, explaining that this chronicle of mendacity, idleness, venality, and ignorance is a splendidly accurate distillation of their calling.

But 'gossip' (or even 'mere gossip') is not one of the terms of abuse genially acknowledged. There are, to be sure, gossip writers enjoyed by the readers. Particularly in England a good gossip page is regarded as a *sine qua non* of such papers as the *Daily Mail* or the *Daily Express* or *The Evening Standard.* More avowedly serious newspapers such as the London *Sunday Times* or *The Observer* acknowledge the need, with gossip columns purged of excessive prurience or outrageous snobbery. These responsible efforts are of course extremely dull. In the United States prurient and snobbish gossip is reserved for the huge mass circulation papers like the *National Enquirer* and sanitized gossip enjoys a brisk renaissance in Suzy's and Liz Smith's syndicated columns, or in *People* magazine or in the ever-expanding column in *The New York Times* also called 'People'.

But although gossip sells papers, the activity of gossip-mongering is still corralled off as an activity with which the 'serious' journalist should not concern himself. The reason is surely that gossip-mongering is at the heart of the psychopathology of the trade, at the center of that 'uncontrollable desire' de Blowitz was talking about. All journalists worthy of the name are gossips, but many of them find this simple urge, central to their calling, too distasteful to recognize. They often prefer to turn matters around and talk about 'the public's right to know' rather than the journalist's need to tell. The gossip's ambition is to discover a secret and the gossip's triumph is to reveal that secret, whatever treachery in the broaching of the secret may be involved. Back in the nineteenth century Robert Lowe, de Blowitz's boss as editor of *The Times*, remarked that the duty of newspapers is to obtain the earliest intelligence of the news and instantly communicate this to the readers. Which is a nicer way of saying the same thing: 'I've got a secret, and here it is.'

All the same the exact psychopathology of the journalist is hard to figure out. No foundation that I am aware of has hired ex-journalists to promote a thoroughgoing inquiry. Journalists themselves are notoriously repressed about the wellsprings of their conduct, merely recognizing that the occupational hazards of their chosen career include alcoholism and a meager and probably impoverished old age.

The great de Blowitz was interested in the tricky business of extracting gossip without being explicitly forced into a relationship where publication of the secret would be interpreted as a direct act of treachery and betrayal.

'I am going,' he wrote, 'for the benefit of younger journalists, to give a hint which a good many of them I know would do well to bear in mind. When a man gives a correspondent an important piece of news, the latter should continue to remain with him for some time, but change the conversation and not leave him until it has turned to something quite insignificant. If the correspondent takes his departure abruptly, a flash of caution will burst upon his informant. He will reflect rapidly and will beg the journalist not to repeat what he has said till he sees him again. The information would be lost, and the correspondent would suffer annoyance that might have been avoided if he had heard nothing. A newspaper has no use for confidential communications it cannot transmit to its readers.'

Only the last sentence of de Blowitz's admirable advice rings oddly. It is after all plain that newspapers constantly find use for confidential communications they feel they cannot transmit. They sit on them, glorying in the possession of knowledge but deterred by reasons of libel or taste or genuflections to national security from letting the readers in on the secret.

There are other reasons why the gossip-monger's excited babble is suppressed. The editors or proprietors may simply feel he is wrong. Official censorship may interrupt the confidential communication. This constant tension between primal gossip and eventual publication is the theme of Phillip Knightley's book on war correspondence, *The First Casualty.* On the whole it is an interesting, if slightly dogged account of how newspaper reports of almost every conflict since the Crimean war turn out, upon examination, to be unrelievedly mendacious. There are varying patterns of distortion. Either, as was often the case during the Russian Revolution, the journalist's own powers of observation were so contaminated by class prejudice that he was literally incapable of understanding what was going on around him. Or, as was famously the case in the Spanish-American war, the proprietor simply wanted a war, whether one existed or not. Or, in almost all cases, the military authorities and the civil government back home did not wish to have the population acquainted with perturbing information. Against such alliances of interest, the triumph of truth – as Knightley tells it – has been rare.

The only problem about the book is what exactly Knightley considers 'truth' to be. This is most conspicuously evident in his examination of the bombing of Guernica during the Spanish Civil War. Knightley starts with the proposition, originally advanced by George Steer in the London *Times,* that, in Steer's words, 'The object of the bombardment was seemingly the demoralisation of the civil population and the destruction of the cradle of the Basque race.' Knightley shows how such an interpretation of the bombing became a potent weapon in the hands of propagandists and sympathizers of the Republican cause. Then he quotes supporters of the Nationalists who claim that the bombing of Guernica was a brilliant propaganda coup by the Republicans.

Finally he calls up two authorities, Professor Hugh Thomas and Professor Herbert Southworth, to give their interpretations. He quotes Thomas as saying that 'the town was bombed by the Germans ... probably not as a shock attack on a specially prized city, but as one on a town where the Republican-Basque forces could regroup.' He quotes Southworth as agreeing that the Germans did the bombing and then as asking, 'Why was it done? This is more speculative. There is nothing to show that the Germans wanted to test civilian morale. German documents tend to show that it was a tactical operation.'

Knightley now mops up: 'So Steer's original accusations, the birth of the legend of Guernica ... now stand contradicted. ... Thus it is clear that the correspondents made Guernica. If Steer, and, to a lesser extent, Holme, Monks, and Corman, had not been there to write about it, Guernica would have passed unnoticed, just another incident in a brutal civil war.'

There seem to be several problems with this triumphant conclusion. First, the quotations from Thomas and Southworth seem much more tentative than Knightley's comment would warrant. Second, Knightley seems to demand some ethereal definition of objectivity and restraint from correspondents like Steer. They would presumably have been allowed by Knightley to report that Guernica had been bombed; that the war factory outside the town had not been attacked, that it was market day and the civilian population had been machine-gunned as it fled to the fields, that the town had been laid open with high explosives and saturated by incendiary bombs.

But there they would had to have stopped, prevented by hindsight from saying that it was a shock attack or that the Germans were trying to test civilian morale. In sum, they should have concluded with the sedate observation that 'this is just another incident in a brutal civil war' and, presumably, 'a war in which many atrocities have been committed on both sides.' The heart of the matter is that the psychopathology of journalism has no place for untoward ideological enthusiasm, and untoward ideological enthusiasm is exactly what Knightley feels he is sniffing in the Spanish Civil War.*

The true journalistic gossip tells his secret, heedless of the consequences. But Knightley's book makes it dismally clear how easily this small pure urge to communicate is extinguished, and how easily it is compromised.

Journalists may start with the pure urge to tell all but their working lives are spent in environments profoundly hostile to this primal desire. Knightley has chosen the most conspicuous environment – that of war,

---

*For the record it should be added that Knightley says that my father, writing under the name Frank Pitcairn for the *Daily Worker*, was 'unfit to report the Spanish Civil War,' insofar as he was writing copy supportive of the Republican cause, to the exclusion of adverse material, and also because he wanted other people to share his belief. So Knightley calls him a propagandist, a label my father would cordially accept. They have different views of the trade – but in the end it's Knightley's quest for the truly 'objective' war correspondent that seems to be vain.

where it may simply be absolutely impossible for the truth to be communicated. Readers may come away with the comforting illusion that things are better in peacetime. But it does not take too long to see that then too the gossip stands in permanent danger of blunting his edge. Can he truly say what he knows about business, about law enforcement, about government? As a gossip, he has to have sources who can and will deceive him, use him for their own ends, reproach him for indiscretions, cut him off from fresh material.

Social gossip is all very well, because the subjects like to read their names in the newspapers, even attached to vaguely disobliging remarks. What about powerful people who do not wish to see their names printed in the newspapers? The gossip moves about his village, but each day faces the neighbors too. He modifies and inflects his news accordingly. I.F. Stone chose, in compiling his own splendid newsletter, a slightly different method, less amenable to contamination. He did not move along the usual gossip circuits, but preferred rather only to read source material, congressional reports, budgetary statements. And in that way he remained immune from the compromises to which his colleagues almost invariably fell prey. Many of them had inside stories, embargoed, off the record, on 'deep background,' too heavy with 'advocacy.' They had the wherewithal to satisfy that basic lust to be first out with the secret, but lacked the freedom, or eventually the inclination, or indeed the moral passion, to satisfy it. Such disappointments do not make journalists cynics, as is popularly believed. They make them despair.

Despair is a central part of the psychopathology. For the handmaiden of gossip is treachery: the record is never off; the tape recorder is always on. Usually the macho of the trade precludes self-awareness, as did the general feeling of journalists that they were a rough, low lot without the leisure for introspection. But journalism seems to be becoming a more respected or rather self-respecting profession. Perhaps more self-analysis is on the way. One hint of this can be found in a book edited by a journalist and his wife called *The First Time*, in which a number of prominent people talked about their first sexual experience.

A couple of journalists are in the collection, giving the inside story on their first times – primal gossip again – and I was much struck by the contribution from the columnist Art Buchwald. Toward the end of it he says,

> I had hang-ups and guilt that didn't help. I put women on a pedestal, but fundamentally I was very hostile to them. I was trying to get even with my mother. Trying to get even with your dead mother is one of the most futile drives. There's no payoff. A lot of revenge fucking of that sort goes on. But I can't do it. I can't be cruel. I can have fantasies about being cruel, but I can't do it. I used to have a lot of rape fantasies, and my being Jewish, they had to do with fucking Wasps,

country-club girls, the girls at Palm Beach or the girls at Smith and Vassar. My fantasies were always of making it with the unreachables, and if you've got a good imagination, your sexual fantasies are always better than anyone possibly could really be. ...

Barney Collier says that Douglas Kiker told him that Buchwald likes him to tell stories of sexual conquest over lunch at Sans Souci. 'Art sits enthralled. When Doug pauses in his story, Art is afraid it's over too soon and goes "Yeah? Yeah?" And Doug, who wrote two long novels, prolongs the climax. "Art loves it," Doug said, "Especially when I get to the fucking part. He keeps saying, Yeah; Yeah; Yeah."'

It's a quintessentially journalistic passage; one gossip relating the gossip of a second gossip who himself is admitting to gossipping to a third person who is quite prepared to gossip about himself to yet another gossip who is putting together a book about first sexual experiences.

It's too early for a complete theory of the psychopathology of journalists but I would commend to investigators Heinz Kohut's essay on narcissism and narcissistic rage in Volume 27 of *The Psychoanalytic Study of the Child.* Kohut talks about the desire among those suffering narcissistic rage to 'turn a passive experience into an active one.' Then he reports the case of Mr. P.

Mr. P. ... who was exceedingly shame-prone and narcissistically vulnerable, was a master of a specific form of social sadism. Although he came from a conservative family, he had become very liberal in his political and social outlook. He was always eager, however, to inform himself about the national and religious background of acquaintances and, avowedly in the spirit of rationality and lack of prejudice, embarrassed them at social gatherings by introducing the topic of their minority status into the conversation.

Although he defended himself against the recognition of the significance of his malicious maneuvers by well-thought-out rationalizations, he became in time aware of the fact that he experienced an erotically tinged excitement at these moments. There was, according to his description, a brief moment of silence in the conversation in which the victim struggled for composure after public attention had been directed to his social handicap. ...

Mr. P's increasing realization of the true nature of his sadistic attacks through the public exposure of a social defect, and his gradually deepening awareness of his own fear of exposure and ridicule, led to his recall of violent emotions of shame and rage in childhood. ...

The New York Review of Books, December 11, 1975

How to be a Foreign Correspondent

Resolving to consider the nature and practice of foreign newsgathering, I originally had it in mind to center attention on CL Sulzberger. It seemed to me, following his intrepid, unending voyage through the capitals of Europe, that in the end one would have a lexicon of cliches – an immense word hoard of all the banalities any man could ever set down about foreign affairs. It seemed to me that CL had become the Mariner 10 of journalism, a typewriter rushing through the vastness of space, pulsing back its twice-weekly message. Perhaps one day the typewriter will fall silent – perhaps it already has – but through a time lag across the light years one feels the messages will still come, datelined Vienna, or Paris, or Rome – and one will feel that although the man himself has departed, his column will adorn *The New York Times* op-ed page forever.

The ground he covers is tremendous. The old files bear witness to his prodigious energies. Here he is in Israel speaking to 'a most authoritative Israeli official' ('I found some interest in both Cairo and Tel Aviv when I proposed the Rafa-Port Suez line which was the actual frontier between Egypt and Ottoman Turkey at the start of World War I ...'); now in Italy ('Italy might be heading towards a Chilean solution ... opening to the left ... nor does much time remain ...'); then briefly back to London ('Democracy need not always abide by what seems to be old-fashioned majority rule') before setting off for Athens and Istanbul ('There is a widespread fear that anarchy and a massive disaster are looming').

Late in 1971, we find him briefly in Vienna, pondering the hundredth anniversary of Stanley's discovery of Livingstone: 'During Stanley's leisurely era, a taste for lonely adventure and for uninhibited literary composition were essential. ... In those nostalgic days the roving reporter was a kind of verbal aristocrat. Boldness of spirit, elegance of style and frequently astonishing knowledge were the assets he combined to prepare literary reports for an audience that depended on newspapers for immediate understanding of the spacious world about it.' It is a poignant cry.

CL is the summation, the platonic ideal of what foreign reporting is all about, which is to fire volley after volley of cliché into the densely packed prejudices of his readers. There are no surprises in his work. NATO is always in crisis. There is and always has been an opening to the left in Italy. *He never deviates into paradox.* His work is a constant affirmation of received beliefs.

CL Sulzberger is much too experienced a hand to avoid the obvious whenever he has a chance to grapple with it. We find him in Nairobi, face to face with the course of events on the dark continent and, sure enough, we find that 'Africans are accustomed to dwelling in tribal societies and respect authority. ... The greatest question for the next generation of leaders is: Can nation-states in the future be maintained over the disintegrating thrust of ancient tribalism?' This is expert stuff, fulfilling *the first law of all journalism, which is to confirm existing prejudice, rather than contradict it.*

So, armed with Sulzberger's Maxim, Never Shun the Obvious, let us see how the foreign correspondent should address himself to the world.

There are certain blank areas one should simply keep clear of. Australia and New Zealand for example: vast territories covered with sheep. Nothing of any interest has ever been written about New Zealand, and indeed very little is known about it. In Australia, if it becomes absolutely necessary to go there, one can touch on (a) convict heritage of the inhabitants, (b) tendency of prime ministers to drown themselves, (c) philistine nature of Australians – see (a) above – and (d) erosion of the Great Barrier Reef. Do not get into discussions of the Japanese invasion and Australian race laws, or even the future of the Australian Labor Party.

Moving north a little we find ourselves nearing New Guinea. This is simple stuff: headhunters *face to face* with the twentieth century. Interview a worried district officer. Speak of the *menace of the modern world* for these simple, yet unpredictable tribes which are usually coated with white clay. Are oil companies about to exploit assets which some geologists speculate may *equal those of the Middle East?*

Indonesia, first of all, is a *teeming archipelago.* It is still shaking itself free of the confused yet charismatic leadership of Sukarno. There was a massacre, but *the wounds are healing* (or, the schisms still run deep and *much bitterness remains*). There are *contrasts.* Wealth *coexists uneasily* with desperate poverty. There are Moslems (a growth subject). The students may be becoming discontented with the rule of the generals. There is much U.S. investment, which so far has done little to adjust the *stark contrast* between rich and poor.

Now we are in Malaysia, where one of the few successful examples of counter-insurgency occurred. Under the wise leadership of Sir Robert Thompson, the Chinese Communists were routed. Relative contentment prevails. Hurry on to Singapore and stay at the Raffles Hotel. Interview Harry Lee; ask him why he has jailed all his political opponents. Singapore is a *fast-growing economic center.* It has a powerful class of Chinese businessmen whose sympathies may well lie with Singapore's *powerful neighbor to the north.*

We are now into southeast Asia proper. Some simple rules for a complex subject: Analyses of Laotian, Thai, Cambodian or Burmese politics are strictly for professionals or addicts. Speak of the *timeless rhythms of the countryside* wherever possible. Never underestimate the Buddhists. Always *revisit* places ('For Lon Tho, a simple peasant, life has not changed . . .'). Be careful about Burma. Most people cannot remember whether it was Siam and has become Thailand, or whether it is now part of Malaysia and should be called Sri Lanka.

Past now, to Hong Kong, a *time bomb,* but also a *listening post. Hideous* contrasts between rich and poor. Highest suicide rate in the world. It teems. Avoid Macao, which is for gamblers only and is *seedy* and *rundown.* Go straight to China. A few simple rules: *always* get an interview with Chou En-lai. He is civilized, but a *dedicated revolutionary.* He has an *uncanny command of detail.*

Be careful about China. It may have peaked as a growth subject. But it still is quite safe to be very favorable about it.

Japan. You can be much more racist about the Japanese than most other people, e.g. they can only copy – albeit superbly – Western inventions. Fearful pollution. No street maps. Workers are intensely loyal to their companies. (Ignore labor militancy.) Tanaka is *dynamic* but *beset by problems.* (The proper adjectival adornment for leaders is a vast and complex subject. If he is one of *our* dictators then use words like *dynamic, strong man, able.* He *laughs* a great deal, is always *on the move, in a hurry.* He *brushes impatiently aside* questions about franchise and civil liberties: 'my people are not yet ready for these amenities you in the West feel free to enjoy . . .' If, on the other hand, he is one of *their* dictators, then use words like *unstable, brooding, erratic, bloodthirsty, indolent.* He seldom ventures out of his palace unless under *heavy guard.* He is *rumored to be ailing.* Oddly enough he is often *charismatic.* At the moment it is particularly dangerous to use any adjectives about Arab leaders. Stick to general concepts in this case, like *converted to Western ways* or *deeply religious.*) Back to Japan. What about militarism? What about soy sauce? Stress unease about Western intentions.

Let us quicken the pace a little, for there is much ground to be covered, and the presses are waiting. Up and away we go, past the Philippines, where Marcos is brushing questions about democracy impatiently aside, ever intent on *dragging his country into the twentieth century* and on *putting an end to corruption*; past Tahiti (where syphilis is *rife*) and down into our All-Purpose Latin American country.

It seems to *symbolize* the problems of a *young continent*, still *scarred by its Conquistador heritage*. An *impoverished Indian population* has little say in the fortunes of a republic scarred by *rampant and soaring inflation*, presided over by an *aging dictator*, backed by a junta. Young officers in the air force are plotting an ill-fated but bloody coup which is deplored by thoughtful but troubled intellectuals, uneasily aware of their great neighbor to the north which they view with *mixed emotions*. The country has *long democratic traditions* which have been *reluctantly abandoned. Armed with a newfound sense of responsibility* the *Catholic hierarchy* is pressing for a return to *cherished democratic norms. Shanty towns* sprawl. Roads cleave the *fast receding jungle* which itself is squeezed between the *long spine of the Andes* and the superb beaches, playground of a *newly affluent middle class.* The *romantic appeal* of Castro can nowhere be sensed. There is, on the other hand, *abundant evidence* of American investment, though *seasoned businessmen* view the future with caution. For though the country *craves strong government,* they *note* the growing power of the trade union movement and *seething* discontent among the students. The university is closed.

Away we go again, high over Canada, conscious as always of its *neighbor to the south,* over Iceland covered with *geysers* and surrounded by *fish,* and down towards Europe.

General features are immediately evident. There is a crisis in the *Common Market:* a crisis in *relations with the U.S.;* a crisis in *NATO;* a huge *immigrant laboring population.* But we relax at once for we are in London where the *civilized pace of life* can be observed. *Class distinctions* are as *subtle but as emphatic as ever,* even though *smiling policemen* constantly pause to give us street directions. The city is stuffed with theaters. We are, however, perturbed by the state of British industry, *disrupted by strikes,* prey to the demands of a *powerful trade union movement* which is supported by *indolent workers.* It is clear, as we observe the *tolerant affection* in which the Royal Family is held, that *Britain has lost an Empire but not yet found a role* and that *thoughtful Britons* still believe the U.S. to be Britain's best friend, and that in the EEC Britain may prove a *valuable counterweight* to French designs.

Spain is afflicted by *the Basque problem.* With its abundant population of *small farmers* and mutinous workers, France seems still enslaved by the heritage of *Descartes* and *de Gaulle.* There's a lot of *Gallic logic* around. The buildings are very clean, but the small markets of rural France seem to be fast disappearing in the face of American-style enterprises. On the whole we leave with a sense of optimism, for it seems that *Gaullist illusions of grandeur* are a thing of the past, even though fervent belief in the destiny and *civilizing mission* of *La France* remain.

Belgium has a language problem, too, as Walloons battle it out with Flems. But Brussels is a soulless city of international institutions so we pass on to Germany. At once we are conscious of a dilemma. Has the country finally *exorcised the nightmare of Hitler*, or does the *new interest in Hitler* presage a return to the ugly passions of the 'thirties. All Germans work extremely hard, leading to *constant trading surpluses* and frequent *revaluations of the mark.*

Italy is a nightmare. *Venice is sinking*; workers are constantly on strike; neo-Fascism is gaining new adherents; corruption is rife and the cabinet is in crisis. The Christian Democrats, in power since 1947, have just closed the door on the opening to the left.

Avoid Austria, home of *Bruno Kreisky*, former center of the Austro-Hungarian Empire, birthplace of Hitler, and, indeed, avoid Scandinavia, too; even Finland, uneasily aware of its *giant neighbor to the east.* There is little to detain the zealous newsman here. Even the passions of Eastern Europe have died down. The *old wounds* of '56 in Hungary seem to be healing and *Cardinal Mindzenty* has left. Poland still has its *drunks* and its *Catholics* and its *openness to modern strains in Western art.* No one knows where Dubcek is. Rumania seems still determined to *steer an independent diplomatic path but shows little signs of any relaxation of the iron grip of the Communist party.* Bulgaria is still *Russia's closest ally* and as befits the homeland of *rose attar* is *always first to toe the Kremlin line.* Yugoslavia is *troubled by Croats* but seemingly gone are *the brave years* when Tito defied its *neighbor to the far north.* We can see only the dim outline of Albania, once the West's *only listening post to the immense enigma of China*, now merely *enigmatic.*

The USSR is for the specialist, but here are a few tips. Try (a) new cities in Siberia, (b) sturgeon poaching in the Caspian, (c) the old men of Azerbaijan invigorated by a diet of kasha and goats' milk, (d) pollution of Lake Baikal, (e) disappointing harvest in the virgin lands, (f) no bath plugs in the old-fashioned Victorian hotels, (g) foreign factories on the Volga, (h) nostalgia for years of Stalin, (i) abiding fears of German militarism.

A quick swing through Turkey, still *heaving itself* into the twentieth century, conscious of the *heritage of Ataturk*, its sky aglow with the gilded minarets of Byzantium.

Outside the *complex* Middle East we are mostly left with India and Africa; the *world's largest democracy* and *a continent in many ways still dark.* There is much to choose from: *sacred cows, religious sects, the Vale of Kashmir, legacy of the Raj, the corrupt Congress party, Jains, Westerners in search of truth, dust, starvation* on an unparalleled scale. In Africa, the *onward march of the Sahara, kwashiorkor, tribalism, President Nyerere, South African labor laws, guerrillas in Mozambique, genocide, famine, still proud Masai, once proud Touaregs* and *still small pygmies.*

We've done it. These are the basic rules. There are many subtleties, of course. The proper treatment of *islands* merits a whole chapter in the novice's manual (*tiny, yet strategically vital; hotly disputed by its giant neighbors*; lying *athwart* what is *possibly* the world's most crucial waterway; *seeking to avoid* the traps and pitfalls of 'modern' life; *threatened* by volcanos/tidal waves/nuclear fallout). Then again, the treatment of a deposed leader: is he *unceremoniously bundled into exile, stripped of his duties, long rumored to be ailing* but dominated by an *ambitious wife* whom many believe to hold the true reins of power? What about allegations of torture? Are they *brusquely dismissed* as fabrications, or *widely accepted* as having some basis in fact?

There are problems of timing: When should one leave the war-torn scene of crisis? After the shooting has stopped; one month after that; six months later? Should one go back ('War still rages in "peaceful" ...')?

By and large avoid the *underdeveloped* or *Third* or *newly emerging* world. Reporting of famine and mass starvation holds little consistent appeal for Western readers, and unrestrained speculation about the probable number of dead (one million, two million, ten million) merely bewilders and depresses people. Stick to the main highways of Western diplomacy and American policy. Remember that your cliché hoard is for *consolation* and *affirmation,* never be *premature* in any criticism of your nation's policy. Remember that the world turns slowly and that almost without exception what was true about a country ten years ago is still true today. *Life goes on as usual.* Bear in mind Lord Northcliffe's sage advice to journalists: 'Never lose your sense of the superficial.' Happy landings.

More, May, 1976

The Pundit

There was a term, nicely indicative of the morbid sensitivity of most journalists, which was much in vogue on the press planes and buses of the recent campaign: 'Bigfoot.' One would hear it hissed in just those accents of horror familiar to fans of Biblical epics, where the sleeve of a mendicant is inadvertently turned back to reveal the diseased skin beneath: Leper!

'Bigfoot' was used to describe any senior officer of the press permitted by status and function to leaven fact with advertised opinion. Whether a Joe Kraft, an Anthony Lewis, or a Hugh Sidey, the reaction provoked among the troops was analogous to that to a general visiting the trenches in the first world war. Among the smoke of press releases, the steady roar of campaign oratory, the screams of the wounded scampering toward daily deadlines, he would make a dignified tour of inspection, briefly confer with the candidate and senior officers on the spot, inscribe a few paragraphs of sagacious observation in his notebook, and return to the soft life in Washington.

When finally published, the Bigfoot's observations would be read by the troops he left behind him with spite and derision. How could the Bigfoot know that the sentiments of the candidate he recorded in Pittsburgh as novel and refreshing insights had been daily staples of the stump for the previous six months, that the 'stumbling and exhausted' campaigner he espied in Austin had merely been suffering from a bellyache and was as fresh as a daisy the following day? The Little Feet, campaign regulars, would thus comfort themselves in some temporary bivouac – a Howard Johnson, a Holiday Inn – before trekking forward to the next deadline.

Most journalists would like to be Bigfeet all the same, enjoying the good life on the op-ed page, with a mind relatively uncluttered by facts and a notebook nicely filled with opinions. The Bigfoot, or pundit, need not be in lockstep with 'the facts' but is permitted by function to move fractionally athwart the prejudices of his publishers, his readers, and of course his regular sources. The Bigfoot is permitted by sociological function not

193

merely to report the lies of others but to contribute some lies of his own. Thus is he a senior officer in what we are pleased to call the 'opinion-forming process.'

The publication of Ronald Steel's *Walter Lippmann and the American Century* concerns the Biggest Foot of them all: a man by the measure of whose perceptions and social utility the opinion-forming profession must stand or fall.

Yet scrutiny of Steel's excellent and pitilessly faithful account of Lippmann's life and works reveals that most of the time he was wrong about everything, consistently receptive to blunder, and that on the rare occasions when he was right no one paid the slightest attention.

Consider the record. In 1914 Lippmann should have seen the writing on the wall. In consort with high-minded colleagues on the *New Republic* he was insinuating himself into the good graces of Teddy Roosevelt, but made the mistake of criticizing one of TR's onslaughts on Wilson. Roosevelt forthwith denounced the editorial board of the *New Republic* as being composed of 'three circumcised Jews and three anemic Christians.' This should have accurately conveyed to Lippmann the constraints of access and the parameters of 'constructive criticism' of the powerful. He was not deterred.

In 1916 he was campaigning for Wilson, and by the following year brought untold suffering on the world by coining the phrase 'Atlantic Community,' a pundit standby ever since. Another lifelong cliché he shouldered at this time was his perception of the 'general slouchiness and distraction of the public morale.' By 1917 he was dressing up the unpalatable in terms of the exalted (traditional pundit task) and justifying U.S. intervention in the first world war by saying that it would lead to a 'transvaluation of values as radical as anything in the history of intellect.'

He was also dodging the draft on the grounds that he wanted 'to devote all my time to studying and speculating on the approaches to peace.' With no trace of self-consciousness he asked Secretary of War Newton Baker for an exemption, for 'the things that need to be thought out are so big that there must be no personal element mixed up with this.' He added thoughtfully that 'I'd rather be under a man [i.e., Baker] in whose whole view of life there is just the quality which alone can justify this high experience.' Lippmann always knew how to flatter his sources and patrons, usually identical.

In October of 1917, just as he was extolling the war as one certain 'to make a world that is safe for democracy,' he discounted the inequities of domestic censorship by saying, 'I have no doctrinaire belief in free speech.' Subsequently engaged in the manufacture of propaganda in Europe, he proposed to explain to German and Austrian troops 'the unselfish character of the war, the generosity of our aims. ... [We] should aim to create the impression that here is something new and infinitely hopeful in the affairs of mankind.' Only in 1930 did he bring himself to confess that the intellectual rationales he had provided Wilson to intervene might have been misguided. 'We supplied,' he brooded comfortably, 'the Battalions of Death with too much ammunition.'

In 1922, in that execrable volume called *Public Opinion*, he produced the fully fledged pundit credo: 'The common interests very largely elude public opinion entirely, and can be managed only by a specialized class.' Lippmann thought that 'intelligence bureaus' – staffed with pundits – would meet the need, and aid 'the outsider' adequately. Simultaneously, amid fears in that year that too many Jews were going to Harvard, he was proposing that Massachusetts set up a state university 'to persuade Jewish boys to scatter.' In 1925 he compounded the damage wrought by *Public Opinion* in *The Phantom Public*, where he concluded it was 'a false ideal' to imagine the voters to be even 'inherently competent' to superintend public affairs: 'Only the insider can make the decisions ... because he is so placed that he can understand and act.'

The Sacco and Vanzetti affair brought forth a characteristic display of mealy-mouthed fence-straddling by Lippmann, who by that time was the chief editorial writer for *The World*. He sedately endorsed the infamous Lowell report, which upheld the conduct of the trial, and finally – the day after the executions – praised Lowell for suffering a 'disagreeable duty bravely.' Measured as ever, Lippmann also doffed his hat to Frankfurter and others active in Sacco and Vanzetti's defense for their readiness to 'uphold the rights of the humblest and most despised.'

In 1928, hot for Al Smith, he naturally discovered a 'new Tammany' that would 'bear comparison as to its honesty, its public spirit, and its efficiency with any other political organization which operates successfully anywhere in the country.' That characteristic plunge into overstatement is, by the way, very common among pundits. But Lippmann also admired Herbert Hoover, which provokes Steel to remark another pundit trait: 'Two virtually identical candidates was Lippmann's idea of a perfect election.'

On the verge of the crash, with a new house and sound-proofed study, and sustained by a higher salary, Lippmann was preaching 'a quiet indifference to the immediate and a serene attachment to the processes of inquiry and understanding.' Democracy, he opined, 'cannot last long; it must, and inevitably it will, give way to a more settled social order.' In 1931, at a dinner organized for him by Thomas Lamont of the House of Morgan, he discoursed on 'Journalism and the Liberal Spirit': 'Who but a political hack can believe today,' he told the assembled businessmen, lawyers, and jurists, 'that the fate of the nation hangs upon the victory of either political party? ... Who can believe ... that the cure for the corruption of popular government [is] to multiply the number of elections? Who can believe that an orderly, secure and just economic order can be attained by the simple process of arousing the people against the corporations?' A luxurious cruise to Greece, courtesy of Lamont, followed two days later.

In 1932 he displayed his usual acuity by attacking FDR as too cautious to take political risks, but came round to him rapidly, sustained by the counsel of one of his banker friends, who wrote to him that 'the hungry and the unemployed might be hard to handle this winter if we were in for four more years of the same policies and the same President.' Before receiving this prudent advice, Lippmann had opposed the child-labor amendment, a federal guarantee of civil rights, and the early payment of veterans' bonuses. When a proposal came up to provide pensions for the widows and orphans of veterans, he said that such special-interest groups posed 'a menace not only to the budget but to popular government itself.'

Nor was Lippmann's attention restricted to domestic unrest. In 1933, just after books were burned in the streets of Berlin, he solemnly wrote that repression of the Jews, 'by satisfying the lust of the Nazis who feel they must conquer somebody and the cupidity of those Nazis who want jobs, is a kind of lightning rod which protects Europe.' A week later he was praising Hitler for 'a genuinely statesmanlike address' that expressed 'the authentic voice of a genuinely civilised people.' The word 'statesmanlike' is the traditional mark of the Bigfoot. No higher term of praise exists in his vocabulary, for it is the attribute of the ultimate insider-executive, who is beyond mere politics or the sufferings of the Jews or other groups of humans, and who works purely for the higher good.

In 1936 he was busy praising the British and the French for remaining neutral in the Spanish Civil War, since neither the legally elected Loyalists nor the Fascists were 'able or fit [pundit word] to organize government.' As the Spanish Republic was forced to turn to the Soviet Union for arms he duly noted that it had 'steadily degenerated into a proletarian dictatorship under foreign guidance.' Chided later for this view he confessed that 'My mind works like a spotlight on things, and it wasn't one of the things I was interested in at that time.' So much for the Spanish Republic.

In 1937 he was at it again, coming away from Europe 'with the feeling that ... the Western democracies were amazingly complacent, distracted, easy-going and wishful.' A year later, concerned with 'distracted' Europe's overpopulation problem, he suggested that a million 'surplus' Jews be sent to Africa.

You may have guessed that Lippmann went for Wilkie in 1940. In 1942, when hysteria about Japanese-Americans on the West Coast was reaching fever pitch, Lippmann concluded after a visit that the whole Pacific Coast was in 'imminent danger' of attack 'from within and from without' and that the enemy could inflict 'irreparable damage' through an attack supported by 'organized sabotage.' His column naturally compounded the panic and helped prompt the relocation of Japanese-Americans into concentration camps forthwith. Later, Lippmann, having partly caused the panic, tried to excuse the relocations on the grounds that they were necessary to protect the victims from the mob.

Though he popularized the phrases 'national security' and 'Cold War,' Lippmann was relatively restrained and sensible in the postwar and McCarthy years. Being athwart official consensus he consequently had no effect. The pundit can never inflect government policy, only explain or excuse it. In his more excitable moments, however, he called, in 1946, for a 'new mighty upsurge of new national economy' to confront Russian aggression; urged the nation to be put on a war footing in the wake of the Prague coup of 1948; approved the dispatch of the Seventh Fleet to the Strait of Formosa in 1950; and concluded in 1952 that it would be a 'catastrophe of enormous proportions ... if Southeast Asia were to fall into the communist orbit.' He approved the Anglo-French attack on Egypt in 1956 with a classic piece of on-the-one-hand-ism – 'we may wish that they had not started,' but 'we cannot now wish that they should fail.'

Love affairs with Kennedy and the early LBJ prompted a defense of the first bombing of North Vietnam as a 'test of American will.' In 1965 he considered retaliatory airstrikes to be wise ventures, since they would put the U.S. in 'a better bargaining position for a negotiation.' Knowledgeable of the corridors of power, he told Eric Sevareid and a CBS audience in that year that war hawks are 'not found in the interior and at the top of the White House.' In the same year, too, he endorsed the U.S.-backed coup in the Dominican Republic.

Then, somewhat late, he discovered that LBJ was a hawk, and that the war in Vietnam was a bad idea. Of the president he said sadly, in the distressed tones of the betrayed pundit, 'He misled me.' He went into opposition and, ultimately, exile in New York. Disillusion did not lead to wisdom. In 1968 he reported that there was a 'new Nixon, a maturer and mellower man.'

The emotions of contempt and mirth natural upon review of this catalogue of misjudgment should of course be tempered by pity. Any journalist who has swung himself into the saddle of punditry and bigfooted it across country will know the temptations of the trade.

It's bad luck on Lippmann that Steel had the energy to excavate the punditry of over half a century and lay out the results for all to see. Opinion columns were designed by God to have the same life-span as a croissant.

The problem is that we do not have – as the Russians do – a press that is self-evidently and admittedly controlled by the state. When the Russian leadership wants to write an op-ed about Zbigniew Brzezinski ('lacks statesmanship') the Central Committee gets around a table, chews a few pencils, and then puts the result in *Pravda* under a collective pseudonym. The column is then carefully studied by *Pravda* readers around the world as evidence of what 'the Kremlin' thinks about Zbig.

The poor Russians have never quite fathomed the complexities of opinion production this side of the Atlantic (though one Soviet commentator did once tell me he thought the Freemasons were behind it all). They viewed Lippmann as someone roughly equivalent to a minister of information and made a great fuss over him when he came to town. They were generally correct in their estimate of him as a bipartisan functionary of the U.S. government, and were consequently bewildered when the U.S. embassy would call up once in a while and tell them that the old sage was speaking for no one but himself, and that – to take one example – his tolerant view of their 'sphere of influence' in Eastern Europe was not shared by John Foster Dulles.

Lippmann was a special case in that he did not graduate to punditry after long years on the police beat, but parachuted into the editorial suite at a young age. He was born with Big Feet anyway, and probably emerged from the womb dictating a measured column on the first Japanese constitution, which was being promulgated around the time he entered the world.

Punditry performs a couple of practical functions for newspapers. On the old principle that comment is free and facts are expensive, it takes care of a couple of pages on the cheap and gives the publisher a proper sense of his own importance to boot. It also provides a stepping stone for those on the way from the newsroom to retirement: a stint as Sage in Residence and then the ink-stained old nag can be quietly let out to pasture.

Clearly there has to be some form of government regulation to cope with the alarming pundit surplus. One answer might be to have a Pundit Supreme Court, with the nine pundits – nominated by the president and confirmed by the Senate – handing down opinions and dissents after all due consideration and consulting of precedent. Their conclusions would then be available to the news media for a modest fee. No other opinion columns would be allowed. In the case of consistent misjudgment – here Lippmann springs to mind – recourse to impeachment would be available.

The only other solution would be to have some sort of primary system and election of pundits, so that every four years they could be answerable to the American electorate. Lippmann would not have liked that, and I doubt whether many of his successors would either. If there is one thing that causes a pundit unease, it's the instincts of the herd in war or peace.

Harper's, December, 1980

The Tedium Twins

(Tease)

ROBERT MACNEIL (voice over): *A Galilean preacher claims he is the Redeemer and says the poor are blessed. Should he be crucified?*

(Titles)

MACNEIL: *Good evening. The Roman procurator in Jerusalem is trying to decide whether a man regarded by many as a saint should be put to death. Pontius Pilate is being urged by civil libertarians to intervene in what is seen here in Rome as being basically a local dispute. Tonight, the crucifixion debate. Jim?*

JIM LEHRER: *Robin, the provinces of Judaea and Galilee have always been trouble spots, and this year is no exception. The problem is part religious, part political, and in many ways a mixture of both. The Jews believe in one god. Discontent in the province has been growing, with many local businessmen complaining about the tax burden. Terrorism, particularly in Galilee, has been on the increase. In recent months, a carpenter's son from the town of Nazareth has been attracting a large following with novel doctrines and faith healing. He recently entered Jerusalem amid popular acclaim, but influential Jewish leaders fear his power. Here in Alexandria the situation is seen as dangerous. Robin?*

MACNEIL: *Recently in Jerusalem on a fact-finding mission for the Emperor's Emergency Task Force on Provincial Disorders was Quintilius Maximus. Mr. Maximus, how do you see the situation?*

MAXIMUS: *Robin, I had occasion to hear one of this preacher's sermons a few months ago and talk with his aides. There is no doubt in my mind that he is a threat to peace and should be crucified.*

MACNEIL: *Pontius Pilate should wash his hands of the problem?*

MAXIMUS: *Absolutely.*

MACNEIL: *I see. Thank you. Jim?*

LEHRER: *Now for a view from Mr. Simon, otherwise known as Peter. He is a supporter of Christ and has been standing by in a Jerusalem studio. Robin?*

MACNEIL: *Mr. Simon Peter, why do you support Christ?*

SIMON PETER: *He is the Son of God and presages the Second Coming. If I may, I would like to read some relevant passages from the prophet Isaiah.*

MACNEIL: *Thank you, but I'm afraid we'll have to break in there. We've run out of time. Good night, Jim.*

LEHRER: *Good night, Robin.*

199

MACNEIL: *Sleep well, Jim.*

LEHRER: *I hope you sleep well, too, Robin.*

MACNEIL: *I think I will. Well, good night again, Jim.*

LEHRER: *Good night, Robin.*

MACNEIL: *We'll be back again tomorrow night. I'm Robert MacNeil. Good night.*

Admirers of the 'MacNeil/Lehrer Report' – and there are many of them – often talk about it in terms normally reserved for unpalatable but nutritious breakfast foods: unalluring, perhaps, to the frivolous news consumer, but packed full of fiber. It is commended as the sort of news analysis a serious citizen, duly weighing the pros and cons of world history, would wish to masticate before a thoughtful browse through the *Federalist Papers*, a chat with spouse about civic duties incumbent on them on the morrow, and final blameless repose.

The promotional material for the 'Report' has a tone of reverence of the sort usually employed by people reading guidebooks to each other in a French cathedral: 'The week-nightly newscast's unique mix of information, expert opinion, and debate has foreshadowed an industry trend toward longer and more detailed coverage, while at the same time helping to reveal a growing public appetite for informational television. Nearly 4.5 million viewers watch the "MacNeil/Lehrer Report" each night during the prime viewing season. . . .'

'A program with meat on its bones,' said the Association for Continuing Higher Education, in presenting its 1981 Leadership Award. 'The "MacNeil/ Lehrer Report" goes beyond the commercial networks' rushed recital of news to bring us in-depth coverage of single issues. . . . There is a concern for ideas rather than video images. . . . and they accord us the unusual media compliment of not telling us what to think, but allowing us to draw our own conclusions after we weigh conflicting views.'

And the handout concludes in triumph with some findings from a 1980 Roper poll: 'Three quarters of those polled said they had discovered pros and cons on issues on which they had not had opinions beforehand.'

ROBERT MACNEIL (voice over): *Should one man own another?*

(Titles)

MACNEIL: *Good evening. The problem is as old as man himself. Do property rights extend to the absolute ownership of one man by another? Tonight, the slavery problem. Jim?*

LEHRER: *Robin, advocates of the continuing system of slavery argue that the practice has brought unparalleled benefits to the economy. They fear that new regulations being urged by reformers would undercut America's economic effec-tiveness abroad. Reformers, on the other hand, call for legally binding standards and even for a phased reduction in the slave force to something like 75 percent of its present size. Charlayne Hunter-Gault is in Charleston. Charlayne?*

HUNTER-GAULT: *Robin and Jim, I have here in Charleston Mr. Ginn, head of the*

Cottongrowers Association. Robin?

MACNEIL: *Mr. Ginn, what are the arguments for unregulated slavery?*

GINN: *Robin, our economic data show that attempts at regulation of working hours, slave quarters, and so forth would reduce productivity and indeed would be widely resented by the slaves themselves.*

MACNEIL: *You mean, the slaves would not like new regulations? They would resent them?*

GINN: *Exactly. Any curbing of the slave trade would offer the Tsar dangerous political opportunities in western Africa, and menace the strategic slave-ship routes.*

LEHRER: *Thank you, Mr. Ginn. Robin?*

MACNEIL: *Thank you, Mr. Ginn and Jim. The secretary of the Committee for Regulatory Reform in Slavery is Eric Halfmeasure. Mr. Halfmeasure, give us the other side of the story.*

HALFMEASURE: *Robin, I would like to make one thing perfectly clear. We are wholeheartedly in favor of slavery. We just see abuses that diminish productivity and reduce incentives for free men and women to compete in the marketplace. Lynching, tarring and feathering, rape, lack of holidays, and that sort of thing. One recent study suggests that regulation could raise productivity by 15 percent.*

MACNEIL: *I see. Thank you, Mr. Halfmeasure. Mr. Ginn?*

GINN: *Our studies show the opposite.*

MACNEIL: *Jim?*

LEHRER: *Charlayne?*

HUNTER-GAULT: *A few critics of slavery argue that it should be abolished outright. One of them is Mr. Garrison. Mr. Garrison, why abolish slavery?*

GARRISON: *It is immoral for one man ...*

MACNEIL: *Mr. Garrison, we're running out of time, I'm afraid. Let me very quickly get some other points of view. Mr. Ginn, you think slavery is good?*

GINN: *Yes.*

MACNEIL: *And you, Mr. Halfmeasure, think it should be regulated.*

HALFMEASURE: *Yes.*

MACNEIL: *Well, I've got you to disagree, haven't I?* (Laughter) *That's all we've got time for tonight. Good night, Jim.*

LEHRER: *Good night, Robin.*

MACNEIL: *Did you sleep well last night?*

LEHRER: *I did, thank you.*

MACNEIL: *That's good. So did I. We'll be back again tomorrow night. I'm Robert MacNeil. Good night.*

The 'Macneil/Lehrer Report' started in October 1975, in the aftermath of Watergate. It was a show dedicated to the proposition that there are two sides to every question, a valuable corrective in a period when the American people had finally decided that there were absolutely and definitely *not* two sides to every question. Nixon was a crook who had rightly been driven from office; corporations were often headed by crooks who carried hot money around in suitcases; federal officials were crooks who broke the law on the say-so of the president.

It was a dangerous moment, for a citizenry suddenly imbued with the notion that there is not only a thesis and antithesis, but also a synthesis, is a citizenry capable of all manner of harm to the harmonious motions of the status quo.

Thus came the 'MacNeil/Lehrer Report,' sponsored by public-television funds and by the most powerful corporate forces in America, in the form of Exxon, 'AT&T and the Bell System,' and other upstanding bodies. Back to Sunday school went the excited viewers, to be instructed that reality, as conveyed to them by television, is not an exciting affair of crooked businessmen and lying politicians but a serious continuum in which parties may disagree but in which all involved are struggling manfully and disinterestedly for the public weal.

The narcotizing, humorless properties of the 'MacNeil/Lehrer Report,' familiar to anyone who has felt fatigue creep over him at 7:40 Eastern time, are crucial to the show. Tedium is of the essence, since the all-but-conscious design of the program is to project vacuous dithering ('And now, for another view of Hitler ...') into the mind of the viewer, until he is properly convinced that there is not one answer to 'the problem,' but two or even three, and that since two answers are no better than none, he might as well not bother with the problem at all.

The techniques employed by the show enhance this distancing and anesthetizing. The receipe is unvarying. MacNeil and Lehrer exchange modest gobbets of information with each other about the topic under discussion. Then, with MacNeil crouching – rather like Kermit the Frog in old age – down to the left and peering up, a huge face appears on the screen and discussion is under way. The slightest discommoding exchange, some intemperate observation on the part of the interviewee, causes MacNeil to bat the ball hastily down to Washington, where Lehrer sedately sits with his interviewee. By fits and starts, with Jim batting back to Robin and Robin batting across to Charlayne, the program lurches along. The antagonists are rarely permitted to joust with one another and ideally are sequestered on their large screens. Sometimes, near the end of the show, the camera will reveal that these supposed antagonists are in fact sitting chummily, shoulder to shoulder, around the same table as Lehrer – thus indicating to the viewer that, while opinions may differ, all are united in general decency of purpose. Toward the very end, MacNeil's true role becomes increasingly exposed as he desperately tries to suppress debate and substantive argument, with volley after volley of 'We're nearly out of time,' 'Congressman, in ten seconds could you ...,' and the final, relieved, 'That's all for tonight.'

It's even important that MacNeil and Lehrer say good night to each other so politely every evening. In that final, sedate nocturnal exchange everything is finally resolved, even though nothing has been resolved. We can all go to bed now.

And so to bed we go. The pretense is that viewers, duly presented with both sides of the case, will spend the next segment of the evening weighing the pro against the con and coming up with the answer. It is, in fact, enormously difficult to recall anything that anyone has ever said on a 'MacNeil/Lehrer Report,' because the point has been to demonstrate that since everything can be contradicted, nothing is worth remembering. The show praised above all others for content derives its attention entirely from form: the unvarying illustration that if one man can be found to argue that cannibalism is bad, another can be found to argue that it is not.

Actually, this is an overstatement. 'MacNeil/Lehrer' hates such violent extremes, and, by careful selection of the show's participants, the show tries to make sure that the viewer will not be perturbed by any views overly critical of the political and business establishment.

> ROBERT MACNEIL (voice over): *Should one man eat another?*
> (Titles)
> MACNEIL: *Good evening. Reports from the Donner Pass indicate that survivors fed upon their companions. Tonight, should cannibalism be regulated? Jim?*
> LEHRER: *Robin, the debate pits two diametrically opposed sides against each other: the Human Meat-eaters Association, who favor a free market in human flesh, and their regulatory opponents in Congress and the consumer movement. Robin?*
> MACNEIL: *Mr. Tooth, why eat human flesh?*
> TOOTH: *Robin, it is full of protein and delicious too. Without human meat, our pioneers would be unable to explore the West properly. This would present an inviting opportunity to the French, who menace our pioneer routes from the north.*
> MACNEIL: *Thank you. Jim?*
> LEHRER: *Now for another view of cannibalism. Bertram Brussell-Sprout is leading the fight to control the eating of animal fats and meats. Mr. Sprout, would you include human flesh in this proposed regulation?*
> SPROUT: *Most certainly, Jim. Our studies show that some human flesh available for sale to the public is maggot-ridden, improperly cut, and often incorrectly graded. We think the public should be protected from such abuses.*
> MACNEIL: *Some say it is wrong to eat human flesh at all. Mr. Prodnose, give us this point of view.*
> PRODNOSE: *Robin, eating people is wrong. We say . . .*
> MACNEIL: *I'm afraid we're out of time. Good night, Jim, etc., etc.*

Trudging back through the 'MacNeil/Lehrer' scripts, the hardy reader will soon observe how extraordinarily narrow is the range of opinion canvassed by a show dedicated to dispassionate examination of the issues of the day. The favored blend is usually a couple of congressmen or senators, barking at each other from either side of the fence, corporate chieftains, government executives, ranking lobbyists, and the odd foreign statesman. The mix is ludicrously respectable, almost always heavily establishment in tone. Official spokesmen of trade and interest groups are preferred over people who only have something interesting to say.

This constriction of viewpoint is particularly conspicuous in the case of energy, an issue dear to the 'MacNeil/Lehrer Report.' 'Economics of Nuclear Power,' for example, was screened on November 25, 1980, and purported to examine why a large number of nuclear utilities were teetering on the edge of bankruptcy. Mustered to ponder the issue we had the following rich and varied banquet: the president of the Virginia Electric and Power Company; the vice president (for nuclear operations) of Commonwealth Edison of Chicago; a vice president (responsible for scrutinizing utility investments) at Paine Webber; and the president of the Atomic Industrial Forum. The viewers of 'MacNeil/Lehrer' did not, you may correctly surmise, hear much critical opinion about nuclear power on that particular evening.

On May 1, 1981, the 'Report' examined 'the problems and prospects of getting even more oil out of our ground.' Participants in the discussion about oil glut included some independent oil drillers, and 'experts' from Merrill Lynch, Phillips Petroleum Company, and the Rand Corporation.

At least on May 1 the viewers had more than one person saying the same thing ('regulation is bad'). On March 27 they were invited to consider the plans of the Reagan administration for a rebuilt navy. The inquiring citizen was offered a trip around the battleship *Iowa* in the company of MacNeil, and an extremely meek interview, conducted by both MacNeil and Lehrer, of the Secretary of the Navy, John Lehman. No dissenting views were allowed to intrude, beyond the deferential inquiries of MacNeil and Lehrer, both of whom, it should be said, are very bad interviewers, usually ignorant and always timid. By contrast, Ted Koppel of ABC's 'Nightline' – a far better show, covering the same sort of turf – is a veritable tiger in interrogatory technique.

The spectrum of opinion thus offered is one that ranges from the corporate right to cautious center-liberal. One should not be misled, by the theatrical diversity of views deployed on the program, into thinking that a genuinely wide spectrum of opinion is permitted. Moldering piles of 'MacNeil/Lehrer' transcripts before me on my desk attest to the fact.

The show would be nothing without Robert ('Robin') MacNeil. Canadian, with a layer of high seriousness so thick it sticks to the screen, MacNeil anchors the show to tedium and yanks at the hawser every time the craft shows any sign of floating off into uncharted waters. He seems to have learned – on the evidence of his recent memoir, *The Right Place at the Right Time* – the elements of his deadly craft in London, watching the BBC and writing for Reuters.

MacNeil is a man so self-righteously boring that he apparently had no qualms in setting down the truth about his disgraceful conduct in Dallas on November 22, 1963. MacNeil was there covering Kennedy's visit for NBC. The shots rang out and he sprinted to the nearest telephone he could find. It so happens that he dashed, without knowing its significance, into the Texas Book Depository: 'As I ran up the steps and through the door, a young man in shirt sleeves was coming out. In great agitation I asked him where there was a phone. He pointed inside to an open space where another man was talking on a phone situated next to a pillar and said, "Better ask him." I ran inside. . . .'

Later, MacNeil writes, 'I heard on television that a young man called Oswald, arrested for the shooting, worked at the Texas Book Depository and had left by the front door immediately afterward. Isn't that strange, I told myself. He must have been leaving just about the time I was running in. . . .'

Later still, William Manchester demonstrated that there was a 95 percent certainty that MacNeil had met Oswald. Any reporter, any human, with anything other than treacle in his veins, would naturally make much of the coincidence and divert children, acquaintances, and indeed a wider public, with interesting accounts of Oswald's demeanor at this significant moment. Not MacNeil. With Pecksniffian virtuousness, he insists that the encounter was merely 'possible,' and that 'it is titillating, but it doesn't matter very much.'

Such is the aversion to storytelling, the sodden addiction to the mundane, that produced 'MacNeil/Lehrer.' Like an Exocet missile, MacNeil can spot a cliché, a patch of ennui, and home in on it with dreadful speed. Witness his proclamation of political belief:

> *Instinctively, I find it more satisfying to belong with those people in all countries who put their trust in Man's best quality, his rational intellect and its ability to recognize and solve problems. It is distressing that the recent course of American politics has caused that trust to be ridiculed or dismissed as some sort of soft-headedness, inappropriate to a virile nation confronting the dangerous world. It will be unfortunate if being a 'liberal' remains an embarrassment, if young Americans should begin to believe that conservatives are the only realists.*
>
> *Each has its absurd extreme: liberalism tending to inspire foolish altruism and unwarranted optimism; conservatism leading to unbridled selfishness and paranoia. Taken in moderation, I prefer the liberal impulse: it is the impulse behind the great forces that have advanced mankind, like Christianity. I find it hard to believe that Jesus Christ was a political conservative, whatever views are espoused in his name today.*
>
> *For all my instinctive liberalism, my experience of politics in many countries has not left me wedded to any particular political parties. Rather, I have found myself politically dining* à la carte, *on particular issues.*

This is the mind-set behind 'MacNeil/Lehrer.' 'I have my own instinctive aversion to being snowed,' he writes at another point. 'The more I hear everyone telling me that some public person is wonderful, the more I ask myself, Can he really be all that wonderful? Conversely [for MacNeil there is always a 'conversely' poking its head round the door], I never believe anyone can be quite as consistently terrible as his reputation.'

Hitler? Attila the Hun? Pol Pot? Nixon? John D. Rockefeller? I'm afraid that's all we have time for tonight. We've run out of time. Good night.

Harper's, August, 1982

Vagabonds and Outlaws

To live outside the law you must be honest.
– Bob Dylan

For noble expression of high ideals we may turn to the editorials written by Robert Lowe for the London *Times* in 1851. He had been instructed by his editor to refute the claim of a government minister that if the press hoped to share the influence of statesmen, it 'must also share in the responsibilities of statesmen.'

'The first duty of the press,' Lowe wrote, 'is to obtain the earliest and most correct intelligence of the events of the time, and instantly, by disclosing them, to make them the common property of the nation. The statesman collects his information secretly and by secret means; he keeps back even the current intelligence of the day with ludicrous precautions, until diplomacy is beaten in the race with publicity. The Press lives by disclosures; whatever passes into its keeping becomes a part of the knowledge and the history of our times; it is daily and forever appealing to the enlightened force of public opinion – standing upon the breach between the present and the future, and extending its survey to the horizon of the world. ...

'For us, with whom publicity and truth are the air and light of existence, there can be no greater disgrace than to recoil from the frank and accurate disclosure of facts as they are. We are bound to tell the truth as we find it, without fear of consequences – to lend no convenient shelter to acts of injustice and oppression, but to consign them at once to the judgment of the world.'

From which exalted sentiments we may turn to the views expressed by Sir Melford Stevenson, who was a British high court judge from 1957 to 1979. To a group of journalists discussing ethical procedures he remarked: 'I think you're all much too high-minded. I believe that newsworthiness is a firm realisation of the fact that there's nothing so much the average Englishman enjoys on a Sunday morning – particularly on a Sunday morning – as to read a bit of dirt. And that would be *my* test of news-worthiness. ... There is a curious synthetic halo around these people who are called "investigative" journalists. Now so far as most courts are concerned – and I think most jurors – the concept of a journalist driven by moral fervour to investigate a public scandal is a lot of nonsense. He enjoys the comforting thought that he has a bit of moral fervour which is filling his pocket as well. And there are few more desirable positions in life than that.'

It is worth noting that it was a judge who expressed these frank senti-ments *à propos* the allure of 'a bit of dirt.' Few journalists would be rash enough to make so succinct a confession, and it is generally the rule that the more squalid the journalistic enterprise embarked on, the more fervent are the professions of high purpose. I would urge anyone who doubts this to study Al Goldstein's editorials in *Screw* magazine.

The occasion on which Sir Melford expressed the pithy views recorded above was one of two conferences organized in 1979 by Granada Tele-vision of Great Britain to brood on the theme of 'The Media and The Law.' These conferences were edited into six programs, broadcast under the title 'The Bounds of Freedom.'

The technique adopted was one originally devised by Fred Friendly for the Ford Foundation, in which journalists and public figures debate hypo-thetical situations where matters of ethics, professional standards, and so forth are discussed under the guidance of a moderator.

As is usual in such proceedings, the air vibrated with protestations of high purpose, even as the participants descended toward the art of the practical. The moderator proposed the hypothesis that 'Lord Runny-meade,' a former British foreign secretary and now a prominent banker, may well have been insane during his term as a cabinet minister. All journalists present agreed that they would have attempted to extract confir-mation from Lord Runnymeade's psychiatrist. The following dialogue then ensued:

> Moderator: *Suppose the psychiatrist says, 'Well, this might do damage to my pro-fession in this community if my patients read that I have breached the relationship. I think I need a few thousand pounds to relocate myself after I tell you this.'*
> Paul Callan (feature writer, *Daily Mirror*): *Give it to him.*
> Moderator: *You'd give it to him?*
> Callan: *Newspapers pay for information.*
> Moderator: *You'd buy the medical record?*
> Callan: *I'd buy the information that the psychiatrist is giving me.*
> Moderator: *Mr. Mangold, would you pay for it?*
> Tom Mangold (reporter for the BBC): *Yes.*
> Derek Jameson (editor, *Daily Express*): *Certainly.*
> Harold Evans (editor, *Sunday Times*): *Yes.*

Moderator (to all present, who include numerous other editors and correspondents): *Everybody would pay for it.* (Silence of general agreement.)

Callan: *Well, the price would certainly go up if we were all bidding.* (Prolonged laughter.)

Later in the series the journalists were confronted with another hypothesis. A television producer receives an invitation. It is from a man who has escaped from police custody. He is thought to be a terrorist leader, responsible for bombings and assassinations. He asks the producer to interview him in a neighboring country and not to tell the police.

Moderator: *Mr. Jameson, would you give them [the police] the note [of invitation]?*

Jameson (editor of the *Daily Express*): *No.*

Moderator: *No – why not?*

Jameson: *He can read about it in my newspaper.*

Moderator: *But the copy of the note that appears in your newspaper won't have fingerprints on it.*

Jameson: *I'll tell you why not. Because never ever must journalists play the role of coppers' narks. It's totally wrong, it is improper.*

All these sentiments passed into the ether without much comment. No one bothered to point out that from time to time lunatics have been at the national helm, without undue curiosity being expressed by the press. It was known to a fairly large number of people that Sir Anthony Eden was 'under great strain,' as they say, when, as prime minister, he embarked on the Suez invasion in 1956. A parallel episode in the United States, also not discussed, was the mental collapse of Secretary of Defense James Forrestal, which led to his eventual suicide. By reason of attacks on Forrestal in his column, Drew Pearson was much blamed at the time for the circumstances of the secretary's demise.

But hypotheses are not always immune to reality. By 1980, when the colloquies quoted above were published, 'real life' was bustling into the discussion. The BBC had interviewed people in Ireland who claimed responsibility for the murder in Westminster of Airey Neave, a Conservative M.P. For this it was very severely censured. And at the end of last year there was much discussion anent the dilemma of Italian editors requested by the kidnappers of Judge d'Urso to print their manifestos, on pain of the judge's death.

Finally, at the end of last year, Conor Cruise O'Brien, then editor of the *Observer* (in the latest twist in a career whose switches between public and private employment would make even Leslie Gelb dizzy), leaped into the debate. First he addressed himself to the matter of the terrorist's request for an interview on condition that the police not be informed. (I should note that Mr. Jameson was not the only person to advertise his willingness to go forward under such conditions. Other editors present said the same sort of thing and one that he would fire any employee who *did* take the note to the police without first informing him.)

> O'Brien: *Let me plainly say that I reject the version of journalistic ethics expounded by [these] people. . . . I think it is dehumanising and decivilising to tell journalists that they are never ever to help the police to catch murderers who are at large. In a democratic society, under the rule of law, journalists have the same civic duties in that matter as everybody else, and are not dispensed from these by some sort of caste ethic. Whether they do their duty is up to them as individuals — as it is in the case of all other citizens — but no employer has the right to fire them, or threaten to fire them, for helping the police catch murderers. If their information was acquired in the course of their professional duties, they should tell their editor first — unless the delay so caused might help the murderer escape. In that case, they should tell the police first, and their editor afterwards.*

A couple of weeks later O'Brien addressed himself to the question of suborning Lord Runnymeade's psychiatrist: 'I'm all in favour of amusing readers, and occasionally attempt that difficult feat, but I wouldn't quite regard the attainment of that end as, in itself, justifying bribery and the instigation of professional misconduct and personal treachery.' He concluded with the general reflection that 'where the ethics of a given profession appear to be diverging sharply from general ethical standards, it might be well to try to bring these professional ethics back into the main stream.' He left no doubt that it was the divergent ethics of the press that he had in mind.

Of course, Dr. O'Brien has strong feelings on the matter of terrorism and 'murderers.' As editor of the *Observer*, he fired his Belfast correspondent for insufficient 'objectivity.' As minister for posts and telegraphs in a recent Irish government, he espoused censorship laws against Irish Republicans fierce enough to make even Chief Justice Warren Burger, let alone the shade of William Douglas, leap up and lament.

But he touched a raw nerve. With none of the constitutional guarantees and few of the legal accouterments enjoyed by their American confrères, British journalists sustain themselves from time to time with the high rhetoric of men such as Lowe. They are simultaneously aware, nevertheless, that aside from this rhetoric there is no safety net and that in some infraction of taste or legality an 'aroused' public, however much it may enjoy its 'bit of dirt,' will applaud their discomfiture in the courts.

Thus in British discussions of journalistic ethics there is, in the end, something of a 'Take me, dead or alive' attitude, the swaggering credo of outlaws, of members of a profession whose social standing – as Auberon Waugh recently remarked – is 'rated somewhat lower than badger gassers.'

The London *Times* columnist Bernard Levin hoisted this Jolly Roger at the end of last year in an article entitled 'The Precise Freedom to be Irresponsible.' Levin was challenging the view of Lord Denning that 'a free press must be a responsible press' and that if it should 'act irresponsibly, then it forfeits its claim to protect its sources of information.'

'It cannot be emphasized too strongly,' Levin wrote, 'nor indeed put too extravagantly, that the press *has no duty to be responsible at all,* [his italics] and it will be an ill day for freedom if it should ever acquire one. The press is *not* the Fourth Estate; it is *not* part of the constitutional structure of the country; it is *not*, and must never be, governed by any externally imposed rules other than the law of the land. The law may demand that a newspaper's sources shall be revealed. The law is perfectly justified (though of course it may be wrong in any particular instance) in deciding as much; if an editor or other journalist then refuses to reveal his sources, he is a lawbreaker, and may quite justly be punished. The press occasionally claims a legal right to keep such confidences, likening itself in doing so to doctors or even priests; my own view is, and always has been, that the claim is not only untenable, but abominable, precisely because it would ... make the press part of the Establishment, which it must not be ... we are, and must remain, vagabonds and outlaws, for only by so remaining shall we be able to keep the faith by which we live, which is the pursuit of knowledge that others would like unpursued, and the making of comment that others would prefer unmade.'

Less eloquently, Derek Jameson, the rugged editor of the *Daily Express* (since removed from that position), remarked to Dr. O'Brien in the course of a television encounter, 'I'm not defending what I'm doing. Sometimes it's right. Sometimes it's wrong. I don't hold with high falutin' talk. I don't claim to be pure ... I'm a newspaperman. I tell stories.'

So much for British empiricism. On this side of the Atlantic it would be an untoward event if the protestations of a Levin or a Jameson were to be voiced at, let us say, the American Society of Newspaper Editors. 'Vagabonds' and 'outlaws' do not shuttle comfortably between the State Department and *The New York Times*. 'Statesmen,' *pace* Lowe, do.

Harper's, April, 1981

Blood and Ink

It was really the enormous mistake of a Nicaraguan national guardsman in killing, on camera, an American reporter from ABC news that sent El Salvador surging out of its Totally Invisible Nation slot and into the category of Strategic Domino. But to appreciate the transformation completely, you have to understand the journalist's way of measuring death.

Any sensible dictator knows that in terms of unfavorable international publicity it is perfectly safe to kill the social entity known to news editors as 'tribesmen' in fairly large numbers – let us say up to 30,000 to be on the safe side. 'Peasants' – a noun with affecting pastoral undertones – are a little trickier. Perhaps one 'peasant' for every hundred 'tribesmen.' Ratios vary from area to area. The murder of priests, missionaries, and nuns is an affair of the nicest judgment, as we shall see in the case of El Salvador. It is really a matter of location, race, and religious persuasion. As a rule of thumb, men of the cloth should be spared, although the elimination of Dominicans, particularly those in rural areas, may be practiced in moderation. Count 200 peasants for one priest.

What our Third World dictator should avoid is the murder of journalists, or at least of those who are citizens of the United States. The penalties – denunciation in Congress and in the news media – are obvious. Count 10,000 peasants for one American reporter; 30,000, if the reporter is from one of the networks; 50,000, if the murder takes place on camera. The moment Bill Stewart of ABC was murdered on network news the fate of Anastasio Somoza was sealed. The United States 'lost,' or at least decided that it could not 'save,' Nicaragua.

And this is where El Salvador enters the picture. With Nicaragua gone, it became a Domino and thus the object of grave concern to the State Department, Defense Department, and cognate agencies, and of interest (intermittently) to the American press and (even more intermittently) to the American news consumer.

As El Salvador crept ever closer to Domino status, life in that unhappy

land was continuing along fairly predictable lines. The oppressors continued their God-given task of oppressing and the oppressed struggled with
increasing vigor to turn the tables. There was a coup in October 1979.
Military men, some of them of moderately reformist stripe, took power,
and civilians from across the political spectrum clambered aboard.

By January 1980 these civilians had clambered off again, denouncing
the junta as both powerless and disinclined to rout El Salvador's traditional
oppressors. Some Christian Democrats took their place, but after another
short interval only the most conservative among them cared to remain. It
was now a case of the junta, firmly under the control of the right, facing the
rest of the country, the bulk of whose members may be conveniently
labeled, after the fashion of the American press, 'extremists of the left,' or,
worse still, terrorists.

From the press El Salvador received your basic coverage (SMALL
MASSACRE IN EL SALVADOR, NOT MANY DEAD). A representative example
of such coverage is the following Reuters dispatch of June 10, 1980. Since
descriptions of El Salvador almost invariably include the information that it
is the size of Massachusetts, I have taken the liberty of substituting place
names from the Commonwealth for Salvadorian equivalents, to 'bring the
news home,' as one might say:

'A wave of bombings shook the capital and at least thirty-four people
were murdered in another weekend of political bloodshed in Massachusetts. Five kidnap victims, including a pregnant woman, were found dead in
Lynn, seven bodies were discovered in Quincy – one with the initials *EM*
carved in his chest; a student was machine-gunned in New Bedford and
twenty-one people were killed in Boston as right- and left-wingers clashed
in the streets. EM is a right-wing group which has declared open war on
left-wing sympathizers who are trying to overthrow the military junta
installed last October.'

Here's another sample of news from El Salvador/Massachusetts, from a
UPI report of October 30, 1980: 'The Rector of the University of Massachusetts died yesterday of a bullet wound received in a street attack, one of
forty-two political slayings reported in the past twenty-four hours in
troubled Massachusetts, authorities said. Most of the victims were found
tortured and shot to death, including a woman with a machete stuck in her
chest, authorities said, apparently the latest in the 8,000 political slayings
(in this El Salvador-sized state) recorded this year by the Catholic Church.
... The junta said it would be willing to open the university, but only if it
gave up its legal protection against police and army raids.'

Such coverage was ratified in traditional weary tones: 'In El Salvador,
trouble never rains but it pours ...' (James Nelson Goodsell, *Christian
Science Monitor*, July 9, 1980) or 'Death and destruction still loom high in
the saddle in El Salvador ...' (editorial in *Miami Herald*, July 12). But it is

important to notice what the editorialists made of all this. For instance, Goodsell continued, 'The country's buffeted junta, weathering almost daily disorders and vicious verbal attacks from both the left and the right, faces its most serious tempest to date.' The phrase to watch here is 'from both the left and the right.' The *Miami Herald* editorialist said the same sort of thing: 'The goals of both the extreme left and the extreme right are inimical not only to the best interests of most Salvadorians, but also to those of freedom lovers everywhere.'

Connoisseurs of 'left/right extremists' coverage will at once recognize familiar terrain. So let me give you a particularly resplendent signpost in the shape of a *Washington Post* editorial quoted in the *Christian Science Monitor* of October 2.

> American policy-makers have been laboring to rally Salvadorians of the center and center-left to the side of the government junta. That is the way to strengthen the civilians' weight in it and to enhance the prospects of effective reform. The going has been rough, but the United States has found it politically more feasible and ideologically less objectionable to support reform, even reform soiled by some repression, than to condone revolution, especially revolution stained by nihilism. . . . It is a difficult policy to conduct and explain, and it may fail: it takes a real optimist to believe that the center in El Salvador will hold. What those who spurn the junta seem to us to ignore, however, is that they are helping spin the country toward a civil war that will make the current carnage look like kid's stuff.

This is vintage thumb-sucking. Note particularly the delicate tilt from 'soiled by some repression' to 'stained by nihilism.' The only trouble with this measured encouragement of juntocentric moderation is that such moderation had ceased to exist several months earlier.

As William Leogrande and Carla Anne Robbins sourly remarked in the summer issue of *Foreign Affairs*, 'What Washington appears to be incapable of grasping is that in El Salvador, as in Nicaragua before it, the centrist forces which the United States perceives as its allies have joined with the very forces which the United States regards as its natural enemy – the radical Left. The centrists are no longer in the center. ... The recently unified Left and Center Left opposition includes everyone but the government and the far Right.'

It is indeed wondrous to observe throughout 1980 how much the press and the U.S. State Department managed to sustain the vision of a centrist junta threatened by dire forces of the (extreme) left and the (extreme) right. Even a casual reader might have gathered that it was the right that seemed to be running amok. The murder of Archbishop Oscar Romero (equals 2,000 peasants) by a right-wing assassin on March 24 was an embarrassment to center boosters. The murder in May of large numbers of peasants (up to 600 in some accounts) by Salvadorian national guardsmen, as the peasants attempted to flee across the Sumpul River into Honduras, added slightly to this embarrassment.

This episode, happily for the junta, was classed by reporters and news editors as an 'alleged' massacre, and hence not worth bothering with. Massacres can stay decorously 'alleged' for years.

Scrutinizing this 1980 coverage one can see clearly enough that the Carter administration decided that the junta it originally endorsed in October of 1979 still represented the middle way in El Salvador. It continued to announce that the middle way was a negotiable thoroughfare long after the junta had become virtually indistinguishable from the business-as-usual military governments of the past. The only entity to take this assertion seriously was the bulk of the American press.

The people most zealously deploying the carefully contrived 'moderate and reformist image' of the junta were adherents and advisers of Ronald Reagan, who announced in the transition period that it seemed to them that the Carter administration had been sponsoring social reform in El Salvador instead of sticking to the basics, as advocated by the Domino School. (For 'Domino School,' see *Wall Street Journal* editorials *passim*: yesterday Cuba, today Nicaragua, tomorrow El Salvador, and before you can say Fidel! the canaille will be stringing up *Wall Street Journal* editor Bob Bartley from a lamppost on Cortlandt Street.*) The basics here are familiar enough: first find your dictator ('firm leadership') and then stick to him ('constancy to our allies'), however many people he kills ('The U.S. cannot afford moral lectures to our friends. Anyway, what about the Gulag?' etc.).

Of course, just about the time that Reagan's men were complaining about Carter-sponsored social reform in El Salvador, uniformed national guardsmen were supervising the torture and murder of liberal and leftist leaders and themselves raping and murdering American nuns. Not too much concern was expressed about the dead politicans ('extremists of the left'). But the nuns were a different matter, even though it is true (good works in Calcutta aside) that the news function of nuns in Third World countries was pithily summed up in the terse cry of a British reporter at Brussels airport when nuns began returning from the Congo in the early 1960s: 'Anyone here been raped and speak English?' The Carter administration suspended aid to El Salvador. Count 1,000 dead peasants for one raped, dead American nun.

It doesn't look as though nun-slaying will be a prime concern of Reagan's men as they ponder policy and possibly direct military intervention in Central America. They, like the press, will denounce 'nun-

---

*Not any more. Perhaps alert to the peril *The Wall Street Journal* has now retreated to a fortress overlooking the Hudson.

slayers of the left and right alike' as they continue to deplore the 'extremist trend to violence.' Once you become a Domino, there's nowhere to go but down. As General Martínez understood in 1932, count 30,000 dead 'extremists' for one stable government. His successors can probably depend on the American press to approve the equation.

Harper's, February, 1981

The Boss

There's an amusing story in *The Annenbergs: The Salvaging of a Tainted Dynasty* (Simon and Schuster) about Lewis Rosenstiel, the Schenley liquor king. Rosenstiel enters the narrative because Walter Annenberg ran off with his wife, Lee. As the author, John Cooney, relates,

> The liquor lord's bizarre behavior resulted in many often-told tales. On one occasion, Rosenstiel was determined to test the loyalty of his subordinates, and he sent word to them that he was dying, requesting that they convene at the townhouse for his final moments. When the men had gathered in a downstairs room [equipped with hidden microphones], Rosenstiel sat in bed wearing pajamas, a robe and dark sunglasses, as was his habit, and monitored their comments. Finally, he had a bodyguard tell the executives that he had died. As his anger mounted, he listened while they expressed their elation in various unflattering ways. When he had heard enough, Rosenstiel stormed downstairs and had his bodyguards throw the men out, telling them they were finished working for him.

Rosenstiel's Jacobean yet finally impetuous way of detecting his critics and then banishing them is a paradigm for the Annenberg story and for Cooney's deferential treatment of it. As befits a saga which stretches from the arrival of a Jewish immigrant – Moses Annenberg – from the Prusso-Russian border in 1885, through his rise to eventual control of most race-track information in the United States, his imprisonment for tax evasion in 1939, and thence ultimately to the appointment of his son Walter as U.S. Ambassador to London by Nixon in 1969, much of the book is about public relations, and of the various ways criticism can be quelled, whether by the primitive device of a straightforward cash bribe or – in the later stages of such American family sagas – the handsome charitable donation.

Behind every fortune lies a crime, as Balzac used to say, and even the polite Mr. Cooney, whose book appears one hundred years after grandpa (Tobias) Annenberg arrived in Chicago, cannot avoid the fact that the

Annenberg fortune was built on some very rugged foundations. No more rugged, perhaps, than the underpinnings of other glorious American houses, such as the Rockefellers, the Vanderbilts, the Duponts and so forth. But with Moe Annenberg one is struck – as in any serious discussion of Joseph Kennedy – that, though charming, here was a very hard and dangerous man indeed.

Joseph Kennedy stayed out of prison, of course, and made it to the Court of St. James at just about the same time that Moe was heading for Leavenworth to begin a three-year sentence for defrauding the Internal Revenue Service of $9.5 million. But then Joe was smarter than Moe, who made the mistake of angering Roosevelt. It took son Walter nearly three decades of what passed as 'wholesome' (a favorite word of his) behavior to make his way to the same Court and thus finally requite his father's disgrace.

The genius presiding over the birth of the Annenberg fortune was William Randolph Hearst, who decided to launch the *Evening American* in Chicago at the turn of the century. Newspaper proprietors have by tradition been a mad and brutish lot, and one of the indices of America's decline has been their growing respectability. The ur-proprietor regarded his paper as a way to accumulate and dispose of political power and, if possible, to make money. Rhetoric about 'a free press' and the right of the public to know was distributed generously, but no one took it very seriously. It is a sign of the sententious respectability of the U.S. press today that Rupert Murdoch, the Australian newspaper proprietor who took over the *New York Post* in 1975, is generally looked upon as a person somehow alien to the American newspaper tradition. *The Annenbergs* is a useful corrective to such unhistorical xenophobia.

Journalism students of our own era, heads stuffed with blather about the duties of a free press, would do well to study some of the implements with which Hearst felt it necessary to accouter himself, in order to do battle in a town which had eight newspapers already. They included platoons of roughs, whose duty it was to secure advantageous street corners for the sale of their own product, to terrorize newsagents too freely displaying the wares of the opposition and to be generally on the alert to combat ploys of the enemy.

Moe's elder brother Max soon became an officer in these battalions. Their toil in support of the First Amendment was unceasing. When Marshall Field canceled an advertisement in the *American*, sixty delivery boys under Max's command surrounded the store, bellowing 'Marshall Field's closed! Marshall Field's closed!' Amid the terror of potential customers of the store, surrender was soon obtained, and the ad shortly reappeared.

Moe had the less violent task of soliciting subscriptions to the paper, and in 1904 he became circulation chief of Hearst's Chicago *Examiner*, with Max fulfilling the same function at the *American*. Many of the city's more notable gangsters – Mossy Enright, Vincent Altman, Gus and Dutch Gentelman, Nick O'Donnell – rode shotgun on Heart's delivery carts, and those of his rival, Colonel McCormick, for whose *Tribune* Max was later enticed to work. Moe, taking a cool look at the escalation in violence – twenty-seven newsdealers killed by 1913, when a truce was called – took himself off to Milwaukee and a quieter life. Here, he expanded his distribution business and speculated successfully in real estate and innumerable other ventures.

Like many great men, he thought of simple ideas and then organized his resources successfully to exploit them. 'Little Woman', he asked his wife Sadie in 1913, 'what do women run out of most often?' 'Teaspoons,' his wife replied. 'Little Woman has just made us a fortune,' Moe shouted to his children. His idea was to sell silver spoons as a promotional gimmick to build newspaper circulation. The spoons, adorned with the official insignia of each state, could be obtained by subscribers' submitting a coupon from a newspaper, along with fifteen cents. A different spoon was offered each week. Newspapers across the country were soon licensing Moe's idea. The *New York Sunday World* sold 150,000 spoons in one week. A billion spoons in all were disposed of and by the age of 36, Moe, who got a cut on the sale of each spoon, became a millionaire.

In 1917, Arthur Brisbane, the prolific Hearst columnist and entrepreneur whose motto was 'Always remember that it is impossible to exaggerate the stupidity of the public,' made Moe publisher of the *Wisconsin News*, where he continued to prosper. Shortly thereafter Hearst hired him to come to New York to be publisher of the *Mirror* and oversee the circulation side of his empire.

Since by this time his brother Max was circulation manager of the *Daily News*, Moe thought it prudent to enlist a strong right arm to assist in the robust business of seizing and holding important street locations. He chose Lucky Luciano, who said later, 'I used to think of the *Mirror* as my kind of paper. I always thought of Annenberg as my kind of guy.' Opponents and victims, tires slashed or legs and heads broken, probably had a less generous assessment.

In 1922, Moe laid a major and still enduring plank in the family fortune. He bought the *Daily Racing Form* for $400,000 in cash. Racing was on the upswing after a wartime slump, and millions of gamblers were thirsting for accurate information. Moe's organizational genius was once again manifest. He split the *Racing Form* into seven separate papers, based in six U.S. cities and Toronto. He improved the information, by recording the positions of the horses at the various stages of each race, thus vastly enhancing the bettors' assessment of how horses had performed throughout their racing careers. Opposing race sheets were effectively terrorized.

In 1927, just as his son Walter was graduating with no particular distinction from the Peddie School in Hightstown, New Jersey, Moe made the fateful decision of his career. He decided to invest in the Central News Bureau, a Chicago operation that used telephone lines to relay racing information to customers. Moe saw the potential in turning a regional into a national service, with the 30,000 or so bookies across the country eager to pay for reliable information.

This was the famous 'Wire' (by the 1930s AT&T's fourth biggest customer), ownership of which would certainly not count among the credentials of a man craving respectability or anything much other than very large sums of loot. But in that engaging style which makes him an infinitely more bracing character than his son, Moe strove to allay Walter's disquiet. As Cooney relates it (and as Walter presumably related it to him) Moe discoursed on the misery of the working man, toiling all week with no distraction from the diurnal grind. Why deny him the tiny thrill of a wager ventured and maybe a wager won? ' "It isn't right to deprive the little people of a chance to be lucky," he told Walter. "If people can wager at a racetrack why should they be deprived of the right to do so away from a track? How many people can take time off from their jobs to go to a racetrack?"' True of course, unless you believe all such gambling is a regressive tax on the poor. Walter used to mention state-sanctioned OTB operations in later years to exonerate his father in retrospect.

All this time, however, Moe was swimming in dangerous waters. A meeting of the nation's major gangsters in Atlantic City led to a proposal by Al Capone to Moe Annenberg that all share in a national wire service. Moe said he was doing just fine by himself, which he was – with the wire eventually stretching across the United States, Canada, Mexico and Cuba and making truly awesome amounts of money for its progenitor. Moe proved resourceful. A New York hoodlum called Waxey Gordon tried to muscle in on the wire and tapped its phone lines to get information for his own service. Moe isolated the section Gordon was tapping, and broadcast only delayed racetrack information over it. During the delay, his men, already apprised of the race results by the uninterrupting News Bureau network, placed bets with the bookies using Gordon's service. Annenberg's men bet on the winners, ruined the bookies and then refunded them their money, warning them that they were 'saps to take second-hand information.'

This is the sort of maneuver people tend to suggest has to be 'run with military precision.' But the military could not have run the Wire, any more than it could have set up the nation's bootlegging system in the twenties. In the twenties the nation's best and most disciplined entrepreneurial talent was probably devoted to such distributive marvels in the service industries.

By 1934, fights over control of the Wire, now known as Nationwide

News Service, were becoming more perilous than usual, and with an annual one-million-dollar payment to the Capone interests as a form of life insurance, Moe thought it expedient to rest up in Miami for a while, a city which had the advantage of being, in Cooney's words, 'under the control of his friend Meyer Lansky.'

With his customary energy, Moe had soon established his *Miami Tribune* as the best selling paper in the area, nourishing the populace with racy pabulum and exercising the traditional prerogative – well illustrated throughout Cooney's book – of a newspaper proprietor, discomfiting his enemies and enhancing his own business interests via the printed pages under his control. Moe wanted to buy an ambitious state senator called Peter Tomasello, who would thus be obliged to fend off the antigambling forces in Tallahasee. His aides warned him that Tomasello had a reputation for passing bad checks. 'That makes no difference to me,' Moe replied. 'We can make up the checks.' His man went off with $2,500 and gave it to Tomasello as 'an initial contribution.' Meeting Moe shortly thereafter, the politician began to outline his political platform. 'I don't care about your political platform,' Annenberg broke in. 'All I want is for you to obey orders.'

It would perhaps have been better for Moe Annenberg to have remained in Florida, peacefully raking in the cash in that baroque state. But in 1937, he sold off the *Miami Tribune* to the Knight interests for $600,000 and bought the *Philadelphia Inquirer*. The purchase signaled the onset of his downfall. His vociferous backing of Republican politicians in Pennsylvania and consequent assault on the Democrats soon aroused the interest and hostility of FDR. J. David Stern, publisher of the *Philadelphia Record* and the *New York Post*, was an FDR backer, and saw the revived *Inquirer* as a threat to his business interests.

The hour of Moe's destruction was at hand. Treasury Secretary Henry Morgenthau Jr. spurred an I.R.S. investigation. The investigation produced indictments. Under a deal that exempted his son from the charges – Walter had been working with no conspicuous talent in the family business – Moe pleaded guilty and was sentenced to three years in jail. He agreed to pay the government $9.5 million in back taxes. Some of the documents read at the trial have a refreshing directness, even at a distance of half a century. In one of them, a letter to his son-in-law, who had proposed an additional business venture in 1936, Moe wrote,

We simply cannot have everything, and, like Mussolini when he started out to grab Ethiopia, he had to very carefully consider what he might be plunging into, but Mussolini had nothing to risk, because Italy was on the bum, and those who might have opposed his ambition had by far and away more to risk than Mussolini. Our position is similar to that of the English nation. We in the racing field own three-quarters of the globe and manage the balance. In other words, the few little nations that are left have to pay us tribute to continue. Now, why isn't that the most beautiful and most satisfactory position to be in, which ought to satisfy even me. ...

There speaks the unfettered voice of nineteenth-century American capitalism, and if the oil companies today were capable of equally forthright brevity in their advertisements on OpEd pages, we would be spared much unnecessary nonsense.

Moe's end makes for painful and even touching reading. He was paroled only to be brought home to his deathbed, afflicted with a brain tumor. 'You know, Walter,' he remarked to his son, 'it all amounts to nothing.' And near the end, he said to Walter, 'My suffering is all for the purpose of making a man of you.'

The rest of Cooney's book is couched largely in the idiom of panegyric, even though he manages to give a pretty good idea of what Walter Annenberg is like. Most moving are Walter's poignant and entirely admirable efforts to exonerate the name and memory of his father. Of less allure is the story of how an idle youth with dim prospects pulled himself together, paid off the I.R.S., and consolidated an empire containing not only the *Daily Racing Form* and the *Inquirer* but subsequent intelligent acquisitions and inventions, including numerous TV stations, *Seventeen* magazine and, of course, the largest-circulation weekly in the country – *TV Guide*.

The narrative is not much fun, all the same. Walter emerges as a stolid, solidly reactionary publisher, supervising an *Inquirer* of steadily declining quality ('Without the *Inquirer* I'd just be another millionaire') until he finally sold it in the 1970s to the same Knight interests that bought his father's *Miami Tribune*.

Walter picked his political allies with more flair than his father: Nixon early on, with a natural gradation to Ronald Reagan, whom – according to Cooney – he found 'wholesome.' He does not appear to have actually called Nixon 'wholesome,' but his admiration is evident in the way the *Inquirer* headlined the disclosure in the 1952 campaign of the Nixon 'millionaires' club' slush fund: 'Friends' Gift to Nixon Draws Demands.'

According to Cooney, Annenberg at first rejected Nixon's invitation to become U.S. ambassador to London. He apparently told the President-elect in 1968 that it would cause him, Nixon, too many problems. Confirmation hearings certainly caused Walter much anguish, since Drew Pearson raked over the embers of his father's disgrace. And just as Moe's final agonies in court and in jail must evoke pity in the hardest heart, so too do Walter's travails when he first arrived in London. His turgid diction and his *faux-pas* caused ceaseless and well-publicized merriment. 'The rain is pouring down with determined resolution,' he remarked as he peered out the window of White's. 'We should get along well. I love spaghetti,' he said to the wife of the Italian ambassador. And in his first audience with the Queen, who asked him how the renovation of the U.S. embassy was progressing, he confided that he and his wife, Lee, were afflicted by 'discomfiture as a result of a need for, uh, elements of refurbishment and rehabilitation.'

Beset by criticism, Annenberg was on occasion discovered by his staff weeping silently in his study. He plodded manfully forward, spending millions on the restoration of Winfield House. Taunted by the elegant Bruces, who had preceded him in the embassy, he cried in the outraged tones of the *arriviste*, 'The Bruces didn't even use finger bowls.' But, if there is anything the British upper classes enjoy even more than laughing at rich Americans, it is eating their food and drinking their wine. The chaffers stayed to quaff and all in the end was well.

And there we have it. A one-hundred-year journey, from Kalwichen, East Prussia, to Palm Springs; from a silver spoon in the hand to one in the mouth; from racetrack tout sheets to walls well covered with impressionist art; from the $1 million in cash once offered by Moe to beat the I.R.S. rap, to innumerable and tremendous charitable donations bestowed by Walter. By the book's end, Walter's wife Lee, now chief of protocol in the Reagan White House, is being chided by the press for curtseying too deeply to Prince Charles. So *The Annenbergs: The Salvaging of a Tainted Dynasty* is worth putting on the shelf, alongside *Centennial*, as a useful parable of the American century and the American newspaper business.

Grand Street, Autumn, 1982

Prizes

Were there ever members of any profession so keen on giving each other prizes as journalists? From the rising up of the sun in the morning until its going down at night they keep at it, ladling out the trophies to each other: 'front-page' awards; 'distinguished service to journalism' awards; 'national magazine' awards, 'best veal picata recipe written under deadline' awards. The list is practically endless, as anyone who has looked at the available prizes set forth in Publisher's Weekly well knows. Then to cap it all, we have the Pulitzer Prizes, the most recent batch of which was announced Monday.

This year followed the usual pattern. Major newspapers got most of the prizes – two for The Wall Street Journal, two for the New York Times, two for the Boston Globe, two for the Los Angeles Times. There are the plucky underdog awards, and this year they went to Peter Rinearson of the Seattle Times for writing about the new Boeing 757, and to Albert Scardino of the Georgia Gazette in Savannah for his editorial writing. I don't know what Mr. Scardino had been editorializing about, and none of the newspapers within my reach on Tuesday told me. For all I know, he's been calling for the death penalty for used-car dealers convicted of misrepresentation. But that's not the point of his prize, which is to tell all the other little guys that if size is almost everything, it isn't always the only thing.

Then there are the prizes achieved by sheer weight of numbers and tedium. In an honest world these would be headlined 'Thirteen articles in search of a Pulitzer.' They usually concern such worthy topics as municipal graft in the awarding of sewerage contracts. This year the Los Angeles Times got one ('meritorious public service' is what this particular prize is called) for an 'in-depth examination' of the Latin community in Southern California that took the form of a 27-part series, conducted by two editors and 11 writers. At the other end of the country the Boston Globe got the 'local reporting' Pulitzer for a series investigating racial tension around Boston. Seven reporters were named here as authors, and I've no doubt at all that they did well in quarrying out the big news that Boston is a town with racial problems and a white power structure.

In fact, if you are searching for a Pulitzer it clearly pays to write about, or take pictures of, people who are not white. Aside from the Latinos in Los Angeles and the blacks in Boston, starving Ethiopians helped photographer Anthony Suau of the Denver Post win his prize, assistance similarly furnished to prize-winning photographer Stan Grossfeld of the Boston Globe by suffering Palestinians in Lebanon. This shows what a wethearted lot of liberals there are on the Pulitzer juries and board. In future they should short-circuit the whole business and give a Pulitzer directly to the starving millions of Africa for consistent, if hungry, service to First World journalism. I hope the Palestinians in Lebanon feel a little better today. Largely misrepresented and racially denigrated though they may have been in the U.S. news media over the past 40 years, at least their sufferings have contributed to the Pulitzer process.

Then there are the dynastics Pulitzers, both institutional and personal. The Washington Post was cut out this year, which makes one think that it will definitely get its dynastic due 12 months from now. So unremitting is the flow of newspaper prizes, however, that the Washington Post was able to console itself in the midst of its Tuesday coverage of the Pulitzers with the news that its own man Ward Sinclair had been named Newspaper Editor of the Year by the National Association of Farm Writers. Los Angeles Times cartoonist Paul Conrad won his third Pulitzer, edging out Don Wright of the Miami News, also in search of his third.

This will not surprise readers of Monday's Wall Street Journal, who were able to find on the editorial page an article by James Squires, editor of the Chicago Tribune and chairman of this year's Pulitzer editorial cartoon jury. Mr. Squires said that there are only about a half-dozen worthwhile political cartoonists in the country, among whom he included Conrad, Herblock and his own paper's Jeff MacNelly, another Pulitzer cartoonist whose record of ignorant and reactionary prejudice is, in my view, unmatched since Sir Bernard Partridge's work in the late 19th-century Punch. At least Conrad thinks better than MacNelly and draws better than Herblock. So why did not the Pulitzer board simply refuse to give a cartoonist prize this year?

Year after year this undignified prizegiving ritual goes on, without any apparent qualms on the part of my profession. Why? If bankers gave themselves prizes ('the most reckless Third-World loan of the year') with the same abandon as journalists, you may be sure that the public ridicule would soon force them to conduct the proceedings in secret.

One answer could be that journalists are, by nature and social function, racked with feelings of insecurity and inferiority; to alleviate those pangs, British journalists turn to drink and American ones to prizes. This may have been true in the days of Daniel Defoe, when newsmen and editorialists were put in the stocks or in jail. Not any more.

The truth is that the Pulitzer business – and, given the promotional uses to which the prizes are put, it definitely is a business – is a self-validating ritual whereby journalists give each other prizes and then boast to the public about them. Each year's ritual proclaims that journalism once again has maintained sufficiently high standards to merit such acclaim. The logical consequence of the boosterism is to have an evening like the Oscars, with all the contestants preening and squirming under the cameras; old stagers like James Reston or C.L. Sulzberger calling for 'the envelope please' and Charlton Heston giving a retrospective reading from the Journal's assault on arms control. Maybe then people would understand that it's all show business.

What else can the Pulitzers be but show business if journalists – supposedly a critical lot – can only get together to tell each other how good they are, but not how bad. Yet, to my mind, much of 1983 was a record of journalistic failure; failure to set forth accurately the issues of arms control and negotiations with the Soviet Union; failure to discuss objectively and accurately the situation in the Middle East; failure to report the political changes in the black community that have stimulated the Jackson candidacy. The list could go on for quite a while.

There is something hugely self-complacent, odiously Pecksniffian about the journalistic profession at the moment. To take one small example, amid all the endless prating about free speech and the First Amendment – has any newspaper found editorial space to lament the case of Hustler publisher Larry Flynt, who was thrown into a federal penitentiary on charges arising out of his refusal to name a source? This is a fate that normally has the editorialists hot with sympathy, but then Flynt is scarcely a shining knight of the Fourth Estate.

Wall Street Journal, April 19, 1984

PART TWO

◆

An Archive of the Reagan Era, 1976–1988

February 23, 1976

Reagan in New Hampshire

MANCHESTER, N.H. – No one can go into New Hampshire without clearly realizing that whether or not he wins, Ronald Reagan is the politician who is boldly putting forward the ideas and framing the debate for the rest of this election year. This is the centrally important fact of the New Hampshire primary.

Reagan represents the most polished expression of political ideas that have been voiced with varying degrees of eccentricity over the last 10 years or so: by Barry Goldwater, by George Wallace, and, of course, most significantly by Richard Nixon. But the crankiness of Goldwater, the uncouthness of Wallace, and the unctuous crookery of Nixon are all subsumed and palatably reborn in the smooth, vigorous style of the Hollywood actor.

Obviously much of what Reagan says is nonsense. But underlying the nonsense – much of which is extremely popular – there is a serious strain of politics. In essence, Reagan is a man of the right-center. In a general election he would attract many votes that would otherwise go to a Democrat of the Jerry Brown variety. At the same time, his right-wing attacks on foreign policy may well attract the adherence of supporters of Scoop Jackson, as well as the right of the Republican party – more or less, the old winning Nixon coalition.

In fact, Reagan's vision of government is very much out of the Nixon mold. It envisions corporate socialism, based on a redirection of the economy.

Reagan's major thrust was his attack on big government. He is, of course, the politician more than any other now active who has defined this term and argued it. The Democrats, in the form of Jerry Brown, Mike Dukakis, and others, merely imitate the genre. In the actual description of his program Reagan is extremely contradictory, but the contradictions between the popular appeal of his attacks on big government and what he is actually proposing show that he is no mere fringe eccentric.

Thus, the weight of Reagan's rhetoric comes down on the side of a powerful corporate state. He says he is for breaking up government, but in fact he is arguing programmatically for a different use of government power, in which the major corporations would occupy a stronger position. He argues for tax reform, very much along the lines of that advocated by the banks and major corporations in the House Ways and Means Committee. He is against emergency unemployment measures and, of course, he has long been opposed to welfare.

Reagan has already placed the Democrats at a disadvantage, and traveling around New Hampshire after the various candidates, you can see how. On foreign policy none of them will do anything other than admit detente has to be watched carefully.

In domestic policy, as any Democrat knows, it is nearly impossible to run without somehow dealing with the specter of 'Big Government.' On the West Coast even Tom Hayden, battling for Senator John Tunney's seat, is making obeisances to fiscal responsibility and expressing his reservations about the sort of bureaucracy that would be involved in nationalization of the oil companies.

Carter remains the main force to be reckoned with. He is without question the front-runner, still weirdly appealing to both the left and right wings of the Democratic party. But his balance in this situation is plainly becoming more and more precarious, as his positions come under scrutiny. Put starkly, he represents Reaganism coming from the other direction, heading for a center-right consensus of the sort that Scoop Jackson always yearns for but has so far completely failed to achieve.

In all of this there is no question but that the Democrats are dancing to the ideas propounded by Reagan. And plainly these are the ideas on the minds of the people who came into the town halls to hear what he had to say. Reagan is indeed the one conspicuous ideologue of the campaign.

The truth of New Hampshire is that after eight years of slump, recession, increasing unemployment, corruption, the dominant political ideas and slogans are coming from the right, and are being articulated by an impressive spokesman. It may well be that Reagan will not win in New Hampshire, but it is hard to imagine that the debate which he has begun in the town halls of this New England state won't be the focus of the entire campaign. It is absurd that a Democratic candidate is not triumphantly conquering all before him with a powerful reforming message. But 1976 does not seem to be 1932, and currently no such Democrat is in view.

Village Voice, with James Ridgeway

April 10, 1976

The Cat's Meo

A couple of weeks ago I noted *The New York Times*'s genial treatment of a couple of war criminals in the shapes of Blowtorch Komer and William Colby, both veterans of the pacification campaign in Vietnam.

The paper, I'm glad to see, is keeping up its efforts to draw a veil over those emotion-fraught events in Southeast Asia. Last Sunday, Steven Roberts had a pleasant piece, filed from Montana, headed LAOTIAN, AFTER YEARS OF WAR, LIKES THE PEACE OF MONTANA. Underneath was a cozy picture of Vang Pao, 'a former major general in the Royal Laotian Army, inspecting cattle feeding on his ranch in Montana.'

Amid his rhapsodies about the Montana creeks 'reborn with melting snow,' Roberts did find space to mention that Vang had been a major general in the Royal Laotian Army, and 'had been an influential leader among a mountain people known as the Meos,' helping 'to organize them into a special fighting force with heavy backing from the Central Intelligency Agency.' Roberts also noted that Vang had left Laos in May 1975 aboard his own American-made plane, along with six wives and 28 children. Roberts said Vang stated that he had managed to pay for his Montana spread with the help of family, friends, and bank loans.

It's too bad that Roberts did not turn for added information to Alfred McCoy's *The Politics of Heroin in Southeast Asia*. Here we find numerous citations: for example, '... the U.S. Bureau of Narcotics has reports that Gen. Vang Pao, commander of the CIA's secret army [to fight the Pathet Lao] has been operating a heroin factory at Long Tieng, headquarters for CIA operations in northern Laos ...' Or, '... In addition to his regular battalion Vang Pao was also commander of Meo self-defense forces in the Plain of Jars region. Volunteers had been promised regular allotments of food and money, but Vang Pao pocketed these salaries, and most went unpaid for months at a time. When one Meo Lieutenant demanded that the irregulars be given their back pay, Vang Pao shot him in the leg. That settled the matter for the moment ...'

According to McCoy, the CIA and USAID helped Vang form his own private airline, Xieng Khouang Air Transport: 'Reliable Meo sources report that Xieng Khouang Air Transport is the airline used to carry opium between Long Tieng and Vientiane.' McCoy's analysis of Vang's alliance with the CIA in purchasing and moving the opium crop is most instructive. With such thoughts in mind, there is something a little moving about Roberts's final lines: 'But now the American land grows his seeds and his children and the morning was slipping away. It was time to get on with the plowing.'

VV

May 2, 1977

Small Talk

The pygmy saga was a welcome relief from the great energy blitz and I followed it closely. The pygmies made their entry into the headlines about a week ago. In *The New York Times* Michael Kaufman reported from Kinshasa that a Zairois government spokesman had announced that the pygmies – 'elite bowmen' – were playing an important role in fighting off the Katangese insurgents. Robin Wright said much the same thing in the *Washington Post*, adding the useful information that 'the few pygmy members of Zaire's army' who had been seen around Kolwezi 'have all been equipped with rifles often as tall as the small tribesmen.' In view of enigmas discussed below, this was an important point, but since Robin Wright's piece was datelined Kanzenze, it is unclear whether she personally observed the rifles and measured them off against the diminutive warriors.

Under the headline 'Bow & Arrow Pygmies Help Rout Zaire Invaders,' the *Daily News* ran a UPI report the same day also quoting a Zairois spokesman, but including his statement that the pygmies were not armed with rifles, only bows and arrows. The UPI man led off with the news that the pygmies were four feet tall and added, further along in the story, the scholarly anthropological information that 'The pygmies are a tiny race living in northern Zaire's dense Ituri forest. They are renowned for their skills in bow and arrow and poison blow-dart jungle fighting.'

The next day Kaufman reported that the pygmies were becoming 'Zairian heroes,' and had been commended in a government newspaper as 'formidably efficient units who can move silently and well against the enemy.' This was all I could find in Thursday's papers. However, on Friday the UPI man in Kinshasa was – as printed in the *Daily News* – in terrific form. 'A force of 300 pygmy warriors,' he proclaimed 'armed with poisoned darts and bows and arrows, was airlifted to the front in Shaba province.' He quoted 'diplomatic sources' as saying the pygmy troops had passed through Kinshasa en route for battle in the southeast. This seems odd, since previous reports already had them in the southeast.

At any rate, the UPI man quoted 'sources' once more attesting that the pygmies 'were dressed in traditional bark skirts and ornate headdresses ... and have thrown fear into the superstitious rebel forces ... the sources said the invaders "have a supernatural fear of the Pygmies" and that reports from the front said the invaders have begun putting good luck charms on their rifles to ward off evil spirits.'

I must say I thought the Zairois minister of propaganda was going a little far. The 'supernatural fear' was a nice touch, as indeed was the accurate-sounding figure of 300. But the business of good-luck charms and evil spirits showed things were getting thoroughly out of hand.

And, indeed, it was as though everyone had begun to agree. The pygmies, that Friday morning, had in fact reached the zenith of their world-wide martial reputation. By the start of this week Michael Kaufman, in a story datelined the Lubidi River, said he'd asked officers about the pygmies, only to receive the grim news that the pygmies had been sent back to Kolwezi: 'Our training was different,' said this unpleasant officer. 'They didn't fit in.' And he added, maliciously in my judgment, that the pygmies could fire arrows only 20 yards, and as there were no close-quarter engagements with the enemy they were superfluous.

Time magazine this Monday even cut down the pygmy force to a mere 150 and said vaguely their average height was 'under 5 ft.' *Newsweek* had the decency to suggest that they were 'barely over 4 feet tall,' but quoted anthropologist Colin Turnbull as saying, apropos their skill with bow and arrow, that 'they are among the world's worst shots.' At least *Newsweek* stuck with the 300 force estimate and called them 'jungle-wise.'

Now, Kolwezi is in Shaba province, so the pygmies are still on active service. Unless – and here is the important point missed by all – they were not pygmies but merely pygmoid.

Your true pygmy, you see, does live in the Ituri rain forests in the north-eastern Congo. His kind are generally known as the Mbuti, a gentle lot subsisting on grubs and occasionally firing off arrows at wild animals or catching them in nets in the manner of the ancient Roman *retiarii.* (A point strangely missed by the UPI correspondent, though perhaps nets are impractical in modern hand-to-hand combat.)

My mother, who spent time among them in 1936, tells me that these Mbuti are three feet six inches on average and 'the most charming people in Africa,' as well as being shy and unwarlike. She strongly opined that the 300 archers were Twa pygmoids, who are ersatz and who furthermore tower above the Mbuti, being at least four feet six inches. These Twa, who come from around Lake Kivu and elsewhere are, she says, 'a low lot', henchpeople for the Watusi (who are very, very tall). The Twa helped the Watusi kill the Bahutu (just after and indeed just before the Bahutu killed those Watusi who were left) in the Burundi bloodletting of recent memory.

VV

May 16, 1977

Small Comeback

I'm glad to see that the pygmies, or pygmoids, are back in action in Zaire.

Now the UPI person in Kinshasa, who has always been sensitive to pygmy news potential, quotes government sources as saying that 'they are spreading panic among the enemy.' This is great news for pygmy fanciers who had been embarrassed by previous stories that the pygmies had been helpless in 'the tall elephant grass of southern Zaire.' Such charges were rank pygmism, since it is precisely under such terrain that the pygmy comes into his own, sneaking deftly through the herbiage before firing off his arrows or, indeed, ensnaring the invader in his net.

VV

Feeling Good Again

'The current pontification about human rights,' Noam Chomsky writes in the new issue of *Seven Days*, 'is little more than an effort on the part of the administration and its propagandists to restore the system of beliefs that was eroded by the Vietnam war.'

'In the course of one of his discourses on human rights,' Chomsky goes on, 'President Carter was asked whether the United States "has a moral obligation to help rebuild" Vietnam. Not at all, he explained: "The destruction was mutual." We bombed their villages and they shot down our pilots. Since "we went to Vietnam without any desire ... to impose American will on other people" but only "to defend the freedom of the South Vietnamese," and since in any event "the destruction was mutual," there is no reason for us to "apologize or to castigate ourselves or to assume the status of culpability." Nor do we "owe a debt."'

This is what's called moral rebirth, or what James Weighart virtuously invoked in the *Daily News* not so long ago as America's moral superiority: something equivalent to a shot of vitamin B-12 before the B-52s are unleashed again on dissidents from U.S. policies in a foreign land.

In the course of this process of rebirth nothing has been more distasteful than the spectacle of American liberals once more scrambling to action stations and in fact stoking up cold war furnaces.

VV

June 27, 1977

The Lavender Hill Mob

On the subject of gays (or 'lavender boys,' as the revolting Pat Buchanan called them in the *Daily News*) amazing scenes were witnessed but unreported in Boston following the Anita Bryant debacle. Gay Pride Day took place there last weekend. First the gays marched past the Granary Cemetery where a wedding party was posing for photographs. 'Two-four-six-eight,' chanted the gays, 'how do you know your wife is straight?' Further coarse scenes involving a transvestite flamenco dancer took place among the tombs.

At the ensuing rally Charles Shively, tenured professor of history at Boston State College and a noted gay, let rip. First he held up his Harvard Ph.D. 'Burn it,' screamed the crowd, and he forthwith did with ceremony, in a bronze wok. Then he read out the letter from Boston State refusing his bid to teach a gay history course. 'Burn it,' etc. His insurance policy suffered the same fate, symbolic presumably of insurance/banker power in Boston. The state laws on sodomy were held up and recited. 'Burn them,' shouted the crowd. Into the wok they went.

Then Shively held up the bible and read from the book of Leviticus. Dead silence from the crowd in Catholic Boston. Finally, a timid mumble of 'Burn it' went up from daring sectors in the throng. Shively tossed the Good Book into the wok. At this, Dignity and other gay religious groups struck back. 'Burn HIM,' they bellowed, and all broke up in disorder.

In the latest issue of that excellent Boston paper *Gay Community News*, I see that Shively has some reflections on the reaction to his speech and his actions.

'The anger directed against me would be more appropriately directed against straight institutions such as the schools, banks, state, and churches. Some have suggested that I personally have scared people back into their closets or made it more difficult to come out. The reason people stay in their closets is not because of a few "dangerous," "flamboyant," or "radical" gay liberationists. They stay in their closets because they correctly fear the straight institutions of this society.

'For instance, I spoke on June 18th. On June 24th the IRS sent me a letter calling for an audit ... Then June 29th the Aetna insurance company canceled my policy. And on June 30th the Customs seized my copy of the Swedish gay liberation publication REVOLT. At my school I have been spied on, my office burglarized, records stolen, and threats made against me.'

This all seems a grim consequence for just a little bit of book burning. As Shively says, 'I only burned one "copy" of the bible; others are free to do what they want with their own copies.'

VV

October 31, 1977

The Sikh's Revenge

John le Carré had a spirited blast about England in last Sunday's *New York Times Magazine*. He flailed away without mercy, pinning much of the blame on the educational system, notably preparatory and public schools to which the prospective elite are dispatched and in which, if one believes le Carré and the immense quantity of other writers who have expressed themselves on the same topic, the wretched denizens suffer the tortures of the damned.

I suppose he is right. I must say I rather liked my preparatory school near Ascot. The fear was not really of bullying or homosexual assault so much as whether one's parents would make public spectacles of themselves on their periodic visits to the school, which was 10 miles across the moors from the nearest point of civilization (Perth).

Once my father had to rush north from London on the night train to conduct vital negotiations with the headmaster on whether – in view of my own imminent expulsion – my brother would be permitted to enter the establishment. I waited by the front gate. Down the driveway came the cab and in it the hunched and gloomy figure of my father. He extended his leg to alight and I at once perceived that he was wearing no socks. Socks are essential to dignified comportment. I protested forcibly and my father, himself terrified at the thought of the impending meeting with the headmaster, babbled an explanation.

It was not convincing. He had, he said, found himself sharing a sleeping compartment with a Sikh who was wearing a magnificent turban. He and the Sikh had 'taken a few drinks.' Later, perched on his top berth, he had watched in the mirror on the opposite wall as the Sikh, in the bottom berth, slowly unwound his turban. He was aware, said my father as we walked towards the headmaster's office, that by spying on the Sikh's turban-doffing he was breaching ancient taboos. But he could not resist further inspection. Just when it became apparent that the handsome young fellow in a turban was – without turban – a very old Sikh indeed, their eyes met in the mirror. 'I passed,' said my father, 'a night of terror, tossing to and fro and awaiting the Sikh's inevitable revenge. I awoke at Perth station from an uneasy doze. The Sikh was gone. His reprisal? The theft of my socks.'

It was a fine try, and as I watched my father hitch his pants down over his naked ankles before stepping into the headmaster's study I felt – not for the first time – the powerful urge to become a journalist, since only a journalist (such as my father) could have conceived such a preposterous story at a moment's notice and within moments recounted it with such vibrant conviction.

VV

November 21, 1977

Poddy on the Threat

Now that it's safely off the stands, and therefore no one can waste a penny on the thing, we can turn our attention to an astonishing essay by Norman Podhoretz in the October issue of *Harper's* entitled 'The Culture of Appeasement.' Podhoretz starts with the sort of ranting one regularly finds in the pages of *Commentary*: namely that the Vietnam debacle left as one of its chief destructive effects 'the undifferentiated fear, loathing and revulsion that the prospect of war now seems to inspire in the American mind ... All one heard about and saw was the horrors of war – unredeemed, as it appeared, by any noble purpose.' Podhoretz, needless to say, thinks this sort of thinking thoroughly bad, since if people don't like the idea of war – noble or not – then they won't stand up to the Russians. And, indeed, he suspects Americans have lost 'the will' to fight Communism.

After more of this sort of thing – the spread of 'native anti-Americanism' and so forth – Podhoretz finally gets down to the real business.

He detects, he claims, resemblances between the United States of today and Great Britain in the years after World War I. Similar distaste for combat occurred then to the extent 'that the Iliad ... could no longer be comfortably read.' England itself was discredited in the eyes of the young; the place seemed drearily middle class. The young rebelled, some of them becoming Nazi sympathisers, others Communists or fellow travellers. 'That Auden and Burgess were both homosexuals,' says Podhoretz, 'clearly had something, perhaps everything, to do with their need "completely and finally to rebel against England."' And indeed it is impossible to read books like *Children of the Sun* or Paul Fussell's *The Great War and Modern Memory* without being struck by the central role homosexuality played in the entire rebellious ethos of the interwar period in England.'

'... Homosexual feeling,' Podhoretz says, 'also accounted for a good deal of the pacificism that rose out of the trenches and into the upper reaches of the culture after the war was over.' One would have thought, actually, that the fresh memory of the most wantonly bloody war in human history might have had something to do with it. Shortly thereafter, we get to the guts of the matter: 'No wonder, then, that so many of those who resented their own country ... should have been or should have chosen to become, homosexuals. For whatever else homosexuality may be, or may be caused by, to these young men of the English upper class it represented – the refusal of fatherhood and all that fatherhood entailed: responsibility for a family and therefore an inescapable implication in the destiny of society as a whole ... they were rejecting their birthright as successors to their own fathers in assuming a direct responsibility for the fate of the country.'

It's but a short leap now to the conclusion: 'Anyone familiar with homosexual apologetics in America today will recognize these attitudes.' That is: England appeased in the '30s; there were homosexuals in England; therefore homosexuals caused appeasement. Watch your ass, Neville Chamberlain. Specifically mentioning Allen Ginsberg, James Baldwin and Gore Vidal, Podhoretz says we 'find the same sort of pacifism [with Vietnam naturally standing in for World War I], hostility to one's own country and its putatively dreary middle-class way of life, and derision of the idea that it stands for anything worth defending or that it is threatened by anything but its own stupidity and wickedness.'

Short of direct charges that Commie faggots are running the State Department, it is hard to conceive of a more hysterical and wilfully demagogic posture: America is getting soft on Communism; America's population includes declared homosexuals; homosexuals are pacifists and soft on Communism: finally (though this is as yet unstated), homosexual Communists run America.

VV

December 5, 1977

Hemingway: The Bald Truth

The absorbing magazine *The Razor's Edge* – a journal crusading for female baldness – has at last published the truth about Ernest Hemingway – to wit, that he was a bald-head freak. In a scholarly article in its fourth issue, Jack Rieux (aided by Robert Singer) comes to this conclusion: 'Just as Hemingway, the revolutionary prose stylist, sought to expunge from literature all unnecessary verbal foliage, stripping his terse, taut narrative down to bare essentials of communications, so he yearned for a female beauty free of cosmetic fluff and reduced to the closely shaven, soft yet firm, gleaming splendor of the clean bald scalp.'

Baseless innuendo, you may say, yet Rieux compiles compelling evidence. Take an early story, *Cat in the Rain*: '"Don't you think it would be good if I let my hair grow out?" she asked, looking at her profile again. George looked up and saw the back of her neck, clipped close like a boy's. "I like it the way it is." "I get so tired of it," she said. "I get so tired of looking like a boy."'

Then we have *The Last Good Country*, another early story. Nick Adam's sister cuts off her hair ('I just held it out and cut it. Do I look like a boy?') and as Rieux comments, the rape of her locks is presented as a moral act: '"It was something we had to do," the sister says. "I should have asked you, but it was something I knew we had to do." "I like it," Nick said. "The hell with everything. I like it very much."'

Keeping up the momemtum, Rieux picks up on Lady Brett Ashley, in *The Sun Also Rises*, with her hair 'brushed back like a boy's' and then speeds on to *A Farewell to Arms*, where Fredrick Henry agrees with Catherine Barkley that it would be 'exciting' if she cut off all her hair. All this of course is prelude to the great sado-masochistic hair-shearing contest of *For Whom the Bell Tolls*.

Rieux really lets rip here, quoting with satisfaction (he is identified in the magazine as combining 'a lifelong interest in the literature of Ernest Hemingway with a similar enthusiasm for balded women') such passages as: ' Her hair was the golden brown of a grain field that has been burned by the sun but it was cut short all over her head so that it was but little longer than the fur on a beaver pelt,' the famous shaving of Maria by the Fascists, and a passage in which Rieux says the erotic elements in head-shaving reach full fruition: 'She curled her legs between his and rubbed the top of her head against his shoulder. "But I would not be so ugly there with this cropped head that thou wouldst be ashamed of me." "No, thou art lovely,"' and so forth.

With a scholarly harrumph, Rieux glosses: 'In the final analysis none of Hemingway's fictional women experience dramatically negative feelings about their cropped heads. Similarly, none of the author's male protagonists react less than positively to the severely cropped heroines of his literature. In fact they eventually prefer the women because of that characteristic. Hence, that sado-masochistic shaving scene of *For Whom the Bell Tolls* is not significant with regard to Hemingway's motivation or basis for appreciating women with little or no hair. He preferred women who were cropped or shaven because of an aesthetic appreciation of the daringly spirited breed of women who would remain confident with such styles.'

Remember that *The Razor's Edge* favors female baldness. Hemingway is dragooned as recruiting agent.

Of course, Rieux makes autobiographical links. Carlos Baker said Hemingway was 'especially conscious of a woman's hair.' All his wives had short hair in the period of their proximity to Papa. And Hemingway shaved his head twice. Once when he got lice in Turkey and once on safari in Africa in 1953, when he 'remained completely shaven for at least four months, going "native" to the extent of hunting with spears and dyeing his hunting jackets a Masai shade of pink while consorting with a completely bald Wakemba girl named Debba.'

I'm not sure of the sex-pol ramifications of all this. I associate shaven heads with fascism, but this may be repression.

VV

February 13, 1978

Bring Back Prohibition

As it casts about desperately for a crusade with which to arouse the American people, the Carter administration would do well to consider one of the great social experiments of the 20th century: prohibition.

At first glance, prohibition, inaugurated with the 18th Amendment in 1919 and ended with passage of the 21st Amendment in 1933, would seem to be a discredited episode in American history. Enemies of prohibition cite the rise of organized crime (including the Kennedy clan), the paralysis of public morals, and the corruption of the political process generally as among the dire results of mass social rejection of the law.

Such denunciation is altogether too hasty. It should first of all be noted that the enactment of prohibition ushered in a decade of prosperity unparalleled in the history of the republic. Repeal of prohibition came hand in hand with the darkest years of the Depression. Prohibition can be directly connected with the boom years of the 1920s. Working- and middle-class savings rose sharply in the first five years of prohibition, since money previously squandered on liquor was reserved for more prudent and useful investment.

But the hidden message of prohibition lies elsewhere and has only recently been excavated by social and medical historians. It is to be found in the field of public health. Epidemiologists in their scrutiny of health trends among the American populace, have detected a downswing in certain kinds of disease during the period of prohibition. The most striking decline was in the death rates due to cirrhosis of the liver, an ailment widely attributed to alcoholism. Consider one startling statistic: For the state of Massachusetts – an area typical of the eastern seaboard – the death rate per 100,000 population from cirrhosis in 1870 was 9.7. By 1900 it had jumped to 16.0. In 1930 (when prohibition was in full force) it declined to 8.2. But by 1968, after 35 years of steady legal drinking, the rate had climbed to 19.0.

Dr. Joseph Eyer of the University of Pennsylvania believes that prohibition had a definite, socially beneficial effect in reducing the cirrhosis death rate. And he goes on to argue that prohibition also contributed to a decline in the accident and suicide rates. He believes that prohibition probably also had an impact on the decline in tuberculosis rates (long before the introduction of antibiotics after World War II). For Massachusetts, the TB death rate per 100,000 in 1870 was 460. It declined to 264 in 1900, and to 68 in 1930. Eyer adds that the prohibition of alcohol consumption may very well have had a cross impact on TB because of diet: alcoholics frequently get calories from liquor, not food, thus lowering resistance to TB.

Indeed, beyond such specific data, the first phase of prohibition until the mid-'20s produced an impressive reduction in alcohol-related statistics in such areas as hospital admissions, police arrests, and the like.

By hindsight, it can be seen that prohibition constituted a dramatic, specific, and successful public-health program and demonstrated that where political leadership and public sentiment combine – as they did in the years immediately following World War I – socially beneficial results can be obtained.

VV, with James Ridgeway

April 24, 1978

Dolls in Gross Act

In a fierce bid to protect the good names of Poppin' Fresh and Poppie Fresh, the Pillsbury Company launched, last Monday, a case against *Screw* magazine claiming damages totalling $1.5 million and enjoining *Screw* against further assault on the reputation of its dolls.

What bothers Pillsbury is that some recent editions of *Screw* have displayed what purports to be a Pillsbury ad showing the dolls engaged in sexual activity, oral and genital.

Pillsbury's lawyers recount how, in 1966, the company began using a 'distinctive trade character popularly known as "Poppin" Fresh, the Pillsbury Dough Boy' ... which trade character has a baker's hat, a neckerchief, and a body with blunted limbs, which is presented in pure white except for his dark blue (in color presentation), or black (in black and white presentation), "pop" eyes.'

Pillsbury, says the complaint, has so far spent at least $70 million in the development and presentations of its Poppin' Fresh trade character. These presentations, they say, have ensured that Poppin' Fresh's 'personality is the best remembered feature ...' Poppin' Fresh has so far appeared on over four billion packages and in 1971 was replicated, as the complaint puts it, 'in three dimensions ... which doll was wrought in soft, smooth and cuddly vinyl so as to appeal to both the eyes and touch of children.' Millions of these dolls were sold.

In 1972, there came into the world Poppie Fresh, the Pillsbury Doughgirl, 'so dressed and configured to be perceived as a female character.' Pillsbury, the complaint says 'has taken care to insure that these characters have always been so presented as to project an image of wholesomeness and decency.'

The tone of the complaint, unctuous in its tender pride on the subject of the dolls, then changes sharply. 'Defendant is a publisher of a periodical entitled *Screw*, which publication is uncompromisingly obscene in its totality, and is thus the antithesis of wholesomeness and decency.' And *Screw*, the complaint reports, ran a purported ad, along with the jingle, 'Nothin' says Lovin' Like Somethin' From the Oven ... and Pillsbury says it best.'

In the ad were, apparently, our old friends Poppin' Fresh and Poppie Fresh. 'The aforesaid damage is exacerbated by the fact that ... in *Screw* Pillsbury's "Poppin' Fresh" character and its "Poppie Fresh" character are indecently portrayed as joining in various sexual activities, including an act which is a crime against nature.'

'... The despicably sordid portrayals,' one count in the complaint runs, 'would have the tendency to tarnish and besmirch the aforesaid copyrighted dolls and would thus diminish both their appeal and their value ...'

Al Goldstein, publisher of *Screw*, did not seem too worried about the suit when I called him on Monday. 'We think,' he remarked briskly, 'that they're full of shit. It's humor. It's a First Amendment thing. They're morons. We will run it again. We'll break their chops.'*

VV

Pillsbury sued Screw *in Georgia and it was only after a long and expensive fight that* Screw *survived.*

December 4, 1978

20 Years On

A perfectly preserved Keynesian has been unearthed by archaeologists investigating the sudden onset of the age of monetarism in the 1960s. The Keynesian was unearthed by excavators from the quadrangle of Kings College, Cambridge, where he apparently had been engaged in digging a hole. The body is in an excellent state of preservation, clad in corduroy trousers and tweed coat. The stomach contains freshly chewed cucumber sandwiches and cinnamon toast.

Archaeologists speculate that diagrams found on the Keynesian, referring to LM and IS, will shed new light on early Keynesian thought. A copy of the *New Statesman*, also found on the corpse, dates the sudden death of the Keynesian to the time of the British devaluation of sterling in 1967. It is believed that the Keynesian, fearing the onset of glacial monetarism, may have fled Whitehall to his old grazing pastures in Kings. But other experts, noting the placid expression on the face of the Keynesian, believe that the catastrophe took him entirely unawares.

A portion of the Keynesian's thigh was flown at once to a banquet held by the Chicago School. 'Tasty and surprisingly fresh,' was a common verdict, though some found the meat 'too fatty.'

VV

September 10, 1979

Death in August

Larry Stern, national editor of the *Washington Post*, died of a heart attack at the age of 50 on August 11. He was jogging, a circumstance to which I will return.

I first recall meeting him in 1974, awakening in a strange house in Washington to hear a noise that sounded as though someone had just dropped a bicycle on top of a dog. This is what had occurred, and I found a shortish man, breathing heavily, seeking to put the situation to rights. With a luminous smile, he introduced himself as Stern, reported that I had come to visit the previous night, had drunk excessively and fallen asleep on his sofa.

The saga, punctuated with abrupt laughs, was related in a species of verbal shorthand, cryptic but full of innuendo and implication. He drew brisk thumbnail sketches of others who had attended the nocturnal revels; backtracked to a kindred revel in Saigon years earlier; moved as swiftly forward to a disobliging anecdote about a noted pundit of the day; and finally fell into silence as he tried to make coffee with the ineptitude and concentrated application of one unfamiliar with the preparation of food and beverages.

As he talked, panting somewhat, the hangover gradually slipped off him like an old familiar dressing gown and he moved more easily through the litter of empty bottles, empty glasses, and well-filled ash trays, inquiring about my business and offering help and counsel. With a few parting words of admonition, a suggestion that I treat his house as mine, he sprang forth to do battle with another day, pausing only to ponder for some minutes where the hell he had left his car.

There were many such evenings, and many such mornings, subsequently conducted in this manner at Larry's house in Washington.

The place was one of those reverse images of a Bermuda Triangle, which journalists always hope to find in some strange city. Writers, lobbyists, reporters, politicians, lovely women, who all previously had been maintaining their own separate, invisible causes, would all suddenly show up on the same radar screen, gathered beneath Larry's generous roof.

To foreign journalists, novices in the nation's capital, he was particularly kind, beaming joyously as Japanese scribes, contorting their tongues painfully round his Christian name, sought inside dope on the 'Rockheed' scandal. Most notable of all was his kindness towards British journalists who became accustomed, over the years, to report directly to his house after arrival at Dulles and then file the facts as they heard them from Larry two or three hours later.

Larry had worked at the *Washington Post* for nearly 30 years, and knew everything about the paper, every skeleton in every closet, just as he knew almost everything one might wish to discover about Washington, and what patch of ground a reporter might tootle in to exhume a body or two. To every piece of inside dopesterism delivered up by one of his guests, Larry could add the extra telling detail.

Since he was an exceptionally good journalist, he could edit as well as he could report or write, and by preference would perform all three activities at the same time. When, in the Watergate aftermath and slight slump at the paper, he became assistant managing editor of the *Post*, in charge of national affairs, the change for the better was – to my eyes at least – instantly detectable. Not least because Larry's heart and head lay on the left side of the political bed. He was not one of those pallidly objective souls who need a route map to get from a gas shortage to Exxon headquarters, or who feel incapable of making up his mind 'until all the facts are in' and till all the evidence has been judiciously assessed.

A Trotskyist in his hot youth, Larry knew what the facts were going to tell him long before he discovered what they actually were, and the route map he carried with him through his life showed the eternal landmarks: the rich man in his castle and the poor man at his gate.

Larry hoped to write books, and if possible to earn large sums of money doing so. In 1976, he did take a year off on a foundation grant to write a book about American foreign policy and Cyprus. It was finished on the usual tight, late deadline, was called *The Wrong Horse,* was very good, and I doubt made him much money at all. I used to find him in the modishly modern Carnegie building on Dupont Circle, confabulating with mysterious Greeks, typing away, and looking rather out of place, a shirtsleeved man in a pinstriped world.

He invited me to a 'seminar,' in which he was to propound the thesis of his book. The audience consisted mostly – so far as I could determine – of his sources, many of them retired, discreet citizens from the CIA and the State Department. Most of Larry's conclusions were far from their own, and only the fact that his mumbling that evening was so spectacular that scarcely a word could be understood prevented them from assaulting him on the spot.

Journalists don't usually write all, or indeed any, of the books they want to; they don't usually earn the fortunes they hope for; and often they don't age happily either. Somewhere after 45, fear enters the soul — for the body so abused by drink, tobacco and late nights, for the bank balance so small, for the middle- to late-age held in no particular respect by the profession.

There was a little of this fear in Larry, as there is in any sane or sensitive person. Between the assaults on the bourbon bottle with genial companions, the justified complaints about the utter incompetence of his publishers, and the romantic entanglements with women – who generally found him most attractive with his crooked teeth, ambitious midriff, and sweet complicit smile – he would try to repair the damage by a spot of jogging or other athletic activity.

His love affair with the running shoe was sporadic, and so I do not imagine that Larry's body, comfortably inured to pleasant abuse over decades, was much pleased when its master instructed it to trot about every couple of days.

He went in early August for a weekend on Martha's Vineyard, with old friends such as Jim Hoagland, Ward Just and John Newhouse. He played tennis, ate a nice lunch with some nice wine, and then went jogging. I wish he had done what he probably wanted to do – would have done in the pre-jogging era – and drunk another bottle of wine. But he went jogging, bent over, grabbed his ankle, remarked to Newhouse that he had been stung by a bee, and died of a heart attack. Autopsy disclosed arterial sclerosis.

I went to the Friends Meeting House in northwest Washington three days later, prepared to say a few words in memory of Larry, feeling almost of singular status as one of his closer acquaintances, and found three or four hundred other people all with the same belief in their privileged relationship to the departed.

For a couple of hours, people from Larry's liquor delivery man, who sang a splendid paean, to a sorrowful Cuban envoy, to many of his colleagues, tried to display what was so special about Larry. I learned new facts. Larry had once been on a boat with George Lardner and two girls, and had successfully proved that the ferry crossing between Edgartown and Chappaquiddick could be swum in darkness by journalists as well as by senators. Larry had, according to Murray Marder, invented the phrase 'credibility gap.' (Marder, with typical journalist's concern for a credit and glory in the afterlife, insisted on retaining 50 per cent of the copyright on the phrase.)

It was one of those times in which the orderly disposition of sorrow achieves the purpose of such ceremonial, the arrangement of grief within tolerable bounds, the fixing of memory and shared affection. It was also, in early August, a time when many attending journalists, briefly returned from vacations, were splendidly bronzed and fit, and thus more resplendent physical specimens than they usually are. Though informal, it was a noble occasion – delightful because journalists' obsequies are so often animated by ignoble, sentimental rites, and speeches too accurately mirroring the ignobility and sentimentality contaminating the profession.

Most of you, who never knew Larry, or who never read his work, may wonder why I should carry on so about him. I have owed a lot to Larry over the years. It's that sense of gratitude that caused a couple of friends to fly out from London for the day of commemoration in Washington. Journalism in America will be affected by his death. He could write the important stories, broker the important stories, which would start in the *Washington Post,* and filter into the *New York Times,* out-of-town papers, wire services and tv newscasts across the country. A progressive force in national journalism is gone, and we will feel the consequences. But aside from all of this, I was most fond of Larry – as so many people were – and the thought of him, no longer stertorously hospitable, now as still as a mouse, is as poignant as it was the day he died.

VV

November 19, 1979

The Greensboro Massacre

The murder of five communist demonstrators by Klan and Nazi gangsters has been greeted circumspectly by what passes for the American left. Though the spectacle of fascism running wild ought to evoke unhappy memories among liberals, most remain unseen and unheard. They are content to let consensus reign, in this case the notion (suggested by Anthony Lewis in a disgraceful column) that the Communist Workers Party brought the hail of bullets down upon itself by its 'provocative' behavior. This leads to a gruesome state of affairs: the *Times* mildly chastises the Greensboro police for lack of vigilance, while those same cops whisper that the commies really fired the first shot. Eventual acquittal of the guilty men seems likely, which will naturally encourage other white supremacist murderers, cross-burners and their kind.

Four of those killed were union activists. Three had organized workers in the Cone textile mills to fight for better conditions with the Amalgamated Clothing and Textile Workers Union, and another, Cesar Cauce, was trying to organize Duke Medical Center workers into the Federation of State, County and Municipal Employees at the time of his murder. Their political views were antagonistic to those of the unions' leaders – who incidentally call themselves socialists – which may be why the labor statesmen haven't bothered to excoriate the killers or those who let the slaughter be done.

Dignity would at least have required labor and its liberal allies to issue some proclamation of grief, some demand for justice if not revenge. Courage would demand issuance of a call for anti-fascist demonstrations in every major city – like the one sponsored by the Spartacists in Detroit. But our liberals are too busy with Teddy, and labor is getting ready to elevate Lane Kirkland as Meany's successor. Action against native fascism is left in the hands of the Trotskyists and other sectarians, who at least can understand the meaning of murder when they see it.

VV

June 9, 1980

Forever Albion

My brother Patrick went to a party in London the other day and bumped into the Duchess of St. Albans. 'What do you do?' she asked. Patrick said he worked for the *Financial Times*. 'Oh good!' the Duchess exclaimed. 'Perhaps you can tell me if Lord Cowdray has got his grouse in yet.'

VV

July 16, 1980

Reagan in Detroit

DETROIT – Behind the purported business of this Republican convention – the forging of harmony, happiness, and the selection of a vice-presidential candidate – lurks the all-important question of whether the enormous gamble that carried Ronald Reagan triumphantly through the primary season and into Detroit will pay off, or explode in his face.

The gamble is everywhere to see and hear: in Reagan's arrival speech at the airport, where he reached out to Detroit's unemployed, made a play for the blue-collar vote, and flayed the government for their problems; in his remarks at the Detroit Plaza hotel as young Reaganites festooned the concrete galleries; in the party's platform; and in the perception here that a new age for the Republican Party might be at hand, rivalling the Democratic turnaround of 1932.

The gamble is this: whether untried economic prescriptions, barely understood by many of Reagan's closest spokesmen and hotly contested by many of his most important advisers, will survive as the engine of the Republican juggernaut, or whether they will shake apart when serious campaigning begins in the fall.

The prescriptions that triumphed in Reagan's mind and in the party platform, amount to the bald assertion that life will improve for all, growth be assured, inflation controlled, production enhanced, and jobs increased and made secure through big tax cuts and a ferocious assault on government regulation.

The Reagan of early 1976 crashed amid much ridicule of his lunges toward fiscal restraint, ill-timed attacks on the Social Security system, and constant volleys at the imprudent and thriftless poor. The Reagan of 1980 is thus far 'The Good Shepherd' of the famous New Hampshire campaign ads, vowing that 'We must go forward, yet none must be left behind.'

The party platform ratified here provides the idiom of the ideological shift:

'To those individuals who have lost their jobs because of the Carter recession, we pledge to insure that they receive their rightfully earned unemployment-compensation benefits.

'The Republican Party recognizes the need to provide workers who have lost their jobs because of technological obsolescence or imports the opportunity to adjust to changing economic conditions. In particular, we will seek ways to assist workers threatened by foreign competition.'

The platform wrap-up is an absolute reversal of the policies normally associated with a Republican government. They have the life-enhancing uplift of New Deal rhetoric: 'We propose to put Americans back to work again by restoring real growth without inflation to the United States economy. ... We must replace the Carter administration's promise of hard times and austerity – one promise which has been kept – with Republican policies that restore economic growth and create more jobs.

'The Democratic Congress and the Carter administration are espousing programs that candidate Carter in 1976 said were inhumane: using recession, unemployment, high interest rates, and high taxes to fight inflation. The Democrats are now trying to stop inflation with a recession, a bankrupt policy which is throwing millions of Americans out of work. They say Americans must tighten their belts, abandon their dreams, accept higher taxes, less take-home pay, fewer jobs, and no growth in the national economy.

'We categorically reject this approach. Inflation is too much money chasing too few goods. Shutting down our nation's factories and throwing millions of people out of work leads only to shortages and higher prices.'

The audacity of all this is breathtaking, and would require nothing less than a miracle from the Almighty God to whom the convention prays almost without cease. (Sample, from the Monday prayer breakfast for 1000 delegates: 'For a greater respect for human life in our country and for the protection of all life, especially for the unborn, let us pray to the Lord.') The same platform that implies reduced revenues from taxation calls for the largest defense increases since World War II. The same platform that speaks with words of understanding and mercy to the poor calls also for attrition in federal efforts to help them, with the proposition that Reagan's tax-cut boom would hurtle a poor black into vigorous self-made prosperity before he had time to crash bankrupt and unhelped into the poorhouse and the grave.

An oft-heard cliché of the convention is that the Republican Party is still uncertain whether it wants to be doctrinally pure, or to win the election. The cliché is based on the anti-ERA and anti-abortion planks developed last week. Yet, a more accurate observation would be, whether the Republican Party will get away with the new premise that it is the party of economic compassion and growth.

The bones of most delgates here ache with ancient verities: that almost everything wrong with the economy and society as a whole can be traced to big government, regulation, and the lack of a balanced budget. This translates into equally ancient verities: a better deal for business, a cutback in social expenditures, and healthful doses of recession and unemployment whenever necessary.

This is traditional Republicanism, and almost all Republicans here in Detroit essentially believe in the faith as devoutly as they ever did. Few of them profess to understand the theoretical ideas behind the New Reagan and his amazing supply-side, tax-cutting life-enhancing schemes. They seem content, all the same, as do the media, to let the hokum roll, and to sit back and enjoy it. The politics of compassion, they realize, has its uses, and it is better to say 'We won't need welfare,' instead of the old version, which was, 'We don't like welfare.'

The group that wrought this sea-change in Reagan's mind, and which has thus far won the battle for it, is that clustered around the congressman from Buffalo, Jack Kemp. It includes the economist Arthur Laffer, the supply-side propagandists, and publicist Jude Wanniski. Kemp's ideological triumph is embedded in the party platform, and his political prestige has been greatly enhanced as a result. By Monday, he was being toasted fondly by many delegates as the preferred conservative running mate to Reagan, the secret favorite of the governor himself, although common sense seemed to dictate the selection of the supposedly moderate and ecumenical George Bush, or a surrogate for same.

The exaltation of the Kemp-Laffer-Wanniski group is sometimes humorous to observe. 'The most important unobserved fact about Ronald Reagan,' Wanniski says, 'is his degree in economics in 1932, when classical economic theory was still in the curriculum. He is now the only global political figure with a certified diploma in supply-side theory.'

But there are Reagan advisers and backers who regard the Kemp group's intrusion into old shibboleths as menacing in the extreme. They sense the dangers of the gamble: that in the fall campaign season, under pressure, Reagan could falter, become torn between conflicting counsel, and crash between Kemp's supply-side boosterism and the old search-and-destroy economic policies of Arthur Burns, Alan Greenspan, George Schultz and the other heavies from Bechtel, the AEI, and corporate America.

Hence the con game. The Republican Party – as anyone interviewing delegates here will rapidly discover – remains, despite 'The Good Shepherd' sentiments, antilabor, anticonsumer, and the spokesman for owners and big business. Between old Nixon-funder and Detroit millionaire Max Fisher, circling a Renaissance ledge party with his bodyguard, and the black Republican delegates – less than 3 per cent of the total – gathered in a chop house four miles up Woodward Avenue, the party's center of gravity lies very definitely with Fisher and his cohort. So much for Lincoln and the new spirit allegedly prevailing.

The sleight of hand, executed by the Kemp faction, is to adorn the visage of Republicanism, red in tooth and maw, with the lineaments of social justice and thus give the old actor his latest role – the savior of the common man.

VV, with James Ridgeway

November 19, 1980

The Present Situation in Israel: Interview with Israel Shahak

'It would be a good thing, I think, for Americans to ask themselves once a year whether the U.S.A. was a democracy before 1865; that is, before the constitutional abolition of slavery ... The situation of the state of Israel and of the territories occupied by it is quite analogous. In the territories there do not exist the smallest vestiges of democracy. Very simply, the military governor is the legislator, the executor of the laws and the judge, and he does what he wants ... Just as the situation of the occupied territories resembles that of the pre-1865 South, so the situation inside the state of Israel resembles that of many states of the U.S.A. some 50 or 60 years ago when racism was popular and when the really influential Ku Klux Klan made and unmade politicians, just as Gush Emunim does now in Israel ...'

The author of these remarks is Israel Shahak, professor of organic chemistry at Hebrew University, Jerusalem, and one of the most uncompromising and outspoken crusaders for human rights in Israel today. Shahak was born in Warsaw in 1933, as a boy was in the Nazi concentration camp of Belsen, and came to Palestine in 1945. 'I lost,' he says, 'my Zionist beliefs in 1956. In 1968 I made my decision to begin acting.' He is chairman of the Israeli League for Civil and Human Rights, and to subscribers around the world he performs the invaluable service of monitoring, translating from the Hebrew press, and dispatching twice a month copious extracts, along with his own commentary. 'I decided,' he recalls 'that what was needed is to publish reliable material from the Hebrew press, whose writers cannot all be described as "self-haters and anti-Semites."'

Dr. Shahak is briefly visiting the United States. He outlines below his profound alarm at the right-wing extremist tendencies accelerating in Israel, the disastrous state of the economy, the status of human rights, the prospects for the future.

'A crisis there must be,' Dr. Shahak remarks. 'Without a deep and serious crisis the majority of Israeli Jews (who are the only ones to count since the idolatry of the majority of American Jews inhibits their power of thinking on this subject) will, very democratically, continue to support the racist system and the oppression of the Palestinians and will agree only to such a peace which will allow the oppression to proceed peacefully. As the experience of 1973 has shown, after a warlike crisis, many of them are capable of change. The awful economic situation of Israel, itself created by the militarization of the economy by U.S. money, brings another possibility: an economic crisis caused by a limitation or cessation of American aid to Israel. However painful such an economic crisis will be, it will be less painful than what the Palestinians in the occupied territories suffer right now, and of course much less so than a war.'

Let's start by talking about the security aspects of retaining, or relinquishing the occupied territories.

Israel Shahak: The manner in which Israelis of all shades of opinion speak among themselves or even seriously discuss these matters in papers or magazines is completely different from the presentation abroad both by the government and by the Labor Party. Therefore I will give you not only my own opinion but serious opinion in Israel about this.

First, all Israelis, by upbringing, are soldiers. I too. We speak as soldiers and only put our military knowledge to different uses. Military danger is danger from an army. Unless a society destroys itself, which happens very rarely, it is only in danger from foreign armies. To put it even more bluntly, if you take the actual number of Israelis killed, the largest number have been killed by Egyptian armies, simply because it was always the biggest army. So the problem is one of danger from armies.

So long as the situation in the Middle East remains as it is now, so long as there are states in the Middle East which may be presumed to be hostile to Israel I quite agree and accept that Israel needs military security which can be achieved exactly on the Egyptian model: patrols, observation posts, observation from the air, and if the Israeli Army says it needs certain anti-tank ditches in Sinai to be observed and kept open by patrols, I accept this.

But we don't need two things: first of all we don't need settlements. Ninety-five per cent of Israelis admit this. It is quite obvious that settlements are a hindrance to military defense. Those who defend settlements, but not for religious reasons, will therefore use psychological factors and argue that if a soldier knows that there is a home inhabited by children behind him he will fight better. To which I as a soldier say this is bullshit. The soldier fights worse, and will fight best when he is relatively near to his own home. Israeli soldiers did not fight well beyond Suez. The second condition is that the soldier must be in open territory. A settlement with families affects his morale worse and not better.

The second condition – here you can read the opinion of General Dan Shomron, head of the southern command, also the commander of the Entebbe operation – is that basically the willingness to fight depends on the state of society.

Israeli society is very obviously being destroyed from within. Shomron, by the way, attributes this more to the settlements than I do. I attribute it more to the economy. But at any rate it is destroyed from within. Israel now has a strong air force, because it is a matter of pilots and they are paid well. It has good elite units, because they are manned from kibbutzim and from graduates of certain high schools and not from the general population; but the general army units are already corrupted, first of all by discontent. The Israeli army itself says that it is now common for soldiers to attack their officers, in cafes, on football fields, on the way to their homes in the cities and so on.

They attack them?

Yes.

Mutiny?

Not mutiny. If officers beat their soldiers and punish them in many humiliating ways, then what will the soldier who has been humiliated by being tied to a bed or to a post do? Five will suffer it, two will grumble, and three will get some friends, and see where it is easy to beat the officer.

If you want another example, a scandal discovered in late October was that many permanent army personnel whose duty was to make routine inspection, servicing and cleaning tank engines, decided that their workload was too great, so they put sand and such into the engines. Thus they were ruined completely, and then – bureaucratically – had to go to another department, and the men did not have to work on it.

An army in which such things have happened many hundreds of times is an army that has been corrupted.

There is no doubt that Israeli society, including the army, is being destroyed from the inside.

You have talked about a renaissance of mystical thinking in Israel today. What do you mean by this?

Jewish mysticism conquered the Jewish world in the 16th century and was a dominant form for about 200 years, until the affair of the false messiah. The mysticism survived among many actinomian sects which believed in the false messiah, which condoned the most extreme forms of sexual license as religious acts and so forth. The mysticism itself was driven underground, and except for very small groups, Jews did not particularly indulge in mysticism in the 19th and 20th centuries. The reason was of course the Jewish enlightenment.

From the '30s on there were mystical tendencies in Palestine. But it suddenly burst forth as a reaction to the October 1973 war and is the ruling principle of the Gush Emunim, 'the bloc of the faithful,' which organizes the settlers. The leaders of this movement really believe that what they are doing is an act of mystical significance, of religious importance, and an act which will override all other things.

In addition they really have eschatological beliefs. They think that their rabbis have had revealed to them by dreams, by portents, by contemplation, the intimation that the end of the world is near. But whether this is a matter of months or decades depends on them. If they are firm, settle more, especially if they come to rule Israel and lead Israel, then not only is the help of God assured to them – and literally they shout, like the crusaders, 'God is with us' – but they are assured of victory in any circumstances.

This mysticism is extremely dangerous. If you accept religiously the validity of the 16th and 17th century mysticism, then you have the basis for their conclusions. It has parallels to fundamentalism. If you accept the idea that Jonathan Edwards was right in the 18th century, many things that Jerry Falwell says now follow.

This Jewish mysticism inflates the coming of the messiah to a cosmic rather than Jewish event. In normal Judaism the messiah will redeem Israel; the Jewish people will conquer the land of Israel, build the temple and that is all. There will be a Jewish state, and the world will go on as before. In Jewish mysticism the coming of the messiah is a cosmic event. The messiah redeems the fall of Adam and Eve. The world is full of the power of Satan – I don't have to give you the parallels – and Satan prevents cosmic salvation. It will be the messiah, with the help of mystic contemplation of right-thinking Jews, who will redeem the whole world. No sacrifice is too great to achieve this goal.

The important thing is that this right-wing minority of 10 to 12 per cent believes and follows orders. In this authoritarian strain, the great rabbis are those who read the portents and issue orders; they are heads of the academies, and scholars even after 10 years follow their orders and indoctrinate.

With people like Begin there is a double sort of attitude to this. On one level he disagrees with them, but on another he respects them – rather like Reagan with the fundamentalists in Texas.

Such attitudes give the Gush Emunim enormous power, and without a Labor victory they will continue to have power.

The right-wing religious fanatics compose the most dangerous group, socially and politically, that has existed in the entire history of Israel.

So what are the opposing ideological strains?

Liberal bourgeois democracy, as a tradition, has remained very strong in Israel. In fact, one of the reasons why things are so different in Israel and the territories is that they have different systems of law. Bourgeois democracy very easily escapes from the reality, as under the British empire, that there is freedom in London and oppression in Bombay.

How would you describe the situation as regards human rights in Israel and the occupied territories?

If you exclude the occupied territories there is no doubt that Israel is a democracy both in its formal apparatus – voting, parliament, government and so on – and, much more important, in freedom of opinion. In the last five years it has increased, and it has also increased under the Begin government. The government – inside Israel – is employing censorship against Israeli papers less and less. In the '60s especially, the Labor government employed a great deal of censorship. Ten years ago the legal office of the government used to try to prosecute poems, leaflets, minority publications. This has ceased. It has something to do with Begin's legalistic nature, and a faction in the Labor Party constantly attacks Begin for allowing extreme groups, especially Palestinian groups within Israel, to publish.

The Israeli public draws a very firm line between what should or should not be allowed within Israel for all Israeli citizens, and what should or should not be allowed in the occupied territories. This public will allow enormous repression of opinion in the territories, but will support an enormous amount of freedom within Israel.

Within this Israeli society, which is very democratic and free, there is a basic discrimination in all systems, legal and social.

Take land and housing. The land is officially divided into 94 per cent belonging to the state of Israel, administered jointly by the Israeli Land Authority and by the Jewish National Fund under regulations which expressly prohibit selling, renting and subrenting to non-Jews. The word 'non-Jew' is operative here. Non-Jews are not allowed to live in this area, buy or rent an apartment, open a business or even raise a tent. The other six per cent is private, and every owner can do what he wants with it. But even here pressure – especially in agriculture, on farmers who own their land not to allow the Arabs they employ to live on the land, not to give them a room or half a room or tents – is applied by cutting their credit. The government holds enormous power by its ability to extend cheap credit. If it cuts credit to a farmer he has recourse only to the higher commercial creditor, is finished and must submit. The Israeli government will persecute a Jewish farmer subrenting to an Arab who then employs other Arabs. For it is claimed that by such means, Arabs are sinking down roots in the land. The impulse here is not economical but national.

Take the question of Palestinian collaborators inside Israel, meaning Palestinian citizens who are jailers in prisons, who serve in special units in the Israeli army, and who are Shinbet (security service) agents. Even a Palestinian who has been an agent of Shinbet or Mossad (external security service) for many years is not allowed to live on Jewish land. He is rewarded by the state financially, receives housing, but the housing must be built on non-Jewish land. In all areas, within Israel there is a division between Jewish and non-Jewish. You can simply look at this Official Statistical Abstract of Israel. Take any statistic. Look at infant mortality. See, Jews, non-Jews. There are no Israelis in Israel. Here we are. Infant death by age, sex and population group. First this table for Jews, which specializes and categorizes in great detail: one month, three months, 11 months and so on, 12 categories. For non-Jews only four categories. Unless you make your own calculations you cannot know from this the infant death rates in Israel, of all Israeli babies. There are no Israeli babies in Israel.

And the situation in the occupied territories?

In the occupied territories the worst thing, to my mind, is the complete lack of democracy and freedom of expression as they exist in Israel. What happened in 1967 was that Israel decided to establish a permanent colony. Because of this, in the occupied territories all books are controlled. The military governor constantly publishes lists of forbidden books. Newspapers and other publications which are openly sold in Israel are forbidden in the territories. Pictures of flowers are forbidden if they are painted in the four colors of the Palestinian flag, white, black, red and green. Another example: a picture of a dove standing in a window was forbidden because the dove was painted with the petals of the kaffiyeh. In the last year the military government has tried to eradicate anything that symbolizes Palestine.

Even worse than this is the absolute power of the military governor. His regulations have the force of law. He can issue any regulations he wants, without any consultation with the Knesset.

Let me omit the deportations, which you know about, and mention a couple of examples, which affect the lives of many people in the occupied territories. Unknown here is the size and scope of administrative limitations imposed on the people, and also the control of the farmers.

The military governor can (and does) forbid Palestinians to move from their own villages or towns without permission. Thousands of Palestinians are now limited to their own villages. I tried to get a man in Ramallah, whose brother-in-law died in Bethlehem, to visit the funeral. Forbidden. None can say this three-hour daytime visit is a matter of security. This is persecution.

All political meetings are forbidden; all assemblies are forbidden; to hold sessions of the municipal council open to the public is forbidden. So when Palestinians want to meet to discuss their local affairs, they use social events, lunches, dinners, wedding receptions. Now under such a system there are spies and informers. So let us say it comes to the local military governor's attention that such and such a wedding reception the next day will really be an occasion on which the notables of the village discuss what to do about land confiscation. Then the normal and usual procedure inflicted on thousands of people is that they are called, usually in the middle of the night, and brought by soldiers to the office of the military governor who says, 'It has come to my attention you are attending a lunch. I hereby define this as a prohibited political assembly and you are forbidden to attend.'

I sacrifice discussion of torture and other things to show by such examples what it means to live under Israeli military occupation, and also how much it differs from Israel itself.

Now let us consider a Palestinian farmer in the occupied territories. Let us say he has some tomatoes. What is the procedure for him to sell his tomatoes in the nearest town, or to send them to Jordan or wherever (and 'wherever' excludes Israel, where the produce cannot be sold)? He must first go to his local mukhtar or headman, nominated by the military governor, and get a blank piece of paper with his personal stamp on it. With this he goes to the nearest military government offices. He then shows them the paper, which is torn, so the next time he will have to bring another. Then he applies for a permit to move or sell his tomatoes, but it is at the absolute discretion of the governor whether he gets the permit or not. Now tomatoes are perishable. I could as well mention grapes, by the way. And so a favorite method of collective punishment of villages or a whole area is to withhold those permits. It works. The notables of the village will go to the office of the military governor and, often in the presence of an American journalist, say what is required.

Such things show that in the occupied territories people are more firmly under the control of the military governor than in any other system I know of, excepting the old Portuguese system, especially in Mozambique. Even the Spanish in the old colonies in Latin America had nothing resembling this.

How efficient is the Shinbet in the territories?

It was my impression, also of others, that the Shinbet was very efficient in the territories until about 1975 or '76. Foreknowledge of demonstrations has now diminished. Palestinian guerrillas stand much less chance of being caught by the Shinbet. Leaflets are widely disseminated, and there is widespread underground political literary activity. Why the change? Two reasons, one Israeli and the other Palestinian. Until '75 and '76 the security agencies, Shinbet and Mossad, obeyed an unwritten rule that extremists from the left and right should be strictly excluded. Now right-wing fanatics, especially religious fanatics are being taken in. The oldtime Shinbet agents, taken from the political center, distinguished between Arab and Arab, and said there are 'good' Arabs who would be favored if, let us say, there was a threat of land confiscation. He would get a certification which would save him from being beaten, which gave him preference on the bridges over the Jordan.

From '75 and '76 but very rapidly after '77 when Begin came to power, with the injection of right-wing extremists, the Shinbet has treated all Palestinians alike, along the lines of a very famous saying now quoted in the Hebrew press, 'the only way to know what an Arab thinks is to break his head open.'

What is your analysis of the Israeli state and the conditions in which it finds itself today?

Historically? I did not understand it when I began my activities. I have understood it in the last four or five years. In the last four or five years I would agree with eighty per cent of the thesis of Edward Said, in his book *The Question of Palestine*, and also *Orientalism*. Basically the state of Israel was founded by people who were not conscious of the rights of non-Western people. Because of this, while very many of them tried to be just within their group, they had absolutely no sense of justice for people outside their group. Since they were Europeans or allies of Europeans, most of the injustices were against people not in this category. To this was added, for many of them, a very dangerous exploitation of certain biblical ideas – 'We are reconquering the land we conquered from Canaanites once.'

So you are saying that an essential strain is fundamentally racist?

It is fundamentally racist, but a combined racism, First Jewish racism and then Western racism: the feeling of Western superiority not habitual now but customary 40 or 50 years ago.

Do you think these trends have accelerated in the last few years?

There have been two periods of acceleration. Slow acceleration between '67 and '73/'74 and very quick acceleration between '74 and '80. You can say that Begin accelerated them even faster, but the basic trends were established in '74 and '75, including settler organization, mystical ideology, and the great financial support of the United States to Israel, whose dimensions have completely changed. Between summer '74 and summer '75 the key decisions were taken, and from that time it's a straight line.

The key decisions? One, increasing the size of what you call the military-industrial complex. Israeli inflation and the economy can be explained in classical economic terms: the pumping of enormous sums of money into unproductive sectors of the population, increasing salaries of unproductive people – army officers, army personnel and so on – increasing the number in uniform. The economic correspondent of the *Jerusalem Post* calculated that 24 per cent of Israeli males in the prime work age, between 18/20 and 45, are in uniform, meaning that they can't do anything for the economy.

The second decision was to keep the occupied territories of Palestine and some small areas of Sinai, the Rafa approaches and the airports near the border, which by the way I'm sure will not be returned – peace or no peace. The decision to hold and keep the territories was taken, and will be held, to keep the territories in the land of Israel, and some small areas around. Meaning apart from the Golan Heights and a small part of Sinai. Those are the key decisions from which everything followed.

Is it possible for the Israeli economy to be in any sense self-sufficient?

Extremely possible. We are really a people and a society which had already by 1967 achieved a high level of technology. Our agriculture is very good, and we export the irrigation techniques we invented to other countries in the world. The chemical industry before 1967 had very great potential. We are perfectly capable of establishing a modern economy based on the most modern technology and inventions, on agriculture and chemistry, also on the very high level of university and other educational facilities.

We were on this road around 1967. It was difficult, but we were on the road. Two things have sidetracked it. First, after '67 the very great influx of speculative capital which was then withdrawn after '73 but which was at the beginning like all speculative capital, as in Egypt, put into tourism, put into quick business, into the army's specialized production of weapons for export and things like this. But this was peanuts. There was still development until '73. From '74 there is no economic development in Israel because there is a flow of cheap money from abroad, from the United States, state controlled. I am afraid you will think I am a Milton Friedman-ite which I am not. But this is common sense. And this money all goes to unproductive things, to the military-industrial sector, to the army, to high salaries in the army so that all manpower is being sucked into the army. Let me give you an example. Under the special conditions of inflation we have two basic credit rates. The commercial rate, as you can imagine, is very high. The state-controlled rate is lower, and this induces every businessman to work for the ministry of defense, as much as he can. These are the conditions for the creation of inflation and the destruction of the productive part of the economy. To use the classical economic example, we are ruined by American money, just as Spain and Portugal were ruined by money from Mexico and Peru. Spain, especially, was a flourishing economy until it conquered South and Central America, and then it became the most decadent country in Europe. All economists attribute this unanimously to an influx of money which was not earned.

Just as Iranian society under the Shah was ruined by the influx of money, so in Israeli society, it doesn't really make a difference if the money is from the sale of Iranian oil or comes from the American congress. Money not earned by productive work, and thrown in vast amounts into any economic system, always creates inflation and ruins society, but makes the government stronger. The same Spanish government under which Spain was ruined in the 16th and 17th centuries was also the Spanish government which sent troops to Italy, to Germany, which carried on the war with the Dutch Republic. The result was that the Dutch Republic became the richest country in Europe and Spain remains the poorest.

And your ideas for a long-term solution?

The idea is more or less for non-discriminatory or non-racist state forms. The most one can hope for in the present situation, even under the banner of Utopia, is for a de-Zionized Israel within '67 borders – an Israel in which all forms of discrimination will be abolished and which will give the right to Palestinians from its territory to return. The right, by the way, can be controlled. Often when I argue about this in Israel my opponent says 'Well, a million Palestinians will enter at the same time.' I answer that it is the principle which is important and then, under realistic conditions, when the principle has been granted, you can say people can enter at the rate of 10,000, or of 50,000 or of 80,000 a year.

And what do you think will happen?

First of all, what may happen is catastrophe. Then I must tell you as a realistic man that the secular fascistic solution may be stable for a decade or so. If right-wingers come to power, you will have a catastrophe.

Here is a practical proposal to you. Discuss the basic facts of the oppression of the Palestinians by Israel as much as you can and going right down to the basics of the racism of everyday. Point out the obvious contradiction between what the majority of American Jews demand for themselves in the USA, and what they defend in Israel. Do not be intimidated in the struggle against racism and for human dignity, equality and freedom, by any demagoguery about peace and democracy, if they are used in the cause of discrimination, and perhaps the words of the prophet (Amos 5. 15) will come true: 'Hate the evil and love the good and establish judgment in the gate, it may be that the Lord God of hosts will be gracious to the remnant of Joseph.'

VV, with James Ridgeway

March 4, 1981

The Network

Right there, Sunday morning, we had *The New York Times* and the problem. On the front page of the main news section there is a report that Argentina's national police have arrested the leaders of that country's human rights movement. Reading on through the story to an inside page we find that the Inter-American Human Rights Commission's November report on Argentina 'supports the view that Argentina's military government has covered up the disappearance of more than 6,000 people who were arrested as suspected subversives between 1973 and early 1980.'

The word 'terrorism' is not used.

That same Sunday morning we had *The New York Times Magazine*. There was a big color picture on the cover of two masked men, one of them brandishing a pistol. And there too was the big word 'Terrorism' with the subtitle 'Tracing the International Network' and the author's name, Claire Sterling. At the start of the article inside an editorial subhead said, 'There is now extensive evidence, says the author, that for the last decade the Soviet Union and its surrogates have provided support for terrorists round the world.'

The story on Argentina did not include any information of backing provided to Argentina by the United States, as for example with the visit of David Rockefeller, post November 4, 1980, in which he told the Argentinian leadership that a new era of understanding of their problems had been launched with the election of Ronald Reagan. The possibility that one of the most powerful bankers in the US was thereby providing 'support' for 'terrorists' who have presided over the disappearance of 6,000 people was not mentioned.

In the bracing atmosphere of the new Reagan-Haig era, the latter's denunciation of terrorism, and his statement that it will replace human rights as the main concern of the administration, we should take a look at some journalistic uses of the word.

Sterling's article is dedicated to the proposition that terrorism in the world today is masterminded by the Soviet Union. It follows hot on the heels of a similar article in the magazine written by Robert Moss. Reading through the article we immediately understand that under the heading 'terrorism' is *not* included such activities as:

– the murder of Orlando Letelier, sponsored by Pinochet's Chile, against which government the terrorism-hating Reagan administration has hastened to drop all sanctions;

– 'disappearances', torture and systematic extermination of political dissidents as practiced in Argentina, Guatemala, El Salvador, Paraguay, etc., etc.

– the extermination, with the help of US weapons, of a significant slice
of the populace of East Timor;

– Israeli behavior in the occupied territories and Lebanon;

– novel techniques in the fostering of human rights as developed by such
US allies and friends as President Mobutu of Zaire, Prime Minister Botha
of South Africa, President Choi of South Korea, President Zia of Pakistan,
etc., etc.

These activities, it cannot be too heavily emphasized, are not terrorist,
but 'regrettably necessary', 'harsh', often 'tragic', sometimes 'authoritarian'
and at worst to be clustered under the label of 'repression' which is to
terrorism as chalk is to cheese.

As a rough rule of thumb, the more ample the scale of elimination of
opponents, the less 'terrorist' the exercise is. Carpet bombing by B-52s in
Vietnam was not terrorism. In fact, in the current spasm of rethinking
Vietnam, this bombing was simply and unfortunately unsuccessful, not per
se evil.

Intellectuals in this country prefer not to think too closely about terrorism or the uses to which the word is put. The best analysis of the semantics
of terror appears in Noam Chomsky and Edward Herman's *The Political
Economy of Human Rights* (South End Press, 1979). This work has not
been reviewed by the *New York Times*, the *New York Review*, nor indeed
by almost every other newspaper and journal in the United States. They
point out, for example, 'among the many symbols used to frighten and
manipulate the populace of the democratic states, few have been more
important than "terror" and "terrorism". These terms have generally been
confined to the use of violence by individuals and marginal groups. Official
violence, which is far more extensive in both scale and destructiveness, is
placed in a different category altogether. This usage has nothing to do with
justice, causal sequence, or numbers abused.'

Undaunted by such matters of definition Sterling proffers her terrorist
network. This kind of journalism is a little like dealing in Maria Teresas.
The currency is rather old. Of nine terrorists depicted on the opening page,
four are in jail, three are dead, one has defected and we are left with the
stand-by Carlos, without whom the terror-analysts would be poorer than
they are today.

Some specimens of Sterling's evidence that terrorism in the late 1960s
and 1970s came under the direction or indirect control of the KGB: the
four West Germans who kidnapped and then murdered the magnate and
former SS officer Schleyer were later discovered on a beach in Bulgaria by
some West German detectives taking a holiday there. Ergo ... the KGB
was behind the Baader Meinhof gang. Sterling does not mention that the
Bulgarian government extradited the four.

In an attempt to prove that Moscow is up to its trouble-making tricks there, Sterling takes a lengthy excursus into the recent political history of Northern Ireland, in which area she displays startling ignorance. For instance: 'they [the Provisionals] helped kill off a power-sharing plan in a new Northern Ireland assembly by planting 48,000 lbs of explosives ... Later in 1973 they helped consign the promising Sunningdale agreements to oblivion by breaking their own cease-fire – the last they would ever agree to – after only three weeks.'

Remembering that the power-sharing plan and the Sunningdale agreements were one and the same, we should bear in mind that a more destructive factor than Moscow guns-and-gold was the Protestant workers' strike of 1974, which was in fact when the agreement collapsed. Of course Paisley could turn out to be another tool of the Kremlin. Sterling doesn't go into this.

Characteristically, Sterling is an addict – as was the unlamented Brzezinski – of the croissant approach to geopolitics: 'More than half the international terrorist attacks since 1968, according to the CIA, have taken place in Western Europe and North America. The most deadly have come in a strategic crescent from Turkey westward through Italy and up to Ireland.'

Purists might quarrel with the honorific 'strategic' appended to the word 'crescent'. Brzezinski's crescent, or 'arc of crisis' lay to the south and east. Other analysts, in the *Wall Street Journal* for example, have detected a 'pretzel of provocation' twisting through Cuba, Nicaragua, El Salvador and Grenada. Others again espy the 'bagel of Bolshevism' surrounding and threatening to engulf Western values. The Hoover, Georgetown and Hudson gangs espouse the 'crumpet of catastrophe', a yeasty confection in which 'holes of subversion' such as the Institute for Policy Studies are linked by constantly circulating melted butter to the solid 'crumpet base' in Moscow.

Let us note Sterling's next paragraph, in which is the amazing statement that 'it is not happenstance that none of the major terrorist attacks have been directed against the Soviet Union or any of its satellites or client states.'

Since 1959 Cuba has sustained one US-sponsored invasion, at least eight attempts to assassinate Fidel Castro and countless acts of terrorist sabotage. Last year a Cuban envoy was assassinated on the streets of New York. Was this terrorism or not?

The word 'terrorism', is one of those immensely useful implements, like the 'Claude glass' or lens once used by landscape artists to focus and rearrange nature to advantage. In the minds of Sterling and innumerable Western journalists and intellectuals, it is not terrorism when a bomb planted by exiles explodes in a Cuban plane and kills 80 or so occupants. It is not terrorism when the South African government dispatches its forces on a raid against the Namibian refugee camp of Kassinga (as it did on May 4, 1978) and wipes out 600 people, more than the combined victims of Carlos, the Baader Meinhof gang and the Red Brigades.

The ideologists of terrorism à la Sterling are a fairly small group of journalists and academics, most, if not all, of them nicely funded by big corporations or sustained by academies and institutions. To use their language, they are tightly knit, dedicated to the overthrow of common sense and any sort of objective analysis. They are captive intellectuals of the state indulging in a spectacular *trahison des clercs*, nourishing the Reaganite vision.

In the network are to be found such operatives as:

– Robert Moss, based in England, has extensive links with the Pinochet regime, British intelligence, Israeli intelligence and the CIA.

– Arnaud de Borchgrave, recently headquartered in *Newsweek*, expelled across the frontier into freelance territory. Wrote *The Spike* with Moss.

– Michael Ledeen. Has received intensive training in psy-war and ideological sabotage techniques at Georgetown Center for Strategic Studies. Observed in close company of master terrorist Henry Kissinger, whose valet he was in the NBC-sponsored trip to Europe.

– Edward Luttwak. Military intellectual in Washington. Close contacts with the Israeli government.

– Brian Crozier, founder of the shadowy, ridiculous Institute for the Study of Conflict.

– Martin Peretz, editor in chief of the *New Republic*. Promoter of Moss, Ledeen et al.

There are others: Rael Jean Isaac, Jeane Kirkpatrick, Ernest Lefever, not to mention the entire *Commentary* gang.

VV

June 17, 1981

Trahison Des Clerical Department

Last week the Freedom to Write Committee of PEN held a meeting at the Public Theater on 'Disinformation, Internal Security and the Writer.' Spirited although meandering discussion between the likes of Arthur Miller, Victor Navasky, Nat Hentoff, Marcus Raskin and Midge Decter took place. There have been reports of the discussion, but as a footnote I would like to quote Sean Gervasi, most recently a consultant to UNESCO on relations between intelligence agencies and the media, on disinformation.

'The background of this discussion tonight is 35 years of institutionalized lying to the public, manipulation and deception of the public. A careful historical analysis of publicly available documentation makes very clear what the problem is and why we are confronted with it particularly now. We have to remember that in the period when the CIA was created, a system of systematic manipulation of public opinion across the whole world was put in place; this system functioned by sending instructions from the CIA to place false, fabricated, misleading or distorted information through assets in the media, through owned news organizations or through individuals who were either paid CIA officers or contract agents, into the world press for the manipulation of opinion for particular purposes.

'We are now paying the piper for having a system of such poisonous capacity function in our society. Disinformation was what was perfected by that machinery, and it is now being introduced into American political life in a way it was never introduced before, because this society is in crisis and because this is a weapon which can be used. We have to guard against it very seriously.

'When Midge Decter talks about free argumentation I have to laugh, because in a political climate which is influenced so profoundly by the constraints placed upon it by this kind of manipulation, we don't have the kind of freedom that we have in many other Western societies. The CIA is the largest news agency in the world today. They define the climate of opinion. By UNESCO estimates in 1978 they were spending almost $300 million a year; they had 1000 men in the field; they had 2000 people at Langley and other places in the US manufacturing lies into reality. The simplest way to explain disinformation is to relate an exchange between my brother Tom Gervasi and Daniel Graham, former head of the Defense Intelligence Agency. My brother cited some statistics and Graham said, "Well, those come from the Center for Defense Information. That's associated with that commie outfit the Institute for Policy Studies." And my brother said, "Since when is the IPS a commie outfit?" And Daniel Graham said, "It's all in *The Spike*." My brother said, "That's a novel." Not to Danny Graham, that's the point. This is the frightening thing about disinformation used on such a systematic scale. It's not simply lying. It's calculated inversion of the truth which now takes place on a massive scale in our society.'

Amid such sentiments, and contrary effusions from other members of the panel, practical reality – and the overall matter of solidarity in the face of assault – was introduced by Bill Schaap, co-editor of the *Covert Action Information Bulletin.*

In recent years this *Bulletin* has made a practice of researching and then publishing the names of CIA personnel. In the present torpor of the Fourth Estate, it must be one of the few investigative operations still under way.

Unsurprisingly, it has become the focus of much congressional, executive, and indeed editorial outrage, and the target of a bill, not yet passed into law, known familiarly as the Agent Identities Protection Act.

Remarking, by way of introduction, that the 'major instrumentality' of disinformation in the world today is the CIA and not the Soviet Union, Schaap asked the panel whether its members thought it proper for a law such as the prospective act mentioned above 'to criminalize the publication by private citizens of unclassified information obtained from unclassified sources.' (Schaap and his colleagues establish CIA identities by just such research into unclassified sources.)

Floyd Abrams, prominent lawyer on First Amendment issues, who has already testified against the act in congressional hearings, agreed that it violated the First Amendment, adding of Schaap's *Bulletin* that 'I do not think [it] serves the public good by what it does.'

Whereupon the following colloquy, richly evocative of New York intellectual life, took place:

Navasky (editor of *The Nation*): Do you think it useful, every time you are commenting on the constitutional right of someone who is basically under attack in our Republic today, to dissociate yourself from their positions in the way you did in the case of *Covert Action*?

Abrams: No, I don't, but so long as Mr. Schaap is here and makes a speech about the benefit to the public, as he views it, of his publication, I thought my First Amendment rights went at least as far enough to respond.

Navasky: They do. My suggestion is that that's one of the things in the past that weakened and fragmented the ability of people who were targets to resist the oppression that occurred.

Abrams: I don't view myself as part of a cause, Victor. I view myself as responding on my own behalf as best I can when I perceive First Amendment interests, including *Covert Action Information Bulletin*, to be interfered with ...

Decter (*inter alia* wife of Norman Podhoretz): ... I think the category of usefulness, as it was used [by Navasky], is a call to close ranks. The call to close ranks is every bit as dangerous as it has been helpful ... that is again an attempt to interdict dissent and discussion. It's not a legal demand but a spiritual demand, and I think it is very bad ... I think it is intellectually about one of the most harmful, deleterious and dangerous things that we can do is to accept that notion and I beg you all not to.

Navasky: Is it useful for a group of people who have reason to believe that they are going to be called before congressional committees and interrogated about their political beliefs, is it useful for those people, to dissociate ourselves from their political beliefs ... I meant to ask that question because my study of the '50s says to me that it was very harmful, to both the victims of that period, and the possibilities of resistance, for everybody who wanted to defend the rights of targets of the congressional investigating committees to have to go through the ritual of dissociating themselves from the positions of the people who were called up there.

Decter: That is why I am against congressional investigating committees. But we are having public debate and discussion ... and if there were no congressional committees, then it would seem to me that we ought to be engaging in public discourse, which is supposed to meet criteria of discourse and not of political convenience or advantage.

Raskin (co-founder of Institute for Policy Studies): Mrs. Decter knows that we live in a situation where Congress and an extremely right-wing government are in control, and where it is the case that books are written for the specific purpose of attempting to destroy individuals. That is something that will be used by the state apparatus ... Floyd Abrams shouldn't withdraw and shouldn't be so frightened. There is a First Amendment, which should be protected, but there is also a state apparatus to be confronted.

Hentoff (*Voice* columnist, friend of the First Amendment and the unborn, noted overkiller): That really is outrageous! I think the point Midge made is exactly correct, that if Floyd has any credibility, it is because he doesn't unify if he doesn't feel like it at the time. He will defend *Covert Action* ... to make him some kind of weak, timorous person is crazy.

Raskin: I am not saying in any way that he is a weak or timorous person. He is obviously quite the reverse, but that is another point. In the history of the 20th century, in terms of the liberal position with regard to the defense of individuals, the view was to take an arm's length relationship to those people. That arm's length relationship gradually redounded not to the poor situation those people were in but to liberalism itself, because liberalism itself turned out to be contentless. That's the danger we now face. Liberalism must be predicated on content. That is what has to be confronted by Floyd Abrams and others of us who call ourselves liberals.

This last remark of Raskin's is, I think, a good description of the liberal community as represented in various sections of the Fourth Estate, complicit with Reaganism until it is too late to behave in any other fashion, bellowing about the First Amendment after the prison doors have slammed.

Contentless liberalism today argues, or even merely reports (in the work of newspapers) on terrain staked out by the right and only produces a liberal passport when questioned closely about its credentials. Thus, whereas in the early '70s the Fourth Estate was, in important sectors, a counterweight to state power, it is today complicit with that power, part – if you will – of the same 'disinformational' network. The true work of the Fourth Estate has once again receded to the margins of the Estate.

VV

August 12, 1981

Working-Class Heroes at Home and Abroad

The New York Times

U.S. Edition, Tuesday, August 4, 1981

'"Maybe we are crazy," said Michael Fermon, a vice president of the striking Professional Air Traffic Controllers Organization. Then again, maybe the controllers, like most everyone else, would just like to work shorter hours for higher pay.

'Whatever the merits of their case – and they appear to be dubious – the air controllers have no right to hold up the nation. President Reagan's tough threat to fire workers who are not back at work by Wednesday is appropriate. A settlement that rewards them for illegally withholding vital services would be a serious mistake ...'

Polish Edition

'"Maybe we are crazy," said Milosz Fermonkiewicz, a Solidarity leader. Then again, maybe the shipworkers, like most everyone else, would like to work less hours for more zlotys.

'Whatever the merits of their case – and they appear to be dubious – the shipworkers have no right to hold up the nation, which, under the leadership of the Polish Workers Party, is striving to raise productivity. Prime Minister Jaruzelski's tough threat to fire workers who are not back at work by Wednesday is appropriate. A settlement that rewards saboteurs of the national economy would be a serious mistake, and would merely offer comfort to the enemies of socialism.

U.S. Edition

'... although their work certainly requires discipline and creates stress, it is hard to feel much sympathy for the controllers. There is no evidence that the work is debilitating. At a time when other Federal employees are asked to accept a 4.8 percent rise, there is little justification in giving them more than twice that much ...'

Polish Edition

'... It is undeniable that the shipworkers occasionally endure harsh conditions, but no thoughtful Pole need feel sympathy for them. There is no evidence that their work is debilitating. And when other comrades are making heroic sacrifices, the shipworkers are not ashamed to demand extraordinary economic privileges ...'

U.S. Edition

'... but beyond that, the equities here are really beside the point. The controllers have no legal right to promote their interests by damaging the national economy. If President Reagan were now to sweeten the deal already cut in June, he would only be inviting other Government employees in key positions to exploit their leverage. Living temporarily without regular air service is a heavy burden. Restoring it on the controllers' terms could be a disaster.'

Polish Edition

'... but beyond that, the equities here are really beside the point. The saboteurs have no right under the Polish Constitution and the principles of socialist legality to promote their own selfish interests at the expense of the national economy. If Prime Minister Jaruzelski were to exceed the agreement already reached, he would only be inviting other groups of saboteurs and friends of imperialism to exploit their leverage. The saboteurs should know that whatever the price in lost production, the Government will never surrender.'

The Washington Post

Union-Busting Edition, Tuesday, August 4, 1981

'The air traffic controllers strike is a wildly misconceived venture that deserves the government's extraordinarily severe response. A strike against an essential public service is always wrong in principle. It is also illegal, and the controllers' attempt to demolish the law is doubly wrong ...'

Freedom-Loving Edition

'The Polish shipworkers strike is an extraordinarily gallant venture and that makes the Polish government's fierce response all the more heavy-handed and abhorrent to all friends of freedom. The right to strike is one of the inalienable attributes of a democratic society. Only in the "workers paradises" east of the Iron Curtain is that right denied. Talk by the Polish regime of infractions of internal "socialist legality" is patently self-interested. The shipworkers' noble attempt to expose such socialist "legality" as a form of slavery is entirely laudable ...'

Union-Busting Edition

'... nor do the controllers seem to understand the position in which they have put President Reagan. He has just bet his presidency on his economic programs. But interest rates won't come down until people see inflation coming down, and economic analysts are currently warning their clients that there's not much evidence yet of any change in the underlying rate of inflation. That underlying rate is, essentially, the rate at which wages are rising. The money markets are watching wage settlements with fixed attention ...'

Freedom-Loving Edition

'... The position in which the shipworkers have placed a government attempting to reform a static economy is one entirely of that government's making. Mismanagement, chronic shortages, and now inflation are all endemic to the ineptly-run socialist economy of Poland. The demands of the shipworkers may seem superficially to place that economy under greater strain, but this is a short term view of crisis. The shipworkers are demanding a greater say in their work schedules, a feeling that they are more than mere robots in a system. The wage demands are symbolic and the symbolism is urgent. This is why all friends of freedom must pray that the shipworkers will prevail.'

VV

October 14, 1981

Death on the Nile

'Magnificent, Poirot!'

Hastings clapped Poirot heartily on the back as the little Belgian delicately touched his magnificent mustaches with a napkin and gazed with disfavor at the half-empty cup of hot chocolate on the hotel breakfast tray.

'*Mon cher* Hastings,' he murmured, 'would you not think that the Nile Hilton could prepare a proper *chocolat*?'

'But Poirot,' exclaimed Hastings, ignoring his friend's complaint, 'to have succeeded where the intelligence services of five countries failed! To have solved the most sensational crime of the decade, the murder of President Sadat!'

Poirot made a lame pretense of modesty. '*C'était pas difficile, mon brave*, if one only uses the eyes and the brain. Let me explain how I came to my conclusions.'

He leaned back and half closed his eyes.

'The first task was to consider the circumstances of the crime. You will recall that the military authorities were quick to announce that the deed had been perpetrated by four members of the Takfir Wa Higra, meaning "Atonement and Pilgrimage", and that this desperate faction of the Muslim Brotherhood had acted independently of any foreign power.

'Now it did not require great exercise of what you, Hastings, like to call the little gray cells, to see that this is obviously what the Egyptian military authorities would say in order to postpone inevitably embarrassing questions about the quality of their own intelligence, and indeed possible complicity of the armed forces in the murder. In our dark century, it is always cleaner to have as our American friends say, "the lone gunman", or in this case four lone gunmen.

'But of course the correct question to ask was why the dog did *not* bark in the night. Who might have known the plans of these four dedicated assassins and not warned Sadat?

'So I had to consider the question of motive, objectively and without prejudice.

'First, who was the immediate beneficiary of the deed? Hosni Mubarak.'

'Great Scott, Poirot,' Hastings burst in. 'Mubarak, the friend, the disciple of Sadat! Surely you could discount . . .'

Poirot raised an indulgent hand.

'*Mon cher* Hastings, you have the feelings the most decent. But I would remind you that we speak of power, of politics. We must not be sentimental. Let us discount Cairo gossip and the stories of Mubarak's relationship with Jihan Sadat. I do not think we have here a case of the eternal triangle. But consider Mubarak's situation. He was the creature of Sadat, as he himself said, the *vache qui rit*, just as Nasser would call Sadat "the black donkey". He was not insensible of Sadat's increasing unpopularity inside Egypt. And he knew of Sadat's occasional suggestions, as for example to Jimmy Carter a few weeks before his death, that he might step down next year and install Mubarak as President.

'Perhaps Mubarak asked himself, why wait? Perhaps in a year the situation would have been beyond recovery. Perhaps on Mubarak's last visit to Washington someone there too had the same idea.'

'The Americans?' Hastings exclaimed incredulously.

Poirot regarded his friend with amusement.

'Always you think with the emotions. As I said, we must consider all the motives, all the suspects, with dispassion. I did not say I thought the Americans were responsible, even if those reports that the American ambassador left the reviewing stand 15 minutes before the attack were, to say the least, tantalizing.

'Of course it is most unlikely that the Americans had any knowledge of the plot. Sadat was their best friend, their tool, in the Middle East. In many senses his death was an American event. It would perhaps have been more appropriate to have buried him in Arlington Cemetery. You will recall their childish predictions that the streets of Cairo would fill with millions of mourners the night of the murder, or the bizarre claim of *le Maire* Koch of New York that Egyptians saw Sadat as a father figure. The Americans had no sense that Sadat was unpopular with his own people, that by the end he was jailing not merely "fanatics" but generals, politicians, people of the left, journalists like Hassanein Heikal, even the leading Egyptian feminist, the *charmante* Nawal el Saadawy. As with the Shah, they could theorize but not actually comprehend that their client's days were numbered.'

Poirot sighed.

'*Les Americains.* Always, always they pick one horse. Always, always they pick the wrong horse. But we must not exclude the possibility that someone in Washington perceived that Sadat was becoming erratic and indiscreet. His boast, for example, to an American journalist that he was helping to supply the Afghan rebels. They cannot have liked that.

'In a sense of course the Americans killed Sadat. He isolated himself in the Arab world and in the eyes of many of his people with the Camp David agreements. And they gave him nothing! *Rien!* They let the Israelis get away with everything. They allowed Sadat to look like a fool, *un idiot!* Then, to make matters worse, they send three Presidents and Monsieur Kissinger to Cairo. So *le pauvre* Mubarak looks like the little lap dog.

'This is to speak in the wider sense. As actual accomplices, they are unlikely suspects. And of course Mubarak himself was in the stand. He was even wounded. If he was implicated he took enormous risks.

'But Mubarak was Sadat's liaison with the Saudis. And with the House of Saud we have a manifest motive.'

Poirot paused to mop the great dome of his forehead with a silk handkerchief.

'The heat, Hastings,' he moaned. 'The dreadful Egyptian heat. Do you not think the air conditioning in this hotel is *atroce*?' He plunged on without waiting for an answer.

'It is no secret that the Saudis had close ties with the Muslim Brothers. They financed some of their literature. You may perhaps not have observed, my dear Hastings, on the ill-furnished bookstalls of this great city,' Poirot made a fastidious *moue*, 'the lurid cover of the magazine *Al Dawa'a*. You do not suppose that the money for this evidently well-financed publication, the organ of the Muslim Brotherhood, comes from the humble piastres of the Cairene poor?'

'Rials from Riyadh, what?' said Hastings.

'They certainly would have had access to Takfir Wa Higra. For them Sadat was anathema, the traitor who flew to Israel. He was also the ally the US most worked with in the Arab world. Sadat, the traitor, they could never embrace. Mubarak, the man they have been in touch with, will be a different matter. Do you not think, *mon cher* Hastings, that the Saudis could have been sending the US a signal during the debate over that foolish plane, the AWAC? A signal saying, "You must deal with us. We, not Sadat, are essential to you in the area."'

He gazed quizzically across the room at Hastings.

'You are baffled, *hein?* For you, *mon cher*, these matters are a little tedious?'

'Of course I follow international events ...' Hastings began, rather stiffly.

Poirot smiled soothingly.

'I am just exercising a little drollery. Do not be offended. To continue with our suspects. We must of course consider the Israelis, the formidable Mossad.'

'My dear Poirot!' Hastings cried hotly.

Poirot continued without pause. 'By April of next year the Israelis would – perhaps still will, though I have my doubts – have had to hand back the rest of the Sinai. Messieurs Begin and Sharon would have had big problems with the Gush Emunim. There would have been bloodshed. Time and again they provoked Sadat beyond the endurance of any man. He accepted everything. He had patience, like a woman. He suffered every slight. Like the Americans, they killed Sadat in the larger sense. So perhaps the Israelis, aware of the *complots* against Sadat, fail in the final crisis to say that not all the conspirators have been arrested. Perhaps they think that without Sadat the "peace process" will finally die and they will not have to surrender the rest of the Sinai. Perhaps they will feel more free to attack in southern Lebanon. Remember, Hastings, I merely examine motives dispassionately.

'On the other side we have the PLO. They too had connections with Takfir Wa Higra. For them Sadat was the great betrayer. Since Camp David, Jerusalem has been annexed, the settlements doubled in number, south Lebanon destroyed. To be sure, they had the motive. It is possible that some PLO leaders saw Sadat as a tiny insurance against more fierce attacks by the Israelis and the Syrians. But when has the PLO leadership ever been entirely logical or consistent?

'*Nom d'un nom!*' Poirot interrupted himself, staring with horror at the shoes proudly deposited by a beaming waiter whom Hastings had just admitted to the suite. 'Hastings, can this be? The *garçon* has administered the polish to my shoes.' Poirot gazed mutely at his cherished patent leather footwear, which indeed bore witness to enthusiastic but misapplied effort.

The waiter was admonished, then dismissed with a look of cold fury from Poirot and a discreet gratuity from Hastings, and Poirot continued.

'I need scarcely speak of the Iraqis, or the Syrians, not to mention the followers of Khomeini. They very much desired to see Sadat dead. The leaders of these Arab countries know well the emotions of their own peoples. You will recall that no Arab diplomat dared attend the memorial meeting in the UN for Sadat.'

'Poirot, you are forgetting the KGB!'

'Always your favorite suspect, Hastings. *Bien sur*, the Russians had no love for Sadat, the man who expelled them from Egypt. They too must be included in the list.'

'And that filthy swine, Q'addafi.' Hastings clenched his fists. 'I'd like to get my hands on that cur!'

'*Pas de zèle, pas de zèle*, Hastings,' said Poirot beseechingly. 'Of course Q'addafi wanted Sadat dead. In his fantasies he probably sees himself as the leader of a united Libyan-Egyptian Republic. His agents too had ties with the Takfir Wa Higra. And Q'addafi knew well that Sadat's emissary, Mubarak, was discussing his overthrow with Washington only days before the assassination. We have here a motivation most manifest.

'And we must not forget the brave General Shazli, whom Sadat fired in 1973. Our friend the American intelligence officer tells us that at a speech in Boston last year at the Association of Arab University Graduates, Shazli more or less openly said he could dispose of Sadat in a coup d'etat, adding that he would be better for American policy in the Middle East than Sadat. Shazli was getting money from the Iraqis as well, presumably, as from the Libyans. And Shazli still had close ties with his colleagues in the Egyptian armed forces. But I think perhaps that there is more bluster to General Shazli than one might think.'

'I must say,' Hastings broke in, 'that as an old army man I find it damned odd how those assassins managed to get their truck in the right lane, get their ammunition and get the job done so efficiently. In my experience, you could train for an operation like that for months and still have something go wrong. Damned odd!'

'Precisely. As usual, you have hit the nail unerringly on the head. Is it not conceivable that commanders in the Egyptian army could have been aware of the plot? The army too was tiring of Sadat, as he had his little chats with *la belle* Walters. He had not only fired Shazli, but since then Gammasy, and Ibrahim Kamal. Sadat liked to disgrace his own pawns and allies, just to show he had the power to do so. Do not forget that the head of the Egyptian general staff and important officers were killed in a crash in the western desert not long before the assassination. The time-honored helicopter method. It was thought then that Sadat's security men, on his orders, might not perhaps have been uninvolved.

'And we have the extraordinary affair of the security guards, ordered to relax their vigilance around Sadat minutes before the *attentat*.

'Does not this arouse one's curiosity about the role of Abu Ghazaleh, Minister of Defense? He did, it is true, sustain some trifling wound. But his composure was much remarked amid that ghastly scene. Does this not suggest a man unsurprised by the sudden turn of events? Consider. Both he and Mubarak stood inches from Sadat while the assassins raked the reviewing stand with machine-gun fire. Do you not think the assassins performed this raking with extraordinary delicacy and discrimination?

'So now Mubarak and the army must coexist together. He will be careful not to displease them. I would not, all the same, much care to be in the shoes of that gentleman.' Poirot cast another sour glance at his own maltreated footwear.

After a moment's reflection, he said absent-mindedly, 'Ratchett.'

'Eh, what's that, Poirot?'

'You will recall, Hastings, the murder of Ratchett aboard the Orient

Express. An intriguing little mystery. But an instructive one, no?'

Poirot raised his eyebrows humorously as he studied the face of his faithful friend.

'Of course, Poirot! That's what gave you the clue!'

'Precisely. *They all killed Sadat.*'*

VV

---

* You have to be a Christie fan to get into this. His admirers may care to know that Christopher Hitchens supplied the line about the Cairene poor's humble piastres.

March 2, 1982

Khmer Chimera

Reading *The New York Times Magazine*, I was particularly struck by Christopher Jones's dramatic story of his journey to Cambodia, which was entitled 'In the Land of the Khmer Rouge'.

This Jones, who is described as 'a freelance writer who has been report-ing on Southeast Asia since 1978,' certainly had an exciting time for himself. Not only was he greeted on arrival in Khmer country by Chhorn May, who introduces himself as Pol Pot's Minister of State of Telecom-munications and Postal Services, but later on – in a somewhat improbable account – he is in a village attacked by Vietnamese helicopter gunships.

At the end of the battle, Jones peers through his field glasses and guess what? '... on the summit of a distant hillside, I saw a figure that made me catch my breath: a pudgy Cambodian, with field glasses hanging from his neck. The eyes in his head looked dead and stony [great field glasses]. I could not make him out in any detail, but I had seen enough pictures of the supreme leader to convince me, at that precise second, that I was staring at Pol Pot ... Thinking back on it now, I am fairly sure it was Pol Pot I saw – whoever he may be.'

Jones clearly has an uncanny knack for being in the right place at the right time. Even his departure from Cambodia across the Thai border has its aesthetic accoutrements, as inscribed in the last paragraph of the article:

'I looked back. By an old Cambodian cemetery a blind man was chanting the Ramayana, a part of Cambodia's cultural heritage, as he twanged a primitive guitar. What better personification of Cambodia could I have found than this old singer, whose heroic and poetic ballad had ceased to have any connection with anything I had just seen? Cambodia, a land possessed, its ancient hymns, like its temples, fallen on evil days. Of all dead lands, the most dead.'

The old singer seems to stimulate that creative imagination of Western writers. Back in 1923 Andre Malraux wrote his second novel, *La Voie Royale*, about Cambodia. It was translated by Stuart Gilbert and published in an American edition in 1935. In a famous passage on page 71, apparently unknown to (*Times* magazine editor) Ed Klein or his henchpeople, Malraux wrote:

'The atmosphere of decay reminded him of something he had seen at Pnom Penh: a blind man chanting the Ramayana as he twanged a primitive guitar. What better personification of Cambodia, of this land of decay, could he have found than that old singer whose heroic strains had ceased to interest any but the beggars and coolie-women squatting round him? Cambodia, a land possessed, and tamed to humble uses, its ancient hymns, like its temples, fallen on evil days; of all dead lands most dead.'

Of course if he was old when Malraux heard him in 1923 the singer must be quite marvelously venerable by now, but I dare say Jones was too enthralled, on his remote frontier crossing, to notice that.*

VV

*This item ultimately led to the exposure of Jones as someone who had made up his entire trip and successfully fooled the Times, *which was much embarrassed by the whole affair.*

January 15, 1982

Catching up with Joneses

'When a newspaper lies, it poisons the community. Every other newspaper story becomes suspect. The lie – the fabricated event, the made-up quote, the fictitious source – is the nightmare of any respected newsroom. It is intolerable not only because it discredits publications but because it debases communications, and democracy.' – *New York Times* editorial in the wake of the *Washington Post* Janet Cooke boo-boo.

'… It may not be too much to say that, ultimately, it debases democracy.' – *New York Times* editorial in the *New York Times* Christopher Jones boo-boo.

VV

20 January, 1982

The Plane That Never Was

Students of threat inflation ought to take a look at a very funny article by John Tierney in *Science 82* about attempts to build a nuclear-powered plane, which lasted from 1945 until they were finally killed by President Kennedy. Cost to the taxpayer: $1 billion. Results: nil.

It all started in Congress in 1945 when a witness at a hearing, J. Carlton Ward Jr., happened to mention the possibility of building a nuclear-powered plane. Ward was the president of the Fairchild Engine and Airplane Corp.

The senators seized on the morsel. 'You see a future for atomic power in an airplane?' cried Homer Ferguson. 'I think so,' replied Ward, who had never thought about it until that minute. 'Would you go so far as to say,' asked Senator Hugh Mitchell, 'that almost any amount of money spent by the government in well-conceived experimental programs in the development of the utilization of atomic energy as a propulsion force would be justified?' 'I think our nation can't afford to do otherwise,' Ward answered.

That was it. The Air Force got behind the idea, despite the fact that Oppenheimer, Teller and many others said it was nonsensical. Fourteen thousand people toiled in seven states. Problems arose: how to shield the crew from the reactor? Answer: use older men, who had already begotten children and who would therefore feel less concern about infertility and conceivably death. And so forth. 'If Russia beats us in the race for atomic bombers,' declared Senator Henry Jackson at an advanced stage of the futile scheme, 'our security will be seriously endangered.'

And so it would have been, but for the fact that there was no evidence that the Soviet Union was taking any interest in atomic-powered bombers. As always, the US press did its best. A cover story in *Newsweek* in 1956 ('The Coming Atomic Plane') reported as 'fact' that 'Soviet respect for the urgency of A-planes has undoubtedly been more pointed than American'. *Newsweek* added that 'Soviet designers probably waste little time on the niceties of keeping a crew well guarded from radiation.' So much for those older men.

Then, on December 1, 1958, *Aviation Week* announced, 'A nuclear-bomber is being flight tested in the Soviet Union.' There was even a little drawing of a long contraption with a red star on the side. *Aviation Week*'s editorial roared its grief: 'Once again, the Soviets have beaten us needlessly to significant technical punch ... How much longer can we "afford" this kind of leadership and survive as a free nation ...'

Senator Richard Russell appeared on television and spoke of the 'ominous threat to world peace'. President Eisenhower said two weeks later that there was not the slightest evidence of the Soviets ever having flown any such plane. It seems that US analysts were construing Soviet reports of US efforts to build the plane as Soviet reports of Soviet attempts to do same. Perfectly natural mistake, really.

It was almost over for the A-plane. When Kennedy killed the project, *Aviation Week* mourned: 'The epitaph now being carved on the tombstone of the program may well be the same as that engraved on our tombstone as a nation.'

VV

March 2, 1982

Adolf Hitler by A.W.

Interview's cover-story interview with Adolf Hitler, over lunch at Mortimer's with Andy Warhol and Bob Colacello, is full of interest for Führer buffs. Hitler is now becoming a fixture on the New York social scene, after some decades of seclusion in Asunción and Palm Springs.

BOB: Don't you wish you'd been able to spend Christmas in Berchtesgaden?
HITLER: Yes, it would have been fun to go along there and see them light the tree and all that sort of thing. Do you spend a lot of time in Europe, Andy?
AW: I have been going to Germany once a month. I think you would find it a bit changed.
HITLER: Blood mixture and the resultant drop in the racial level is the sole cause of the dying out of old cultures; for men do not perish as a result of lost wars, but by the loss of that force of resistance which is contained only in pure blood. All who are not of good race in this world are chaff.
AW: Gee. Maybe we should get a waiter and order.
HITLER: Just a salad for me, thanks. What about you?
AW: I'd like a medium cheeseburger and french fries and a lot of ketchup. Tom Enders was saying the other day that the Polish thing shows what a lot of trouble the Russians are in.
HITLER: Here fate seems desirous of giving us a sign. By handing Russia to Bolshevism it robbed the Russian nation of that intelligentsia which previously brought about and guaranteed its existence as a state. For the organization of a Russian state was not the result of the political abilities of the Slavs in Russia, but only a wonderful example of the state-forming

efficiency of the German element in an inferior race ... For centuries Russia drew nourishment from this Germanic nucleus of its upper, leading strata. Today it can be regarded as almost totally exterminated and extinguished. It was replaced by the Jew. Impossible as it is for the Russian by himself to shake off the yoke of the Jew by his own resources, it is equally impossible for the Jew to maintain the mighty empire forever. He himself is no element of organization, but a ferment of decomposition. The giant empire in the east is ripe for collapse. And the end of Jewish rule in Russia means also the end of Russia as a state. We have been chosen by fate as witnesses of a catastrophe which will be the mightiest confirmation of the soundness of the folkish theory. I was saying this sort of thing back in the 1920's. In the mid 1940's I thought I might have been wrong, but now I think time is proving the essential soundness of my arguments.

BOB: Did you enjoy being Führer?

HITLER: Well, it was wonderful, mostly. First of all, to have been there and had that sense of history was very exciting and interesting. And you had a chance to meet some wonderful people, interesting people that you wouldn't have met otherwise. You were in a position to become involved in things and do things that you wouldn't have done ordinarily. So it was great.

BOB: It must have been hard, though. I suppose you have more time for shows and movies now. Have you seen Taxi zum Klo?

HITLER: No. If a proletarian tells me what he thinks, I can cherish the hope that some day this brutality can be turned toward the enemy. When a bourgeois indulges in daydreams of culture, civilization and aesthetic joys of the world, I say – at least I used to say – 'You are lost to the German nation! You belong in Berlin's West End! Go there, dance your nigger dances till you're worn out, and croak!' Just let me peek at the dessert cart. Andy, do you want some strawberries?

AW: Oh, not for me.

HITLER: I'll just take one helping of chocolate mousse. Just one. God, not that much.

AW: The Shah used to worry about the Russians too.

HITLER: Can't you see that Bolshevism is a conception of the world which is on the point of subjecting to itself the entire Asiatic continent, and will gradually shatter the whole world and bring it down in ruins? Bolshevism, if it proceeds unchecked, will transform the world as completely as in times past Christianity did. Thirty or 50 years count for nothing where fundamental ideologies are at issue.

BOB: At least the new Administration recognizes this.

HITLER: Up to a point. But there is this stupid lip service to democracy. It is absurd to build up economic life on the conception of achievement, on the value of personality, and therefore in practice on the authority of personality, but in the political sphere to deny the authority of personality and thrust into its place the law of the greater number: democracy. In the economic sphere communism is analogous to democracy in the political sphere. We find ourselves today in a period in which these two fundamental principles clash in all areas where they meet. Fortunately, some of your leaders recognize this.

BOB: Have you found that unfair treatment by the press hurts in a very personal way? Or have you found yourself becoming immune to that?

HITLER: It hurts sometimes. But let me finish the point. Today we stand at the turning point of America's destiny. If the present course continues. America must one day land in Bolshevik chaos, but if this development is broken, then this people must be enrolled in a school of iron discipline. Either this nation's leaders will succeed in forging out of these parties, associations, ideologies, upper-class conceit and lower-class madness an iron-hard national body, or America will finally perish because of this lack of inner consolidation. You're too young to remember, but I said that about my own country to the Dusseldorf Industry Club in 1932. Most of those businessmen were too stupid to understand, though Fritz Thyssen did shout 'Heil, Herr Hitler!' What goes around comes around, as they say. We should recognize quite clearly that if Marxism wins, in Italy or in El Salvador or wherever, we will, in the end, be annihilated. Nor should we expect anything else. But if we win, Marxism will be annihilated. And totally. We too should know no tolerance and not rest until the last Marxist is converted or exterminated. There is no middle course.

A W: Do you miss the Third Reich? I mean, where do you think you made a mistake?

HITLER: Well, obviously I took a big gamble with the invasion of Russia. I remember the day very well. It was June 22, 1941, and the night before I said to someone, 'I feel as if I am pushing open the door to a dark room never seen before, without knowing what lies behind the door.' There was more than I bargained for, what with Churchill refusing to make a separate peace and that damned Russian winter.

But I said it to Martin Bormann in 1945 and I'll say it now. What choice did I have? We had lost hope of being able to end the war by a successful invasion on English soil. For Britain, ruled by stupid leaders, had refused to grant our hegemony in Europe and would not conclude a peace without victory with us as long as there was a Great Power on the continent which in principle confronted the Reich as an adversary. Consequently, the war would have had to go on forever, with, moreover, increasingly active participation by the Americans. Time – and it was always a matter of time – would necessarily have been working more and more against us. In order to persuade the English to surrender, in order to *compel* them to make peace, we consequently had to dispel their hope of confronting us on the 'continent with an enemy of our own class, that is, the Red Army.

We had no choice; for us, it was an inescapable compulsion to remove the Russian piece from the European chessboard. But there was also a second, equally cogent reason, which would have been sufficient for the tremendous danger that Russia meant for us by the mere fact of her existence. Russia was – and at least your leaders now seriously recognize this – a plague center for humanity. So I dreamed of an ethnic catastrophe, that would deprive not only Bolshevism of its centers, but wipe out the Muscovites. When I see that the species is in danger, my feelings give way to ice-cold resolution.

BOB: It must have been a strain at the time, all the same.

HITLER: It was, it was. After 1942, I was taking a lot of downers. Dr. Morell had me on 28 different drugs by the end of the war. I'm off all that now. Just a eucalyptus candy once in a while. Want one?

AW: No thanks. Those are great boots.

HITLER: Aren't they! An old friend of mine sends them up from Asunción, or has a pair waiting for me when I go down to Paraguay for my annual check-up. Anyway, to return to 1942 for a second, we did our best, the *Einsatzgruppen* took ruthless and energetic measures against Bolshevistic agitators, guerrillas, saboteurs, Jews and the Slavic subhumans. Oh, there was a fuss about it at Nuremberg, but no one worries much now about what happened to the Russians, do they? Times have changed, as they always do. What is on the agenda of history now, Andy? I'll tell you. The issue of German re-unification will not forever be postponed. And maybe here at last you have a leadership, for the first time in a generation, which will not shirk the fundamental task. If I had had the means then that you have now! A nuclear war can be fought and won! If the American people are no longer so strong and ready for sacrifice that they will stake their own blood on their existence, then they deserve to pass away and be annihilated to another, stronger power. And if that is the case, I would not shed a tear for the American people, any more than I did for my own.

BOB: Is there still pressure for you to think of your image and act a certain way?

HITLER: I don't think of image so much anymore. I really don't, Bob.

BOB: Well.

HITLER: Have I stopped you cold?

*AW: Well, no. It's just that it's interesting to be here, that's all. This is very exciting for us.**

VV

---

* *This 'interview' was provoked by the rising fortunes of the late Andy Warhol's* Interview, *its exaltation of the 'fascist chic' style and its moral indifference to its heroes and heroines.*

March 30, 1982

Their White Paper ... and Ours

Last Saturday the State Department put out another White Paper-type report on the Cuban and Nicaraguan roles in guerrilla activity in El Salvador. It crawled with facts, factoids and innuendoes. Ploughing through it, probing for blunder and false assertion, I began to ruminate on the absurdity of having to take seriously the essential US premise: that external support for revolution in El Salvador is something shameful, irrefutable evidence for which will allegedly discountenance US supporters of El Salvador's popular resistance.

But of course external material support for resistance in El Salvador should be proudly proclaimed from the rooftops, or would be in a rational world not geared to Reaganite political syntax. Supporters here should not be putzing about with medical-aid teams, but volunteering to form part of an International Brigade ready to carry guns as well as bandages. Must support for national liberation be confined to caring for refugees if it is to retain any so-called 'credibility' or respectability in the first world?

Take the latest State Department document, then turn it on its head and write a similar sort of Report – our White Paper, or Pink Paper, or whatever – about the US role in El Salvador's turmoil:

I. Introduction. There has been a lot of debate and controversy about US support for terrorists running so-called governments in Central America, particularly in El Salvador. This paper does not contain sensitive intelligence. Such intelligence cannot be made available publicly, because such publication might endanger the lives of some brave people who believe it is important that the people of the United States know what is going on. The purpose of this paper is thus not to produce new revelations but to describe the general pattern of outside support for El Salvador's government terrorists inside and alongside that government.

II. The Pattern. US support for terrorism in El Salvador takes many forms, as it does elsewhere in Central and South America. Clear, irrefutable and damning evidence for such support comes in many guises, including: publicly available government data on direct US financial aid, both military and civil; congressional testimony by US government officials; innumerable photographs of US government officials conferring with representatives of its terrorist network in El Salvador, Guatemala, Argentina, Chile and other countries.

'Evidence for US intervention can, for the purposes of this paper, start in 1932 when US frigates stood off El Salvador, while General Martinez put down a peasant uprising. In 1941 a US officer took over the military school in San Salvador. Throughout World War II, the US armed El

Salvador's terrorist dictatorship through Lend Lease. US Military Assistance to El Salvador's police force began in 1956. Similar US Military Assistance continued through the 1960s and 1970s. US arms and materiél have been openly transported to El Salvador's government terrorists.

III. Training Camps. Within the United States the government operates training camps, at Fort Benning and Fort Bragg, where El Salvador's terrorists receive instruction; 2,000 Salvadoran terrorists, so-called 'military officers,' were trained in this manner between 1950 and 1979, with another 1,900 being similarly trained since that date – in itself overwhelming evidence of stepped-up US backing for internationally condemned Salvadoran government-sponsored terrorism.

IV. Command and Control. The internationally denounced terrorist Roberto D'Aubuisson was welcomed in Washington DC in 1980, conferring with many government figures. Two weeks ago General Jaime Abdul Gutierriez visited Washington after a visit to another staging post in the international terror network: South Korea.

IV. The Terror Network. Innumerable intelligence and media reports confirm the existence of a network operated by the US to foster and maintain government terrorism in the region. Under US guidance, support from Argentina, Chile and other outlaw regimes is being recruited for El Salvador's terrorists. Known veterans of international terrorism such as Thomas Enders, Deane Hinton and Vernon Walters have been traced on many missions to foster this international conspiracy. Shown evidence of such activity by the US, officials of many governments have agreed that US-sponsored terrorism and murder are intolerable. The "election" on March 28 is clearly a carefully stage-managed affair, designed to whitewash and ratify such US-backed terrorism in El Salvador, where all objective observers agree that the thousands of dead of the past two years have been the victims of the US-backed junta of terrorists.

VV

April 13, 1982

Will the Freeze Movement Be More Than a Fad?

From President Reagan down, no politician can ignore the growing popular alarm. Television programs, teach-ins, seminars, town meetings, and city council debates concern themselves almost daily with the horrors of nuclear apocalypse. On Capitol Hill itself, Congress has allocated special time to consider nuclear peril.

The accelerated growth of the movement against nuclear weapons, which has coincided with Reagan's presidency, bulks ever larger on the political agenda.

In a way, in this apolitical frenzy of interest, nuclear apocalypse merely becomes more rooted in the national psyche, refreshed by the tears of its possible victims.

Everyone is against the bomb, with degrees of passion and with various strategies to avert mass extermination. Reagan is against the bomb, and calls for a military build-up followed by sharp reductions to be agreed upon with the Soviet Union at some later date. Many senators and congressmen favor a freeze. Organizations such as Ground Zero – sponsor of Ground Zero Week to be held April 18-25 – focus on educating the public in graphic detail, through talks and seminars, about what nuclear war would be like.

Around the country, groups nurtured by traditional peace organizations such as SANE and the American Friends Service Committee are loosely linked in a freeze campaign. Local town councils, on the Western European model, are refusing to participate in civil defense plans.

On the surface the swell is impressive, and bears every sign of being a potentially vast grass-roots movement, based largely in the middle class, with some urban minority involvement. But those with memories of the Ban the Bomb campaign in Britain in the late 1950s, or who took part in the efforts toward the 1963 nuclear test-ban treaty, know well how quickly such swells can subside, their moral fervor finally extinguished by quotidian political reality and expediency. A lack of politics or of clear political objectives beyond the rhetoric of hellfire, laid them low.

By the early 1960s the British CND movement had all but disappeared. The 1963 ban on nuclear testing in the atmosphere, in outer space, and underwater, signed by the US, USSR, and Great Britain, was hailed at the time as a significant first step toward general disarmament. Columbia Professor Seymour Melman, long a critic of military spending, took part in that campaign on behalf of SANE. He recalls: 'It [the treaty] proved to be the first step toward disaster in Vietnam. President Kennedy bought off the generals and civilian hawks, the military industries, and the weapons scientists by dramatically escalating the arms race on every front. The nuclear weapons crowd agreed to take their tests underground in exchange for a vastly increased level of research and testing.'

Arms limitation, or 'freezes,' should be examined with much skepticism. To take one example, Kennedy's secretary of defense Robert McNamara decreed that there should be no more than 1000 Minuteman ICBM 'delivery vehicles.' Hence the development of multiple independently-targeted re-entry vehicles – the Pentagon's answer to the McNamara freeze. So instead of 1000 Minuteman delivery vehicles with 1000 warheads, we now have 1000 delivery vehicles with more than 2000 warheads, with up to three warheads on each vehicle.

SALT treaties or proposed treaties have never *reduced* the nuclear inventory by so much as a kiloton. They have merely arranged the terms on which nuclear escalation is to be conducted.

Professor Melman recently argued that a freeze, say in 1986, would leave many problems unsolved: 'What have we actually frozen? Certainly not the 25,000 to 30,000 nuclear warheads in the U.S. arsenal in 1982, when the freeze campaign began. In that year President Reagan had already set in motion plans to increase the nuclear arsenal by some 17,000 warheads, which, allowing for retirement of some older warheads, would bring the total up to 40,000 to 45,000. Thus we would be freezing the arsenal at a level roughly 50-60 per cent higher than what prevailed in 1982, which was already adequate to destroy every Soviet city of 100,000 or more population forty times over. So now we can destroy them 60 times.'

Only two nuclear devices have, so far in human history, been used in acts of war. It should be conceded by disarmers that, to some degree since World War II, deterrence as a strategy has actually worked. It is foolish to argue otherwise. What has to be combatted is deterrence as an ideology governing the geopolitics of the world, with linkage stretching from southern Lebanon to worldwide nuclear holocaust. In the period since World War II, in which no nuclear weapons have been used, there have been 25 million war deaths in 140 'conventional' wars, fought for the most part in the third world.

A nuclear freeze, without consideration of where wars are actually being fought, or with what – napalm, 3-4-5 D, airburst munitions and other near-nuclear 'conventional' weapons – represents a stunted acquiescence in the present relationships of the first and third worlds, or, more bluntly, of neocolonialism and movements for national liberation.

Obviously everyone should press for a Comprehensive Test Ban. Indeed a CTB treaty was being successfully negotiated at Geneva during Carter's presidency until the battle over SALT II and the president's succumbing to domestic political pressure blasted all hopes. A ban on all nuclear testing would certainly slow the momentum of the nuclear arms race, as would a ban on in-flight testing of the vehicles carrying such nuclear payloads. These are the absolutely minimal demands of an antinuclear movement, portions of which will quite rightly press much further – in the direction of unilateral disarmament demands, and so forth.

But as the British socialist Raymond Williams has said in an essay on the European disarmament campaign in *New Left Review,* 'To build peace, now more than ever, it is necessary to build more than peace. To refuse nuclear weapons, we have to refuse much more than nuclear weapons.'

A resolute disarmament movement must come to grips with the consequences of its demands for the national economy. About a quarter of the visible U.S. budget is now spent on defense, and this $220 billion figure is a very large understatement of the true state of affairs. The country is in a long-term recession, and its basic heavy industries – steel, autos, and aircraft – are tied to military procurement. In the years since 1946, when military Keynesianism was more or less proposed as national policy, critics have convincingly argued that the Keynesian effect of increased defense spending has eroded rapidly. Spending money on high-tech weaponry, which removes scarce engineers from the civil sector, and reducing productivity through DOD cost-plus contracts is different from building factories employing thousands to make army boots or bullets.

But even so, if the prime heavy industries were wrenched away from the defense spigot in this time of recession, the consequences could be extreme, and disarmers should face such consequences. In response they can argue, with some truth, that in real growth industries, like some sectors of the computer market, civilian application or 'conversion' has been a boon. Conversion (the substitution of civilian for military production or function) is not the simplistic equation disarmament advocates sometimes propose. In fact, Admiral Hyman Rickover presided over a long and arduous effort to convert military nuclear technology to peaceful uses. It is true that he was presiding over the military side at the same time. End result: disaster for the civilian side.

Think for a moment of basic industries. From the Industrial Revolution onward, innovation and mass-production in such industries have been largely war-related. The Bessemer process itself, instrumental in the creation of the steel industry, was an offshoot of the French effort to build a better gun. Thereafter its fortunes were tied increasingly – and particularly in times of crisis and economic recession – to armaments.

The so-called strategic-metals industry, seen as a source of uplift to the metals industry as a whole, is tied to warfare and dependent upon military expenditure and oppression of the third world producers.

In industry after industry, from oil, through pharmaceuticals, through rubber, through airlines, the Defense Department is the customer of last resort. Good will, spasms of alarm about nuclear apocalypse, and some large demonstrations will not be enough to discommode this nexus.

The question for months to come will be whether a broad movement against the nuclear arms race can have much more fuel than a somewhat faddish preoccupation with global catastrophe. And if anyone thinks this is a cynical way of putting it, let us remind them once more that simple horror and moral affront are at the same time often too intense yet too vague to translate into useful political results.

Twice in the last 20 years in the United States, we have witnessed the emergence and growth of large middle-class movements animated by outrage: the antiwar movement of the middle to late 1960s, and the environmental movement of the 1970s. They achieved great successes, but in the end fell short of the potential once hoped for them. The reason was a failure often to confront and certainly to change the economic and political underpinnings of the evils they were combatting.

VV, with James Ridgeway

May 19, 1982
The Kelpers

I once met a former governor of the Falkland Islands. He stood at a 45-degree angle out of sheer habit, owing to the unremitting fury of the winds that howl across that barren little archipelago.

The Falklands must be included among the more appalling spots ever to have subsisted under the Union Jack. The islands represent a sort of parody of British weather and of the British class system. The sky is perpetually the color of a mud-stained sheep. It rains 250 days in the year. And the natives, 1,800 in all, spend most of their time knee-deep in icy water harvesting seaweed. Readers of *Das Kapital* will recall that this is the condition to which the Duchess of Sutherland reduced the Scottish peasantry at the end of the Highland clearances. The Falkland Islands Company does not permit the wretched kelpers (gatherers of seaweed) to own their homes or indeed to enjoy a pension. Thus, after a lifetime of kelping, the aged and bankrupt serfs are compelled to live out the sunset years in Australian poor houses.

Wild life is attenuated. Seasoned kelpers recall seeing an occasional small wolf or loup renard of the sort espied by Bougainville, and even the wild hog, formerly abundant, is a rarity now. The king penguin and the mollymauk are also sparse. In their desperate situation the kelpers seek eagerly almost every stimulant or narcotic, and Falklanders tending their flocks are often to be found behind some tussock grass inhaling *Bolar glebaria* or 'balsam dog', a greenish vegetable material emitting an aromatic scent. Incest is almost impossible to avoid, though the genetic logjam will surely now be broken by the rough Latin soldiery.

The Falklands throve in distant obscurity until the First World War, at which point they leapt into prominence. The German General Staff, devising the Schlieffen plan, had forgotten that all the nitrates essential at that time in the manufacture of explosives came from Chile, and that athwart the sea lane to Chile was a British coaling station and garrison, in the form of the Falkland Islands.

Undeterred, and with munitions factories ravenous for nitrates, the German armada set off towards the southwest Atlantic. The British studied their route but failed, just as the German General Staff had, to make the connection between war in Europe and nitrates in Chile. Generals and admirals were not trained to know what gunpowder was made of and where it came from. So the Admiralty thought the Germans had simply gone mad. Nonetheless the two fleets met. Admiral Von Spee battled for Germany with the Scharnhorst and the Gneisenau. For Britain there was Admiral Sturdee and H.M.S. Invincible and H.M.S. Australia. On December 8, 1914, in the battle of the Falkland Islands, the pride of German sea power plummeted to the ocean floor. In the nick of time the Germans learned how to manufacture synthetic nitrates.

The Falklands lapsed into obscurity once more.

VV

May 26, 1982

Hell-Spawn

Argentinian plans for Antarctic domination continue apace. Jeff DeRome tells me that 'the Argentinian military is setting up bizarre breeding farms where they intend to mate large Emperor penguins (*Aptenodytes forsteri* – to four feet in height) with particularly fertile Argentinian peasant stock. Their object: to create an oily breed of feathered mestizo which will be all but impervious to the cold. This hell-spawn will then be used to swell the ranks of the Argentine military to provide the occupation force for the entire Antarctic continent, which they openly covet.'

VV

'Mad Dog' Barks

Anyone suffering a lapse in imperial self-confidence would do well to peruse Sam 'Mad Dog' Huntington's essay, 'American Ideals Versus American Institutions', in the spring issue of the *Political Science Quarterly*. Much of this astonishing tract – clearly a bid for employment by Reagan – is dedicated to the proposition that there has arisen since the Second World War the 'myth of American repression'. So far as Huntington is concerned, the impact of a US Marine's boot, a CIA officer's poison pistol or cash bribe in foreign climes invariably led to an expansion of human liberty: 'The conflict between American power and American principles virtually disappears when it is applied to the American impact on other societies.'

Huntington's impudence is breath-taking. Try this one: 'The impact by United States Marines in Haiti, Nicaragua, the Dominican Republic and elsewhere in these years often bore striking resemblances to the interventions by federal marshals in the conduct of elections in the American South in the 1960s: registering voters, protecting against electoral violence, ensuring a free vote and an honest count ...'.

Huntington remarks a little later that 'If ... the United States had been as active in the popular election of 1970 as it had been in that of 1964, the destruction of Chilean democracy in 1973 might have been avoided.' Here is a man, presumably esteemed within his profession and a member of the National Security Council during the presidency of Jimmy Carter, arguing with a straight face that if the US had been successful in the coup it tried to promote in 1970, it would not have been necessary to arrange some of the circumstances and provisioning of the coup of 1973!

When US academics are finally placed on trial for betrayal of intellectual principle, I hope the editors of the *Political Science Quarterly* will be brought to book for all this, and for Huntington's conclusions: 'Contrary to the views of both "realists" and "moralists", the contradiction arising from America's role in the world is not primarily that of power and self-interest versus liberty and morality in American foreign policy. It is, rather, the contradiction between enhancing liberty at home by curbing the power of the American government and enhancing liberty abroad by expanding that power ... When American power was clearly predominant, such legislative provisions and caveats were superfluous: no Harkin amendment was necessary to convey the message of the superiority of liberty. The message was there for all to see in the troop deployments, carrier task forces, foreign-aid missions, and intelligence operatives ...'*

VV

*Revenge cometh in the evening. In 1987 Huntington was denied entry into the American Academy of Sciences, on grounds of specious claims to scientific objectivity in his methodology.

July 27, 1982

The Camp Follower

Poor Lebanon has been spared no travail or indignity. First the Israeli tanks, planes, and cluster bombs, and then Martin Peretz, editor of the

New Republic and camp follower of the IDF, prancing northward in the wake of the tanks, planes and cluster bombs.

'I was there,' says Peretz proudly at the start of an enormous article in the current *New Republic.* And indeed he was, but not for long, before he dashed back to Washington to write a paean to Israeli military comportment during the invasion, giving the general impression that between the military operation of the last six weeks and rush hour on the IRT it was hard – so far as brutality is concerned – to choose between the two.

'I was there', says Peretz proudly. Other people were there too, including the Norwegian and Canadian doctors whose accounts of the beating and murder of Palestinian prisoners in a convent courtyard in Sidon I mentioned a couple of weeks ago. Both the Norwegians, Dr. Stainar Berge and Dr. Oyvind Moeller, and the Canadian Dr. Giannou had been in this country testifying about their experiences during the invasion, and what they subsequently observed after being taken prisoner by the Israelis.

Moeller was a social worker. He and his wife had been working for nine months in a rehabilitation center for handicapped children, in the Palestinian refugee camp of Ain El Hilweh outside Sidon. The program was partly financed by the Norwegian government, trade unions and the refugee council.

There were seven armored personnel carriers with a machine-gun trained from each personnel carrier on the crowd of prisoners. Thirty to fifty soldiers with sticks, chairlegs, staves with nails sticking out of the end, surrounded the prisoners. They had ropes with knots and nail clusters at the rope ends. They had stiff plastic hoses. Five prisoners had their hands tied behind their backs and were blindfolded.

'One soldier kneed a man in the groin with all his strength. He hit the man on the back of the neck as hard as he could and then kicked him in the stomach. Then he kicked the prostrate man hard in the head. This was then done to the four other prisoners of the group of five. In variation this treatment was then given all these prisoners.'

On another day, Moeller says, 'There was a man, sixty some years old. He was now desperate. The heat was unbearable. We had had no water. He got up and staggered forward. He tried to kick an Israeli soldier in the leg to get his attention. Four or five soldiers jumped him and kicked and beat him. They used plastic hoses, sticks, the ropes with knots and then kicked him with their boots. They kept this up for ten minutes. Dr Berge was with me and we both agree it was at least ten minutes. It was terrible to watch. It seemed to go on forever. This took place in front of everybody. Such savage beating went on constantly in the yard but not in front of the entire group. For ten minutes they pounded and beat him everywhere: in the groin, the stomach and the head. Yes, all over his body. When they were finished beating him he lay still.

'Then they tied his heels together and tied the rope to his wrist so he was trussed up in an arch, lying on his stomach with his head pulled up by the tautness of the rope around his heels and wrists. It was sickening ...'

Later, says Moeller, 'I saw him. He was no longer trussed up. He lay motionless in the sun with three others. They all seemed dead. They were piled on top of each other, their motionless limbs intertwined. They were swollen, none moved. That was the last I saw of that old man.

'I later saw the ambulance with the back door open. Inside I could see a pile of bodies. I couldn't determine exactly how many. Stainar saw at least six at a later time. We know many of the prisoners died from their beatings.

'Whenever prisoners started to ask for water, the soldiers began the beating. We heard prisoners had been without water in the broiling sun for three days. Whenever a prisoner cried for water he was beaten.

'At one point some soldiers brought a few cups of water. Some prisoners got up on their knees and tried to crawl forward. Their handcuffed hands were stretched out in front of them in a posture of prayer, begging for water. Many had lost all pride and pleaded: "Please, please give me some water". Now soldiers came forward.

'They had cups and let a couple of prisoners have a few meager drops of water. The soldiers were taunting the prisoners. The prisoners now pleaded for water even more frantically. Now the soldiers moved forward and began to beat the prisoners fiercely with sticks. The prisoners tried to retreat to the group and to sit down again, but the soldiers moved after them and struck them repeatedly with staves. The prisoners were collapsed to the ground. The soldiers seemed to have their pretext for doing the beatings again ...'

Moeller adds that Colonel Arnon Mozer, Israeli commander in the Sidon region, was two meters away from him at times when beatings were going on and did nothing to stop it.

So Moeller was there, and Peretz wasn't. But I suppose that Peretz, just like the Israelis, will hint that Moeller and Berge and Giannou were all terrorists, or had 'links' to terrorist organizations. Organizations unspecified of course – with the ascription 'terrorist' intended to nullify their words.

VV

September 28, 1982

The Beirut Massacre and the US Press

The massacre in Beirut will not make much of a difference in US reporting on the Middle East; nor will it signal the dawn of a new era in the US-Israeli relationship or in the history of Israel. Those still incredulous about Israeli complicity in the massacre will ask for 'more details', even as the details minutely described this week dim in the memory. The *de facto* annexation of the West Bank will not stop because the US press is at long last – though who knows for how long – doing a better job. The lot of the Palestinians will not necessarily be improved if Begin falls or Sharon is disgraced. People who presage a new dawn, born suddenly from 'tragedy', remind me of those who used to ask back at the end of the '60s when the Northern Irish problem would be resolved. In their brisk demeanour they seemed to be thinking of next week, or at the outside next month. History is more sluggish and less pleasant. Lars-Erik Nelson, Washington Bureau chief of the *Daily News*, wrote on Monday:

'It is disingenuous for Reagan to lay the responsibility for the slaughter of the Palestinians at Israel's door. Yes, the Israeli Army, which seized West Beirut to preserve order after Gemayel's death, immediately opened the refugee camps to Christian gunmen seeking to avenge the death of their leader, Gemayel. And yes, the Israeli Army was encamped outside the gates of the refugee camps and did nothing while gunshots rang out and women screamed hysterically for 12 hours.

'"We do not really know who has been in there pulling the trigger" a senior administration official said Saturday as the magnitude of the horror was unfolding.

'But we do know who provided the guns and bullets used in the massacre: Israel, with a defense budget subsidized by the United States.

'We do know who assured the Palestinian guerrillas that, if they evacuated West Beirut, their wives and children would be safe from having their throats cut and their brains blown out by vengeful Lebanese Christians. President Ronald W. Reagan of the United States of America provided those assurances. They were worthless.

'American honor was at stake in West Beirut. Israel was the guardian of that honor. And then Israel put its own honor in the hands of a blood-thirsty band of savages, renegade Christians who, with pictures of the Blessed Virgin taped to the stocks of their Uzi submachine guns, committed an atrocity that will rank with Lidice and Babi Yar and My Lai.

'For this, shame on who? On Menachem Begin? He will not accept it. Shame on us for letting him lead us on.'

Shame to the press for having been, for so long, complicit in this process. Shame to those who reveled in terror scenarios à la Claire Sterling and in international conspiracy-mongering. They were as credulous recipients of propaganda as those Haddad militiamen described by Thomas Friedman who accused foreign doctors being marched down the main street of Shatila refugee camp of being a 'Baader Meinhoff gang', even as they snatched away a Palestinian among them, took him behind a cinder block wall and, it seems, summarily murdered him. From 'terrorist', to 'terror nest', to mass murder: you can't kill the Palestinian idea without breaking some eggs. The US press assisted for years in that confiscation of identity and humanity which, for those Palestinian men, women and children, culminated in that final confiscation of life.

VV

October 26, 1982

Anti-Semitism

Michael Kramer, fanzine booster of Arik Sharon, writes in *New York* magazine about 'Israel's No. One joke: "One Palestinian in the sea equals pollution; all Palestinians in the sea equals [sic] solution."'

First, I will give a dollar to anyone who convincingly demonstrates to me that he or she heard this joke in Israel in the last six months. Secondly, I wonder if *New York* magazine would have so blithely printed a sentence reading 'One Jew in the sea equals pollution; all Jews in the sea equal solution'?

VV

Smears Exposed

For those who have long been following with distaste the intellectual motions of the *Washington Post* editorial page, some of its recent gyrations are not without a certain grim interest.

On October 9 the *Post* ran an editorial titled 'Hot Words for the Freeze.' The first three paragraphs of this particular piece of punditry were run-of-the-papermill criticisms of President Reagan and Senator Jeremiah Denton for saying that the freeze movement is manipulated by the international Communist conspiracy.

Wearying of such worthy themes, the editorialist then tacked on a final paragraph, as ripe a piece of red-baiting as you might find this side of

Commentary or *Human Events*, not to mention the *New Republic*: 'It is true, however, that one Peace Links advisory group, Women's International League for Peace and Freedom, is a Soviet front, and another, Women Strike for Peace, has connections to a second front, the Women's International Democratic Federation. They have the right. But why does Peace Links abide the taint that even the slightest connection to a Soviet stooge group imparts? Its judgment is in question. Mr. Denton should have left it at that.'

Connoisseurs were uncertain whether these revolting sentiments were written by Meg Greenfield or Stephen Rosenfeld, respectively editor and deputy editor of the editorial page. Some thought that it was Greenfield; others pointed out that her mind might be more occupied with South Africa, whither she had recently jaunted with Katharine Graham, big-game hunting for a rarely seen but oft-described creature known to zoologists as 'Moderate Progress.'

In the event, the author seems to have been Rosenfeld. Two days later the *Post*'s letter columns bulged with three gigantic epistles from: (a) Yvonne Logan, national president of the US section of the Women's International League for Peace and Freedom; (b) Ethel Taylor, national coordinator, Women's Strike for Peace; and (c) Norman Dorsen and Ira Glasser, president and executive director of the ACLU. Logan and Taylor lengthily described the origins, aims and irreproachable credentials of their respective organizations.

Dorsen and Glasser asked pertinently, 'The Post questions the "judgment" of Peace Links in "tainting" itself with such organizations. The implication is that Peace Links should dissociate itself from such organizations, and question its other associations, so it does not invite the kind of attacks made by Mr. Reagan and Senator Denton. Is The Post suggesting that Peace Links should impose a loyalty oath: "Are you now or have you ever been a 'Soviet-front' group or 'connected' with one?" Should this test come in the form of a list of suspect groups – drawn up, for example, by the attorney general so Peace Links will know who to avoid in order not to be branded a "Soviet stooge" by Senator Denton or President Reagan or The Post itself? Will The Post publish its own list, as it has already partially done?'

On the same page as the letters was another editorial, strewn with broken branches, torn foliage and other evidence of an editorialist climbing down: 'We now believe that the available evidence does not support our calling the WILPF a Soviet front ... We do not mean to suggest that any of the groups advising Peace Links is a Soviet stooge.' Of course the editorial two days earlier had suggested exactly that. 'Certainly there is no question ... of questioning someone's loyalty ...' Although the earlier editorial had, quite plainly, carried just that innuendo.

Finally, on the following Tuesday the *Post*'s ombudsman, Robert McCloskey, a tireless Polonius of the Either/Or, plunged in. First, McCloskey hailed the climbdown as 'a class act.' It was not a class act. It was a somewhat half-hearted gasp of contrition for a piece of outrageous McCarthyism. Then McCloskey made the interesting disclosure that the first editorial had 'lost its bearings by relying too literally on a State Department report that, among other things, attempts to keep book on "front groups" ... Both Meg Greenfield and Stephen Rosenfeld ... acknowledge "tripping over names and institutional associations ... that drew us to faulty conclusions ..."'

VV

They Smear, We Expose

Since we are on the smeary end of the spectrum, did you catch the footnote in Sidney Hook's article about Einstein in *Commentary* for August? Look not to what books a man might read or idea he might hold. Look rather to his pedigree and whom he went to school with. '... When I was no longer chairman of the American Committee for Cultural Freedom, I learned that when it was unable to pay its rent, Norman Thomas,* a member of the executive committee, telephoned Allen Dulles of the CIA and requested a contribution. Subsequently, when I questioned Thomas about this, he said that he and Dulles had been friends and classmates at Princeton – both being protégés of Woodrow Wilson – and that he had solicited the contribution purely on the basis of his personal friendship.'

VV

* *This was the 'socialist' Norman Thomas, of course.*

October 28, 1982

The Entrepreneur

Perhaps because they represent brief, comet-like streaks of hope against a background of unremitting decline, the British have a great fondness for entrepreneurs who might seem to most objective observers to be unwise investments. Turned down by Puerto Rico and the Irish Republic, John De Lorean was welcomed with open arms by the last Labor government, which showered him with taxpayers' largesse (almost $100 million) and which remains impenitent about the investment to this day.

One has the impression that if De Lorean had short-circuited his alleged business operations and proposed erection of a cocaine-refining factory in Northern Ireland, the British government would have issued a rousing welcome and tactful suggestions that the subsidized facility be called a dust reprocessing plant.

Given this fondness for far-out investors, De Lorean's fall was big news in Britain and since I was there last week on a brief visit I was able to sample some of the press coverage firsthand. The Daily Mirror had a front-page banner headline, 'Shame of De Lorean,' and a stirring story from its U.S. correspondent: 'He was born with the fumes of exhaust pipes streaking through his veins. ...' De Lorean's former colleagues at GM will be interested to know that, according to the Mirror, 'In 1969 he took over as general manager, turning General Motors back from the brink of disaster.'

The Sun ('De Lorean's Tears in the Dock') provided similarly racy prose: 'Poor Boy John De Lorean roared to the top of the tough world of motor moguls by driving himself flat out – with his foot hard down on the accelerator. ...' But George Gordon, New York correspondent of the Daily Mail, won the day with a riveting description of 'high society' in the United States.

'The white-powdered derivative of coca leaves blows through the corporate offices and inner sanctums of banking institutions with almost blizzard force,' Mr. Gordon reported, adding by way of illustration, 'On Madison Avenue a small dish on the board room table sets the scene for a weekly conference. While the notepads and pencils lie on the table, the executives neatly roll a $100 bill in order to sniff a two-inch line from the polished surface ... on the ski slopes of Aspen, maids in the luxury apartments expect a spoonful of the powder as a tip.'

I came back to the U.S. over the weekend to find local pundits hard at work, boiling up nutritious commentary from poor De Lorean's bones. The richest concoction undoubtedly came from Pete Axthelm, columnist for Newsweek. 'No,' Mr. Axthelm exclaimed, 'this American downfall belongs less to Fitzgerald and Dreiser than to Nietzsche and Ayn Rand. De Lorean was a philosophical superman in the Nietzschean mold, a self-made capitalist superstar Rand might have applauded. ... It took a De Lorean to demand a door that flaired [sic] upward, simulated flight, defied gravity. Whatever the cost.'

Heart-stopping stuff, albeit a bit off the mark in the reference to the gull-wing doors, supposedly first demanded by Nietzschean John. The first production vehicle to have gull-wing doors was the Mercedes 300 SL in 1954. In the early 1970s Malcolm Bricklin went broke trying to sell his gull-wing car. The fact is that gull wings have about the same success rate as the contraption Daedalus strapped on Icarus.

What occurs to Joseph Kraft, ruminating on the De Lorean affair is that 'high rollers are on the loose. Greed at the top has been systematized and even sanctified.' And starting with De Lorean, Mr. Kraft starts ticking off big blips on the greed graph: William Agee, 'a promiscuous bidder for other companies,' football owners and players, bankers lending to Zaire and Poland, oil companies doing business with Libya, Bert Lance, Jerry Ford, Richard Nixon, the Tylenol case, the Reagan administration, the elite universities, business schools, press, television and Jerry Falwell.

He seems to have left almost no one out, but the argument is extremely unfair to De Lorean who was trying to save his company, in rather more daring and innovative a fashion than goody-goody Lee Iacocca who has been resourceful enough thus far to entrap rather than be entrapped by Big Government dollars.

Mr. Kraft's grave observations on the new age of greed must have been infectious, because the Washington Post ran an editorial shortly thereafter, lamenting that 'tragically, in some areas, cocaine, not cars, is the growth industry. ... The case of John De Lorean ... is a reflection on an economy and a culture where creative business enterprise can fail and the soul-destroying corruption of drug addiction thrives.' Having thus hammered down the coffin lid on the cadaver of the American Way we can imagine our editorialist leaping clear of the typewriter and hurrying off for a bracing cocktail. Editorialists regularly write off the American Way by about 5 p.m. and never seem to express surprise at finding it still in place the following day.

There is no need to sound the knell for capitalism, in brooding on the De Lorean case. Aside from the foolishness of his alleged final attempts to organize a bailout, De Lorean's main mistake in launching his entre-preneurial venture was to do it during an administration dedicated to the entrepreneur.

Reagan rhetoric, back in the good old days when sage mariners were predicting that a flooding tide would raise all boats, nailed its colors to the mast of the new entrepreneur, who would avail himself of supply-side surplus and make America great again. The whole thing went wrong of course, and now the new entrepreneur, doomed by interest rates and economic conditions, lies with a stake through his heart.

The same thing happened over in Britain, once that other friend of the entrepreneur, the Thatcher government, came to power. One of Prime Minister Thatcher's greatest enthusiasms was Freddy Laker, and poor Sir Fred was one of her first victims. Soundly weighted with the Thatcher plaudits and the Thatcher economy, he sank like a stone to the bottom.

Nor is cocaine a symbol of America's decline. It is an emblem rather of capitalism's great resourcefulness, and I am somewhat surprised that the achievements of the cocaine industry have not been properly hailed in the editorial columns opposite this page.

In the first place cocaine is a plucky inflation-fighter. The Drug Enforcement Administration informs me that the 'street' price of approximately $100 a gram has held since President Reagan took office. The DEA also reckons that the retail value of cocaine sales (in 1980) was $29.5 billion, to an estimated 10 million regular U.S. consumers. This puts it well ahead of tobacco, with total retail value of sales in 1981 at $20 billion, and even ahead of alcohol sold outside of saloons and restaurants ($27 billion).

Now it does not take the coincidence of a Nobel Prize to Professor Stigler, analyst of the costs of regulation, to realize that if the cocaine industry can reach such a level even though hogtied by government interference and red tape, what levels of business-enhancing potential might it not ascend to once government is prized off its back! This is the lesson libertarians should hammer home, even as they rally behind De Lorean, who should become one of their most honored martyrs.

Wall Street Journal

December 2, 1982

Mount Kissinger Erupts

Halfway through November, spewing smoke and cliche hundreds of feet into the air, Mount Kissinger entered a peculiarly active phase. Though no actual loss of life seems to have occurred, 'Kissinger Alerts' were broadcast on an hourly basis, warning the populace to beware of falling platitudes and other detritus from this semi-extinct volcano.

The first eruption took place in the London *Economist*, dated November 13-19, and took the form of a 'conversation' between Mr. Kissinger, coyly described as 'a private citizen,' and the editor of the *Economist*, a long-term Kissinger disciple, Andrew Knight. Over five interminable pages the two K's rambled through the politics of the Levant, leisurely seeking out and successfully locating the obvious: the 'fresh beginning' now to be descried beneath the rubble of Lebanon; the hopes but yet the perils offered by the Reagan plan; the possibility for moderate advance, yet the ever-present menace of extremism.

Hardly had the basso rumblings died down before Mount Kissinger burst into activity once more. The eruption came this time in Newsweek, in the edition that went on sale on November 22. That magazine's new young editor in chief, William Broyles, seemingly as eager an acolyte as Mr. Knight, spread Mr. Kissinger across four inside pages and gave him the cover as well: 'How to Deal with Moscow – An Exclusive Report by Henry Kissinger.'

Once again, for those foolhardy enough to embark on the text, there was the exhausting trek through slowly cooling statesmanspeak: 'To bring about a genuine change – expressed in substantial reciprocal arms reduction and restraint in international conduct – requires American leadership founded in firm purpose, clear concept and steadfast strategy. ... Our policy must be based on strength to discourage adventurism yet at the same time offer a vision of a better world for all peoples. ...'

At first I took all this volcanic activity to be part of a normal pattern: Mr. Kissinger's perennial need to keep his name in the public eye as a senior statesman, and thus maintain his exchange value. In a decently ordered world Mr. Kissinger would have at some point endowed himself with legal credentials and thus could now – like Cyrus Vance or William Rogers – have retired to the powerful obscurity of an obscurely powerful law firm. The alternative, for which no known credentials are required, would be an academic position of the sort now enjoyed by the Brzezinskis, Rusks and Bundys of the world. The Kissinger imperial ego evidently regards this latter course as unthinkable.

I had thought that Mr. Kissinger's chosen mode, that of international superstar, cafe society's preferred oracle, would not for long endure; that the decline would be rapid, from special adviser to NBC, to guest on the Johnny Carson show, to final apotheosis on the Hollywood Squares. Not so.

Needing, by the look of his appurtenances and domestic requirements, at least a million a year in income, Mr. Kissinger has lived by his wits with amazing success. There is now a whole range of semi-extinct volcanoes, including Lord Carrington and R.O. Anderson, grouped under the generic title 'Kissinger Associates' and charging $250,000 entry fee to each client. There are business consultancies to Goldman Sachs and Chase and advisory functions at ABC and Newsweek.

Necessary in the success of this type of operation is the belief of client or public that the relevant retired statesman has anything to offer, beyond gallon jugs of 'wisdom' and 'experience.' The trick here is to ensure at least the appearance of 'briefings' or 'consultancies' by those actually in power, and of course the possibility that the retired statesman might one day get back into power himself. Mr. Kissinger, hinting that he might have had a hand in the formulation of the Reagan plan for the Middle East, perennially bathing himself in rumors of an emissary or more substantial role, and at a pinch proffering sagacious public advice, is a master at giving the volcano at least a semblance of life.

Yet there was more to the November eruptions than such considerations. Oddly enough, Anthony Lewis provided the tipoff. Normally this liberal columnist is so quick to leap on his moral high horse that he clears the saddle by a couple of feet, but on November 22 he hailed Mr. Kissinger's utterances on the Middle East, while adding cautiously that 'on such issues as Vietnam and Chile he used power beyond the limits of decency. We can expect to learn more about his role in Chile from a forthcoming Atlantic Monthly article by Seymour Hersh.'

The commotions of Mount Kissinger were at once, in my view, satisfactorily explained: a preemptive strike. If a volcano is bursting ponderously into life, you have less time to inspect the pool of sewage spreading across the backyard. The issue of the Atlantic with Mr. Hersh's article in it went on the newsstands a day or two after Newsweek grandly promulgated Mr. Kissinger's views on the Russians.

Mr. Hersh's article has not caused much of a stir. The Washington Post said it contained 'no smoking gun.' These are times, or course, when a gun has to explode in your hand for anyone to pay attention. Wounds are being healed, Vietnam memorials unveiled and ex-presidents rehabilitated at such a rate that they'll probably be reappointing Spiro Agnew soon as secretary of commerce.

Mr. Hersh's examination of the actions of Messrs. Nixon and Kissinger immediately before and after the popular election of Salvador Allende in September and October 1970 seems to me to establish as solidly as available historical evidence will probably ever permit that orders for the overthrow – and, Mr. Hersh implies, the assassination of – Allende came out of the president's office and were urged by his national security adviser. Mr. Hersh also deduces that CIA operatives were dispatched to Chile and that their mission culminated in the murder of Gen. Rene Schneider, commander in chief of the Chilean army. Mr. Hersh's investigation demonstrates that Mr. Kissinger subsequently lied repeatedly about his and his master's attempts to bring down the legally elected Chilean president. The article shows in detail Messrs. Nixon and Kissinger conspiring with U.S. executives to subvert Chile.

You could argue that a man who tried and may indeed ultimately have succeeded in engineering the overthrow of Allende is well qualified to assess the best manner of dealing with the former head of the KGB. But that is not quite how Newsweek presented Kissinger's expertise. For the opinion-forming elite, as represented by the editors of the Economist and Newsweek, the smoking volcano seems permanently to overshadow the smoking gun, which shows you can survive anything, provided you are statesmanlike about it.

WSJ

December 21, 1982

White Mischief

'Why not a Martin Luther King Day?' the *New York Times* asked editorially last Friday, and answered, 'Dr. King, a humble man, would have objected to giving that much importance to any individual. Nor should he be given singular tribute if that demeans other historical black figures like Sojourner Truth, Harriet Tubman, Frederick Douglass, Booker T. Washington, W.E.B. Dubois and Malcolm X. ...' Give one of them a holiday and they'll all be wanting one. Muhammad Ali Day, Kareem Abdul-Jabbar Day. Where would it all end? Better, the *Times* suggests, to give King a statue in the Capitol, presumably in white marble to blend in with the rest.

VV

Tender Offer

'The lower organs of the party must make even greater efforts to penetrate the backward parts of the proletariat.' Such was the directive from Moscow, scrutinized by my father at British Communist Party headquarters just after the war. When he pointed out to the Russians that the toiling masses would take such a directive, if printed unaltered in the *Daily Worker*, as a rather dirty joke, he was told sharply that such reflections were out of order.

My father recalled the 'lower organs' episode in his memoirs, which are on my mind since it is now exactly a year since their author died, and a week since the *Manchester Guardian* reported on an interesting set of documents recently declassified in the national archives in Washington.

These documents, dating from the start of the Second World War, consist partly of reports from the US Embassy in London revealing that the British security services kept a central index of suspicious persons, with 'the name of every person ever suspected in any part of the world of anti-British activity – a total of 4,500,000 names. The index is freely used by British industry and government departments.' The British made the list available to the Americans in the London embassy, who were much impressed by the whole operation and told Washington: 'The English have done a very smart thing in connection with counter-espionage, which might well be copied by the United States. Unknown to the British public, unknown to the newspapers and unknown even to most of the Government officials there has been in existence in this country for 31 years an elaborate organization for the detection and prevention of the activities of foreign governments ...'

The British spooks apparently attributed their success to 'the fact that they have operated in absolute secrecy. They declare that no British newspaper has ever discovered the scope of the organization ... the public is completely unaware of the existence of the super-machine of which MI5 is merely one cog.'

All this burnishes, at least retrospectively, the reputation of the British secret service, whose donnish majesty – hymned by Le Carré – has been reduced somewhat by the exposure of Prine the cipher stealer, who did not elegantly shove secrets across All Souls high table along with the port, but likes to stick his hand up little girls' skirts.

Anyway, these documents in the national archive apparently have much material devoted to the investigation of my dear father. In a letter dated March 5, 1937, to the American embassy, Colonel Sir Vernon Kell, director of the Imperial Security Service, describes my father as a man 'whose intelligence and wide variety of contacts make him a formidable factor on the side of Communism.'

VV

January 27, 1983

'The Bipartisan Appeal' or More Mush from the Wimps

It is axiomatic that methodical use of the word 'bipartisan' indicates that some gross deception is about to be practiced upon the persons (and usually the pockets) of the citizenry and that the perpetrators wish to indicate by the deployment of 'bipartisanship' that normal democratic procedures and alternatives have been suspended.

But whereas President Reagan, in his State of the Union address, invoked the term almost mechanically, in the spirit of defensive political maneuver, it was being more substantially employed in another State of the Union address, printed in this paper on the same day that Mr. Reagan faced Congress.

This was the 'Bipartisan Appeal' mounted by Peter Peterson and signed by many of the crowned heads of corporate America.

Mr. Peterson's Bipartisans claim that vast deficits, modishly termed 'structural,' now loom and threaten 'to lock the economy in stagnation for the remainder of this century.' They call for cuts in entitlement programs, cuts in defense spending and more taxes. If such measures are not adopted, they claim, the ship of state will move into 'uncharted fiscal territory,' presumably strike a rock and sink to the bottom.

To evoke the famous Boston Globe headline about President Carter: More mush from the wimps. Many of the people who got the economy into its present mess and who have been profiting vastly under present conditions signed the appeal with a shamelessness that would be irksome in a child but is repulsive in persons of mature years.

Among 'founding members' of the appeal, are a couple of seasoned helmsmen-for-disaster in the shape of William Simon and W. Michael Blumenthal. One presided over the slump of the mid-70s and the other surrendered to the bankers and the Fed in 1978-79 and launched the country into its present depression. They are accompanied by Henry Fowler, co-conspirator in the fueling of Vietnam-era inflation.

Signatories of the appeal include the chief executive officers of the Bank of America, Bankers Trust and the Chase Manhattan Bank, and indeed David Rockefeller himself. In a decently ordered moral universe they would shun the light of day, knowing full well that the taxpayer will be sustaining the eventual cost of their lunatic loans of the last decade, for which they managed to shuffle off responsibility while raking in the profits.

But even the bankers' hypocrisy is outstripped by the platoon of arms-makers who have signed up as Bipartisans. Ingratitude, thou marble-hearted fiend! Here, howling for cuts in defense spending, we find the chief executive officer of Martin Marietta, a concern President Reagan is valiantly trying to bail out with the Pershing II and the MX. We find the boss of Grumman, fat with the F-14 and providing high employment in Long Island, yet strangely yearning for restraint. We find the heads of RCA and Textron, seemingly heedless of the rewards of the Aegis system or the beneficence of Navy Secretary John Lehman. And we find Adm. Elmo Zumwalt, prime tom-tom pounder for bigger defense dollars.

It's not the way I would personally wish to order things, but defense spending (and the Bipartisans don't actually wish to cut much) is about the only thing saving this country's economy from looking like Canada's. If the Bipartisans' calls for spending cuts and deficit reduction are actually heeded, the bloodied economy will take another lurch toward the tomb, and the Social Security system, which they have the impudence to claim they are trying to save, will be truly imperiled.

Why the panic of the Bipartisans? Many of them, along with Democratic and Republican economists, pushed for a dollar defense package in 1978-79 and launched Paul Volcker on his tight-money, high interest rate course. They called for increased defense spending. Now they have an overvalued dollar, trade imbalance and a world depression. They called for an end to inflation and now they complain about high interest rates and unemployment.

The hysteria about the deficits is bunk. Last year the states showed an overall surplus. 'Passive' in nature, the federal deficits would, in an expanding economy, soon wither even in the fevered imaginations of the Bipartisans. The talk of 'uncharted' waters is bunk too. As Prof. Lynn Turgeon of Hofstra University points out, the national debt of about $250 billion in 1945 actually exceeded the gross national product of $212.3 billion. Right now, debt is about 30% of GNP. But after the war interest made up 4% of all types of income. Now it makes up 15%. Since 1951 the money supply has been growing more slowly in real terms than GNP.

What does this suggest? A reverse clue is another signatory to the appeal, in the person of the swivel-hipped Lester Thurow, a quasi-Keynesian who now apparently has no compunction in signing the Peterson recipe for a crash. The real Keynes would have no trouble identifying the real culprit, in the form of the independent Federal Reserve and the policies of Mr. Volcker. The real Keynes is properly described by Paul Sweezy in an editorial in January's Monthly Review called 'Listen Keynesians!'

This is the Keynes of the 'General Theory' who would call for the 'euthanasia of the *rentier*' and suggest that capitalism's endemic problems of accumulation might only be solved by the 'somewhat comprehensive socialization of investment,' and equalization of income distribution through the elimination of interest and rent.

I doubt if even Mr. Thurow and certainly the rest of the Bipartisans have the kidney for this kind of analysis. Abolition of *rentier* income is scarcely what Peter Peterson or co-signatory Henry Kaufman have in mind. In the whole of the Bipartisan Appeal, the role of the Fed is not even mentioned. The president did not indict the Fed in his address and, though I fell asleep halfway through their television spectacular, I doubt if the Democrats did either. The Democratic candidates content themselves with obeisances toward protectionism. Is there not one just man or woman in America who can launch a *partisan* appeal to impeach Mr. Volcker and bring the Fed under the full control of government? It's either that or the gold standard of the supply-siders.

WSJ

February 1, 1983

Orwell's 1984

It's interesting to go back and see how *1984* was received when it was published in 1949. V.S. Pritchett and Lionel Trilling reviewed it on the same day, June 18, 1949, for the *New Statesman* and the *New Yorker* respectively. Both liked it. Pritchett wrote that 'the purges in Russia and later, in the Russian satellites, the dreary seediness of London in the worst days of the war, the pockets of 19th century life in decaying England, the sordidness of bad flats, bad food, the native and whining streak of domestic sluttishness which have sickened English satirists since Smollett, all these have given Mr. Orwell his material.'

Trilling predictably thought *1984* momentous, adding carefully, 'Despite the impression it may give at first, it is not an attack on the Labor Government.' Trilling venerated the book's weakest aspect, namely its analysis of power – its supposed theme.

Orwell himself said, 'My novel *1984* is *not* intended as an attack on Socialism or on the British Labour Party but as a show-up of the perversions to which a centralised economy is liable ... I do not believe that the kind of society I describe necessarily *will* arrive, but I believe that something resembling it could arrive.'

Orwell was influenced, among many others by, James Burnham, Von Hayek, and H.G. Wells. A story called *Cloud Nine* by his old school chum Cyril Connolly, printed in the *New Statesman* in 1938 and later in the *Condemned Playground*, was obviously influential. Isaac Deutscher stated flatly in 'The Mysticism of Cruelty,' his essay on *1984*, that Orwell 'borrowed the idea of *1984*, the plot, the chief characters, the symbols and the whole climate of his story from Evgeny Zamyatin's *We.*'

This was probably overstating the case a bit, even though Orwell was a keen and avowed admirer of *We.* Deutscher's essay, to be found in *Russia in Transition*, is well worth reading: '[Orwell's] distrust of historical generalizations led him in the end to adopt and to cling to the oldest, the most banal, the most abstract, the most metaphysical, and the most barren of all generalizations: all *their* conspiracies and plots and purges and diplomatic deals had one source and one source only – "sadistic power hunger". Thus he made his jump from workaday, rationalistic common sense to the mysticism of cruelty which inspires *1984*.'

Deutscher added a footnote:

'This opinion is based on personal reminiscences as well as on an analysis of Orwell's work. During the last war Orwell seemed attracted by the critical, then somewhat unusual, tenor of my commentaries on Russia which appeared in *The Economist, The Observer*, and *Tribune*. (Later we were both *The Observer*'s correspondents in Germany and occasionally shared a room in a press camp.) However, it took me little time to become aware of the differences of approach behind our seeming agreement. I remember that I was taken aback by the stubbornness with which Orwell dwelt on "conspiracies," and that his political reasoning struck me as a Freudian sublimation of persecution mania. He was, for instance, unshakably convinced that Stalin, Churchill, and Roosevelt consciously plotted to divide the world and to divide it for good, among themselves, and to subjugate it in common. (I can trace the idea of Oceania, Eastasia, and Eurasia back to that time.) "*They* are all power-hungry," he used to repeat. When once I pointed out to him that underneath the apparent solidarity of the Big Three one could discern clearly the conflict between them, already coming to the surface, Orwell was so startled and incredulous that he at once related our conversation in his column in *Tribune*, and added that he saw no sign of the approach of the conflict of which I spoke. This was at the time of the Yalta conference, or shortly thereafter, when not much foresight was needed to see what was coming. What struck me in Orwell was his lack of historical sense and of psychological insight into political life coupled with an acute, though narrow, penetration into some aspects of politics and with an incorruptible firmness of conviction.'

Fair enough. Deutscher concluded, 'It would be dangerous to blind ourselves to the fact that in the West millions of people may be inclined, in their anguish and fear, to flee from their own responsibility for mankind's destiny and to vent their anger and despair on the giant Bogy-cum-Scapegoat which Orwell's *1984* has done so much to place before their eyes. "Have you read this book? You must read it, sir. Then you will know why we must drop the atom bomb on the Bolshies!" With these words a blind, miserable news vendor recommended to me *1984* in New York, a few weeks before Orwell's death. Poor Orwell, could he ever imagine that his own book would become so prominent an item in the program of Hate Week.'

He probably could, and may not have been displeased. As even Irving Howe pointed out, *1984* is silly about power, about sex and about the proles. On Orwell and the proles, Wyndham Lewis is good: 'The Orwell picture is of a long outdated socialism. His two humanities contrasted in *1984* of, on the one hand, a virgin virile world of workers, bursting with potential leadership, on the other, a ruling class in the Stalinist party pattern, is really socialism in one of its nineteenth century forms (probably medieval and guildish, confronting the stream-lined efficiency-socialism of today). I for one would have considered *1984* a better book had the Prole business been left out, and a more realistic treatment of the probable condition of the mass of the population been employed.'

VV

Peacock Souvenir

Iran lies in the darkness of Khomeini's regime, even more atrocious and barbaric than the one it overthrew. Does that mean, therefore, that we must grant the Shah retrospective absolution and concur with his supporters that the electrodes of *his* Savak were somehow more beneficent than the clubs and goads of the mullahs?

No. The Shah pandered to Islamic fanaticism, called himself the 'shadow of God,' and was propelled back into power in 1954 with the help of the ancestors of Khomeini's clerics. Over the years his regime tortured and persecuted the left. The Shah and his US backers contrived and ushered in the present darkness, even though they were among its first victims. There is no retrospective absolution for having curried favor with the Peacock Throne.

VV

February 8, 1983

Red Horror

Discussing the politics of 1948 last week, I mentioned an article that appeared that year in *Look* magazine, titled 'Could the Reds Seize Detroit?' A couple of readers expressed disbelief that such an article could have appeared, even in the first flush of the Cold War.

Indeed it did. It was written by James Metcalfe and illustrated (courtesy of men from the police department) with dramatic though staged pictures of rifle-wielding Bolshie scum. Metcalfe's narrative began, 'Detroit, home of mass production, city of assembly lines, maker of weapons in time of war, is the industrial heart of America. Today, a sickle is being sharpened to plunge into that heart.'

A trusted prop of terror fantasies about the Red Octopus is the 'strategic waterway'. In recent years this waterway has usually been a 'crucial sea lane' or 'tanker route'. Metcalfe made eloquent use of the Detroit River. For it 'gives Detroit's position strategic value, controlling as it does an essential link in a vital inland waterway'. He added laconically that 'factories alone would make Detroit a magnet for Communists'.

Grasping the nettle firmly, Metcalfe asked, 'Do a mere three-to-six-thousand Reds constitute a threat to a metropolitan area of nearly two-and-a-half-million inhabitants? The answer – *Yes, if the time and conditions are right.*'

Metcalfe then plunged into racy terror-porn: 'The first few minutes would be busy ones for the Communist flying squads. On split-second schedule, groups would be liquidating certain civic and political leaders. Other units would take previously selected hostages into custody.' At the same time 'equally ruthless units' would be seizing broadcasting facilities, and sealing off the city. 'Rabble-rousers, using sound trucks, would roll into those sections of the city where years of preparation had conditioned the people to Communist leadership. Now, caught in the madness of the moment, emboldened by the darkness, intoxicated by an unbridled license to kill, loot and destroy, mobs would swarm in the streets.'

Metcalfe swept to a conclusion thrilling enough to have brought Lenin bouncing out of the mausoleum: 'Now, using the straw-man technique of creating a crisis, then solving it, the Reds would utilize captured press and radio facilities to urge a restoration of calm and order. City officials, either at gunpoint or to avoid further bloodshed, would caution the populace against resistance, advising them to bow to Red leadership. Quislings would take their appointed posts, top-flights agents would arrive to master-mind further developments and Detroit could conceivably become another Prague.'

How quaintly all this reads now, or if you prefer, how ironically, when considered in the light of the riots of the 1960s. Metcalfe envisioned another scenario, whose preliminary outlines are rather familiar to anyone contemplating Detroit today. 'Visualize,' he urged his readers, 'conditions during a great depression when factories are idle, when hundreds of thousands of men – all normally employed by Detroit's auto plants – are out of work, bitter, disillusioned and susceptible to influence by subversive agents who offer them an antidote for despair.'

In 1980 the subversive agent was Ronald Reagan, who offered those idled UAW workers an antidote. But that wasn't quite what Metcalfe had in mind.

VV

22 February, 1983

From Vietnam ...

Suddenly everyone is 'rethinking' Vietnam. They've just had a conference about it in Los Angeles. The *New York Times Magazine* even ran a cover story last Sunday on 'The New Vietnam Scholarship,' by Fox Butterfield. The picture on the cover showed Douglas Pike, formerly of RAND, conducting a seminar at Berkeley. On the blackboard behind him the word 'ideological' is misspelled as 'Idelogical.' This is fair evidence of the quality of the new scholarship.

In the course of Butterfield's article I read these sentences: '... specialists are revising even their views of the Phoenix program, the scheme sponsored by the CIA to destroy the Vietcong apparatus in the villages by arresting or killing local Communist cadres. "The conventional liberal wisdom at the time was that it was a terrible thing," says Mr. [Stanley] Karnow. "It killed people indiscriminately and was subject to corruption by the South Vietnamese who turned people in for the reward money. But the people I talked to on my trip to Vietnam said it had wiped out many southern cadres and helped cripple the N.L.F."'

Now, recalling that on former CIA director (and executive of the Phoenix program) William Colby's own testimony 20,587 'suspected' NLF cadres were killed in the first two and a half years of Phoenix, let us look again at Butterfield's approving citation of Karnow.

The first knee-jerk word is 'conventional.' This epithet, yoked to 'wisdom,' alerts the reader that once again the liberals, in protesting a program of rural assassination as a 'terrible thing,' were making fools of themselves. Presumably the 'unconventional liberal wisdom' would have been that virtually indiscriminate murder was a 'good thing.' Karnow evidently believes this to be so, for he counterposes to the 'conventional liberal wisdom' the news that many southern cadres were 'wiped out' and the NLF crippled.

So now, not even a decade after the Americans left Vietnam, we have an alliance of old mass-murderers, new scholars, neo-conservatives, neoliberals, ex-radicals, and no doubt neo-leftists proclaiming that the US was morally justified in its intervention in Vietnam, militarily victorious in its conduct of the war and, stayed from triumph only by stabs in the back administered, according to taste, by the press, the protesters, the Congress or indeed the President.

But just for the record let us remember that the US was wrong to go to Vietnam, perpetrated unspeakable atrocities while in Vietnam and was finally thrown out of Vietnam because it was defeated by Vietnamese. Thank God. The liberals and ex-radicals now say that Vietnam is not a paradise flowing with honey and the milk of human kindness. The Pentagon refuses to give Vietnam maps of where landmines were placed. Each week peasants tread on these mines, and on unexploded bombs dropped from US planes, and die. My colleague Bob Brewin, ex-veteran, goes to the Vietnam memorial and records the pleasant emotions he felt on seeing General Westmoreland. I read in a newspaper of a friendly account of a former POW now teaching a course on survival. The article treats at length his unpleasant experiences in a Vietnamese prison camp. It mentions only in passing that he was a navy bomber pilot. The author of the article clearly did not think it worth asking him how he felt about dropping cluster-bombs on men, women and children from a height of 40,000 feet. He got to go to a prison camp. They got to go to a graveyard (assuming their relatives could pick up the pieces).

The nation that forgets its massacres and atrocities this quickly is certainly going to repeat them. The Sunday *Times Magazine* runs a cover article on 'The New Vietnam Scholarship' – basically as a signal to readers that it is very definitely okay to stop feeling bad about the war. Self-flagellation unparalleled since the Middle Ages breaks out at such venues as the Los Angeles conference, rethinking Vietnam. Now why don't they have a conference to rethink Chile? Why doesn't the *New York Times Magazine* run a cover on 'The New Chile Scholarship'? It could discuss such exciting items as the real-life consequences of the monetary theories of the Chicago School in Chile, 1973-83.

VV

To Amritsar ...

One massacre a lot of people have been thinking about over the last few weeks occurred in Amritsar, India, on April 13, 1919, inflicted by the British on the Indians and graphically depicted in that excellent movie *Gandhi*. In *Gandhi* General Harry Dyer is shown marching white soldiers towards Jallianwallah Bagh. According to Louis Fischer's *Life of Gandhi*, Dyer had with him as riflemen 25 Ghurkas and 25 Baluchis. The firing, at point-blank range upon the unarmed crowd, lasted about 10 minutes, with an expenditure of 1,650 rounds. Dead amounted to 379, and 1,137 were wounded. Total: 1,516 casualties. Only 134 bullets went to waste.

Three days earlier, in revenge for an assault upon Miss Sherwood, headmistress of a girls' school in Amritsar, Dyer had ordered anyone passing the street where she was assaulted to crawl on all fours. At Jallianwallah Bagh, somewhere between 10,000 and 20,000 people had gathered peacefully when Dyer gave the order to open fire. 'I had made up my mind,' he later told the Hunter Commission, 'I would do all men to death ... I was going to punish them. My idea from the military point of view was to make a wide impression.'

Dyer, who concluded that he thought he would be doing 'a jolly lot of good,' was reprimanded and asked to resign from the army. He was allowed to retain full pension rights. The British in India took up a collection for him, amounting to £26,000, a very large sum in those days.

Exactly a hundred years ago, Dyer was receiving the rudiments of education at Middleton College, County Cork, Ireland, not 20 miles from where I grew up. I learned this from Fischer's book, almost at the same time in this last week that I received a wonderful excerpt from a speech made last summer by William Whitelaw, British Home Secretary, at my old school of Glenalmond in Perthshire, Scotland.

Whitelaw's words are stewed-up Buchan, fragrant with imperial esprit of the sort that made Dyer feel he had done a jolly lot of good in Amritsar:

'I suppose,' Whitelaw said, 'I meet as many people in all walks of life as most people today, from prisoners at one end of the scale to very many skillful people at the other, and the Home Secretary is always talking and meeting people. I have over the years developed one very simple test, which I always carry with me – I don't think it's an unfair test because it has never been seen to be wrong. If you look very firmly and straight at anybody who comes to talk to you and look straight into their eyes, will they look at yours? If they will, you are nearly always on sound ground. If they won't, then you know you are on very bad ground. That test I always apply if I am lucky enough to be asked to a school prize-giving. I used that test today and I can only say that Glenalmond came out of the test with the highest possible rating I have ever found at any time when I have given the prizes away anywhere else. And that I do think is something. If it is my test I don't think it's a bad one and if you win on it, well, then I think that's a very good thing.'

The thing is, you see, that *white men* looked you in the eye. Indians didn't look you in the eye. They looked at the ground and their eyes slid away, and you knew that they would slide a dagger between your ribs as soon as your back was turned.

VV

... To Shatila and Sabra

The Vietnam Rethinkers say the US would have won if Westmoreland and the soldiers had been given their heads. The problem, or rather the disaster, say the Israeli investigators, came because Sharon was given his head. So Sharon takes the rap but gets off rather more lightly than Dyer. Sharon is no longer Defense Minister but remains in the cabinet.

Massacres may be symbolic but they are also distracting. My Lai and the guilt or otherwise of Rusty Calley diverted attention from the fact that tremendous massacres went on day after day, month after month, year after year. The horror of Amritsar and the reprobation of the Hunter Commission are more dramatic but less telling than other statistics: after nearly 200 years of British rule, with a population of approximately 380 million, India in 1939 had only 1,306 students of agriculture, 2,413 of engineering, 719 of veterinary science, 150 of technology, and 3,561 of medicine in its colleges and universities, according to the Statistical

Abstract for British India. The British debauched Indian industry and transformed it into an agrarian country whose villages could not produce sufficient food. According to a British source, deaths from famine in India between 1800 and 1900 amounted to 21,400,000.

All of which makes Dyer's murders seem diminutive. The dramas of accusation, condemnation and exoneration surrounding the massacres in the refugee camps are compelling yet they distract attention from the violence being inflicted upon humans, day by day, yesterday, today and tomorrow, on the West Bank. By his refusal to permit US grain shipments to Bangladesh in 1974, Henry Kissinger very definitely murdered, by forced starvation, many thousands of people, huge multiples of those killed at Amritsar and Shatila. Yet somehow it wasn't a 'massacre' in the journalistic sense of the term. Kissinger, after innumerable horrifying crimes, is still honored by people who would not regard themselves as accomplices to murder. Indeed he gave, by invitation, a rousing speech about the Communist menace at *Newsweek*'s 50th anniversary binge. No one among the hundreds of journalists present saw fit to leave the room in shame that such a man should have been summoned to sanctify the anniversary of a major American journalistic enterprise.

VV

Down Memory Lane

Around the 50th anniversary of the accession of Hitler to power on January 30, 1933 (Gandhi was assassinated on the same date in 1948), the newspapers hinted that coverage at the time was not entirely satisfactory. This is a serious understatement. An excellent article in the Boston *Globe* magazine for January 30, by M.R. Montgomery, had some extraordinary quotations. As usual, the newspapers tended to hope for the best from national leaders, especially when they were declaredly anti-Communist. Thus the *New York Times* for April 4, 1933: 'It may be fair to Hitler himself to say that in all probability he did not himself sanction either the violence directed towards the Jews or the boycott plans. His anti-Semitism is understood to have been mainly rhetorical.'

The London *Times* said, 'Herr Hitler has, in fact, like Signor Mussolini ten years ago, made a great reputation in opposition. He has now to show that, like his great Italian prototype, he is capable of constructive leadership.'

After Kristallnacht, in 1938, in which thousands of Jews were beaten, murdered or taken to concentration camps, the *Chicago Tribune* chided the Nazis severely: 'If it is the policy of the German state to eliminate Jews from business, the government is presumed to have means to accomplish it in legal forms and by its own agencies. To turn the task over to unrestrained private fury is the negation of civilized political responsibility. It is chaos rather than government.'

Of Austria, after the Anschluss, the *Los Angeles Times* ran a headline: 'Culture Hub Seen Here Due to European Crisis' and, noting the exiling of liberal and Jewish artists in the Reich, saw the chance of 'a great festival of the arts in California before the year is over.'

A signed editorial-page column in the L.A. *Times* a few days later discussed Austrian events and concluded: 'Even if we owed them no debt of gratitude we so-called Christians can scarcely justify any persecution of the Jews. There is always "noblesse oblige," rank imposes obligation.'

VV

Life Follows Art

'Suddenly, the President addressed him: "And you, Mr. Gardiner? What do you think about the bad season on The Street?"

'Chance shrank ... He stared at the carpet. Finally, he spoke: "In a garden," he said, "growth has its seasons. There are spring and summer, but there are also fall and winter. And then spring and summer again. As long as the roots are not severed, all is well and all will be well." ...

'"I must admit, Mr. Gardiner," the President said, "that what you've just said is one of the most refreshing and optimistic statements I've heard in a very, very long time."' (Jerzy Kosinski, *Being There*, 1971)

'Economic recovery is something like a seedling. For a while it grows underground and you don't see it above ground. And then it shoots up and seeds are sprouting all over the place. And that's what we're starting to see around the nation right now.' (Ronald Reagan, January 1983)

VV

March 24, 1983

The 'Judeo-Christian Tradition'

At the risk of offending religious sentiment – the American Spectator recently pronounced the Enlightenment to be 'over' – I must enter a protest against the use of 'the Judeo-Christian tradition' as an advertisement for freedom or uplifting human values. To take the 'Judeo' part first, we need only glance at the Old Testament to find a deity of savagery, urging his chosen people to acts of genocide. It is a saga of unremitting ferocity rivaled only by that other foundation stone of Western culture, the Iliad.

Need we recall the fury of Moses that Midianite children were spared? 'Now therefore,' he roared, 'kill every male among the little ones, and kill every woman that hath known man by lying with him.' Readers whose memories of Holy Writ have grown hazy may care to consult the disgusting 10th chapter of the Book of Joshua ('So Joshua smote all the country of the hills, and of the south, and of the vale, and of the springs, and all their kings: he left none remaining, but utterly destroyed all that breathed, as the Lord God of Israel commanded') or the crazed 28th chapter of Deuteronomy, with 54 verses of curses from God on those straying from his word.

After perusal of these episodes I would recommend the account in Numbers, Chapter 25, of God's outrage at racial intermingling between the children of Israel and the hosts of Midian. Phineas, son of Eleazar, having risen up with a javelin, 'went after the man of Israel into the tent and thrust them both through, the man of Israel, and the woman through her belly.' God is delighted: 'So the plague was stayed from the children of Israel. And those that died in the plague were twenty and four thousand.'

It could fairly be argued that two of the greatest blots on what the president would no doubt call 'the Judeo-Christian era' were slavery and the subjection of women. For a detailed inspection of the Judeo-Christian record I commend G.E.M. de Ste. Croix's magisterial 'Class Struggle in the Ancient Greek World,' but it can be stated in brief that Christianity failed to improve Greco-Roman society. Becoming the official religion in no way tempered its excesses, and in many ways made it worse in terms of violence and extremes of wealth.

Christianity did not oppose slavery. Jesus accepted it and so did Paul, whose political outlook was most famously expressed in his view that 'the powers that be are ordained of God.' Paul told Ephesian slaves, 'Be obedient to them that are your masters according to the flesh, with fear and trembling, in singleness of your heart, as unto Christ.' Augustine cited the instruction approvingly, adding that slavery was God's punishment on mankind for the sin of Adam. St. Leo I wrote passionately in 443 against slaves being accepted into Holy Orders, which would be 'polluted by such vile company, and the rights of owners ... violated.'

From the birth of Christianity, Prof. Ste. Croix asserts, no outright Christian condemnation of slavery can be found until the petition of the Mennonites in Germantown in 1668. This sect was founded by an Anabaptist and we need only glance at the 38th of the 39 Articles of the Church of England to see what orthodox Christians thought of *them*. In fact Christianity was a powerful buttress to slavery, just as Joshua's treatment of the Gibeonites ('hewers of wood and drawers of water') is often used as a justification for apartheid.

Jesus was anti-property, but this was soon twisted by socio-political realities. The Christ of Luke ('Blessed are ye poor, for yours is the Kingdom of God') became the Christ of Matthew ('Blessed are the poor *in spirit*, for theirs is the Kingdom of Heaven'). Indeed Christian advocacy of alms and charity invested wealth with a moral aura, a stratagem familiar today, as those studying Michael Novak's paeans to the modern corporation know well.

Nor has the 'Judeo-Christian tradition' much to offer women, whether in Genesis ('In sorrow thou shalt bring forth children; and thy desire shall be to thy husband, and he shall rule over thee') or in the Epistles ('The head of every man is Christ and the head of the woman is man; and the head of Christ is God'). Woman came from man, woman was responsible for the fall. The Judeo-Christian concept of sex and marriage is unhealthy and often psychopathic.

We may add to this the Christian tradition of persecution of heresy, which produced some of the bloodiest pages in human history. And those progressive forces in Catholicism and Protestantism that have recently emerged as a footnote to the Judeo-Christian tradition are denounced by Pope and Reagan administration alike.

Against such a tradition there is something to be said for the man who died 100 years ago and who wrote that 'Religion is the sigh of the oppressed creature, the heart of a heartless world,' and that criticism of religion meant not that man should bear the chains of oppression without fantasy or consolation 'but so that he shall throw off the chain and pluck the living flower.'

WSJ

March 29, 1983

Koestlers: Exeunt Omnes

Peering at the fashion photographs of Norman Parkinson, a man who would have made even the cellar at Ekaterinburg look like the studio for a modelling session for cossack boots, I was surprised to see a photograph of Helen Trefusis, described as Mrs. Arthur Koestler. I thought of the recently suicided Mrs. K and looked at the 1935 glamour snap with added interest.

It turns out that Helen Trefusis was but the first of three Koestler consorts and therefore was not able to assist at AK's final exit. But the Koestler affair still sticks in one's mind. Cynthia Koestler was 56 to

Arthur's terminally ill 77 and had many years of pottering about the planet still ahead. There was probably money too, in reasonable quantities. Why did she down the barbiturates at the same time as her husband?

An interesting piece by Peter Osnos in the *Washington Post* set forth some of the details. She joined Koestler as his secretary in the late 1940s, answering an ad he had placed in a French paper for a temporary secretary.

She was born in South Africa, Jewish on her mother's side, Irish on her father's. When she was 10 she heard the bang, as her father blew his head off. She worked as a secretary for Koestler through his second and her first marriage and finally married him in the early '60s. Before that she had adopted his name.

All sources say she slaved for K, typing his manuscripts and performing all the other tasks necessary to keep an intellectual on active duty. He got sick with leukemia and Parkinson's disease. Life got harder. One silent witness to the stressful situation was the Koestlers' dog, a Lhasa apso called David. Cynthia dragged the wretched hound off to the vet and had it 'put to sleep', then told the maid she had given him away. Poor David. I can imagine the worried mutt hearing the Koestlers discussing rational suicide and barking his profound disagreement.

On February 28, Osnos reports, 'the day before the couple probably died, she called one couple to postpone a visit and sounded agitated. The same day milk and newspaper deliveries were cancelled.'

I was never much of a fan of Koestler, probably influenced by my father, who loathed him. During the siege of Madrid, when it looked as though the Fascists were going to come storming in, Koestler suddenly found good reason to attend to revolutionary affairs in Paris. The siege was lifted, Koestler returned and the comrades made some disparaging remarks about his fortitude.

Then they were all in Malaga and once again the Fascist foe was advancing. Time to flee, said my father to Koestler. Not on your life, Claud, said Arthur. Last time I ran you all called me yellow. This time I stand. So they all ran away and Koestler stood. The Fascist foe advanced, entered Malaga, shoved him in jail and prepared to advance the date of his exit by nearly half a century. The Communists organized a worldwide campaign to save him. He was released and returned to England to issue a savage denunciation of communism. His name was always mud around the Cockburn household.

I called up my mother to check whether she thought that Mrs. K had somehow done the noble thing and was delighted to find her outraged. 'Claud always said what a bastard Koestler was,' she shouted down the international phone line indignantly, yet with the satisfaction of someone finding a point well proved at last.

VV

April 5, 1983

Reagan's Mousetrap

In the summer of 1980 General Daniel Graham, former head of the Defence Intelligence Agency, told James Ridgeway and my brother Andrew that the future way to combat the Russian threat was to position laser weapons in space above the North Pole. Any missile arching its way from Siberia towards the United States could be zapped at will. As Andrew and Jim listened agape to the general's allocution, he pressed on to discount the danger of nuclear munitions. If the three of them were told at that precise moment that a one-megaton bomb was going to land on the office in one hour, they could walk 4.2 miles and hide behind a lilac bush. (One megaton equals one thousand kilotons. The Hiroshima A-bomb was 12.5 kilotons.)

From Graham to Reagan, who unleashed the space laser concept last week. The insane proposition has received much respectful commentary in the press. I imagine that if Reagan had solemnly announced the deployment of a 200-mile-high mousetrap on the North Pole, equipped with magnets to divert and then crush Russian missiles, the press would have been just as respectfully assiduous in weighing his proposal. 'Mousetrap Scheme Under Fire, But Some Scientists Don't Scoff' etc., etc. The president proposes and the press sweeps up. Next week Reagan will probably announce that American scientists have discovered that the entire US agricultural surplus can be compacted into a giant tomato one thousand miles across, which will be suspended above the Kremlin from a cluster of US satellites flying in geosynchronous orbit. At the first sign of trouble the satellites will drop the tomato on the Kremlin, drowning the fractious Muscovites in ketchup.

VV

The E.H. Carr Case

It's scarcely surprising that the age of Reagan and Thatcher should be witness to the most violent diatribe of postwar British academia. Its object was the great historian of Soviet Russia, E.H. Carr, and the perpetrator was a fellow of Carr's old Cambridge college, Trinity, who had the audacity to attend Carr's funeral while actually putting the finishing touches to his assault.

Carr died on November 3, 1982, at the advanced age of 90. The issue of the *London Review of Books* for January 20 carried on its cover the simple words 'Against E.H. Carr'. Inside, beneath the heading 'Grim Eminence', were several thousand words by Norman Stone.

Every now and again, from the mephitic swamps of British academic life, come the poison bubbles of a long-nourished hatred. Previous to this, the single most abusive essay I can remember was one by John Sparrow, Warden of All Souls, assailing the scholarship of an American edition of Housman. In abuse, if in nothing else, Stone far outstrips the Warden. Housman at least could not be recruited to the Cold War. Stone is part of a conservative group of historians long hostile to Carr for his temperate attitude towards the Soviet Union.

Here's an early sample of Stone's spleen: 'It would appear that [Carr's] own parents did not much care for him either. It is said that they farmed him out to live with an aunt, one of these sad Edwardian spinster-dependants. She adored him; she even learned Latin so as to help him with his homework. Once he reached Trinity College, Cambridge (as a student, not a fellow), he dismissed her and she died in loneliness and penury some years later. It was not the last act of cruelty which Carr was to perform. There were three Mrs Carrs (not one, as the Times obituary claimed), and each marriage ended in hideous circumstances: one wife was left when she already had terminal cancer, another abandoned, when Carr was almost ninety, because she was "depressing". He died in an old people's home, the matron of which he would ask, piteously, to hold his hand. For Carr very greatly wanted to be loved, and he much preferred women's company to men's, although he treated his women so badly ... He was also, it is said, very mean.'

This is a fair specimen of what followed: Charges of adultery and miserliness are succeeded by denunciations of Carr as an appeaser and a coward, all in an idiom of spiteful venom that becomes strangely oppressive.

'The curious thing about Carr, the historian of power, was that he never had much himself. He did not become editor of the Times. After the war, he lost his chair at Aberystwyth: the Nonconformists among the governors objected to his affair with one (or perhaps more) of their professors' wives ... As a reviewer Carr was sometimes just and never fair. He resembled a remote, irascible potentate who would not hesitate to put a whole town to the sword if one of its inhabitants ate peas with his knife. ... Carr was not a good teacher. In conversation, he never gave much away, and he disliked talking to anyone with whom basic principles had not been agreed. He was a very ungenerous reviewer of research-fellowship dissertations ...'

Such summary judgements are combined with extended attacks on Carr's fifteen-volume *History of Soviet Russia* and other volumes (*Romantic Exiles, What Is History*) on which his reputation was based.

Stone's diatribe provoked much indignation: four successive waves of letters in subsequent issues of the *London Review*. First came a letter from

Carr's daughter, Rachel Kelly, which suggested that Stone's researches into his subject had not been taxing. Her father, Mrs. Kelly wrote, had never been 'farmed out.' 'He spent his childhood and school years in the family home of which the spinster aunt had formed a part.' Nor had the spinster died in pathetic and impoverished circumstances. Nor had Carr's first wife died of cancer, abandoned in her terminal throes by Carr. She had been cured of cancer ten years before the marriage broke up, and lived a further fifteen years before dying of pneumonia. 'We are appalled,' Mrs. Kelly said on behalf of herself and her half brother, 'that a historian, in writing of a colleague lately dead, should publish defamatory untruths which he could have researched. He has caused distress to the family.' Stone apologized for the inaccuracy.

The following week Stone sustained severe punishment from heavy-armored academic divisions. Carr's collaborator, R.W. Davies (praised by Stone) concluded his letter with the remark, 'Stone stigmatises Carr as "something of a coward". It seems to me this phrase would be better applied to a man who published a vituperative attack on the most eminent historian of his college a few weeks after his death, while praising his still-living collaborator.' Two other supporters of Carr reminded readers that Carr had reviewed Stone's book in the *New York Review* and referred to the author's 'slap-dash impressionism'. Further refutation of Stone's charges and a weak defense by Stone have followed.

What lies behind this strange eruption? Part of the story is Stone's bile at Carr's review of his own *The Eastern Front, 1914-1917*. Part is his rage, and those of his clique, at the dominance established by Carr over book-reviewing policy at the *Times Literary Supplement* in the '50s and '60s – when, incidentally, all reviews were unsigned. He says Carr and Isaac Deutscher jointly controlled reviews of books about Russia and enthusiastically praised each other.

It is true that at the *TLS* all books about the Soviet Union were, at least in the mid-1960s, packed off to Carr. I know, because I helped toss the volumes into the Carr pile. It saved much time. All American books went to D.W. Brogan. Deutscher scarcely wrote for the *TLS*. Stone triumphantly said that Carr was dropped when John Gross became editor. Gross was and is a timid little reactionary, and so this story is likely too.

It seems that Stone, twice-married himself, has been through personal upheavals that scarcely afford him a moral vantage point from which to belabor Carr. His own removal from Jesus College to Trinity recalls – in consequence if not in precise nature of provocation – Carr's precipate removal from Aberystwyth (which, as one letter announced, is to establish an E.H. Carr Chair).

It is true that Carr, heavy with years, did indeed remove himself from his wife, Betty Behrens, when he was 89 and she some 20 years younger. As

Carr lay in the nursing home, Stone insinuated himself into the graces of Behrens (whom Carr refused to see), picking up much of the personal material deployed and then refuted in the *London Review.* Nor does he seem to have avoided research missions to Carr's rooms in Cambridge in the latter's terminal decline.

One view is that Stone has permanently damaged his own academic career.* Another is that not least in the extraordinary aspects of the affair is the willingness of the *London Review of Books* and of its editor Karl Miller to print the Stone farrago, unchecked, defamatory, chock to the gunwales with turbid innuendo. So much for the British literary scene, so different from the high-toned Parnassus on view this side of the Atlantic, where the Podhoretz can lie down with the lamb in perfect amity.

VV

*He did not. He is now Professor of Modern History at Oxford.

May 3, 1983

Secret Conversations with Hitler

The enigma of the Hitler diaries was solved on Friday when a man called identifying himself as Adolf Hitler and requesting an interview. Hitler told me he had been doing part-time political consultancies and translation work in recent years, most recently on US Ambassador to the UN Jeane Kirkpatrick's staff, and as a rewrite man and headline writer on a New York newspaper he declined to identify.*

In subsequent interviews and examinations, Hitler's authenticity was verified by a number of experts retained by the *Voice,* including a German-born Brooklyn dentist, an accountant who worked for *Der Stürmer,* and Madam Sosostris, the famous clairvoyant much favored by the Nazi high command in the late 1930s, now working in the West Village.

Voluntarily submitting to a series of tests gruelling to a man of his years, Hitler passed with flying colors, effortlessly chanting passages from Wagner, the battle order of the Wermacht in 1939 and substantial portions of the works of Gobineau.

In our meetings Hitler dressed casually, but with a certain panache. He

*The New York Post

betrayed little sign of the physical disabilities – palsy, motor inhibition, drooping eyelid, slurred speech – noted by intimates in the bunker.

He had, he said, decided to come forward in order to expose the 'degenerate drivel and outright forgery' sponsored by *Der Stern* magazine. In three frank interviews, interspersed with copious readings from the journal he intermittently dictated, Hitler set the record straight on a life that, as he said, 'has been grotesquely misunderstood.'

It was after a late-night dinner at Elaine's that Hitler admitted the existence of his journals, kept on an occasional basis from the late 1920s, bringing out the transcripts and several manuscript pages over schnapps. These pages have been authenticated by handwriting experts. Spectrographic analysis reveals the paper to have been made from linden pulp of the correct period.

Some entries:

January 30, 1933: 'Chancellor at last! I am very excited! This is the biggest day in my life so far! I had feared that after the tumultuous events of the morning and afternoon, twilight would bring with it a spasm of that *Weltschmerz* which has afflicted me since the shameful provisions of the Treaty of Versailles were imposed upon the Fatherland. But my spirits held up. Göring is very jolly though I mistrust him, particularly for his gross drug-taking habits about which the cunning Himmler keeps me informed.'

June 30, 1934: 'Night of the Long Knives, as historians will call it. Rid of Röhm at last! I shall be accused of excessive ruthlessness, but R was a sexual pervert and a security risk ... I shall be Führer and Reich Chancellor by the end of the summer. Eva looked wonderful tonight. I pray she will soon be pregnant. Perhaps then we could abandon the world-historical stage and retire to a little hamlet in the mountains where I could get on with my novel and Eva devote herself to the joys of motherhood.'

September 3, 1939: 'England has declared war. Frankly, I'm surprised and not a little perturbed. I wouldn't put it past Churchill and the war party to get America into the war, with some trick like the Lusitania routine.'

Looking up from this diary entry, Hitler sighed:

'That was my mistake, my greatest mistake. I should have invaded England in 1940. I had no idea how weak the place was until I read Churchill's memoirs after the war. What about the Eastern Front, you are going to ask. Well, if I had sent the Gross Deutschland Division farther forward, redeployed the Hungarian and Rumanian units and allowed Von Paulus to make a break for the west earlier, things might have been very different.'

'What, aside from Stalingrad and the failure to invade in 1940, were your greatest disappointments?'

'Leni Riefenstahl not getting an Oscar! We were all shattered by that. That was a very personal disappointment of course. The reason was obvious, naturally. The Jewish émigrés in Los Angeles.'

'What achievements of yours have been underrated?'

'Schacht could teach Volcker a thing or two. Low interest rates, heavy government funding, large scale public works ... that's the way forward. After the Autobahns we had them build the Siegfried Line. That's how to keep the lumpen lice loyal.'

Hitler says he misses Berlin but finds New York 'the most exciting city in the world' and intellectually 'very stimulating.' 'Culturally,' he says, 'the trend has been encouraging over the last decade as the irresponsibility and defeatism of the late '60s is replaced by a new sense of destiny. New York is obviously a genetic garbage dump, but every garden needs its compost heap. I study the trends and I am content.'

Hitler laughingly discounts suggestions that he will enter politics. 'I am too old and even now too controversial.' He hints though that he will soon be giving his agent a new, updated version of *Mein Kampf* and a postscript about the final days of the Reich. Simon & Schuster is 'very interested.'

'The time is just about right,' Hitler ruminated aloud as we stood outside on Second Avenue. 'The cataclysm of 1945 was only prelude to the cataclysm that must inevitably come soon.'

VV

May 12, 1983

Springtime for Hitler

I must confess some regret that the Hitler diaries weren't genuine. For if Hitler had kept a journal perhaps his notations would have forced people to revise misconceptions about the German economy between Versailles and the Second World War. These misconceptions continue to exercise a dire effect to this day.

From the vantage point of the mid-1930s Hitler would have been able to reflect in his diary that there was nothing wrong in principle with the $30 billion worth of reparations demanded by the victors at Versailles in 1919. Late Keynes was right and early Keynes was wrong. Properly paced and administered, they would have been of great benefit to the German economy, just as the reparations paid by the defeated French after the

Franco-Prussian War were a great stimulus to the French economy, and a bane to the Germans.

Reparations present a problem for those on the receiving end. After World War I the Germans were to pay reparations to the French and to the British, who were in turn to repay loans to the U.S. Both British coalminers and French construction workers protested passionately as German reparatory goods began to arrive, and in New York in 1921 John Foster Dulles wisely pointed out that the U.S. economy would not be able to absorb the goods flowing west as a consequence of the reparatory process.

The $15 billion worth of 'reparations' paid after World War II under the Marshall Plan was a great boon to the U.S. and not troublesome to those on the receiving end, given the destruction of capital plant in Western Europe. By the 1970s the lesson had been lost and Congress foolishly rejected the idea of U.S. reparations to Vietnam, which would have been a useful shot in the arm for the American economy.

There is no illusion more widespread than the notion that inflation led to Hitler. This myth has been used relentlessly by economic reactionaries for as long as I can remember. People seem automatically to associate those heaps of worthless currency in the hyperinflation with the accession of the Nazis. Hitler would certainly have been surprised to learn that the hyper-inflation of 1923 led to his triumph as chancellor a decade later. His diaries would no doubt have recorded the fact that the Weimar economy in the 1920s, until April 1929, was the third most vibrant in the world, after those of the U.S. and Canada.

Indeed the 1923 hyperinflation stimulated the German economy, by wiping out savings and thus accelerating consumption. In contrast to the bouncing Weimar economy, Britain limped its way through the 1920s, shackled by a return to the gold standard and an overvalued pound.

Genuine Hitler diaries would undoubtedly have referred to the Bruning government's decision in 1931, at the urging of its economists, to cut wages 10%. This foolish move would no doubt be applauded today by those in the U.S. pushing for a lower minimum wage and other reductions in workers' pay. Herbert Hoover was sensible enough to see that it would scarcely benefit the U.S. economy to diminish workers' purchasing power.

In 1933, when Hitler became chancellor, unemployment in Germany stood at 40% and prices were falling, as they had been since 1929. Savage deflation was in progress. By 1936 German unemployment stood at 1%. His diaries would no doubt have outlined the policies producing this extraordinary recovery – achieved, contrary to undying popular belief, without the stimulative effect of arms spending.

Hitler's desire for a larger German population led to substantial subsidies for construction and hence a housing boom. Massive public works – most famously, the Autobahns – boosted the economy. Hitler paid little attention to the deficit or to the protests of the banking community about his policies. Interest rates were kept low and though wages were pegged, family income increased by reason of full employment.

German military spending remained far lower than is now imagined, right up until 1939. Genuine diaries would certainly have recorded Hitler's alarm over the British declaration of war, his lamentations over German military unpreparedness, and his satisfaction that the phony war allowed him time to build up resources for war. The one-time-only lunge of *Blitzkrieg* was dictated as much by scarcity of these resources as anything else.

Thus genuine diaries might have recorded economic history as well as the monstrous plans of a mass murderer. Not the least abhorrent aspect of the Hitler hoax was the speed with which publishers and would-be publishers of the bogus diaries seem prepared to believe in the sanitized Hitler touted therein.

WSJ

May 31, 1983

Squalid

On the subject of Vietnam let us pause to consider a cover story, the Sunday before last, in *Parade* magazine. The story concerned the famous picture, taken by Eddie Adams, of General Loan about to kill a captive during the Tet offensive. An advance publicity bulletin from *Parade* announced that 'The photograph, which won a Pulitzer prize for photographer Eddie Adams, ruined the life of its subject, Vietnam chief of police General Nguyen Ngoc Loan, Adams has revealed.'

You might have thought that Adams would say that the life of the other person in his picture was more than ruined. But Adams seems to entertain no such thoughts. He very decently explains that 'General Loan had become a man condemned both in his country and in America because he had killed an enemy in war.' And he reports of Loan that 'Today he runs a small coffee and pizza shop in Virginia. When I visited him there he told me, "You were doing your job, and I was doing mine."'

So much for revisionism.

VV

June 21, 1983

The Revolution Betrayed: An Open Letter

It's all the rage these days to claim fidelity to left principles while joining the ranks of the cold war. It's also all the rage to justify the subversion of Nicaragua on the grounds that the Sandinistas have 'betrayed' the revolution. I am glad, therefore, to be able to publish the following letter:

As leftists we, the undersigned, wish to express our outrage at the ongoing betrayal by the Sandinista leadership of the original high ideals of the Nicaraguan revolution.

Abundant reports make clear that private enterprise – that is, the rule of capital – continues to dominate Nicaragua's political economy. Reactionary religious functionaries who, in any *authentic* expression of the popular will, would have been swinging from every sapling in Managua, are permitted to subvert the people's cause in pulpits and confessionals across the land.

The grim catalogue of betrayal continues: we have before us eyewitness accounts of *campesinos* tending their *own* plots – painful testimony to the absence of any vigorous push towards collectivization. The Sandinista leaders boast too easily of the absence of a 'bloodbath' in the wake of Somoza's overthrow. Do we have to remind them that a revolution is not a tea party and that enemies of the revolution, permitted to survive and even to prosper, will proliferate like weeds and choke the revolutionary blossom?

In their defense, the Sandinista leadership speaks in the language of Cavour, of the '*tacte des choses possibles*'. But when in history have the 'objective conditions' ever been perfect? When has the moment ever been ideal to open the revolutionary engine to full throttle?

Some of us would plead guilty to the charge of anarchism, of 'ultra-leftism'. Others have been steeled in the libertarian populist fires of American nativism. All of us have caught upon the wind the strangled cries of millions who, amid the dark night of compromise, yearn only to be as radical as reality itself and to urge upon their leaders that word at once magical and peremptory: FORWARD!

Signed: Ronald Radosh, Ronald Reagan, John Judis, Paul Berman, David Denby, Charles Krauthammer, Martin Peretz, Morton Kondracke, Morton Janklow, Morton Salt, Stephen Rosenfeld, Meg Greenfield, John Corry, Bruce Cameron, Aryeh Neier, Ed Bradley, Morley Safer, Marvin Kalb, Pam Hill, Pope John Paul II, David Owen, Harold Evans, Hodding Carter, François Mitterrand, Regis Debray, Bayard Rustin, Ben Wattenberg, David Jessup, Al Shanker, David Horowitz, Peter Collier, Michael Kramer, Idioticus, etc.

VV

July 19, 1983

The Death of Herman Kahn

More than almost any other person in the postwar period, Herman Kahn symbolized the defense intellectual, both in his depraved role as conceptualizer of mass murder and in the cap and bells of the court jester fooling about on the battlements while the 'serious' war criminals checked out the utility of his blueprints.

Herman Kahn's great 'achievement' – if one can use such a word about so evil an intellectual venture – was to domesticate nuclear war, to invent a vocabulary for discussing it, to persuade many, including the men now surrounding Ronald Reagan, that nuclear war need not be viewed as Apocalypse but could be a controlled continuance of foreign policy by other means. Terms such as 'civil defense,' 'window of vulnerability,' and 'nuclear blackmail' all began with Kahn and his colleagues at the RAND Institute in Santa Monica.

We are fortunate in having the recently published *The Wizards of Armageddon* by Fred Kaplan for an incisive encapsulation of Kahn's career as nuclear guru. Anyone wishing to study the military-intellectual complex should put this book at the top of the list – along with case studies of Kahn, Bernard Brodie, Sam Cohen, and their associates.

Kahn was born of Jewish immigrants in Bayonne, New Jersey, and moved soon thereafter to the Bronx. At age 8 he rode on a bus on the Sabbath and noted that God did not punish him. An agnostic thereafter, he became interested in man-made rather than divine modes of retribution, and at a socialist Jewish summer camp he was discovered, at age 10, to have four military aviation magazines – which were confiscated forthwith – among his personal effects.

His parents were divorced about his time, and Kahn moved with his mother to Los Angeles. When he was in the 7th grade his teacher announced to the class that wars never settle anything. During next day's lunch hour, young Herman crept into the classroom and covered the blackboard with incidents when, in his belief, wars had settled something. He expounded his views to the class when it returned.

He went to UCLA and the California Institute of Technology, and began looking for a job in 1948. He had almost settled on a career in real estate when his friend Sam Cohen – subsequently the 'father' of the neutron bomb – said he should try for a job at the RAND Corporation, which had been set up by General 'Hap' Arnold after the Second World War as a way of retaining some intellectuals to think about such matters as nuclear war.

According to Kaplan, Kahn knew he had come to the right place when he was put to work on a technical advisory board studying nuclear-powered planes. And indeed the application of 'rationality' to such a demented project does sum up Kahn's function. Kahn played a role in the mathematics of early-'50s efforts to design an H-bomb. He also joined with such colleagues as Albert Wohlstetter – another peculiarly baneful military intellectual of the postwar period – in pondering nuclear strategy. As Kaplan puts it:

'Bernard Brodie had first conceived the idea of avoiding Soviet cities in nuclear strikes, but when Victor Hunt and others in the RAND Strategic Objectives Committee extended that concept to avoiding cities *and* going after Soviet military targets Brodie expressed pessimism about its feasibility. Calculations suggested with a purely counter-military attack, two million people would still die, a horrifying high number. But Kahn ... put a novel twist on this observation. To Kahn such a calculation made the two types of targeting all the more distinctive: as Kahn phrased it, *only* two million people would die. Alluding almost casually to 'only' two million dead was part of the image Kahn was fashioning himself, the living portrait of the ultimate defense intellectual, cool and fearless, asking the questions everyone else ignored, thinking about the unthinkable.'

The RAND intellectuals were at this time embarking on the project of trying to conceive of nuclear war as something other than a spasm of mass destruction. Such intellectuals – many of them the same people – are to this day trying to dream up ways of fighting 'winnable' nuclear wars with deaths of 'only' two million, or six million.

Bernard Brodie – who was undergoing psychoanalysis at the time – had written a paper which, as Kaplan says, was for private circulation in RAND, comparing war plans and sex. Brodie equated the all-out nuclear assault on the Soviet Union planned by Strategic Air Command to 'going all the way.' He likened the notion of avoiding cities and 'withholding' full nuclear assault to withdrawal before ejaculation. Kahn ridiculed the SAC plan as not 'a war plan but a war orgasm' and parodied it by proposing a Doomsday Machine, a vast computer wired to H-bombs which would automatically detonate when the Soviets did something deemed intolerable.

Kahn became the systematizer of this bogus military science, proposing no less than 44 'rungs of escalation' from 'Ostensible Crisis' to 'Spasm or Insensate War' – Brodie's G Spot.

In ideological formation Kahn was probably a cold-war social democrat – that virulent breed which has taken up permanent residency in the AFL-CIO and elsewhere. At the time of the bogus 'missile-gap' of the late '50s he was talking about the threat of Soviet 'nuclear blackmail' (the Soviets, it turned out later, had just four ICBMs at the time and the U.S. had hundreds). To counter 'nuclear blackmail' Kahn began arguing for 'first use' of nuclear weapons under provocation, backed by a civil defense program. For Kahn civil defense was not about anything so mundane as protecting the lives of the citizenry. Kaplan quotes him as saying, 'The whole purpose of the system is to enable the U.S. to take a much firmer position,' to engage in first strikes and cliff-hanging threats. With that retrospectively comical ability to get the future utterly wrong, Kahn reckoned that full-scale urban evacuations might well occur three times a decade and that 'insofar as the civil defense program gives us the ability to convert [from conventional to nuclear war] *at our discretion* it would be a good thing.'

Kahn served as a consultant to the Gaither Committee – which called, in the late '50s, for a huge expansion of U.S. nuclear capability in preparedness for a Soviet assault. He sought a $200 billion shelter program over the next 15 years, and was turned down. Finally, in 1960, he set forth all his ideas on controlled nuclear war-fighting and thinkable Apocalypse in *On Thermonuclear War*, published in 1960 and correctly described by the mathematician James Newman in *Scientific American* as 'a moral tract on mass murder: how to plan it, how to commit it, how to get away with it, how to justify it.'

At the time it had an enormous effect. It is surreal to look back now at a volume that should properly have caused the sequestration of its author under psychiatric care and find such sentences as these on the beneficial aspects of the increase in human tragedy after nuclear war: 'The increase would not preclude normal and happy lives for the majority of survivors and their descendants ... we can imagine a renewed vigor among the population with a zealous, almost religious dedication to reconstruction exemplified by a 50-to-60 hour work week.'

Kahn had hoped for a job in the Kennedy administration as director of civil defense efforts. Paul Nitze told Kennedy that Kahn was more useful on the outside. Kahn left RAND and set up the Hudson Institute, an even more disreputable lazar house for military intellectuals. In 1964 Kubrick's *Dr. Strangelove* came out, clearly indebted in parodic form to *On Thermonuclear War*. Kahn later told Kaplan that 'Dr. Strangelove would not have lasted three weeks in the Pentagon ... he was too creative.'

As befits the director of a think tank with corporate clients and government contracts to fulfill, Kahn began to plunge into the modern version of an ancient necromancy: futurology. He also proffered, for a price, helpful advice to the Pentagon on how to fight the Vietnam war. In what he described later as 'one of the best single ideas I've ever had' he suggested that the U.S. military build a stretch of 'freeway canals' in the Mekong Delta, along which patrol boats would move at high speed, commanding the countryside and aiding the economic development of that countryside – a project which nicely symbolizes his moral/intellectual regions.

Immensely respected by the defense establishment until the day he died,

Kahn's apogee came with *On Thermonuclear War.* His later books, *Things to Come, The Year 2000, The Japanese Superstate,* and *The Coming Boom* are of interest now mainly as evidence of how you can sell almost anybody on anything, provided it is dressed up as modern thinking. In *Things to Come* in 1972, Kahn and his co-writer, B. Bruce-Briggs, were looking at the next two decades and asking if the war in Vietnam would end by 1985.

Kahn died at the age of 61, having apparently transferred to his doctor his own inability to predict the future accurately, since the doctor had – just before Kahn expired – concluded a medical examination with the pronouncement that he had nothing to worry about.

VV

July 26, 1983

Cuba at 25: Was It Worthwhile?

Thirty years ago this July 26, Fidel Castro and his companions attacked the Moncada Barracks in Santiago, Cuba. Twenty-five years ago, on December 31, 1958, Fulgencio Battista fled into exile, and the Cuban guerrillas swept into Havana. Since that day the Cuban Revolution has survived the U.S.-backed invasion at the Bay of Pigs in 1961 and over 20 years of economic and paramilitary subversion. No other country in the socialist bloc has faced such unremitting pressure. For many of these years, it should never be forgotten, highly placed U.S. officials actively conspired to murder Castro. Today, 22 years after the so-called Khrushchev-Kennedy accord, it is unclear whether the Reagan administration is once again actively pursuing the dream of rolling back the Cuban Revolution.

How would the world look today if that very first assault on Moncada had been wiped out, or if the U.S. had managed to extinguish the revolution thereafter?

Consider the price being paid by citizens of other countries in Latin and Central America and the Caribbean where dictator clients of the U.S. hold sway, where capitalism is maintained by death squads, U.S.-trained officer corps, and Chicago-trained economists.

Guatemala, led by an evangelical exterminist much favored by U.S. corporations, has, at a conservative estimate, seen at least 40,000 state-sponsored killings in the last decade, and practical application of an overused word – genocide – against the Indians.

At least 40,000 were murdered in Chile in the first year after the overthrow of Salvador Allende in 1973. Death squads in Brazil, Paraguay, Uruguay, and Argentina have 'disappeared' scores of thousands more. Today the U.S.-backed junta in El Salvador presides over a charnel house.

The junta the U.S. is attacking in Nicaragua demolished another such charnel house, erected by Anastasio Somoza. Against such a bloodstained backdrop, the Cuban revolution remains a triumph on the level of the most elementary human justice.

Without Cuban help, the map of Africa would not be the same today. The revolutions in Ethiopia and Angola would probably have been destroyed, with Angola in the same condition as its neighbor to the north, the fiefdom of a murdering bandit, sustained in power by U.S. corporations and U.S. dollars.

At the time of the revolution about half the Cuban economy – including all public utilities and half the sugar industry – was owned by U.S. corporations. Middle-class prosperity went hand-in-hand with scarcity and grim prospects for a worker or a peasant. Today, under siege conditions, the economy and the material of this section of the population have been vastly improved.

Illiteracy in Cuba fell from 20 per cent to just 3.3 per cent between 1960 and 1975. World Bank statistics tell us that in 1975, among people 15 and over, Cuba ranked first of all Central and Latin American countries in literacy. Against Cuba's 3 per cent (and the U.S.'s 1 per cent), Costa Rica's illiteracy rate in 1975 stood at 12 per cent, Jamaica's at 14 per cent, and the Dominican Republic's at 30 per cent.

Between 1961 and 1962 – according to CIA reports – the number of schools in Cuba increased from 2482 to 22,458. This was at the start of the campaign against illiteracy. The number continued to increase after that, although more slowly. Student enrollment in medicine, agriculture, and technology doubled.

Some other simple indices: life expectancy in Cuba increased 9.3 per cent, from 64 in 1960 to 70 in 1977. (In the U.S., over the same period, the numbers went from 70 to 73.) Infant mortality in Cuba decreased from 36 per 1000 in 1960 to 25 per 1000 in 1977. The U.S. figure in 1977 was 15. Deaths per 1000 went from 15.4 in 1967 to 12.2 in 1978. An average Cuban's daily calorie intake increased from 2414 in 1961 to 2866 in 1980. CIA statisticians compare this with Jamaica's 2715, Costa Rica's 2645, and the Dominican Republic's 2246.

Tom Enders, when he was riding high at the State Department, used to proclaim regularly that the Cuban Revolution had 'failed.' By what standard? Compared with almost every country in Central and Latin America, it is a haven of economic stability, personal security, and cultural and intellectual pluralism. Readers might care to contemplate the destiny of Cuba over the last quarter-century with that of the U.S.'s most closely held Caribbean puppet Puerto Rico, and draw their own conclusions.

The victory of the Cuban Revolution ushered in the heroic decade of the 1960s. A decade after Castro and his movement overthrew Battista, the

Tet offensive exploded the myth of U.S. invincibility in Southeast Asia.

The 1980s are not 'heroic.' Yet the Cuban Revolution continues to reverberate throughout Central and Latin America and the Caribbean. In 1959 the plans for a Bay of Pigs were already on the drawing boards. In 1983 a Nicaraguan Bay of Pigs is on the drawing boards. The antagonists remain the same: justice versus infamy and exploitation. After a quarter of a century, the beacon of that Cuban Revolution remains as powerful as it ever was.

VV

August 4, 1983

The Myth of the Mob

There they go again, another commission on organized crime. This, in case you are getting confused, is not the body headed by Henry Kissinger and required to clarify U.S. policy toward Latin America but a platoon of worthy citizens, headed by Judge Irving R. Kaufman, now allocated three years and a few million dollars to analyze 'organized crime' in the U.S. and advocate ways of combating this supposed cancer in our midst.

Indeed, Judge Kaufman, seeking an image for the high purpose of his commission, actually likened its impending labors to 'cancer research,' thus demonstrating the status 'organized crime' holds in the hierarchy of America's afflictions, shoulder to shoulder with cancer as Public Enemy No. 1.

It isn't hard to predict what will happen. The commission's report will lead to hearings in which members of Congress, mindful of the publicity earned by such crime battlers as Estes Kefauver and Robert Kennedy, will eagerly participate in the traditional ritual: a gentleman of Italian-American descent (sometimes wearing a paper bag over his head) testifying (in return for local immunity from prosecution for his atrocious crimes) that the American capitalist system is run by five gentlemen from a Sicilian village, usually Castellammare del Golfo, which is to crime what the Harvard Law School is to the opposition.

The congressional committee will eventually conclude that significant sections of the economy are now 'controlled' by 'organized crime,' and the Justice Department, seeing its chance, will finagle through new conspiracy laws, injurious to our freedom. Crime will continue, reflecting as always the state of the economy and the degree of legal impediment to human desires and the motions of the marketplace.

The myth of 'organized crime,' in the form of a kind of super-directorate supervising illegal activity in the U.S., combines two pathologies. One is racism and the other the paranoid belief that 'we' are being secretly controlled by 'them' – 'them' being variously the Freemasons, the Council on Foreign Relations, the Trilateral Commission, the homosexuals, the Catholic Church, the KGB or the Mob.

The lobby maintaining the 'organized crime' myth in existence is probably unbeatable by now. Just as the absurd antitrust laws now survive only as a rationale for the antitrust bar, 'organized crime' persists as a splendid vehicle for professional advancement and profit for journalists and prosecutors, 'strike forces' and publishing houses, the FBI and the entertainment industry.

'Organized crime,' whether known as the Mob, the Mafia, Cosa Nostra, 'This Thing' etc. was engendered, so far as I can remember, by a headline-seeking DA in New Orleans somewhere around the turn of the century. He found people he suspected of perpetrating crime and fomenting sedition, noted that they were Italians and launched the American 'Mafia' on its career forthwith. The simultaneously burgeoning FBI and motion picture industries weren't slow to perceive the usefulness of the Mafia myth. The childish mumbo jumbo about blood oaths, Sicilian brotherhoods and the like was naturally absorbed by young criminals who then sought to live up to the image vouchsafed them by society. The inconvenient fact that many criminals noted for their 'links' to 'organized crime' were Jews and not Italians was explained by another piece of racism – that the Jews were there to do the bookkeeping. Meyer Lansky was always described as the Mob's 'accountant,' as though the race that invented double-entry bookkeeping couldn't add or subtract.

After the dislocations of the 1960s, Americans needed a strong image of the family and thus turned with relief to the Family invented by Mario Puzo in 'The Godfather.' Criminals, always insecure about their image and role, regarded the book as a guide to manners and correct social comportment. Thus, a few years ago, the Irish police lieutenant directing a 'sting' operation in Washington studied 'The Godfather' for tips on etiquette in his guise as an Italian *capo*, and so did the Polish-American thief who was uncertain whether he should kiss the *capo*'s ring. Both pretended to be Italian.

For journalists and prosecutors, the allocation of the opprobrious 'linked to organized crime' subclause upon a victim has the wonderful advantage that the victim can do almost nothing about it. It is like, in another context, being called 'an enemy of Israel.' The enemies of organized labor, in particular, have never been slow to realize this.

This is not to say that all crime in America is entirely 'unorganized' or even 'disorganized.' That would be a terrible slur upon the national character. Obviously neighborhoods, cities and states have gangs and gangs have turf. These gangs will seek monopoly or, where they cannot attain it, combination. If crime were permanently and absolutely unorganized, there would be social anarchy, with much unnecessary bloodshed and inconvenience to the consumer. The pastoral myth of the allegedly beneficent properties of 'small business' apply as much to criminal as to 'legal' commercial enterprises.

It is particularly surprising, all the same, to see President Reagan launching the Kaufman commission on its path. In many ways 'organized crime' is his economic ideal. Unburdened by taxes it is Venture Capital, swashbuckling and inventive, ever seeking fresh opportunity in the marketplace. It, like Reagan, is hostile to bureaucracy. It, like Reagan, would like to get Big Government off our backs.

Just as true Keynesians particularly honor counterfeiters for courage (and often self-sacrifice) in the face of the Fed and tight money, so too should Reagan praise rather than blame such organized crime as we have, while thanking its representatives for stabilizing the system in time of recession and unemployment. Without criminals there would be fewer than the million private police and million lawyers currently trimming unemployment at either end of the social scale.

WSJ

August 9, 1983

War Is Good For You

Politicians and journalists, upon manly confession of error, sometimes say that they are having to eat crow. None of them ever does. But I have eaten crow. The experience swam back into my mind's nose while reading a review by Kingsley Amis in the *TLS* about English food. Amis rightly praises the effect upon English health of rationing during the Second World War. This rationing was planned by Lord Woolton and a nutritional biochemist called Jack Drummond, who was murdered along with his wife and daughter by a mad French peasant in 1952 in a very famous case.

Amis says that with the launching of rationing, 'the British were given the high-extraction National Loaf, kept short of fats, starved of sugar both as such and in jam and sweets, encouraged both by deprivation and in broadcasts and advertisements to make soups and use green vegetables cooked and in salads. So far from going short, the nation ate more healthily than ever before.'

There was almost no protein though, just about one meat cutlet a week, and although I was convinced recently by Dr. Andrew Weil that America's ills stem in part from excess protein, we did need some. So my mother bought crow and stewed it like pigeon. We did better than the cat, which had almost no milk. Only cats 'engaged on work of national importance' (i.e. mousing in warehouses) got their special quarter-pint ration. Cats had a sense of patriotism in those days.

VV

September 20, 1983

Press of Parrots

You can say that the Russians were wrong to have shot down the South Korean jumbo jet and killed 269 snoozing passengers, but I still don't see that this proves Russians enjoy blowing up commercial airliners or that every Soviet leader stood a little taller in his boots the next day and shouted, 'One, two, three, many jumbos' into the shaving mirror.

The Sunday after the plane went down Leslie Gelb wrote in the *New York Time*'s Week in Review that 'Ever so rarely, something happens that cuts through the ambiguities of politics and proves a point. Last week, a Soviet fighter plane shot down a South Korean passenger airliner that had strayed over Soviet territory, killing 269 people. The point, if it needed reaffirmation, was that the leadership of the Soviet Union is different – call it tougher, more brutal or even uncivilized – than most of the rest of the world.'

Now Gelb is alleged to be something of a middleperson on the political spectrum, so you know things are bad when he steps onto the same logical escalator that has already carried the late Larry McDonald, the Moral Majority crowd, the New Rightists and the social democrats to the conclusion that since the Soviet Union is an empire of evil, a pariah state, inherently untrustworthy and morally *different*, you may as well prepare to get them before they get us. Get ready to drop the Big One.

Across the political spectrum all hands turned out to assist in the verbal holocaust, with nouns like 'barbarism,' 'atrocity' and 'massacre' on 24-hour alert. Amid the tumult it has been futile to expect much in the way of interesting journalism, but boiling down 10 days we seem to be left with these theories in descending order of kookiness:

• *The Soviet Union wanted to kill Larry McDonald, and was not bothered by the inconvenience of having to send 268 other souls to perdition alongside him.*

This is the theory voiced by close supporters of McDonald who, as head of the John Birch Society, could be reckoned as one of the Russians' most implacable foes. Variations on this theme include the view that

McDonald's presence on Flight 007 was publicly announced by the Reagan administration, to alert the Russians. Why would the Reagan administration want McDonald dead? Because the Reagan administration is really controlled by Trilateralists such as George Bush and James Baker, who regarded McDonald as their fiercest adversary. A sub-sub-variant, voiced by one former intelligence officer, is that the CIA was involved in the downing of the plane because the agency knew that McDonald had key information about its involvement in drug trafficking. A sub-sub-sub-variant is that the Russians' true target was Scoop Jackson, knowing full well that news of the incident would give him a fatal heart attack.

• *The Russians wanted to kill 269 passengers on a jumbo jet to test American reactions and American will.*

This is the basic theory of the Reagan administration and retains wide popularity. The normally unreliable Niles Lathem, Washington bureau chief of the *New York Post*, reported on September 2 that a 'high intelligence official' had said, 'What they were trying to do, we think, is show them [the South Koreans and Japanese] how powerful they [the Russians] are and how little can be done in the face of the Soviet military machine.'

Reagan himself likes this theory and makes much of the fact that Soviet pilots must have known the plane was a civilian 747 since it was a moonlit night (variously described as half or three-quarter) and the Russian was only a mile away and therefore would have known that the plane was a 747 from its telltale forward humps. Thus he knew he was killing innocent men, women and children. No reporter has seen fit to question this view, which is in fact entirely wrong. Any fighter pilot will attest that it is very hard to make visual identification of planes, particularly at night, through the distorting glass dome of a cockpit a mile away. Stand on top of the Empire State Building and try to figure it out for yourself.

• *The entire affair was, in origin, a South Korean caper.*

At the simplest level, this theory holds that Flight 007 was involved in a KCIA espionage operation.

More elaborately, it is proposed that South Korean fanatics wished to provoke an international incident, and that Flight 007 captain Chun Byung In was part of the plot. In an interview with the *Seattle Times*, reported by UPI, Chun's widow said that he considered the Soviet Union 'to be the enemy of the whole world' and had told her that he encountered a Soviet plane while in flight last year and the incident had made him 'real nervous'.

A sub-variant of this view is the theory advanced by *Hustler* publisher Larry Flynt in the full-page advertisement inexplicably turned down by the *New York Times* but published in the *New York Post*. The entire advertisement, replete with learned references such as to the 'arch fascist Metternich', is rousing stuff, essentially arguing that Flight 007 was contrived by the US as a Gulf of Tonkin incident: 'A man like McDonald is so nuts that his martyrdom cannot be ruled out as a motive. In his world the sacrifice of 268 other people would be nothing compared to eliminating the 'incomparably' greater evil of communism. With the help of the pilot, or other CIA operatives (contacted through the John Birch society) who were just as weird as McDonald and who could have replaced the pilot, he could have caused the flight to take its fateful course, causing the Russians to shoot down the plane. With the help of even higher authorities on the inside (possibly the President), there would have been no problem at all. Knowing that the accusatory finger would be pointed at the Soviets, he could be assured of escaping any suspicion. And the US could maintain an appearance of "innocence".'

• *The SNAFU theory, which deduces that the Koreans were crooks trying to save on gas and the Soviets drunks following orders.*

According to this theory, when the plane first entered Soviet airspace the Russians scrambled but could not find the intruder visible on the radar screens. Conscious of the farce of 1978 when it took Soviet fighters many hours to locate another Korean airliner, the Soviets this time were determined to put up a better show. With the South Korean jumbo about to leave Soviet airspace, and ignoring warning bursts of tracer fire, with fuel in the Soviet fighters running low, the local commander went by the book – fatally for 007.

• *The US was using the South Korean airliner as a tool of espionage, and thus the Russian claim is correct.*

This is the view rather surprisingly taken by, among others, the noted right-wing commentator Dr. Martin Abend, who apparently announced both on CNN and Channel 5 that he had information that the relevant South Korean jumbo had been the subject of last-minute technical alteration in Alaska. The US, and ultimately President Reagan, Abend said, bore direct responsibility for the deaths of 269 people.

Newt Royce of Hearst Newspapers reported on September 4 the admission of intelligence officials that civilian airlines are routinely used for spying. Aeroflot does it for the Russians and, inter alia, Finnair for the US.

The objection to this, most recently raised by Drew Middleton's US intelligence 'sources' in the *New York Times* last Sunday, is that there is nothing 007 could have 'seen' that cannot also be seen by US satellites. This argument, again mostly unchallenged in the US press, is untrue. For one thing satellites overfly at regular times, known to the Russians, and therefore concealing measures can be taken at the appropriate moments. Secondly, photographic intelligence obtained at 35,000 feet will be superior to photographic intelligence obtained at greater altitude. Given the importance of infrared photography, this holds true at night as much as in daylight.

No one has yet provided anything approaching a satisfactory explanation of why the South Korean airliner was so many miles off course, given three computer systems, radar beacons and other monitoring devices. Furthermore, 007's transponder was also shut off. Either with or without the participation of the US RC-135 (the US spy planes that regularly fly around the Sakhalin area) whose presence in the area was disclosed by the White House two days later, the jumbo could have been provoking and monitoring Soviet radar activity and other reactions following its entry into Soviet airspace and flight over important military installations.

I have teetered between the last two theories myself, but come down in favor of the espionage theory on the grounds that the South Korean pilot does not sound the sort of man to have drifted off course by mistake. A Soviet military test was scheduled at the time of 007's overflight. Obviously it's not to the Russians' credit that they shot 007 down. On the other hand, anyone studying Russian history in the 20th century need not be particularly surprised that they did.

The world is definitely becoming a more dangerous place. In 1955 the Bulgarians shot down an Israeli plane that had drifted into their airspace, killing 56. This was right after Eisenhower's Geneva summit (and open-skies proposal) with the Russians. The *New York Times* editorialized that 'At Geneva last week Soviet leaders went all out to impress the outside world with their desire for friendship and peace. This murder in Bulgaria gives a hollow ring to such words. For friendship and peace the Communist countries must be willing to behave in decent, civilized fashion. There is nothing either decent or civilized about this barbarous incident, and public opinion in the West will draw the appropriate conclusions.' Fairly soon after the Bulgarians said it was a bad business, its gunners had been trigger-happy, and paid compensation to the relatives of the victims.

On February 21, 1973, the Israelis shot down a Libyan airliner, a Boeing 727, killing 106 people. At first the Israelis claimed that the plane had acted in a highly suspicious manner, ignoring warning shots and making a final dash for safety. Later, confronted with transmission recordings between the cockpit and the Cairo control tower, as well as the black-box flight recorder, the Israelis conceded a rather different sequence of events. It seems that the plane had got lost during a sandstorm. The crew thought the Israeli fighters buzzing it were Egyptian MIGs. The plane was leaving Israeli airspace over the Egyptian border (thus obviously not heading for a kamikaze run on Jerusalem or Tel Aviv) when the Israelis fired without warning.

It seems that the Israeli O.C. Air Force Mordechai Hod contacted chief of staff Lieutenant-General David Elazar for orders. Elazar was freshening up at home after staying up all night supervising an Israeli terror raid on two Palestinian refugee camps near Tripoli. He was in the shower, and

338

according to the Israeli journalists who wrote *Kippur*, Elazar 'tried to find [Defense Minister] Moshe Dayan and consult him, but he wasn't to be found, though he later contended he was at home – and though he had at his disposal one of the most sophisticated communications systems in the world.' So Elazar shouted from the shower the order to shoot down a civilian airliner leaving Israeli airspace. After a good deal of covering up, including an attempt to blacken the French pilot's reputation by contending he was not licensed to fly 727s, the Israelis agreed to compensate relatives of the victims, and Dayan admitted it had been a bad show.

The international political and press reaction was markedly different from the uproar following the 007 disaster. No one called for suspension of landing rights for El Al. The International Federation of Airline Pilots' Associations decided against any action. Leslie Gelb did not write an article declaring that the leadership in Israel 'is different – call it tougher, more brutal or even uncivilized.' In fact the *New York Times* editorialist took a most understanding attitude. The first such editorial was headed 'Tragic Blunder' ('At best a horrifying blunder. ... At worst ... an act of callousness that not even the savagery of previous Arab actions can excuse'). Most of the editorial was devoted to a sympathetic analysis of possible Israeli motives. On March 1, after earth had been shovelled over the Libyan and Egyptian victims, wogs when you come right down to it, a second *New York Times* editorial declared that 'No useful purpose is served by an acrimonious debate over the assignment of blame ... the basic fact illustrated by this tragic incident is that clashes ... are inevitably going to occur over and over again so long as the two sides remain in the rigid stand-off which has produced such a sterile stalemate all these years.'

VV

October 26, 1983

A-B-C

There is a surreality to this kind of stuff in *Time*, whose reporters recently visited Nicaragua:

'On the surface the Sandinistas have done little to alter the basic three-R's curriculum in the country's elementary schools. Still, there are disquieting signs that the educational system is being used as a propaganda outlet for the government. The government's newly issued primer at first seems to be little more than a Dick-and-Jane clone. But one of the examples of words beginning with the letter *D* is *defense*, and it is accompanied by a photograph of soldiers. "Valiant militias march into the plaza," the caption

reads. "The militias are from the people, the pueblo is ready for defense."
... Even a natural science class at one of Managua's largest public schools
includes a lesson on the alleged exploitation of the Third World by multinational corporations.'

It must take a truly remarkable moral detachment from reality to worry
about '*D* is *defense*' and kindred devilish Sandinista propaganda, when
US-paid contras are disemboweling young teachers in the countryside who
are trying to teach peasants to read and write. Note also the phrase 'alleged
exploitation of the Third World by multinational corporations.'

VV

November 1, 1983

The Rosenberg Debate

I wish people would show some respect for McCarthyism – at least as a
word that once carried some emotional weight. At the Rosenberg debate at
Town Hall on Thursday night Marshall Perlin, lawyer for Michael and
Robert Meeropol, the Rosenbergs' sons, shouted at Ron Radosh, with
perhaps excessive enthusiasm, to 'answer the question, yes or no.'
'McCarthyism of the left,' Radosh shouted back. This is preposterous.
Radosh is not some political martyr being hounded by the custodians of a
repressive society. To the contrary, he is the widely hailed co-author of a
book received with resounding plaudits by these same cultural custodians.
He appears on television shows. The *New Republic* permits him to conduct
a searching examination of democracy in Nicaragua. In other words he is
doing just fine. These days you can hardly belch in public without someone
using 'McCarthyism of the left' to kill debate. Susan Sontag, who did
herself no harm by saying that communism is fascism on the same Town
Hall (it should change its name to Canossa) platform last year, tries
sometimes to contrive the same sense of martyrdom amid her evident prosperity. Jeane Kirkpatrick has used the 'McCarthyism of the left' plot to
great effect as well.

Not having grown up with it, the Rosenberg case has never carried the
same weight for me that it plainly did for many people at Town Hall. At
one point James Weinstein, who was bustled off the stage for not adhering
to the prescribed format of the evening, said that many CP members back
in the '40s would have thought it quite right and proper to have transmitted
secrets to the Soviet Union: proletarian internationalism, you might say.
That's always been a view about the Rosenbergs. If not, why not? But
that's too glib toward the Meeropols and all the other intelligent people

over the years who have labored to show that the Rosenbergs were the victims of horrible injustice.

One does get edgy, all the same, hearing Radosh talk about Rosenberg as a traitor and hearing Joyce Milton say that he 'paid for his crime'. I don't mind talk like that from right-wingers, but Radosh claims to be a 'democratic socialist'. Now let us suppose that a US citizen today obtained information that a CIA-controlled agent in Managua was planning to shoot Daniel Ortega with a sniperscope on a certain day. Let us suppose that the only way that this concerned US citizen and sympathizer with the Nicaraguan revolution could convey this information to the Sandinistas was via a friend in the Cuban mission in New York. Let us suppose that the CIA agent was prevented from his deed, but that a defector later disclosed to the FBI the action of the US citizen, and the US citizen was subsequently indicted for espionage. Where would Radosh stand on this one? We would probably end up saying that no decent democratic socialist should have anything to do with the concerned US citizen and that those who supported this same concerned US citizen were dupes of Stalino-Andropoid barbarism polluting the nativist, innocent course of the American revolution.

Neoliberals or neoconservatives – the two strains have virtually merged by now – are always concerned that revolutions are being 'spoiled' or 'betrayed'. You can never find them actually supporting *any* revolution anywhere, so profound is their fear that some primal, virtuous festival of the oppressed will be besmirched by the Stalinist contagion. Both Ron Reagan and Ron Radosh worry about Nicaragua's deflection from true revolution. Both Ron Reagan and Ron Radosh think that the Communists and the fellow travellers betrayed America in the '50s and after. Both, I assume, think the same of them today. Both of them play the politics of the loyalty oath. Preferable to both is the tradition of the French Communist facing a Nazi firing squad, who shouted with his last breath, 'Long Live the German Communist Party!' (It's the international socialist tradition I'm talking about; not the present or even past policies of the PCF or the KPD.)

In an interview about the Rosenberg case in the November/December issue of *Socialist Review*, Michael Meeropol says this:

'The whole issue of being willing to convict an entire movement and an entire group of people on the basis of unsupported and in some cases very flimsy allegations of a most extreme sort is pertinent today. We laughed in the 1960s when people said that the movement against the war was Communist-inspired from Russia or Cuba or China. Similarly, we have to say to ourselves that the American Communist Party, for all its acceptance of the Moscow line on everything and for all its rather slavish support for everything the Soviet Union has ever done, was a group of Americans interested in radical change in the United States.

'They were not traitors; they were not spies. Any effort to suggest that is what the American Communist Party was in the 1930s and '40s is exactly the same kind of effort that was made in the 1960s to connect the anti-Vietnam-war movement with some dangerous foreign power, and exactly the same kind of effort that's being made now to say that if five people in the hundred thousand who were involved in some peace activity are also members of the World Peace Council that proves that Moscow is pulling the strings of the American peace movement. It was absurd to suggest that in the 1940s and '50s and it continues to be absurd to this day. People should learn that from my parents' case.

'If people come to believe what Radosh and Milton have suggested, then it will help the government today to isolate left elements of the peace movement for example, and turn the peace movement into a house-cleaning organization. Theirs is just the kind of attitude that destroys movements. One of the things that was good about the 1960s is that people who really had dislike for each other politically worked together on the anti-Vietnam-war movement. I thought that was very good. It helped make our movement stronger and helped make it impossible for the government to shut us up. So that's what we have got to do today. We've got to refuse to let the lesson that Radosh and Milton offer shut us up.'

VV

November 8, 1983

The Press and the Grenada Invasion

With considerably less resistance than that displayed by the Grenadian militia, important sections of the US media surrendered without much of a struggle in the face of the US invasion of Grenada and the Reagan administration's propaganda barrage to justify this outrageous and illegal venture.

It's true that editorials in the *New York Times*, the *Boston Globe* and the *Washington Post* – to mention three important papers – indignantly denounced the invasion, its legality and its rationales. It's true that an assiduous reader of the papers would have had a fair amount of infor-mative material against which to assess the claims of the administration. But even after last weekend fundamental Reaganite assumptions remained entirely unchallenged in the mainline media.

A crucial moment for the Reagan administration came with the network newscasts on the first Tuesday, the day of the invasion. These, more than any editorial or report in the *New York Times* or *Washington Post*, set the basic terms for public perception. The CBS, NBC and ABC newscasts were all, by and large, ill-informed, if not actively misleading. They accepted most Reaganite assumptions and, particularly in the case of Bill Moyers on CBS, actively endorsed them.

Consider the famous airstrip. For over a quarter of a century the Grenadians have been hoping to lengthen their airstrip, which cannot accommodate the large passenger planes that could bring tourists so necessary to the island's economy. The airstrip has been favorably viewed by the World Bank. At least half its financing comes from western European countries. The British firm of Plessey has been advising on its construction. There is an enormous difference between a civilian airport – which is being built on Grenada – and a military one.

It is not as though such reflections were kept from the highly paid reporters, anchormen and producers who put out the network news. Serious attempts to deflate to sensible proportions the dreaded airstrip were made at the time of Maurice Bishop's visit to the United States this summer. Yet, last week, it was as though such informed assessments had never been made. On CBS, Bob Simon reported jauntily, 'The Grenadians said their new all-weather night-and-day airport, with its 10,000-foot runway built by Cubans was for jumbo jets carrying tourists. Washington said, "Nonsense." The Grenadians said the new port facilities under construction were for banana boats. Washington said, "No Way." Washington believed this tiniest Caribbean country was being redesigned from a tourist haven to a Communist airbase and a way station, a stopping-off point for Cuban soldiers on their way to Africa, for East Bloc supplies on their way to Nicaragua.'

For ABC, Jack Smith faithfully parrotted Reaganite claims about the airstrip and the deep port. NBC was somewhat more restrained. Unchallenged on all three programs was the fundamental premise that Grenada could be of immense military and strategic value to Cuba and the Soviet Union. Why? This was never satisfactorily explained, aside from some astounding bosh promulgated by former CIA director Stansfield Turner on *Nightline* to the effect that a Cuban/Soviet controlled Grenada threatened crucial oil tanker lanes.

What is always astounding is that these networks, and indeed these newspapers and newsmagazines, equipped with incredible sums of money and enormous staffs, apparently find it impossible to find anyone who knows *anything* about the Caribbean, anything about the economy or politics of the region beyond the *New York Post*-size headlines which apparently substitute for thinking inside Reagan's head.

In an entire week, an American citizen would have found it hard to discover that the 'democracy' allegedly overthrown by the New Jewel

Movement on Grenada was a corrupt and fraudulent regime run by Eric Gairy in which ballot boxes were routinely stuffed, political opponents killed and the economy sold to criminal interests.

Since the press prates on ceaselessly about the public's 'right to know', you would have thought that the media would have tried to cater to this same right. Instead of which, we had this revolting homily from Bill Moyers:

'In a world where freedom has enemies, the use of force can be justified. The question is always when and where ... You can argue that a tiny island with a leftist government could scarcely have been more than a nuisance, if that. But then that huge airstrip appeared, built with Soviet and Cuban help, and harder-line Marxists trained in Cuba threw out the hard-liners already in power. There followed a blood letting similar to the one Marxists had already inflicted on opponents in nearby Surinam.

'You can hardly blame the peaceful islands around Grenada for being alarmed, or an American president for imagining the strategic consequences of yet another Soviet base in the Caribbean. John Kennedy almost went to war to get Soviet missiles out of Cuba; and Lyndon Johnson sent some 20,000 troops, of whom 28 died, to prevent a Communist takeover in the Dominican Republic. So it's not surprising that Mr. Reagan would also consider the use of force legitimate in the Caribbean.

'Whether the price was worth it depends on whether the result is to replace their "thugs" – as Mr. Reagan calls them – with our thugs, as happened in Guatemala, in Chile, or whether the people of Grenada really get their freedom. If this happens, there will be no less grief for the next of kin of the troops who died in Grenada than for those flown in Beirut; but at least they can say, "mission accomplished".'

Notice, inter alia, the mechanical repetition 'trained in Cuba' as a way of categorizing opponents of the US. The technique – which has nothing to do with truth, since neither Bishop, Coard nor for that matter Austin were 'trained' in Cuba – is kindred to the Israelis' systematic use of 'terrorists' for Palestinians. Persistent use of 'Cuban-trained' or 'Cuban presence' or 'Cuban support' gradually induces a pathological response, in other words, brainwashing.

Note above all the distortion of Lyndon Johnson's intervention in the Dominican Republic, for which Moyers may indeed have had a soft spot, since he was in the White House working for Johnson at the time.

Johnson used the excuse of a threat to Peace Corps volunteers in the Dominican Republic to try to prevent not a Communist takeover but the overthrow of a rightist junta by a group of nationalist junior officers with a reformist bent. The Peace Corps volunteers met later to protest LBJ's use of them as a rationale for intervention with 21,000 marines, which tells you the difference between 1965 and 1983, with those medical students slobbering over US soil after being rescued by marines from the consequences of a US attack.

Notice finally that none of these law-abiding commentators actually care a fig for the law. Not Moyers, who simply says that the end can justify the means and hang the consequences, nor James Reston who said the same thing. I exclude here such predictable desperados and ardent supporters of the Reagan administration as Norman Podhoretz ('Grenada points the way back to recovery and health') or the *Wall Street Journal* editorial page, which declared exultantly that the world was the better for this display of US military might.

The media had some problems with the first of the Reagan administration's excuses for intervention – the 'appeal' from the Organization of Eastern Caribbean States. The flouting of the UN and OAS charters, not to mention the famous section 8 of the OECS charter, was too blatant. But even so, you had to read long and hard to discover that the US almost certainly backdated the so-called appeal for intervention of Governor General Sir Paul Scoon and in effect kidnapped him onto the USS Guam – where legally he had no standing as governor general, since he was not on Grenadian soil.

After a brief moment in which Dr. Modica, representative of the St. George's medical school in New York, maintained that intervention was unnecessary and might indeed endanger the students, the press collapsed, along with Modica, and accepted the Reagan line.

My colleague Jason Salzman talked on Monday to Alice Palatnick, who had just got back from Grenada where she had been visiting a friend in the medical school. Palatnick says she felt in no danger during the curfew period. 'Half the med students didn't like the Grenadians. Students called them FIGS – Fucking Ignorant Grenadians. This is indicative of their attitude, especially the ones who came back and who were kissing the ground. From Tuesday to Friday when we were lifted out we just viewed the war. The only time I felt endangered was when the Americans bombed nearby. Jim Brubacher, a med student who lived in the area, had his house totally destroyed by a bomb on Tuesday. The whole time I was there not once did I hear of Grenadians or Cubans threatening any students. The attack put us in incredible danger because the Americans did not know where we were the first days. It was thanks to the good will of the Cubans and Grenadians that I didn't get hurt. The American soldiers didn't even have maps to the island. They borrowed all our maps and binoculars.'

With the US military's censorship, which produced howls of outrage, the story turned into a rather self-regarding saga of how the US press tried to invade Grenada on its own. Of course the censorship did have a purpose which the press, amid all its indignation, did not point out – perhaps because the networks were too busy running DoD film and the editor of

Newsweek, Maynard Parker, too occupied denouncing his photographer, who let the side down by breaching army rules and staying beyond his appointed term. The point was that the US invading force was hosing down Grenada with 20 millimeter rounds from its AC-130 gunships, in salvos which, if Vietnam is anything to go by, produced large numbers of civilian casualties. Simultaneously, artillery salvos were leveling such institutions as the mental hospital, as Paul McIsaac in this paper and others have described. The *New York Post* was decent enough to call this one of the 'misfortunes' of war. So it was, but one can imagine what the *Post* would have said if some force other than the Americans had been responsible? The 'accident' would speedily have become a war crime.

By now the Reagan administration had cast aside the student/hostage rationale and was claiming that it had got there 'just in time' to prevent the conversion of Grenada into a Communist version of Guantanamo. Once again, before journalists such as Loren Jenkins of the *Washington Post* actually took a look at the famous warehouses with their venerable guns and the Cubans provided full lists of their people on the island, the networks and papers bought the story.

'American military sources say they were staggered by the depth and strength of the Cuban military presence,' ABC's John McWethy reported on Thursday night. He went on to speak of our old friend 'sophisticated communications equipment' and 'what one intelligence source described as an enormous supply of ammunition and weapons'. This all turned out to be lies of course, but by then the damage, or rather the good — if you look at it from the Reagan administration's point of view – had been done.

Very late on Thursday night, too late for the Friday morning headlines, the US ended up isolated in a Security Council vote – a solitude reminiscent of French and British isolation in the wake of Suez. But US media, which could hardly keep out of the Security Council for an instant when it was a matter of condemning the USSR for KAL 007, had far less to say on this occasion.

It's not that there was no decent reporting at all, though television was by and large disgraceful. It's more that the Big Lie techniques of the Reagan administration, now in full and menacing flower after three years growth, overwhelm conventional journalistic techniques with sheer volume of arrogant mendacity. In one of the few really tough pieces, Robert Kaiser pointed this out in the *Washington Post* Outlook section last Sunday:

'But if the limitations of Reagan and his team are widely accepted by the expert community in Washington, the experts mostly keep still. Reporters who also realize that many officials in this administration are less than wizzes don't know how to put that into print. ... Lou Cannon, the *Post*'s White House correspondent wrote the other day that according to a congressman who heard him discuss the invasion of Grenada, Reagan displayed "an unusually detailed grasp" of the issues involved. A reader from Mars might have thought that this meant that in absolute terms Reagan had a splendid mastery of the material. But every insider in Washington knew what Cannon acknowledges was pretended – that this time, Reagan knew something about what he was discussing.

'"Everybody in this town has known that the emperor has no clothes," said a former cabinet member, but there has been a polite silence not to say so.' Polite or foolish? Perhaps, once again, the American people will have cause to complain that the "establishment" which is supposed to know the most about these things failed to warn its countrymen of the dangers it faced. If those who know most say nothing, what is the good of having the freedom to speak out?'

VV

November 22, 1983

Reagan and Lies

The reason Nixon took a beating from the press and Reagan always lives to smile another day seems simple enough. Nixon thought it necessary to tell lies. The press, after a longish interval, began to point out that the president was not telling the truth. Nixon got mad and insisted that he *was* telling the truth. Sensing it was on to a good thing, the press pointed out some more Nixon lies and so, in the end, the president resigned on August 8, 1974.

Reagan, on the other hand, doesn't mind telling the truth. He doesn't mind telling lies either. The truth is that he cannot tell the difference. Nixon knew when he was lying and – since he sweated and twitched when he was telling the lies – most other people knew when he was lying too. Reagan, the actor, has absolutely no moral sense about truth or falsity. Truth, to him, is what he happens to be saying at the time. Even when he is repeating some hoary old lie about welfare cheats which has been exposed in the press a hundred times, he still looks as though he is telling the truth and I'm sure he thinks he is telling the truth.

The problem for the press is that Reagan really doesn't care that he's been caught out with another set of phony statistics or a bogus anecdote. How do you deal with a president without guilt? Reagan has gone one better than George Washington. He cannot tell a lie and he cannot tell the truth.

VV

November 29, 1983

Double Your Standard

A civilian airliner downed by a ground-to-air missile ... all 126 persons aboard killed ... a guerrilla group claims credit. We may surely expect a spontaneous welling up of denunciation, in the press and Congress, at this atrocious crime. Actually we may not expect it. For one thing the passengers were sub-Saharan Africans and therefore not really recognized as people at all in the Western media. For another thing, the plane belonged to Angola, that is Marxist in orientation and guarded by Cubans. And the group which claimed credit for shooting down the airliner as it took off from Lubango in southern Angola was UNITA, which is certainly financed by South Africa, probably financed by the United States (covertly) and which has the support of outfits such as Freedom House, which has hosted UNITA's leader Jonas Savimbi in this country.

UNITA claimed proudly to have shot down the airliner, which belonged to the Angolan airlines TAAG. The official Angolan news agency Angop says that the plane crashed due to a technical fault. The London *Daily Telegraph* quotes Western military sources as saying that UNITA probably did bring it down with a SAM 7 captured from government forces.

VV

December 13, 1983

On the Importance of Being Paranoid

Since this week, indeed this very day of December 7, happens to be the anniversary of the attack on Pearl Harbor, *The New York Times* might have done slightly better than the small headline on page A14 of last Sunday's edition, which said 'Sailor Identified in War Warning'. What those five words indicated and what the story confirmed was fresh evidence of the fact that the surprise attack by the Japanese on Pearl Harbor 42 years ago was not a surprise at all; that the White House and more specifically Franklin D. Roosevelt, General Marshall and a few others knew very well in the first week of December 1941 that a Japanese naval task force was moving towards Pearl Harbor and that an attack was impending.

The attack that finally came over the Waianae Hills at dawn left over 4,000 Americans dead. The United States immediately entered the war. Thus the Roosevelt administration not only undertook the blockade and the embargoes that forced Japan into war; it also knew that Japan was about to attack and waited for it to do so, so that Roosevelt could at last outmaneuver the isolationists and enter the war against the Axis powers on a tide of popular feeling.

It is one of the great conspiracy stories of the 20th century, and it was masterfully told by John Toland in his great book *Infamy*, published by Doubleday last year. For those who do not know it, the thesis that Toland in my view proved is that although Roosevelt and his closest counselors knew that a Japanese force was about to attack Pearl Harbor, they were so convinced of the impregnability of the base that they did not believe that this attack would have any serious effect. They thought a surprise Japanese raid would do little damage, leave a few casualties, but would supply the essential *casus belli*. In *Infamy* Toland quotes from labor secretary Frances Perkins's diary an eerie description of Roosevelt's ravaged appearance at a White House meeting the night of December 7. He looked, wrote Perkins with extraordinary perception, not only as though a tragedy had occurred but as though he felt some more intimate, secret sense of responsibility.

It has taken over 40 years for the Pearl Harbor story slowly to unravel. The US military commanders – Kimmel and Short – on Honolulu were pilloried, destroyed, set up to bear the major responsibility. For many years they fought to vindicate themselves, only to face hidden or destroyed evidence and outright perjury from their superiors. The cause became one espoused particularly by the isolationist right.

In May of this year following publication of Toland's book, an officer from the Naval Security Group interviewed one of Toland's sources who had previously insisted on remaining anonymous. It was the release of this four-hour interview and the name of the source that prompted the *New York Times* story last Sunday. The person in question was Robert Ogg, who had been an enlisted man in Naval Intelligence during the war. He had been one of those who had detected the presence, through radio intercepts, of a Japanese task force working its way towards Pearl Harbor in the first week of December 1941. This force had been under radio silence, but such silence had been broken on a number of occasions.

Both Ogg and his immediate superior, Lieutenant Hosner, reported their intercepts and conclusion to the chief of intelligence of the 12th Naval District in San Francisco, Captain Richard T. McCullough. McCullough was not only a personal friend of Roosevelt's but had assured access to him through Harry Hopkins's phone at the White House. Ogg confirms today that McCullough had said at the time that the information about the Japanese task force had been passed to the White House.

Thus it seems that Toland has been vindicated. Roosevelt, I suppose, remains vindicated by the indisputable fact that it was a good thing that the US entered the war and that if, towards this end, it was necessary to allow the Japanese to attack Pearl Harbor, so be it. Ask Winston Churchill about the sinking of the Lusitania in 1915.

The lesson here is that there is no construction too 'bad' or too 'outrageous' but that it cannot be placed upon the actions of powers great and small, though usually great. When Toland's book was published, there were many who scoffed at the 'inherently implausible argument,' the 'outrageous innuendo,' the 'fine-spun conspiracy theory'.

VV

December 27, 1983

Fact Finding

MANAGUA – Experts here say that the shortest known 'fact-finding mission' to Nicaragua was that undertaken by Senator Jeremiah Denton. Desirous of testing the proposition that a US citizen can enter Nicaragua without a visa, he did so, found the proposition to be true and departed forthwith. On his way home the plane touched down briefly at the airport in San Salvador. So, in a matter of some five hours the senator had, as they say, 'seen at first hand' the Marxist-Leninist contagion in two central American nations at extremely modest expense for the US taxpayer.

You can always tell that the US is up to something bad by the number of fact-finding missions undertaken by the country's elected representatives to convince themselves to the contrary. The usual congressional tour to Nicaragua lasts anywhere between eight and 24 hours; a very generous allocation of time, considering that the main objective of the US – as always since the intervention of 1909 – has been to destroy the slightest vestige of independence or progress in this charming and beautiful country.

The usual tour goes something like this. The congressional delegation lands at Managua airport, is hastened through Protocol and whirled off to the US embassy for a briefing. 'Facts' about Nicaragua in the possession of the average congressman are these: Nicaragua is a country in Central America. It may or may not border on El Salvador. There is widespread congressional confusion on this important point. It once was ours and is now run by Marxist-Leninist thugs. The Pope doesn't like it. Priests are Communists. It has Russian tanks in it, and a wonderful newspaper called *La Prensa*, which is a beacon of freedom amid darkness. There was an earthquake there and one of our fellows in charge, called Somoza.

After the briefing the US embassy throws a dinner. At the dinner will be a representative from COSEP, which is basically the Nicaraguan chamber of commerce, and some people from the political opposition. Archbishop

Obando y Bravo, hostile to the regime, will also be there wolfing down the viands, along with a member of the Permanent Commission on Human Rights though not the Nicaraguan Commission for the Promotion and Protection of Human Rights.

A good night's sleep gives way to a demanding schedule. First, a visit to the offices of *La Prensa* and a discourse by Pedro Joaquin Chamorro. Unlike his progressive brother, Carlos Fernando, who runs the Sandinista paper *Barricada,* Pedro Joaquin is no friend of the regime, indeed hates it with undiluted passion. It comes as no surprise to learn that on the old *La Prensa* run by his father before he was assassinated by Somoza, young PJ used to sell advertising. Hearing him for an hour, you understand where many US journalists get their news.

Braced by Chamorro's retailing of Sandinista horror, the delegation heads on for another session with the archbishop, or perhaps, an encounter with Obando's stand-in, Bismarck Carballo.

At this point some congresspeople give up and go home. Others then enter the Sandinista half of the program. They get an army briefing, a session in the foreign affairs ministry, a meal hosted by the Council of State and finally a meeting with one of the commandantes, very often Co-ordinator of the Junta Daniel Ortega. Then it's home, and another vote for covert CIA funding.

Nicaraguans tell stories about these US fact-finders with a certain wry incredulity. One congressman listened to a commandante outlining the murderous rampages of the contras and then burst out, 'Suppose 5,000 contras cross your border. Suppose you are invaded by the entire Honduran army, why should you worry. Are you *that* insecure?'

Another congressman was at Managua airport just as a contra bomb exploded on the baggage carousel on February 21, 1982. It was on the part of the carousel on the baggage handler side and thus did not kill a large number of passengers. But four handlers were blown apart, their remains gruesomely spread over the carousel. The congressman, irate at the delay caused by the US taxpayer dollars financing this act of terror, called his wife in the States who spoke with newspapers which duly ran a headline 'Congressman Being Held'. Daniel Ortega offered his plane but the congressman refused, afraid – as he said – to put his life in the hands of the Sandinistas.

The arrival of the Kissinger Commission for an afternoon provoked much resentment at the great man's astounding arrogance. 'We come here with an open mind,' intoned Kissinger, before berating the Sandinistas for backing the Soviet invasion of Afghanistan. It was quietly pointed out to him – just as it had been to him a few days earlier in Washington – that the Nicaraguans did *not* support the Soviet invasion, and had gone on record in the UN with this position.

Daniel Ortega outlined the Nicaraguan case and the Kissinger group displayed low interest in the proceedings. Some lolled, others yawned or chatted among themselves. Finally former Texas governor William Clements passed Kissinger a note saying, 'We don't have to put up with this son of a bitch.' At the end of Ortega's remarks Kissinger said abruptly, 'With your permission we'll board the plane.' As he turned to leave, Ortega tapped him on the shoulder and said, 'You are bothered by our words and we are bothered by your bombs. We are limited in our capacity to respond. We respond to bombs with words. So I ask you which hurts more – our words or your bombs?' 'I myself am highly offended both by the content and tone of your remarks,' said Kissinger and turned on his heel.

VV

Life at the Inter

The Inter-Continental Hotel in Managua was built by Somoza. Nearby was his bunker. The hotel is '50s Aztec in style and houses the press office for foreign journalists. Sit there long enough with the agreeable and cooperative staff and you'll see most of the international press corps trundling by. Down by the pool there's a curious amalgam of well-off Nicaraguans hostile to the regime, correspondents and a smattering of the local Sandinista-supporting US community, a pleasant group reminiscent in style of those portrayed in the early scenes of Costa-Gavras's *Missing*.

A Nicaraguan in the press office describes the main interests of the visiting correspondents. As with the congresspeople, Obando y Bravo is in keen demand. Many wish to observe him celebrating mass. Similarly in demand is the editor of *La Prensa*. So is anyone from COSEP. 'Three days for the contras,' a Nicaraguan says sourly, 'and one day for us. With us they ask for interviews with Ortega, Borge, Ernesto Cardenal and Miguel d'Escoto. Then they want to see militia training and visit the front.'

With exactly the same wry incredulity used in discussing the US congresspeople, a Nicaraguan described the performance of a photographer from the *Providence Journal*. In 1980 Nicaragua had been conducting its literacy campaign and the Soviet Union kicked in with a couple of helicopters to get the literacy workers around the back country. The helicopters were openly parked at the airport and as the photographer landed he took a picture out of the window which was duly printed on the front page of the *Providence Journal*, headlined 'Secret Soviet Aid'. Then the photographer went off to the Camino Real hotel, and took some pictures of the Soviet helicopter pilots in the country to teach Nicaraguans how to fly. The news of these 'Soviet advisers' was soon alarming the citizens of Rhode Island.

The truth is that most US reporters, consciously or even half consciously, are frightened of saying anything particularly positive about the Sandinistas. Much of this stems from Shirley Christian's attacks on Alan Riding of the *New York Times* and Karen de Young of the *Washington Post* as having failed to communicate to US readers the true nature of the Marxist-Leninists in the FSLN. Christian, formerly of the *Miami Herald*, modishly anti-Communist, loves to talk about 'Marxism Leninism' in a theologico-technical way, as though she were an expert in ideological rabies. But the mainline reporters, chicken-hearted at the core, have been cowed by the (Shirley) Christian assault and steer clear of anything that could be traduced as being soft on, or duped by the Marxist-Leninist conspiracy.

VV

Sandinista Safety

Privately, every journalist this side of Christian will admit that Managua is one of the safest cities in Central America, and that the country – despite the massive arming of the population against invasion – is the only one in the region where you can look at a policeman, a soldier or a militia person swinging a machine gun without jumping out of your skin. Nicaraguans are a friendly, un-macho bunch, and the place, according to veterans of the region, is without the pervasive violence of El Salvador, where even the movies on offer tend towards grotesquerie and nun rape: sublimation by violence both in life and art.

The rates of exploitation were somewhat different in the two countries and besides, Nicaragua, compared with El Salvador, is a relatively empty place, so far as population per acre is concerned. Of course the country has been plagued by horrible violence. The Spanish conquerors behaved in predictably monstrous fashion towards the Indians. Of its five earliest rulers in the Spanish conquest the British explorer and historian Boyle wrote in 1868, 'The first had been a murderer, the second a murderer and rebel, the third murdered the second, the fourth was a forger, the fifth a murderer and rebel.' Direct US intervention began in 1909 in exactly the same manner as many speculate will occur today. A US puppet regime was installed on the Miskito coast. The National Guard, trained up by the US, were the praetorians sustaining the Somoza family in power until final departure of the gang in 1979. Fifty thousand Nicaraguans died in the war to overthrow Somoza – an immense number in a country with a population of under three million. The US tried to save Somozism until the last, prolonging the agonies of the country as it (in this instance the Carter administration) sought a compromise in its interests. The delay probably meant the deaths of 10,000.

VV

Cock and Bull

As Foreign Minister Miguel d'Escoto greeted us he remarked to me, 'Of course the name Cockburn is well known in Nicaragua.' I puffed out my chest a bit and began to Oh-I-say-not-really when he added, 'Yes, the explorer John Cockburn wrote a most amusing book about his adventures back in the 17th century. I have three editions of it.' He showed them to me. My ancestor John and companions had been washed up on the Miskito coast. Naked, they wandered into a village where women observed with horror and fear their reddish blond beards and hair and concluded they were monkeys. I think this may have been the same Cockburn who named an island after himself in the Arctic. Some other explorer in Australia didn't like him much, to judge from the names of a mountain range. The first is Mount Despondency, the second Mount Despair and the third, in a climax of misery and disappointment, Mount Cockburn.

VV

Tumbling Down

God brought the earthquake, man the revolution. The earthquake hit Managua just after midnight almost exactly 11 years ago, on December 23, 1972. Up to 20,000 died, and 75 per cent of the city's housing was destroyed. Today you can look down from the Inter-Continental Hotel towards the lake across open land which was once downtown Managua. It's as though you stood on top of the Plaza Hotel on Central Park South and saw only two or three buildings between you and 14th Street: central city clearance taken to its furthest extent.

The shell of the cathedral and the Bank of America building survived, showing who gets the best bricks and mortar. Somoza used earthquake aid money to enrich himself, but the earthquake intimated his end. In a curious way the absence of a downtown, a middle-class focal point to the city, symbolized what happened later: 'Somozism without Somoza'; a national bourgeoisie failed to consolidate; the future passed out of their hands to the Sandinistas.

VV

December 29, 1983

The US in Central America

In which Central American country has the jackboot of tyranny crushed the fragrant flower of freedom, as symbolized in that bastion of democracy – a free press? Answer: El Salvador, where two opposition papers – La Cronica and El Independiente – closed, their editors and publishers terrorized into silence by the death squads of the right-wing government. In which country has a systematic program of genocide been practiced against the indigenous Indian population? Answer: Guatemala.

Which country has welcomed the money, advisers and matériel of a foreign power, seeking to destabilize an adjacent country? Answer: Honduras, in which U.S. dollars, military officers and equipment proliferate, launching the *contras* of the FDN against Nicaragua. Which other country lets terrorists use it as the base for aggression against a neighbor? Answer: Costa Rica, whence Eden Pastora and his ARDE forces also menace Nicaragua.

And which Central American country has drafted a treaty proposing to: end the presence of foreign advisers in the region; offer guarantees against the destabilizing of other countries; prohibit the introduction of sophisticated military technology; negotiate the size of standing armies; offer mutual guarantees against the use of countries in the region as foreign bases? Answer: Nicaragua.

This is what Nicaragua proposed last fall, and the State Department, put on the spot by the fact that such a treaty would stop the export of violent counterrevolution in El Salvador and Honduras, tried to say nothing.

The basic trouble is that the Nicaraguans made one big mistake in their relations with the U.S. On a recent visit I found many of them prepared to admit the mistake frankly: they had a revolution.

What is it that the U.S. has against their revolution? Where did the Nicaraguans go wrong? For nearly half a century they were robbed blind by the Somoza clan. Then, after a war in which Somoza's U.S.-founded national guard and U.S.-supplied planes killed 50,000 people, 4% of the population, the dictator and his henchfolk saw the writing on such walls as were left standing by the earthquake and their own artillery. They fled to Miami. Their fugitive planes were overweight with plunder from the national treasury, and to lighten the load they jettisoned bombs on the Nicaraguan factories and towns along their flight path, thus slaughtering a few extra thousand by way of farewell.

Well before this stage, the U.S. was worried things were getting out of hand. It would be helpful, the Carter administration told the Sandinistas, if the national guard were not disbanded and if the political topography of pre-revolutionary Nicaragua, minus Somoza, were kept intact. The U.S. plan seems to have been to return Nicaragua to its mid-19th century status as a primary producer where a thin stratum of businessmen, ranchers and planters could carry out the rituals of a sham democracy while everyone else sank in the ooze of underdevelopment. This was the 'revolution' the Sandinistas quite rightly betrayed, though the 'betrayal' the Reagan administration invokes pre-supposes commitments the Sandinistas never made.

WSJ

January 3, 1984

Bad Start

MANAGUA – North Americans have been coming to Nicaragua for a long time. Back in the 1850s the struggle in Nicaragua was between 'liberals' and 'conservatives' a fairly bogus contest which extended down the decades and which seems to have had a good deal to do with who was to control the customs and excise department. When the 'liberal' Francisco Castellon suffered defeat on the field of battle before the troops of the 'conservative' Frutos Chamorro (yes, same family) he looked for outside help.

It came in the form of William Walker, a journalist hailing from Tennessee and backed by Cornelius Vanderbilt's Accessory Transit Company, which was transporting emigrants to California via Nicaragua. Walker raised a 'phalanx' of Americans which captured the Conservative capital of Grenada in 1855.

Walker soon got ideas above his station, turned against his liberal sponsors and seized power. As the account in Henri Weber's useful *Nicaragua* has it, Walker was an ardent supporter of slavery and dreamed of forging the five isthmus states into a single white republic. Walker hoped that the model slave state of his dreams would bolster Southern morale against the abolitionist cause. On June 10, 1858, he had himself 'elected' president of Nicaragua and you will not be surprised to hear that his government was at once recognized by US president Franklin Pierce. English was declared the official language and slavery reintroduced.

Walker's theory was laid forth in his *War in Nicaragua* quoted by Weber: 'The necessary consequence of the triumph of free labor will be the destruction, by a slow and cruel process of the colored races. ... The labor of the inferior races cannot compete with that of the white race unless you give it a white master to direct its energies; and without such protection as slavery affords, the colored races must inevitably succumb in the struggle with white labor.' In other words, *It's for their own good.*

Walker dreamed his dream, which included takeover of the other Central American states. His flag bore the motto 'Five or None.' Walker fled back to New York in the face of a collective force. Four years later he tried a comeback and seized the Honduran town of Trujillo. The British, who feared his designs on the Miskito coast of Nicaragua (always a zone of interest to them), nabbed him and handed him over to the Hondurans, who shot him on September 12, 1861.

From 1893 to 1909 the country was run by the liberal nationalist General Jose Santos Zelaya, whose name now designates the eastern, Atlantic half of Nicaragua. Zelaya's ambitious plans, particularly his relations with British capital, greatly perturbed the U.S. Matters came to a head with the U.S.'s decision to dig a canal through Panama. Zelaya began to work out plans with Germany and Japan for an alternative route.

Guess what? In 1909 Juan Estrada, governor of Bluefields on the Atlantic coast, rebelled against Zelaya. In Weber's words, 'he was advised and financed by Adolfo Diaz, employee of the Luz and Los Angeles Mining Company. The US secretary of state, one Philander C. Knox, who as it happened was a legal adviser to Luz and Los Angeles [and apparently the main stockholder], broke off relations with the Zelaya government and gave full support to the rebels.'

From then on, Nicaraguans got used to US marines. In 1912, 1700 arrived. Over the ensuing years Nicaragua was carved up, greatly to the advantage of the banking houses of Seligman and Brown Bros. Defiance finally came from Nicaragua's national hero, Augusto Cesar Sandino, in 1927. The Pentagon today, pondering plans to invade Nicaragua, might do well to study the defeat of US forces by Sandino over six years of guerrilla warfare. US counterinsurgency used such honored techniques as population transfers, systematic terror bombing, 'strategic hamlets' and widespread torture.

Sandino became an international hero. Famously, Kuomintang troops held up Sandino's portrait as they entered Peking in 1928. Nicaraguanization of the war, via the National Guard, which the US had created in 1927. Chief of the Guard was Anastasio Somoza. With the complicity of the US ambassador, Sandino was lured into a trap by Somozo and, on February 21, 1934, shot down.

The dictatorship of the Somoza dynasty then began and lasted until July 19, 1979.

Did we find in those long years that passionate concern which now so animates opinion in the United States about social, political and human rights in Nicaragua? Did we find indignant editorials in the *Washington Post,* the *Wall Street Journal,* the *New York Times* and innumerable other publications? Did the nation's representatives from Congress make 'fact-finding' missions on a weekly basis? Or was Nicaragua a pleasant playground for the rich, and – assuming the unlikely distinction – the criminal associates of the Somozas? Take a trip through the newspaper files and find out for yourself.

VV

January 17, 1984

Nigerian Newspeak

The Nigerian coup took the US press by surprise. An article by Robert J. Rosenthal put out on the Knight-Ridder news service was fairly representative. It began: *'The military coup in Nigeria, coming just four months after the reelection of President Shehu Shagari, is a crucial defeat for democracy in black Africa and a significant blow to U.S. interests there. ...'*
Translation: This looks bad for us.
'Americans in Lagos believed strongly in Shagari and had high hopes for his second administration. They believed that with a mandate to govern and without the stigma of his military-controlled first election, Shagari would institute reforms and attack corruption effectively. ...'
Translation: We thought we had Shagari in our pocket and, with his image cleaned up a bit, would be able to do what the IMF and the banks told him to.
'Shagari's wide open, freely contested political campaign, involving five opponents was not without corruption or violence. But it was the first democratic and Western-style presidential election held in black Africa. ...'
Translation: The election was a bit of a farce, but we tried.
'Orderly challenges to leadership are not culturally accepted in Africa. In independent Africa, power has changed hands most frequently as the result of coup or assassination. Thus the Nigerian experiment with democracy was tremendously important. ...'
Translation: Africans are a bunch of bloodthirsty savages. They always will be.
Unstated Fear: Maybe the Nigerian military will try to make itself popular with the people by increasing revenues by slashing the price of its oil on the international market, thus undercutting OPEC. This could add up to another credit crunch for countries already gasping from reduced oil revenues. And this could cause more problems for the U.S. banks and their rickety loans. Hence the 'significant blow to U.S. interests.'

VV

January 26, 1984

Campaign Cliché Crisis

We are in January of an election year and what we have on our hands is a first-rate crisis: If Walter Mondale really does have the nomination locked up and Ronald Reagan is a sure bet in November, what's going to happen to the election industry?

There's no sense in underestimating the gravity of the situation. It's as though the Russians suddenly opted for 100% unilateral disarmament. What would the military-industrial complex do?

We are talking, don't forget, about a hefty slice of the economy: four-star pundits plus native bearers to carry their afterthoughts, reporters, photographers, anchormen, makeup artists, television crews, media advisers, campaign managers, software consultants, advertising firms, direct-mail operations, political action committees, motel operators, catering firms, balloon manufacturers, button merchants, political platform assemblers and the estimated 11% of the population conducting polls on a full- or part-time basis between now and the end of the year.

All this adds up to an immense interest group known as the Post-Industrial Political Complex, dedicated to the empty but profitable ritual known as the Permanent Campaign.

Much of 1983 was spent staging the Mondale-Glenn contest, amid mounting evidence of consumer apathy and dissatisfaction. Jesse Jackson had to be rushed on as a stopgap measure to try to hold the crowd. And now there are other signs that the strain is beginning to tell. On Tuesday, for example, The Wall Street Journal had a story about the brief but potent influence wielded in the days before the Iowa caucus by the political correspondent of the Des Moines Register. Traditional fare for this time of year, but on the very same day the WSJ had a front-page story on the billowing cost of Mr. Mondale's campaign promises. Now this story usually comes during the election campaign proper, somewhere in early October. The Permanent Campaign is getting out of control.

As I understand it, the stories should go more or less as follows. Turn of the year through first primaries: The front-runner 'commands wide but shallow support' and is often charged with 'shading his opinions to please different interest groups.' Depending on the prejudices of the reporter, he is either 'encumbered with essentially meaningless endorsements' or 'has won significant support that brings with it a lot of organizational clout.' He is naturally reminded with increasing frequency that 'no one who has not first won in New Hampshire has ever gone on to win the presidency.'

As the primary nears, the Democratic front-runner begins to experience trial by Evans and Novak: 'Aghast at the stunning news contained in a top-secret poll conducted by the Newt organization, distraught campaign strategists took the desperate step of urging their candidate onto a do-or-die course that could very well deal his faltering bid for the presidency a fatal blow.'

Meanwhile, the other candidates are sharing other traditional coverage. The second runner usually is suffering the consequences of 'deep divisions within his staff' and attempting to 'recover from what local political observers judge to be serious organizational deficiencies.' If things are very bad, he is 'trying desperately to re-animate his flagging campaign with a new theme in what aides are describing as a "major address".'

Long-shot candidates get adjectives like 'dogged,' 'stubborn' and 'lonely.' They command 'a small but intensely loyal following' and often grow 'increasingly petulant at what they regard as the biased press coverage.'

First primaries to early summer: Some trusted stratagems by the Permanent Campaign to sustain consumer interest. Best known is the slip or blunder. Slips usually occur in this period because this is the time when the candidate deems it necessary to produce an idea. Previous to that, he has had a theme, drained of all nutritious content, such as industrial policy. Ideas are dangerous. The press distrusts them, finding them mysterious and inappropriate to a political contest. Mr. McGovern had an idea with his $1,000 plan in 1972, with disastrous results. Mr. Reagan suffered the same fate over the $90 billion shift in 1976, and then, with amazing effrontery, actually had another idea (supply side) in 1980. These are the only ideas that I can remember.

In the slip season it's best that the serious candidate has no ideas, jokes, feelings or any other significant personal attribute that might protrude above the tundra-like wastes of the banal and attract unwelcome attention.

Summer is convention time: The season for delegate counts, for 'healing the bitter divisions of the nomination struggle,' for platform fights and, of course, for the search for a running mate. We may note here the traditional 'eagerness to avoid the Eagleton fiasco' and the hallowed reflection that the vice presidency is 'not worth a pitcher of warm spit.' From then on it's clear sailing, past Labor Day into the final campaign, the 'awesome advantages of incumbency,' the 'October surprise', and the 'last-minute appeal to the voters.'

The basic effect of the Post-Industrial Political Complex and of the Permanent Campaign is to extirpate the slightest trace of original thinking on the part of either the candidates or the electorate. Any aspirant from the left is speedily banished from discourse with reference to his 'eccentric' appeal. From the right, Ronald Reagan only made it by grace of Jimmy Carter and the movies.

As for the voters, they are simply incorporated into the Permanent

Campaign. The average New Hampshire family contains a grandfather interviewed by Teddy White in 1960, a father who participated in an Ann Arbor attitudinal survey in 1968, a son who helped process NBC questionnaires in 1976 and a daughter on standby for exit-polling this year. Weighed with New Hampshire's 'historic responsibility,' none of them thinks his or her own personal views of much consequence.

WSJ

February 23, 1984

A Real Democrat Would Run Against Paul Volcker

The way things are going, I fully expect to see Paul Volcker make a celebrity appearance at the Democratic convention, rather as Colonel Sanders did in the old days. As the band plays 'Hail to the Chief,' the chairman of the Federal Reserve will be escorted down the aisle by a flying wedge of Democratic candidates, past picketing supply-siders and assorted bully boys led by Jack Kemp, all howling for his blood.

Then, with the chairman comfortably seated and many fine speeches made in his honor, the real fun of the evening will begin, in the form of a new Democratic game called Bait the Deficit. The poor old thing is dragged in on the end of a chain while Democratic picadors torment it with spears. Secret plans for the San Francisco convention envisage an exciting climax when Walter Mondale, in toreador cape and hat, dispatches the deficit with some cleanly delivered campaign promises while the crowd chants the '84 campaign slogan, 'Raise taxes, raise taxes.' That will make Mr. Reagan shake in his boots.*

What's going on here? A few years ago when you saw someone running down an alley and screaming for help, it usually turned out to be the chairman of Federal Reserve fleeing a mugging from liberal Democrats. These same Democrats pampered the deficit shamelessly, tossing it a couple of billion dollars whenever it rattled its cage. Not any more. The night of his success in Iowa, I heard Mr. Mondale describe the deficit as 'obscene' – a word Democrats used to reserve for denunciations of oil company profits.

Mr. Mondale is not alone in this execration of the deficit. His rivals fall over themselves to echo the same theme. Not just Ernest Hollings, who

This was an accurate prediction. At the Democratic convention five months later, Mondale pledged to raise taxes, thus dooming his campaign as it began.

wants to take the Attila approach and kill the economy right off with a budget freeze: not just Gary Hart, who wants to chloroform it with neo-liberalism; not just John Glenn (the one for poison gas, Mr. Mondale likes the natural stuff), but George McGovern and Jesse Jackson, each so pleasing in other ways.

It's not so much the opportunism of all this deficit-bashing that dismays one, but the foolishness of it. Take the Mondale pitch to the voters. 'What has Reaganomics brought us?' he shouts (and I paraphrase). 'Why, Reaganomics has brought us fearful military spending, horrible social injustice and these damnable and ever-to-be derided deficits. Ronald Reagan has brought the economy to its knees!'

The Democrats seem to have got it the wrong way round. Reaganomics has had a certain success on its own terms: inflation is dead and the military spending-cum-tax cuts have produced the only halfway vigorous economy in the advanced capitalist world, one still growing despite an import surplus. And Reaganism has made the U.S. a haven for fearful capital. But just as the Democrats underestimate Reaganomics' past, they overestimate its future. Each recovery gets shorter; each time, air leaks more rapidly out of the balloon. As Reaganauts seem to be realizing much more rapidly than Democrats, the recovery may well abort before the election.

And, even as the Democratic candidates jabber on about the deficit, the Reaganauts know exactly where to put the blame: the monetary policy of Chairman Volcker.

It's hard to know how Mr. Mondale could do it without the most extraordinary feat of historical gymnastics, but any Democratic candidate would be well advised to run against both Mr. Reagan and Mr. Carter and take his stand with the John F. Kennedy of 1962, on monetary policy and a relaxed attitude towards deficits (and, for that matter on arms control). Our candidate would flay Mr. Reagan for unfairness and for military spending, not because we can't afford it, but because we don't need it.

Our candidate would ask what sort of a 'recovery' it is that sees real interest rates at an unprecedented 7%. He would remind his audience that in 1942 we thought it more important to beat Hitler than cool off an over-heated economy and thus put the Federal Reserve back under the control of the Treasury. Interest rates stayed at 2% until 1951, when the Fed broke free again.

Our candidate, throwing in some populist rhetoric, would ask who exactly these high interest rates are benefiting. By now he would have the crowd baying for blood as he pledged to tame the Fed, force it to monetize the debt and bring interest rates down. With the fall in interest rates, our candidate would conjure forth the real recovery. He would scoff at the 6.5% unemployment now defined as the 'inflation threshold.' The baby boom, he would remind the crowd, ended in 1964. The demographic consequences 20 years later are the only reason Mr. Reagan can point to a fall off in unemployment.

Our candidate would talk about full employment at 4%. He would talk about Humphrey-Hawkins. He would talk about the growth that would bring down deficits. In short, he would sound like a real Democrat instead of like the merchants of pain and planned shrinkage now chasing votes in New Hampshire.

WSJ

March 17, 1984

Jackson and His Slur

Form and custom demand that at least one Democrat speak to the disen-franchised, the have-nots, the underclass, the wretched of the earth – in other words, the electoral cannon fodder which has to be marshaled briefly at the polling booths in November to propel the consensus candidate into office. This was to be the role of Jesse Jackson, given media sanction to animate the masses with his Baptist eloquence, register them wherever possible and then take a back seat to a 'serious' candidate.

Well, not only had Jackson been doing rather more than that, overstep-ping his role in fact, but then he had to go and make opprobrious racist slurs, the stupid *schwartze*. Now, Jackson's use of 'Hymietown' and 'Hymie' was racist speech which should be condemned every time, anytime. What does seem odd to me is that the 'ethnic slur' has become practically the only connecting rod between politics and morality so far as the liberal opinion-forming elite is concerned. Without undue perturbation this elite tolerated the agricultural policies of Earl Butz – policies which induced the starvation of large numbers of people in the Third World – until he was rash enough to make his tight-pussy/loose-shoes remark in front of John Dean. James Watt was a monster, polluting and pillaging, yet he was regarded as acceptable until he made a remark that in and of itself hardly warranted his eviction from government.

President Reagan's policies are racist to the core, causing misery, depriv-ation and shortened lives for poor blacks, beyond all others. But he would be in serious trouble as a racist only if he matched words to deeds and called them 'worthless niggers.' At least Menachem Begin suited the motion of his lips to the movement of his tanks and called Palestinians 'two-legged beasts'; his Chief of Staff, Gen. Rafael Eitan, likened them to 'drugged roaches'; and in neither case did the slur seem particularly to distress polite opinion here.

None of which excuses Jackson for his Hymie-talk, but they sure were lying in wait for him, were they not? Newspapers that have been racist in their hiring policies, racist in their coverage, racist in their newsrooms, racist in their accounting departments, clambered up their high horses, hitched him to a rope and dragged him round the ring. He should not have afforded them the opportunity, which does not in the least vitiate the hypocrisy of the entire spectacle.

The Nation

May 6, 1984

Crossing the Line

'If I were a real woman, I would never know the ecstasy of being a man being a woman. If I were a woman, I could never experience the joy and pleasure of preparing myself to change roles.' Thus does Ed Cottle explain his transvestism in the May 5 issue of *Gay Community News*. This is an exquisite evocation of the dialectic.

The Nation

May 12, 1984

Mr. Chou Changes Planes:
Tales of Terror Continued

The coincidence of Reagan's horrible antiterrorism proposals and his visit to China reminds me of an episode that was certainly not raised amid all those toasts in Beijing last week.

In 1955 the nonaligned nations gathered for a great conference in Bandung, Indonesia. Among those leaders heading toward the town was Chou Enlai, Foreign Minister and Premier of the People's Republic of China. The Chinese delegation flew in two rented Air India planes. Chou and his party stopped over in Hong Kong before the final leg to Bandung. Gamal Abdel Nasser, who was stopping over in Rangoon, invited Chou to visit for private consultations. At the last moment Chou took a regularly scheduled flight to Rangoon and his party left for Bandung.

Seven hundred miles from its destination one of the rented planes, the Kashmir Princess, blew up; the shattered fragments, along with fifteen people, eight of them Chinese diplomats, fell into the South China Sea. The British sent divers to examine the wreckage and concluded that the plane had been blown up with a sophisticated device of Western manufacture. The Chinese intimated soon after that they thought the United States had been behind the attempt to murder Chou.

On November 22, 1967, *The New York Times* reported that American defector John Discoe Smith had published an article in the Soviet periodical *Literaturnaya Gazeta* claiming that the CIA had been involved in sabotaging the Air India plane and that he had delivered the timing device – later recovered by the British – to Chinese Nationalists in Hong Kong. The Hong Kong police described the affair as 'carefully planned mass murder.'

There is the strong possibility that the CIA had been involved in an attempt to assassinate Chou. In the mid-1970s more than a hundred staffers on Senator Church's Intelligence Committee toiled away, but none of them ever bothered to look into the Bandung incident. At the time of the furor over the CIA and assassinations, someone who remembers the Bandung episode well asked Chinese officials why they did not press the matter. They smiled, saying the situation had changed since those difficult times.

The Nation

The US and the Death Squads

The Reagan Administration, echoed by many editorialists, continues to claim that 'progress' is being made in reducing the activities of El Salvador's death squads, a name that misleadingly suggests bands of psychotics randomly roving the streets and countryside. Although the press was alerted to Allan Nairn's explosive report in the May issue of *The Progressive*, no major newspaper has publicized his important findings. As a result of a courageous investigation in El Salvador – which included interviews with many death squad organizers and participants – Nairn establishes that the very death squad apparatus the Reagan Administration denounces was built up by the officials from the State Department, A.I.D., CIA and other agencies and managed with their cooperation through six Administrations over the last twenty years.

The construction of El Salvador's national security edifice began, unsurprisingly, with President Kennedy's Alliance for Progress and, specifically, with a series of meetings following the Declaration of San José, Costa Rica, in 1963, when Kennedy told six Central American presidents that 'Communism is the chief obstacle to economic development in the Central American region.'

Through interviews with the relevant U.S. and Salvadoran officials Nairn shows that U.S. advisers subsequently set up Orden, the rural paramilitary and intelligence network out of which came the Mano Blanco, paradigm of the death squads. Around the same time they conceived and organized Ansesal, 'the elite presidential intelligence service that gathered files on Salvadoran dissidents and ... relied on Death Squads as "the operative arm of intelligence gathering."' These same U.S. officials 'supplied ANSESAL, the security forces, and the general staff with electronic, photographic, and personal surveillance of individuals who were later assassinated by Death Squads. According to Colonel Nicolas Carranza, director of the Salvadoran Treasury Police, such intelligence sharing by U.S. agencies continues to this day.'

Nairn reveals that the United States gave Roberto d'Aubuisson the intelligence files that he used in his 1980 television broadcasts denouncing many trade unionists, peasant leaders, Christian Democrats and clergy as Communists or guerrilla collaborators. Many of those named were subsequently assassinated. The broadcasts launched d'Aubuisson and his Arena Party. U.S. officials, writes Nairn, also 'instructed Salvadoran intelligence operatives in the use of investigative techniques ... that included, according to a former Treasury Police agent, "instruction in methods of physical and psychological torture."'

Far transcending the recent revelations of Roberto Santivanez (who once headed Ansesal), Nairn shows that the death squads are the prime instrument of counterinsurgency in El Salvador, organized and still abetted by U.S. agencies. The Phoenix program rises again. Previously it was possible to propose this as a theory. Nairn establishes it beyond all doubt.

The Nation

June 14, 1984

Guatemala: 'The Whole World Is Watching'

In the beginning of June top U.S. officials stepped up their denunciation of the Communist beachhead in Central America. The president himself warned that the Communists were trying to export their revolution to El Salvador. Meanwhile the CIA continued its training and supply of the contra-invasion force based in Honduras. The aim: to seize a port on the Atlantic coast and declare it a 'liberated area.' The scheduled invasion date: June 18.

The June in question could, right down to the invasion date, belong to 1984, but it was in 1954 that President Eisenhower said that 'the Reds are in control and they are trying to spread their influence to El Salvador as a first step to breaking out of Guatemala.' The CIA organized an invading force in Honduras and hand-picked its leader, Castillo Armas. Almost 30 years ago, on June 18, 1954, Mr. Armas led a convoy of trucks over the frontier into Guatemala. Within two weeks the legally elected government fell.

It would be a shame if President Reagan, fresh from his outing to the Normandy beaches, were to ignore this anniversary. Though evidently less grand in scale than the D-Day landings, the U.S.-organized *Putsch* in Guatemala was every bit as significant in setting the entire post-war tone of U.S. dealings in Central and Latin America. To this day, though the names vary – Nicaragua for Guatemala – the script remains the same.

And what was the justification for the toppling of the regime headed by Jacobo Arbenz? The best account of the entire shameful episode is that provided in 'Bitter Fruit' by Stephen Schlesinger and Stephen Kinzer, published in 1982. In sum, Mr. Arbenz's crime was to have tried to implement some modest land reforms in the course of which he mightily offended the United Fruit Co. And he did not help his reputation in Washington by having Communists in his government.

So President Eisenhower instructed the CIA to go to work. It mounted 'Operation Success' forthwith, and by the end of June 1954 Mr. Arbenz had been forced into exile, a counterrevolutionary regime installed and vigorous bloodletting under way against labor leaders and other noisome elements in Guatemala. In the U.S. the editorialists came down from the hills to shoot the wounded. Noting that 'genuine' agrarian reforms were needed, a New York Times editorial writer observed that 'The answer to communism in Guatemala and other countries is not reaction but liberal reform. The road is a long one. This country may have made mistakes over the years past and in this particular episode. Now it is for us to show ourselves warm and intelligent friends of all the people of Guatemala.'

This suggestion that it was now up to the U.S. to demonstrate the superiority of the American way was reiterated by Vice President Nixon when he visited Guatemala in 1955. This, he said, was 'the first instance where a Communist government has been replaced by a free one. The whole world is watching to see which does the better job.'

It's hard to say what sort of job the Arbenz government would have eventually done, but there seems to be remarkable unanimity about the performance of its successors – to whom the U.S. has been so sympathetic. Down the years Guatemala has been consistently denounced as one of the most savage violators of human rights in the world. In the late 1970s the Carter administration went so far as to suspend aid (despite the ban, levels of military assistance never actually diminished) though the Reagan administration has restored it. Most recently Americas Watch has called the Guatamalan government 'a pariah,' most notably for its persecution – which some have called genocidal – of Guatemala's four million Mayan Indians, who form the bulk of the population.

Aside from the massacres following the coup against Mr. Arbenz, the most appalling slaughter came with the U.S.-organized counterinsurgency beginning in the middle 1960s. A 1981 Amnesty International report concluded that in the 15 years after 1966 more than 30,000 people were 'abducted, tortured and assassinated' in Guatemala.

In the manner now familiar to those following events in El Salvador, government-organized death squads reached into every nook and cranny of Guatemalan life, exterminating opposition.

Has this savage repression been administered to protect the liberal reform urged by the New York Times in 1954? At the end of the 1970s, 25 years after such reform was supposedly given its chance, the World Bank reported that 10% of Guatemalan landowners still owned more than 80% of the land, only 15% of the population had access to piped water and 4% had electricity. Malnutrition and paucity of medical care exacted a dreadful toll. Figures from the Guatemalan government indicated that 83 out of every 1,000 children born alive did not survive their first two years. Four out of every five children were said to be undernourished. The death rate from all causes – 11 per 1,000 – lagged only behind Haiti and Nicaragua (where the situation has improved immensely since the overthrow of Anastasio Somoza in 1979). The illiteracy rate was 70%.

Guatemala in other words, is a conspicuous and absolute failure for 'liberal reform.' The bulk of its population lurches forward in misery and deprivation, governed by one military government after another – which obtain power by fradulent means and hold it by force – all with the unremitting support of the U.S., some of whose business corporations profit mightily from the cheap labor and freebooting environment of Guatemala.

This is the counterrevolution that the U.S. hopes to export to Nicaragua, whose people are now making heroic efforts to haul themselves out of the darkness of the Somoza years.

At the start of this June, President Reagan and the other Western leaders celebrated D-Day – the opening of the long-awaited second front against Nazism. President Reagan spoke of the high responsibilities of defending freedom. That same month of June 1944, after fourteen years of the Ubico dictatorship, the people of Guatemala began at last to rise in opposition. They were in part stimulated by Franklin Roosevelt's 'Four Freedoms,' those invocations to liberty to which they listened on the short-wave radio. On June 29, 1944, Guatemala saw the largest popular protest of its modern history. On July 1 President Jorge Ubico resigned and the liberation being enjoyed in Western Europe also began in Guatemala. A decade later the U.S. aborted that liberation and night still reigns. Are these the sort of anniversaries that Americans in the U.S. wish to celebrate?

WSJ

June 23, 1984

Therapeutic Nihilism

Presumably sensitized by Bolivia's unilateral debt moratorium and the quivers in the banking system, the Reagan Administration now admits that there are some economic problems that the magic of the free market may not be able to cure. Previously, its stance had been similar to what was known in nineteenth-century Viennese medical theory as therapeutic nihilism: that is, letting nature takes its course. As William Johnston describes therapeutic nihilism in *The Austrian Mind,* 'By 1850 skepticism toward traditional therapy had so taken root that the only medicament used in the General Hospital was cherry brandy. For fear of distorting symptoms, doctors refused to prescribe any remedies.'

Johnston follows with an amazingly apt description of Reaganism. In the view of the therapeutic nihilists, 'disease comprised part of life: the task of doctors was not to eradicate it but merely to understand it.' (Shades of Marx's thesis on Feuerbach!) 'The poor dreaded entering the hospital, fearing that they would never leave ... patients had to pay in advance.' One doctor who visited the General Hospital in 1898 offered this description:

> A party of students [were] sounding a woman who was dying of pleurisy or pneumonia, in order that they might each hear the crepitation in her lungs as her last moments approached. She expired before they left the ward. [I] said something about treatment in another case to the professor who was lecturing these young men. The reply was, 'Treatment, treatment, that is nothing; it's the diagnosis that we want.'

The coincidence is not fortuitous. Therapeutic nihilism in the medical field in Vienna was paralleled, as Johnston points out, by the reluctance of Austrian economists like Carl Menger and Ludwig von Mises to tamper with an unimpeded market economy. And von Mises, God to our economic libertarians, is one of the fathers of Reaganism.

Associated with the Reaganite version of therapeutic nihilism is a wild Reaganite voluntarism about results. After doing nothing to cure the patient, the Reaganites declare him alive and well, even if he is dead and rattling through the gates of the graveyard. This is why lying – the relentless

accretion of mendacity, tirelessly repeated, impervious to rebuttal or
rebuke – is so central to Reaganism. Since the Reaganites' vision of the
world bears no relation to the world that exists, and since their policies
achieve precisely the opposite of what they intend, the world has to be
recreated as a creature of the will and of effusive imagination. War
becomes peace; ruin is reborn as recovery; the world is safer and not more
perilous.

This cut-price, ESTian mutation of Schopenhauer and Nietzsche is
naturally popular. In hard times everyone wants a Siegfried.

The Nation

July 21, 1984

The Left, the Democrats and the Future

With hardly a backward – or forward – look, the bulk of the surviving
American left has blithely joined the Democratic Party center, without the
will to inflect debate, the influence to inform policy or the leverage to share
power. The capitulation of the left – a necessarily catchall word, here
covering the spectrum of progressive politics from old socialism to recent
radical activism – is almost without precedent. This time out there is no
McCarthy of 1968, no McGovern of 1972, no Kennedy of 1980, not even
a John Anderson or a Barry Commoner to raise a standard of dissent or
develop an alternative vision against a Democratic Party whose project is
overwhelmingly conservative in attitude and action. The excuse for submission is easy to discern: Anybody But Reagan. But the consequences are
likely to be dire, and they are already taking shape. By accepting the
premises and practices of party unity, the left has negated the reasons for
its own existence.

In the beginning, of course, there was a certain Somebody within the
Democratic fold who was a candidate not only of principle but of opportunity for the left. Jesse Jackson, and the Rainbow Coalition he proposed,
represented the historical base, the organized movement and the radical
program for which the left has been hunting the last thirty-five years.
But ... no. Jackson is usually taunted for failing to broaden his coalition,
but when he made personal pitches to each likely constituency, the invitees
almost invariably declined.

Long before Louis Farrakhan slouched into the headlines, white leftists
had run through every excuse to withhold support from the black candidate. First there was the argument that only a respectable black with a
significant white following should be allowed to swim in the Democratic

mainstream. Then there was the notion that any black candidacy would provoke a backlash from white voters. Next came charges that Jackson was, in turn, a charlatan, a crook, an anti-Semite, a capitalist roader, a poor administrator, a divisive force. Quickly the dark motif of Campaign '84 changed from Anybody But Reagan to Anybody But Jackson. Once again, racism destroyed the promise of a populist, progressive, internationalist coalition within the Democratic Party.

As had to happen, Anybody became Walter Mondale, and he arrived promoting a platform as immoderate and regressive as any to be found in the Democratic Party archives since John W. Davis's unremembered candidacy of 1924. With substantive objections only from Jackson's under-represented contingent, the party's preconvention committees adopted policies and accepted planks that contained the essential elements of Reaganism: continued military expansion, support for Reagan's allies in Central America, the Caribbean and the Middle East, further degradation of the welfare system, denial of black demands for equity and unqualified submission to the imperatives of the corporate system.

Complicit in the first formal expression of Mondaleism are those who early and often endorsed Mondale without reservation: leaders of the National Organization for Women, organized teachers, democratic social-ists, black officeholders, labor hierarchs, Hispanic leaders. They must now be foot soldiers in a campaign whose captains are implacably antagonistic to the principles and concerns of their constituencies. What can Mondale's tame left flank do, for instance, to rescue poor women, blacks, service workers and the young and old from the ranks of the growing underclass impoverished by economic policies and structures Mondale endorses? How can socialist leaders save socialist politics from the isolation, irrelevance and ultimate extinction ordained by complaisant submission to Democratic Party practices? How can union chieftains get more power for union members when the point of Mondaleism is the expansion of management control? How can black politicians win from Mondale what they have been denied by the party machinery for years on end?

Where does the left – the white left, that is, which refuses to concede Jackson's validity and hardly acknowledges his existence – stand now? It has given up on class struggle, black liberation, the Third World, even détente. It can hardly remember the nuclear freeze. Its only live demand, settled last week, was the promotion of a woman as the Democratic vice-presidential nominee: the transubstantiation of politics into symbolism.

Is this bleak prospectus the inevitable consequence of what Michael Harrington recently extolled as the necessary strategy for any left in America today: that 'the Democratic Party, with all its flaws, must be our main political arena'? Harrington, co-chair of the Democratic Socialists of America, and Irving Howe, editor of *Dissent* and avatar of democratic socialism as an unhyphenated ideology, chatted at great length recently in *The New York Times Magazine*, which touted them as 'Voices From the Left.' The import of their conversation, which ran 8,000 words without one mention of the difficult name Jackson, was the denial of any vital role for the left in current politics.

They are wrong. There is a way to salvage something of the left's presence even this late in the year, to broaden its constituency and sphere of action, to begin building a role for the next decade – and still engage the realities of the two-party system. But the left must first accept the invitation of history.

Heedless of the seismic convulsions in the American economic and social landscape during the last two decades, the left continues to read old history, the chronicles of the New Deal and its successor deals in the postwar boom. In that long time, the Democratic coalition offered industrial workers, the new urban and suburban middle class and white ethnic minorities (overlapping categories, to be sure) a certain measure of economic security, social mobility and political influence in return for their cooperation in the governing strategies of state and business in the American Century. The bargain gave labor wage security in exchange for docile acceptance of management supremacy in all significant economic decisions.

The bargain began to unravel in the early 1960s, when the underclass mutinied. The Democratic response was the War on Poverty, a kind of Federal trust fund for the civil rights revolution. But the war was lost. A few statistics illustrate the size of the rout. In 1965 the poorest 40 percent of the population earned 11 percent of the total U.S. market income; nearly a decade and a half later, that same group's share had shrunk to 8.5 percent. From 1945 to 1983 black male participation in the labor force fell from 80 percent to 60 percent. The poor got poorer, and the blacks got unemployed.

In his trenchant résumé of postwar American history, Mike Davis, writing in the January-February 1984 *New Left Review*, stresses that the civil rights revolution

> fundamentally failed in its ultimate goals of achieving the mass incorporation of black labor into the high-wage economy, or of surmounting the barriers of *de facto* segregation in Northern schools and suburbs. A generation after the first March on Washington for Jobs and Freedom, black unemployment remains double that of whites, while black poverty is three times more common. Sixty percent of employed black males (and 50 percent of Hispanics) are concentrated in the spectrum of the lowest paid jobs.

The number of working women doubled between the Eisenhower and Reagan Administrations, though in the same period their earnings declined to 59 percent of the average wage for men. In 1980, one-third of all full-time women workers earned less than $7,000 a year, as against a white male median of $17,000.

A populist, progressive Democratic Party could have entered the 1970s with a renegotiated social compact, an expanded coalition and a renewed vision. It could have proposed to bring women and blacks into better-paying jobs; to reform tax and spending policies to expand public services and collective consumption; to apply Keynesian theories to a peace-building rather than a warmaking economy; to answer increasing demands for better health care, education, recreation and a clean environment. And, indeed, there was a ready-made activist base and an eager constituency for change in the civil rights, black liberation, women's and peace movements of that period.

It was the road not taken. The Democratic Party leaders and their allies – Hubert Humphrey, Henry Jackson, George Meany – were unprepared to accept the necessary conditions for the directional shift. They could not imagine converting to a peace economy when the war economy (and the ideology that rationalized its expansion) had been the foundation of Democratic fortunes since 1939. Labor leaders could not countenance the threat to their power implicit in the demands a militant and unified work force would make for integration, participation in management decisions and conversion. And finally, the party bosses would not allow a broad alliance of disenfranchised blacks, poor people, women and low-wage workers to challenge their hold on the party and its agenda. In short, the Democrats would not accept a transformation of their party.

The party traditionalists counterattacked. Labor leaders forced blacks out of training programs, bucked affirmative action and literally assaulted those who protested the war system. In 1972, Democratic hierarchs and their labor lieutenants decided to defect from the campaign of their party's candidate – standard-bearer of the popular alliance at its strongest hour – rather than permit a new politics to develop. On that scorched earth was built the political architecture of the next period.

With its crumbling coalition and its old commanders, the Democratic Party now faces an entirely changed landscape. The road the country did take as the postwar boom ended led to the famous split-level economy, with its vast low-wage ghetto (containing a third of the labor force), its newly employed and scandalously underpaid female component and its powerful echelons of the new rich.

To sustain and expand their privilege, the new rich have mounted one of the most successful campaigns in American political and economic history. From the tax revolts of California to the tax programs of the Republican Administration and the Democratic Ways and Means Committee, the large upper class has devised schemes to make a better living for itself at the expense of the even larger underclass. Despite spasms of opposition to one or another policy or piece of legislation in the assault, the Democrats are incapable of challenging the basic corporate campaign. For it is an attack in which those who beat back the new politics in 1972 have a large stake. They cannot meet the enemy; they are it.

The Democratic weakness is much more structural than spiritual. For instance, the present phase of military expansion, from 1977 to (at least) 1986, is the longest in U.S. history. Amid long-term stagnation, it is the engine of what vigor remains in the economy. To cut back on such spending in any substantial way would be to assail steel, machine tools, aerospace, shipbuilding – all of which are, in labor terms alone, core parts of the Mondale coalition. Mondale could no more allow antimilitarist sentiment to threaten the war industry than he could let insurgency threaten Third World regimes in hock to the American banking system.

Mondale pretends to include members of the newly expanded underclass in his old coalition, but the programs he espouses leave no place for them except as voters on election day. Gary Hart could have undercut Mondale by embracing the popular alliance that the old Democrats ignored. Instead, he chose to clothe his neoliberalism – the politics of lowered expectations – in bogus generational rhetoric. In the end, his only issue was the difference between Mondale's birth-date and his own, whatever that may be.

So, in control are the Democratic 'pragmatists,' as the pollsters and pundits call them, the ones who argue for party unity at the expense of movement and who propose that the way to beat Reaganism is to denounce its excesses while accepting its premises. The pathos of their opportunism lies in its shortsightedness. As every tactician attests, the key to defeating Reagan is turnout. But turnout has political content and context. People will not simply vote for Anybody But Reagan; they want somebody who speaks to their interests, who promises them more than they've got and who offers them hope.

The enormous nonvoting constituency of today is located in the lower precincts of the split-level economy. Its participation in the election is by no means assured. But it is there that the left must look for its opportunities and discharge its responsibilities in the next period.

The only way the left can work within the Democratic Party is to act without it. That is, the future of the party will be determined by the development of forces operating on its margins or beyond its boundaries (just as the developing American political economy – late capitalism – faces its most serious challenge at the hands of the Third World, both within and outside the national frontier). The constituency that formed in response to Jackson's campaign is a prime example. Its votes are absolutely necessary to defeat Reagan, but its priorities set it directly against the power and position of the Democratic mainstream. The pragmatists who want the votes will soon see that those votes don't come free and that without a significant reordering of the Democratic agenda, the new voters will not stream to the polls.

To address the concerns and accommodate the needs of the female proletarians, a political party and the political economy itself would have to undergo change considerably greater than the existential *frisson* engendered by the nomination of a woman as Vice President. Because NOW asked only for that gift, there is no reason for Mondale to move toward the changes that could materially improve the lives of the mass of women whose votes he expects.

The left has a history of attachment to a political logic that admits two equally unacceptable alternatives: isolation in purist parties (activists and intellectuals doomed to life on the margins of social practice) or total immersion in the belly of the Democratic beast. Once the left sees that party as the only possible vehicle, it is trapped in the lesser-of-two-evils paradox and ends up as a cheering section for the most reactionary elements in it.

To see a way around the paradox, and escape the logic, the left need look no further than the Jackson campaign's project to form a popular coalition of people who need change most and can be counted on to fight for it hardest. It offers an example of how an alliance of the disenfranchised can approach the Democratic Party, use it when necessary and work at some remove when that seems propitious. Symbolic of that complex relationship, Jackson's trips to Syria, Cuba and Nicaragua stand out in high relief against the kind of foreign policy pronouncements other candidates have made. Jackson posed himself squarely against the cold war policies and imperial attitudes that the Democrats have maintained for years.

There are other opportunities as well. An election campaign, it should be stressed, is only one avenue of action in the process of empowerment. The methods developed by Ralph Nader to organize coalitions of consumers at the point of consumption, aggrieved citizens at the point of their grievance and workers in the context of their workplace make enormous sense for left activism. Parties are important but they are not all-important. The Democratic Party is a vehicle, not the only vehicle. It can be used for its power and commanding position in the society.

As the fall campaign begins, the left should remember that there's more to politics than is suggested by that self-deprecating formulation of *Realpolitik*: hold one's nose and vote for Mondale. Barbarism with a human face is still preferable to barbarism with a barbaric one, but there are hundreds of other campaigns, scores of local coalitions in formation and numerous activist projects which carry greater weight in an electoral year. Voting for Mondale, the old in/out on November 6, does not necessitate giving up on all those activities.

The Democratic call for unity is a guilt trip when party whips – the ones in the press as well as in power – use it to extinguish all signs of life on the left side of the universe. It is not the left's business to shore up the party and cheer on its candidate every four years. There is a bigger job to do in creating radical alternatives to dead-center politics – and that means regarding the Democratic Party without sentiment or illusion.

The Nation, with Andrew Kopkind

August 4, 1984

Regrets Only

Being black means always having to say you're sorry. First Jesse Jackson and then Vanessa Williams issued apologies to the American people. Americans like apologies. It's a cheap way of feeling good, as the apologizer gets down in the dirt and grovels. Then you can either be big about it and accept the apology or say you are adopting a 'wait and see if he means it' attitude.

Jackson was, of course, the progressive voice in San Francisco, and the commentators gleefully reported the crushing of his platform demands. They'd reel off his calls for enforcement of the Voting Rights Act, diminished military spending and so forth, and then say, in a curve of rising petulance, 'What does Jackson *want*?'

In the end all the spleen against Jackson and all the suppressed male rage against Geraldine Ferraro got displaced on poor Vanessa Williams. Men had coped with the Ferraro threat by making her into a man, calling her 'ballsy.' The Freud memorial couch cushion in this category goes to Representative Tony Coelho, who said Ferraro 'isn't a threat; she is not a feminist with wounds.' Men are mad and by extraordinarily bad luck, Williams came into the line of fire at precisely the wrong moment. And she was not posing with just anyone. *She was posing with another woman.* I doubt if even a full repudiation of Louis Farrakhan and all he stands for would have got Williams off the hook at that point.

It's the essence of a witch hunt that the past is re-created as guilty secret. Williams took off her clothes in a Mount Kisco studio and, years later, was 'unmasked' for that unclothing. Alastair Reid spoke offhandedly to a seminar and, years later, was unmasked in *The Wall Street Journal.* And now the supposedly Hispanic novelist Danny Santiago is unmasked as the Commie Anglo Daniel James, by John Gregory Dunne, in *The New York*

Review of Books. The New York Times picked up the story and, just as it did the Reid affair, ran it on the front page.

It's true that James sanctioned Dunne's article and – so Carl Brandt, his agent, tells me – is relieved to be freed from the constriction of his false identity. But the way *The Times* ran the story from *The New York Review*, it seemed a re-enactment, a mime, of the ritual of naming names. McCarthyized in 1951 and forced into pseudonymity, James has been McCarthyized all over again in 1984. Dunne's narrative, self-regarding, contrived and conservative in the patented Didion-Dunne manner, had the whiff of the witch hunter while purporting to be something else. Edwin McDowell's piece in *The Times* reeked of it.

Of course, since there is hardly a left in America to be extirpated, the witch hunter must turn to ever more ludicrous substitutes, and verbs like 'admit,' 'confess' and 'disclose' are pressed into ever more trivial service. Mark Twain will soon 'admit' that this was not his true name. George Sand will 'disclose' her true sex. Beauty queens, recruited to a degraded and fetishistic ritual called a pageant, will be denounced for having exploited their sex on terms other than those laid down by a bunch of promoters in Atlantic City.

The Nation

August 18, 1984

Kowtowing to Reagan

The TV networks are kowtowing to the Reagan Administration in the most craven fashion, none more zestfully than ABC, whose Riefenstahlian coverage of the Olympics – interspersed with heavy-breathing promos for its movie *Call to Glory* – finally provoked protest. These Olympics frighteningly evoked the rising tide of American chauvinism and self-regard. It was not in 1936 in Berlin that the camera caught a ferociously partisan local crowd attempting to intimidate the umpires in the gymnastics competition with cries of 'Ten! Ten!' as the local heroine – Mary Lou Retton – strutted, preened and courted the baying mob.

Leigh Montville in *The Boston Globe* had a fine column from Los Angeles about the late-night bus from the press center to the hotels winding its way through the inner city: 'I look at the bums on Pico, standing in the doorways. I look at the iron gates on Crenshaw, every store locked and covered, made into a fortress to withstand attack in the night. I know the ride will take almost an hour and the landscape will not change.'

Montville tried to imagine what it would be like if he were a foreign journalist covering the games:

I would be looking to see my native son or daughter go to work. All I can see is American flags. Everywhere. On shirts. On hats. On banners. On the flagpoles. ... It would be as if my player, my team, my country did not exist ... this time they are America's games. No one else seems to matter. The pleasant, spontaneous cheering of 1980 in Lake Placid for the US hockey team has become a manufactured mania for 1984. Every crowd exults for every American.

The Nation

September 15, 1984

Questions About Reagan

President Reagan has now been in office nearly four years. He seeks re-election and stands a good chance of being the first Chief Executive since Dwight D. Eisenhower to serve out two full terms. Following are some questions and answers about President Reagan:

Is the President mentally infirm?

In recent times Mr. Reagan has been unable to recall the name of his dog or of some of his Cabinet officers. One of his staff has conceded that he dozes in Cabinet meetings. Other world leaders have had similar lapses of memory, particularly with respect to their subordinates. Experts acknowledge that it is exceedingly rare for a politician to forget the name of his dog.

Is the President deaf?

Increasingly so, but White House aides have marshaled sophisticated technological equipment to compensate for this affliction, common in people of Mr. Reagan's age. For example, after each question at press conferences, the interlocutor's name and inquiry are flashed on the podium miniscreen in front of the President. He can answer, 'Well, Bob ...,' thus deluding the public into thinking he is on a first-name basis with the entire press corps, when in fact he has not the slightest idea who they are.

Does the President know the difference between fact and fiction?

There is overwhelming evidence that he does not, or – at the very least – that he sees no utility in distinguishing between them. Thus on two separate occasions he has claimed to visitors that he accompanied a unit that filmed the Nazi death camps at the end of World War II, although actually he never left the United States.

Does President Reagan believe the end of the world is at hand?

On a number of occasions in the recent past the President has indicated his belief that Armageddon could well occur in this generation, most likely in the Middle East. To take two examples, in the 1980 campaign Mr.

Reagan told preacher Jim Bakker of the PTL Television Network, 'We may be the generation that sees Armageddon.' He said almost the same thing to Thomas Dine, executive director of the American Israel Public Affairs Committee last October. The Rev. Jerry Falwell has confirmed that Mr. Reagan's concept of Armageddon is that of the fundamentalist Christian: the Second Coming, damnation for the wicked and paradise for the good. Texan journalist Ronnie Dugger, who has made the most determined investigation of the subject, cites a 1978 broadcast in which Mr. Reagan asserted his belief in the literal truth of the Bible, including Christ's walk on the Sea of Galilee and the parting of the Red Sea for Moses. Secretary of Defense Caspar Weinberger has expressed his own belief in the prediction of the world's end made in Revelation 16:16, where the final struggle will be fought near the Hill of Megiddo in the area about fifteen miles southeast of Haifa.

The Nation

September 29, 1984

Minnesota, Mondale and the Tempo of Doom

They keep saying that the best reason to vote for Walter Mondale is Ronald Reagan. But since Mondale filed to change his name and political identity to Reagan halfway through September, this argument doesn't carry quite the weight that it once did.

Reagan claims that Nicaragua is exporting revolution to the rest of Central America, and so does Mondale. Reagan says Nicaragua should be 'pressured' until it mends its ways, and so does Mondale. Reagan says he will invade Nicaragua if it buys twenty-eight-year-old Soviet MIG-21s to protect itself, and so does Mondale. Reagan says that he supports the policies of Salvadoran President José Napoleón Duarte, and so does Mondale. Reagan justifies the invasion of Grenada by claiming falsely that its purpose was to save endangered Americans, and so does Mondale. Reagan blames the missile crisis in Europe on the Russians, and so does Mondale. Reagan is for increases in military spending, and so is Mondale. Reagan is bad on the Middle East, and Mondale is worse. And finally, Mondale promises to raise taxes and cut social spending.

The Nation

October 27, 1984

Balancing Acts

Are you more likely to tolerate drivel than you were four years ago? I think the answer is yes. Four years of Reagan has deadened the senses against an uninterrupted barrage of nonsense. I finished reading one of William Safire's columns last week and was contemplating a run through Anthony Lewis's when I suddenly realized that I had experienced none of the feelings of intellectual distress, outrage, misery, fear, loathing, contempt, abhorrence, indignation and overall pissed-offness that are the inevitable consequences of reading Safire's prose. I had ingested his column in a sort of synesthetic equilibrium in which my mind had automatically abdicated its normal functions.

I took another look. Sure enough, Safire's column was a piece of ripe insanity. He used the I.R.A.'s Brighton bomb to argue in favor of President Reagan's Star Wars program. The idea seemed to be that the 'terrorists' of the future (by which Safire did not mean governments holding the world for ransom with their nuclear arsenals) would probably use nuclear devices to blackmail mankind but would be outwitted by the Star Wars defense. The column concluded, 'A generation from now, the Reagan Presidency will be remembered for sinking the socialistic Law of the Sea and for launching the world's counterterror space defense. How many of us will be able to say we supported him in his greatest moves?'

Now that is raving, pure and simple. But if you asked Punch Sulzberger about it, he would probably say that those who dislike this kind of talk were able to turn on the same day to Anthony Lewis whacking away at George Bush. This is what Op-Ed intellectual discourse has got us into. So long as you can strike some sort of 'balance,' it doesn't matter that on one end of the seesaw sits a man saying things that in a rational world would have him held by doctors for observation.

The Nation

November 24, 1984

Hello History, Get Me Rewrite

The way the newspapers are these days, it's getting harder and harder to remember what the supposed advantages of a free press are. I opened up my *Washington Post* on Monday, November 12, and found this in an editorial about Chile:

A myth of American responsibility for the collapse of Chilean democracy spread in the 1970s. We say myth because the ever-expanding record makes it clear that Chileans were the architects of their own disaster, and the American role was, though often unwise and unhelpful, finally peripheral.

Unwise and unhelpful, eh? The United States contrived to starve Allende's Chile of multilateral and bilateral economic aid. It sent teams that successfully organized the assassination of Gen. René Schneider and that plotted the murder of the President himself. It financed the opposition newspaper *El Mercurio*, fostered labor disruptions and enthusiastically promoted the tyranny that survives to this day.

As the World Turns

'Could the officer have aimed to warn or wound rather than to kill? Could the team have used Chemical Mace or tear gas?' This was in a November 2 *New York Times* editorial, apropos the N.Y.P.D.'s shooting of Eleanor Bumpurs, the 66-year-old Bronx woman who was behind in her rent. I love liberals when they try to think constructively.

The Nation

December 8, 1984

You Just Mugged My Heart

The new Jarvik heart pack is only nine inches square and weighs eleven pounds. The heart is worn on the shoulder, in the manner of a camera bag or ghetto blaster. This is a giant step forward in the commodification of the human body, whereby the corporeal infrastructure becomes a hatstand for corporate merchandise in the form of various life-extending or life-enhancing impedimenta.

It won't be long before the discount stores will be carrying hearts of varying price and quality, from the Sony Hart-Pak, with detachable ventricles, to the cheaper South Korean Eezi-Thump. In the case of malfunction, return device with guarantee to your nearest authorized dealer.

We can see now that the big ghetto blasters, carried mostly by blacks and Hispanics, and the tiny Walkmans, carried mostly by whites, were cultural prophecies of the portable heart, alternatively booming or whispering their life-asserting beat. Somewhat along the same lines, the gigantic technological breakthrough represented by the new stand-up toothpaste dispenser was harbinger of Reagan's America, newly erect.

There on the washbasin is no longer the squeezed-out tube of toothpaste, abject and shrunken, but a puissant dildo, some seven inches tall. When the pump tip is pressed firmly, the paste oozes from its nozzle. The tube remains erect and ample, no matter how often it is used. I don't know how feminists feel about having to grab hold of a dildo every time they clean their teeth, but the plain fact is that the new road to gum pride in Reagan's America comes by way of the simulacrum of a male Caucasian sexual member, or – if you want to be overdetermined about it – of a nuclear missile.

It turns out that the new device was launched on its test-market career around the time of the invasion of Grenada, just when America was learning to stand tall again. It went into national markets in May. Sold here under the brand name Check Up, the pump dispenser began to be imported by Minnetonka Inc. in cooperative agreement with Henkel of West Germany just about the time that the Pershing 2s were heading the other way. Henkel put out its pump-dispensed product, Thera-med, about ten years ago, when West German missile frenzy was beginning to gather force, culminating in Chancellor Helmut Schmidt's request for the new NATO missiles.

Larry Wilhelm of Minnetonka tells me that the non aerosol technology was a 'difficult problem' demanding 'precision tolerances' of the utmost refinement. In the United States the pump dispenser is extremely popular. Colgate was soon in the fray with its version, exhibiting a bit more throw weight than Check Up (it stands taller) but without the latter's saucy label, 'Adult Tooth Gel.' Lever Brothers has its Aim rival; Crest is testing one, in cooperation with Procter & Gamble. These are the true technological triumphs of the Reagan years.

The Nation

January 26, 1985

Jackboot Liberals

Now that four more conservative years have been officially inaugurated by Ronald Reagan, we may as well remember that much of the damage associated with the rightward swerve of the *Zeitgeist* is not being inflicted by Birchers or kooks from the Moral Majority but by upstanding members of the supposedly respectable intellectual community. Anyone who doubts this should look at the 'Thanksgiving Statement' issued by twenty-seven academics toward the end of last year, urging schools to instill good character in students and warning that 'schools in general are not doing enough to counter the symptoms of serious decline in youth character.'

This is reminiscent of the muscle-and-blood authoritarianism preached by Thomas Arnold and by subsequent, more explicitly fascist educators. 'Character,' said the report, 'is often revealed in the concern and affection we display toward other members of our group or country. These traits are fostered through the learning of what Sidney Hook called "the history of our free society, its martyrology, and its national traditions." Such learning encourages students to be patriotic; to be loyal to our society, and to care about the welfare of their fellow Americans.' The report recommended frequent and high-quality ceremonial activities, stressing 'contribution.'

An article by Charles Claffey in *The Boston Globe* for November 25 quoted local notables enthusing about this horrible document. Nathan Glazer – one of the report's signatories and professor at the Harvard School of Education – attributed part of the problems of the young to, in Claffey's evocation of his views, 'an overpermissiveness arising from the fear of being considered intolerant.' David Riesman, professor emeritus of social sciences at Harvard, said that he was heartened by the report and that 'critical concerns of character and quality' had to be addressed. 'The problem is how – in our delirium of due process and the ACLU – to carry this out.'

These rude views were capably matched by another 'liberal,' Dr. Robert Coles, child shrink on the Harvard Medical School staff and recently self-appointed flagellator of 'elitist' freezeniks, on behalf of his good blue-collar buddies on the faculty. Coles told Claffey he liked the report, adding, in reference to a 17-year-old girl's refusal to salute the flag at a school in the Boston area: 'There's something wrong when you can't salute the flag in a school classroom without creating a constitutional issue. Things like reciting a school prayer and saluting the flag are part of belonging to a society ... we are creating a state of anarchy when what kids need are control and discipline.'

By an illuminating coincidence, the *Times Literary Supplement* for November 30 contained a review by Gordon Craig of Christa Kamenetsky's *Children's Literature in Hitler's Germany.* Craig cited the Nazis' plan to emphasize 'the duties of the individual to the state and the imperatives of racial awareness and upon character-building and physical training.' The proto-Nazi critics of modernist Weimar thought its educational system was 'sadly deficient in recognizing its responsibility for promoting a sense of national identification and loyalty among students.' Nazi educational theorist Ernst Krieck argued, apropos folklore, that, in Craig's words, 'the comparative dimension ... must give way to an emphasis upon the specifically German folk community, and folklore and saga must be made to serve as a kind of political science for contemporary Germans.'

The Nation

February 28, 1985

Telling Lies About Nicaraguan Policy

The president and Secretary Shultz are campaigning to persuade Congress to restore $14 million in 'covert' funds to the Nicaraguan contras. 'Covert' in this case means 'overt,' only it's more difficult to do a field audit to find out who's stealing the money.

The technique adopted by the president to restore the funds is one he perfected long ago: erect a mountain of lies, and as members of the press examine each new falsehood they find themselves on a foundation of older lies taken for granted as natural features of the landscape.

Let's look at these lies, many of which the editorial writers and network pundits take as gospel.

Nicaragua is exporting revolution to the rest of Central America, and most particularly to the guerrillas in El Salvador.

For almost as long as it has been in power, the Reagan administration has been trying to prove that the Salvadoran guerrillas survive and fight courtesy of arms shipments supervised by Nicaragua. Some newspapers have made the effort at persuasion easier by printing maps showing Nicaragua and El Salvador with a common border. The two are separated by Honduras, loyal ally of the U.S.

Now a 23-page draft report called 'Soviet-Cuban Influence in Latin America,' put together by the Pentagon, with a foreword by Cap Weinberger, opts for Stealth Canoes. It says that 'seaborne delivery of arms and supplies is carried out by 30-foot ocean-going canoes, powered by 100-horse-power engines. These canoes are difficult to detect on radar because of their low profile and wooden construction.'

The Gulf of Fonseca, whose waters these canoes would have to cross, is 20 miles wide at its narrowest point and 30 to 40 miles wide in the bay bordering on Honduran territory. The gulf is under intensive U.S. surveillance from ships and from the watch post on Tiger Island. Anytime Mr. Weinberger wants to demonstrate that hauling arms and ammo in a pirogue at night through open waters, heavily surveilled, is a good way of transporting war materiel in significant bulk I'll be happy to attend and throw him a life preserver.

Last year David MacMichael, an intelligence analyst attached to the National Intelligence Council, disclosed that, after reviewing all relevant data, he had found no evidence of arms shipments from Nicaragua to El Salvador. In fact, the Salvadoran guerrillas are nicely equipped by the U.S., whose rifles, dispatched to the Salvadoran army, are then sold by corrupt officers to their opponents in the field.

The Sandinistas betrayed the Nicaraguan revolution, and violated promises and written guarantees made to the OAS that they would implement speedy elections and move forthwith to democracy. The government is not chosen by the people.

Everyone from Mr. Reagan to the New York Times editorialists agrees on this one. The State Department is now circulating to Latin American diplomats a document claiming that 'Nicaragua violated a written agreement that it contracted with the OAS in July 1979 to hold democratic elections "within a few months."'

This is falsehood and, in the State Department's case, outright forgery. On June 23, 1979, when Somoza was still clinging to power, the 17th Consultative Meeting of OAS foreign ministers passed a resolution calling for a peaceful solution and democracy in Nicaragua. On July 12, 1979, five days before Somoza fled, the provisional revolutionary government sent a telex to the OAS secretary general outlining a 'Plan to Achieve Peace.' Point 5 of this plan expressed an intention 'to call Nicaraguans to the first free elections that our country will have in this century, so that they may elect their representatives to the city councils and to a constitutional assembly, and the country's highest-ranking authorities.'

So much for the actual words, which promise the Sandinistas have fulfilled. What standing did this telex have? To listen to Mr. Reagan and Mr. Shultz and to read the editorials, one would think that this message, rushed off in the climactic moments of a revolution, had the same standing as the U.N. Charter. As one high OAS official last year told the Central American Historical Institute, based in Washington, it was simply 'a telex sent by a group trying to reach power to the secretary general, which he communicated and made public to the member states.' Commitments to the OAS must be made in the context of official meetings. When Mr. Reagan first started playing the 'broken promises' card in 1983, an OAS official said he was entirely mistaken.

In 1980, the Nicaraguan government announced a program of literacy campaigning, along with laws concerning political parties and constitutional structure, and pledged elections by 1985. Elections were held on Nov. 4, 1984, on which day there was a 75.4% turnout of the 93% of all Nicaraguans who had registered. The Sandinistas got 67% of valid votes, the Conservative Democratic Party got 14% and the Independent Liberals 9.6%. Of the 96 seats in the National Assembly, 35 are held by the opposition. A multitude of observers from around the world testified that the elections had been free and fair, though a Conservative politician said that some of his constituents had been harassed by the contras not to vote. The U.S. embassy tried to persuade opposition parties to withdraw and thus make the election into the farce for which the Reagan administration was praying. In the case of Arturo Cruz, such efforts were successful, just as U.S. efforts to sabotage Contadora via Honduras, El Salvador and Costa Rica were successful two months earlier.

The Sandinistas should let the contras, or 'freedom fighters,' participate in their revolution.

But as a political entity, who are these contras? Thus far, efforts by the CIA have failed to hand-stitch their clients into a 'Democratic Alliance' or a kindred trumpery cabal vaguely espousing freedom in a manner calculated to delight Congress. The real military leaders of the FDN, men like Enrique Bermudez and – at least until recently – Ricardo Lau were officers in Somoza's National Guard. The president is urging resumption of aid to a gang whose sole record of achievement is the bestial murder or kidnapping of more than 3,000 Nicaraguan civilians and whose sole known purpose is the overthrow of a democratically elected government recognized by the U.S.

WSJ

March 9, 1985

Collapse of Free Press

'Reagan wants to remove the Sandinistas in Nicaragua, not oust them.' This was Connie Chung on an NBC 'Newsbreak' the night of Reagan's press conference, when he gave up pretending and said straightforwardly he wanted to invade.

The Nation

What Did You Do in the Cold War, Daddy?

I sit down and draft a preposterously long telegram – some eight thousand words, if I remember correctly ... I wonder uneasily what the reaction will be at home. To my amazement, it is instantaneous and enthusiastic ... I seem to have aroused a strain of emotional and self-righteous anti-Sovietism which in later years I will wish I had not aroused.

This is George Kennan, describing in *The New Yorker* for February 25 how bad he feels about helping start the cold war. He is still vaguely surprised that the U.S. ruling elite in 1946 was not displeased to get an 8,000-word telegram urging 'containment' of the Soviet threat. Now, like Adm. Hyman Rickover and William Colby and all the other reformed souls going back to Gen. Smedley ('I was a racketeer, a gangster for capitalism') Butler, Kennan says he's sorry. But he was a bad guy when it counted, and 'self-righteous anti-Sovietism' has never been in better shape.

These self-righteous anti-Sovietists have a tricky moment coming up on May 8, the fortieth anniversary of the defeat of Nazism. The problem is how to avoid mentioning that the Soviet Union had more than a little to do with that defeat. The easiest way is to do just that – avoid it. The way the fortieth anniversary of the Yalta agreement was handled in the press and on TV a few weeks ago is a pretty good guide to what will happen in May. The burden of this commentary was basically that the meeting between Roosevelt, Churchill and Stalin was one in which a trusting Roosevelt, over the protests of Churchill, was duped by Stalin into ratifying the enslavement of millions.

This absurd thesis has always been advanced by the merchants of rollback, but it's being advocated with more than usual intensity by those who contend that all arms-control negotiations with the Soviet Union are a mistake. 'Look on Yalta,' they say, 'and beware.'

There seems to be considerable ignorance about what actually happened at Yalta. In *The Wall Street Journal* for February 7, the erratic Paul Johnson – the only man I know with clenched hair – wrote, 'At Yalta the Western powers agreed (at Stalin's request) to deliver their devastating double air strike on Dresden, Germany, precisely to encourage the Soviet armored thrusts.' As a matter of fact, Stalin took the sensible view that bombing was of little military utility ('Bombs and rockets rarely find their target,' as he put it) and would scarcely have been militarily 'encouraged' by the terror-bombing of the hundreds of thousands of refugees who were crammed into Dresden when the Allied planes struck, or by the U.S. Mustangs that returned the following day to machine-gun the fugitive survivors. The Americans and the British bombed Dresden to demonstrate to the Russians, who were bearing the brunt of the fighting, what would now be called by the Reagan gang 'resolve' and 'will.'

On *NBC Nightly News* for February 4, Tom Brokaw announced that in the view of 'critics,' the agreement at Yalta was a 'brutal division that gave Joseph Stalin and the Russians an advantage they could never have won on their own.' That was an odd way of putting it. The truth is that the Russians had fought the Germans back through Eastern Europe and thus had won an advantage entirely on their own.

Brokaw then introduced Garrick Utley, who announced that he was 'here in Torgau, on the banks of the Elbe.' Forty years ago, Utley said,

Europe was divided by the superpowers, and 'the people of Torgau had no voice in that.' Considering that the people of Torgau had been led up to then by Hitler and had suffered the misfortune of being on the losing side, this was scarcely surprising.

The notion that Stalin behaved in a beastly fashion to the Germans was also suggested by a February 8 news story in *The Wall Street Journal*: 'After World War II Stalin politically terrorized and economically exploited Eastern Europe, especially East Germany. Whole factories were disassembled and sent back to the Soviet Union.' What did they expect, goodwill visits from the Bolshoi? Germany had just claimed at least 20 million Russian lives. The shipment of factories, reparations agreed to by the Allies, seems a rather genteel penalty, and perhaps in better taste than the West's idea, which was to ship Nazi war criminals in good working order – not even disassembled – to safety in the United States or Latin America.

'By agreeing to divide a defeated Germany' at Yalta, Utley said, 'the deed was done.' The problem here is that they didn't agree to divide Germany at Yalta. There were zones of military occupation. Formal division came much later. Gen. Lucius Clay's decision to institute a separate currency in West Germany in 1948 and the establishment of the Federal Republic of Germany the following year are more relevant than what Utley imagines happened at Yalta.

Roosevelt was no dupe bamboozled, despite Churchill's efforts, by Stalin. He saw the Yalta agreement as a realistic acknowledgment of postwar spheres of influence in which the United States did very well, the British less well and in which Soviet hegemony in Eastern Europe was duly recognized. The Western allies came out of Yalta justifiably pleased with the results, which included the Soviet Union's agreement to enter the war against Japan and thus deal with the near-million-strong Kwantung Army in Manchuria. The idea that Roosevelt and Churchill had a profound interest in democracy, in contrast to Stalin's brutish designs, is grotesque, as a scrutiny of their efforts to save the pro-fascist monarchies of Italy and Greece speedily attests.

The founding of the United Nations was also settled at Yalta, but Brokaw, Utley and Johnson did not mention the fact. It is not fashionable in the American media to say anything civil about the United Nations.

It is hard to know what the denouncers of Yalta would prefer to have happened. If you start by refusing to accept that the Soviet Union bore the brunt of the fighting, and was mainly responsible for the defeat of fascism, then you end by ignoring the realities of the war and prating nonsense about 'betrayal' and Roosevelt's 'innocence' at Yalta, as if Churchill had not already accepted those realities a year earlier in Moscow in the famous agreement with Stalin on spheres of influence. Of course, many in the Reagan gang agree with West German Chancellor Helmut Kohl that the best way to remember Yalta in 1985 is to encourage Silesian Germans to recover the 'lost territories' in Poland and that the way to arouse the masses in Eastern Europe is to transmit anti-Semitic broadcasts, as Radio Liberty has been doing with such zest.

The Nation

March 23, 1985

Contraprop

Sometimes I wonder which side *The Nation*'s editors are on. In the issue for March 9 an article on the efforts of the Nicaraguan *contra* factions to form a broad alliance was titled 'A Fragile Unity Is Born.' Whoever wrote that headline must be secretly working for Arturo Cruz. The word 'fragile,' with its aura of virtuous vulnerability, is linked to 'unity,' another positive attribute. The rhythms of hope are rounded out with 'born,' a word replete with fecund optimism.

Let's get this straight. *Our* side gives birth to fragile unity, *their* side *cobbles together a makeshift coalition. Our* people *strive to sink their differences*; in *their* case, *strains mark C.I.A.'s ill-assorted bedfellows.* Jon Lee Anderson and Lucia Annunziata's article was quasi contraprop anyway; there was no need to do it the favor of a moist headline.

The Nation

April 6, 1985

The Value of A Free Press

With the sale of ABC to Capital Cities Communications, the largest non-gas-related takeover in the history of the world, attention focused on Warren Buffett, the Nebraska-based investor. Buffett was a major player in the deal and already owns hunks of media stock, including about 13 percent of the B shares of *The Washington Post.*

The New York Times Business section ran a flattering article about Buffett. This is not surprising. If reporters from the *Times* Business section were to put out a new edition of Engels's *The Condition of the Working Class in England,* they would call it *Deregulatory Innovation: Productivity in the British Textile Industry.* In Buffett's case the *Times* reporter sought the views of Carl Spielvogel, an executive in the advertising business. Spielvogel brought the purpose of the Fourth Estate and First Amendment into sharp focus: 'Long ago Warren identified communications companies as the bridge between the manufacturer and the consumer.'

The Nation

May 2, 1985

The US and the Nazis

Amid the uproar over President Reagan's little outing to the Bitburg military graveyard, one particular concern has been that he might thereby be paying homage to SS men involved in the massacre of 86 U.S. prisoners of war at Malmedy during the Ardennes offensive. Of course we don't need Malmedy or the extermination of the villagers of Oradour to demonstrate that the 49 SS men buried at Bitburg belonged to a criminal organization, but the story of what actually happened to the massacre's perpetrators deserves to be remembered. It gives a useful perspective on the celebrations this week of the Allied victory over Nazism 40 years ago.

The bleak sequel to Malmedy is set forth in Charles MacDonald's book on the Battle of the Bulge, 'A Time for Trumpets.' By spring 1946 the U.S. Army had rounded up 73 suspects from the First SS Panzer Corps and charged them with the torture and murder of U.S. soldiers and unarmed allied civilians. The trial began at Dachau in May and ended on July 11 with the sentencing of all the accused: Forty-three, including Col. Joachim Peiper, the commanding officer, were condemned to death; the others drew terms ranging from life to 10 years. Subsequent review by the Advocate for War Crimes caused 13 convictions to be dismissed and 30 of the 43 death sentences to be commuted.

This review came in 1948, when U.S. hostility toward its recent opponents was being rapidly displaced onto the Russians. The chief defender of the SS men in the Dachau trial had been Col. Willis Everett Jr. and now, back in the U.S. as a civilian, he opened a fierce campaign on their behalf. Eventually the SS men's cause attracted the attention of a junior senator eager for exposure, a man for whom, as Mr. MacDonald remarks, the affair was tailor-made, since some of his constituents in Wisconsin were 'wealthy, right-wing and pro-German': Joseph McCarthy.

It was his first circus and he made the most of it. He bellowed about the supposed maltreatment during interrogation of the SS '16-or-17-year-old boys' and viciously assailed the motives and integrity of one of the German-Jewish interrogators who had fled Hitler to the U.S. before the war. On May 20, 1949, McCarthy denounced the U.S. Army for 'Gestapo and OGPU tactics,' declared the hearings 'a shameful farce' and stalked out of the hearing room. The uproar placed additional pressure on the U.S. deputy military governor in Germany, Lucius Clay. In the end no SS man was executed and the last of them, Joachim Peiper, was released in 1956. (Twenty years later he died amid the firebombing of his house in Alsace.)

Anti-communism and a forgiving attitude toward the Nazis have been a constant of the Cold War ever since Allen Dulles commenced his friendly parleys in early 1945 with Gen. Karl Wolff of the Waffen-SS about a German surrender in northern Italy. There is no doubt that Gen. Clay supervised a vigorous de-Nazification campaign in the U.S. Zone in the year following victory, and when supervision of the campaign was handed over to the Germans in 1946 he urged diligence. But the temper of the changing political situation bore on him. In his own memoirs he recalls an unidentified U.S. congressman refusing to sit in on a de-Nazification meeting and denouncing the Germans running it as traitors to their fellow countrymen.

While the SS men charged with the Malmedy crime sat in Dachau, U.S. intelligence operatives from the Army and proto-CIA were offering sanctuary in the U.S. to members of the SS Einsatzgruppen and Nazi White Russians, Byelorussians and others who had eagerly assisted in the extermination of Jews, gypsies, communists, etc. on the Eastern front. The rationale was the Cold War, and it has never been set forth more clearly than by Lt. Col. Eugene Kolb, a retired U.S. Army counterintelligence officer who justified postwar cooperation with, and protection offered to, Klaus Barbie by writing in a letter to the New York Times in 1983, 'To our knowledge, his activities had been directed against the underground French Communist Party and Resistance, just as we in the postwar era were concerned with the German Communist Party and activities inimical to American policies in Germany. ... His skills were badly needed. ...'

Just as it did not take Col. Kolb and his fellows long after the victory over Nazism in May 1945 to see the French Resistance as the enemy and Barbie, the scourge of that Resistance, as the friend, so too did the Western Allies change step. By 1947, according to writer Richard Barnett, 40% of all higher civil-service positions in the zones that became West Germany were occupied by former Nazis and 30% of the ownership of private industry. By 1950 two-thirds of the top jobs in the Bremen judicial system and two-thirds of the teaching jobs in West Germany were occupied by people with more than trivial Nazi pasts.

In the rapidly changing postwar climate some major U.S. corporations were prominent in urging a spirit of charity toward German business stained by Nazi associations. In his book 'The Crime and Punishment of I.G. Farben' the late Joseph Borkin describes in detail such urgings, culminating in a final forgiving by Attorney General Robert Kennedy of what had been I.G. Farben, a corporation that had once suggested to the SS that it would improve productivity by beating the slave laborers to death in the prison quarters at Auschwitz – a site selected by I.G. Farben – rather than at the rubber factory there.

On Tuesday night, NBC reported that Exxon's efforts to lift the postwar ban on doing business with the vestiges of I.G. Farben were being viewed with sympathy by the Reagan administration.

So it's been live and let live almost as far back as the Nazi surrender, and President Reagan may be forgiven for wondering at the commotion over his excursion to Bitburg. He sees history entirely in symbolic terms and for him the date of May 8, 1945, appears to represent the moment when the Russians were finally stopped at the Elbe by the Americans, the British and the good Germans. He effortlessly translates the war against fascism into the Cold War against Russia.

An optimist could have hoped that this 40th anniversary of the victory over fascism along with the 10th anniversary of U.S. withdrawal from Vietnam might have prompted a more constructive reading of history than that deduced by the administration and its admirers from these two benchmarks in history: excuses for rallying cries for NATO, for Star Wars and for the overthrow of Nicaragua.

WSJ

May 4, 1985

The Horror, the Horror

Almost without exception, the special issues of magazines – *Time, Newsweek, The New York Times Magazine, The New Republic,* etc. – devoted to the tenth anniversary of the American defeat in Vietnam find it impossible to discuss the central aspect of the war: what Americans did in Vietnam before 1975. This is a closed book, along with the memory of the nearly 3 million Vietnamese the Americans managed to kill.

As one might have expected, *The New Republic*'s issue was by far the worst, so infinitely vile that for twenty-four hours I thought I had eaten rat poison. 'Our allies in South Vietnam,' writes the *TNR* editorialist, 'were not worthy allies. And it was they who lost the war to the Communists.' That one line tells the whole story.

The Nation

May 23, 1985

Murdoch's Long Shadow

It's hard to believe that Rupert Murdoch truly intends to sell the New York Post. It would be like Dracula selling his coffin. The New York Post made Mr. Murdoch famous. It's the lengthened shadow of the man. When he bought it everyone said he would turn it into a sensational and inaccurate tout sheet for his political prejudices, and so when the New York Post swiftly became a sensational and inaccurate tout sheet for Mr. Murdoch's political prejudices all were delighted to find their prophecies confirmed. Mr. Murdoch had lived up to expectations and he became a big man around town.

But now Mr. Murdoch has said that he will sell the New York Post, as he must if he is to comply with Federal Communications Commission rules that render it impossible for him to own a newspaper and a TV station in the same town. With Marvin Davis, the Denver-based natural-gas entrepreneur, his equal partner in Twentieth Century-Fox, Mr. Murdoch is buying a string of TV stations from Metromedia which includes Channel 5 in New York. Hence the promised sale of the Post.

Now with Mr. Murdoch, promise made and promise redeemed do not always march in lock step. I was working at the Village Voice when he took it over and was impressed to hear him issue solemn vows that he would not change the paper's editor. He hired a new editor instantly. I dashed to his apartment with a colleague to remonstrate and he gracefully backed down, but expressed no contrition for the breach of promise. I think he regarded the promise as purely ceremonial speech, devoid of substantive meaning, like saying 'have a nice day.' In the wake of the Metromedia purchase he has pledged thus far that he will stop being Australian (a foreigner cannot own more than 20% of a TV station) and stop owning the New York Post, and I'm sure that if the FCC asked him to stop breathing for a couple of months he would signal promptly his eagerness to comply.

A few years ago, leftists and people of a generally populist disposition would warn about growing conglomeration of the media, the attenuation of public debate, the capture of the means of expression by the rich and the right. Those were the days when public TV, funded by the taxpayer and by public contributions, was seen as the little guy's alternative to big media. In the late 1960s, under the urgings of Commissioner Nicholas Johnson, the FCC vetoed a bid for ABC by International Telephone & Telegraph on the ground that ITT would be an unsuitable owner for the network.

Everything the left and the populists warned about has turned out to be true. Conglomeration has proceeded rapidly. Public TV is now a quality advertising outlet for corporations such as American Telephone & Telegraph and Mobil, and the spokesman for the little guy is William Buckley. And a successful campaign by such lobbyists as Reed Irvine has shoved the gutless TV medium even further to the right than it was in the first place. Just to take the three major news programs, on ABC George Will acts as Ronald Reagan's spokesman beside Peter Jennings; on CBS the indubitably liberal Bill Moyers has not been allowed a commentary in months; and from NBC it would be fair to say both the Kalb brothers now work for the administration. The leftmost end of the political spectrum given regular or even intermittent access to the airwaves is to be found among the Scoop Jackson Democrats.

One of the reasons that there has been so little commotion about this accelerating conglomeration is that the leading parties have been relatively bland-looking corporate entities. It's hard to get riled up at names like Gannett or Capital Cities, and in this growing tolerance toward the Money Power, people barely ask whether it is seemly that NBC should be owned by a major defense contractor or that CBS's chairman, Thomas Wyman, should allow himself to be nominated to the board of General Motors when one presumes that one of the functions of his network is to make objective and possibly hostile assessments of GM's products. CBS also owns Car and Driver, which is also supposed to make objective assessments of the new GM models.

The onslaught of high-stakes players with well-publicized ideological convictions like those of Mr. Murdoch and Mr. Davis disturbs this tranquil apathy. If TV stations are merely regarded as properties whose purchase and sale have the same relevance to democratic debate and communication as a trade in pork bellies, then it scarcely matters who owns the station. But if ownership is taken as a matter of vital concern in a democracy, then presumably it is right for the FCC to ask Mr. Murdoch not about his sudden enthusiasm for U.S. citizenship but about the way he views his communications properties as political and commercial instruments. It might also be appropriate to probe into Marvin Davis's exuberant career in the oil and gas industry and ask him why he thinks he should own a TV station. Vigorous FCC hearings would be instructive. Mr. Murdoch and Mr. Davis may be caricatures of the norm, but being such, they highlight the norm, too.

WSJ

June 1, 1985

Remember El Salvador?

Over the past two years the United States has been organizing, supplying, overseeing and in many cases actually executing the heaviest bombing and most ferocious aerial war ever seen in the Americas – and not one coherent report of the extent, viciousness or consequences of this campaign has appeared in any major U.S. newspaper or magazine.

Since the middle of 1983, this aerial war has been responsible for most of El Salvador's 500,000 internal refugees and for many of the 750,000 refugees outside the country's borders. It reached a particularly savage level during the country's presidential election campaign of 1984, when almost as many U.S. reporters were in El Salvador as were in New Hampshire during the primary season. Yet these reporters let it pass without a word of description or protest. It is as if 750-pound bombs were being dropped on the White Mountains, the farmers of New Hampshire being regularly machine-gunned from the air and their families being mutilated and slaughtered, and the press corps in Concord on primary night said nothing about it.

As noted in the September 1984 issue of *Alert!*, the monthly newspaper of the Committee in Solidarity with the People of El Salvador:

> The fact that this unprecedented bombardment is *completely* absent from press accounts is all the more astonishing as the carpet bombing of the Guazapa volcano at times literally shakes the residences of the international journalists, safely ensconced in the capital city.

What is taking place is a 'secret war.' A secret war may be defined as a military enterprise carried out by the United States and known to its victims, international observers, humanitarian organizations, foreign journalists and the domestic radical community but, for reasons of collective internal censorship, not reported in the mainstream media of the United States. In this sense, the U.S. bombings from the early 1960s through the early 1970s of South Vietnam, Laos and Cambodia were 'secret,' until circumstances permitted this collective censorship to be relaxed, though in the case of South Vietnam much of it is still in force.

Anyone who doubts that such a war is being waged in El Salvador should obtain two reports from Americas Watch: 'Free Fire' was published last August; 'Draining the Sea ...' appeared this March. Equally valuable is 'U.S. Aid to El Salvador,' a report presented to the bipartisan Arms Control and Foreign Policy Caucus by Representatives Jim Leach and George Miller and Senator Mark Hatfield. There has been some fine reporting by Chris Hedges in *The Christian Science Monitor* and the *Dallas Morning News*, by Mary Jo McConahay for Pacific News Service, and by Bob Ostertag in *Alert!* and *The Guardian*. So far as I and my colleague Maura Sheehy, who assisted in the research for this column, could determine, that is more or less the full story for a nation of more than 226 million people, whose journalists give each other more prizes each year than the press of the rest of the world put together.

The report to the bipartisan caucus puts the aerial war in its proper perspective. El Salvador – by which I mean the elite that seeks to retain power – is now an aid junkie, courtesy of the United States. The elite needs the war to get the aid that prevents the economic disintegration of the country, which would otherwise be bankrupt. Of the $1.7 billion in U.S. aid that has gone to El Salvador since 1981, no less than 74 percent has been devoted to war and war-related activities. An increasing amount of the present $500 million annual stipend is used for the aerial war. The last thing the Salvadoran elite will ever want is peace negotiations.

In October 1983, El Salvador's military overseers in the U.S. Defense Department switched to aerial terror after repeated successes by the Farabundo Martí National Liberation Front. The basic techniques of the air war are: demolition and fragmentation; the dropping of 500- and 750-pound iron bombs, many fitted with nose rods to convert them to 'anti-personnel' devices; incendiary bombing, using Israeli-supplied napalm and U.S.-supplied white phosphorus; machine gunning, with A-37 fighter bombers, AC-47s (those 'Puff the Magic Dragons' of Vietnam infamy), Huey and Hughes helicopters. A U.S. intelligence battalion based in Honduras flies OV-1 planes over El Salvador on frequent intelligence missions. Its observations are processed by the Pentagon and fed within two hours to the Salvadoran Air Force by the local U.S. supervisors. U.S. pilots oversee the resulting missions and frequently take part in them.

The bombing is indiscriminate, designed to terrorize the people it has not killed into taking flight. The Salvadoran Army contributes regular massacres to accelerate this flight. In honor of South Lebanon in 1982, Colonel Sigifredo Ochoa speaks of an 'Israeli solution': establishing free-fire zones which, journalists are told, contain no 'people,' only 'terrorists.' Conforming to this inhumanity, Ochoa's troops have prevented relief organizations from getting food and medical supplies to the desperate victims trapped inside those areas. Ochoa is frequently given respectful treatment by U.S. journalists because he exemplifies the younger, more efficient breed of Salvadoran officer.

At all times the U.S. Embassy in San Salvador and the Administration in Washington have lied about the uses of its aid, the increasingly grotesque evasion of the fifty-five-person limit on military advisors, the use of AC-47s in combat and the rate of fire of the guns installed in them, and about the war crimes being committed. The facts are there. There are towns and villages in ruins. La Escopeta is a 'ghost town,' Chris Hedges reported in *The Christian Science Monitor* for April 6. 'Every structure appears to have been hit at least once by a bomb and many show signs of being strafed by machine-gun fire.' According to Hedges, parts of Cabanas province look like a wasteland. Americas Watch observers have described hearing the Salvadoran Army's 105-millimeter howitzers blasting away through the night.

The mainstream press typically gives upbeat stories about President José Napoleón Duarte's progress toward defeating the rebels. He is hailed for ordering the Salvadoran Air Force to avoid indiscriminate bombing. In January, James LeMoyne of *The New York Times* provided a straight-faced account of such an order given last fall, with absolutely no discussion of what the air force had been doing before that time and whether the order had any purpose, or result, other than to be faithfully transcribed by the U.S. press corps. In many reports, notably the admiring ones by Edward Cody in *The Washington Post* on the 'bigger, tougher' and 'trim' Salvadoran Army, one almost gets the sense that the war is winding down, that the 'problem' has been solved. The concentration on Nicaragua by the U.S. left and left-liberal community has contributed to this mood.

An article in the *St. Louis Post-Dispatch* for May 12 by Ambrose Evans-Pritchard, Central America correspondent for the London *Spectator*, put it quite simply:

> If the bright mood in the capital suggests that El Salvador is returning to the fold of civilized nations, it is a consummate deception; it is just that the war has moved from assassinations in the cities to indiscriminate bombing in the country-side. ... The strict rules about aerial bombardment [Duarte] introduced last September are scoffed at by the army high command and particularly by Gen. Juan Rafael Bustillo, the tough air force chief. That is the price Duarte has to pay to keep the loyalty of the armed forces and to stay in power.

The supervisory criminals are ensconced in the Defense Department and the upper echelons of the Reagan Administration, fully cognizant of what their executors – Salvadorans working shoulder to shoulder with U.S. instructors – are doing on the ground or in the air, bombing, machine-gunning and massacring. All you need is a complicit or cowed press and a mendacious State Department, and the American people need scarcely know that not far south of Miami their government is sponsoring the repeat of My Lai and Operation Speedy Express.

The Nation

June 15, 1985

True

'The revolution advances like a bus, with its difficulties. When it changes speed, there are some who fall off. That's natural. ... So we say that the petty bourgeoisie is always pulled between two interests. It has two books. On the one hand Karl Marx's *Capital,* on the other a checkbook. It hesitates: Che Guevara or Onassis? It is necessary to choose.' Those excellent sentiments were expressed by Thomas Sankara, chair of the National Council of the Revolution and President of Burkina Faso (formerly known as Upper Volta), in the course of an interview given to Ernest Harsch in Ouagadougou and published in *Intercontinental Press* on April 29.

The Nation

July 6, 1985

The Gospel According to Ali Agca

At precisely the moment the United States is lashing itself into a state of incoherent paranoia about the ambit and menace of terrorism, one of the prime exhibits in the pantheon of 'terrorism' is collapsing before the eyes of the world's press assembled in Rome.

From the moment, in September of 1982, that a Bulgarian connection in the bid to kill the Pope was first proposed to a wide American audience by Claire Sterling in *Reader's Digest* and by Marvin Kalb on NBC, the presumed KGB-backed plot has been taken as the weightiest evidence for the existence of a Terror International sourced in Moscow. Agca's 'confession' was of immeasurable help to the Reagan Administration in its denunciations of the Evil Empire.

But ever since the most keenly anticipated show trial of our time began in Rome, on May 27, what has been emerging in outline is the story not of a KGB-inspired plot but of a right-wing conspiracy to bring off a major propaganda coup in the cold war, throw some more dung on the already putrefying corpse of détente and, specifically, discredit the left in Italy. If the witting executors of this conspiracy are found in official and para-governmental organizations in Rome and Washington, the unwitting – to put it most charitably – agents are located in the offices of *The New York Times, The Wall Street Journal,* NBC, PBS and *Reader's Digest.* It will be instructive to see how all these outfits deal with the proceedings in Judge

Severino Santiapichi's courtroom in the next few weeks, now that Agca has only to open his mouth for everyone there to start laughing.

At this point, *The New York Times*, NBC and others have become so heavily committed to the Bulgarian connection that it is difficult for them to extricate themselves from the wreckage without grave loss of credibility. Meanwhile, the premise and bogus methodology of the 'terror connection' have taken firm hold. The terror model to which the media automatically turn in their hour of need is the one fashioned by the ideologies of the new cold war, with special input from Israel in such forums as the Jonathan Institute.

Part of the problem is that too many careers and reputations, including those of almost everyone who ever buffed Kissinger's boots at C.S.I.S., depend on the terror connection and on punditry about 'terrorism,' the new mother lode of grant contracts and gravy by the barrel. This industry will survive despite Agca's collapse.

'Terrorism' has been a central preoccupation of the Reaganites. The concept is truly totalitarian. It avoids moral responsibility (who was the greater 'terrorist' in El Salvador or South Lebanon?), rejects logic (the 'terrorist act' never has a cause) and, in the end, produces the mentality and morality of the war criminal, as was made apparent in the disgusting June 19 CBS documentary, *Terrorism: War in the Shadows.* Kissinger henchman Lawrence Eagleburger called for assassination to become official U.S. policy, and Robert Kupperman (C.S.I.S.) said that the war against terrorism would involve 'charred babies.' These charred babies would be on TV. 'Can we withstand that?' asked Kupperman. 'Do we have enough confidence in ourselves as a nation and are [we] willing to take enough risks, and don't have this incredible guilt from Vietnam days?' Mr. Rambo, please light the grill.

The Nation

September 7, 1985

Dead Fish, Live Souls

Almost by definition a newspaper prefers to write about the day before yesterday on the ground that the present is too disturbing. In the August 25 *New York Times Magazine*, an exceptionally foolish piece by James Atlas about the 'changing world of New York intellectuals' gave the general impression that the most important phenomenon this side of the Rocky Mountains is Hilton Kramer's *New Criterion.* The article's subtitle said that 'the old school has been overtaken by dispersal and a drift to the right.'

Gosh fellows, *a drift to the right*! The fact of the matter is that the so-called New York intellectuals, both then and now, from William Phillips through Lionel Trilling to Sidney Hook and such comic side acts as Norman Podhoretz and Midge Decter, were always irrelevant by any realistic measuring of the history of world consciousness or even of culture and politics between the Azores and the Hudson. The lunge of a tiny, self-promoting segment of the New York intelligentsia to the far right is scarcely news today, and Hilton Kramer's miserable little magazine is of interest only to its corporate patrons such as the Smith Richardson Foundation and those who, like Atlas and the editors of *The Times*, wish to sustain the myth that Kramer, Podhoretz and the others represent anything more than a paragraph or two in the history of public relations.

The New Criterion is the only magazine of its kind that arrives at the bookstore covered in cobwebs. If Atlas had cared to, he could have found plenty of evidence across the terrain of American political culture that such life as is visible scarcely confirms his thesis.

In terms of politico-cultural journalism, it seems that the cycle begun by *The Village Voice* in the late 1950s and, at various levels of exploitation and cynicism, carried forward by *Rolling Stone* and even *New York* is now well and truly dead, both in style and content. *New York* has long been without interest even as a model for regional magazines; *Rolling Stone* is a fanzine; and *The Voice* is so spavined with Democratic reform politics and self-regard that it needs crutches to get out to the paddock. The publications that have vitality are poor and semiunderground, still – and perhaps always – at the most basic level of production.

The Nation

October 3, 1985

Terrorism Is as Terrorism Does

> DUSTY: How about Pereira?
> DORIS: What about Pereira!
>   I don't care.
>   – T.S. Eliot, Sweeney Agonistes

As France's guilt in the sinking of the Rainbow Warrior, the ship belonging to the environmentalist group Greenpeace, became increasingly manifest, I awaited with interest the considered views of The Wall Street Journal. On the face of it, the sinking seemed to be a terrorist act: two bombs, one death – adding up, one would surmise, to a fairly thoroughgoing attempt on the part of the French government to terrorize those who would challenge its practice of testing nuclear devices in the South Pacific.

All through September the French gave ground. The Tricot report, designed to exculpate the French secret service, quickly became inoperative. Then, just as the French government was nerving itself to 'fess up, the Journal showed the way to the unmodified hang-out posture, in an editorial on Sept. 20 with another catchy title, 'The Wogs at Tahiti.' The WSJ solution to the question of guilt allocation was breathtakingly simple: Blame New Zealand.

New Zealand! Of course. How could we have missed it? The editorial laid it out, fair and square: 'Nonetheless, the bottom line in the Greenpeace episode is that New Zealand Prime Minister David Lange wants nuclear tests to leave the South Pacific, and to take the French with them.' The writer went on to make some dutiful bow to 'alleged French complicity' but then let *le chat* come frisking out of the bag with the thought that 'however stupid an event may be uncovered, France has not been moved to similar desperation in the harbors of more supportive nations.'

And this forgiving spirit from a page that edged in black its editorial in memory of the U.S. serviceman murdered in the recent TWA hostage affair. There was a man aboard the Greenpeace murdered by the French. He was a Portuguese photographer, his name was Fernando Pereira, and he leaves a wife and two children.

At this point we must welcome Jeane Kirkpatrick to our story. Six days after the Journal editorial about 'Wogs at Tahiti' ('Frogs at Tahiti' wouldn't have been respectful of the *force de frappe*), the press reported that the former U.S. ambassador to the United Nations had discussed the Greenpeace sinking with Vice President Bush and apparently found an important distinction between international terrorism and the action of the French intelligence service, in that 'the French clearly did not intend to attack civilians and bystanders and maim, torture or kill.'

I'd like to hear her outline this view to Mrs. Pereira. Let's see. The French government authorizes the attack on the Greenpeace ship. The ship is manned by civilians. The ship is not simply disabled by one explosive charge attached to its propeller. To the contrary, two bombs are used, with no warning given either before or between the two explosions. When bombers don't want to maim or kill, they use the telephone. One civilian is killed and a great many more would have been either maimed or killed had not a strategy meeting of the Greenpeace crew been moved ashore at the last minute. If this isn't terrorism, what is it?

Perhaps Mrs. Kirkpatrick's point was that since the French government is not in the habit of exporting terrorism, it should be given the benefit of the doubt in the case of the Rainbow Warrior. The problem here is that the French secret intelligence service has been practicing terrorism for years.

Mrs. Kirkpatrick can bring her discriminating moral intelligence to bear on such episodes as the poisoning of a Cameroonian opposition leader in Geneva in 1960; the abduction of the Algerian Ben Bella in 1956; the kidnapping of the Moroccan Ben Barka in 1965 and his subsequent delivery to the late and unlamented Col. Oufkir, who tortured and then murdered him.

WSJ

October 19, 1985

Down With Evenhandedness

The defeat sustained by Jesse Jackson at the hands of Jerry Falwell in the September 4 *Nightline* debate on South Africa provides a number of lessons. First, our side has simply got to stop apologizing. Every time Falwell invoked the Communist menace and asked the audience if it would care to see the red flag flying over Cape Town, Jackson ran for cover. Lesson number two: Defy their premises.

> FALWELL: If there is a Soviet-Cuban takeover in South Africa —
> JACKSON: Stop right there. Standards of health, education and nutrition are higher in Cuba than anywhere on the Latin American continent, Reverend Falwell. If the average South African black were to wake up in Cuba, he would think he had gone to heaven.
> FALWELL: What about Ethiopia, Reverend Jackson?
> JACKSON: Well, what about Ethiopia, Reverend Falwell? Let's talk about conditions in Ethiopia when the U.S. supported Haile Selassie there. Let's talk about Uganda after your friends in Israel had installed Idi Amin. Let's talk about Zaire, shall we, Reverend Falwell?
> FALWELL: Who does Bishop Tutu represent?
> JACKSON: Who do you represent?

The trouble with progressives is that they always panic at the sight of the Red-baiter's paintbrush. This is what finished off the nuclear freeze movement.

Lesson number three: Evenhandedness becomes a degenerative disease. Consider Tom Wicker on September 9. He wrote, 'Beginning with the Soviet leader's proposal for a moratorium on nuclear testing –' Hold it right there, Wicker! Gorbachev didn't *propose* a moratorium. He *initiated* a unilateral Soviet freeze on testing. Later on, Wicker wrote, 'The test proposal might be tricky and propagandistic.' This, once again, is the sound of two even hands clapping. Why not say that the Soviet Union has commenced a unilateral testing moratorium for a period consequent on U.S. actions? The Wicker mindset leads to people writing: 'In a deft propaganda victory, black youths placed themselves at the mercy of white South African police whips, under the eyes of the Western media.'

The Nation

October 19, 1985

The Best Tunes

I open my mail. I find a letter from the International Socialist Organization. It begins:

> Dear Sir or Madam,
> The future looks bleak: Racist repression in South Africa. Mass starvation in Ethiopia. Near-record poverty rates in the U.S. ... Racist and sexist oppression is a fact of everyday life. Is there any way out?

What's the matter with the left? How about:

> Dear Sir or Madam,
> The future looks great: White slavers on the run in South Africa. The opening of a revolutionary era in Ethiopia. Popular rage in the U.S. Racist and sexist oppression under attack everywhere.

You don't get far by making people feel bad. My father used to quote sadly the old Communist Party recruiter back in the 1930s: 'Brothers and sisters, even as I speak our comrades in Latin America are writhing in the torturers' thumbscrews, our comrades in India starving in the stinking jails of British imperialism, our comrades in Africa groaning under the boot of the oppressor. Brothers and sisters, join the Communist Party.'

Editor's Note

The New York Times now promises to issue corrections for the sake of balance. So:

A *New York Times* Business Day report published two days ago quoted sources confident of America's continued economic expansion, but the report failed to provide adequate balance to these optimistic views. The report markedly failed to represent the views of the Marxist school.

According to the Marxist school, the capitalist economy of the United States will suffer increasing crises of accumulation and a falling rate of profit. These phenomena will aggravate social and economic contradictions to a degree that will be ultimately fatal to capitalism. Failure to note the theories of the German economic and social critic Karl Marx violated *Times* standards of fairness.

The Nation

November 24, 1985

The Liberal Hour

'What is the right and effective way now for Chile – with its history – to fight terrorism? ... Would not the Chilean government do better to act in a way 1) to isolate the violent 1,000 on the left as the only practitioners of terrorism in Chile and 2) to earn the good faith of the great democratic majority of the country by allowing an open political system to be restored?' This is our old friend *The Washington Post* editorialist trying to think constructively again.

The Nation

December 12, 1985

Excusing US Capitalism by Denying Its Presence

Here we are, right on the edge of the season beloved by demagogues and socialist agitators, the season of stark contrasts between rich and poor. On the one hand the swag-bellied plutocrats, on the other the needy and the desperate; here the shop windows of Fifth Avenue with their costly Christmas goods, there the squalor of the soup kitchen and the city shelter. At this point the agitator springs to his soapbox and, pointing to these same stark contrasts, denounces capitalism and says there has to be a better way.

I've been doing this for years, but this time around, just as I was hauling the soapbox out from the bottom closet, Ron Paul launched a sneak attack that momentarily left me floundering. Mr. Paul, you may remember is the fiery libertarian and former congressman from Texas. In November right here on this page, he said flatly that as a consequence of such evils as easy money and excessive government spending the U.S. economy is not capitalist. This crafty ploy by capital – of which Mr. Paul is an assiduous agent – to escape responsibility for the starving, the homeless, the needy and the desperate has to be answered by any agitator worth his soapbox. So let's settle this issue right here. Are the basic elements of a capitalist economy still in place?

What about the Stinking Rich, a traditional ingredient of capitalism much denounced by the demagogues of yesteryear? In recent years this concept of a small and wealthy elite, fatly feasting off the labor of the exploited masses, has been dismissed as caricature, distorting the urbane reality of a vast, property-owning middle class, fragrantly wealthy in a decent, almost populist fashion.

The old caricaturists and rabble-rousers can rest easy. Little has changed. Data collected by the Federal Reserve two years ago tell the story well. Only 19% of all families own even a single share of corporate America, and the richest 2% of all households hold 71% of all shares outstanding. Ownership of other forms of financial wealth such as government and corporate bonds is even more concentrated. Only 4% of all households hold any of these. Just 1% of all households own any U.S. government securities and indeed 97% are held by the richest 2% of these households.

Right away I can hear Peter Drucker shouting that pension-fund socialism has already come to America and that by their assets in these funds the laboring masses have, willy-nilly, gained control of the nation's economic destiny. But this is another ruse of capital. The masses have no control over these funds, as any union person speedily discovers when he tries to protest their investment in anti-labor enterprises here and abroad.

So, on the one hand the Stinking Rich, sleeker and more noisome than ever; on the other hand the exploited masses – the twin poles of genuine capitalism. What else can we find wherewith to refute Mr. Paul?

These same old socialist agitators used to insist that capitalism could not survive without a reserve army of the unemployed. The great late Polish economist Michal Kalecki, hardly a demagogue, explained this point eloquently in 1943: 'Indeed, under a regime of permanent full employment, the "sack" would cease to play its role as a disciplinary measure. The social position of the boss would be undermined and the self-assurance and class consciousness of the working class would grow. ... It is true that profits would be higher under a regime of full employment. ... But "discipline in the factories" and "political stability" are more appreciated by the business leaders than profits. Their class instinct tells them that lasting full employment is unsound from their point of view and that unemployment is an integral part of the "normal" capitalist system.'

This ingredient of capitalism, excellently defined by Kalecki, is as conspicuous as it ever was and indeed is getting more potent as the years flit by. Unemployment and underemployment have increased in each business cycle since the mid-1960s. In the depths of the last recession of 1982-83, official unemployment rose to more than 10% of the work force, more than at any time since the 1930s.

Wealth ... unemployment ... and, of course, crises. Where would capitalism be without them, even though there are those indomitable zealots who assert that U.S. capitalism has never been in crisis? Robert Lucas, high priest of the right-wing 'rational-expectations' revolution in economics, hails the 'incredible amount of stability' he detects over the history of U.S. capitalism and, with a jolly laugh, predicts 'unending growth.'

Today, sitting in his office at the University of Chicago writing book reviews such as the one that appears in today's Wall Street Journal, Prof. Lucas can throw one of his treatises out of the window and hit a genuine capitalist crisis right on the head, the head in this instance belonging either to one of Chicago's 23% officially unemployed blacks or to one of the bankrupted 20% to 25% of all farmers who, as the Journal's Alex Kotlowitz reported on Dec. 3, have been driven off their land since 1981. And if Mr. Lucas tells the jobless black or the former farmer that his troubles stem from mere 'frictional adjustment' within the capitalist economy, he must be prepared to experience a frictional adjustment between the fist of this interlocutor and his own nose.

Capitalism has to endure crises, the better to purge itself and fulfill its ancient commitment to give the lion his predator's share. As Kalecki noted, there is a capitalist solution to crises and the other ills – falling rate of profit, weak markets for goods and so forth – that plague any capitalist system. This solution is war, or military spending in preparation for war.

Here again Mr. Paul and other doubters can restore their confidence in the functioning reality of U.S. capitalism by noting the level of U.S. military spending and the vigilance of the arms contractors – merchants of death, as they used to be called – in guarding against the true threat to capitalism, namely peace.

In sum, peering from the soapbox across today's economic terrain, past the massed platoons of the Masters of Capital and the Stinking Rich, past the bread lines, past the crises that desolate the inner-city streets and the Midwest prairies, can I or Mr. Paul or anyone else doubt that it's capitalism and no other economic system that has this country by the throat?

WSJ

February 1, 1986

Here Is The News

My brother, Andrew, dug up the BBC's first report, at 6 pm on Monday,
August 6, 1945, of the dropping of the A-bomb on Hiroshima. This
newscast seemed a good example of how the state's imagination can work,
given half a chance:

> Here is the News:
>
> President Truman has announced a tremendous achievement by Allied scientists.
> They have produced the atomic bomb. One has already been dropped on a
> Japanese army base. It alone contained as much explosive power as two-
> thousand of our great ten-tonners. The President has also foreshadowed the
> enormous peace-time value of this harnessing of atomic energy.
>   At home, it's been a Bank Holiday of thunderstorms as well as sunshine: a
> record crowd at Lord's has seen Australia make 265 for 5 wickets.

The Nation

February 15, 1986

The No-Fault Presidency

The 'news spasm,' more frequent and more intense as the Reagan years
progress, is becoming a frightening feature of the national political culture.
Particularly memorable spasm events include the downing of K.A.L. 007,
the destruction of the U.S. Marine barracks at Beirut airport, the T.W.A.
and the Achille Lauro hijackings and now the explosion of the space
shuttle.

These news spasms are totalitarian in structure and intent, obsessively
monopolistic of newsprint and the airwaves, forcing a 'national mood' or
consensus in which rituals of grief and vengeance can be carried forward,
with President Reagan as master of ceremonies in electronic equivalents of
a Nuremberg rally. The cries of grief, the howls for vengeance, all obscure
the fact that President Reagan has almost invariably been to blame for the
events provoking the spasms.

In the latest tumult over the loss of Christa McAuliffe and the others the
quest for vengeance centers on some faulty piece of equipment, such as the
solid fuel booster. But if the long-term blame can be traced back to

Kennedy and NASA officials complicit in the utterly pointless manned space program, the short-term blame must certainly be laid to President Reagan. It was his idea to give space, the zone of Star Wars, a cozy, Rockwellish 1950s tinge by sending up a small-town American school-marm. And it was presumably the thought of President Reagan tilting his words up to McAuliffe in his State of the Union Message that prompted NASA officials to send up the Challenger even though they were well aware that the freezing temperatures were perilous in the extreme, particularly to the solid fuel boosters.

All such unpleasing questions were overwhelmed by the spasm, which, as usual, was evangelical in its fervor to establish a mood of national unity and unanimity. Words ('tragedy,' 'heroes') were voided of meaning. Schoolchildren, we were told, would need special 'counseling' (that is, brainwashing). As a lad who survived the death of Buddy Holly without the need for emergency therapy, I say that children are tougher than that. A *New York Times* poll further implicated the nation's youth in the spasm, reporting that they still 'favored' space exploration. These were the pollsters who told us right before Christmas that 87 percent of all children between the ages of 3 and 10 believe in Santa Claus.

The spasm, in short, deflects blame and, by the obsessive narrowness of its focus, reasserts priorities: this is a society that mourns, to a point well past hysteria, Leon Klinghoffer but not Alex Odeh, Christa McAuliffe but not that true heroine Samantha Smith, U.S. Marines killed by Moslems but not Nicaraguan teachers killed by U.S.-backed *contras*.

The Nation

March 15, 1986

More Swill From Marty

Writing about the bloody events in South Yemen, Martin Peretz, editor in chief of *The New Republic*, writes in his 'diary' for March 10 at the back of that deplorable journal: 'The causes of the coup are not readily grasped by Westerners. What do we know of the fratricide bred by antique tribal hatreds?' To judge by the paragraph preceding the material quoted above, Peretz himself is testimony to the potency of tribal loathing. He writes: 'Nonviolence is so foreign to the political culture of the Arabs generally and of the Palestinians particularly. It is a failure of the collective imagination for which no one is to blame.'

The time has long passed since such racism comes as a surprise in the pages of *The New Republic*, but familiarity should not breed indifference. The magazine's pages shame all who write in them. Actually the restraint of the Palestinians enduring Israeli occupation has been remarkable. On the subject of violence and nonviolence in the Levant let me once again cite some numbers. According to B. Michael, writing in *Ha'aretz* in July 1982, 282 Israelis were killed by Palestinian violence between 1967 and 1982. During that time the rest of Palestine was occupied; 200,000 Palestinians expelled; Jerusalem annexed; thousands of Palestinian houses blown up on the West Bank and the Gaza Strip; and, according to Meron Benvenisti, approximately 52 percent of Palestinian land in those areas expropriated. Beginning in the early 1970s Israel systematically bombed Palestinian refugee camps in South Lebanon and Beirut and as far north as Tripoli, killing many thousands. And during the summer of 1982, the Israeli Army, conservatively, killed about 19,000 people in Lebanon, mostly Palestinians.

The Nation

April 12, 1986

Say Hi to History

I jumped out of bed at 4:30 am last week and drove down to the Key West state beach to look at Halley's comet. About twenty people were already there. My friend Irving Weinman was at the center of an admiring group, bellowing authoritative instructions: 'Down from the bright star on top of the Teapot constellation, left a bit from the dim one,' and so on. I couldn't see a thing but everyone else said they'd spotted the comet, so I let out a few affirmative yips. Then an earnest fellow in wire-rim glasses who had been laboriously assembling a telescope pointed it at a different bit of the sky from Irving's favored patch and said, 'There it is if you want to see it'.

'It' was thoroughly dissatisfying – a milky blur in the eyepiece – but I went home feeling I'd got my money's worth. The comet's appeal is presumably that its interim appearances give people a sense of intimacy with protracted time, at an angle to our normal experience of minutes, weeks, years and so forth. It's like being asked to a party with all the other watchers of Halley's comet throughout human history.

I like skipping across the decades like that. My brother Andrew and I made a point last year of calling on Joe Vesel at his home near Carmel, California. Vesel was a witness to the murder of the Archduke Franz Ferdinand in Sarajevo on June 28, 1914, which prompted the outbreak of World War I, hence determining the destiny of our century. Vesel also had gone to school with the assassin, Gavrilo Princip. Vesel is bursting with vim at 85, and he plunged into a detailed lecture on Balkan politics at the time of the assassination, with much edifying incidental detail, such as how Emperor Franz Josef had kissed him on the forehead when he, Vesel, was 10. Franz Josef had as a young man surely known people who had listened to Mozart play at the Viennese court.

I later told my mother that I had shaken hands with this particular chapter of history, and she riposted with the information that as a little girl, her grandmother Edith Blake had met an elderly Frenchman who as a little boy had been one of Marie Antoinette's pages. Edith asked him if Marie Antoinette had been pretty. He said, 'Very,' and drew a sketch of the Queen, which I can remember looking at when I was a youth.

The Nation

April 17, 1986

Bombing Libya

In the face of the negligible threat posed to U.S. interests – and to the world – by Muammar Qaddafi we now witness the U.S. tossing aside elementary dictates of law, evidence, morality, compassion and proportion; all discarded in a gust of national self-congratulation.

Law: Since the raids against Tripoli and Benghazi would quite clearly have been illegal had the U.S. invoked a principle of retaliation, President Reagan cited Article 51 of the U.N. Charter claiming the right of self-defense against future attack. But this piece of legal justification is equally without foundation. The purpose of Article 51 was to give the right of self-defense to any U.N. member state actually sustaining attack, until the Security Council could take appropriate action.

But, of course, since the U.S. was not under attack by Libya at the time of the bombing raids, it has become necessary to invoke the threat of future attack, equipped with the usual convenient 'intelligence report' of imminent Libyan conspiracies. Is the Reagan administration now raising prophecy to the level of international juridical principle? If so, the Nicaraguan government, very reasonably determining that the U.S. is planning an attack on its territory, has the right to bomb Washington. Denis Healey, shadow foreign secretary in Britain's Labor opposition, pointed out to ABC's Ted Koppel on Tuesday night that by this same rationale of defense against future attack, Britain could bomb apartment blocks in New York and Chicago on the ground that they contained people sending money and military supplies to Irish Republican Army members in the UK.

Evidence: Although he cannot legally claim the right of retaliation, the president has invoked the bombing of the Berlin nightclub as justification for the attacks on Libya, saying the evidence of Libyan guilt is 'irrefutable.' The U.S. media now echo him with similar talk of 'overwhelming' evidence. But how overwhelming is it? As late as April 14, U.S. and West German officials were speaking of 'suspected' Libyan involvement. Only later came predated assertions of certainty by April 5.

Nothing in the history of the Reagan administration – whose relationship to veracity has been spasmodic at best – gives one any encouragement to credit such claims. The administration's idea of 'irrefutable evidence' is anything CIA Director William Casey chooses to put under plain brown wrappers. And, on Reaganite logic, if the Libyans were implicated in the nightclub bombing, they could no doubt similarly claim this was retaliation for U.S. military activities in the Gulf of Sidra in the last week of March: the London Sunday Times has quoted a British engineer in Libya as having said that on the basis of his radar observations, U.S. planes overflew Libyan soil before the Libyan missile batteries opened up. More than 50 Libyans apparently died in those attacks.

Would not the evidence as easily suggest that for the second time the Reagan administration sought a (politically popular) confrontation with Libya on the eve of a congressional vote on funding of the Nicaraguan contras, and that the eccentric interpretation of Article 51 could be designed as an excuse for future bombing of Nicaraguan installations?

Morality: That so many prominent citizens of a large and powerful country now delight in calling the leader of a small country a 'mad dog' indicates that dignity and self-possession have yielded to childish, brutish emotions. To hear and to watch politicians and commentators talking with abandon about 'taking out' Col. Qaddafi, even 'nuking' him, in the name of 'self-defense,' is to be reminded of the way the Nazis used to speak. Hitler liked to talk about self-defense just before he attacked a small nation. Is it really now the policy of the U.S. to attempt aerial assassination of leaders it opposes? A dead Qaddafi would render all the more weighty the charges addressed against the U.S. act.

All the talk about efforts to limit 'collateral damage' by bombing strikes of 'surgical precision' is the purest flimflam, made all the more squalid by subsequent shifting of blame to 'hung' fuses or Libyan missiles. If you bomb a city at night – or by day for that matter – you are going to hit civilians, as the Reagan administration knew well. The U.S. military certainly knew. With the use of infrared viewers and laser-guided equipment, at least 20% of the bombs would go wild.

Compassion: The president exults and the people exult with him. They speak of a victory over terror. Let them remember what they have wrought. 'In the wreckage of what had been a comfortable two-story villa,' went an

Associated Press report, 'rescuers found the body of Mohammed Ibrahim al-Shirkawy, an elderly merchant. His body still dressed in nightclothes was buried in rubble on the top floor bedroom. Across the street in a one-story villa ... reporters walked through pools of blood on the marble floor. In one room where neighbors said children had been sleeping, bed sheets soaked in blood lay strewn about the floor. ...' Think of Mr. al-Shirkawy before you dance in the streets.

Proportion: How is it that the Reagan administration could, without any apparent sense of irony, proclaim its duty to wage war on terrorism at the very moment it was seeking millions from Congress to export terrorism, via its contra clients, into Nicaragua? How is it that Col. Qaddafi can be enlarged from a figure of puny consequence into the world's premier contriver of terror? Amnesty International reckons his unfortunate political victims in two figures. Since 1980, more than 50,000 people have died in El Salvador, largely as a result of right-wing violence condoned by the U.S.

In the shadowy world of the Reaganite imagination, Col. Qaddafi is a figure of immense utility, an easy demon, in pursuit of whom all common sense may be abandoned, just as a war against 'terror' substitutes the geography of political paranoia and prime-time posturing for the geography of the real world. Is terrorism the main enemy, as opposed to famine, disease, underdevelopment? Is it a matter of national self-congratulation that when it comes to the map of paranoia, the U.S. inhabits the same latitudes in which it locates its foe Col. Qaddafi, though with infinitely more consequence for the world, and thus deserving of far greater censure?

WSJ

April 26, 1986

Superfiend

It is not surprising that the Qaddafi obsession should have sprouted so luxuriantly in the mulch of President Reagan's imagination. Reagan thinks almost exclusively in terms of myth and symbol and has identified Col. Muammar el-Qaddafi as the latest incarnation of that ancient and familiar stereotype in popular culture, the superfiend. His instinct was sure. Only when we examine the roots of the Qaddafi obsession can we understand why press coverage of the Libyan leader has been so consistently appalling.

The function of the superfiend is to act as receptacle for fantasies of an imperial, military, racist and sexual nature, with the fantasist experiencing no moral qualms about his reveries, reasoning that when it comes to absolute evil, normal standards of behavior cease to apply.

This moral self-absolution is nicely represented by the phrase 'mad dog,' which the President used in his last press conference to describe Qaddafi. Everyone knows what happens to a mad dog. George Will stated the theme back in 1981: 'Can the Western world be taken seriously in its rhetoric about terrorism, and indeed in its determination to survive[!], if a mad dog on the streets of the world, such as Gadaffi, is allowed to go on like this?'

Stress on Qaddafi's 'madness' has the added function of reminding people about evil. Any devotee of trash culture over the past hundred years knows well that the dividing line between evil and madness is all but invisible, and superfiends are absolutely evil or absolutely mad or absolutely both depending on ethnic origin, religious faith and the exigencies of the plot. Chinese superfiends tended to be horribly rational, as did the Jewish villains in anti-Semitic fiction. Constantine Schuabe, the Jewish superfiend in the British best seller of 1903 *When It Was Dark*, had eyes that were 'coldly, terribly *aware*, with something of the sinister and untroubled regard one sees in a reptile's eyes.'

Chinese and Jewish villains were superfiendishly cold. Arab superfiends were, and are, hot, as befits men of fanatic faith, desert origin and uncertain but ardent erotic preference. Back in 1973, Shana Alexander touched on some of those attributes in a column in *Newsweek*: 'Kaddafi, son of a barefoot Bedouin, dreamed as a child of overthrowing the evil King and leading his people out of poverty and back to the fierce purity of Islam.' The phrase 'fierce purity' has the correct ethno-sensual *frisson*, which sends us back to T.E. Lawrence's reflections on Bedouin sexuality in *The Seven Pillars of Wisdom* and to that great best seller of the 1920s *The Sheik*, by E.M. Hull. The theme of *The Sheik* was the subjugation of proud, upper-class, Western Diana Mayo by a fiery son of the desert, himself of impeccable lineage, as memorably established in Diana's tumultuous self-discovery:

> Quite suddenly she knew – knew that she loved him, that she had loved him for a long time, even when she thought she hated him. ... her heart was given for all time to the fierce desert man who was so different from all other men she had met, a lawless savage who had taken her to satisfy a passing fancy and who had treated her with merciless cruelty. He was a brute, but she loved him, loved him for his very brutality, and superb animal strength. And he was an Arab! A man of different race and color, a native; Aubrey would indiscriminately class him as 'a damned nigger.' She did not care ... she was deliriously, insanely happy.

The superfiend has, naturally enough, a superplot. And where Qaddafi is concerned, Western popular culture has not failed its task. In an article titled 'Qaddafi, Man and Myth,' in *Africa Events* for February, John Haiman and Anna Meigs make some incisive observations. There is, for example, the close identification of Qaddafi the superfiend with the superfiends of James Bond movies and similar stereotypes in the great tradition. They cite recent comic strips that seem to have been mandatory reading in the National Security Council. In one of them King Cybernoid plots world domination. His plan: kidnap the greatest minds of the free world – the commander of NATO, the chief F.B.I. agent, the United States' top nuclear scientist and Dr. Gustav Nemhauser, 'the bacteriologist genius.' The kidnappings go well, and it takes all Dr. Solar's ingenuity to rescue the cream of the military-industrial complex and thus save Western civilization. As Haiman and Meigs points out, 'The extreme puerility of the pseudo-sci-fi trappings of this tale accords with the equal puerility of its political and social assumptions. Yet, while we dismiss the first as merely silly, we find, surprisingly, that with the second we are on familiar and thus respectable ground.' Qaddafi, as in *The Fifth Horseman*, becomes the 'nut with the bomb,' stand-in for all the nuts in the world who actually have the bomb.

Qaddafi's great contribution to the anatomy of superfiendishness has been his deliberate and indeed joyous acceptance of the role thrust upon him by Western fantasists, right down to a cultivation of sexual ambiguity. Sometimes he gives interviews only to women journalists or makes a pass at Imelda Marcos; at other times he dashes about in campy military attire or unisex caftans. (Imelda Marcos told George Bush about the pass, and Bush urged her to give Director of Central Intelligence William Casey a 'debriefing,' or blow-by-blow account. Finally, Casey and his men asked her whether she'd gone all the way with the superfiend, at which – according to William Deedes's report in the London *Spectator* – she laughed and said, 'What a question to ask a girl.')

Bottom line, in terms of myth and symbol, Qaddafi is a youthful portrait of Reagan, the aging Dorian Gray, embodying in his eccentric person the old actor's own characteristics: off-the-cuff braggadocio, a highly personal and romantic conception of the nature and state of the universe, and a demagogic relationship, though socially far more constructive, with the masses.

The U.S. press has given the Administration free rein in deploying Qaddafi fantasies in the past few years. There was no scrutiny of the circumstances under which two Libyan planes were shot down in 1981 after firing at U.S. jets, although there is evidence that the United States contrived a provocation. A few months later the press gleefully accepted the concoction of a Libyan plot to invade the Sudan across 600 miles of desert. The absurd scenarios of Libyan hit men infiltrating from Canada to murder President Reagan were given serious credence by the press, which then refused to print the facts, as exposed in the *New Statesman* of August 16, 1985, that the 'assassins' on the official U.S. list were prominent members of the passionately anti-Libyan Lebanese Shiite Amal.

The press partook in, and indeed willingly fostered, the Administration's hypostatizing of terrorism as an expression of its own paranoid vision of the world and also its magnification of Qaddafi, a diminutive figure on the world stage, into master terrorist and superfiend, a monster in racist fantasy whose end has to be achieved by any means, with the delirious hatred that is the mirror image of Diana Mayo's delirious love.

The Nation

The Private Use of Public Space

The architect I.M. Pei supplied his usual grin in a photograph accompanying a respectful article in the November 24 *New York Times Magazine* about a pyramid he designed now being erected in a courtyard of the Louvre. What is the point of this ridiculous structure? Pei told *The Times*: 'You need to be welcomed by some kind of great space. ... That space must have volume and it must have light and it must have a surface identification. You have to be able to look at it and say, "Ah, this is the entrance."'

As far as I know, visitors down the years have not been experiencing enormous difficulty in discovering the entrance to the Louvre. What Pei really meant was that in our unfolding *fin de siècle*, public institutions need an area with 'volume' and 'surface identification' where rich people can assemble for cocktail parties, banquets and kindred functions, to which the word 'charity' is attached to satisfy bodies such as the I.R.S. Consider Pei's last essay in triangular form, the East Building of the National Gallery in Washington, which was completed in 1978. The museum's pictures are secreted in tiny closets. Voluminous space is given over to an immense area whose sole function is to contain the fetes and galas mentioned above. In the same spirit Mies van der Rohe's 1929 Barcelona Pavilion is now being restored solely for cocktail parties and allied festivities. The main purpose of the Metropolitan Museum in New York these days is to supply its various courts and arbors for black-tie affairs and at the New York Public Library we find the same dismal story.

The Nation

May 1, 1986

Tipping in America

Hovering somewhere between charity and a bribe, the tip is one of our most polymorphous social transactions. At its most crude it can be a loutish expression of authority and disdain. At its purest it can approach a statement of love. At one end of the scale we had the foul decorum of those old lunch places where the men thought it their right to pat the waitresses on the backside. If a waitress objected to these caresses the tip would be thrown into the dirty plate. And at the other end we have the elevated *snobisme* of Marcel Proust, for whom the tip was a profound and complex form of social expression. 'When he left,' writes Proust's biographer George Painter of one meal in the Paris Ritz, 'his pockets were empty, and all but one of the staff had been fantastically tipped. "Would you be so kind as to lend me fifty francs," he asked the doorman, who produced a wallet of banknotes with alacrity. "No, please keep it – it was for you"; and Proust repaid the debt with interest the next evening.'

Hanns Sachs who grew up in Vienna at the same time as his 'master and friend' Sigmund Freud wrote a memoir of life in that city in the late nineteenth century in which he devoted some testy pages to the growing complexities of *trinkgeld*, complexities which he took to be evidence of the decadence of the Austro-Hungarian Empire. Everybody had their hand out for prescribed portions of *trinkgeld* – the coachman, the doorman, the hatcheck girl, the waiter, the wine waiter, the headwaiter, the maître d'hôtel:

> Every door which you had to pass was opened for you by someone who demanded a tip; you could not get into the house you lived in after 10 p.m. nor seat yourself in the car in which you wanted to ride without giving a tip. Karl Kraus, Vienna's witty satirist, said the first thing a Viennese would see on the day of Resurrection would be the outstretched hand of the man who opened the door of his coffin.

Doctor Sachs' indignant portrait is clearly reminiscent of today's taxi driver, doorman, hatcheck lady, waiter, and so forth, all of whom, from Manhattan to San Francisco and from Chicago to Corpus Christi expect and usually receive similar *trinkgeld.* Is America therefore in decline? Visitors to the young republic found to their surprise that coachmen and waiters refused their tips. An organization called the Anti-tipping Society of America, founded in 1905, attracted some hundred thousand members, most of them traveling salesmen. But anti-tipping laws were declared unconstitutional in the same year that Congress passed the Volstead Act, and Americans entered the twenties buying bootleg liquor and tipping big.

Tipping is even bigger money now, with some five billion dollars per annum being left on plates, scrawled on credit cards, squirmed through taxi partitions, and slapped into outstretched palms. This is not so much an art as an item in the federal budget serious enough to provoke certain provisions in the Tax Equity and Fiscal Responsibility Act of 1982, designed to insure that the U.S. Treasury gets its tip too.

That's the trouble. Tipping is a paradox: formal yet informal, public yet private, commercial yet intimate, voluntary yet in reality so close to compulsory that most people, across the years, have little difficulty in remembering the times they felt compelled to leave no tip at all. If tipping becomes an entirely mechanical act, beneath government supervision, it loses its vitality.

A tip must, however fleetingly, be the acknowledgement of a personal relationship, which is why the process can instill such panic in people plunged into a ceremony where much is uncertain and where only a special familiarity will teach one the proper mode. Due contemplation of the appropriate tip, in size and allocation, discloses not only what sort of place you are in but what sort of person you are: the sort who self-righteously calculates fifteen percent of the pre-tax total and gives fifty cents to the hatcheck girl, or the sort who bangs down a big tip with the vulgar flourish that says, 'There! I've bought you!', or again someone like Proust, who saw the tip as a perverse gift. At the conclusion of an excellently cooked but badly served meal at Boeuf sur le Toit, Proust (in Painter's words) ignored the person who served him so badly and 'Summoned a distant waiter and rewarded him regally. "But he didn't do anything for us," protested [Paul] Brach and Proust replied, "Oh, but I saw such a sad look in his eyes when he thought he wasn't going to get anything."'

The tip can become a bond between tipper and tippee, leagued in a transaction against absentee ownership. We tip waiters, doormen, hat ladies, taxi drivers, and hairdressers. We don't tip airline hostesses. Bank clerks, no; croupiers, yes. The modalities are complicated, ever-expanding. The service economy, exploding decade by decade, will affect the tipping process. Seen more darkly, this could mean two increasingly divergent classes, one rich and one poor, with the latter increasingly dependent on tips, gratuities, presents, and other pretty expressions of the master–servant relationship to get by. Tipping in America may therefore become an ever more complex and fraught affair, approaching the status of necessary alms-giving as for the well-heeled traveler in India.

It would be better, some argue, to give up tipping altogether, as they have tried in Eastern Europe and China. Tipping is, after all, about the relationship between served and servant and should play no part in a free society of equals. It depends on what one thinks the origin of tipping is. It can be traced to the primitive gift exchange, the amiable and generous distribution of surplus goods and cash which, in its most abandoned expression takes the form of the potlatch, where the surplus was either disposed of by common consumption or heaved over the side of a cliff. In a perfectly equal society everyone would exchange equivalent gifts – portions of the surplus. Everyone would tip and everyone be tipped in universal rhythms of generosity and gratitude. But, of course, modern society is not equal and the surplus wealth is unequally controlled and allocated, so the distribution of surplus wealth must always be an expression of power and of domination.

All this was understood perfectly by P.G. Wodehouse who approached the intricacies of the served–servant relationship more boisterously than Proust, but who expressed it with equal realism as in the scenes at the end of so many of the Wooster-Jeeves sagas, in this case *The Inimitable Jeeves.*

> "Jeeves!" I said.
> "Sir?"
> "How much money is there on the dressing table?"
> "In addition to the ten-pound note which you instructed me to take, sir, there are two five pound notes, three one-pounds, a ten shillings, two half crowns, a florin, four shillings, a six pence and a half penny, sir."
> "Collar it all," I said. "You've earned it."

House and Garden

May 23, 1986

A Prince of Sycophancy

The death of Theodore White provoked a predictable torrent of lamentation about the passing of a man one obituarist called 'the chronicler of U.S. politics.' White's greatest journalistic fame came with his first *Making of the President* account, of John F. Kennedy's campaign against Richard Nixon in 1960. He kept on churning out *Making* books right up until 1980 and was an enduring fixture of TV convention coverage, chatting cozily about the wayward wonders of the democratic process.

In many ways White represented, at a potent level of distillation, almost everything wrong with U.S. journalism, on screen and in newsprint. He approached unfolding history with an ecstatic sentimentality that ignored process and caressed the powerful in a way that, as Lenin once remarked of an opponent, would be touching in a child but was repugnant in a person of mature years. Inside Teddy White there was a Barbara Walters struggling to get out, and such efforts at self-liberation were almost invariably successful. He was the spiritual father of the present panjandrums of screen and newsprint, careless of truth and servile to power. It is not surprising that in the wake of her husband's assassination, Jacqueline Kennedy was successful in persuading him to use the term 'Camelot' in his *Life* magazine article describing the White House in the Kennedy years, and that famous PR man's touch is a true emblem of his function.

Twenty years ago I.F. Stone caught White perfectly. He quoted a typical White paean: 'To a Rockefeller all things are possible. This is a family ... that examines a rotting tenement area ... and begins there to realize such a dream as the Lincoln Center of Performing Arts, designed to be the most fantastic monument of man's spirit since Athens.' Stone remarked that 'a writer who can be so universally admiring need never lunch alone.' The kind of flattery at which White was so adept has now become so pervasive throughout U.S. journalism that it passes almost without comment. But perhaps future generations will gaze back at the present grotesque cult of Reagan's personality with the same wonder as we do now at the passages in *The Making of the President 1964* in which White wrote that abundance and peace were the legacies Kennedy left Johnson and that 'it was as if Kennedy, a younger Moses, had led an elderly Joshua to the height of Mount Nebo and there shown him the promised land which he himself would never enter but which Joshua would make his own.'

What 'Moses' had actually shown 'Joshua' from the top of Mount Nebo was the promised land of Indochina and a decade of horror leading to the expenditure of about 2 million lives. Here again White knew the language that would serve power. Of the Tonkin Bay reprisal raids that stampeded Congress into giving Johnson carte blanche to wage war, White wrote, 'The deft response of American planes to the jabbing of North Vietnam's torpedo boats had been carried out with the nicest balance between bold-ness and precision.' The last long piece of his I can recall reading was a racist distortion of reality on the 40th anniversary of the end of the war in the Pacific, printed in *The New York Times Magazine* and titled 'The Danger From Japan.' Now White is dead, but his influence on the corrup-tion of language and thought survives in the TV chatter, still fresh in our ears, about the 'boldness' and 'precision' of the bombing raids on Libya.

LA Weekly

May 24, 1986

An Ear For An Ear

Representative Charles Wilson's offer of Soviet ears to members of his entourage as they toured near the Afghanistan border is solidly within the American tradition, as is the demonization of Colonel Qaddafi. I urge anyone appalled by the idiom of the Reagan years to read John W. Dower's excellent book *War Without Mercy: Race and Power in the Pacific War,* published by Pantheon. This is a blood-chilling anatomy of racism and the fomentation of hatred, in which state-sponsored intellectuals played their usual shameful and willing role.

Apropos ears, in April 1943 *The Baltimore Sun* told of a local woman who had petitioned authorities to let her son mail her an ear he had cut off a Japanese soldier. She wanted to nail it to her front door. Dower writes of thousands of Japanese prisoners of war or survivors of submarine sinkings being routinely machine-gunned to death, of bodies looted, gold fillings torn from the living, and the dead exhumed for plunder. On March 15, 1943, *Time* reported that 'low-flying fighters turned lifeboats towed by motor barges, and packed with Jap survivors, into bloody sieves.' One reader questioned the morality of such 'cold-blooded slaughter,' provoking outraged letters, including one that said, 'Thoroughly enjoyed reading of the "cold-blooded slaughter." ... Another good old American custom I would like to see is nailing a Jap hide on every "back-house" door in America.'

In 1945 the U.S. Office of War Information noted that 84 percent of one group of Japanese prisoners said they had expected to be killed or tortured when taken prisoner. The U.S. analysts commented that their fears were not irrational. Rhetoric at home matched savagery in the field. There was enthusiasm for genocide, with 13 percent of respondents in one 1944 poll wanting to 'kill all Japanese,' and the chair of the War Manpower Commission, Paul V. McNutt, saying he favored the 'extermination of the Japanese in toto.' The pathological Admiral Halsey had as his motto, 'Kill Japs, kill Japs, kill more Japs.'

The Nation

June 7, 1986

The Likes of Sobran

William Buckley, editor of *National Review* and no slouch at imputing racism to others, such as myself, may wish to have a serious word with his columnist Joseph Sobran. On May 13 *The New York City Tribune*, a Moonie newspaper, carried an article by Sobran in which he observed:

> Our ethnic etiquette makes our ethnic problems pretty nearly insoluble. ... I know of only one magazine in America that faces the harder facts about race; a little magazine called *Instauration*. ... [It is] an often brilliant magazine covering a beat nobody else will touch, and doing so with intelligence, wide-ranging observation and bitter wit. It is openly and almost unremittingly hostile to blacks, Jews, and Mexican and Oriental immigrants.

Quite a testimonial. *Instauration* (the word means 'renewal') is a monthly looking somewhat like *The New Leader*, published by 'Howard Allen Enterprises' out of a box number in Cape Canaveral, edited pseudonymously, according to Sobran, and carrying unsigned articles. Its sense of humor recalls *The American Spectator* and *The Dartmouth Review*. The January 1982 issue had a story titled 'Rev. Jerry Falwell – Majority Renegade of the Year.' The word 'renegade' is explained by Falwell's companion in the accompanying photograph, Menachem Begin. As Sobran said, the magazine doesn't like Jews. An article in the same issue announced: 'We are pro-abortion, despite the aesthetic horror of it, because it is the only effective way to cut down on nonwhite proliferation, both here and abroad. Unfortunately, a greater proportion of whites in this country practice abortion than blacks.'

Instauration for February 1984 carried a reproduction of Sully's painting of a blond boy with a hat, with the line, 'In Praise of Fair Children.' The June issue of that year hailed the war criminal Archbishop Valerian Trifa. The following year, in June, an article denounced the Heritage Foundation and *Policy Review* for being run by Jews ('most of them without any conservative identity or credentials. The table of contents exudes such names as Robert W. Kagan, Midge Decter, Oscar Handlin ...'). Burton Pines, Heritage vice president, is singled out as a Jew, and the foundation's director, Ed Feulner, is identified as being the husband of 'the former Miss Linda Leventhal.'

Sobran's modesty in failing to disclose the fact is understandable, but the September 1985 issue of *Instauration* carried a three-page article on him, titled 'The Brave Pen of Joseph Sobran,' in which he was praised for his support of Reagan's visit to Bitburg: 'The man has repeatedly defended white racial pride and solidarity, despite the mounting campaign to get him.' In the same issue of *Instauration* we find racist cartoons of 'Marv,' a Jew, and 'Willie,' a black. Marv is saying: 'Not everyone at the Last Supper was Jewish. I am working on a book that will prove Judas was a goy.' This is the brilliance, intelligence and bitter wit Sobran recommends to his readers.

The Nation

June 19, 1986

Marilyn and the League of Decency

When the headlines told me at the start of this week that by persuading 8,000 convenience stores to stop carrying 'adult' material Attorney General Edwin Meese and his men had scored some victories in their war on porn, I hurried along to my news agent to check whether worried smut hounds were laying in emergency supplies.

Over at Valladares, the news agent on Duval Street in Key West, Fla., people seemed calm. Make no mistake, Valladares is a serious news agent, so serious that the very first thing you see is David Stockman's book, right by the counter along with Time, Newsweek and U.S. News & World Report. Opposite are piles of The Wall Street Journal and the other daily papers. All along one wall are magazines of unimpeachable decency; great racks full of magazines catering to home furnishers, wrestling fans, electronics buffs, diet freaks, and so forth. Round the corner of the newspaper racks is a secluded section with a little signpost saying 'adult material.' Here the shelves have labels on them saying '15 minutes only' and publications with such titles as Honcho, Hot Dream, Oral Hots, Forum, Overload, Coco Cups and Iron Horse.

As I scouted along these shelves the woman at the counter called over to me that they had never had any trouble from agents of Mr. Meese's commission on pornography. A few years ago a Baptist minister from Stock Island, just north of Key West, had come by and removed, without making any payment, more than $100 worth of the adult magazines and taken them down to the police station. The court had determined that the adult material was properly secluded, that persons under 18 were denied access to it – and so the Baptist minister lost the day. About 10% of the magazine titles in the store were 'adult,' even though they count for a far more substantial portion of the revenues. No, she didn't think porn led to violence.

While we were talking. Frank Taylor entered the store. After listening for a while, Frank, who has enjoyed a distinguished publishing career in New York and two bouts of producing in Hollywood, told a story illustrative of the folly of porn commissions and the hypocrisy of bluenoses.

In 1961 he had, Mr. Taylor said, been the producer of 'The Misfits,' a film directed by John Huston, which had starred Marilyn Monroe, Clark Gable and Montgomery Clift. Gable had died 10 days after completion of the film, and United Artists was eager to release the film world-wide as rapidly as possible. But first it had to be cleared by the Legion of Decency, an avatar controlled by the Roman Catholic Church.

'I rushed the film to New York,' Mr. Taylor recalled, 'and ran it first for a rather informal group from the Legion. If there were any questions, the film was to be referred to a more august body. In this first screening they found something that bothered them. In one very beautiful scene Marilyn, in a mood of benign drunkenness set off by Gable, stumbles into the yard and embraces a tree. I was told, without explanation, by the Legion people that this scene would have to be viewed and questioned by higher authority.'

Mr. Taylor pondered his strategy. About halfway through the shooting of 'The Misfits,' Monroe had remarked that the world was waiting for one thing in this movie, which was for Gable to kiss Monroe, but that so far they had barely touched one another. Gable agreed with her analysis. With some reluctance Huston was persuaded to add the desired embrace between the two great stars. But Monroe, Taylor recalled, took things further: 'In this scene where Gable is cooking her breakfast he walks over to kiss her awake. Marilyn opened her eyes, sat up in bed and did not hold the sheet up to herself when she did this. Marilyn argued that she was with a man she loved and had just slept with, and this was the natural and normal thing to do. Well, there was great horror on the set as well as titillation. When we ran the scene it was very beautiful, but Huston insisted that we had to have a different version, and he re-shot it with Marilyn holding up the sheet to cover herself. So we had these two takes, the naked one and the discreet one.

'After my conversation with the first group of Catholics, when I knew I was in trouble, I cut in the original bare-breasted scene of Marilyn so I would have something to negotiate with, since I'd used the covered-breast version at the first screening. At the second screening there was a Catholic bigwig, maybe a monsignor, and a highly placed Catholic woman. They were both salivating somewhat, and when the tree embrace came they knew what they were looking for. They asked me to stop and when I asked why they said, "Marilyn is arousing herself against that tree, and we don't allow that in films." I said, "What do you mean? She's embracing the tree in the darkness." So they said to run it back in slow motion. The two of them were fixed on Marilyn's beautiful behind and the tree in the lovely yard. "See right there," they cried, "she's pushing her pelvis up against the tree. That means only one thing."

'"Let's put this on one side," I said, "and go forward with the film." On we went and we got to the naked-breast scene. Now no one had seen a naked breast on film since Hedy Lamarr in 'Ecstasy' and that was underwater. They were incensed and said, "If you don't cut this, we won't give you the seal and it won't be released in this country." The UA lawyers said we'd have to capitulate. But because I had used the bare-breasted version we had a negotiating posture, and after we'd bargained for two hours the church agreed that if we covered Marilyn up we could have the tree [scene]. All of which proves that pornography is entirely in the eye of the beholder.'

Frank bought his newspapers and went about his business. I continued to paw my way through the adult racks. It was all soulless, tedious stuff. But it seemed on closer inspection that Reaganite concerns have had an effect, though perhaps not quite in the way Ed Meese has in mind. One magazine offered a labored little fantasy called 'The Red Hot Woman Terrorizes The Terrorists'; another had the headline, 'Machine Gun Chic: Giving it Back to Qaddafi.' Sex is getting increasingly militarized, in accord with the ideology of the '80s.

I walked down Duval past further testimony to the darker side of fantasy: a shop full of T-shirts with 'First Strike Now!' and 'I'd Rather Be in Central America Killing Commies' written on them. I recalled the late Herbert Marcuse's remark in his 1965 essay on 'Repressive Tolerance': 'The authorities ... are vociferous against the increase in juvenile delinquency [pornography]. They are less vociferous against the proud presentation, in word and deed and pictures, of ever more powerful missiles, rockets, bombs – the mature delinquency of a whole civilized nation.'

WSJ

June 20, 1986

By the Walters of Babylon

When a deposed dictator flees into retirement, can Barbara Walters be far behind? The Duvaliers faced her halfway through June for a *20/20* interview devoted mostly to unsparing small talk about their finances:

> WALTERS: We then showed Mrs. Duvalier a check from her foundation for $60,000, made out to 'cash' and deposited in her personal account. Mrs.

Duvalier insisted that it was for her foundation work.

Madame, who is Monsieur Jean Sambour?

MRS. DUVALIER: He is the one that decorated our apartment, and a good friend of ours.

WALTERS: We have another document from the Bank of the Republic of Haiti, showing over $4 million being given to M. Jean Sambour on various government accounts.

MRS. DUVALIER: Jean Sambour is a friend of ours, and he decorated our apartment. He decorated our little villa that we had in the mountains, and he was also the one in charge of buying – because I couldn't travel myself – things for the official house, and also he's the one that decorated the airport when the Pope came.

WALTERS: And that money would also have come out of the National Defense account?

DUVALIER: It couldn't come out of my own pocket, because it wasn't for my own purpose.

WALTERS: But the National Defense account, one would think, was for defense of the country, not for decorating airports. And $4 million ... Isn't that a little high?

If Mrs. Duvalier had been on the ball at this point, she'd have said, 'Well, Barbara, you know how interior decorators are: a chair here, a chintz there – it soon adds up to real money. How much did it cost to decorate your apartment, Barbara?'

After about two minutes of this I felt a profound sympathy for the Haitian exiles, stained with larceny, cocaine and blood though they may be. As always, Walters managed to be both cringing and arrogant at the same time, an imperial plenipotentiary slapping around the help, recently retired after years of faithful service. And naturally enough, Walters played up the Dragon Lady theme, the sexist inference that misrule in Haiti and the Philippines can be traced to shoe-crazed 'strongwomen' dominating their compliant mates.

One day, after a bloodless seizure of power by the Revolutionary Committee, I hoped to see an interview conducted in the south of France with the exiled Barbara Walters and Hugh Downs.

INTERVIEWER: Mr. Downs, forgive me for the impertinence, but while apparently 'anchoring' the *20/20* program you seemed to have surrendered real power to the Dragon Ladies, Barbara Walters and executive producer Pam Hill.

DOWNS: I have no regrets. If I had to do it all over again, I would change nothing about my behavior.

INTERVIEWER: But we have here copies of checks showing that you were paid more than $750,000 a year. For what? A few banal words a week for only a part of the year.

DOWNS: I distributed much of the money privately around Christmas. And besides, the government took so much of it in taxes!

INTERVIEWER: Ms. Walters, you were paid well in excess of $1 million per year. Let me ask you, do you think you were worth it?

WALTERS: I ...

INTERVIEWER: And we have records here of your accounts with a number of fashion designers and interior decorators. Did you deduct the cost of your dresses as a professional expense, thus making the common people pay for your wardrobe?

WALTERS: I ...

INTERVIEWER: More than $1 million a year, Ms. Walters! Did you feel any pang that within two miles of your door on the Upper East Side of New York there were people surviving on pet food?

WALTERS: I ...

And so on. The U.S. – to use a phrase coined by Edward Herman and Frank Brodhead – sponsors 'demonstration elections' from time to time, as in El Salvador in 1982, which are devoid of real democratic content. In the same manner, Walters conducts 'demonstration interviews' designed to show her as probing, incisive, pitiless in her inquisitions. In practice, Walters trembles before the powerful and is impudent only to those unable to defend themselves with much conviction. 'I can't believe why they would agree to do this interview,' cried Walters to Downs. Of course the Duvaliers agreed to be interviewed by Barbara Walters. She's a star.

In the Third World, the big question is how many pairs of shoes Barbara Walters has. In the U.S., the news interview – and this is not true merely of Walters – is not designed to elicit information but to be a mime show, displaying the star-as-interviewer. To the Duvaliers, an interview with Barbara Walters was ratification that they existed, that they still meant something in the real First World of network stars and network TV.

In the same manner, towards the end, President Anwar Sadat communed with 'Ba-ba-rr-ra' in those showcase interviews about the 'peace process.' In their total seclusion from reality Sadat and Walters were probably equally surprised when the assassins struck and scarcely anyone in Egypt shed a tear. As much as anyone, Walters helped kill Sadat, and when I see her I am reminded of some words by Edward Said in *The London Review of Books* of May 8, 1986, reflecting in the wake of the U.S. raid on Libya:

'The gigantism and inflation of the current impasse is not only due to the media's gross distortions, it derives from a sort of ideological surplus, an unhealthy swelling which, on the one hand, is the effect of history avoided and transgressed and, on the other, of the failure of rational secular politics. ... We can now see the imperialist legacy in its interdependent aspects on both sides of the great cultural divide between the West and the Third World. Domination of non-whites by whites simply didn't end, and it won't go away with decolonization or independence. It persists with extraordinary tenacity, and with much generosity it animates all those institutions designed for violence and forgetfulness.'

LA Weekly

June 21, 1986

From AIDS to Old Maids

First *People*, then *Newsweek* sank its teeth into the season's best-chewed bone, 'the marriage crunch.' The crunch clamor stems from the suggestion of a couple of sociologists at Yale and an economist at Harvard that college-educated women who are still single at the age of 35 have only a 5 percent 'chance' (the idiom of the lottery is popular in these stories) of getting married. *People* put the unpublished study on its cover of March 31, with pictures of Donna Mills, Diane Sawyer, Sharon Gless and Linda Ronstadt under the title 'Are These Old Maids?' Translation: If these people aren't married, what hope have you got? *Newsweek* put the same study on its June 2 cover.

The uproar over the Yale-Harvard study is just another twist on a favored theme of the 1980s: women have liberated themselves into lonely, unfulfilled, childless lives; the modern girl can't get a man. The motifs of the *Newsweek* article were indignity and desperation, emblems of failure reminiscent of the sagas of 'bad girls' gone to ruin I used to read about in the 1950s, desperate myself to become a bad boy and hoping to meet a bad girl to accommodate me. Last year's version of the modern-girl-can't-get-a-man theme was a cloudburst of articles plus the usual supporting studies on the perils of combining work and motherhood. Work in this case was restricted to middle-class career echelons, with the usual permapress moral about the pitfalls of feminism. Next year they'll be saying that modern girls make boys gay, and follow it up with stories showing how exercise dries up your ovaries.

Contrary to the 'Marriage Is Back' stories, also a staple of the 1980s, there were fewer marriages in 1985 than in 1984, all of which is causing heartache to the marriage apparel industry and to all the other magazine advertisers who see the married state as the catalyst for the all-important circulation of commodities. In fact, census figures (quoted in a *Wall Street Journal* article for May 28, titled 'Staying Single') show that the proportion of never-married men and women in their late 20s and early 30s doubled between 1970 and 1985. There are now 4.2 million such women and 6.1 million such men. *The Journal*'s story, by Joann S. Lublin, dealt in a reasonably dispassionate way with the decline of marriage as an economic institution. It was *People* and *Newsweek* that festooned the statistics with black crepe, converting mere numbers into a sermon and fostering the notion that demography is taking a timely revenge on women's absurdly heightened hopes for life, just as other lethal cover stories on herpes and AIDS used those afflictions to take revenge on the spirit of liberation.

Turn then to the masthead of *Newsweek* to see how it reflects women's hopes heightened over the last fifteen years and find that of the top fifty-two names, eight are women and of these one is 'chairman of the board.' All twelve domestic bureaus are headed by men except for the U.N., which traditionally ranks as womanish in the executive mind, since it is concerned with peace. So much for the famous *Newsweek* sex-discrimination case of the early 1970s.

The Nation

June 21, 1986

Amnesia

The imperial imagination thrives on amnesia. On May 18 *The Washington Post* published an article on Chile by Bradley Graham, which contained the news that the Chilean Communists are now endorsing violence because of the Sandinistas' example of successful armed struggle and because 'Chilean Socialists had gone through their own soul-searching after the coup and emerged more moderate, embracing democracy and repudiating Marxism-Leninism and the violent road to power.' It will be recalled that Salvador Allende was the constitutionally elected candidate of the Socialists, whose scrupulous adherence to democratic procedures was violently terminated by Gen. Augusto Pinochet.

The Nation

July 3, 1986

After the Contra Vote

At the Nuremberg trials Robert Jackson of the U.S. Supreme Court stated, 'If certain acts and violations of treaties are crimes, they are crimes whether the U.S. does them or whether Germany does them. We are not prepared to lay down a rule of criminal conduct against others which we would not be willing to have invoked against us.'

Nine days before 'Liberty Weekend,' and one of the most conspicuous displays of bad taste in human history, the U.S. House of Representatives voted $100 million in military aid to the contras. The 221 legislators who voted for the measure should take care to study Article 6 of the Nuremberg Laws:

> a. CRIMES AGAINST PEACE: namely, planning, preparation, initiation or waging a war of aggression, or a war in violation of international treaties.
> b. WAR CRIMES: namely, violations of the laws or customs of war. Such violations shall include, but not be limited to murder [or] ill treatment ... of [a] civilian population ... [or] murder or ill treatment of prisoners of war or ... killing of hostages ...
> c. CRIMES AGAINST HUMANITY: namely, murder ... and other inhumane acts committed against any civilian population ...
> Leaders, organizers, instigators, and accomplices participating in the formulation or execution of a Common Plan or Conspiracy to commit any of the foregoing crimes are responsible for all acts performed by any persons in execution of such plan.

And having read Article 6, they should then read the Treaty of the Organization of American States and the United Nations Charter:

> No State or group of States has the right to intervene, directly or indirectly, for any reason whatever, in the internal or external affairs of any other State. The foregoing principle prohibits not only armed force but also any other form of interference or attempted threat against the personality of the State or against its political, economic and cultural elements.
> – OAS Treaty, Chapter 3, Article 15

> All Members shall settle their international disputes by peaceful means in such a manner that international peace and security, and justice, are not endangered.
> All Members shall refrain in their international relations from the threat of use of force against the territorial integrity or political independence of any state ...
> – UN Charter, Article 2, Sections 3 and 4

Ours is a lawless administration, which is now being given free rein in its barbarous policies by a Congress that has a similar disdain for law. In the deliberations before the vote there were speeches saying that the $100 million might not do the job, and that the contras were incapable of launching a real challenge to the government of Nicaragua. Scarcely a congressperson had the elementary principle to protest that what was being proposed and what has now been passed is simply illegal.

Did the newspapers and television channels offer a corrective to this blindness? Scarcely. The unanimity with which the anti-Sandinista consensus has been carried forward is truly totalitarian. Of the 85 columns and op-ed pieces discussing Nicaragua in *The Washington Post* and *The New York Times* in the first three months of this year, not one was anything but hostile to the Sandinistas. Precisely two conceded that the Sandinistas had carried out social reforms.

To be sure, the papers will carry stories of contra drug-running and there may even be hearings about it in the Senate Foreign Relations Committee. But the Rubicon has been crossed: the way is now clear to steady escalation of war in Central America, to increasing direct CIA and other U.S. military participation in organization of the contra war. The media will take an intermittent interest, but at the crucial moment they have failed in their proper role. The consequences will be with us – and with Central America – for many years to come.

LA Weekly

July 10, 1986

The Ban on Irish Divorce

ARDMORE, Ireland – Far into the night a week ago we sat up in Gallagher's Bar here and poked about amid the ashes of the Irish government's failed attempt to alter the constitutional ban on divorce.

Nuala, a young woman of progressive views, down from Dublin on holiday, attributed the defeat to priestcraft, the power of Rome. Her friend Helen said it was the turnip-snaggers, Ireland's conservative rural voters. In Dublin the voters split 50-50 on the referendum; in the rest of the country 69% to 31% against. A local Ardmore man asked the group why in heaven's name a man would vote for divorce if he could enjoy himself in Gallagher's Bar while his wife minded the home. And my friend Tony the fisherman said the effect of American television should not be discounted. 'Everyone watches "Dallas" and "Dynasty." They watched and they said, "We don't want those morals here!"'

Handing me a couple of aspirin the next morning and admiring the 10-pound salmon that had been Tony's parting gift, my mother said there was no need to talk about priestcraft or turnip-snaggers and reminded me that she had correctly predicted the result two months earlier. 'By and large, women voted against divorce for entirely logical reasons. The more they listened to what the government was saying, the more they felt that though they might be badly off now, they would be even worse off if the law got changed.'

In fact the Irish divorce referendum is an instructive parable on the stupidity of sticking derisive labels on people for adopting a supposedly 'reactionary' position on a social issue. Americans looking across the Atlantic should feel no special glow of superiority at their more advanced legal state. And in their present debates on the future course of the feminist movement, American women should study the Irish divorce campaign and ponder anew the ways in which it is possible to be liberated into slavery as well as out of it.

The bid to end the constitutional ban on divorce was very much a personal commitment of Garret FitzGerald, leader of the Fine Gael Party and prime minister in the coalition government. Aside from Malta and Andorra the Irish Republic is the last national entity in Europe to forbid divorce. If the Protestants in Northern Ireland were ever to support any form of federal association with the republic, then they must be satisfied that there would be legal sanctuary in the united 32 countries for a religious or social minority. Besides, argued Mr. FitzGerald and his associates, there are an estimated 70,000 people in the republic now trapped in broken marriages. Should not the state exhibit compassion toward them?

So a change in the constitution was duly drafted. It proposed that the courts could dissolve a marriage, provided that the partners had been separated for five years, that there was no hope of reconciliation, and that adequate provision was made for the dependants. Battle was joined. The Roman Catholic Church was obviously opposed to it. Charles Haughey, leader of the Fianna Fail Party, declared that for his party's members (which polls now show likely to prevail in the next election) the vote would be a matter of individual conscience.

Irish women began to ask about the fine print. In the main, they saw themselves left rather than leaving. They raised some very pertinent questions about succession rights, about property. And about maintenance. Who would stay on the family farm? Who would run the farm? Which widow would inherit a pension? Since, under Irish law, no heir can be disinherited, would not this mean that the farm would have to be sold off to satisfy the claims of two sets of claimants? Besides, said a substantial proportion of the women of Ireland, no man can support two families, so where does the maintenance come from?

Here was the government's decisive failure. It mumbled about 'provision being made' by grace of 'suitable arrangements.' From these noises many voters construed that the provisions would be worthless, the arrangements would fail, and the taxpayers would end up footing the bill. Thus, the day before the referendum on June 26, polls showed that opinion had shifted sharply against the proposed change. The polls were right. And if, of the 63.5% who voted No, many opposed divorce on principle, there were many more who felt quite simply that under the terms of the government's proposals the first family, stranded by divorce, would get the dirty end of the stick.

It's not as though the Irish Republic is immune to the notions of the heart or to the moral climate of the late 20th century. For those who can afford it, state-sanctioned divorce can be acquired by establishing a two-year foreign domicile, getting divorced and remarried abroad, and then moving back to Ireland. The chuch can and does accord annulments, which many erroneously construe as being annulments under law and therefore sanction for what are in practice bigamous second marriages. Others, aware of the legal block, enjoy a second church marriage following annulment, but don't sign the register and change their names by deed poll. The state also provides annulments, though in the wake of the referendum the Irish Times cautioned editorially that this cannot, without fostering cynical disrespect for law, be expanded into an alternative to constitutional sanction of divorce.

As an informed look round the village of Ardmore attests, some of those to whom love beckons, but who haven't the money or the time for the expedients outlined above, simply move in together and have done so without scarlet letters being painted on the walls of their bungalows. As in other villages and towns there are girls with illegitimate babies living happily with their families, for whom the $75 per week single-parent allowance is a welcome addition to the family income. The government is trying to abolish the status of illegitimacy as far as inheritance is concerned, provided the presumptive heir can prove the paternal connection. Such a prospect terrifies many a farmer who fears the by-blows of a misspent youth will come charging down from Dublin to claim a slice of the family farm.

In other words, it is certainly foolish to underestimate the power of the Catholic Church in Ireland, but there's no reason either to detect nothing but the fingerprints of its hierarchy on the ballot boxes of late June. And this is the reason why Americans should not adopt a patronizing posture. Granted that people should have a right to divorce, such freedom should be rooted in reality. There are millions of American women bringing up children alone, for whom legal provision has been made but who are not getting a penny in child support. Many of them, particularly feminists, should listen with sympathetic understanding to their Irish sisters who might say that marriage can indeed be a contract of injustice, with their unpaid labor and sexual services exchanged for economic security, while at the same time adding that 'freedom' could, under the terms of the constitutional change offered by the Irish government, mean fresh injustice, shambling forward in the trappings of modernity.

WSJ

July 25, 1986

Remembrance of Cocked Snooks Past

There seem to have been remarkably few signs of disrespect evinced by the British people toward the costly nuptials. It was not thus in the old days. My father Claud used to describe in triumph his successful intervention in the hugely pompous Silver Jubilee of George V's uninspiring reign. He and a fellow conspirator studied the intended route of the procession of carriages traveling through central London. Then, attired as workmen employed by the city of London, they entered a newspaper office on Fleet Street – which was on the route – carrying a banner they announced had to be strung across the street in company with the profuse bunting already deployed. The newspaper's staff gazed with satisfaction upon the banner's patriotic message, 'Long Live Our King', and watched with pleasure as my father and his friend managed to get it hoisted over the road.

On the day of the procession the crowds in Fleet Street were vast, and it was only with difficulty that the two were able to reach the string running down from the banner and round a corner into an alley. Choosing their moment by the enthusiastic bellowing of the throng, they pulled the string. After a slight pause there was a rolling howl of outrage, and they took to their heels. The banner had opened in timely fashion right in front of the royal coach, to reveal the words '25 years of Hunger, Misery and War.' The movie news cameras traveling right behind the coach caught the moment satisfactorily, and it is thus preserved on film.

George V did have a humane side. Aides once came upon him peering gloomily at a report indicating that a senior police officer of whom the King was fond had been discovered in St. James Park in compromising circumstances with another man. 'He had it in his hand,' the King sighed regretfully. 'That looks bad; that looks bad.'

LA Weekly

August 15, 1986

Mailbag

J.W. writes from Livingstone, Montana, 'You seem to use the word "liberal" as a term of abuse, loaded with negative overtones. But surely liberals are more on our side than theirs. (I am an anarchist myself.) Please explain.'

Dear J.W.: It is true that there are many decent liberals in the world with whom we should be glad to make cause against the common foe. But very often the 'liberal' is nothing much more than an ideological policeman working on behalf of the right. His or her crucial function is to mark off the acceptable limits of political discourse and pronounce anathema on all those who transgress them. Thus the liberal is the right's watchdog, alert for signs of lefty infiltration. Consider this very fine example of liberal-think, culled from the *Fence-Straddlers' Gazette.* Noted syndicated columnist Anthony Lewis, doyen of the liberal pundits, is discussing Ronald Reagan's disgusting recent speech on South Africa, in which the President denounced the African National Congress for its communist ties: 'There are communists on the ANC executive,' Lewis writes. 'Anyone who cares for South Africa must be aware of the fact and concerned with it. But the question is how to deal with it.'

Note the classic contours of liberal think here. No matter that South African communists have been part of the backbone of the ANC for decades, heroically and in conditions of great peril, advocating a multiracial strategy for political change. Lewis chooses to make common cause with Reagan against South African communists, differing only on the means whereby their influence can be annulled. The net effect is therefore to endorse the president's position on the ANC.

The same sort of liberal, dismayed by Sandinista curtailment of civil liberties, concerned by Nicaragua's growing reliance on the Soviet Union, disturbed by tales of religious persecution, and scared shitless at the prospect of being caught out on a limb, sees *some* merit in maintaining *some* carefully monitored aid for the contras, if only to place pressure on the Sandinistas to bring them into a peaceful, negotiated solution.

LA Weekly

August 16, 1986

Sods on the Road

I am in receipt of mail from intending vacationers, perturbed by the Supreme Court decision upholding the Georgia sodomy laws and anxious about their travel plans. For many of them the question comes down to this: Can you drive coast to coast across the United States without entering states that have legal sanctions against the practicing sodomite, remembering that the Georgia law defines sodomy as 'any sex act involving the sex organs of one person and the mouth or anus of another'?

The news is bad. Assuming you are traveling west to east, the problem comes with an impenetrable moral barrier: the tier of states stretching from Arizona, up through Utah, to Idaho. All of these have laws against both heterosexual and homosexual sodomy. You can either bypass via Canada or Mexico – both of whose laws in this instance are unknown to me, so best consult your travel agent – or abstain for this portion of your trip. In the event that lust is virtually ungovernable, heterosexual sodomites can take Highway 2 through northern Idaho, a matter of some fifty chaste miles, before arriving in the comparative safety of Montana.

Homosexual sodomites will have to be more prudent if they do not wish to fall foul of Montana law. Hold off till you get to Wyoming, which, like the states to its immediate south and east, smiles upon the polymorphous and the perverse. The sods' gateway to the east is Iowa, which is as liberal as Wyoming; from there it's a clear run through Illinois, Indiana, Ohio, Pennsylvania and into the Big Apple. Stay out of Michigan, Minnesota and, of course, the South. Heterosexual sods can freely frolic in Arkansas and Texas.

In sum, law-abiding heteros and homos intending sodomy should watch it in Ida, Ut, Ariz, Mo, Okla, La, Miss, Tenn, Ky, Ala, Ga, Fla, S.C., N.C., Va, D.C., Md, R.I., Minn and Mich. Heterosexual sodomy is O.K. in Nev, Mont, Kans, Tex and Ark. Happy holidays, and thanks to *Workers Vanguard,* 'Marxist working-class biweekly of the Spartacist League of the US,' which published a useful map. I didn't know the Sparts were into that kind of thing.

The Nation

September 11, 1986

Fighting Drugs

Crack is in every headline; it's hard to say why. Perhaps it is because the cocaine that many journalists, politicians and businessmen shove up their noses sells at around $100 a gram and therefore can be regarded as an upscale commodity of privilege, less vulgar than crack, which is a people's drug retailing for as little as $5, thus offering a lift for the price of a six-pack of beer.

These have been years when Americans have rushed from one symbol to another of 'malaise,' to use the word that got President Carter into such trouble in the late '70s. A paroxysm of concern for teen-agers and alcohol stiffened the drinking laws, and stimulated a boom in fake IDs. Alongside of this came the sudden discovery of child abuse, which sometimes produced persecution similar to that of the witch trials, as children were compelled to denounce entirely innocent schoolteachers or people in day-care centers, whose lives were ruined as a result.

The same sort of hysteria is now mounting over drugs. People are being thrown into jail for life for offenses that, a year ago, would have earned them probation. This is part of what Mrs. Reagan has urged as 'a climate of intolerance' for drug abuse. Drug testing is advancing steadily through offices and plants; the computer checkup, the lie detector and the urine sample are fast becoming the sine qua non of gainful employment.

Suddenly drugs have become the objective correlative of everything that is wrong with society. Benjamin Ward, the New York City police commissioner, says in all seriousness, 'I believe the crime problem in America today is the drug problem,' thus proposing the absurd thesis that if there were no drugs there would be no crimes.

Do illegal drugs have any social utility? At one level I suppose one could argue that the wholesaling and retailing of these drugs have had a beneficial countercyclical economic effect. Many a depressed main street in America today can boast stores and restaurants set up to wash drug money or to shelter it.

At a deeper level, drugs are useful in the subjugation and atomization of the dangerous classes, meaning the potentially disruptive poor. A narcotized underclass can be comfortingly defined solely in terms of its addictions. The current Time magazine, in its cover story on drugs, features a large photograph of a black youth spray painting an 'X' on the door of an abandoned building used as a crack house in Harlem. There's another picture of an abandoned house two pages later. The social problem, as perceived by Time and almost everyone else, is the drug rather than the building, the symptom rather than the cause, for these abandoned houses are testament to the political and economic injustice of which the ghetto drug culture is a consequence.

The government and corporations don't have the moral authority to wage a righteous war against drugs because they promote a culture in which many addictive, harmful substances are perfectly legal. The medical establishment is badly compromised in this regard. Many addictions can be considered what San Francisco journalist Fred Gardner calls 'medically or governmentally induced.' Former Los Angeles Dodger pitcher Steve Howe told Mr. Gardner he was put on the drug Ritalin as a hyperactive schoolchild in Michigan and was later drawn to cocaine because it seemed to have the same pseudo-calming effect.

The American people are not going to make a revolution or effect significant change in the status quo while stoned and half-lobotomized by drugs and alcohol. The bottom line is that the notion of a drug-free society is a subversive idea. Right now we face an option: a punitive policy of social regimentation on the one hand and on the other a fully cooperative, socially transforming approach that could pose a more radical challenge to the evils of modern industrial society.

WSJ

September 26, 1986

The Unutterable Swine

'Mr. Ortega spoke faster and his eyes narrowed. He moved forward in the rocking chair, and the Marxist zeal that in 1960 he first put at the service of the Sandinistas formed on his face.' Thus did Bruce Olson of UPI describe Ortega as he spoke at a gathering in Manhattan in late July. Bad guys' eyes always narrow, and they usually speak rapidly. The other thing they do is stab the air with an urgent/angry finger, and I was glad to see Olson didn't miss out on this: 'We cannot have chaos in our country when we are at war with the aggression of the United States,' he said, his finger stabbing the air.' Those Sandinistas will stop at nothing.

LA Weekly

September 27, 1986

Upholding the Shutdowns

On August 12 the Israeli Interior Ministry closed *al-Mithaq*, a Palestinian Arabic-language daily published in Jerusalem, on the ground that it was financed by the Popular Front for the Liberation of Palestine. The Israelis shut down the weekly *al-Ahd* for the same reason. *Al-Mithaq* is the first Palestinian daily to have lost its license to publish on a permanent basis. At one point in the course of this episode the Israeli authorities said, 'Although we offer them freedom of expression ... it is forbidden to permit them to exploit this freedom in order to harm the state of Israel.' After a hastily concluded legal battle the Israeli Supreme Court upheld the shutdowns. Evidence allegedly linking the two papers to the P.F.L.P. had been presented to the court in a closed session, from which lawyers for the papers had been barred. According to *al-Mithaq*'s editor and publisher, Mahmoud al-Khatib, the two publications are financially independent and have no connection with any Palestinian organization, although they do tend to reflect the views of opposition circles within the P.L.O. There has been no stir in the U.S. press over the suppression of the right to publish in this case.

The Nation

November 11, 1986

Pull the Plug

About twice a month someone asks me what sort of word processor, and even what sort of program, I use, and I answer that I don't have a word processor or a program and I rely on a variety of typewriters, both manual and electric. When I tell my fellow writers or editors with whom I do business that I don't have a word processor, they wag their heads and register the surprise appropriate to an admission that I prefer to go about town with no trousers on. They become earnest and advise me on the sort of machine I should buy. They have the zeal of evangelizing Christians, and only when I start seriously to explain my reservations about the role of word processors and video display terminals in intellectual production do they turn to outright ridicule. They stare at me with the severity of a 19th-century English judge transporting Luddites to Botany Bay and say heavily – this is always their final shot – 'Once you try it, you'll never want to use anything else.'

I've put up with this for about six years now, almost always – particularly in the early days – slightly on the defensive. The Left has always been in something of a quandary about technology: thumbs up to the machines that relieve us of drudgery, increase productivity, and release mankind into cultivated enjoyment of the social surplus; thumbs down to machines that degrade quality, deny – without appropriate compensation – employment, attenuate experience. On the one hand, the pastoral gentility of the mixing bowl and the wooden spoon, on the other, the time-shrinking whir of the Cuisinart; here the robot, there the unemployment line.

The trouble is that the Left, or what I might call 'our crowd,' usually doesn't know very much about technology and therefore manages either to overestimate or underestimate the quality of its specific applications. When it comes to military affairs, our crowd has a touching faith in the precision and reliability of the electronic gadgetry developed by the arms companies, solemnly parroting their salespeople's preposterous claims (such as that a submarine-launched ballistic missile can hit a Russian silo at a range of

5,000 miles). And on the other side of the ledger, our crowd is often oblivious to the more subtle threats technology poses. No one wants to look as though he or she is opposed to progress. When Alf Landon ran against FDR in 1936, Landon and his supporters hotly denounced Social Security. 'Those numbers,' they said, 'are the numbers of the modern police state. They will follow you from cradle to grave. They are the emblems of totalitarianism.' How our crowd laughed!

And just as our crowd welcomed transistorized amplifiers, which produce worse sound than the old tubes, and now hurry to buy compact discs, which produce worse sound than the old records, so too have they – or those with the remotest occasion to use them – welcomed the word processor and the computerized office almost without reservation.

I suppose I should add for the record that I am not against *any* use of computers; nor am I hostile to some time-saving, knowledge-expanding data bases. I am not an enemy of the 20th century, but we have to retain the necessary discrimination. It goes without saying that there has always been a strong element of cargo cult among devotees of the word processor. Poorer by some $2,000 or $3,000, writers crouch reverently before their new deployment of screen, computer, and printer as though the mere arrival of this equipment, massive and unsightly on the desk, will prompt an effortless flow of literary production. By way of justification, they then launch into the familiar patter. I heard it just the other day from my friends Ellen Ray and Bill Schaap, publishers of *Covert Action Information Bulletin*, and mustard-keen on their word processors. With pity, Bill eyed the five typewritten pages of a column I happened to have with me. 'With a word processor,' he cried, 'you could *move paragraphs around.*'

They always say this. To which the answer is twofold. With scissors and Scotch tape, the same miracles of paragraph transfer can be achieved, and indeed achieved far more easily. Suppose I am reading over a draft of a 15-page typewritten article. I can glance rapidly from page to page, from beginning to end and back. The word processor doggedly 'scrolls' his or her article on the VDT screen in a process that is far more cumbersome and time-consuming, and if he or she wants to get an overview of the article, it has to be printed out, thus turning it back into a despised typewritten product. So then the writer makes marks on the printout, enters these corrections into the word processor, prints the article out again, thus deriving the dubious gratification of being able to furnish his or her editor with *an entirely clean manuscript*, which this editor has now been conditioned to expect as his or her due.

All the while our word processee is writing worse than he or she did before. Computers degrade the prose style of those who use them. The syntax takes on a listless quality and, as they do in extemporaneous human speech, the rhythms become nerveless. The reason is surely that what is produced is not script but transcript, the self-indulgent flow of someone assured that the cursor, bustling about the screen, emending, transposing, obliterating, is emulating the justice and finality of properly accomplished prose. But the emulation is spurious. There is never finality in the display terminal's screen, but an irresponsible whimsicality, as words, sentences, and paragraphs are negated at the touch of a key. The significance of the past, as expressed in the manuscript by a deleted word or an inserted correction, is annulled in idle gusts of electronic massacre.

Thus far we have been talking of the writer, now immobilized in the garret by this supposedly time-saving machinery. But the essential function of the computer is revealed in group production, as on a newspaper or magazine. Over the past few months I've been observing all the usual depressing signs of conversion to electronic procedures at *The Nation.* The villain of the party here is, as always, the publisher or office manager who has nothing better to do with his time than attend computer courses and spend long days in confabulation with salespeople and advisors from the industry. It is he who speaks of the 'inevitability' of conversion and who wags his head comically at anyone saying everything seemed to be working OK in the first place. So at *The Nation,* first the accounting was computerized, with the result that it took longer to get paid.

The aim in view is of course productivity, in whose cause are recruited the procedures of de-skilling typical of the development of mass production in the early 20th century. At the moment I, a *Nation* writer, furnish my copy to an editor, who gives it scrutiny, comments on external and internal contradictions, logical fallacies, libels on the Catholic church, and processes it on to the typesetter, who punches it in on his or her Computron. The galley proof is then perused by intern-researchers, by the copy department, by me, and finally by the editor, who assembles all the corrections and returns the proof to the typesetter, who inserts the corrections and produces a fresh text that is pasted up on the sheets awaiting the photographer and ultimately the printer.

The dream of the publisher is naturally to abolish these varying and important functions unpleasantly reminiscent of a medieval guild by having the article punched once, preferably by the originating writer, after which point all changes are made on the screen in a series of electronic interpolations. To the dismay of union representatives and the joy of management, role and function become blurred as the galley ceases to have a history, revealed in the discrete markings of the various parties. Instead the galley becomes a notation of an electronic collective, which views the article as a series of VDT screen bytes, thus perceiving it in a manner entirely different from either that of the writer (until he or she becomes a puncher) or the reader (until he or she in the end becomes part of the electronic collective by reading the article on a television screen).

Thus is the mind industrialized. The form of the article is emended by the dictates and limitations of the tiny viewing screen. Its syntax and spelling are supervised by the appropriate program. The producers are chained to terminals that are physically dangerous, and indeed susceptible of being monitored by supervisors for evidence of productivity, worker enthusiasm, and so forth. On an amplified scale we have here the mode of production of a modern newspaper, whose reporters in the field carry smaller terminals with tiny display screens, through which they communicate to headquarters. Under such conditions they cease to be writers in any traditional sense of the word and become information inputters, in a properly industrialized fashion. Extended syntax and narrative structure become a thing of the past and with them disappears the possibility of any ample individual vision. The editor's authority is vastly increased. The collective – with obscured lines of individual responsibility – gains power at the expense of the individual writer. As Hans Magnus Enzensberger remarks in *The Industrialization of the Mind*: 'The mind industry's main business and concern is not to sell its product; it is to "sell" the existing order, to perpetuate the prevailing pattern of man's domination by man, no matter who runs the society and no matter by what means. Its main task is to expand and train our consciousness – in order to exploit it.'

The day I bought my sixth typewriter, my daughter and I visited the Huntington Library near Pasadena, California. Halfway down the spacious public gallery, replete with its Gutenberg Bible, Shakespeare folios, early maps, and other testaments to the rise of capitalism, there is a case containing a scrap of paper on which is a letter written by Andrew Jackson. Dated November 2, 1813, Major General Jackson's note is an injunction to massacre. He commands General John Coffee to destroy the Creek Indians in Tallahatchie, in the Mississippi Territory, and 'under a discreet officer ... to envelop any Indians that may be spying on the south east bank ... you will in performing this service keep the greatest order and observe the greatest circumspection.' Coffee descended upon the Creek Indians, murdered the braves, 186 in all, and captured 84 women and children. President Jackson adopted one of the orphans. There, in the case in the Huntington Library, is the order, with deletions and rephrasings scored on it by Jackson. Down the years it has carried the testament of individual responsibility and, though the author did not see it that way, individual guilt. It is not a record that, in the age of electronic, industrialized consciousness, would have ever survived.

Mother Jones

November 8, 1986

After the Press Bus Left

Back in May of this year, nine months into the strike of Local P-9 of the United Food and Commercial Workers against Hormel, some workers and artists dedicated a magnificent mural. Measuring eighty by sixteen feet on an outdoor wall of the Labor Center in Austin, Minnesota, it depicted the enduring struggle of workers. It showed a woman swinging with a cleaver at the serpent of exploitation wrapped around the smokestacks of a factory. It showed faceless workers going in one end of the factory and coming out with their features delineated and their fists raised. It showed scenes from the 1933 Austin meatpackers' strike and from farm protest movements. A banner with a verse from a turn-of-the-century poem read, 'If blood be the price of your cursed wealth, good God we have paid in full.'

The mural was conceived by Denny Mealy, a P-9 member and self-taught artist, and Mike Alewitz, a professional muralist from Virginia who went to P-9's national solidarity rallies in April and stayed to work on the painting without pay. You can see one of Alewitz's political murals in León, Nicaragua. Mealy lined up support from other unions at the Labor Center and from the Twin Cities; they donated time and – from the St. Paul's Sign and Display Local 880 – forty gallons of paint. More than one hundred P-9 members were involved in the project. The final product was dedicated to Nelson Mandela.

As many in this sad world know, P-9 found an enemy as remorseless as Hormel in the form of its own international union, the U.F.C.W., which finally forced the local into trusteeship, signed a contract with the company, and then began a purge of the strike movement. Determined to extirpate the memory and culture of P-9's struggle, the U.F.C.W. ordered sandblasting of the mural. No union shop would do the job, so the U.F.C.W. had to use its own organizers for the dirty work. A court order has temporarily halted the destruction of the mural, but too late to save the first targets of the sandblasters' attack: the word 'Solidarity' and the faces of the hitherto faceless workers.

The Nation

November 13, 1986

Is Press Awakening to Reagan's Deceptions?

President Reagan and his news handlers must be wondering what hit them. After nearly six years of brilliant success in making, shaping and faking the news to suit their interests, a string of misfortunes has put them on the defensive. On Oct. 2, disclosure of the White House disinformation campaign concerning Libya. On Oct. 5, the crash in Nicaragua of the C-123 cargo plane containing the voluble Eugene Hasenfus and documents linking officials including Vice President Bush to an illegal arms-smuggling operation. In the weeks that followed, the confusions at Reykjavik and, most recently, Robert McFarlane's 'guns for terrorists' mission to Iran.

The press, emboldened by this sequence of mishaps and also by Republican reverses in the midterm elections, is now showing some signs of coming to life. Is it conceivable that the charmed existence – so far as critical coverage is concerned – enjoyed by this president is coming to an end, that the lap dogs will at last become watchdogs? It is not as though the press has been uniformly and utterly bad. There's usually someone, somewhere trying to tear the lid off the bad news and expose the evil men. But what's one watchdog on the edge of town? It's the steady canine chorus that restrains government and serves the public weal. What we need now is a bit of pack journalism, baying along the fragrant spoor, but judging by present form we have a while to wait.

Disinformation: When Bob Woodward of the Washington Post disclosed the program developed in August under the supervision of Adm. John Poindexter of the National Security Council and designed to bamboozle U.S. journalists and Muammar el-Qaddafi in equal measure, there were bellows of outrage in the press, and State Department spokesman Bernard Kalb rushed for the gangplank holding his nose. From most of the coverage you would have thought that disinformation from the Reagan team began and ended in late 1986. But it would have required no more investigative zeal than a trip to the clip files to see that this administration has been practicing disinformation a lot longer than that.

Back on Aug. 3, 1981, Newsweek reported that CIA director William Casey had approved 'a large scale, multiphase and costly scheme to overthrow Kaddafi and his government' by means including a 'disinformation program designed to embarrass Kaddafi and his government.' At whom was the disinformation program to be aimed? Col. Qaddafi, certainly, but also at the U.S. press. In December 1981 headlines trumpeted out the news, leaked by the administration, that Col. Qaddafi had sent a hit team to assassinate President Reagan. By the end of the year, after a spate of Demon Libya stories, the hit-team scare disappeared as suddenly as it came.

(Even if the watchdogs could be pardoned for ignoring the ancient history of 1981, one might reasonably have expected them, pondering Mr. Woodward's story, to scrutinize once more the rationale for the bombing raids on Tripoli and Benghazi. Did those famous intercepts really show that Libya had ordered the bombing of the West Berlin discotheque? Maybe not, and indeed on Oct. 29 John Lawrence of ABC News reported that top West German officials were now blaming the outrage on Syria. So much for the irrefutable evidence cited in April.)

An administration prepared to lie to the press about Libya would surely have no compunction in adopting the same tack about Nicaragua. But when Alfonso Chardy of the Miami Herald carefully documented just such a disinformation campaign, the pack was silent.

Mr. Chardy reported on Oct. 13 that the president had authorized this campaign at the start of 1983, calling for a 'public diplomacy' (i.e., disinformation) program superintended by the National Security Council and 'designed to generate support for our national security objectives.' He ordered it to be merged with an incipient effort then called Project Truth. The public diplomacy program seems to have consisted mostly of leaking anti-Nicaraguan material to journalists who faithfully relayed it to their readers without saying where it came from. The usefulness of this operation, subsequently transferred to the State Department, was best demonstrated by the great disinformation coup of election night 1984, when television reporters – Bernard Kalb's brother Marvin among those in the lead – breathlessly cited White House tips about a shipload of Soviet MIG fighters nearing Nicaragua. With tremendous Reaganite bluster about worrisome escalation filling the airwaves, any remote possibility of benign coverage of Nicaragua's first elections in history two days earlier was successfully averted.

Hasenfus: There's been some bracing journalism about the mechanics of how the Reagan administration, under the supervision of Vice President Bush and Lt. Col. Oliver North, has been funneling arms to the contras. But the pussyfooting has reached comical extremes. The trail of evidence linking the contras and their White House suppliers is as broad as in interstate highway. The breaches of the Boland Amendment, the Neutrality Act and the Arms Export Control Act are plain for all to see. Congress banned arms to the contras in 1984, and the White House promptly went into the gun-running business. But yet the press talks about the 'perception' that the administration 'may have broken the law.' Short of a signed confession from Mr. Bush, what does it take to call a spade a spade, or a broken law a crime?

Reykjavik: The press found itself in the painful position, a few days after the summit, of having to turn to the Russians for an acceptable, non-disinformational account of the proceedings. Might this not prompt the watchdogs to ask themselves about misrepresentations of Soviet proposals in the past, including the disinformation campaign mounted by the White House in late July 1985 to counteract the effect of the unilateral Soviet test ban?

The McFarlane mission: The press is hot on the trail of this one, but it's hard to understand the surprise being voiced at the administration's arms supplies to Terror Central in Iran. The story has been around for a while. In October 1982, Moshe Arens, then Israeli ambassador to the U.S., told the Boston Globe that Israel had been supplying arms to the Khomeini regime 'in coordination with the U.S. government ... at almost the highest levels.' The next day he informed the Globe that he'd 'caught a little flak from the State Department' for his indiscretion and then confided that 'the purpose was to make contact with some military officers who might one day be in a position of power in Iran.' The administration may have been trying to buy back a hostage. It has certainly, in partnership with Israel, been trying to buy into a future Iranian government down the post-Khomeini road.

This is an administration that has thought as much about news management, and practiced as much disinformation, as any in peacetime history. The milestones of its progress – yellow rain, the El Salvador White Paper of 1981, the 'Pope plot,' KAL 007, Sandinista drug-running – stretch back through the years. The pack slumbered and only a few watchdogs rattled their chains. Now perhaps amid the brave cries of 'lame duck' we can expect the pack to start doing its job.

WSJ

November 22, 1986

'Whose Deficit Is It Anyway?

The great Reaganite trap, all baited and set for the years 1986 through 1992, is to have the Democrats supervise fiscal and budgetary shrinkage following Reagan's deficits incurred in the service of the military and the rich. The populist counterattack is to ask, Whose deficit is it anyway? Interest on the debt, which is a swelling portion of the budget, is raised by taxes on the many and repaid to the few. It's a form of transfer payment to the rich. So the answer is not to take the Mondale route of 1984, signposted toward raising taxes and slashing deficits (the Reagan trap mentioned above), since cutting the deficit will bash the economy into even worse shape than much of it is already. The populist way out is to urge socialization of the debt, deficit spending for the common good through public housing and the like. The corollary, redistribution of wealth through progressive taxation, is, thanks to Bill Bradley et al.'s pre-emption of true tax reform, off the agenda.

The Nation

December 6, 1986

The Shit Hits the Fan

Critical mass in a scandal is achieved when half of the wild rumors turn out to be true, and people start giving the other half their undivided attention. This is when official denials have the same effect as matches on gasoline.

Up to the amazing Reagan/Meese press conference of November 25, the turmoil over the Administration's dealings with Iran had not yet spilled over to its Central American operations. In all the uproar over McFarlane's mission, scarcely one of the clamant pundits and politicos bothered to point out that when it came to disdain for U.S. law, the record of Vice President Bush, Director of Central Intelligence Casey, Secretary of State Shultz and his equerry Elliott Abrams was already a matter of public knowledge, as were many of Lieut. Col. Oliver North's dealings with the *contras.* All of them have been deeply involved in the illegal supply of money and arms to the *contras,* despite a Congressional ban in the form of the Boland Amendment, not to mention the Neutrality Act and the Arms Export Control Act.

The mathematics of the illegalities have never been complicated. Military funding of the *contras* was illegal between November 1984 and April 1986, but the *contras* continued to operate militarily, and clearly had the money to do so. For two years the press mostly solved this equation by speaking of 'private' funding or of aid from other countries (generally unnamed but in fact Saudi Arabia and Israel). In short, the lawless behavior of the Administration – not just Poindexter, North and the so-called cowboys in the N.S.C. – has been evident for months.

Another indication of critical mass is that the press stops ignoring the obvious. This is why the present scandal has swollen so rapidly. The press had a lot of the obvious to catch up on.

Today it's the shady career of Oliver North that holds the attention of the press. But what of tomorrow? How about a detailed account of the dealings and influence of the Pentagon's Richard Perle and such associates as Stephen Bryen? When it comes to sagas of arms and technology transfers, there are years left in the story.

The Nation

More Shit, More Fans

I consider the fall of Ivan Boesky to be a benchmark signaling the demise of the Roaring Eighties and the vindication of the notions of Uncle Whiskers, *a.k.a.* Karl Marx. Boesky, Goldsmith, Pickens, Icahn and others have flourished by takeover, greenmail, junk bonds, leveraged buyouts and the rest because their corporate targets have often had a stock price below the value of their fixed assets. Why has this been so? The stock prices have reflected the poor performance of these companies, consequent upon the falling rate of profit, which Uncle Whiskers reckoned to be prominent among the symptoms of capitalism's final slide toward the dustbin of h.

Contemplating Boesky, those with a mind for historical parallel may recall the fall of Clarence Hatry. Hatry was a British entrepreneur of the late 1920s, highly esteemed for his financial acumen. They said the same sorts of things about him that they later said about Boesky. He soared higher and higher. Then he tried to buy United Steel for £8 million sterling. His collateral turned out to be fraudulent. His fall, in September of 1929, led to the tightening of the British money market, the withdrawal of call loans from the New York market and, as an assisting fact, the topping out of the stock market and, in October 1929, the crash.

The Nation

January 24, 1987

Dolan and AIDS

The right, never famed for its protective zeal in this regard, has developed a veneration for privacy where conservative AIDS victims are concerned. When Roy Cohn, a lifelong gay-basher, died of AIDS, there was much murmuring in conservative circles about the indecency of reporting what the man had died of. It's been the same with Terry Dolan, the right-wing organizer who died at the age of 36 of congestive heart failure after a long illness. *The Washington Post* said it was AIDS. *The New York Times* merely quoted Dolan's doctors as saying the heart failure could be attributed to diabetes and pernicious anemia. Conservatives rushed in, shouting *The Post* had no right to print unfounded rumor. The paper is sticking by its story.

It certainly seems relevant to say how Dolan met his end. For one thing, it cannot be conducive to proper public sensitivity to the AIDS crisis if the disease seems – at least in the news headlines – to strike down only the poor and obscure, Rock Hudson notwithstanding. And for another, Dolan spent his active political life promoting vicious conservatives of the New Right, whose favorite pursuit is to bait gays and whose dearest ambition is to throw homosexuals in jail and otherwise persecute them. During his life-time, so far as I know, no journalist challenged Dolan seriously on the hypocrisies intrinsic to a life in which he seems to have made no particular secret of his preferences.

The Nation

February 5, 1987

The Real Soviet Challenge

Back in 1948 some imaginative fellows scripted a miniseries about invasion and gave it the catchy title 'Operation Bushwacker'. The notion was simple enough: How could the U.S. take over the Soviet Union? The answer given in the treatment was excitingly bloodthirsty, full of tough-minded talk about smashing the Soviet state: 'The destruction of ... governmental and control facilities would be given high priority ... [and] would be accom-plished along with the destruction of the industrial urban areas.'

'Operation Bushwacker' never got made into a movie. Its authors never intended it should. They were working for the Pentagon and charged with preparation of a whole series of true-life invasion scenarios, requested by President Harry Truman and his Secretary of Defense, James Forrestal.

That same year, over at the National Security Council other scriptwriters were hard at work on NSC Document 20/1, which addressed the question of political control of the Soviet Union subsequent to a U.S. invasion. This script had a similarly tough-minded lilt to it, talking about 'decommuni-zation' and proposing that 'one of our major war aims would be to destroy thoroughly the structure of relationships by which the leaders of the All-Union Communist Party have been able to exert moral and disciplinary authority over individual citizens or groups of citizens.'

One worry of the drafters of NSC 20/1 was the emergence, subsequent to invasion, of communist partisans and guerrilla bands. To deal with this they proposed a quisling government, under the control of the Allies and consisting of exiled White Russians and members of the czarist aristocracy.

These scenarios have been unearthed recently by Michio Kaku and Daniel Axelrod, who have made thorough use of the Freedom of Infor-mation Act to compile their excellent new book, 'To Win A Nuclear War: The Pentagon's Secret.' They make interesting reading in light of the current commotion over the ABC miniseries 'Amerika,' which is due to start Feb. 15. Hollywood writes treatments of what They would like to do to Us: Ivan on Main Street; thus inverting the fantasies of the U.S. government, which invariably concern what We would like to do to Them: GI Joe on Nevsky Prospekt. (After all, the U.S. did once invade the Soviet Union, and the Soviets are now planning a miniseries about it.)

During the Korean War there was the same inversion. Armed Forces Radio Service ran a series of half-hour shows titled 'Springfield, U.S.A.', supposedly set in the future – 1960. The Russians had taken over, and each episode dealt with the forced communization of defenseless America and the torture and killing of courageous but outgunned Americans. While the AFRS scriptwriters were hard at work on this series, the Pentagon was outlining its own plans, as expressed by Gen. Curtis LeMay's briefing officer in 1954, when he told a group of visiting Navy officers that the war plan of the U.S. (i.e. LeMay's Strategic Air Command) was to reduce the Soviet Union to a 'smoking, radiating ruin in two hours.'

The public-relations aspect of this scenario had already been contemplated by President Dwight Eisenhower and Secretary of State John Foster Dulles a year earlier when, according to minutes of an NSC meeting, quoted by Messrs. Kaku and Axelrod, they 'were in complete agreement that somehow or other the taboo that surrounds the use of atomic weapons would have to be destroyed.'

So now we have 'Amerika,' about a Russian takeover in the Midwest, which echoes by inversion the bountiful disclosures concerning Pentagon dreams in the Reagan era on how best the U.S. could fight and win a nuclear war with the Soviet Union, right down to nuclear 'decapitation' of the Soviet high command.

The trouble with 'Amerika' is that it is coming to the nation's TV screens about four or five years too late. Back in 1982 and 1983, Pentagon war fever was at its height. The political coordinates of the cold war have changed drastically. In Mr. Reagan's first term you could hardly open a magazine or newspaper without reading gloating material about the last days of the Soviet Union, plagued with an aging leadership, a sluggish economy, drug and alcohol abuse, and an unpopular war.

And now? We don't need the eavesdroppers of the National Security Agency to tell us the sort of dispatches the Soviet ambassador is sending back to Moscow: 'Aging president increasingly out of touch ... efforts at glasnost over Iran/contra scandal thwarted by powerful interest groups in the government, much of whose operations remain entirely secret ... economy toiling along at rates of growth half those of the Soviet Union ... problems of addiction pervasive throughout national life ... public deeply opposed to miring of country in an unpopular war. ...'

Everything is changing around and one can detect a certain air of panic in the cold war impresarios here as they start looking at the ledger: over here a sickly president and becalmed administration wallowing in scandal; over there a healthy Mikhail Gorbachev bringing Andrei Sakharov back from exile and calling for the injection of some vitality into Lenin's concept of democratic centralism, a vibrant Soviet press rooting out corruption. Things could get worse. The Russians actually could withdraw from Afghanistan, thus leaving the U.S. defenders of the 'Afghan freedom fighters' to justify their heroes, whose program is the restoration of feudalism and the flogging of every Afghan woman who has had the temerity to give up the veil or get a job.

The Russians are confident enough to call for a conference on human rights in Moscow this year. They have got a lot of explaining to do, no doubt about it. But so has the U.S., particularly when its hosts give readings from Articles 23 and 25 of the Universal Declaration of Human Rights, with their embarrassing language about the right to work and to protection against unemployment; the right to equal pay for equal work; the right to a standard of living adequate to health and well-being, including food, clothing, housing, medical care and necessary social services; and the right to security in the event of unemployment, sickness, disability, widowhood or old age. This is not to mention the language in the United Nations civil and political covenant outlawing material likely to provoke war fever.

So what may we expect with these changed terms of ideological trade? 'Amerika' is one response, but it's already out of date. No, I think there is a more encouraging prospect. A revitalized Soviet Union could provoke a revitalization of politics and ideals in the U.S. At the end of the 1950s came Sputnik and a bustling Nikita Khrushchev, talking of reform and vying with John Kennedy for the admiration of the rest of the world. That challenge prompted some of the most creative years the U.S. has ever seen. This is the scenario all the political scriptwriters should now be working on.

WSJ

February 26, 1987

Reagan's Reversals Uplift the Left in the Northwest

I have bad news for President Reagan. Having spent many evenings in my life addressing left-of-center audiences, I think I'm not too bad a judge of morale, and on the evidence of six straight nights of podium pounding this past week to crowds in Southern California, Washington and Oregon, Mr.

Reagan's misfortunes have come as a splendid tonic.

Too often, alas, it is the fate of a radical speaker to gaze out at a sea (or sometimes, to be frank about it, a sprinkling) of faces doleful at the size of the obstructions in the path of a successful march toward the commonwealth of enlightened ideals. And over the past six years, amid the incense of the Reagan cult wreathing the mainstream media, it has sometimes been hard to strike a convincing note of optimism. But now the mood, as I've encountered it in San Diego, in Eugene, in Seattle, in Spokane and in Moscow (Idaho, to be sure), is one of positive exuberance. And to the cry from the platform, 'Does anyone here think the nation can ill afford a stricken presidency or the trauma of another Watergate?' there is always a gratified silence.

There are some sound reasons for this gratification and the kindred sense that the Reagan administration has had it coming. The groups inviting me to talk about the press and the scandal have Central America as their focus, and the background of the Iran-contra scandal is familiar to them. For the past two years they've been importuning their local newspapers and their congressional representatives to take a hard look at illegal shunting of money and arms by the Reagan administration to the contras. They've been waiting for the stories of contra drug-running to the U.S. to get serious attention and, overall, for the press and Congress to stop genuflecting before the Great Communicator and start scrutinizing secret government and abuses of power. Now that the mainstream press and the congressional overseers are paying attention, if only momentarily, these groups feel with some justice that they were right all along.

Of course there is nothing so uplifting as having history whisper in your ear, 'You were right all along.' These are people who have been listening in frustration and anger as the president has set the terms of debate, lashing at the Sandinistas for having ties with Iran. He came up with this particular charge last March, just a few weeks after he had signed one of his 'findings,' authorizing a supply of arms to Iran and the men of terror there who supposedly paid $1 million to blow up the U.S. Marines in Beirut.

There's another reason why the people I was talking to feel good. Many think that if it were not for the scandal, a U.S.-backed invasion of Nicaragua would by now be under way and that such an invasion would, if successful, shape the political agenda for years to come. Indeed, the only check to unalloyed rejoicing is the fear that the administration might, cornered rat-style, try a quick invasion of Nicaragua to get itself out of its present mess, just as the invasion of Grenada stopped people talking about the 242 Marines killed in their Beirut barracks.

So there, across the Northwest, were all those audiences of gratified people welcoming the new political environment, and the sight of them reminded me once again of the illusion, zealously fostered by the apostles of Reaganism in the media and politics, that this country has plunged irreversibly to the right and that a progressive political culture has shriveled to the very margin of public life.

Now the Northwest has a long radical, progressive tradition. In the Spokane meeting I met Morey and Margaret Haggin, a spry couple still highly active in political life who fondly recalled organizing a local chapter of the National Association for the Advancement of Atheism back in the early 1930s and mounting at the Masonic Temple in Spokane a debate between Clarence Darrow and the evangelist Aimee Semple MacPherson.

Alongside the Haggins were people who have fought the good fight down the years and, like the Haggins, are still fighting it. Guy Burton, my host in Eugene, now working for Clergy and Laity Concerned, had long done organizing work in the Northwest and before that, in the style of the '60s, had had a spell of back-to-the-land farming in the Ozarks. The people from Seattle Central American Media Project who work with the mainstream press to try to get them to address their concerns, have rich lineages of political activism over the past couple of decades. These encounters confirmed something I've long observed nationally: that the 60% and more of the American people who oppose intervention in Central America haven't arrived at that position en masse by accident or purely by cause of instinctive isolationism or dreaded Post-Vietnam Syndrome.

What can be called the Central American solidarity movement in this country is far broader and better informed than its equivalent during the Vietnam era. Community after community has a 'sister city' project with Nicaragua. There is a vigorous sanctuary movement for protecting refugees from Central America. Thousands of people have visited Nicaragua and returned to recount their experiences to church groups, labor unions, community coalitions and the like. In Spokane, for example, at least 50 in the town have made journeys to Nicaragua, and the day I was there, one of them, Kevin Baxter, published a vigorous and well-informed account of his experiences in the local paper, the Spokesman-Review. There is a level of knowledge and of direct experience of Nicaragua that no amount of thunder from Elliott Abrams and the others can dispel.

The breadth of this Central American solidarity movement, rooted in the mainstream of the political culture, is a clue to the size of the progressive movement in this country overall, a movement largely disenfranchised by the media and by politicians. Someone incensed by Reagan's war on Nicaragua is most likely an activist in the fields of arms control or the environment, and is eager to defend social programs at home.

They are the people, millions and millions of them, who got upset about the 'Amerika' series. I kept looking at the panel on Ted Koppel's Viewpoint program broadcast from Minneapolis Monday night to see if they were represented. I saw Ted Sorensen, lawyer for the United Nations, and I saw Jeane Kirkpatrick. I saw Ted Turner, who did much the best job of articulating their concerns. In the audience I saw Reed Irvine of Accuracy In Media, who seemingly gets summoned to the mike wherever these Viewpoints are held.

But I didn't see on the panel anyone from the churches, the unions or the left. You almost never do on such panels (except for conservative evangelicals, of course), which is why the people I've been meeting may be gratified now, but are basically still angry. About half this country's political spectrum, from the middle out to the left, is systematically excluded from what passes for public dialogue, and this is something far more dangerous to this nation's political health than even the abuses now hitting the headlines.

WSJ

March 7, 1987

The Coup d'État

The Reagan Administration is not the first to have decided that the public rituals of democratic elections were only necessary prelude to the actual seizure of power, institution of secret procedures and evasion of accountability. Such seizures have become riskier. Nixon's coup d'état produced Watergate, and the Reaganites its sequel. But in both cases, despite abundant evidence of criminal behavior and abuses of power, the mainstream press persisted in keeping its eyes firmly shut while trumpeting the supposed popularity of the *caudillo* either truly or notionally in charge.

What did the press know, and when did it know it? Take Libya. Into the headlines last week shot the news that Acting President Oliver North along with N.S.C. and C.I.A. officials such as Director of Central Intelligence designate Robert Gates, devised and promoted a plan for a joint U.S.-Egyptian invasion of Libya. This plan should not have come as a surprise to U.S. journalists based in Paris or Cairo, assuming that either they or their in-house interpreters were capable of reading the local newspapers. On March 31, 1986, the Egyptian daily *Al-Ahram* reported that U.S. officials had suggested a joint attack on Libya no less than three times. *Al-Ahram*'s director, Ibrahim Nafaa, denounced the proposal with the words 'Egypt will never take up arms against another Arab country, even if the country is Libya.'

That episode occurred in the tense period culminating in the Reagan Administration's effort to murder Col. Muammar el-Qaddafi and his family while they slept. A few days later, on April 2, *Le Monde* reported

Al-Ahram's disclosure on its front page, again without arousing much interest in the U.S. press.

In *The New York Times Magazine* for February 22, Seymour Hersh outlined the plot, approved by President Reagan and unchallenged by the bureaucracy or by Congress, to murder Qaddafi. The intention was entirely obvious at the time, since nine F-111s were targeted on Qaddafi's tent and, as *The Washington Post* then reported, the White House had prepared a statement for the President before the raid anticipating Qaddafi's death and asserting that it had not been planned. There is little doubt that Qaddafi's assassination and official protestations that it was accidental would have been accepted uncritically, just as the U.S. press had obediently swallowed the government's refusal to acknowledge Qaddafi's daughter as a bomb victim, despite the pitiful evidence in Tripoli, and had also bought the claims of 'irrefutable' proof of Libyan complicity in the disco bombing in West Berlin.

Unless there are serious divisions in the ruling elites, the press will always defer to the assertions of government and relay its propaganda without much challenge. In the Reagan era there have been no such divisions. The coup d'état had bipartisan backing in Congress, and no institutional force in American society outside the progressive churches (given no strenuous coverage by the press) challenged it. Anyone looking for examples of this bipartisan complicity need go no further than Walter Mondale and Frank Fahrenkopf Jr.'s ringing defense of the National Endowment for Democracy in *The New York Times* for February 23, or the response of Representative Lee Hamilton, then chair of the House Intelligence Committee, to the president of Common Cause, who was inquiring about possible illegal funding of the *contras* by the Reagan Administration. In a letter dated November 7, 1985 (after his committee had gratefully heard a denial by Robert McFarlane of such funding efforts) Hamilton wrote: 'I would need to be shown credible evidence that Colonel North violated the Boland Amendment. At this point, I am unaware of such evidence.' This was after Lieut. Col. Oliver North had been mentioned by name in sixty-two separate stories about *contra* aid in leading U.S. newspapers, magazines and wire services between 1983 and 1985.

Apt to this bipartisan complaisance to the coup d'état, the press swallowed month after month, year after year, the claims of the Reagan Administration that it would conduct good-faith negotiations with Nicaragua, provided Congress lubricated such parleys with military aid for the *contras*. Time after time the editorialists and reporters rallied to Reagan. Take your choice from the archives of credulity:

Notwithstanding the Sandinistas' quick and defiant rejection of it, President Reagan's new Nicaragua plan marks a step forward in one important respect. It points a way to suspension of the war for at least two months in order to give negotiations a better chance.

This was an editorial in *The Washington Post* for April 7, 1985, duplicated remorselessly throughout the press. The eruption of the scandal slightly discommoded this willing suspension of critical faculties. On January 1, 1987, Joanne Omang, an experienced reporter for *The Washington Post*, reviewed the evolution of government policy toward Nicaragua: 'First, the idea of negotiating a peaceful settlement with Nicaragua was rejected in early 1983 after a fierce struggle within the administration. Any agreement that would leave the leftist Sandinistas in power has not been seriously considered since.' That is, everything the left in this country said about Reaganite intentions was true, and everything the editorialists and reporters have written since 1983 was bunk.

There's a powerful urge in Congress and in the press to see the scandal in procedural rather than substantive terms, and this is reminiscent of Watergate. When the articles of impeachment were being prepared in 1974, the secret bombing of Cambodia was considered in the moral candlelight of the question, Why had Congress not been properly consulted before the United States showered Cambodian peasants with high explosives? The crime of killing those peasants was not in itself on the agenda. Today, the fact that the United States breached international law in attacking Nicaragua and then fled the World Court has not caused Congress or the press to charge the Administration with piracy. Once again the concerns are couched in procedural terms.

Nor does there seem to be much desire to prowl down some of the darker alleyways of the coup d'état. In *The New York Times* for February 15, Joel Brinkley reported the Tower commission's uncovering of this coup's pulsing engine: the secret side of Project Democracy, a bipartisan affair if ever there was one. He wrote that in 1982 and 1983 there was much discussion in government of how to get rich people to contribute to Project Democracy:

> In March of 1983, Charles Z. Wick, the U.S.I.A. Director, arranged a White House meeting with the President for several millionaires and billionaires, including Sir James Goldsmith, publisher of L'Express, the French magazine; W. Clement Stone, a Chicago businessman, and Rupert Murdoch, who owns newspapers and other publications in the United States and other countries.

Those are men not famous for selfless generosity. They are also men in constant contact with regulatory bodies such as the Securities and Exchange Commission and the Federal Communications Commission – to take the cases of Goldsmith and Murdoch. With what expectations did they attend those White House fund-raisers? Who else was at those meetings?

How many other magnates in the communications sector had quiet conversations with the executives of Project Democracy? We speak, remember, in a period when all three networks have changed hands beneath a benign regulatory eye and when mergers, buy-outs, joint operating agreements and the like have proceeded on well-greased wheels.

Let's end with a forthright expression of where power in the press lies, as described in Walter Isaacson and Evan Thomas's book, *The Wise Men.* In 1943, *Newsweek* had the temerity to raise questions about the efficiency of daylight bombing of Germany. One of the artificers of that policy, Robert Lovett, then in the War Department, asked Averell Harriman, then in London, to help out. Harriman, who at the request of his friend Vincent Astor had invested in *Newsweek,* laid down an editorial line for his brother Roland, who sat on the magazine's board of directors, to impose:

'Tell Roland that I am in dead earnest and will brook no compromise,' Harriman wrote Lovett in April of 1943. 'I have not supported *Newsweek* for ten years through its grave difficulties to allow our hired men to use the magazine to express their narrow, uninformed or insidious ideas. ... Roland has my full authority to use any strong arm measures he considers necessary ... The other directors can be asked to resign if they do not go along.'

This is the ruling class talking to itself, and it should be pasted on the front gate of every journalism school as a pithy statement on the realities of the business.

The Nation

March 13, 1987

Can the Press Save the Presidency?

Since the fundamental role of the official press is to provide reassurance, reassurance has been provided in ample measure. Barely had the president gabbled his way through his speech on March 4 before pundits and politicians were on hand to say that yes, Reagan had adequately demonstrated contrition for deeds of the past and determination to do better in the future and now the nation had best put the whole sorry scandal behind it.

In fact the president demonstrated no such contrition and had nothing at all to say about the Nicaraguan end of the scandal. But the mesmerized urge to sustain the Reagan cult for two more years proved overwhelming. In his commentary the day the Tower commission's report was released,

NBC's John Chancellor caught this servile idiom perfectly:

'But the Tower commission accuses him of no actual crime, only the sin of inattention. And Ronald Reagan, with all his skills, ought to be able to handle that accusation. He has one very big thing going for him: Nobody wants him to fail. Nobody wants another Nixon. He should be able to build on that, as he reshapes his image and his administration ... He has been wounded, but not crippled, by the Tower commission ...'

This is more or less the line served up on all the networks and in most of the editorial columns. The most glaring misconception is obviously contained in the line 'Nobody wants him to fail.' Who can Chancellor have been talking to? Millions of people in the United States want Ronald Reagan to fail. They want him to fail in circumstances of utter humiliation both for himself and his co-conspirators. They want the delicious drama of another Watergate to last, day by day, hour by hour and minute by glorious minute, till the curtain finally falls on his odious administration.

But the people, like Chancellor, who say that no one wants Reagan to fail are the same people who insist, night after night on the TV screens, day after day in the newspaper editorials, that the president 'still commands enormous affection on the part of the American people.' Who says? According to *Newsweek*'s poll, published in its March 9 issue, more than half of the American people disapprove of the way he's handling his job; less than half have personal confidence that he would 'do the right thing' (i.e., tell the truth or avoid blowing up the world). Another poll shows a majority thinking him a liar. This is enormous popularity?

LA Weekly

March 27, 1987

Buckley's Confession

Prime among the mysteries of the Iran/contra scandal is the question of William Buckley's possible confession. Buckley was the CIA station chief in Beirut, kidnapped in 1984 and presumed murdered by Islamic Jihad. On November 17, 1986, Islamic Jihad issued a statement saying it had 90 written pages along with six videotapes of Buckley telling all he knew about CIA operations in the region, including which major Middle Eastern figures worked for the agency.

Islamic Jihad then said, 'We are waiting for the proper time to release these dangerous facts about CIA operations ... We are warning the U.S. government that their only choice is to satisfy our demands.'

At the time no one in the U.S. seems to have picked up on this, aside from columnist Jack McCarthy in *Florida Flambeaux* for December 8, 1986. The matter of Buckley's confession is alluded to in the Tower commission's report, and a number of rumors are circulating in Washington to the effect that the content of Buckley's confession after torture was one of the reasons why the Reagan administration remained eager to deal with Islamic Jihad's sponsor in Teheran.

What could Buckley have said? Revelation of CIA assets in the Middle East would have been, would still be, embarrassing, but scarcely enough to prompt panic in the CIA or in the White House. Buckley had previously been station chief in Mexico City, and therefore might have had much to reveal about U.S. skullduggery in that area. He might also have been in a position to discuss what Reagan's people might have been up to in 1980 when President Jimmy Carter was desperately trying to achieve an 'October surprise' by bringing back the Teheran embassy hostages before the election. He failed, and eventually the hostages came home just in time to grace Ronald Reagan's inauguration. One version is that in those battle-fraught final weeks of the campaign, Reagan's operatives, headed by campaign chief William Casey, offered Iran a better deal – over arms, oil or frozen assets – than anything proposed by Carter, thus toying with the hostages' lives in return for domestic political advantage. This is not so much a smoking gun as a stack of dynamite waiting for lightning to strike.

LA Weekly

April 4, 1987

Afterglow: All the President's Men

Senator Robert Dole called the White House after President Reagan's March 19 press conference to tell him that he 'hit the ball out of the park.' Dole is noted for drollery, but I wonder if he had studied the transcript:

> Q: Mr. President, is it possible that two military officers who are trained to obey orders grabbed power, made major foreign policy moves, didn't tell you when you were briefed every day on intelligence? Or did they think they were doing your bidding?
>
> A: Helen, I don't know. I only know that that's why I've said repeatedly that I want to find out. I want to get to the bottom of this and find out all that has happened and so far I've told you all that I know. And you know the truth of the matter is, for quite some long time, all that you knew was what I'd told you.

This is fun to read, particularly if you rearrange it in blank verse, but it suggests a high score on the Alzheimer graph, unless you happen to be David Broder, senior political correspondent of *The Washington Post.* He hastened to tell the readers of his nationally syndicated column that the press conference 'provided the strongest evidence yet that the proprietor of the shop has regained a good measure of his emotional balance and is ready to reclaim his role at the center of government. ... he showed the steadiness and confidence that has been so conspicuously missing in the final months of 1986.'

This is the most startling example yet of the official press's determination, against all the available evidence, to fulfill its fundamental role of providing reassurance rather than news. Broder was not alone. I came brow to brow with this mind-set back in December, when I appeared on the *Donahue* show with Richard Cohen and Mark Shields, two columnists for *The Washington Post*, both of liberal reputation. They hastened to defend Reagan. Cohen insisted that the President had been surrounded by a 'closed circle of advisers ... who have made foreign policy,' and Shields agreed that the President had been the victim of 'a bloodless coup in the White House,' which he 'didn't know about.' They firmly maintained that Reagan had never been involved in such distasteful activities as attempting to murder Col. Muammar el-Qaddafi by targeting nine F-111s on his tent. When Seymour Hersh later published a long article in *The New York Times Magazine* for February 22 underlining that this is exactly what Reagan had done, I was interested to see a remarkable coincidence between the excuses offered by the Reaganites – that Qaddafi's death would have been welcome but had not been specifically sought, that he was nomadic and hard to locate – and what Cohen and Shields had to say on the matter. The best apologists need no briefing.

This instinctive flackery for Reagan diminishes sharply once one gets clear of the editorial pages of *The Washington Post* and *The New York Times* and the analysts on the networks. On March 23, four days after the press conference, *USA Today* had a strong editorial, saying:

> At his prime-time press conference, President Reagan showed he was unable to answer the questions that would help us get to the bottom of this mess. Many in the USA think he's unwilling. Polls show that most voters think he has got his head in the sand.

Two days earlier, on March 21, the Cleveland *Plain Dealer* was even tougher. Its lead editorial said that the reporters' questions at the press conference 'sounded too mild' and that

> they [press conferences] no longer are opportunities for the public to gain added understanding of the President's thoughts. Instead, they are opportunities for Reagan to deploy his patented look-good, feel-good defense. Several questions

deserved special attention, especially those dealing with the President's obvious misstatements regarding the role of Israel, and the nature of the arms deal itself. His answers to both were unsatisfactory. . . . But again, answers weren't the point. Appearance was, and for the most part, the press seemed alternately crippled by fear that it would look bad, and driven by some atavistic urge to ignore that fear.

The Nation

April 10, 1987

Detente and Dirty Tricks

Now that *People* magazine has visited the Soviet Union, we can say definitively that detente is back in style again. The cold warriors must be getting desperate, since detente is bad for arms companies. Every time Raisa Gorbachev smiles, the Senate Armed Services Committee gets heart failure. And the Soviets have thrown themselves into peaceful competition with a will. We have Fawn Hall – and before you can say 'Tovaritch,' they have Violetta Seina, the Messalina of the Marine Corps.

Expect the CIA to try to make Boris look bad. Back in the mid-1960s, when the Vietnam War was giving Uncle Sam a poor image across the world, the CIA, as *Time* magazine revealed a few weeks ago, performed the exceptionally dirty trick of telling the KGB the true identity of a couple of dissidents who had smuggled material out to the West, where it had been published under pseudonyms. The KGB promptly did exactly what the CIA hoped it would, arresting Andrei Sinyavski and Yuli Daniel, placing them on trial in 1966 and then giving them lengthy prison terms.

When the Soviet poet Yevgeny Yevtushenko visited the U.S. shortly thereafter, he called on Robert Kennedy, then a U.S. senator. 'To my surprise,' Yevtushenko wrote in *Time*, Kennedy 'invited me into his bathroom, turned on the shower and in a lowered voice he said, "I would like to tell you to tell your government that the names of Sinyavski and Daniel were given to your agents by our agents." I was amazed, and I asked him why they would have done that. He smiled at my naivete and said, "Because our people wanted to take advantage of the situation, and your people took the bait. Because of Vietnam, our standing had begun to diminish at home and abroad. We needed a propaganda counterweight."' The *Time* story was confirmed by Dusro Doden of the *Washington Post*, who got extra corroboration from Kennedy's Russian translator, Professor Albert Todd of Queens College.

LA Weekly

Straight Bull from Biden

Coming your way in the near future will be Senator Joseph Biden, one of the many awful Democrats planning to seek the presidential nomination of his party. Since you may have only glimpsed Biden on prime-time network newscasts posturing in some congressional committee hearing for the benefit of the TV cameras, you may be wondering who he is.

Biden is the senator from Delaware who took over chairmanship of the Senate Judiciary Committee when Senator Edward Kennedy chose to lead the Labor and Human Resources Committee instead. Thus, if a seat on the Supreme Court becomes vacant, Biden will be bathed in the limelight as he grills any Reagan nominee. The Senate Judiciary Committee – Democrats included – has over the past six years been mostly complaisant about Reagan's appointments.

As to Biden's world view, it was adequately represented by a speech he gave in early February at Northwestern University in which he hailed the 'triumphs' of the invasion of Grenada and the bombing of Tripoli. He said the Democrats must now 'cure the paralysis of the Vietnam syndrome' and must not 'cringe at the use of force to protect American lives.' As Garry Wills remarked in his column, Biden is still making the Democratic Party safe for the Reagan era.

What else? Biden assured his audience he would not stand 'idly by while tyrants impose their will' in Nicaragua. He hailed the way Kennedy defied international law in the case of the Cuban missile crisis. In other words, Biden is another cold war Democrat proving he's got hair on his chest and sawdust in his brain. You have been warned.

LA Weekly

May 16, 1987

The Assassination of Ben Linder

I left Nicaragua on the morning of April 28, the day Ben Linder was killed. The next morning I woke up in Florida to find that the most prominent story on the front page of *The Miami Herald*, from its correspondent in Managua, Sam Dillon, was headed 'Sandinistas Limit News On Contras.' *The Herald*'s report of the first killing of a U.S. peace volunteer in Nicaragua was tucked in below this dispatch about the difficulties of a journalist's life and was uninspired, ill researched and therefore emblematic of much of the mainstream newspaper coverage concerning Linder's assassination.

Under the headline 'American Died in Rebel Ambush, Nicaragua Says,' Stephen Kinzer's dispatch from Managua in *The New York Times* made it clear that Kinzer had concentrated most of his energies on calling Miami and Honduras to get the reactions of *contra* spokespersons, whose self-serving remarks were quoted early and at length.

Kinzer reported that Linder had been living in El Cuá, and stated: 'Several land mines have exploded under vehicles passing through the area, including one on July 3 that took 34 lives. According to diplomats, the mines were planted by *contra* squads.' The episode to which Kinzer was referring here was the horrifying U.S.-inspired *contra* murder of men, women and children that took place just as the Reaganite orgy known as Liberty Weekend was getting under way last summer. Kinzer preferred to stay in Managua rather than visit the wreckage of the truck and the bodies of the thirty-four, and fell back on his old friends, diplomatic sources. And what did he quote them as saying then? On July 11, Kinzer wrote:

There are ... reports circulating in the diplomatic community here that at least some of the victims of the explosion last week were members of the Sandinista militia who may have been wearing olive green clothing.

Neither diplomats who believed the Sandinista version [that the mine had been the work of *contras*] nor those who doubted it could offer concrete evidence for their theories. They said their conclusions were based solely on speculation and deduction, and they agreed that the truth would be almost impossible to determine.

Most mainstream papers rapidly gave up on the Linder story, omitting any account of the arrival in Managua of his parents and brother and their denunciations of President Reagan and his policies. By the weekend many of these newspapers, like the *Los Angeles Times*, had already made the usual speculations as to whether Linder had been armed or not. This is a propaganda ploy that the Administration has instilled into the U.S. press with near-total success, as indicated by the reaction of Alberto Fernandez, the press attaché at the U.S. Embassy in Managua. 'We don't know anything about this man,' Fernandez was quoted by *The Miami Herald* as saying, 'Was he armed? Was he unarmed?'

The U.S. journalists in Managua invariably ask this same question, as if the crime of blowing up or shooting people is somehow mitigated if they were imprudent enough to have met their end in the company of a militiaman or within eyesight of a weapon. And because it is usually impossible to prove that a weapon was not in the vicinity, the journalists dutifully raise the contingency that it was. Now, let us suppose that a gang of U.S. neo-Nazis commissioned by Gen. Augusto Pinochet of Chile blew up a busload of men, women and children trundling along a U.S. highway. Would the press pause to ask whether there had been a gun on the bus, or whether a U.S. serviceman had been present? Would the press have regarded it as relevant? Of course not. They would say that it was a terrorist crime, an outrage under national and international law, which is exactly what these *contra* attacks are in Nicaragua, specifically categorized as U.S.-sponsored crimes by the World Court.

The full laxity of Kinzer and his colleagues was strikingly revealed in the coverage of Linder's death by a newspaper whose reporters were several thousand miles from the scene of the crime. *The Daily*, a student paper at the University of Washington in Seattle, from which Linder graduated in 1983, carried in its issue for April 30 a detailed reconstruction of the attack, complete with a diagram illustrating the position of Linder and his companions beside a stream at the time of the ambush. I quote from the story by Kurt Jensen:

> Now, as he sat recording the readings from the weir [a device used for measuring the rate of water flow] in the minutes before eight o'clock in the morning, a group of between seven and 10 men, U.S.-backed Contras, crept up a small outcropping of rocks that rose behind Linder and the six Nicaraguan civilians seated in a small circle beside the weir.
>
> 'There's no doubt these were the Contra,' said Mira Brown, a close friend and colleague of Linder's, recounting the attack which had occurred 15 miles away and 36 hours before. 'Ben was in a kind of gully, and they came from above and behind him.'

> Speaking from a room adjacent to the one which held the coffin of Benjamin Linder, Brown continued. ... As Linder fell beside the weir he had installed earlier that morning, two other Nicaraguans – 'people that considered Ben family, who called him brother,' Brown said, collapsed nearby. Sergio Fernandez and Pablo Rosales, both of whom worked with Linder for some months on the hydroelectric project the 27-year-old engineer was supervising, died shortly after the initial grenade attack, presumably as a result of the gunfire which followed.

The paper interviewed Laurie McQuaig, a member of Witness for Peace in Managua and one of the first to arrive at the scene. It also reported that earlier last month two of Linder's assistants, Frederico Cortavanao and Oscar Blandon, were the objects of death threats from the *contras*; that on March 24 the dam Linder had built in El Cuá was attacked by 'roughly 100 Contra rebels using heavy machine guns, artillery, hand grenades and grenade launchers'; and that a week before Linder's death, just hours after he had left the village, El Cuá was attacked by *contras*, who shot several Nicaraguans. None of the Managua correspondents for the major U.S. papers I saw bothered to tell their readers any of this in the days immediately following Linder's death. None of them managed to speak with anyone who had been at the scene or with any of Linder's associates. As Bruce Barcott, the news editor of *The Daily*, wrote in a letter, 'If a

goddamn college paper in Seattle can get ahold of these people, why can't
The New York Times?'

The Nation

The Modern Rasputins

Although the Iran/*contra* hearings will not frame it this way, what is now
under gentle scrutiny on Capitol Hill is the terrorist culture of Reaganism.
James Petras has an interesting article about this culture and the implications of its rise in the March-April issue of *Against the Current* (available
from 17300 Woodward Avenue, Detroit, MI 48203).

Petras suggests that the United States' declining economy and weakened
global hegemony are the sources of the corrupt culture of 'covert action'
and profiteering now under investigation in the Iran/*contra* scandal:

> With the decline of productive capital, the reason for empire – domination of
> productive resources – changes. The clandestine intelligence apparatuses,
> initiated as the instruments of capital, become more institutionally autonomous.
> The ascent of the repressive apparatus at a time of declining hegemony and
> increasing use of state-terror has created a new historical conjuncture, and
> evoked a new political type: the military adventurer as Presidential adviser; the
> ideologue and political thug as under-secretary of Latin-American affairs. North
> and Abrams embody the new political ethos, the lumpen-intellectuals. ... The
> ascent of speculator capital and the decline of productive capital in the economy
> is based on the same ... illegal, clandestine, insider strategy and activities so
> characteristic of the lumpen-intellectuals who occupy the nether world between
> the White House and the Central American jungle airstrips of the narco-
> contras. ...
>
> The ascent of the modern Rasputins and the routinization of terror, the
> increasing tendency to submerge ideology to illicit transactions defines this
> critical juncture in the slide of U.S. power.

The Nation

May 22, 1987

The Smoking Gun That Doesn't Smoke

The hearings are frustrating – much more so than their Watergate equivalent – because their structure permits no sustained offensive. What is

actually going on is something akin to vaccination against disease. Vaccination is essentially a process of habituation, in which the patients are inoculated with safe doses of the disease against which they are to be protected. Thus, in the case of the Iran–contra scandal, the public has to be inoculated against the idea that the president is a liar who knowingly broke the law over a protracted period. Inoculation takes the form of revealing that the president is indeed a criminal liar, while at the same time stoutly maintaining that no proofs are available for this conclusion.

The first stage in this particular program of vaccination was the report of the Tower commission. It published abundant material showing that the president had day-to-day knowledge of the illegal activities and had authorized them. Simultaneously, the commissioners and the press announced that the report showed that the president did not have day-to-day knowledge of the illegal activities and had *not* authorized them. Thus we have the familiar spectacle of the politicians, editorialists and commentators examining a gun from whose barrel smoke is visibly leaking, while unanimously announcing that the weapon has not been fired in years.

So Secord's and North's testimony, see-sawing between frank admission and coy retraction, slowly habituate the public to the paradox that although the president knew everything, he knew nothing. The end result will be a conditioned response, wherein North will say he spent 10 minutes each day with the president getting authorizations for each weapon and dollar transfer. The White House will issue a denial, and the Congress and the press will agree that the s.g. is nowhere in sight.

This is what happened in the Watergate investigations, and by midsummer of 1974, after an avalanche of evidence of Nixon's guilt, *Time* magazine had solemnly asked the question, 'Is the press going too far?' and answered, 'Yes.' Then a tape surfaced that was so incriminating, so palpably the s.g., that all normal vaccination procedures were useless and Nixon had to resign. But this time it is unlikely that such a tape exists, and the public has already been inoculated against the idea that Reagan's written authorizations might have been physically destroyed. McFarlane's disclosure of the 'shredding party,' which did precisely this destruction, can now be dismissed as 'not another s.g.'

The Reagan administration has always had a particularly sophisticated grasp of these procedures. Consider the degrees by which the press was conditioned to accept the idea that President Reagan is hoping to 'restore' democracy in Nicaragua, even though the press would also concede, if pressed, that democracy never existed in Nicaragua prior to the revolution of 1979 and the elections of 1984, and therefore by definition cannot be 'restored'; and that, furthermore, Reagan wants to return a bunch of former National Guardsmen to power.

In *The New York Times* of May 14, Elaine Sciolino solemnly reported 'a discussion of a plan drafted by President Oscar Arias Sanchez of Costa Rica. ... President Reagan expressed concern about whether it could guarantee a process of democratization in Nicaragua.' She asserted later in the same story that the Arias plan 'calls for an end to American aid for the contras in return for the creation of a democratic system in Nicaragua' and that Guatemala 'favors re-establishment of a democratic system there.' All of this is untrue, but Sciolino would probably react angrily to the charge that this is a piece of shameless publicity for the White House on the occasion of a visit by Guatemalan President Vinicio Cerezo Arevalo, though this is exactly what it was.

Another piece of classic inoculation was the Reagan administration's assault on the ABM treaty, with claims that a piece of treaty language outlawing the testing of space-based systems could in fact be broadly interpreted as permitting the testing of space-based systems. There are innumerable other examples that propel us toward the inevitable conclusion that almost all reporting, whether about the Iran–contra scandal or the ABM treaty or the homeless or the unemployed, is both inoculation against reality and reassurance that despite all appearances, the world is not what it seems.

LA Weekly

May 30, 1987

Invisible Man

'Who is the front-runner?' asked the columnist Robert Novak of Democratic Party chair Paul Kirk on a recent edition of *Crossfire*. With a sly grin Novak waited for Kirk to fall into the trap, which Kirk duly did by answering that there was no front-runner in a field so richly endowed with human and political talent. Wrong, said Novak. 'There is one front-runner, ... Jesse Jackson. Isn't it a fact that you just don't call him a front-runner because he's black?' Kirk rather feebly tried to haul himself out of the hole by suggesting that Jackson himself had said there was no front-runner, which is, of course, what all front-runners say.

The inability of the political and journalistic establishments to state straightforwardly that Jackson leads in the race for the Democratic presidential nomination grew even more comical with a *New York Times* survey, published on May 17. It showed that out of a field of eight candidates Jackson led with 17 percent, six points ahead of the beau of Route 128, Michael Dukakis. But *The Times*, eager to cast a whiter light on the worrisome implications of those numbers, crowned the survey with the headline 'Jackson Tops Poll (Not Counting Cuomo).' Adam Clymer's story announced that if included in the list of candidates, Governor Mario Cuomo, who has formally withdrawn his name from contention, comes out ahead, with 25 percent – over Jackson, with 12 percent, and Senator Bill Bradley, another noncandidate, with 6 percent.

Poor Jesse. These contortions must remind him of the coverage of his victory in Louisiana in 1984, the first by a black in any state presidential primary contest in the history of the United States. *The Times* headlined that one 'Jackson Takes Louisiana Vote in Low Turnout' and belittled the victory as the result of a voter boycott of the election. The week before, Jackson had won the primary in Washington, D.C., a triumph the *Times* reporter Ben A. Franklin attributed to the aberrant demographic makeup of the District. If Jackson's fortunes continue to wax, he must expect more of that sort of thing, with headlines such as 'Jackson Ahead (Not Counting F.D.R. and Christ)' and stories like this:

> The Rev. Jesse Jackson today held a commanding lead in states participating in the crucial Super Tuesday primary contests, but when asked to state their preferences if other, undeclared, candidates were included, a substantial number of those polled voiced enthusiasm for Franklin Delano Roosevelt and even for Jesus Christ, an evangelist popular across the South. 'Of course I'd vote for F.D.R. if he was running,' was one typical response from a 75-year-old citizen. When pressed at length by a reporter about alleged irregularities in the funding of Mr. Jackson's Operation PUSH, along with allegations of anti-Semitism, sexual misconduct, logorrhea, arrogance, satanism and capitulation to Moscow, the senior citizen conceded that had she been aware of those charges, they 'might have qualified [her] support for the black candidate.'

If people think the preceding quotation a somewhat far-fetched parody, I forgive them. I thought so myself until, the day after writing it, I came across a couple of columns by our old friends Mark Shields and Richard Cohen in *The Washington Post* for May 19. Shields simply refused to recognize that Jackson is a contender, as indicated by this observation: 'As the leader, Hart had defined the race; the message of every other candidate was "I'm Gary Hart, only different and better."' Cohen preferred to have it both ways, saying that it was not racist to deny that Jackson is the front-runner, but that even the fact that he is the front-runner 'ain't worth much.' (Cohen apparently thinks the vernacular is appropriate to discussion of Jackson.) The man who once argued that shopkeepers in Washington have every right to refuse entry to blacks then produced this dialectical masterpiece: 'Of course, some of the reluctance to acknowledge Jackson as the front-runner has to do with race – although not necessarily with racism. It is simply not likely that a black person will be elected president in 1988.

Acknowledging the reality of racism is not in itself racist.' That is, journalists are not necessarily being racist when they are being racist. I presume the pro-Jackson people in the *Times* survey were not journalists. Cohen spent the rest of his space reminding his readers of Jackson's indulgence of anti-Semitism, his 'dash to Cuba' (something the liberal Cohen found particularly offensive), the fact that Operation PUSH was 'hardly run with IBM-like efficiency' and, needless to say, the fact that Jackson had once hugged the leader of the organization that killed Leon Klinghoffer.

The Anyone-But-Jackson coalition, teetering between Cuomo and Bradley, extends clear across the political spectrum, nowhere more snappishly than in the tendencies associated with the Democratic Socialists of America and *In These Times*. On January 21 of this year John Judis, the political correspondent for *In These Times*, dismissed Jackson as the 'black candidate' ('Not simply a result of the fact that he is black. Not being a politician, he has never represented a broad constituency') and directed his readers' attention to the following robust political vista:

> The Democratic ticket that I believe has the best chance of winning and governing is Hart as president with Sen. Sam Nunn (D-Ga.) as vice president. Nunn, the chairman of the Senate Armed Services Committee, would be a good choice because he is a Southerner, a conservative by reputation and also a man of great intelligence. If ever given the chance of representing the entire nation, he could surprise.

With social democrats like this, who needs Chuck Robb?

Heading into Election '88 there will be those like Judis to remind us that there is such a thing as the lesser of two evils, and, besides, there is the Supreme Court to think about. So think about it. If the Democratic invocation of the lesser-of-two-evils argument had been heeded in 1948 and voters for Henry Wallace had supported Harry Truman, we would have been spared Thoms Dewey. This Republican President gave the go-ahead to the H-bomb, plunged the United States into Korea, stoked the anti-Communist witch hunts of the period and, by so doing, distorted the politics of a generation.

The Dewey years led to the rabid interventionism of President Adlai Stevenson, and in disgust some Democrats went for Richard Nixon in 1960. Had John F. Kennedy become President in 1961, we would have avoided involvement in Southeast Asia and the horrors of the Alliance for Progress. And so on down the years. Would not Jimmy Carter have been better able than the victorious Gerald Ford to resist the late-1970s push for a military buildup? As things stand, with Walter Mondale in the White House we have a vast improvement over a second Reagan term. Mondale, by refusing a meretricious treaty of medium-range missiles, has successfully finessed Gorbachev's attempts to split the NATO alliance. His refusal to abandon the Nicaraguan *contras* has been balanced by eloquent rhetorical support for the idea of a Contadora treaty and, latterly, the so-called Arias plan.

The Nation

Reagan and Hegel

Recall that at the time of the release of the Tower commission's report the President's claims of having been on permanent mental vacation were taken at face value, and he was chided for his 'management style.' The hearings have established that, to the contrary, Reagan exercised a hands-on attention to detail that would have been the envy of Jimmy Carter. He personally approved the mining of Nicaragua's harbors, personally urged the President of Honduras to release one arms shipment to the *contras*, personally urged King Fahd to double his donation to '*contra* freedom fighters,' as Judy Woodruff cravenly called them a couple of weeks ago.

So are the editorialists now calling him a liar? No, they are noting with scholarly detachment the White House's repositioning, away from the question of knowledge and toward that of legality: whether he is conditionally bound to give a fig for Boland or any of his amendments. This is tactically sound, since it urges the press back toward the reflexive flattery of pre-scandal times. Remember what Hegel said about flattery in *The Phenomenology of the Spirit*: 'Through this process the indwelling spirit of the power of the state comes into existence – that of an unlimited monarch. "Unlimited," since the language of flattery raises power into its purified generality. ... "Monarch," since flattering language likewise puts individuality on its pinnacle. ... By giving the monarch his proper name, flattery elevates the particularity of its own ego, which otherwise is only imagined into its pure essence.'

The Nation

June 27, 1987

Sans Merci

On the night of Margaret Thatcher's victory in the elections of June 11, Sir James Goldsmith threw a huge party, costing about $750,000, at Cliveden, onetime home to Lady Astor and symbolic headquarters of pro-Nazi appeasers in the 1930s. The revels paid for by Goldsmith were, by all accounts, exuberant and prolonged, with the jollity animated by a sense of relief. On election eve had come tidings that Labor was making spectacular gains, that there might even be a hung Parliament. Financial markets experienced a slight shudder, which was not subdued until, with almost the first returns, it became clear that Thatcher's absolute majority was assured and that, with this third straight victory, she had obtained a triumph unprecedented since the early nineteenth century.

By dawn on June 12, just as the last of Goldsmith's bleary guests were tottering home, traders were heading into the City to pick up the action from the markets in Tokyo and Hong Kong. By the close of business more than $10 billion had been added to the value of quoted shares, and the wine bars around the City were awash with champagne at the prospect of another term of what is tactfully described as 'stability '.

Joy on the Conservative side was more than matched by consternation and grief amid the opposition. To believe one's own propaganda is easy at any time, and never more so than in the hours before voters enter the polls. In the final days of the campaign, commentators left and right were unanimous in their opinion that the Labor leader, Neil Kinnock, had fought a model campaign, eschewing socialist dogma and exuding compassion like sap off a maple tree. The trouble was that though many voters saw in Kinnock a pleasing contrast to the hypnotic goofiness of former leader Michael Foot, they still concluded that the party had no convincing economic strategy and that they would be worse off if it got back into power. This was an entirely rational calculation. Social democracy as promulgated by the Labour Party is a fraud, and the voters can scarcely be blamed for rejecting it.

The Nation

What's In It for Me?

The rich – at least those who wish to be sure of remaining in that happy state – would obviously vote for Thatcher and her party because she has been very good to them, just as Ronald Reagan has been good to their associates on the other side of the Atlantic. The British journalist John Rentoul shows in his book *The Rich Get Richer* that since Thatcher came to power, in 1979, there has been a sharp increase in the income share of the top 10 percent of the population, with the top 1 percent doing best. The gain of these top people has come at the expense of the middle third and, most damagingly, the bottom 10 percent of the population. Rentoul reckons that income in Britain is now spread as unequally as it is in the

United States, which has one of the most unequal distributions in the industralized capitalist world.

So Thatcher has delivered for the rich. The two determining episodes of her sojourn have been the victory of the state in the battle with the miners in 1984-85 and the renaissance of London as entrepôt for international finance capital and launching pad for British finance capital. Between 1979 and 1987, Britain exported about $175 billion in capital invested around the world; between 1979 and 1983, when Britain became a net importer of industrial goods for the first time in its history, investment in British industry fell by two-fifths, and by the end of that period the volume of overseas investment was double that at home; in the past eight years manufacturing has declined by about 38 percent, and financial services now engage one-tenth of the work force. Britain remains, overwhelmingly, the largest investor in the United States, much of it new capital since 1979. An indicator of London's success as entrepôt for the great speculative boom is that in the past three years assets controlled by London-based financial institutions have doubled, to just over $1.5 trillion. The lubricant for these developments, so congenial to the Goldsmith crowd, has been North Sea oil, which has prevented internal decay from swerving the whole pantechnicon into the ditch.

But Thatcher has not delivered merely for the rich. The single most chastening figure for Labor was the Conservatives' 36 percent share of the manual-working-class vote, the largest in any postwar election. Those workers who live in the south gave the Conservatives a larger lead – 46 percent to 28 percent – than the electorate as a whole. This slice of the working class undoubtedly includes many of Britain's 6 million new stockholders, who have snapped up the carefully undervalued shares in such privatized industries as British Telecom and British Gas. In this slice too were those homeowners and tenants of once publicly owned housing, who have all seen property values double in the past couple of years. Beyond real estate, people of all classes in the south have, in the past nine months, been enjoying the pickings of a boom in services and in the undocumented economy.

The boom stops at Birmingham. North and west of there, apart from strategic hamlets of wealth, the scene gets rapidly worse, and Labor's strength grows in proportion. The Conservative Party no longer has any seats in Manchester, Leicester, Bradford, Liverpool, Newcastle and Glasgow. You could pack all the Conservative M.P.s in Scotland into a couple of taxis. Labor gained in the north and thus is becoming, in the words of Ivor Crewe, a professor of government at the University of Essex, the 'party neither of one class nor one nation' but 'a regional class party.'

The unemployed and the desperate voted Labor because to vote Conservative would be to embrace the hangman, but even they had no self-interested reason to vote for Kinnock-style social democracy. For them, as for anyone else, a Labor victory would have meant a strike of capital in the form of a slump in the value of sterling, disinvestment by multinationals and, in the end, less money for such emblems of the welfare state as the National Health Service. All of those unwholesome consequences could be endured if the Labor Party was committed to the principle of full employment. But its manifesto this year displayed no such resolve, and recent archives contain full proof of the capitulation of former leaders Harold Wilson and James Callaghan to the International Monetary Fund and the supposed imperatives of the Phillips curve, with its trade-off between inflation and unemployment. It was Wilson and Callaghan who paved the way for Thatcher, just as the Carter of 1978-80 oiled the hinge for Reagan.

The Nation

Is Social Democracy Done For?

It's true that Kinnock's notion of a social crusade was, aside from his compassionarias, to promise, in the manner of Walter Mondale, to raise taxes, but could a more mettlesome socialist advocate have done any better? Are there now, across the face of the Atlantic alliance, too many haves, too vigilant a SWAT team of custodians of international capital? The model here is what the Swedish social scientist Göran Therborn, in *Why Some Peoples Are More Unemployed Than Others*, calls the 'Brazilianisation of advanced capitalism': the twinning of war Keynesianism and monetarism, with mass unemployment a permanent fixture; at the top, the hyper-rich and the elite managers; in the middle, the stably employed; at the bottom, the underclass of permanently and marginally unemployed, facing a future of reduced benefits with concomitant waves of desperation and passivity, riots, repression and contempt.

This, as Therborn points out, is the society envisaged, designed and blueprinted in Reagan's America and Thatcher's Britain. The draftsmen have been at work since 1973, the dawn of the present era of mass unemployment. After Thatcher won a second term, in 1983, *The Times* of London said, 'Surely this election victory has shown that the tired attempts to invest the phenomenon of unemployment with some statistical morality have not taken in the electors ... Nevertheless, statistical unemployment is here to stay. It is necessary therefore to discover a different language in which to explore the profound changes which will affect the whole pattern of work in society in the 1980s and the 1990s.'

In fact, mass unemployment is not ineluctable. Five countries in the advanced capitalist world have managed to keep unemployment low: Austria, Sweden, Norway, Japan and Switzerland. Those societies differ in political and economic texture, but they all share an institutionalized commitment to full employment. Austria, Sweden and Norway score high on unionization and social democratic political weight. Japan and Switzerland do not, but, Therborn suggests, they have a strong precapitalist component – quasi-feudal in the former, petit bourgeois in the latter – which contributes to a politico-economic perspective broader than the rate of return on invested capital. None of the five is a member of the E.E.C.; all are peripheral to the Atlantic alliance. Thus, national roads to full employment are possible. They require progressive control of the policies of the national bank; low real interest rates; direct government intervention in the economy; reflation geared to investment, both public and private; active labor-market policy measures; emphasis on productive over finance capital and the payment of dividends. None of this is particularly socialist, but, as Therborn says: 'As long as a large part of the potential working class is unemployed and marginalised, no further advances are likely. People on the dole will not bring about socialism.'

The Nation

The Old Mole

Thirteen percent of the British workforce is on the dole. Socialism or barbarism, said Rosa Luxemburg. As the results of the elections came through, a lot of people sadly watching their television sets said barbarism seemed to be having the better of it, and what was there left to do but take an exceedingly long view of history and hope that the Old Mole of revolution was out there somewhere, tunneling away with pick and spade? But it's not a very dialectical way of looking at things to tell people to hang in there quietly until late capitalism fails and a new depression offers opportunity. In the elections' aftermath analysts were pointing to a couple of significant molehills.

It would be hard to find three men who have been more vilified in the British press than Tony Benn, Ken Livingstone and Arthur Scargill. Benn has been the excoriated leader of the 'hard left'; Livingstone was the militant leader of the Greater London Council, subsequently destroyed by Thatcher; Scargill led the miners. Amid Labour's disaster, candidates supporting their political traditions of militancy all did well. In the south a rainbow coalition saw four blacks entering Parliament, the first time in many years. Women, including an old-age pensioner, entered Parliament in greater numbers than ever before. The only self-declared gay member of Parliament, Chris Smith of Islington, increased his majority. In the north the hard left did well. In other words, those who said they would personally be overjoyed to see the ruling class swinging from the gibbet of history prospered. Those who said that reasonable people should sit down and discuss their differences in the prudent fashion did not.

The left presence in Parliament – the so-called Campaign Group, associated with Tony Benn – will now have a membership of about fifty, much stronger than the S.D.P., beloved of columnists but crushed in the elections. That presence has developed out of intense struggles and coalition building in such towns as London and Liverpool and such national campaigns as the miners' strike. It has been seasoned by ferocious witch hunting by the press. Its core members are a tougher lot than the Labourite rebels of yesteryear and have no problem identifying the City, finance capital and NATO as the enemy. The next phase will see battles at the regional, national and European levels.

And the overall lessons, particularly for (rainbow) coalition and movement builders in the United States? Without a coherent movement, militant leadership is nothing; and without a coherent and militant program, a movement will soon fall apart. All serious campaigns are long term, as the Old Mole knows so well.

The Nation

July 4, 1987

Its Ugly Head

It was strange to get back from England, home of the political sex scandal, to find that, several weeks after the downfall of Gary Hart, the morals of both Democratic and Republican candidates are prime topics of journalistic investigation.

The obvious candidate for these self-righteous probes is the Rev. Jesse Jackson. The mainstream press mostly hates Jackson, because he is black, because he is unafraid to express radical sentiments and because he is doing well in Iowa and could make a strong showing in the primaries. When he first ran, in 1984, the fire hoses were directed at Jackson for anti-Semitism and the origins of his finances. This is happening all over again, with allegations about his sex life thrown in for good measure. The moral contortions required to justify this kind of sex-police journalism are considerable. In Gary Hart's case, the fact that he had a long-term relationship with a woman in Washington was well known to journalists in town, including some at *The Washington Post*, long before Donna Rice entered the picture and Lynn Armandt rang up *The Miami Herald.* Hart, indeed, used to share a house with *The Post*'s Bob Woodward. When Hart ran for the Democratic nomination in 1984 none of these witting journalists taxed him in print with his extra-marital relationship or declared that it rendered him unfit for office. But with the scandal at flood tide *The Post* entered the sex-policing business, apparently at the vehement urging of managing editor Len Downie. The useful idiot was *Post* reporter Paul Taylor, who informed a Hart aide that the newspaper had detailed evidence of Hart's affair with a woman in Washington. It was subsequently alleged that this evidence took the form of a report by a private detective, but the private eye's dossier is a red herring. Those knowing reporters had simply decided to change the rules on Hart.

If *The Post* thought the woman's identity was newsworthy, it should have published her name. If it thought her identity was not newsworthy, it should not have published the information regardless of whether or not Hart stayed in the race. By sharing the knowledge with Hart but not with the public, *The Post* sought to force Hart from the race, which is not, supposedly, the role of a newspaper. All this makes Ben Bradlee and Downie blackmailers. Once the press gets into the sex-policing business, journalism will inevitably be brutalized to the level of the F.B.I. agents who put a bug under Martin Luther King's bed.

Since most male politicians have overtime libidos, perhaps, as Moore remarked to me, we will end up with an all-woman ticket, which would be no bad thing. So far, at least one Democrat has declined the race because he feels his personal life could not withstand scrutiny. On the other side the stories are even wilder. I was hardly off the plane when I heard that a leading Republican contender had an illegitimate child in 1981 and that *The Chicago Tribune* was about to report that George Bush has had no less than three mistresses. It will be a sad day for human values when they nail Bush for adultery rather than complicity in the murder of hundreds of Nicaraguan men, women and children.

The Nation

July 18, 1987

The Tricoteuse of Counterrevolution

When historians come to trace the rightward swerve of mainstream journalism in the United States over the past decade, they will certainly want to take a long and unloving look at Shirley Christian, recruited to *The New York Times* in the final phase of A.M. Rosenthal's tenure as executive editor. But though she has promulgated fantasies as egregious as those of another recipient of Rosenthal's patronage, Claire Sterling, Christian is today regarded in many quarters as a reporter and not a batty pamphleteer in the Sterling mold.

One of Christian's most effective coups as a right-wing propagandist was an article in the *Washington Journalism Review* for March 1982 which charged that U.S. reporters had been soft on the insurgent Sandinistas before their triumph, failing to disclose the rebels' true nature as cold-blooded Marxist-Leninists with hot lines to Havana and Moscow. This was widely read by publishers and editors, with the result that many reporters in Central America went through shameful contortions to avoid accusations that they were agents of a communist conspiracy.

All in all, in her stints at *The Miami Herald* and *The New York Times*, Christian has proved herself to be as rapturous an apologist for Latin American fascism as you will find writing in a major U.S. newspaper. By way of evidence, consider a June 7 report in *The Times* devoted to the proposition that the Argentine officers who murdered more than 10,000 people in the late 1970s were merely doing their best under trying circumstances and are now 'under siege' by a society reacting 'ungratefully.' Consider also her horrifying June 21 article about Chile headed 'An Unlikely Lab for Free Markets.'

Christian's theme in the latter piece was that the 'Chicago boys' – economists associated with the conservative school of Milton Friedman – have finally turned Chile around and thus their 'free-market policies' have been 'vindicated.' Readers probably nodded approvingly at the bland recitation of auspicious data: G.N.P. up 5.7 percent last year; unemployment down, at 8.8 percent. Christian noted decorously that 'some analysts question the merits of some of the free-market policies and wonder whether Chile's poor have actually shared in the economic revival,' then moved on to quote such Christian Democrats as Andrés Zaldivar, to the effect that the economy is 'successful,' and such ultrarightists as Pablo Barahona, who said that the situation in 1973 was 'so chaotic' that '80 percent of the people found it completely legitimate for the armed forces to take power, and completely legitimate that the armed forces put down the centers of resistance.'

What one would not know from this love poem is that the Chicago boys ran the economy into the ground with such effect that G.N.P. sank 15 percent in 1982 and another 0.7 percent in 1983. It had nowhere to go but up. And that was Chile's second depression, since G.N.P. had crashed by 13 percent in 1975. Essentially the Chilean economy has been stagnating for fourteen years, with national output per capita 20 percent lower than it was at the time of the U.S.-supported coup. Consumption levels have fallen 8 percent since 1973. Per capita income, adjusted for inflation, has dropped sharply, and the manufacturing sector has grown at a rate of 1.1

percent since the coup, as opposed to 4.1 percent in the eight years preceding the coup.

What is happening is that the World Bank, the I.M.F. and Chile's private creditors are financing a short-term boom to help Gen. Augusto Pinochet's 'pre-election' campaign, Chile's debt having just been renegotiated on extremely generous terms. As a flack for Pinochet, Christian naturally excludes from the unemployment figures the 11 percent who are underemployed – that is, skilled workers selling trinkets on street corners. She cites a stingy public works program as accommodating 4 percent of the work force, a statistic considered low by sources consulted in researching this column (the Center for International Policy and Americas Watch were particularly helpful). Unemployment in some poor neighborhoods of Santiago is running at 40 to 60 percent, and 10,000 people rely on soup kitchens. Thirty percent of the city's population has inadequate housing. Throughout the country 46 percent of children under the age of 10 are malnourished. More than a quarter of all Chileans live in extreme poverty.

The economic miracle touted by Christian has been the familiar one of a transfer of income from poor to rich. The slice going to the richest 20 percent has risen by almost one-third since 1970; the poorest 40 percent of Chileans make half what they did then. Between 1973 and 1980 the minimum salary was halved in real terms and has declined markedly in the past five years. Annual social spending has dropped about 20 percent from what it was in 1970, and the military budget has soared.

The Barahona quotation was particularly offensive because he was a prominent member of the right-wing campaign to discredit and sabotage the economy under Salvador Allende, whose coalition, despite that campaign, increased its votes from 36.3 percent in 1970 to 43.4 percent in 1973, only a few months before the coup. As my colleague Ken Silverstein, who assisted me with this item, remarked, talking to Barahona about the Allende years is like interviewing Goebbels about the Weimar Republic. Torture, unmentioned by Christian, is widespread. Last year 20,000 people were arrested in raids in the shantytowns.

This is not the first disgusting apology for fascism in Chile produced by Christian. In *The Miami Herald* for November 16, 1980, she hailed Chile's 'burgeoning, free-market economy' and declared that Pinochet's 'plebiscite' on a new constitution, held in early September of that year, fairly reflected the views of the Chilean electorate and that 'most Chileans like their ruler.' This, it should be recalled, was a plebiscite in which there were no lists of registered voters and in which blank ballots were counted as votes for the constitution. The Interior Ministry printed the ballots, and Pinochet's officials handled all vote counting. As a reporter for the *Los Angeles Times* commented at the time, 'The main challenge to the government was to take care not to announce more votes than there are Chileans.'

Imagine what Christian would have made of such conduct if it had occurred in Nicaragua. And this is the reporter *The New York Times* rushed to Washington to do a glowing interview with Lieut. Col. Oliver North shortly after he was fired. Maybe *The Times* and the joint Congressional committees should ask Christian what she knew and when she knew it.

The Nation

October 20, 1987

Rene's New Legs

MANAGUA – Young Rene, a few weeks short of his 18th birthday, was riding in an open truck with 24 companions last September 14 when he had direct personal experience of the diversion to the contras of profits from the sale of U.S. arms to Iran. As the truck rattled along the road from Pantasma to Wiwili in northern Nicaragua, the truck hit a land mine.

Rene was blown more than 100 feet away from the road, and when he was found he was thought to be dead. He opened his eyes in a wagon carrying the bodies of four of his friends. One of his legs was amputated right away and the other shortly after his mother arrived following a two-day trip from Managua by bus.

Rene grew up in a very poor neighborhood in Managua called San Judas, and by last Christmas he was back there to recuperate after spending the previous three months in a hospital four miles north of Jinotega. Then, two weeks ago, he went to the Hospital de Rehabilitacíon Alido Chavarria, which is where I saw him Monday.

Rene's legs end just about where he puts his hands in his trouser pockets. He's a few inches shorter than he used to be because the false limbs he is now perched on are designed to lower his center of gravity. On Monday he was doing well. In the previous two weeks he had graduated from beginners' stumps, low to the ground, through knee-high limbs, to his present eminence. Now he was strutting awkwardly through parallel bars to the applause of the physiotherapist, Rosa Olivares, who handles 40 patients a day.

As Rene clomped about, he crossed paths with Melba Campo, a woman in her late 30s trying out her new legs. Melba, mother of eight children ranging from 4 to 22 years of age, had been riding in a truck last September when she, too, had firsthand experience of the efforts of President Reagan,

Lieut. Col. Oliver North and others to outflank the Boland amendment. The truck she was in drove into an ambush, and a bullet went through her knee. Amputation followed soon after.

Watching Rene and Melba from the sidelines were four other Nicaraguans minus one or more of their limbs. They looked somewhat surreal since, resting after their exertions with the therapist, they had unstrapped their false legs and arms and held them casually, like soldiers at ease on the parade ground.

In fact, some of them were soldiers. Rene, for example, had been doing his two-year stint of militia duty, incumbent on all young Nicaraguans, when he was blown up. The truck Melba was in also had contained some militia people, which, in the bizarre value system of many North American observers of contra conduct, somehow makes it OK for Melba to be now less one leg as she looks after her ample family.

The rules of this particular game dictate that if Nicaraguans drive along the back roads unarmed, and not in the company of anyone who might protect them, they may die or be maimed at the hands of the contras, but they can at least be confident that in the eyes of caring North Americans their human rights were abused. Melba, on the other hand, made the fateful mistake of climbing into a truck with militiamen rather than setting off along the moonlit road, alone and on foot.

Francois Muller and Esteban Barahena, a Dutchman and a Guatemalan who run the only leg and arm factory in Nicaragua, at the Alido Chavarria Hospital, under the auspices of the Red Cross, are now working hard to train a permanent Nicaraguan staff to turn out prosthetic devices and make their country self-sufficient in this regard.

They are making good progress. A metal knee joint from the United States used to cost $250 and took a year to get to Managua. The locally made one costs $25. Over in the foot shop, Juan Loche was bonding rubber and cedar wood and producing 40 prosthetic feet a week, as nice an example of import substitution as one could hope to see, at a fraction of the cost of the American product.

The arm and leg factory is already working at full tilt, and even if the U.S. Congress kills funding for the contras tomorrow, Juan and his colleagues will have lifetime employment to look forward to, since Rene and Melba and the others will need to replace their false limbs every four years. Children, some 10 percent of the factory's clientele, need a refit every six months.

I asked Rene how he felt about the men who had blown his legs off. He said they were dung, and he had the same view of the ultimate sponsors in Washington of his misfortune. He said he wasn't surprised though. Rene smiled so much that he almost made one overlook the mutilation of a life now back in the wheelchair.

Later that day, I drove down to the old town of Granada where, for the past few weeks, the British director Alex Cox has been filming 'Walker,' the life of the mid-19th-century filibuster from Nashville who briefly became president of Nicaragua. It was a big night, for they were going to burn Granada, or at least the film-set edition of it erected in the main square. The flames spurted satisfactorily. A few hundred yards down the road was the church that William Walker actually had burned.

Such terrorism had been excitedly hailed in the United States where, for example, *Leslie's* magazine had said in late 1856, 'Walker ... is at last drawing unwilling praise from those not heretofore disposed to believe he was a man of successful destiny.... We have no mawkish sympathy with any semi-barbarians, whether they live on this continent, China or Japan. The only way to purify and enlighten such people is with powder and ball; they are the great corrective and reformatory measures of the age. Walker has done more for Nicaragua, for its real independence and final success as an independent country, than could have been accomplished by the ordinary "moral suasion means" in a century.'

I had asked Rene as I left whether he had any final message for the readers of *The Wall Street Journal,* and he said to tell them that Nicaragua will prevail, that the moral will always outweigh the material forces. These days journalists are rambling about the Nicaraguan-Honduran border with publicity-seeking contras, and obediently sending back promotional material to foreign editors who want only pictures of contras with guns in their hands and not anything of what the contras might have in mind for the future of the country they are being paid to attack.

A visit to the leg and arm factory and a talk with Rene and Melba offered a sounder perspective on this latter-day emulation of Walker, who was finally executed in 1860 in Honduras in the town Trujillo. The town is one of the sites of the U.S. military maneuvers and rehearsals for possible invasion of Nicaragua in mid-May, around the time Rene will be leaving the hospital with his new legs.

WSJ

January 29, 1988

Glasnost Turns Upside Down

In Moscow this week, under conditions of official sanction that have remained open to doubt until the very moment the participants are brought to order, a momentous gathering is taking place: the first conference of the

Federation of Socialist Clubs, which saw its public political birth at the end
of last summer.

Back then, between August 20 and 23, in a hall provided by officials of
the Moscow branch of the Communist Party, a conference of independent
left-wing reformers was held, the first such meeting to be sanctioned in
more than 50 years. It brought together about 600 representatives of 50
ecological, cultural and grassroots socialist groups. The proceedings were
tumultuous and at the end various associations emerged, among them the
Federation of Socialist Clubs, the core bodies being the Club for Social
Initiatives (CSI); Obshchina, a student group; and a youth group called the
Forest Folk. Also under the Federation's umbrella came such clusters as
the Young Communard Internationalists, the Che Guevara Brigade and
Red Sails.

Among the leading activists of the Federation is a 29-year-old socio-
logist called Boris Kagarlitsky. He was jailed in 1982 for advancing Euro-
communist notions and released 13 months later under Andropov. His
father is an expert on Kipling and Wells, and Boris speaks English fluently.

The intellectual and cultural distance of Kagarlitsky and his comrades
from the previous generation of dissidents has already been clear from a
long article he published in *New Left Review* in October/November 1987.
(His book *The Thinking Reed: Soviet Intellectuals, 1917–82* has been
published by Verso.) I first talked to Kagarlitsky in Moscow in the fraught
days after Mikhail Gorbachev's speech to the central Committee in
November. People were prowling through Gorbachev's speech, trying to
gauge the shifts and eddies in the political winds. The affair of Boris
Yeltsin, the Moscow party leader, was on every lip. Would he fall, and if so
what would that presage?

In those anxious moments Kagarlitsky and his association were active in
supporting Yeltsin. They were on the streets collecting signatures in his
support; calling for the minutes of the meeting that disgraced him to be
made public. Kagarlitsky was frankly pessimistic about the consequences of
Yeltsin's dismissal if it came. On the eve of this week's conference we
talked again. In what follows we can discern the stance – novel, portentous
and precarious – of an emergent socialist revival in the Soviet Union.

AC: *It's now nearly three months since Yeltsin's enforced resignation.
What changes has his fall produced?*

BK: There are contradictory signals. In some ways the situation is not
good. We can't get the level of *glasnost* that prevailed before November.
It's not that the conservatives are gaining the upper hand, but they are
more efficient and active than they were three months ago. But in another
way the situation is better, as witness the possibility of this conference.

AC: *What are you hoping for from your conference?*

BK: We want to democratize and formalize the structure of the Federation of Socialist Clubs, and produce a document to be used for its legalization. This is very important. Right now the state is drafting a law concerning 'voluntary organizations' that is actually worse than the existing law, which was promulgated under Stalin in 1932, so you can imagine how bad it is. We want a return to the revolutionary law of 1926, and the conference will be a venue to agitate for that. Also we want to plan practical actions concerning education, prices and so on. Official, or unofficial, either way, it is going forward.

AC: *I'd like you to go back now to Gorbachev's speech of November 2.*

BK: It was disappointing. People were waiting for more on Bukharin and something positive about Trotsky. Without saying something about Trotsky's participation in the establishment of Soviet power and the Red Army, you can't have a real history, which is very important in a country where people are crazy about history and are eager to get the empty parts of the past filled in. Trotsky is treated as a criminal for saying something about the peasantry that was really wrong, but Stalin is not treated as a criminal for putting the same outlook into actual practice. The solution should be to say, Trotsky made a lot of mistakes, but Stalin was a criminal. But we have the reverse situation. Another thing, there's an anti-Semitic campaign that says Trotsky was responsible for all the evils in Soviet history. It would have been important if Gorbachev had said something to counter the anti-Semitic arguments of fascist groups. There was one favorable mention of Bukharin, but all the major criticisms of him resurfaced in the speech. All the same, you mustn't say that it was a Gorbachev speech. It was a speech of the Central Committee delivered by Gorbachev. There had been many versions, but the final one was dominated by conservative thinking.

AC: *Could you draw a politico-intellectual map of what is going on?*

BK: One current that is gaining ground now is the neo-Stalinist one. It's a very real danger which under *perestroika* is becoming much more popular than it was under Brezhnev. Stalinists are trying to become populists. Traditional Stalinism was simply manipulation of the people by bureaucratic means, and propaganda was simply a matter of explaining orders to the people. Now hard-line Stalinism, for the first time in its history, is trying to conquer the hearts and minds of the people.

AC: *What is hard-line Stalinism today as a political project?*

BK: The Stalinist project states, first, we must re-establish the initial values of the system, not liberalize it, not change it, not democratize it, but recognize that the only way to solve our problems now is to turn back to the initial stage of the system, of the 1930s, to restore the same structures and the same mode of operating inside the structures. Second, as one Stalinist author wrote, we need a whip. That is, to make functionaries and workers more productive, democratic elements in the system should not be nurtured; per contra, some kind of moral terror should be established. Their economic project is simply to limit consumption, to destroy western patterns of consumption, thus to free up resources for the second industrialization, which means scientific breakthroughs with computers and so forth. What is interesting is that, psychologically and ideologically, these Stalinists have a lot in common with Reagan's neo-conservatives. They're always talking about national pride, traditional values, moral climate, while at the same time urging struggle against subversive external influences, liberal tendencies of an allegedly counterproductive nature. So, psychologically, neo-Stalinism is more like Reagan neo-conservatism than like old-fashioned Stalinism. Now, that kind of propaganda is very efficient – not among the youth but among the older age groups.

AC: *That's a strong intellectual current?*

BK: You can't find too many self-respecting intellectuals in this camp, but you do find these ideas at the popular level. Then there is a liberal, westernizing current, which, naturally, is better than neo-Stalinism but, all the same, is rather out of touch with reality. Its adherents want to copy western modes of management, thinking, behavior, without considering how ordinary people would react. They don't think about traditional Russian or Soviet culture. Not ideology but culture. Russian culture is not consumer-oriented or profit-oriented. Even Russian capitalism was inefficient because the capitalists were always more interested in the moral influence they could have on the workers than in the simple business of profit.

Then there is a current called cultural democracy. Those of this mind say they aren't interested in capitalism or socialism. They say, that's not our problem. They say they want free culture; under which system is a matter of indifference.

AC: *They don't think about the relations of production?*

BK: Not at all. It's a kind of historical liberalism. There's also a current – weakening – of liberal communism of the Twentieth party Congress genre, which is simply trying to say once again everything said during the Khrushchev period. It's influential among people in their 60s, for whom the Khrushchev period was very important, their shining hour. It has absolutely no influence on youth. There's also a growing nationalist tendency. It's not 100 per cent Stalinist but there is a de facto alliance between the two.

AC: *You're talking about Pamyat [the far-right nationalist, anti-Semitic group]?*

BK: They're anti-Semitic, saying the Jews are responsible for things that go wrong, force them to pay and so on; but the most important thing is that it is based on some feelings of frustration, especially among the petty bureaucracy – engineers, bureaucrats who are underpaid but not qualified for raises. They don't want competition, especially with Jews.

AC: *You're 29. What was formative for your generation – people from 25 to 34, say?*

BK: What was very important for my generation was the failure of 'official dissent', meaning the dissident movement of the sixties and seventies. It failed not only to change anything but also to establish any kind of ideological alternative. People ended up just saying that in principle you can't do everything in this country, so the only thing you can do is criticize it, for reasons of pure criticism – which means recognizing that you are a complete failure politically. They were as intolerant as the Stalinists. It became clear that this wasn't the way forward. If you read dissident materials, you find a lot of inverted Stalinists. For example, Stalinists say socialism is what exists in the Soviet Union now; the dissidents said the same thing. No democratic socialism is possible, say the Stalinists. Agreed completely, said the dissidents. So on theoretical points the dissidents agreed 100 per cent with the Stalinists. They simply changed plus to minus, 'good' to 'bad'. When Solzhenitsyn wanted to criticize western left-wingers, he always quoted Stalin.

So an alternative had to be discovered. We began to study Marx and Lenin, and other thinkers like Bukharin. Some people were interested in the role of Trotsky. People suddenly came upon the Gramscian tradition and discovered that there is a whole culture of the western left, as well as eastern European reformism. That was the first stage, which came about ten years ago. Now the problem is not to copy western models of thinking and acting but to find out the Russian way of being a left-winger.

AC: *How would you describe the crisis that produced such developments as glasnost, perestroika and so on?*

BK: Essentially, as the failure of the Brezhnevite historic compromise. Soviet society was never monolithic in the sense required by theories of totalitarianism developed by western Sovietologists. The Soviet system always included different social and political tendencies. The problem was, how to balance the different forces within the system? The Brezhnevite compromise was in a sense based on over-exploitation of the country's resources. Every group got its slice.

AC: *Not a zero-sum game.*

BK: No victims. Russia is resource rich, but there are limits. The Brezhnevite system arrived at its own limits, which accounts for the emergence of *perestroika* even before Brezhnev's death. With the start of the 1980s the limits were evident.

AC: *What sort of limits are you talking about?*

BK: Money, for example. You can't just print it. I'm not talking merely about salaries but about the costs of running the apparatus and the enterprises. If the enterprises – industries and so on – are losing money, then you have to subsidize them more heavily. And if each enterprise or sector wants to expand, and thus acquire more bureaucratic influence, you have to find even more money. So there was a financial crisis.

AC: *What does economic reform really add up to?*

BK: There are two concepts of economic reform. One is a kind of technocratic imposition of capitalist elements onto the existing system.

AC: *Material incentives?*

BK: Material incentives are not necessarily capitalist. When you think that human beings are animated *only* by material incentives, that is capitalism. For that matter one could ask, what is the alternative to the material incentives of the westernizers? The major incentive for Russian workers should be more free time.

AC: *That reminds me of a West Indian organizer in London, Darcus Howe, who once said to me, 'Less work, more leisure'.*

BK: People should have some say in how much they work. Given the choice, they may not work more but they will work better. The quality of their work will improve tremendously. Free time, incidentally, means a better quality of life, which in itself is much more than a matter of living standards.

AC: *What do the technocratic reformers want?*

BK: More power to managers, more strength to market forces but without abolishing the system of centralized bureaucratic planning, centralized distribution of resources. They just want to give managers more power in establishing prices for the final product. That's a bureaucratic-capitalist mix. The technocratic conservative faction says, let us do everything we did before, but better – better managers, better computers. One of our people said that these reformers are 'serf-owning liberals', as in the nineteenth century. They want some kind of feudal capitalism; that is, manipulative elitism. This means forcing ordinary people to pay for the crisis produced by bureaucratic management. If you don't abolish the central elements of bureaucratic management, the crisis will be reproduced again and again.

AC: *And the other currents?*

BK: A growing left-wing current expresses the necessity of democratizing not only the political system but also the relations of production, giving people more say in decision-making; more possibility for workers to elect their managers and also have direct democracy on the enterprise level. There are a few people in the official groups who support those ideals.

It's strange that the most radical people in the official sphere are culturally oriented. They are not thinking about enterprises and economic reforms. We have generated a lot of papers on the economy, but the intelligentsia is generally more interested in social and cultural problems, thus, surrendering the economic sphere to the conservatives. It's an important point about any cultural radicalism or liberalism. You try to establish cultural hegemony, but when you think you've got somewhere you find, finally, that the decision-making centers are inside the economy and you can't reach them. That's why the socialist club movement is important; we're trying to cross that gap between the socio-cultural and the economic spheres.

AC: *On the economic front what thinkers influence your group?*

BK: Internationally, some Hungarian economists, like Janos Kornai, though now we consider him to be moving to the right. Many are disappointed with his recent work, but his earlier work, from the fifties, on overcentralization influenced a lot of people. Also Vladimierz Brus, a Polish professor at Oxford. Some are interested in Scandinavian social democracy, though I don't know whether anything can be learned from that; I should stress that the people looking at Sweden are not social democrats. More broadly, people are very influenced by Marcuse and by Gramsci. Among the members of Obschchina [the student organization under the Federation of Socialist Clubs], Bakunin is very important. People are information-hungry and seize on any left-wing thought.

AC: *So how are you bringing your ideas to bear in the economic sphere?*

BK: For example, we've set up a group called the Campaign for Just Prices, trying to show that price rises are not only unnecessary and unjust but also anti-reformist. So, first, give more power in decision-making about prices to the local authorities – since they are more sensitive to market pressures and also to local needs, and will be forced to find a balance between the two forces – but at the same time democratize those local authorities. Second, you need to have differentiated prices functioning as a redistributive force, making richer people subsidize the consumption of those poorer than themselves. That means higher prices for luxury goods, restaurant meals and so on.

So far as distribution is concerned, we must move toward the market, which is the natural framework because it's the only way to establish the sovereignty of the consumer over the producer in the Soviet economy, which is producer-dominated. So in that sense some movement toward the market is needed. But the problem is to accompany that with a movement toward producers' democracy, toward more participation of the people in decision-making, with some redistributive mechanism which should be democratic.

AC: *There's a tendency in the west to read all recent Soviet developments in terms of Gorbachev's initiatives, which is surely a naive way of looking at events?*

BK: Under Brezhnev there was already some kind of bureaucratic pluralism, and today the power struggle is not more intense than in Brezhnev's last years, but it is more visible, because now we have *glasnost.*

There are bureaucratic institutions and groupings that have different political concepts. It's rather more of an American than a western European type of pluralism. We have a one-party and the Americans a two-party system, but in the sense that interest groups are more important than the formal political machinery, a certain similarity becomes evident. In that way the Soviet system is evolving toward an Americanized system, with much more weight attached to lobbies, political groupings inside the structure, which impose political constraints on the elite. What is truly new is that grassroots left-wing and right-wing tendencies are trying to influence that structure.

AC: *So the present plan of the clubs is to develop reinvigorated socialist concepts and try to circulate them?*

BK: Yes, and to become a real factor, a real pressure group, in the decision-making process. In local issues the groups can have great effect. With global problems it's not so easy. We've managed to get a lot of people at the official level to accept our role as a pressure group and to recognize that under *perestroika* it is normal for such groups to exist. Even those who don't identify themselves with us see that it's necessary to have forces on the left to counterbalance the right.

AC: *What are your hopes for the future? Are you optimistic or pessimistic?*

BK *(laughing)*: I should say I'm not completely pessimistic. The balance of forces is moving slightly toward the more conservative end. If you try to change things you always get some kind of polarization. So the left is growing stronger, as are the extreme right and the conservatives, and the liberal-moderate tendencies are going to be weaker.

AC: *Some dialogue between your group and people in western European and US left movements could obviously be important.*

BK: Often we are disappointed with the western left. It is pragmatic and de-ideologized, whereas Russian culture is ideological and value oriented. We're interested in the history of the New Left, also in the present peace groupings and the Green movement, because they are also value oriented. Of course, to those western value-oriented movements the Soviet left-wing groups must seem rather pragmatic, since we must necessarily avoid demagogy and formulate concepts engaging seriously with economic shortcomings and contradictions. Value-oriented groups in the west sometimes forget about practical contradictions. In principle we're open to dialogue with the western left.

The Nation

January 30, 1988

War on Peace

'Where were you hurt?' a journalist asked six-year-old Kenia Rodriguez, who was lying on a stretcher waiting to be evacuated to Managua on the same plane on which he and his colleagues had arrived.

'In my feet,' she answered calmly. Under the sheet covering her, she had no feet, only carefully bandaged stumps at the ends of her legs. 'My grandmother was killed, and my aunt was injured,' she added, still very solemn, as photographers crowded in for a shot.

Kenia lost her feet when *contras* mortared the town of Siuna on the Sunday before Christmas and hit her house. Residents said the mortaring was indiscriminate. Beside Kenia lay someone whose face was speckled black and gray with shrapnel wounds and who could not speak. Next was a young doctor shot when *contras* sprayed the ambulance in which he was riding with automatic rifle fire. The doctor with him had been killed. All were being taken for better care to Managua.

The Nicaraguan government called the attack on this and two neighboring mining towns in the northeast of the country 'propagandistic', meaning that it was intended to impress Congress rather than to have any lasting military impact. Phyllis Oakley at the State Department called the attacks a 'one-hundred per cent success'.

Anxious to answer the Reagan Administration, which applauded the strike as a signal of *contra* military effectiveness, the Nicaraguan government started flying journalists to the site early Tuesday morning, December 22, two days after the attack. It need not have bothered, for it was Siuna's misfortune to be hit twice that week. The second attack came on Friday, Christmas Day, when James LeMoyne landed a story on the front page of *The New York Times*. The *contras*, he wrote, had launched their 'largest and most successful military operation of the war', occupying the mining towns of Siuna for a whole day and of Bonanza for 'almost two'. This was news indeed, including for many of the journalists who were there at the same time as LeMoyne.

The Reagan Administration had clearly hoped that the long-awaited occupation of a town would shake loose votes in Congress from those who, not bothered by the provision of the Guatemala accords that specifically rules out aid to the *contras*, wonder whether the *contra* war yields value for money. 'Why can't they take a town?' senators demanded insistently last February in Foreign Relations Committee hearings. LeMoyne's story therefore announced exactly what the Administration had wanted to hear and assisted in the US politico-military attack on the accords.

Before continuing any further with the fateful conjunction of the *contras*, Siuna and LeMoyne, we should step back and look at the larger picture, in which, with the summit in Costa Rica over the weekend of January 15, the Reagan Administration tried to finesse – though 'finesse' is scarcely the word for the strong-arm tactics actually employed – the possibility that the Guatemala accords might inconvenience its plans in Central America. This would have been impossible without the supportive role played by the mainstream US press and, above all, by *The New York Times*. It is one of those moments in history, as in the reporting of the Paris accords on Vietnam in 1973, when the performance of the press as accomplice and handservant of the state can be discerned in every turn of phrase.

Start with the signing of the Guatemala (or Arias) accords on August 7 of last year. From that instant, when the usually nebulous concept of a 'peace process' began to assume concrete outline, *Times* reporting became increasingly attuned to the interests of the Administration and its *contras*. Remember first of all that a central feature of the accords was *simultaneity*, the stipulation that all five countries in the region would move jointly on implementing the provisions on reconciliation, cessation of support for insurgencies and so forth. Any serious reporting of the progress of the accords would therefore have looked at the performance of all five countries. But a search through available *Times* files from August 7 through January 18 found about one hundred stories on Nicaragua's compliance with the accords; half a dozen on El Salvador's; two on Honduras's; and none on Guatemala's.

This ignoring of simultaneity, and the corresponding stress on Nicaragua, was congenial to the Administration, since it suggested that everything depended on unilateral actions by Nicaragua. On October 26 Stephen Kinzer wrote, 'Pressure is building on Nicaragua's Sandinista leaders to take two key steps' in order to comply with the plan: (1) to release large numbers of prisoners; (2) to open cease-fire talks directly with the *contras*. On January 18, after Nicaragua had submitted to those two key demands, LeMoyne wrote, 'Mr Ortega responded with a shrewd tactical move by making what were probably the minimum concessions he could offer'. That same day Kinzer had a story remarking that 'Mr Ortega took the new steps toward compliance less than three weeks before Congress is scheduled to vote on new aid for the contras'. So submission is translated into cynicism, and unilateral moves not even required by the accords – which do not call for blanket amnesty or for talks with armed irregular forces – are translated into compliance.

The fervent coverage of the *contras* in *The Times* has been widely noted. There was LeMoyne's October 4 meditation in the Sunday *Magazine* on the obstacles large and small – childlike faith in US resolve, lack of political program – impeding the passionate but simple peasant fighters. A month later there was Lindsey Gruson's cover story on the welcoming emotions aroused by the *contras* on their forays into Nicaragua. And on December 29 there was LeMoyne's evocation, boxed and given special prominence by the editors, on the daily miseries of life for the Nicaraguan masses, 'for whom strong belief, except in God, seems largely to have fled'. Now we have the deep-sixing by *The Times* and almost all the mainstream press, with the exception of Peter Ford in *The Christian Science Monitor* for January 15, of the International Commission on Verification and Follow-up (CIVS). This was the body charged with monitoring compliance with the accords.

Right before the Costa Rican summit the CIVS issued a unanimous report markedly sensitive to the delicate terrain over which it was proceeding. As one non-Central American official of the commission quoted by Ford said, 'Our conclusions are vague because the Central Americans were involved in drawing them up, and Honduras, El Salvador, and Guatemala were watering them down all the way'. For example, the report originally said that amnesties in El Salvador, Guatemala and Honduras were not effective because of the practice, in all three countries, of killing prisoners. This was ultimately changed to say that killing of prisoners was the practice of the countries' 'previous governments', a phrase inserted at the insistence of the three culprits.

The commission did make one unequivocal statement:

> In spite of the exhortations of the Central American presidents the government of the United States of America maintains its policy and practice of providing assistance, military in particular, to the irregular forces operating against the government of Nicaragua. The definitive cessation of this assistance continues to be an indispensable requirement for the success of the peace efforts and of this Procedure as a whole.

This was reported by Ford, and Julia Preston made a slight mention of it in *The Washington Post.* LeMoyne, in an incredible lie, had only this to say about the CIVS report:

> A meeting of the verification commission ended last weekend with little agreement. The commission is made up of members of the United Nations, the Organization of American States, the so-called Contadora Group of Latin countries and the five Central American signers of the peace treaty.

That was it: completely false on the matter of 'little agreement', since the document was a unanimous release; reprehensible in its failure to mention the explicit statement against US aid.

The final CIVS report should not have discommoded the Administration's four proxy states in Central America, yet they have effectively put an end to the commission by rejecting its chief operational recommendation – namely, the institution of verification procedures that could be somewhat objective in evaluating all the countries' compliance. The report suggested that teams from the UN and the OAS might be set up to carry out on-site inspections. This is unacceptable to the United States, so it is unacceptable to its dependencies; therefore, the summit in Costa Rica ended with El Salvador and Honduras refusing any outside presence and saying that only the presidents of the countries could decide whether they were complying. With the burial of the international commission the Administration has succeeded in eliminating every independent actor who might mediate in Central America, this campaign beginning with the scuttling of Contadora and ending with the total exclusion of non-client states from the 'peace process'.

So much for the larger picture; now back to Siuna.

LeMoyne was not the only journalist to visit the town just before Christmas. Among those making the trip was Mark Cook, the person inquiring of little Kenia Rodriguez where she had been hurt. Cook has been living in Nicaragua off and on since 1982, and permanently since 1985. He is a freelance journalist, *inter alia* sending reports to WBAI's 'Contragate' program. What follows is essentially his commentary on the attack, and on LeMoyne's coverage of it.

Problematic for LeMoyne was that there is no material evidence that the *contras* did occupy the town, and plenty that they did not. 'For reasons that are not clear', LeMoyne wrote, 'they did not destroy several heavy trucks and the mine works here. They also failed to attack or shell the headquarters of the 366th Sandinista Army Brigade, even though it was immediately in front of them'.

The reason was clear enough to residents whom Cook and other journalists interviewed. The *contras* did not occupy the town; they mortared it from surrounding hills. They did enter two barrios and briefly passed one entrance to the huge mine during the fighting, but fled when shooting picked up. They forced terrified people who had taken refuge in the La Luz church to chant *contra* slogans while a film crew recorded the event, residents report. (Most in Siuna's population of 7,500 are mine workers, and strongly pro-Sandinista.)

LeMoyne quotes one of his sources as saying that people 'implored the rebels not to destroy the mine works, a major source of work here'. Probably they did. Did the Sandinista Army commanders also implore them not to destroy the army command post, which is in the center of town?

'Ten residents said in separate interviews,' LeMoyne goes on, 'that the rebels held the town for about eight hours and walked around the center talking to civilians. They said there was no looting or abuse of civilians.'

What was the Sandinista Army doing during all this time? LeMoyne's article doesn't say, but on the plane taking him and the other reporters back to Managua, he said he had been told that forty Sandinistas had been killed on the outskirts of the town and the rest had fled, leaving the *contras* to have the run of the town. But how could they have fled, since, according to LeMoyne, the *contras* had attacked the village from five directions? Witnesses other journalists spoke with said fighting continued without interruption.

As for abuses, LeMoyne conceded at the end of the story that 'the rebels appear to have won few friends in the towns by causing so many civilian casualties' – nineteen killed and one hundred wounded. He did not report that people living in an isolated cooperative a few miles outside of town told journalists that the *contras*, unable to find the residents, who were hiding, destroyed most of their food supply, setting fire to bags of rice and bayoneting cans of lard that went rancid in the heat. In another incident, they opened fire on civilians hiding in a tunnel, killing two adults and five children.

'The rebels occupied Siuna and Bonanza, where they engaged government troops and destroyed an important radar station, a large arms and munitions warehouse, ... among other targets,' LeMoyne wrote. Those two targets, however, were not, as is implied, inside the town. The radar was on a high hill almost a mile from Siuna, from which the *contras* were raining down mortars, and the weapons warehouse, which he did not visit, was about three and a half miles outside the town. Their destruction does not support his claim that the *contras* occupied Siuna. On the contrary, the extraordinary violence inflicted by the *contras* on the outskirts of the town and the indiscriminate mortaring of residential districts suggests the usual *contra* tactic of molesting relatively unprotected areas. LeMoyne's claim that Siuna was occupied is rendered all the more bizarre given that residents were burying *contra* bodies in common graves while the journalists were in the town. Cook says that had *contras* been even temporarily in control they would have followed their invariable practice of burying the bodies separately and secretly, in respect for their fellows and for the sake of military security.

LeMoyne claims that reporters could not go to Siuna until Wednesday. Untrue. One batch of reporters flew from Managua to the site early Tuesday morning and were there when Cook, LeMoyne and the others arrived. That second contingent left Managua Tuesday afternoon, but because the landing strip at Siuna cannot handle a jet, the reporters had to fly to Puerto Cabezas and there wait for a propeller plane to go the rest of the trip. The government was trying to evacuate the wounded and fly in troops to pursue the retreating *contras*, thus the delay until Wednesday is hardly surprising.

LeMoyne also says that reporters were not allowed to visit Rosita or Bonanza and were permitted only a few hours in Siuna. Completely false, says Cook. The journalists, offered the opportunity to visit all three towns, asked to visit only one because they wanted to get back to Managua to file their stories on an already old event. The military imposed no restrictions on the visit to Siuna and provided trucks to take journalists where they wanted to go. Several asked and were taken to the destroyed arms and ammunition shed, considering it the best photo opportunity.

Despite the mortar attacks that 'inadvertently' hit a lot of homes, LeMoyne considers it 'credible' that the *contras* have 'extensive support in this area' and that 'local peasants provided them with key intelligence' to prepare the surprise attacks. 'Accounts by soldiers and villagers indicate that the guerrillas dominate this zone of Zelaya Department.' This is typical of *The Times*'s propaganda on behalf of the *contras*, recommending itself with the word 'dominate' and avoiding any distracting facts: that Zelaya is thinly populated, thick with virgin forests, relatively undefended by Sandinista Army regulars and near to the *contras*' Honduras lifeline; also that in exercising their dominance the *contras* have twice kidnapped Sister Sandra Price, a Catholic nun from the United States in Siuna; that last year they kidnapped a pro-revolution lay churchworker, later found castrated and otherwise mutilated; that at about the same time they burned a Catholic mission to the ground.

Cook says that sympathy with the *contras* among what rural population there is has been declining, not increasing. Much of the rural area around the mines is populated by Sumo and Miskito Indians, whose support for US-controlled forces has dropped off in recent years because of the government's Atlantic Coast autonomy project, which encompasses the mining region, and because of *contra* abuses, including those by the now virtually defunct Indian *contras*.

Every now and again the artful accomplices of the Reagan Administration do a minor course correction to show an independent turn of mind. On January 20, LeMoyne cited 'diplomats and Government officials' in Costa Rica as contending that the 'peace treaty is in danger[!] of being converted into a series of demands directed only at Nicaragua'. This is what Noam Chomsky calls 'safe criticism', salve on a reality already savaged beyond recognition. Thus the occasional proposition that US 'plans' to continue aiding the *contras* 'appear' to inhibit peace. Remember that since August 7, amid the near total silence of the mainstream press, the US government has stepped up surveillance flights and dispatched, courtesy of the CIA and in direct defiance of the Guatemala accords which it has pledged to uphold, cargo after cargo to the *contras* – two to three airdrops per day. One small component of those supplies probably blew off Kenia Rodriguez's feet. As she hobbles through life on her wooden stumps, she will have every right to blame the Free Press of the United States for being among those responsible for her condition.

The Nation

April 9, 1988

What Did You Say He Wanted?

Mulling the situation over the day after Super Tuesday, Jerry Roberts, political editor of the *San Francisco Chronicle*, proposed that 'Jackson's vote in black districts resembled the totals that dictators pile up in no-opposition elections.' *Sic semper tyrannis.* Mulling further, a *New York Times* editorial at the end of March said that support for Jackson amounted to political alcoholism, ruinous to the Democrats, who had been twelve-stepping along nicely since the McGovernite bout with the bottle back in 1972. That same day Anthony Lewis said it was 'moving' to see Jackson triumph over racism, then urged Democrats to vote for a white man. That's liberalism for you. Viva Mondale!

   The designated candidate of drunks and party wreckers, quizzed still about what he wanted, could remember Michigan, where he pulled an average of 2,000 people a rally, outside Detroit. The Democratic Party did its best to keep democracy at bay. In Flint, there are normally 91 polling places open. On caucus day, March 26, there were nine. Voting could take place only between 10 a.m. and 4 p.m., when many auto workers were on shift down in Pontiac. There were absentee ballots only for Jews and Seventh Day Adventists, so the shut-ins – poor, frail and mostly for Jackson – could not vote.

   Coleman Young, Mayor of Detroit, backed Dukakis, and this got respectful play in the press as a sign that mature Afro-American opinion knew on which side its bread was buttered. Earlier in the week the mature Irish-American William Shannon offered the view in *The Boston Globe* that maybe sometime soon a black candidate's day would come, but 'he would have to be a candidate with a cool, conservative style and a message that was mainstream and not threatening to the status quo'. In other words, that noted Afro-American Al Gore. The UAW's candidate had been Richard Gephardt, and the poor man kept asking in bewilderment why the union that had written his protectionist bill and virtually invented his candidacy had suddenly deserted him. Former UAW president Doug

Fraser endorsed Dukakis. Gephardt stood in Flint, eyed curiously by about a hundred people while the UAW officials kept a prudent distance, knowing that the man was doomed and that a graveside nod from Solidarity House would only highlight the union's inability to sway its members. Those members were busy cheering Jackson, in rallies at Local 600 in the Rouge plant or outside the closed Fisher Body plant in Flint, where the sit-down was held in the winter of 1936–37.

By early afternoon many caucus centers in Flint had run out of ballots. The turnout was much larger than expected. Voters waited patiently, an hour or even two. Then came the preliminary results: in the first ward, Jackson, 2,050; Dukakis, 67. Michael Moore, who's originally from Flint, says that the car horns started sounding in triumph when the magnitude of the victory became known. it was a giant Fuck You to the system, to received opinion, to the experts, to Coleman Young, to the UAW and to all the motions and devices of Business as Usual. The auto plants in Flint have lost 40,700 jobs in the past ten years. The official rate of unemployment is 15.2 per cent; the real rate is at least double that, with the rate for blacks at 50 or 60 per cent and more than 80 per cent for black youth.

The message Jackson had been bringing to these angry and desperate people was the same one he had brought to the AFL–CIO in Austin, Texas, back in January: 'Are the South Koreans and Taiwanese taking jobs from the US? Let's look at that, friends. GM announced it was closing seven plants and 30,000 jobs last November, then announced 30,000 jobs in Korea. The South Koreans are not taking jobs from us. GM took jobs to them. The number one exporter from Taiwan is not the Taiwanese. It's GE, which owns RCA, which owns NBC, which advertises "Buy American". Makes you feel guilty if you don't. While they take jobs from America to Taiwan, make the product with cheap labor there, sell for high prices here.'

The evening Jackson wiped out Dukakis and Gephardt in Michigan, one could feel the air literally quiver with agonized appraisals, as the opinion formers finally took heed of the here and now, and then hurried to oppose it. While the horns were honking in Flint, a few hundred miles southeast in Washington the political and journalistic elites were resplendent in white ties and long dresses at the Gridiron Club dinner, poking decorous fun at one another. The vote from Michigan came as the finger writing on the wall at Belshazzar's feast: 'Mene, mene, tekel, upharsin,' which translates roughly as 'The game is up'. The first thought was to inject Dukakis with powerful rhetorical vitamins; the second, that this was impossible and that the only viable Democrat with enough blarney in him to save the day was Mario Cuomo, god from the machine.

In their agony, the Gridiron Democrats urged journalists to turn up the heat on Jackson. In this endeavor there are a number of approaches. First, urgent stress on the fact that Jackson should never have been born. For by being born, he ultimately ended up winning the Michigan caucuses, thus facing the Democratic leadership with the prospect of denying the nomination to the most popular candidate or, supposedly, losing in November to George (Just Fly Low) Bush. The second approach is to stress that Jackson has thus far been the beneficiary of racial politesse, with reporters too sensitive to his ethnic identity to give him the same sort of pitiless leathering accorded Dukakis or Gore. *The Wall Street Journal* quoted Mark Siegel, a Democratic National Committee member, as saying, 'It's time for the press to scrutinize Jackson as a serious potential nominee'. Siegel is an Israel-right-or-wrong man, and his remark translates as 'It's time to give Jackson another serious going-over as an anti-Semitic malfeasant of Federal funds whose campaign platform has been drafted by Arafat and Soviet moles working in the Institute for Policy Studies.' This approach, by traditional dialectical entrechats performed by the Ben Wattenberg corps de ballet, becomes the third line of action against Jackson: serious Red-baiting as a Castro-loving comsymp who will, if blessed with any further irresponsible support in the polling booth, cause the Dow Jones index to drop 200 points just as a warning of what could happen if he continues his mad chatter about raising marginal and corporate tax rates. Wall Street has not been deeply uneasy about any candidate for a long time. If Jackson continues to prosper, the uproar at Belshazzar's place all those years ago will be mild by comparison, however many times he appears at a window with Clark Clifford and even though the more farsighted strategists of capital should realize that, given the new terms of global competition drawn by Gorbachev, a populist black candidate, safely lodged in the Democratic Party, is exactly what the US system needs for renewed validation in the eyes of the world.

The Nation

April 23, 1988

The Kiss of Death

It should not, at least in theory, require a Democratic presidential primary to remind one of the foulness of New York City's political culture, which is now of unmatched toxicity. New York is, after all, a city that boasts among its spiritual guides Ed Koch, Al D'Amato, Daniel Patrick Moynihan,

Cardinal O'Connor, George Steinbrenner, Morton Downey, Jr., Howard Stern and A.M. Rosenthal. No other town in the United States condemns its inhabitants to listen to men like these on a virtually daily basis. Hardened though one might be, seasoned by the memory of similar primaries in years gone by, the effect of New York on the campaign has been striking nonetheless. The place really does bring out the worst in people.

Only New York provokes, at this most morally degraded intensity, the sickening rhetorical rituals mandatory in grubbing for the Jewish vote. First came the grotesque spectacle of Al Gore baiting Michael Dukakis for insufficient fervor toward Israel. Everyone knows that Dukakis has been a model of traditional Democratic cowardice on this issue, though less craven than Gore, who openly went begging to pro-Likud contributors, from whom Dukakis kept his distance. Then Gore got respectful attention in the press for proclaiming that Jesse Jackson had disqualified himself from pretension to high office by placing Israeli and Palestinian aspirations on the same moral plane.

Was it not possible for one of those editorialists, columnists or reporters to ask Gore and Dukakis how they felt about Israeli soldiers forcing an Arab up a telegraph pole until finally he was electrocuted? Or to ask if Gore or Dukakis was prepared to condemn the Israeli Army for blowing up houses in the village of Beita *after* the army had established that Tirza Porat had been killed by a shot from the Gush Emunim fanatic Rumam Aldubi? Does anyone feel any qualm that here are men seeking high office who have nothing to say about the forcible internment without trial of almost 5,000 people; who have felt themselves unable to criticize the Israeli Prime Minister, Yitzhak Shamir, for calling Palestinians 'grasshoppers'? Why doesn't the press, eager to remind the world for the millionth time about Jackson's 'Hymietown', challenge the two white candidates to speak out on this or any of the innumerable racist statements from Israeli leaders about Palestinians?

In the end New York showed that in a crunch Jackson could be as spineless as his rivals. On *Face the Nation* on April 10 he was asked by Lesley Stahl, 'Would you sit down with Arafat?' Jackson: 'I would not. It is not necessary to do that. We must not equate Arafat and the PLO with a sovereign people – the Palestinian people. ... We have to search for the quality and combination of leadership on both sides, whether it's Abba Eban or Peres on the one hand, or more sensitive Arabs or Palestinians on the other.' His concern, Jackson told Stahl, was 'that we must somehow get Israel beyond the burden of occupation, and the Palestinians beyond the pain of being occupied'. Jackson made these evenhanded observations shortly after Porat's funeral, at which Israel's Minister of Religious Affairs, Zevulun Hammer, said, 'Beita does not exist on the map of Israel. A settlement should be built there and be named Tirza Porat'. Shamir said the killing strengthened the determination to hold on to all of the 'land of Israel'. Some burden.

If Jackson ends up talking like a *New York Times* editorial, then what is the point of the Jackson campaign? A lot of American Jews have supported Jackson precisely because he has – though decreasingly so in recent weeks – refused to abide by the moral double standard endemic to all discussion of Israel and the Palestinians. Which is the more morally compromising embrace for an American politician: a hug from Arafat or one from Shamir? It is Shamir and his Likud associates who speak of obliterating Palestinians, of deporting them. It is Labor's Rabin who approves the internments, curfews, mutilations, blowings up, deportations. How many US politicians feel compromised by their embraces?

Jackson told Lesley Stahl he would not talk to Arafat until the PLO leader voiced explicit recognition of Israel's right to exist. A few weeks ago I wrote here that Arafat should be clearer about this, if only to overwhelm by repetition the refusal of the US press to recognize recent PLO statements on this subject. (I also suggested he might shave so as to look better on network TV, which was cheap. If he looked like Pat Boone it wouldn't make any difference.) But Arafat was explicit shortly thereafter in an interview on March 12 with Youssef Ibrahim and Anthony Lewis, both of *The New York Times*. As Ibrahim wrote, 'When Mr Arafat was asked again if he was prepared to make peace with the Israeli government he responded, "Yes"', definitely reiterating respect for the relevant UN resolutions. Anthony Lewis confirmed this the following day. Jackson may be short on advice, but surely someone can clip the papers for him. When the candidates sitting in the *New York Times* offices urge Arafat to accept 242 and 338, why don't their interviewers remind them of Arafat's recognition of same, recorded in the questions' own newspaper?

The candidate's miserable performance with Stahl provoked a hail of furious phone calls to the Jackson campaign. Hani Masri, an Arab-American and Republican, debated whether to cancel a big fundraiser for Jackson in Washington. James Abourezk, head of the American-Arab Anti-Discrimination Committee, said, 'If you're going to give up your principles, get something out of it. Jackson got nothing. He can't just slowly back away from what he said to Stahl; he has to make a substantive correction.' By the next morning Jackson had invited Edward Said to stand by his side at a political breakfast and subsequent press conference, and when asked by Gabe Pressman of the NBC affiliate in New York whether he supported the idea of a Palestinian state, Jackson said 'Absolutely,' without equivocation. But neither then nor in subsequent debates did he correct his statements on *Face the Nation*.

The Jackson campaign should stop being defensive and remember some important points. A Gallup poll in March showed that 58 per cent of all

Americans believe that Israel should recognize the PLO; 53 per cent say the United States should deal with the PLO; 42 per cent say US aid to Israel should be decreased, while only 7 per cent say it should be increased. Second, as a sovereign people, which Jackson says they are, the Palestinians should be able to select their own representatives. No one tells Israel who should represent it. Third, on the issues of land for peace and self-determination, the United States is outside the world consensus of Common Market countries, the African bloc, the Islamic bloc, the Non-Aligned countries, the Socialist bloc. Finally, Jackson should remind the country that it is the Palestinians who are being interned, expelled and tortured.

The Nation

May 26, 1988

'Death Squads' in Northern Ireland

Say the words 'death squad' in Ireland and people won't automatically conjure up Central America. Chances are they will think about Northern Ireland and Mrs Thatcher and what her government has been sanctioning and condoning. Writing as one who grew up in County Cork, I don't think there have been many moments in my lifetime, certainly not since Bloody Sunday 1972, when troops shot unarmed people in the streets of Derry, that the British state has been held in lower esteem by Irish people.

Why is Britain so unpopular? Three words – Stalker, Birmingham and Gibraltar – gesture to the reasons. First, the British policeman John Stalker has said that the inquiry bearing his name turned up evidence that a policy of state-sanctioned murder – death squads in fact – was operating in Northern Ireland, in which suspects were being gunned down without benefit of arrest, interrogation or trial. A British government official conceded to Parliament the disturbing implications of the inquiry but proclaimed that 'national security' compelled it to be closed off.

No less infuriating to Irish people was the refusal by Britain's judicial system to acknowledge that men and women in all likelihood innocent – the Birmingham Six – remain in prison. They were arrested after a bomb explosion had killed twenty-one people in Birmingham. Subsequent investigation has shown that confessions were consequent upon beatings, that forensic evidence was dubious, that the guilty parties are at large. But a British judge rejected convincing indications of a terrible miscarriage of justice. The Birmingham Six remain behind bars and many Irish people think 'national security' is the decisive factor in their continued incarceration.

The killings in Gibraltar are freshest in mind. Three members of the Irish Republican Army, two men and a woman, were shot to death by British security forces, who claimed their victims were about to detonate a terrorist bomb. But the British government's account turned out to be false. A British TV network aired – over fierce pressure from Mrs Thatcher and her forces – eyewitness accounts indicating that the unarmed trio were murdered, and the BBC, increasingly gagged and servile in the Thatcher years, has come up with similarly disturbing accounts.

The fury in Ireland is echoed by Irish Americans, who are baffled by the extraordinarily genteel way these episodes have been handled by the press here. Now the role of the US press is of great importance, as the British well understand. An alert press means an alerted public, hence responsive politicians and ultimately pressure on the British government to clean up its act. Any equitable political solution in Northern Ireland depends in part upon the confidence of all parties – Catholic as well as Protestant – in the lawfulness and impartiality of government. As the foregoing material suggests, no such confidence now exists; nor will it till the British government stops flouting elementary justice, whether with a shoot-first, ask-questions-afterward policy, or with its Diplock courts where people in Northern Ireland can be bundled into prison virtually without due process.

Well aware of the importance of the US press, the British run an efficient public-relations campaign, blessed with great cooperation on the part of American journalists, as a remarkable account by Jo Thomas in the May/June issue of the *Columbia Journalism Review* (and reprinted in the June issue of the more widely circulated *Irish America*) underlines.

Ms Thomas, now teaching at a journalism school in Illinois, was previously a correspondent for the *New York Times* and a journalist for eighteen years. From 1984 to early 1986 she was based in the *Times*'s London bureau, making forays to Northern Ireland. Ms Thomas narrates how she began investigating the involvement of police and British Army undercover units in what she calls 'questionable shootings'. She completed two stories before, as she says, 'I was abruptly ordered home'. By her count, between 1982 and 1987 there were at least forty-seven suspicious shootings by police or undercover army units. At least twenty-one of the victims were unarmed and the rest, in Ms Thomas's opinion, were probably given no opportunity to surrender before being killed.

Why was she suddenly recalled? Ms Thomas says a senior editor told her it was because she had been paying too much attention to Northern Ireland, and she sets this charge in context. It is easy, she writes, for American journalists in London to feel important and well informed. They get their weekly confidential briefing at 10 Downing Street. They are invited to dinner at the best places: 'No one understands hierarchies better than the British, and they are careful to make close personal friendships with members of important American news organizations. It makes us reluctant to offend, especially to bring up the touchy subject of the war, which they refuse to call a war, in Northern Ireland.'

Anyone following US reporting from Britain will recognize the accuracy of this. Anthony Lewis, a former *New York Times* bureau chief in London, still visits Glyndebourne every year and remits to his readers paeans to the British Way of Life of a sentimentality unrivaled since Rupert Brooke's World War I poem 'Grantchester'. A subsequent bureau chief, R.W. Apple Jr., seemed as determined as Mr Lewis to savor an England perfumed with fine claret and the values of an eighteenth-century squire. When American journalists meet British bobbies ('smiling and unarmed', of course, though the opposite is usually true) or members of the upper classes, their backbones and prose turn to the neuro-physiological equivalent of a British nursery pudding staple, junket.

Ms Thomas says that the good favor of her colleagues and hosts subsided abruptly as she embarked upon her inquiries in Northern Ireland: 'A senior editor, who kept a home in London as well as New York ... began telling me to stay out of Northern Ireland. A high-ranking British official, who in the past had close ties to the intelligence community in Northern Ireland, took me to lunch and suggested that I drop my investigation in exchange for a lot of access to the secretary of state for Northern Ireland.' Her mail arrived opened. Finally she was recalled.

Reflecting upon her experience, Ms Thomas analyses acutely the biases afflicting most American reporting on Northern Ireland, from the political reverberations of using 'Ulster' to denote six counties, to the way in which a crime by British security forces is often described not as such, but as 'a propaganda victory' for Sinn Fein. It is rare for a mainstream journalist to be so forthright, and perhaps it will have an effect. 'If a police force of the United Kingdom could, in cold blood, kill a seventeen-year-old youth with no terrorist or criminal convictions, and then plot to hide the evience from a senior policeman deputed to investigate it, then a shame belonged to us all,' former Deputy Chief Constable John Stalker writes. 'This is the act of a Central American assassination squad – truly of a police force out of control.' Mr Stalker took his responsibilities seriously and so, too, should the US press. It would make a difference.

WSJ

May 27, 1988

Where Was George?

'Now, you can deny US government involvement in drugs all you want, but the patterns are there and the players are there popping up again and, you know, eventually somebody's going to realize what the truth is.' Ramon Milian-Rodriguez, PBS, *Frontline*, May 17.

These are difficult days for Vice President George Bush. Even as he goes about the country promoting the administration's anti-drug campaign, evidence rolls forth demonstrating the involvement of his office and, informants vigorously suggest, himself with drug smugglers in the efforts to supply the Nicaraguan contras. Last week, Darryl Gates, the police chief of Los Angeles, accompanied Bush and platoons of photographers to a 'crack house' recently stormed by the LA police. Bush peered earnestly at the wreckage (as an earnest peerer there are few to beat George) and claimed that in the war with the narco-terrorists there would be, at least from him, no quarter, no truce. But the headlines from Washington the same day carried more news to the effect that the Reagan administration was trying to extricate something from the far more serious wreckage of its efforts to unseat General Tony Noriega, by offering Tony a deal whereby he leaves office for a brief spell, having nominated his own successor.

The trouble is that far too many people in the United States for the Vice President's political comfort think that somehow he's been involved in monkey business with the same narco-terrorists he denounces. Pollsters chatting to their cluster groups found about a month ago that Bush and drugs seem somehow to have got unwholesomely welded in the popular mind. This helps explain why he is now ten points behind Michael Dukakis, the likely Democratic nominee, in the polls, though I don't think it needs the drug smuggling imputation to explain Bush's low standing. I've never met an audience that likes the man. Right-wing Republicans think he's a stooge for the trilateralist banking conspiracy. Liberal Republicans think he's a sell-out to the right.

Bush's spirits cannot have been refreshed by a story in the US edition of *Newsweek* for May 23, partly echoing a piece by Allan Nairn in *The Progressive* a couple of months ago. Richard Brenneke, an Oregon businessman with previous connections to both the CIA and the Israeli Mossad, has now publicly disclosed that he was a point man in an operation called the 'Arms Supermarket'. In this affair, the Colombian Medellin cocaine cartel, hoping for political advantage, put up money and planes to fly arms to the contras. The arms came from Eastern Europe, acquired there by Brenneke, and were flown to Panama under the supervision of General Noriega's confidant, the former Mossad man Michael Harari.

The drug cartel used the same planes to fly drugs to the United States. In a sworn deposition Brenneke has told a Senate Foreign Relations subcommittee, headed by Massachusetts senator John Kerry, that Bush's 'National Security' aide Donald Gregg was the Washington contact for the operation, and that when he first queried the Israeli contacts on the propriety of the deal they gave him Gregg's office number to call. Brenneke – who says that one of the reasons he is surfacing this information is because of a young relative's drug addiction – discloses that he flew with one such drug shipment to Amarillo, Texas, in mid-1985 and tried to tell Gregg what was going on, but received the curt response, 'You do what you were assigned to do. Don't question the decision of your betters'. Kerry's investigators say they have corroborated part of Brenneke's story from Noriega's former head of political intelligence, José Blandon, and from another former Mossad agent.

In his personal notebooks Oliver North made frequent references to the 'Arms Supermarket'. An entry for July 12 1985, recently released by a congressional committee reads, '[White House deletion] plans to seize all ... when Supermarket comes to a bad end. $14 M[illion] to finance came from drugs.' The denials from Gregg that either he or the Vice President knew any of this are looking increasingly bizarre, particularly given Bush's term as CIA director in the mid-1970s when, as he himself likes to put it on other topics, he surely came to know the world as it is, not as it should be. Noriega was on the CIA payroll for a long time. CIA agents tipped off Noriega and his men to the whereabouts of Noriega's foe Hugo Spadafora. Spadafora was soon thereafter found decapitated in Costa Rica just over the frontier from Panama. When the finger of suspicion naturally swivelled towards Noriega, the CIA sent one of their people to Panama from Costa Rica to claim publicly that evidence disclosed that Spadafora had been done in by the Salvadoran FMLN.

As usual it is Noriega, who has done his bit in coarsening the tone of international diplomacy, who put the matter most pithily. Noriega's former sidekick, Col. Roberto Diaz Herrera, says Noriega told him gleefully, 'I have Bush by the balls'. The problem for Bush is that the historical record suggests an intimate relationship between drug smugglers and US covert operations, and this brings us back to Ramon Milian-Rodriguez, whose remark stands at the head of this article.

Milian-Rodriguez, who is now serving a 43-year sentence in a US federal prison for money laundering on behalf of the Colombian Medellin drug cartel, was first recruited as a brilliant young accountant by Manuel Artime in Miami in 1972. Artime was one of the CIA's favorite Cubans, running operations for the Agency out of southern Florida. One of Milian-

Rodriguez's early assignments was to arrange the payments for the Water-gate burglars, and one of his last tasks, before going behind bars in January 1986, was to pass just under $10 million from the cartel to the contras, via Vice President George Bush's man-on-the-spot, an old CIA colleague Felix Rodriguez.

One of the virtues of a recent public television documentary, com-missioned by WGBH and written and directed by Andrew and Leslie Cockburn (for the record, brother and sister in law to the present writer) is that it approached the always interesting matter of the consanguinity of drug trading and covert operations in a structural rather than purely anec-dotal fashion. The activity of drug smuggling draws together people of criminal disposition who are philosophically and pragmatically devoted to the 'free market' in its fullest amoral stretch, generates large amounts of 'unregistered' money, and is at a strategic angle of contact between the First World and the Third, like slavery and the strategic spices in an earlier era. These are all properties alluring to secret services, who will therefore gravitate towards the illegal drug trade unless detained by powerful bureaucratic or ideological considerations.

The first half of 'Drugs, Guns and the CIA' clarifies long-held alle-gations about CIA involvement in opium and heroin trafficking in South-east Asia, amplifying and hardening the pioneering work done in this area by Al McCoy in his book *The Politics of Heroin in South East Asia.* The mathematics of the CIA's 'secret war' in Laos are compelling. (A 'secret war', remember, is a US martial enterprise known to everyone, but for reasons of tact kept from the American newspaper-reading and TV-watching public.) By 1970 the Pentagon's contribution to the war in Laos was running at $146 million, but the same secret document furnishing that figure also noted that the CIA was spending up to $60 million more than its official appropriation. Thus the question put to Victor Marchetti, who as a CIA officer helped assemble the Agency's official budget:

Q: 'Is it conceivable the CIA would fight a war with dope money?'

Marchetti: 'Well, yes, in the sense that they would not sell dope to earn money to support an operation, but they would look the other way if the people they were supporting were financing themselves by selling dope.'

This 'looking the other way' included provisioning the CIA's client Vang Pao with an airline (Xieng Kouang, aka Air Opium) to ship opium from Long Chen, in Laos, to sites further south. The airline was entirely controlled by the CIA. As former AID official Ron Rickenbach says, 'I was in the areas where opium was transhipped; I personally was a witness to opium being placed on aircraft, American aircraft; I witnessed it being taken off smaller aircraft that were coming in from outlying sites'.

Part of the aftermath is supplied by the legendary CIA officer Tony Poe, who was the prototype for the Brando character in *Apocalypse Now*. Poe lives in Thailand and has hitherto kept his mouth firmly shut. He describes how Vang Pao would load up a DC3 with heroin: 'They were flying it in a big wet-wing airplane that could fly for 13 hours, a DC3 and all the wings were filled with gas. They fly down to Pakse, and then they fly over to Danang, and then the number two guy to President Thieu would receive it.'

By the end of 1970 there were 30,000 Americans in Vietnam addicted to heroin, and President Nixon asked the CIA to get involved in limiting the drug traffic. In 1972 a US intelligence agent in South-east Asia sent a secret field report to Customs, suggesting a serious conflict of interest: 'It was ironic,' the agent wrote, 'that the CIA should be given the responsibility of narcotics intelligence, particularly since they were supporting the prime movers. Even though the CIA was, in fact, facilitating the movement of opiates to the US, they steadfastly hid behind the shield of secrecy and said that all was done in the interest of national security.'

Among those who began to realize the moral perspectives of what was going on was Rickenbach, who finally woke up to 'the rather horrible implications of what we were doing' and stopped working for the government.

By this time, in the wake of Watergate, the CIA had allowed Artime and his network to go to an independent, consultative status, and Milian-Rodriguez was working for the Medellin cartel, supervising the washing and investing of $200 million a month, with a total capital fund of $11 billion. At the time of his arrest in 1983 he was carrying $5 million, a fact that brought Vice President George Bush to pose with what the money launderer called his 'petty cash'. In 'Drugs, Guns and the CIA' he is asked:

Q: 'How much money was actually contributed by you or through you to the contras, total?'

Milian-Rodriguez: 'It was a little under ten million dollars.... It was delivered on a per need basis.'

Exactly as in Laos, the drug money filled the funding gap. The documentary then turns to Noriega's former aide José Blandon:

Q: 'When General Noriega told you Felix Rodriguez (a Cuban exile and CIA agent allegedly involved in the capture and murder of Che Guevara) was friendly with Ramon Milian-Rodriguez, were you surprised to hear that Felix Rodriguez would be involved with a drug trafficker?'

Blandon: 'Surprised? Why?'

According to Blandon, while Felix Rodriguez was supplying the contras from Ilopango base in El Salvador he was getting arms shipments with the help of Mike Harari, the former Israeli intelligence agent and key aide to Noriega.

Then, once again some problems arise for the Vice President.

Q: 'Who was Felix Rodriguez working for, or with, when he approached you?'

Milian-Rodriguez: 'Well, the only government mention he made was Vice President Bush.'

Q: 'And what was his relationship with Bush as you understood it?'

Milian-Rodriguez: 'He was reporting directly to Bush. I was led to believe he was reporting regularly to the Vice President.... The request for the contribution [i.e. drug dollars from the cartel to the contras] made a lot more sense *because* Felix was reporting to George Bush. If Felix had come to me and said I'm reporting to anyone else, let's say, you know, Oliver North, I might have been more sceptical. I didn't know who Oliver North was and I didn't know his background. But you know, if you have a ... let's say we'll call him an ex-CIA operative, even though it's not true you know, he's a current operative ...'

Q: 'Who is?'

Milian-Rodriguez: 'Felix ... Yeah, there's nothing ex about him. But if you have a CIA, what you consider to be a CIA man coming to you saying "I want to fight this war, we're out of funds, can you help us out? I'm reporting directly to Bush on it", I mean it's very believable.... Here you have a CIA guy reporting to his old boss.'

In fact Felix Rodriguez's relationship with Bush goes back to when Bush was CIA director in the mid-1970s. A February 1985 memo from General Paul Gorman said that Rodriguez 'is operating as a private citizen', but his acquaintanceship with the Vice President is real enough, going back to the latter's days as Director of Central Intelligence. During the 1980 campaign Felix Rodriguez was in contact with Bush, who was particularly active campaigning in southern Florida, both in the primary race against Reagan and in the election battle with Carter. As is well known, the first call Rodriguez made after Eugene Hasenfus was shot down on a contra supply flight in October 1986 was to a staffer of Vice President Bush, whose office subsequently admitted to seventeen meetings with Rodriguez, including three between the latter and the Vice President himself.

Right now election considerations are prompting an escalation in the 'war' on drugs. After twenty years of resistance, the California state assembly is giving way on a bill allowing the police to tap telephones, supposedly confined to drug investigations. The US Congress is giving the military vast new powers of interception, surveillance and seizure in civilian areas. The US customs service can now find, or plant, a few marijuana seeds and confiscate a car or a boat. Meanwhile the US government is experiencing humiliating defeat at the hands of the drug smuggler and military strongman in Panama they have been paying for years. For the Vice President to say he was ignorant of such goings on is to say – as the documentary demonstrates – he has been in a coma for the last 20 years. How otherwise could he have been unaware of such an important component of the US government's relationship with the rest of the world?

Footnote: 'For seven and a half years I've worked alongside him, and I'm proud to be his partner. We've had triumphs, we've made mistakes, we've had sex.'

This was George Bush describing his relationship with President Reagan, at the College of Southern Idaho on May 6. As the audience roared, Bush quickly corrected himself: 'Setbacks, we've had setbacks.' Bush then amplified the motions of his own unconscious by adding, with a little smile, 'I feel like the javelin competitor who won the toss and elected to receive.'

New Statesman

July 1, 1988

The Duke: History and Psycho-history

We've reached the stage in the US electoral cycle when a potential nominee spends most of his time reassuring relevant constituencies that if elected president he won't adversely affect their interests. This process differs from the earlier phase, in primaries and caucuses, when the candidate has to excite activist groups sufficiently to get them into the polling booths. So Michael Dukakis, the nominee-designate of the Democratic Party, now voyages from one podium to the next projecting an aura of optimistically mature responsibility, like an insurance executive on a swing through branch offices.

The headline in *The New York Times* that lies before me on my desk says 'Dukakis Seeks to Assure Allies on Support for NATO'. Of course no ally needs any such assurance, or believes that US commitment to the Atlantic alliance is anything other than what it has always been, so the headline is actually a code for something else, namely 'Dukakis Assures Military-Industrial Complex It's Business as Usual'. Addressing the Atlantic Council Dukakis called for a CDI (Conventional Defense Initiative) and proclaimed that 'while we negotiate, we must strengthen the alliance as well, beginning with our conventional forces'. Thus Dukakis signals his acceptance of that whiskered myth, presumed NATO deficiency in conventional might wherewith to confront the Slavic hordes in their race to the Bay of Biscay.

Polls show that though people think that Dukakis is not a bad fellow and maybe better than George Bush, which isn't saying much, they are unclear about his views. Dukakis was lucky here. The press and party leaders were so keen to find someone to save the Democratic Party from Jesse Jackson that Dukakis was spared much inconvenient scrutiny about what his ideas and policies might actually be. So who is the governor of Massachusetts?

There is a book partly by Michael Dukakis and a couple of books about him. The book by him, *Creating the Future* (co-authored with Rosabeth Moss Kanter) must rank as one of the most unreadable pieces of political literature ever to creep from a printing press. Its theme is the 'Massachusetts miracle', being the story of how the fiscal and industrial slum of the early seventies flowered into the success story of today. And if you ask whether the price of success has to mean turning Cape Cod into a parking lot and having a lot of open-face brick arcades selling candles and pot-pourri, you are probably the sort of negative type who does not understand the price of progress.

The prose style of *Creating the Future* is a particularly horrifying example of the shrunken linguistic universe inhabited by almost all economists and politicians, who between them now establish the canons of public speech. This was once a function shared by bards and priests, who at least had a sense of style and occasion. Clichés march shoulder to shoulder down the grey pages, as italicized:

> '*Economic growth requires fiscal stability* and Massachusetts *has put its fiscal house in order* – a lesson of *particular urgency* to a nation *facing record deficits.*
> When I first took office in 1975, Massachusetts was *a financial basket case....*
> *Tough choices* followed – including *deep cuts* in social welfare programs and an income tax surcharge. The choices may have cost me my re-election in 1978. But I *believed then and now* that *tough decisions had to be made* – that's what *governing and leadership are about.*'

The so-called 'miracle of Massachusetts' is central to Dukakis's self-advertisement as a man to lead America towards a better future. The proposition he and his admirers advance is that the Massachusetts economy is the paradigm of what a post-industrial economy can be. A generation ago the state and indeed the whole north east was gray in the embers of a declining manufacturing economy, with high taxation and policies guaranteed to repel business investment.

Under Dukakis's leadership, so the story goes, the education/high-tech industry centered on Boston and along Route 128 became the fulcrum for an expanding partnership of state government and free enterprise, in which fiscal and investment policies allied to produce jobs and a flourishing economic environment.

Like most such claims of having been the architect of economic renewal, Dukakis's pretensions have less in them than meets the eye. There is no doubt that the economy of Massachusetts and of the area of which it is the hub (southern New Hampshire, northern Connecticut) 'recovered' to a certain extent from the consequences of a decline of its old manufacturing base, which saw plant closures and plant flight – to the non-union south or overseas – throughout the 1960s and early 1970s. By the late 1970s union strength in Massachusetts had been severely eroded and the cost of labor substantially lowered.

But the role of high tech in the recovery of the late 70s and early 80s has been overestimated. There's no doubt that high technology does play an important part in the state's economy, but it is one that has nothing to do with Dukakis and everything to do with the presence of the Massachusetts Institute of Technology, which in 1946 in association with Harvard, the Federal Reserve of Boston and several insurance companies created American Research and Development Inc. This company became famous for financing the start-up of such successful enterprises as Digital Equipment Corporation. In the late 1950s the Bank of Boston agreed to let start-up high-tech companies use their federal contracts and grants as collateral against loans from the Bank, which had predictable results. In an interesting paper, 'Reassessing the "Massachusetts Miracle"' the MIT economists Bennett Harrison and Jean Kluver have calculated that by 1973 high-tech manufacturing accounted for 6 per cent of all employment in Massachusetts. Between 1979 and 1984 it rose to 9 per cent, but has now started falling back.

A significant fraction of this high-tech employment may be engaged in producing goods and services for the military, which brings us to another aspect of the miracle that does not have too much to do with Michael Dukakis. Massachusetts has always been one of the top defense contracting states, particularly in proportion to its population, with a tradition of arms production stretching back to the American Revolution. Part of its economic decline between the end of the Second World War and the mid-1970s can be attributed to the closing of military bases, and corresponding credit for revival must be laid to the arms build-ups initiated by Jimmy Carter in his last two years and continued by Reagan. From 1980 to 1985 Massachusetts's prime military contracts rose from $3.7 billion to $7.7 billion, accounting for 7 per cent of gross state product in 1987, which was more than the share back in 1968 at the height of Vietnam war spending.

In sum, much of the Massachusetts miracle is, in miniature, a paradigm of what happened in the national economy. An 'encouraging' business climate (cheap and cowed labor, plus state incentives), along with a regional postwar tradition of high-tech activity, was reflected in economic prosperity, aided by Pentagon dollars. But such growth has been lopsidedly at the eastern end of the state, around Boston, and there have been growing disparities within a wage structure that is now at about national levels, having been lower for many years. There is low unemployment in Massachusetts, but it can be chiefly traced to the very low rate in expansion of the labor force. Workers aren't flooding into the Boston area to find jobs, in part because housing is extremely expensive.

This points us to an important component of the famous miracle, particularly since 1984. Nearly all the growth in Massachusetts associated with local advantage – what Dukakis would invoke as the consequence of his wise leadership – has been concentrated in business and legal services, finance, insurance, real estate and especially construction; a process that the economist R.D. Norton has called 'Manhattanization'. So the 'miracle of Massachusetts' is the miracle of Boston, and a miracle that most working people will be unable to afford in terms of rents or actual house purchase. The competitive advantage of the state relative to others has disappeared and with it Dukakis's claims to be a miracle worker. His other great pride and joy – a state 'work-fare' scheme – takes some people on welfare and puts them in very low-paying jobs, thus supposedly schooling them for self-betterment. This too depends on an expanding economy.

For insight into Dukakis's personality we must turn to the books about him. One of these, *Dukakis*, by a couple of Boston reporters called Charles Kennedy and Robert Turner, is reasonably informative. The governor emerges as your average politician seeking the presidency: driven, repressed, compulsive, anal-retentive, megalomanic, self-deceiving, somewhat of an iceberg, with seven-eighths of his personality submerged in psychic darkness. On his paternal side Dukakis is Lesbian in origin, his grandparents having hailed from that delightful island. His other side originally came from the Epirus, though his mother Euterpe was born in Larissa. The values imbued in this son of immigrants were frigidly petit-bourgeois: reverence for education, all-important adjunct of assiduous self-betterment; manic thrift; rigorous purging of dysfunctional emotion; reverence for the self-made man; contempt for failure. The end impression is of a cloistered, somewhat Robespierrean virtue occasionally adorned with lunges at the common touch, whether with Zorba-like caperings at ethnic feasts or confessions of new-found humility and respect for the opinions of others, particularly after the traumatic defeat by Ed King in the Massachusetts gubernatorial race in 1978.

Jimmy Carter, another person who took failure very, very hard, says in *Nothing But the Best* that he burst into tears after losing an early political race. Tears seem to be elements unfamiliar to Michael's countenance. Mothers' tales of the early characteristics of their offspring are always revealing. The one about the infant Mike is of first Greek words being *monos mou* ('by myself') and of high-octane 'self-confidence' otherwise known as thinking you are right all of the time. He did well at school in the classroom and on the playing field and was in general the sort of son self-betterers dream of having. The strain took its toll on Michael's elder brother Stelian, who had a 'nervous breakdown' in his late teens and tried to do himself in with pills. 'Incredibly,' Kenney and Turner rather naively write, 'Michael says he does not remember whether Stelian tried to kill himself.' Michael also doesn't remember whether or not Stelian was at the 1960 Democratic convention in Los Angeles working for Adlai Stevenson while he, Michael, was naturally working for the Great New Frontiersman.

Stelian was, as they say, 'never quite the same' after the breakdown and bobbed along in Michael's triumphant wake, trying to keep on an even keel. One time he let it all hang out and during one of his brother's campaigns started stuffing mailboxes with leaflets suggesting that people voting for M. Dukakis should have their heads examined. Finally the poor man was knocked off his bicycle by a hit-and-run driver and, after a period in coma, died. As one might expect from such a positivist, Michael now thinks his brother's problem may have been physiological in nature, and thus presumably amenable to a rational fix-it solution with a squirt of lithium or some hi-tech equivalent.

Dukakis's Robespierrean self-assurance sufficiently pissed off the voters of Massachusetts for them to turf him out of office in 1978, and after a period of lying low at the Kennedy School – where he alienated students with his mad reformer's insistence that every problem MUST have a solution and only one solution (being the solution he had in mind) – he came back into the public arena with unconvincing assertions that he would henceforth be humble and court the opinion of others. He returned to the State House in 1982 and was reelected in 1986.

There's not much sign of the new Dukakis at any level beyond the gestural. Aside from the fate of Stelian, big blips on Michael's psychograph come when his relationship with his political intimates is displayed: all of them have departed abruptly, mostly because Dukakis gave no sign of rewarding them for their efforts on his behalf, an ascetic expression of megalomania. One of them, Fran Meaney, now tells Kenney and Turner that Dukakis is 'the number-one master of self-delusion I have ever met in my life'. John Sasso, Dukakis's most recent political advisor, left because he apparently failed to be frank with his boss about distributing a disobliging tape concerning Joe Biden on the campaign trail. Sasso took the fall while Dukakis proclaimed that no dirty trick would mar his cause. Back during his late 1970s exile at the Kennedy School he urged an aide to plant a compromising story about Ed King in the *Boston Globe*, later claiming he had no memory of having done so. Repression is a big item with Michael, as one might gather from this terse description of his father's death: 'It was just a long, slow process. It was sad to watch, in a way. We were all very supportive and were as helpful as we could possibly be.'

At one time I thought the fact that Dukakis failed to notice for 25 years that his wife Kitty was on speed did not bode well, but again there may be less to this than meets the eye. She apparently started taking 'diet pills' during her first marriage, and I kept up with a reasonably spartan daily regimen of amphetamine down the years until she went off for a detox session at a place in Minnesota in 1982. That's the story anyway. Call it Michael's admitted flaw (he talks about it a lot), though it has the convenience of being his wife's. Kitty – half Jewish, half Irish – seems to have performed with ability the usual wifely role of ego-buttressing and general care and upkeep of the crazy man of the house. Kenney and Turner say she's a keen shopper, thus balancing the prodigious stinginess of the Duke.

So much for clues to Dukakis's personality. What about his political destiny and that of the Democratic Party? In an interview with Jesse Jackson published in the *Los Angeles Times* on May 27, the reporter Robert Scheer had the following exchange with the candidate:

> Scheer: 'If I understand you, you're saying that in this presidential campaign the Cold War wing of the Democratic Party and the anti-affirmative action people, the neo-liberals and neo-conservatives have lost.'
> Jackson: 'They all lost. They were stung in Iowa, stymied in New Hampshire, lost at home on Super Tuesday, and after Super Tuesday, they just disintegrated.'

But they didn't disintegrate, even though their ideas suffered popular rejection. To the extent that they got Jackson to announce he would not meet with Arafat they managed to integrate him. The first third of this year of the campaign for the presidency showed that the American people were ready for radical change. The second third is being spent ensuring that radical change does not make it onto the agenda and the final third will be the traditional 'democratic' *coup de grace*: two candidates espousing mostly similar positions, battling it out for leadership of the free world.

Jackson is now vowing to try and extend Phase One at least into Phase Two. Culturally the Jackson campaign has been an unqualified plus. It's been good for the country, good for the left and especially mobilizing and empowering for black people to have a black man taken seriously as a presidential candidate. Jackson has been uncompromising about his blackness. No Ralph Bunche he. But institutionally the main meaning of his campaign has been to reinforce the hold of the two-party system by bringing disaffected people into the Democratic Party. Hence the contradiction. To be taken seriously, Jackson had to run as a Democrat. This contradiction resides in the power the mass media have over American culture.

In a companion, and very revealing, interview with Dukakis, Scheer elicited two particularly conspicuous intellectual traits of the governor, namely unconditional support for whatever Israel may decide in the matter of situating its capital in either Tel Aviv or Jerusalem, and refusal to reject a 'first strike' nuclear policy. On the latter issue the best he can offer is the pledge of 'no *early* first use' (my italics) of nuclear weapons, which is no doubt a source of encouragement and comfort to one and all.

Liberals, trying to like Dukakis, say hopefully that at least he is not a cold warrior. This seems to me to be far from clear. His speeches are, when the occasion calls for it, studded with alarmist phraseology about Soviet beachheads, and to Scheer he said flatly that so far as the western hemisphere is concerned 'if you have a Soviet satellite – at least as that phrase is commonly defined – then you'll have both a foreign military presence, which threatens our security, and an ideology which systematically attempts to subvert neighbors. We can't tolerate either one.' Oliver North would find little to object to there, and neither would the 2506 Brigade. Pressed by Scheer on whether the Soviets have an equivalent right to announce a principle of non-toleration of foreign military bases on their borders, Dukakis declined any such equivalence. Perhaps one of those advisors from the Kennedy School can lend him a copy of the UN Charter.

On Israel Dukakis was cravenly outrageous, with such remarks as 'If Israel wants its capital in Jerusalem, then as far as I'm concerned, its capital is in Jerusalem'. For a notion of the moral range of the likely Democratic nominee, consider this answer to Scheer's enquiry as to whether the internment without trial of 5,000 Palestinians violated their civil rights: 'Dealing with civil disturbances – some of which are being encouraged and supported from outside the occupied territories – is not an easy job, as anyone who's ever tried to deal with them knows.' Pressed twice more by Scheer, Dukakis finally conceded that rights had been violated.

The bottom line on Dukakis is that it is not really relevant whether he is or is not, at the instinctual level, a cold warrior. Since he exhibits no belief that the system is in crisis, or that the war economy can be challenged only in a structural fashion, his inevitable role will be that of attempting to make the war economy work just as he tried to make the state budget work in the mid-1970s by throwing people off the welfare rolls.

In that context it is now quite clearly the present historic destiny of the next Democratic President to avert or finesse the threat to the war economy presented by Gorbachev's appeals for peaceful co-existence, which in fact look more and more like desperate attempts to get breathing space during which the wrenching dislocations of *perestroika* can be endured without the added burden of a huge arms budget. The effect of a large arms budget is of course completely different in the US and Russia, since the former has excess capacity in the economy and the latter does not.

Liberal Democrats are in their usual dilemma, arguing that if Bush refuses to rule out first use of nuclear weapons and Dukakis does the same, with the proviso that he might be first but he won't be an *early first,* then Dukakis is obviously the guy to put in the Oval office. This is not self-evident. Like all Democrats seeking the presidency Dukakis has to demonstrate that he is not secretly in favor of Russians taking over Western Europe, that he's not an appeaser. Like all Democrats in the White House Dukakis will have to go on doing that. This is why the cold war usually gets worse under Democrats, as in the case of Truman, Kennedy, Johnson and Carter. Under Republicans, like Eisenhower, Nixon, Ford and Reagan, relations between the US and the Soviet Union get better.

It's particularly likely that Dukakis will use the White House as a post-graduate course in cold-war fighting, since he has the mystifying reputation of being a *liberal* Democrat to contend with, in contrast to *moderate* Democrats like Senator Sam Nunn, chairman of the Armed Services Committee, much loved by *pragmatists* like John Judis of the 'socialist' *In These Times* and the editors of the *Wall Street Journal.* Therefore Dukakis will have to 'reassure' the ruling class that he agrees with its axioms in foreign policy, as set forth earlier this summer in *Newsweek* and subsequently in *Foreign Affairs* by Henry Kissinger and Cyrus Vance in their joint statement of the 'bipartisan' agenda. Vance, it should be remembered, was installed by Carter as secretary of state and then, because he was somehow regarded as 'liberal', immediately balanced by the crazed Brzezinski as national security advisor. Kissinger–Vance bluntly advise that 'future agreements' with the Soviet Union will be 'difficult to conclude'; agree that research and devewlopment of SDI should continue; and reject the notion of a pledge against nuclear first use or of the denuclearization of Europe. Both agree that 'our economy and consumption have become so overextended that the remedies will involve sacrifice and slower growth in our standard of living'.

There is no evidence that Dukakis has the intellectual background or the political coalition necessary to contest such an agenda. His prime foreign policy advisor is Madeline Albright, a former assistant to Brzezinski, and he is surrounded by many best-and-brightniks. His chief economic advisor is the utterly conventional Lawrence Summers, who is even more orthodox than Bush's man, Martin Feldstein, who at least says that real interest rates are a problem.

Liberal admirers say that Dukakis believes in the rule of law, thus distinguishing him from Reagan's Bush, who went along with defiance of the World Court, abuse of legality in Central America and complicity with drug runners, contra murderers and the CIA. But Dukakis has also said that a Soviet base in the western hemisphere would be an unacceptable threat to US security. (Dukakis, it should be said, has also spoken strongly about South Africa and has accepted Jackson's insistence that it be termed a 'terrorist state'.)

George Bush's economic strategies will be essentially the same as those of Dukakis so it's a question of which party you would prefer to take the blame for economic contraction in the wake of Reagan's super-defense budgets and exchange rate mercantilism.

I do think that at times there is a lesser and a larger of two evils. If Carter rather than Reagan had won in 1980 I doubt there would have been such an immediate and exuberant paroxysm of slaughter by the right in El Salvador in 1981, though of course Carter would have been as assiduous a promoter of Duarte as figleaf for the army and treasury police. The figures are as follows: 10,000 killings in El Salvador by the right in Carter's last year, 1980; 13,000 killings in Reagan's first year, 1981; 10,000–11,000 killings in 1982. In 1983 some decent reporting by Ray Bonner in *The New York Times* helped fuel congressional threats to stop funding unless death squad activity diminished. Bush flew down and told the generals to cut out killings in El Salvador, which they promptly did and, once again with US patronage, started bombing the countryside instead.

In Nicaragua it's less likely that Carter would have worked so unstintingly at creating the contras or at promoting their cause with the same demonizing energy. Carter's strategy would have been, indeed already was, to undermine the Nicaraguan economy. You could argue that such a strategy might in the end have been more successful in undermining the Nicaraguan revolution than Reagan's approach, which resulted in thousands of deaths and mutilations, but also probably firmed up revolutionary fiber, not least in the training of thousands of young cadres in the army and militia. This is of course all in the area of the Grand Perhaps.

Africa? Hard to say. Invasion of Lebanon in 1982? Who knows. It should be noted that Reagan's defense spending is more or less – maybe a little less – in line with Carter's budgetary projections, even though the curve is differently shaped. SDI is plainly better than impending substitutes since it has no useful military application and therefore was purely a device of military Keynesianism. Would Carter have been as successful, even as eager, to distribute income upward, to the top 20 per cent? Probably not. On the other hand it was Carter who installed Volcker, thus unleashing the contraction of the early 1980s and high real interest rates ever since. Reagan's budgets have stunted lives, shortened them, despoiled them, whether by ketchup as lunch on a schoolkid's plate or by toxins sanctioned by Reagan's EPA seeping into the groundwater. But then again, Volcker's interest rates, multiplying through the Third World's debt burden, have ruined lives in the Third World too.

Truth be told, under two-party rules you get Carter and you get Reagan. Over two or three terms there's no either/or, only both/and.

New Statesman

July 7, 1988

Great Balls of Fire*

Not for the first time in the career of the Reagan Administration, physical disaster and political set-back have come in the form of a fiery explosion in the heavens, followed by the grim culling of human remains and mechanical debris from the sea.

The explosion of the space shuttle Challenger spelled the end of the heroic phase of the space fantasy engendered in the Kennedy era. And if some blame for that catastrophe attaches to the political pressures surrounding NASA's eagerness to get the shuttle up in time for President Reagan's 1986 State of the Union message, the direct cause lay in the contractual procedures and bottom-line priorities of the aerospace industry and its contract-issuing opposite numbers in government.

The destruction of Iran Air Flight 655 provokes a similar set of consequences and conclusions: the definitive end of a particularly high-strutting phase of American moral self-righteousness, stoked to white heat in the post-Afghanistan invasion period by the downing of Korean Air Lines Flight 007. Attachment of blame must go to the US government for sending the missile cruiser Vincennes to those troubled waters, but the primary responsibility rests with the military-industrial complex that produced the equipment that caused an entirely avoidable loss of 290 lives.

Nine hours after either one or two missiles from the Vincennes disposed of the Iranian A-300 Airbus, Adm. William J. Crowe, chairman of the Joint Chiefs of Staff, proposed the official line, which was that the Iranians – those flying the Airbus carrying 290 people and those who let it ply between Bandar Abbas and Dubai under such conditions – brought it on themselves. The Airbus was off course. It was descending toward the Vincennes on a presumptively hostile flight path. Its transponder, designed to identify its civilian status and course, was not switched on. The crew failed to respond to seven distinct warnings on both civilian and military radio channels. There were electronic indications suggesting that an attack by an F-14 was starting.

On such analysis, regrets but not apologies were in order and this, so far, has been the Reagan administration's posture. The press, mostly performing its fundamental role of offering support to the government and reassur-

---

*This column, written within two days of the event, was mostly on mark. In fact, however, the Airbus was not off course at all, but well within its recognized air corridor. Also, the Airbus was at an altitude of 12,000 feet and, as Dubai air-traffic control insisted, ascending when shot down. Finally, the GAO report referred to has now been released and confirms that the crewmen involved in the May 1984 test knew in advance the speed and direction of the 'surprise' targets.

ance to the public, has duly followed along, with the exception, from what I've been able to read, of good coverage by Fred Kaplan in *The Boston Globe*.

But how is the official story standing up?

The Airbus was 'off course'. Yes, but by about four or five miles, which is not in the least unusual, and on the far side of the corridor of the Vincennes. By comparison, KAL 007 was 365 miles awry, and this was not at the time taken by the Reagan administration as being an exonerating factor. Adm. Crowe also made much of the fact that the plane was at an altitude of 9,000 feet, unusually low for a commercial flight. And he claimed the plane had a 'threatening flight profile', notably in the alleged fact that it was descending.

He was correct in saying the plane was at 9,000 feet, but this was not peculiar, given that the Airbus had taken off only seven minutes earlier, and thus the normal flight profile would have been to keep climbing steadily to 25,000 feet before leveling off. Assertions of a menacing descent notwithstanding, there is nothing to suggest the Airbus was doing other than what it intended, which was to fly straight from Bandar Abbas to Dubai.

This suggests a panicky response from the Vincennes, particularly since a Pentagon air-combat specialist quoted by Mr Kaplan in *The Boston Globe* said that an attacking F-14 probably would be traveling 'at at least 550 to 580 knots', 100 knots faster than Adm. Crowe says the Airbus was flying, and 'well under 1,000 feet.... Someone flying straight and level at 9,000 feet ain't hostile'. It seems, by the way, that the height-finding ability on all radar systems is their weakest function.

Much has been made of the fact that the Vincennes sent four warnings on a military radio channel and three on a civilian one. The military warnings are irrelevant since only a military aircraft would have been monitoring such a frequency. A common thread to such shoot-down incidents is that the attacker always claims to have given plenty of warning. It's not rare for pilots to be lazy about listening to emergency channels and the Airbus pilots could have had the relevant equipment down or off. The Russians made similiar sorts of efforts to contact KAL 007.

The transponder is an automatic device that gets queried by air-traffic control and responds automatically with pertinent data. The Vincennes was equipped with the same querying device. If transponder and interrogator are both working there can be no misidentification. The US's initial claim that the Airbus's transponder was off was acceptable in all US press accounts, but there was no compelling reason for such credulity. The A-300 Airbus is equipped with a back-up transponder and the chances of both being either turned off or broken are remote.

Indeed, US government officials are now sending out clouds of uncertainty on the matter of the transponder. Maybe it wasn't off, after all. Maybe the ambiguous signals were coming from another plane. And on the crucial matter of whether the plane was going up or down, Dubai air traffic control insists it was ascending.

Suppose we abandon the theory very naturally espoused by the US, that the Iranians and their Airbus were either incompetent, malevolent or both and instead consider the theory that the Vincennes' equipment is an extrusion of the corrupt, inefficient and profiteering system now under major investigation by the FBI.

The Vincennes is an Aegis-class cruiser, billed by the Navy as the last word in high-tech wizardry in its ability to track and identify dozens of planes and missiles at the same time. But congressional suspicions of the Aegis radar system was once so high that the whole program was in trouble. Just in time for a major funding vote in May 1984, a test showed miraculous results in detecting low-altitude surprise attack. Critics at the time said the actual element of 'surprise' in this test was highly questionable, and the General Accounting Office recently concluded a report on the matter that hasn't yet been declassified. The joy of Aegis from the contracting point of view is that it is extremely expensive. Along with associated systems, it accounts for half the $1 billion cost of the ship on which it is installed.

The Aegis system is known to be unreliable, and the allied electronic warfare system, the SLQ-32, whose job is to sort out incoming transmissions and determine which aircraft are Friend or Foe, is notoriously unreliable. The Vincennes couldn't tell the difference between the Airbus and an F-14, despite being loaded with equipment for high-tech fighting via radar screen, supposedly more reliable than a man standing on the bridge with binoculars announcing the passage of an Airbus flying south at 9,000 feet. But then, in military Keynesian terms, or in the brusquer language of the arms companies' bottom line, binoculars don't count for much.

Another point not being discussed is that even if it had been an F-14, this should not necessarily have provoked a speedy missile launching, as the F-14 is not designed to carry anti-ship missiles. Here we get to our old friends the fog of war and the actual circumstances of the men on the ship. They were in the midst of an engagement with Iranian gunboats. They no doubt also remembered the fate of Capt. Glenn Brindel of the USS Stark, forced to resign after an Iraqi Exocet missile killed thirty-seven of his men. Capt. Brindel has complained of the unreliability of the SLQ-32.

The Reagan administration is urgently contesting parallelism between flights 655 and 007, but there are many parallels too evident to mention. On the matter of such terrible incidents in general, President Reagan is no doubt already rescinding his view that only an Evil Empire could accomplish such a vile deed, preferring to say the incident is closed. But the Soviets made major changes in their air-defense system after they shot down KAL 007. The best way to requite the 290 victims of Flight 655 would be to reform the corrupted technology and procurement system that almost certainly did them in.

WSJ

July 27, 1988

After Atlanta: The Politics of Street Heat

The strangest thing about the Democracts' political convention in Atlanta was the sense of utter isolation from the normal ingredients of political life. Everything – Gorbachev, NATO, the corrupt arms contractors, Nicaragua, death squads in El Salvador, the CIA, control of the economy, insurance companies, landlords, toxic waste, empowerment of ordinary citizens – vanishes and is replaced by about three operating cliches, repeated thousands and thousands of times. I would drift off to sleep in my Holiday Inn bed with their cadences still squirreling away at my synapses: 'Make America number one again. . . . Invest in our youth . . . curb the monstrous deficit'.

In four days sitting in the Omni auditorium I don't think I heard anything resembling a realistic description of what is going on in the world today, even in simple silhouette. Language ceases to be an instrument of intelligent communication and becomes, rather, a kind of inchoate, dispiriting odor, like the smell you get these days from opening up a glossy magazine.

The level to which the rhetorical poverty line has sunk is almost beyond belief and should excite pity in the hardest heart. Many of the nation's most prominent politicians support themselves with as few as one idea (make America great/make way for competence/make life hard for Bush) and one joke. Sample from Senator Edward Kennedy: 'Some people say don't count your chickens before they're hatched. Well, the Republicans have already hatched their chickens this campaign – and George Bush is a dead duck.'

The reason for this desperate state of affairs lies not in the fact that several thousand citizens had suddenly lost the power of substantive thought or speech, but that they feared the slightest manifestation of intelligent discussion on the issues of the day would provoke the far larger number of journalists in attendance to start denouncing the convention as a typically infantile Democratic zoo of the sort nominating George McGovern in Miami in 1972. Having thus induced the panic-stricken Democrats to avoid saying anything interesting the journalists duly – in the manner of Roone Arledge of ABC – denounce the convention as boring and demand that in future it be confined to four hours' prime-time viewing across – at most – two nights between the hours of 8 and 11 p.m.

The other remarkable thing about the coverage of the convention was the evident horror of the press that anything might mar the unity of the occasion. Listen to Lesley Stahl of CBS interviewing Jesse Jackson the day before the convention opened:

Stahl: 'I thought the [private] negotiations were aiming towards one platform. I thought you were trying to resolve these very questions in these talks, so you wouldn't have the minority votes on the floor [of the convention].'

Jackson: 'Let it be known that our minority planks are not for the most part a minority position. For example, most Americans do not want any more taxes on middle income and poor people. The corporations and wealthy must pay their share.'

Stahl: 'But Dukakis doesn't want that in the platform, and this is supposed to be his convention.'

Jackson: 'That is an illusion. This is a convention of the people. This is the delegates' convention. They will determine who the nominee will be. They will determine what planks will be agreed upon. They will determine who the vice president will be. I guess I must say to you, I do not see this convention as show business but as serious business.'

This is supposed to be his convention. The totalitarian impulse is very strong.

I was standing on the convention floor by the Vermont delegation as Senator Lloyd Bentsen approached the rostrum on Thursday night to commence his own narcotic observations. Some of the Jackson delegates in said Vermont delegation had caused the printing of 2,000 placards saying 'No Contra Aid', and distributed them throughout the hall. The idea was to remind the world that Bentsen, described in the *Atlanta Journal* as 'courtly' and 'happier drinking Chassagne Montrachet than long neck Lone Star beer', had been a keen supporter of the use of US dollars to pay for contras to kill Nicaraguan civilians. I'm glad to see that some of the Vermonters – Cindy Milstein, Lisa Kiley, Liz Blum, Ellen David Friedman and Mike Korczykowski (the minority member of the Vermont Jacksonian fraction in that he is a man, white and not Jewish) – made a terrific din, holding up their placards and shouting its message. Theirs was almost the only exhibition of the placards throughout the hall. Neighboring delegates were visibly and audibly angered, trying to block the cards from view with their own loyal advertisements for the Dukakis/Bentsen ticket.

Thus took place the only audible public objection, in plenary session, to the selection by acclamation of a man partially responsible for the deaths of thousands of innocent people in Nicaragua, not to mention Angola.

I should note here, as have others, that the recent Soviet Communist Party conference in Moscow was far more democratic – at least in the public airing of disparate points of view – with substantive intellectual and political brawling, as between Ligachev and Yeltsin, taking place in open session.

But what about Jesse Jackson's performance, you might ask. His vocabulary before the convention, with its phraseology about 'baling up' the black vote and taking it up to the big house, seemed to me to be patronizing to the point of racism. Very objectionable, unless you argue there was a Brechtian objectivity in Jackson's parodic account of what the white bosses wanted him, as underboss, to do. About half his speech on Tuesday night was very fine, always excepting the appalling nonsense about needing two wings to fly and the hawk lying down with the dove. No bird I've ever heard of flew with wings of different sizes, trying to flap at different speeds. Most sensible doves would never dream of going to bed with a hawk.

This was Jackson's effort to sketch in the dialectics of unity and coalition. He did a much better job the morning after Mike Dukakis's speech accepting the Democratic nomination. At breakfast time 1,200 Jackson delegates, most of them running on three hours of sleep for the fourth night in a row, gathered at the Marriott Marquis for a meeting with their candidate. Finally Jackson walked in with Dukakis and Bentsen to argue the case for working with the ticket, for working within the Democratic party, for accepting the Bentsen nomination without terminal uproar, and to show Dukakis and Bentsen that here were 1,200 activists with minds of their own.

The rhetoric was more relaxed than the prime-time style as Jackson, in front of Dukakis and Bentsen, made his case for a dialectical relationship to power: 'close enough to serve, far enough to challenge.' Martin Luther King, Jackson said, had asked Lyndon Johnson to put through civil rights legislation. Johnson told him he could never get it through Congress. Then came the marches and the violence and Johnson moved. So there were the ingredients of change, Jackson said: 'The White House on the one hand and street heat on the other.' Each time Jackson played with the idea of 'street heat' the delegates roared. Dukakis, Bentsen and Paul Kirk creased their faces into a somewhat strained jocularity at the idea. When they took themselves off to a victory breakfast at the other side of the hall Jackson started talking about the practical consequences of his position of qualified support for the Dukakis/Bentsen ticket.

With Bentsen the running mate, he said there was now one fewer in favor of contra aid, on the eve of an important vote. Another consequence of not breaking open the convention was support by the Democratic leadership for Rep. Ron Dellums's bill on South Africa, Rep. John Conyers's proposed legislation on same-day registration, for D.C. statehood (two more good senators), improvement on government set-asides and legislation on children. He made the case eloquently, though it's also true to say that no one spoke from the other point of view.

There are obvious questions: how much of a substantive Rainbow organization will survive Jackson's 1988 campaign, or would survive if Jackson were to go into permanent exile? The answer is that it's clearly wrong to say no form of long-term structure is in place, and that it's clearly too early to see how much building will be done or how interested Jackson really is in urging it along. One thing seemed far clearer than I had imagined: Jackson has absolutely no interest in anything other than the Democratic Party as the vehicle for any agenda he considers to be within the realms of practical consideration. He is clear in his own mind that he truly can and will one day be president of the United States.

The man most visibly thwarting that ambition on the Democratic side is of course Michael Dukakis. He is now hailed in the mainstream press as the cool political engineer who skilfully managed the political pirouettes required to allay the anger of the Jackson camp and forge unity without prompting this same mainstream press to announce that he had sold out to the Black Jacobins. The papers were well disposed to Dukakis after his 'realistic' choice of Lloyd Bentsen as running mate – 'realism' or 'pragmatism' being words traditionally attached to blatantly crude, usually short-sighted, acts of political self-interest.

There was nothing skillful about the handling of the Bentsen announcement, as the world now knows. The famous 'missed phone call' – failure to give Jackson advance warning of the announcement – allowed Jackson just the opening he had been waiting for: one in which he could efficiently guilt-trip the Dukakis centrists into the mindframe appropriate to deal-making in Atlanta.

The rosy afterglow now flushing the faces of Democrats should not obscure the realities of what a Dukakis presidency would portend. Neither in the primary campaign, nor in his speech at Atlanta, nor in his subsequent stump oratory (this last being essentially Reaganesque in timbre) has Dukakis given the slightest sign of understanding that the problems of late capitalist America are not going to be solved by competent management, his sole plank. *Within the terms of the system*, the United States has been run pretty competently for the last eight years. The country is in its 67th month of continuous growth. Granted the average rate of growth is 2 per cent, but even so the line has gone gradually up rather than down. Deficit spending permitted the surge in military appropriations that have been the engine of this – indeed of the capitalist world's – economy. What George

Gilder has termed 'exchange rate mercantilism' – fixing exchange rates relative to West Germany and Japan in particular to the US's advantage – has once again worked well, even producing signs of revival in the rust belt, notably in the steel industry.

Such 'success' has been accompanied by the unpleasant consequences much touted in Atlanta: transfer of wealth from poor and middle-income to rich; the injustice of beggar-thy-neighbor exchange rates; the immorality of running the economy as a war machine. Competence won't fix the war economy or reform the international economic system. Dukakis has developed neither the ideas nor the constituency that would allow him to arrive in Washington in January, 1988 and embark on the necessary major programs. These are easily as far-reaching as anything Roosevelt did in the 1930s – redistribution, public financing, roll-back of corporate control, restructuring of relationships with the Third World – but are essential if he is to do anything but continue to tinker with the system, probably to its detriment, while allowing it to proceed on its own terms. Nothing said or proposed in Atlanta challenges such a conclusion.

So what do progressives, leftists, left-liberals, radicals – take your ascription of choice – make of the world after Atlanta, as it tilts towards November and beyond? After Jackson's talk to his delegates I spoke to a radical delegate who's been active in the Democratic Party and the Jackson campaign. 'I'm a career leftist, from a white affluent background,' she remarked, 'and the notion of ever agreeing to serve with a bourgeois politician [i.e. Dukakis] feels like a defeat. I have extraordinary faith in Jesse, and in the nature of his movement. After the session I went for a long walk in a black working-class neighborhood, talking to people on the streets and in the stores. They were uniform in what they said: "Jesse has made us so proud of ourselves. We can't let George Bush be elected." It reminded me of what the Cubans said when I was part of a group that went there in 1981: "You American leftists are so sanguine about there being no real difference between Carter or Reagan. But we would rather send to Miami for something than wait six months to get it from Yugoslavia." So here I am thinking that if I want to be part of a mass political movement led by black progressives, I must accept that leadership. The major reformation of power has to be led by people of color.'

Part of what she meant was that coalition with the Dukakis crowd had already entailed compromise. That moment before Bentsen spoke on Thursday night, when only a handful of delegates, mostly in the Vermont section, put up their Stop Contra Aid signs, could have been very different. When the Vermonters earlier handed out 2,000 such signs they were enthusiastically received by many delegates who later sat on them. Why? They sat on them because a well respected member of Jackson's staff sent out word to the floor that this is what they should do. In other words, part of the deal made between Dukakis and Jackson was that there would be no perturbing demonstrations from the floor; in effect, no 'street heat'.

The argument justifying such a deal and compliance by the would-be demonstrators is being put like this: white New Left activists need to redraw their political maps. A radical agenda has been pressed by a movement with a mass base, said movement and mass base being led and largely inhabited by people of color. For such a base, concessions demanded and bargains won from Dukakis are not the intimations of co-optation but the tokens of survival. First principle: protect your people. Same-day registrations, 'as demanded' in the Conyers bill, would change the face of American politics by enfranchising the poor. Already the party structure is being changed and the platform along with it. A Dukakis victory in November would bring a share in power.

The riposte to this, no doubt being made to many a Jackson delegate back home from Atlanta and explaining what went on, is that historic compromises with power usually turn out to be historic co-optations. The first thing power always asks is for the signs to come down. Ask the Populists what happened when they met up with the Democratic Party. Those delegates should not have put away their No Contra Aid placards whatever the Jackson camp asked them to do.

The dilemma is not insoluble; one only has to listen to Jackson's own dialectic about power and street heat. If Jackson, by his campaign, his oratory and his political skills, has provided the progressive wing with an exponent and a national presence undreamt of in years then the progressive movement – in labor organizations, Central American activism and so on – has provided Jackson with important parts of his base. 'I'm accountable to you,' Jackson told his delegates Friday morning. 'I work for you. I don't need another job. You can trust me behind closed doors.' Trust is not particularly necessary, since the proof of the pudding will be there on the menu for all to read. If Jackson shows no sign of any desire to foster structures – such as the National Rainbow Coalition – to survive his campaign this year then the trust will be commensurately diminished. The same thing is true in the relationship of Jackson and his forces to Dukakis and to power.

The first act of one of the Jackson appointments to the Democratic National Committee was to demand that Bentsen make a commitment to honor the party platform. This meant not merely absenting himself from Congress during the upcoming contra aid vote, but being present and voting against contra aid. Every Central American peace group can doubtless urge him to take this stand, or let the ticket take the consequences. This, presumably, is what street heat is all about.

Anderson Valley Advertiser/New Statesman

List of Articles Included in Part II

Index